STATE OF THE PRISONS IN ENGLAND, SCOTL.
JAMES NEILD

OF THE
prison
ENGLAND, SCOTLAND, AND WALES,
EXTENDING TO VARIOUS PLACES THEREIN ASSIGNED,
NOT FOR THE DEBTOR ONLY,
BUT FOR FELONS ALSO, AND OTHER LESS CRIMINAL OFFENDERS.
TOGETHER WITH SOME USEFUL
Documents, sDiweruationg, ano Eemarfeg,
ADAPTED TO EXPLAIN AND IMPROVE
THE CONDITION OF PRISONERS IN GENERAL.
BY
JAMES NEILD, Esa.
TREASURER OF THE SOCIETY FOR THE DISCHARGE AND RELIEF OF PERSONS IMPRISONED FOR SMALL DEBTS; ONE OF HIS MAJESTY'S ACTING JUSTICES OF
THE PEACE FOR THE COUNTIES OF BUCKINGHAM, KENT, AND MIDDLESEX; AND
FOR THE CITY AND LIBERTY OF WESTMINSTER.

Like Sailors Tired, The Happy Port 1 Gain:
HOW SWEET THE PLEASURE, AFTER TOIL AND Paix!
LONDON:
PRINTED BY JOHN NICHOLS AND SON, RED LION PASSAGE, FLEET STREET.
M,DCCC,XII.

Not having received the Freedom of the Royal Burgh of Inverness early enough for Insertion in its proper Place, (Page 292,) I here avail myself of the opportunity to express my grateful Acknowledgements, for the Honour so liberally conferred upon me by the worshipful the Provost, Magistrates, and Council.

TO THE RIGHT HONOURABLE AND HONOURABLE THE PRESIDENT AND VICE-PRESIDENTS, AND TO THE AUDITORS, AND OTHER GOVERNORS AND BENEFACTORS OF THE SOCIETY FOR THE DISCHARGE AND RELIEF OF ersons gmpu-

s ...nsiiiuieD IN FEBRUARY 1772, THE FOLLOWING WORK, CALCULATED, ON AN ENLARGED AND GENERAL PLAN,
FOR THE IMPROVEMENT OF PRISONS, AND COMFORT OF THE PRISONERS,
IS
MOST RESPECTFULLY DEDICATED,
BY
THEIR FAITHFUL SERVANT, THE AUTHOR
Chelsea.
Nov. 1811.

TABLE OF CONTENTS.
Page
Dedication v
Observations on Civil Imprisonment ix
Remarks on Courts of Conscience xx
Observations on Crimes and Punishments xxvi
General List of Prisons, distinguished in Alphabetical Order lx
State of Prisons in England, Scotland, and Wales 1
Conclusion 617
Portsmouth And Langston Harbours 619
No. I. Report on the State of the Convicts in Portsmouth Harbour, 1802 620
II. Report on the State of the Convicts in Langston Harbour 623
III. Report on the Hulks at Portsmouth, 1807 627
IV. Report on the Hulks in Langston Harbour 630
V. Report on the Hulks on the Thames 632
Statements Respecting Criminals 634
1. An Account of the Number of Criminals executed in the City of London and County of Middlesex,
from the Year 1749 to the year 1806, inclusive; shewing the Proportion in each Seven Years,
and distinguishing Years of War from Years of Peace 635
2. An Account of the Number of Criminals executed in the City of London and County of Middlesex,
between the First day of January 1749,

Publisher's Note

The book descriptions we ask booksellers to display prominently warn that this is an historic book with numerous typos or missing text; it is not indexed or illustrated.

The book was created using optical character recognition software. The software is 99 percent accurate if the book is in good condition. However, we do understand that even one percent can be an annoying number of typos! And sometimes all or part of a page may be missing from our copy of the book. Or the paper may be so discolored from age that it is difficult to read. We apologize and gratefully acknowledge Google's assistance.

After we re-typeset and design a book, the page numbers change so the old index and table of contents no longer work. Therefore, we often remove them.

Our books sell so few copies that you would have to pay hundreds of dollars to cover the cost of our proof reading and fixing the typos, missing text and index. Instead we usually let our customers download a free copy of the original typo-free scanned book. Simply enter the barcode number from the back cover of the paperback in the Free Book form at www.general-books.net. You may also qualify for a free trial membership in our book club to download up to four books for free. Simply enter the barcode number from the back cover onto the membership form on our home page. The book club entitles you to select from more than a million books at no additional charge. Simply enter the title or subject onto the search form to find the books.

If you have any questions, could you please be so kind as to consult our Frequently Asked Questions page at www.general-books.net/faqs.cfm? You are also welcome to contact us there.

General Books LLC™, Memphis, USA, 2012.

and the Thirty-first of December 1806; shewing
the various Crimes of which they were Convicted 63d

3. An Account of the Number of Criminal Offenders committed to the several Gaols of England and
   Wales for Trial in the Years 1805 and 1806, together with the result of their Commitments 638

4. An Account of the Population of each County, according to the Population Returns; the
   Number of Offenders committed within the same respectively in the Year 1805; together
   with the Amount of Paupers in each County, and the Number of them in each Hundred of the
   Population, arranged according to the Circuits of the Judges 543

5. A Statement of the Number of Persons charged with Criminal Offences, committed to the different Gaols in England and Wales, for Trial at the Assizes and Sessions held for the several
   Counties and Places therein, during the Year 1810; shewing the Nature of their Crimes, and
   the Sentences of those Convicted; and the Nature of the Crimes respectively of such as were
   Acquitted; and of such as were Discharged by reason of no Bill being found against them,
   and by reason of no Prosecution; and the number Executed of those who have received Sentence of Death 642.

OBSERVATIONS ON THE LAW OF CIVIL IMPRISONMENT.

AN esteemed writer, on the "subject of our Penal Laws, considers imprisonment, when inflicted for punishment, as not according to the principles of wise legislation. If this position be true, in respect to crimes committed against positive institutions, (and it seems too firm to be shaken,) how much more forcibly will it apply to civil arrests, and imprisonment for debt, when the multiplied and intricate concerns of extended society make the path of the most intelligent, in matters of trade, a course of considerable uncertainty. If then the political wisdom of confining the *persons of debtors* for debt be matter of doubt, how important is it that, whilst the practice is allowed to continue, it should be subjected to such general regulations, as are best calculated to lessen the resulting inconveniences; and prevent the necessity of resorting, at least so frequently as of late years, to the legislature, for acts of parliament to relieve insolvent debtors; which, while they do honour to the feelings of those friends of humanity who introduce and promote them, it must be admitted are too often perverted, to screen a fraudulent debtor from the just demands of his injured creditors. It is the fate of whatever is human to be slow in its progress to perfection; nor is it matter of surprize, when rightly considered, that the laws of a country should move the slowest, where rectitude is their aim.

In the early ages of society, the mind of man is less complicated, than when advanced into the refinement of older governments. The laws at first laid down for his regulation are, like his habits, plain and intelligible to the most ordinary capacity, being little more than moral rules or maxims, against which he is not to offend; and having few temptations to lead him astray, he readily forms himself to their government: But, when luxuries, the never-failing attendants upon successful commerce, break in upon his primitive habits, new laws become necessary, to restrain the too free indulgence of his acquired propensities. These laws are not b framed in the anticipation of new events, which a prospective eye may view as likely to arise in the progress of society, but to check what have already taken place, and to prevent their recurrence. Hence it follows, that laws so formed will always be somewhat behind the actual state of the people, their proneness to vice considered; and it frequently happens, that laws, calculated to suit one state of society, are permitted to continue in another; and to remain as law at a period, in which, if they were then introduced for the first time, they would be unanimously rejected, as impolitic, and inapplicable to the condition of the people to be governed by them. In this view of the subject, arrests for debt may be considered: and although, when England was the lowest amongst the commercial nations of Europe, arrests for debt might have been less impolitic, it can hardly therefore be argued, that their continuance should be suffered, when England, as at present, is the first trading country in the world.

In a commercial country, the hazards attendant upon justifiable commerce entitle the unsuccessful adventurer to greater indulgences, than a debtor, under almost any circumstance, could have a right to expect, in a country purely military. But leaving the policy of the question, as to whether arrests for debt ought or ought not to be continued, to the judgment of those who are better able to consider it; and without venturing to anticipate what would be the decision, it seems a more useful appropriation of the time of an humble individual, to consider the law as it stands at present: and to inquire, Whether a superstructure may not be raised, to answer many good and salutary purposes, without materially affecting the fabric; which, whatever may be its defects, has the venerable shield of time to protect it against the grasp of hasty innovation? Secondary causes, or inducements, to cast the unfortunate debtor into prison, or to continue his confinement when there, beyond what naturally arise between him and his creditor, should be watched with jealousy, and removed, if possible: and it would be desirable indeed, when a returning gleam of liberty presents itself to the prisoner, if he could be found no further encumbered with debt, than when he first became the inhabitant of a gaol. At this moment of hope the *debt* can be arranged for; but, alas, the *costs* are perhaps of equal amount, and present an insuperable bar to his liberation! It would be deemed a wicked oppression, on the part of a government that transported a subject to slavery for a period of years, to say, at the end of the term, "Your labour was ours, by the offence which you committed: We have now a demand upon you, both for the clothing we have supplied, and for the provisions you have consumed; and as you are unable to pay us, you must return again to slavery for the debt you have contracted." His reasoning, that the origin of the debt was involuntary on his part, would be of no avail: the hand of power is against him: and as well might the debtor say, the costs were not incurred by his act, nor with his consent, and he ought not to be detained for them. When a disappointed and offended creditor LAW OF CIVIL IMPRISONMENT.

Applies to his attorney, he hardly desires his advice, but rather directs the proceedings to be taken with his debtor; and, indeed, if he did otherwise, what answer could be expected? Is not law the business of the attorney? and is it found that men, generally speaking, who have the greatest temptation thrown in their way, are the best? Individuals may be, and are not unfrequently, so found; because from temptation alone can self-denial and forbearance be discovered: but experience proves that it is not so with the great bulk of mankind. "Just debts ought to be paid, or the laws must be enforced for their recovery", is the language of the irritated creditor, re-echoed by his attorney; with this only difference between them, that the one is unconscious of the result of what he directs; while the other, with the knowledge, has the satisfaction also of knowing, that the plaintiff is-a solvent man, and that, be the event what it may, the attorney must be paid. Thus, regardless of their operation on the unfortunate debtor, proceedings commence: in-a short time considerable costs are incurred: the already angry creditor finds himself exposed to a new loss, which he never anticipated; and becomes not only confirmed in his first resentments, but furnished with fresh occasion for their inveteracy. Is a man so circumstanced fit to judge in his own cause? Is he capable of deciding, with moderation and temper, upon the portion of imprisonment his debtor ought to endure? It will be readily answered, "Certainly, no P The hardened creditor will triumph in the imprisonment which he has power to inflict; regardless of the sufferings of the victim, whom perhaps he at first solicited to take the credit he has abused, and equally unmindful of the wretched complainings of a forlorn wife and starving children: while the man less cruel, or perhaps indolent in his nature, as also the man basking in the sunshine of prosperity, will put away the prisoner from his thoughts. But, should his complaints or humble solicitations be obtruded upon him, he will endeavour to excuse his want of humanity by the pretence, that the confinement of the prisoner is an act of the law, for which he is under no responsibility. Can a more wretched state of an *honest* man be conceived? Nay, more, does even *the fraudulent* debtor merit this perpetual, undefined punishment, in all the wantonness of its tyranny?

In further pursuit of these observations let it be supposed, that an unfortunate man, unable even to pay a debt of 10/. is arrested on the eve of a law term, and thrown into prison for his inability; and that, in the same number of days as he owes pounds, he will be involved in a fresh debt, of equal or greater amount, for the costs of his detainer in prison: What will be the exclamation of the voice of Reason? But, carry the inquiry a little further, and let us suppose that his attachment by one creditor alarms the rest, (nor is it unnatural that it should do so,) and that he has ten detainers laid against him, for debts of the same amount; what will then be his situation? Why, he will in a few days be incumbered with additional debts, for costs of a greater amount than all his original debts put together, at the very time that he is immured in prison; without subsistence, or the meaJns of earning any for himself, or the wretched dependants on his affection; and without having done a single act to occasion the expences, which he is wholly unable to prevent. What, then, will be the exclamation? and where, as the law now stands, is he to look for mercy? The Bankrupt Laws, which to the fair trader, who has had the good fortune to deal with humane creditors, afford relief, are not open to his assistance: he has been too modest in all his transactions in trade, to have ventured sufficiently to come within their purview: his debts are not of the required amount to entitle him to their relief. His creditors,—most probably of the same class in life with himself, and who can but ill afford to pay the expences that have been incurred,— will *they* commiserate his sufferings, and restore him to liberty? or will they not rather be acted upon, in the fulness of their resentments at the loss of their claims; and (having, as they experience, thrown away good money after bad, and apprehensive, if they liberate the prisoner, that they can have no pretence for suspending the payment of their attorney's costs), will they not be more likely to extend his confinement, and endeavour to throw the odium of the expences incurred, upon the pretended obstinacy of the unfortunate victim, for whom no one considers it his interest, or feels any incitement, to drop a word of kindness or mitigation? And yet, in a Country boastful of its laws and of its freedom, these are the persons who are to pronounce on this imprisonment of their fellow subjects, perhaps for the period of their lives, without a right of appeal to their country, or the hope of relief! Power, in the hands of man, is always subject to abuse; but what is to be expected from him, when he is suffered to judge his own cause, under the influence of conceived injuries, and agitated by resentment? The highest advocates for the dignity of human nature must admit, that, in practice, a result of this kind will not be found to elevate their subject.

In support of what is thus stated, the ordinary and allowed Bills of Fees and Disbursements, in cases of arrest for 10. are here made out: By which it appears, that at the commencement of a Term they will, within ten days, if in London, amount to near *Twelve pounds!*

In the case of a *City Arrest,* where the defendant is taken to prison.

Hilary Vacation.

s. d.

J,9th April. Instructions and warrant to sue-------o 12 0

Affidavit of debt-0 7 2
Drawing Precipe' for original, fol. 25-----150
   Copy for the Cursitor----0 12 6
   Paid for original-----------0-" 6
   Fee thereon-------------06 8
Paid the King's fine, and attending to compound it-0 10 0 s. d.
Returning and filing original--------024
   Capias and Fee------------016 0
   Warrant and messenger----------030
   Attending to instruct officer--------034
Paid officer for arrest 0 10 6
Letters and messengers---------020
Hilary Term.
23d April. Motion for a rule to return the writ------034
   Paid for the rule-----------0 66
   Copy and service-----------020
   Instructions for declaration---------068
   Drawing same, fol. 25----------0l6 8
   Entering on the Roll, and paid Prothonotary---1 5 0
Copy declaration on stamps to deliver to defendant, and duty 0 9 8
Attending to deliver same---------034
   Affidavit of service, duty, and oath------072
   Copy declaration to annex to affidavit, and duty--0 9 8
Copy affidavit and declaration, and stamps----013 4
29th, Paid filing affidavit and declaration------020
   Attending to file same----------034
   Term fee, letters and messengers------0120
   Total---.11 15 8

And *in the Country,* if the arrest is made at a considerable distance from the county gaol, they will perhaps amount to Twenty Pounds, within the same period!

The *Lords' Act,* which subjects the creditor to make his prisoners an allowance while he detains them in prison, may be considered by some as a sufficient check on the inconveniences here described; But, upon investigation of the practical effects of this Act, it is feared that it will not be found to possess those Benefits which some humane advocates may imagine. Five terms are allowed to the plaintiff to proceed to judgment against his debtor, and to charge him in execution; and, until the proceedings against the prisoner are in this advanced state, he cannot apply for the benefit of the Lords' Act. The creditor, informed of this operation of the Act, instructs his attorney to do no more than comply with its directions. The attorney, within the course of the first ten days, having secured the greatest part of his expected harvest, is found obedient to his instructions; and, slowly protracting the remaining forms of proceeding against the unfortunate prisoner, spins out the five terms, by measured distances, to retard his application for relief as long as possible! Thus the Debtor pines at least a twelvemonth in prison, under the heavy afflictions of poverty and grief, by the protracted course of *legal* proceedings; which might, and would be completed against him within the first term, but for the provision (it may almost be said the *tantalizing* provision) made for him by this kindly intended Act of the British Legislature.

What is here stated seems chiefly applicable to the *unfortunate,* yet *honest* sufferer. But we will now turn to the *fraudulent* and *designing* debtor, and see how the Act operates with respect to him, and to his injured plaintiff. Conscious of the time, which he thinks will elapse, before he is put into a situation to seek the benefit of the Statute, he takes care to retain to himself the means of subsistence during the protracted period; then, covertly, makes over the rest of his property, to put it out of the reach of his creditors; and when the time arrives, for making his claim under the Lords' Act, he audaciously takes the oaths prescribed, and is ordered to receive its benefit.

The duty of the Judges, it is possible, may sometimes clash with their judgment, whilst ordering the relief intended by law for the impoverished debtor, to many applicants of another sort; whose conduct, even in the face of the Court, almost amounts to a conviction, that their applications are made in the confident expectancy of their plaintiff's neglecting to make his due payment at the appointed times. It is the natural consequence attendant upon the order for this due payment of an allowance to the prisoner, that it should not only be made in the current coin of the country, but punctually also, on a fixed day, and at a stated period; and that any any omission, or non-compliance with that order, should be followed by the prisoner's liberation. Hence it may be seen, that the payment of a counterfeit six-pence, (and who, in the present state of the silver currency of England, can be certain that their money is not counterfeit?) or the forgetfulness of the plaintiff to make his payment, at the prison, on the appointed day, or till one minute after the prison is shut for the night, must be followed by an immediate discharge of the debtor. What a promising speculation is this, on which a fraudulent debtor may realize his hopes! A plaintiff, situate many miles from the prison, will but in few cases continue his payments for several weeks: most likely he may fail in the first week; and the greatest rogue be thus cast upon society, to renew his depredations on the fair trader, without being in the least reclaimed by his imprisonment. Voluntary confinement, the basis of a contrivance to defraud, can produce no improvement in the moral habits of a prisoner.

From this view of the Lords' Act it seems fairly deducible, That the honest debtor may be starved, before he can have the benefit of its provisions; whilst the fraudulent debtor finds in it a very probable, if not the certain avenue to his liberation.

To remedy this evil, so far as circumstances will admit, Insolvent Acts have been devised. But, highly as the principle of these acts must be admired by every friend of society, and great as is the care of our legislature to govern their operations by wise and numerous provisions; yet still it must be admitted, that though productive of much general good, they will at times be found to extend an injurious influence, in favour of the profligate and designing debtor.

A modification of the existing Statutes for debtor and creditor, would, it is conceived, afford a remedy of the present inconveniences, without any necessity, in the first instance, of framing a new code of laws.

The practice of the Courts may, in all cases, remain the same as it now is: But, surely, it will not be too great a boon for the *unfortunate* debtor to solicit of his country, that, whilst he remains in actual confinement, through incapacity to pay his debts, he should stand excused from contributing to the necessities of the state; and that all legal proceedings against him, when a prisoner, should be exempted from stamp-duty.

The Judges of the land, not more elevated by their wisdom than their humanity, and, mindful of the liberal and well-bestowed salaries they receive from the country, can have no hesitation in ordering the subordinate proceedings of the courts, conducted at their chambers, to be transacted gratuitously, without taking any fees for the same.

The Barristers, educated to fill, and in the hope of discharging, at some future period of life, one of the most important trusts in human society, can be influenced by no mercenary motives. It is but justice, therefore, to the acknowledged liberality of the Bar, to conclude, that they will, with one voice, consent to a privation of their fees, in all cases, where proceedings are to be taken against the *unfortunate* debtor, whilst in custody.

The Officers of the Courts, amidst the multiplicity of their other business, will And a remuneration fo: their trouble, sufficient to put them beyond the desire of taking any thing from a prisoner, who is absolutely denied the means of protecting himself and family, through the heavy inflictions of poverty. t

The Attorney,—who principally labours in the business,—must perhaps receive some reward for his personal trouble; but he should be removed, far as possible, from the influence of interested views. The best mode of securing so desirable an end seems to be, the reducing his fees to half their present amount, in all proceedings against debtors under actual confinement. By this means the mercy of the plaintiff will not be restrained by the recollection of considerable law expences, in addition to his debt; and, his resentments having subsided, he may in time think more favourably of his unfortunate debtor, and restore him to the blessings of Liberty. Nay, it seems not too much to apprehend, that the adoption of this plan, alone, would reduce the number of prisoners confined for debt, at least in the proportion of six out of ten.

But, to guard against the effect of a contrary temper in any plaintiff, who, care, less or unmindful of his debtor, may incline to leave him to the laws of his country, and the imprisonment which they inflict,—a further remedy presents itself; under which an Apportionate Imprisonment might be inflicted, according to the nature and extent of the debts, and of the particular circumstances under which they were contracted.

The first feature of a plan, professing to allow of Temporary Imprisonment for debt, should be the providing necessaries of life for the impoverished *Debtor,* hi order to protect the *Man,* now rendered unable to protect himself, against the painful claims of unsatisfied Nature. This allowance might be created out of the countyrate; and, to prevent its misapplication, might only be furnished to those prisoners, whose necessities oblige them to live on the *poor side of a prison!* (deprived of all association with other prisoners, whose better circumstances, or whose friends, place them above the necessity of seeking so humble a relief;) and who are, also, in a situation to declare themselves, upon oath, not to be possessed of the value of *20l.*

This would prevent the recurrence of what humanity dreads to record; although it may be asked, "What else can be expected, when certain prisons in Great Britain, for the confinement of Debtors, are without any allowance *of food* whatever; nay, some even without access to *water!* and have no more than the keeper, or his servants, may think fit to bring them?—In one place they paid a halfpenny for a jug of water; in another, a penny was demanded for a pailful!

The next object to be considered is, At what period of time the prisoner for debt, against whom no imputation can be brought of dishonesty or intentional misconduct, may, with safety to the state, be restored to his liberty. How obligatory soever it may be upon every man to pay the debt which he owes to another man, there is still a higher duty which he owes to his country at large, in the application of his labour and talents for the general good of the community; and of his power to perform which, no man, under any circumstances, ought to possess the means of arbitrarily depriving him. It seems difficult to reconcile to any principle of sense or policy, that a man, to whom a debt of only *lol.* is due (a sum very inadequate to the claim, which, in these times, the country has upon the annual exertions of the humblest of her individuals) shall possess the power of depriving the state of his debtor's services for a long course of years—nay, for ever, without limitation of time in his favour to restore him to liberty. Surely, as the less atrocious the nature of a man's crimes is, who offends against the Criminal Law, the lighter is his punishment; so the smaller a man's debts *bond fide* contracted are, the shorter should be the period of his confinement. And here it may not be amiss to observe, that, generally speaking, the man who is cast into prison for a debt of 10/. may really be a more useful member of the country, by the due application of his labour, than the prisoner who is confined for 10,000/. A period of three months may reasonably be considered as a sufficient length of confinement, to induce a more cautious conduct in the future dealings of a man, whose debts do not exceed *lol.* Progressive scales of time, and money, might also be formed, to produce the same good effect with those persons, whose debts are from that sum up to 2000/. And after these, perhaps, it might be as well to suffer all debts of a higher amount to be placed in the same scale.

But, as the creditor ought not to possess an nncontrouled power over the *person* of his debtor, so perhaps the debtor should not be enabled to determine the quantum of punishment in the power of his creditor to inflict upon him: And, for this reason, his liberation at the periods proposed might not stand as matter of right, but only times assigned, when he may have the power of submitting his conduct, (in regard to the contracting of the debts for which he is charged in custody,) to the consideration of a Jury, summoned by the proper officer, at the instance of the prisoner, and upon notice to be duly served on the plaintifFs attorney.

If, upon this investigation of the prisoner's conduct, nothing should transpire to induce the Jury to remand him back to prison, their verdict might give him his liberty; and the law might thereupon vest his property in the clerk of the peace, or other officer, for the benefit of his creditors, in like manner as the insolvent's property is now vested, under the acts for relief of insolvent debtors. But should the jury be of opinion that the conduct of the debtor merits a prolongation of his imprisonment, it might be safely left with them to determine the extent of its continuance, according to their judgment, founded upon the facts disclosed in evidence; and for this purpose the plaintiff might himself be examined on oath. Or, the power of the jury, in case of their remanding the prisoner, might be modelled according to the better judgment of Magistrates, or other still more experienced persons, so as to do justice between the country and the parties.

The operation of such a plan as this upon the *fraudulent debtor,* is too obvious to require explanation. He would be remanded to an increase of punishment, proportioned to his misconduct; while the honest, though unfortunate debtor, would be restored, by the voice of his countrymen, to his liberty, to his family, and to those social blessings, of which perhaps the becoming security for a friend in an unguarded moment, may have most unhappily deprived him.

Another advantage also might be made to result from an appeal to a Jury. The fraudulent debtor, who prefers remaining in gaol to the payment of his debts, and who lives in confinement, surrounded with luxuries,—whilst his plaintiff may pine without, scarce able to provide himself and family with the ordinary necessaries of life,—might be summoned before a jury, at the desire of any of his creditors, after he had remained the apportioned time in confinement, according to the amount of his debts: and, unless he could shew a satisfactory reason why his effects should c not be assigned for the benefit of his creditors, the jury might by their verdict, find for, and direct such assignment to take effect, and that the prisoner should be set at large. Thus the fraudulent debtor would be prevented from wasting that substance in confinement, which his creditors would gladly receive in satisfaction of their debts; but upon which, (as the law at present stands,) they can have no claim.

If the principles here humbly laid down were approved of, a Bill, with no more clauses in it than are ordinarily introduced into an Insolvent Act, would furnish all the requisites needful for carrying it into effect. And this, it is imagined, would at once render Insolvent Acts unnecessary; deprive the fraudulent debtor of the means of diverting the Lords' Act from its humane object, to the worst of purposes; enable the unfortunate debtor to turn his talents to the pursuits of industry, for support of himself and family; and deter the evil-minded from levelling their fraudulent practices against the fair trader. Or, in case these should be found hardy enough to continue their evil courses, it would teach them, by an exemplary and not indiscriminate punishment, to adopt a better plan of life when liberated, and to cease from defrauding their neighbours, under a daringly-pretended sanction of British Law!

A TABLE of 'Bailable ptOCeW against Debtors, for ONE YEAR,
from *Michaelmas,* 1801, to *Michaelmas,* 1802.
DIVIDED INTO FOUR CLASSES.

Note, The disproportion against the first and lowest class, on a comparison with the second, is two to one; on a comparison with the third, is increased; and on a comparison with the fourth class, is twenty to one. Middlesex is reckoned only at one fifteenth of the whole kingdom.

The number of Debtors, consisting of the capital Merchants and Traders to all parts of the world, is reckoned greatly to exceed the number of those, whose credit is limited to the sums of Thirty Pounds: the disproportion is therefore much greater against the lowest class than is apparent.

In 1793 the number of bailable writs and executions for debts from ten to twenty pounds, in Middlesex only, amounted to *Five thousand seven hundred and nineteen;* and the aggregate amount of the debts sued for was £. 31,791.

It will scarce be credited, yet is most unquestionably true, that the mere costs of these actions, although made up, and not defended at all, would amount to,68,728.; and if defended, the aggregate expence to recover s£S1,791. (strange and incredible as it must appear) can be no less than *two hundred and eighty-Jive thousand nine hundred and fifty pounds;* being considerably more than three times the amount of the debts sued for or defended!

For this Table of Calculations I beg leave to express my acknowledgements to Joseth Burchell, Esa. the present worthy Under-Sheriff of Middlesex.

J. HE Observations hitherto made on *the Law of Civil Imprisonment,* have been restricted to those Arrests for Debt, where the cause of action amounts to ten pounds or upwards, and where the plaintiff asserts upon oath to that effect; and also to Executions, issued upon actions that have been instituted in the superior courts.

But there is yet another sort of confinement for debt, which, notwithstanding the cause of action is comparatively inconsiderable in amount, deserves, if possible, the more serious consideration of every reflecting person; as chiefly falling amongst labouring husbandmen and working mechanicks, the very strength and sinews of the country; but who, having no visible estates of their own wherewith to support themselves and their families, are unacquainted with the bread of idleness; who can only be maintained by their daily toil; and who, in this respect, may be truly said to come most immediately within the letter of that divine, infliction upon the first offenders of mankind: "In the sweat of thy face shalt thou eat bread-J-."

It is not easy to conceive a case more distressing than that of a father of a family taken from this class of life, unprovided with the smallest store of any kind to answer his growing wants, or (what is not unlikely), without ever having had an opportunity of enabling himself to provide any; and immured within the walls of a prison, where no allowance is made, to meet the necessities of his nature.

The description of so deplorable a situation in adequate colours is beyond the power of the author; and he must therefore leave it to the humane reader to depict to his own heart the wretched plight of so devoted a victim: without food, without "The Court of Requests bad originally and properly the cognizance of all poor men's suits, which were made to his Majesty by supplication; and upon which they were entitled to have right, without payment of any money for the same." Smith's Commonwealth.
f Gen. iii. 19. firing, without bedding; with only his thread-bare garments to cover bis shivering limbs; and with the painful reflection, that his wife and helpless offspring are starving without; or else, seeking relief from parish officers, a picture of human woe shall there present itself, such as imagination could never have formed: It is drawn from *combinations* of misery, which extend themselves far beyond the walls of a prison: they reach the mournful dwelling of many a wretched family, reduced to the extremities of want.'
When the maxim of our Laws, that "Idleness is an offence against the publick Oeconomy," is duly considered, it cannot fail of creating surprize to every reflecting person, that the same laws should, under any circumstances, take a man from that class in society wherein his personal labour is of the most essential value to the community, and *compel him to be idle;* for such is most distinctly the situation of a prisoner who is confined for debt. It would rather be expected that the same legal polity which induced the adoption of so wise a maxim against idleness, should have extended the principle to the case of a debtor, unwilling or unable to pay his debts; and have required that he should be obliged to work for increased periods of time, and not remain incarcerated, not only without work being provided for him to perform, but without the conveniences, or, it may nearly be said, without being suffered to exercise his calling, if capable of being carried on in a prison. To the great jealousy of our ancestors for the preservation of their liberties under all circumstances, can alone be attributed this favourable consideration of prisoners for debt: But, as our laws, in their present form, do not allow such prisoners to be set to work, and the situation in which they are placed under the laws as they exist, being more immediately the object of the present enquiry, the policy of their being set to work will not be further pressed; though it seems certain, however, that it might humble the pride of some of the dashing adventurers for this distinction in life, that it would be less injurious to their healths and their morals, than the extreme of idleness, with confinement, to which they are constrained.

To form a just conclusion of the good or ill effects which result to the community from the imprisonment of debtors, for the payment of debts which do not, separately taken, amount to *forty shillings;* it will be proper, in the first place, to take a view of the persons by whom, and with whom, such debts are most commonly contracted; the general nature of the debts; the constitution of the courts in which they are to be recovered, and the steps to be taken for their recovery: and, lastly, the coercion directed by the law, to enforce its own ordinances, and the consequences produced by such coercion, as it is now exercised.

With respect to the persons by whom and with whom such debts are in general contracted, it has already been observed, that the labouring classes of society present the mass of prisoners found in the gaols of this country for debts under the amount of forty shillings; and it may readily be concluded, without the hazard of error, that the persons with whom such debts are contracted will be found amongst the lowest class of shopkeepers and inferior tradesmen; not omitting the publican; who, (however his debt may have been contracted, in breach of the laws against tippling, and in defiance of those for better regulation of publick houses,) considers himself equally entitled, with the dealers who may have supplied the necessaries of life, to recover his demand, of which he has been the only *score-keeper;* and upon its being verified on his own oath, and confirmed by the commissioners, (persons; invested with large discretionary powers, and selected from his own rank in life), to immure his unfortunate debtor without mercy, in a prison; to the great injury of the community at large, by the loss of his labour, and the increase of the poor's rates in his particular district, by the maintenance of his family; the certain consequence of the father's absence.

Debts under 40. it may be said are, and they certainly are sometimes, most fairly contracted, for a supply of the absolute necessaries of life; and these should therefore, in point of strict morality as well as of law, be scrupulously discharged. But, notwithstanding this truth, which is most implicitly subscribed to, the situation of the contracting parties, the power of influence, and the manner in which the labouring man and the mechanick receive the reward of their labours, deserve to be taken into consideration; and it will from thence be readily seen, that in sound policy, credits of this nature should be as limited, as the returning payment of the poor man's wages; it being an undeniable position, that longer credits are the certain bane of his future well doing.

A prudent labouring man, (and, thank God, there are yet many amongst us in that class of life who merit the commendation) so arranges the expenditure of his little income, that he is able to square it with the necessities of his family, and with his weekly wages, so as to pay every one their due; and to put a small.pittance by, or to make some other regulation, for the payment of his landlord. But, give to this man an easily acquired or a protracted credit, and he will soon get into such difficulties, as it may be out of his power ever after to overcome.

A Debt of only a single Pound in amount, to the person from whom the working man buys his bread, will make him the Baker's slave for life; and oblige him to purchase his bread from *him* only for ever after, or subject him, in case of his refusal, from the badness of the article he buys, or other circumstances of more evil tendency, to encounter his Creditor's resentment; and this, by the experience he has learnt from his unfortunate neighbours, the latter has but too much reason to think, can only, from the principles on which he carries on his trade, be satisfied by an Appeal to the Court of Conscience, and the final Imprisonment of his Debtor. The same Remarks equally apply to the Chandler-shop Man, and in some degree to the Butcher, though not so generally; as from the high price of meat, the great bulk of the labouring class of people are debarred the means of purchasing it; and what they do purchase is chiefly, and in many cases can only be bought with ready money. Of all the creditors which the poor man can have, there are none who seem so little entitled to a favourable consideration as the Publicans: And yet it is believed that in general they are not the least numerous class of complainants at the Courts of Request. Debts contracted with the Publican are seldom for the use of the Debtor's *family,* and never, it is apprehended, for their comfort or benefit. The effect of such debts, therefore, in the course of their being contracted, leads to a dissolute life, an inattention to consequences, and a contempt or utter defiance of the laws of his country: And ought the non-payment of them (in the contracting of which the Creditor appears more than an accessary to the poor man's error, in which he is often in fact the principal, who leads him to destruction) to give *such a Creditor* the power of immuring his unfortunate Victim in a prison, when he has no more money to spend? debarred of medicine in the hour of sickness, and of every necessary which the preservation of life requires? and at the same time to injure the community, by depriving it of the labour of a man, from whose services, if employed, the Country would receive more solid advantage, than from the whole class of Publicans within the Kingdom, in their licensed capacities?

When an Englishman is considering the Courts of Justice of his Country, it is natural for him to look with partiality to the wise Institutions of Alfred the *Great,* the founder of the English Laws, and the framer of that valuable prerogative, the Trial by Jury: And never can he observe so glorious an Institution intrenched upon by modern improvements, without a pang of regret, and justly conceived alarm, from an apprehension that ill consequences may arise, from new-created jurisdictions dispensing with this invaluable British blessing.

"The policy of the Great Alfred," as Mr. Justice Blackstone expresses himself , "was to bring home Justice to every man's door." With this view he appointed the Court-Baron, The Hundred Court, and The County Court; gradually ascending from the lowest Jurisdiction up to the supreme Courts, and investing them, among other powers, with the power to hold pleas of Debt, not amounting to forty shillings. These Courts were of limited Jurisdiction; but were dispersed universally throughout the Kingdom, and were held at short intervals of time; the freeholders of the respective districts forming the Juries, who decided the Questions that were brought before them.

One of the great advantages which resulted to the people from the formation of these Courts, arose out of their Proximity to the Abode of those persons whose Interests could be affected by them, and the Prevention of that loss of time and expence, which, under the present order of things, takes place, in travelling to a See mere, in my Statement of the Boeou&h Compter, pp. 65, *66.* distance of many miles, (frequently not less, and sometimes more than three times.in succession,) for the recovery of a small debt, and which, if recovered, will seldom repay the Creditor for his loss of time, and necessary maintenance during his absence from home: whilst the frequency of the Court's being held in ancient Times, prevented the possibility of any material delay taking place in the Administration of Justice; and called forth that commendatory observation of our great Lawyer, Sir Edward Coke, who describes them as " formed for the ease of the people; that they might have justice done them at their own doors, without any charge, or loss of time."

As the King was ever considered by the Laws of England to be the great fountain of Justice, and general conservator of the Peace, it was not the design of the Great Alfred, by the institution of these inferior Jurisdictions, to shut out his people from the natural right they possessed, of seeking Justice in his presence, (in the *Aula Regia,* or great Court of the Kingdom,) whenever the magnitude, or the difficulty of the case to be decided, was too great for the obtaining of Justice in the inferior Courts. In some cases, also, it was permitted, for either of the parties a common suit to remove the proceedings, in the first instance, by the Writs of *pone,* or *accedas ad Curiam;* and even after Judgment pronounced, to stay the issuing of Execution by Writ of false Judgment, and then rehear the Cause in the superior Court.

It is the fate of all human institutions, however founded in wisdom and the best intentions, to be subject to error or abuse. The Great Alfred, when he allowed of this Appeal to himself from the inferior Courts, felt no apprehension that it would be perverted to the embarrassment and vexation, instead of the ease and benefit of his people. Sitting in person in the great Court of the Nation, it was not to be apprehended that any one would be sufficiently hardy to remove a Cause of insignificant or small import, merely for the purpose of delay, or to harrass his feebler adversary: Such a conduct would be sure to experience immediate and exemplary punishment. But, when the Kings of England ceased to be really present at the Administration of Justice in their Great Court, and when the Court of *King's Bench,* in its present form, became completely established, various circumstances concurred, to induce the Judges not to frown away Appeals which came from the lower Courts. Hence the removal of suits became at length so frequent, that it was soon found expedient to institute them in the upper Courts, in the first instance, rather than be subject to the circuitous mode of a removal; and this circumstance combining with the neglect of the Great Men of the provincial districts, in not attending to assist at the inferior Courts, has occasioned their having generally fallen into disuse.

The increase of Trade and Manufacture in the Country was, of course, attended with an enlarged population in particular districts; and the disuse into which the inferior Courts had fallen was soon felt as a serious inconvenience: Upon which the City of London, in order to substitute a remedy for itself, obtained an Act of Parliament, to enable two Aldermen and four Common-Councilmeu to sit twice a week, in order to hear and determine all Causes of Debt arising within the City, not exceeding the value of Forty Shillings.

In this manner summary redress was obtained for the Citizens of the Metropolis at a moderate expence; and if the establishment were not subject to exception, in regard to its intrenchment on the Trial by Jury, it might, from the elevated rank in commercial life of the persons appointed to preside at it, be considered, in other respects, a tolerably good substitute for the disused, but more ancient, and, in fact, better Courts of the Country: And the more so, as from its Restriction to the Limits of the City, it answered, in that point of view, the intention of the HundredCourt, by bringing home Justice to the Citizen's door, without loss of time.

The Example thus set by the City of London has been followed by other trading and populous Districts; and sundry Courts of Request, or Courts of Conscience, for the recovery of Small Debts, have been sanctioned by the Legislature, and are at present pretty generally in use. But these Courts, in addition to the fundamental objection against the Court for the City of London, do not now possess a single trait, in their formation or practice, that can merit a favourable consideration.

The Commissioners who there preside, and determine the causes brought before them, are little otherwise than self-elected; and, when once appointed, may be considered as Standing Commissioners for the purposes of the Act. They are, generally, too near in rank of life to the parties whose causes they decide; and it is no unusual thing for a Commissioner to pass on one side, whilst his brother Commissioners determine a question to which he himself is a party. The wide limits of the jurisdiction of these Courts of Conscience are also another source of vexation, as embracing districts of many miles in extent, which greatly harrass both the suitors, as well complaining as defending: while, in fact, they do not possess a single advantage for the people, that would not be infinitely better, and more constitutionally answered, by a revival of the antient Hundred-Court; which would preserve the Trial by Jury, and bring home justice to the door of every man, without any considerable loss of time, and at the least possible expence.

The Sheriffs', or County Court, as established by Alfred the Great, is still, in some respects, preserved, though greatly impaired, from the loss of that antient dignity and consequence which prevailed, when the bishop and great men of the county attended, with the Sheriff, to preside in it. This court, though similar to the Court-Baron and Hundred Court, is not a Court of Record; and yet it has the same power as possessed by them, to hold pleas of debt, not amounting to forty shillings; and (by virtue of a court, called "Justice's") to hold pleas of all personal actions to any amount.

Thus the County Court possesses all the requisite d powers to administer justice between party and party, as to debts under forty shillings; and maintains, through its trial by Jury, that best prerogative and boasted right of Englishmen, which is alarmingly infringed by the substitution of Commissioners in the Courts of Conscience; so as to afford precedents in practice, the evil consequences whereof no man can foresee, nor the extent to which they may in time be carried.

The County Courts, it must be remembered, are only a branch of the political institution of our English Justinian, Alfred; and were framed by him at the same time with the Courts-Baron and Hundred-Courts: thus, by the immediate locality of the lesser Courts, continuing to preserve the beautiful symmetry of his excellent system, and bringing home justice to the door of every man. But, deprived of these lower Courts, a chasm is created; and the only possible objection that seems capable of being now taken to the institution of County Courts, presents itself in the remoteness of the situation, in which, wherever they may be held, they must be far distant from some parts of the County over which they preside. Let but the Courts-Baron and the Hundred-Courts be restored, (or at any rate the latter,) and the chasm will then be filled up; the harmony of plan again rendered complete; and Justice may revisit the door of every man, without loss of time, or the accumulation of unnecessary expence.

The Remarks above mentioned are solely confined to the inferior Courts established amongst us for the recovery of Small Debts: and it may not be hazarding too much, to conclude, that, if compared with a *Trial by Jury,* our *Courts of Request,* or of *Conscience,* do not present an equal certainty to the honest Creditor, or the poor Debtor, of obtaining Justice: But, on the contrary, that many of them, from the extent of their jurisdictions, and the description of persons who are too often found to preside at them, are, not unfrequently, the very bane of those principles which they profess to support, and which led originally to their institution.

It now remains to consider of the Coercion directed by the law, to enforce its ordinances for the recovery of small debts; and the consequences produced by such coercion, as it is now exercised.

The plaintiff may have many miles to go, to swear to his debt, and obtain a summons for his debtor; and when this is obtained, it is more than probable that he will have the same journey to repeat on a fruitless errand, because the defendant may not think proper, or be unable to attend. An order will then be issued for a future day, and this too, in like manner as the summons, must be served upon the defendant. At the time appointed the plaintiff is obliged to renew his journey; and if he then establish his debt to the satisfaction of the Commissioners, whether the debtor attend or not, be obtains a warrant of execution against his body. Thus armed with power, the Officer of the Court endeavours to arrest the Defendant; but his natural apprehension of the loss of liberty occasions him to forsake his house, and skulk about as a fugitive vagrant, until at length he is taken by surprize, and carried to prison.

It will not be dealing fairly by this class of Debtors, to attribute their conduct, as here described, solely to dishonest motives. The sentiments of liberality and truth require that great allowance should be made, for their situation in life, and their want of knowing better: and to this, it is conceived, with their incapacity of being absent from their daily labour without injuring their families, may more properly be attributed their neglect of the process of the court, and the seeming apathy with which they view the unfortunate situation to which they are thus reduced.

The Plaintiff will have had some fees to pay at the Court, and to its officer, for the arrest; and, still smarting with the trouble and expence attending the many journeys he has been obliged to undertake, for establishing his demand, he of course is but little disposed to compassionate his debtor; to whom he applies, perhaps most wrongfully, the harsh epithets of Rogue or Swindler, with the charge of incorrigible obstinacy, instead of the truer and more applicable terms of "unfortunate, and ignorantly-confined poor man."

The time of a prisoner's confinement may be temporary, perhaps forty days; a period which, in the ordinary course of life, may not be considered as of long duration. But who, possessing the mild sentiments of humanity, and the invaluable blessings of Christian Knowledge, can contemplate the forlorn and wretched condition of an unhappy prisoner, and thus venture to consider it, as applying to him? If there be such a person, let him but picture to himself a man, torn from his family, which can only live by the efforts of his daily labour; hurried to a prison, without a change of garments, and those which cover him of the most impoverished and thread-bare kind: where no medicine is provided against the hour of sickness, which so frequently attends his altered situation: without a bed to lay himself upon, in the dark and loathsome cell of a damp, unhealthy prison; without the least firing, whatever may be the extreme of cold; without food; nay, without any corporeal provision of the humblest necessary, to support his fainting nature, or the aid of a spiritual comforter, to sustain his failing Christianity in the day of trial! Let him, I say, contemplate a picture of this kind, and it may then with confidence be asserted, that he will be a convert from his opinion, and deem the term of incarceration, even for forty days only, an age of woe! a sufferance, infinitely transcending the cause which occasioned the unhappy situation of the prisoner, even though it were admitted that his debt had been originally contracted by an excess of heedless dissipation. The distracted sufferings of the prisoner's wife, whose affections, though unable to bring him relief, induce her daily to travel from her offspring, amidst cold and wet, over a dreary road, to soothe their father's care;—for the pinching cold and hunger of *the children* need not be noticed here, to heighten this scene of wretchedness, as they must be presumed to receive some parochial relief, to save them from perishing. These are the certain and immediate consequences of a poor man's confinement for a Court-of-Conscience debt!

But, to pursue the inquiry a little farther, (and it will be found that the above is only a faint description of the personal sufferings of the afflicted individual;) Nothing so effectually corrupts the morals, or debases the mind, as *Imprisonment;* and the bad effects produced on society by the consequences of such confinement, remain yet to be disclosed.

Shut up in a *Bridewell* (for of this sort are the prisons to which such debtors afe frequently sent), in common with the most abandoned criminals, amongst whom, as of necessity, he must associate, an intimacy will soon take place: and which, strange as it may appear, (provision being made for the hardened *criminal,* however he may have outraged the laws of God or man, though withheld from the *debtor,)* will be cemented into friendship by the very influence of gratitude, the most honourable tie in nature, in return for the pittance which is spared him, by *a Felons sympathy,* to support his famished frame. A friendship thus formed (and its existence can hardly be questioned or condemned) will soon be extended beyond the donor, to the companions and associates of the criminal, who visit him in his confinement. His mind becomes thus prepared for the commission of those crimes, which *feed his fellow prisoner*: And where is the sanguine friend of subordination, whose zeal will hurry him to conclude, that it will not be continued after the liberation of the Debtor; nor attended with all those fearful consequences, which experience has confirmed as the never-failing retinue of Evil Associations?

The internal *regulation* of Bridewells, with an indiscriminate mixture of prisoners, are so notoriously bad, that the poor man who enters within their walls as an *unfortunate debtor,* must possess more resolution and fortitude than can be expected from persons in his rank of life, if he be not dismissed with those habits of vice and idleness about him, which may soon return him to his dreary abode, as a *formidable felon;* charged with the commission of crimes, that subject man's life to the offended laws of his country!

The object designed by the publication of this Work, does not admit of my entering into an enlarged detail of the irregularities and bad management of the Prisons in question. But, if the Reader's curiosity is excited by the foregoing remarks, (which he will do well to consider, not as an effect of fancy, but as the result of the Author's personal observation;) and if he be desirous of pursuing the subject, he may find it but too faithfully delineated by that admirable writer, *Henry Fielding,* in his " Enquiry into the Causes of the Increase of Robbers," &c. a most authentick and interesting narrative of the hideous scenes of vice which there take place; a detail of the alarming consequences that result to Society, from the permission of such abominable practices against good order and morality; and of which, (subject to little or no modification,) the Author cannot hesitate in opinion, that they actually and fully exist at the present day, in all their horrid enormity.

Having thus, in a hasty sketch, gone through the proposed Inquiry, it remains to be discussed, "whether the permitting the body of a Debtor to be taken in execution, for a Debt not amounting to *Forty Shillings,* will not be found, under the best laws and best arrangement that human wisdom can frame, an impolitick measfore; likely to defeat its own end, and calculated materially to injure the interests tf publick oeconomyr" To form a just opinion upon this head, let the price be considered, which is paid to a labouring man for his hire, at the lowest possible rate by which the value of his time can be estimated. The produce of his labour might, indeed, be taken as a truer criterion; but, as this would lead to calculations not so readily elucidated, and be open to some cavils from inventive acuteness, the former is preferred, and made the basis of the following remarks; which are submitted by the Writer, with an earnest hope that they may excite the attention of some more efficient and able pen, in justice to the important subject.

A labouring husbandman, for instance, may be considered to receive one shilling and sixpence *per* day, or nine shillings *per* week, for his hire. Now this, for the space of forty days,— the supposed term of his confinement, excluding the intervenient Sundays,— will amount to the sum of two pounds eleven shillings; and, considering his debt to be one guinea, will be more than double its amount. On the most moderate computation, therefore, the loss sustained by the publick will be found to exceed twice the amount of the sum sought to be recovered by the individual Creditor.

It may be advanced, that if you take away the Debtor's liability in his *person* for such debts, the poor man will get no credit; and that this circumstance will subject him to greater inconveniences than those he sustains under the law, in its present form.

The first part of this apprehension, it is admitted, might in some cases take place; but that it would produce inconveniences greater, or even equal to the consequences of imprisonment, is most earnestly denied.

The loss of credit, if it should happen, would produce one of these two effects: either that a labouring man should live within his means, or apply to his parish, in the first instance, for parochial relief. And, surely, should the latter event occur, it will be found materially in favour of the parish, (upon a decent representation being made out, entitling the applicant to relief,) that they should contribute something, in aid of his labour, for the support of himself and family; rather than be obliged wholly to maintain the family during the confinement of the father, with the certainty of his returning to his hamlet a disgraced man, "a man forbid!" as our great Poet phrases it; a man, deprived of his former habits of industry, and fitted only to rank with the idle poor, than whom there cannot be greater pests to Society. But, while the attention is engaged about confining the *Persons* of Debtors, is it to be supposed that an execution against their *Goods* is a thing without influence? Is there not a commendable pride, amongst the humblest cottagers and occupiers of rooms, to have their little places set out with domestick conveniences, equal if not superior to their neighbours? Will not the preservation of these objects of their regard from the execution of the Law, sufficiently stimulate them to pay their debts? Nay, even should this not be the case, will not the depriving them of their Goods be of *less injury to the Country,* than the confinement of their Persons? And, supposing they have no effects, what good can result from their imprisonment, when they avowedly have not the means to pay their debts?

Let this power of the Law be done away: let it be concluded that thus they will obtain no credit; and it will then be seen, that they must work, or seek parochial relief: and what then will be the next result? If they apply for the latter improperly, they may be sent to prison, not as *debtors,* but as *vagrants;* and, instead of idleness and *no allowance,* (the lot of a debtor, subjected to the discipline of a prison,) they must be kept to hard labour, and fed on the poor, yet life-supporting food of a place of confinement. It seems paradoxical, to treat of the relative duties we owe to society, and at the same time admit a creditor's right to destroy the exercise of those duties, by shutting up his debtor in prison for a sum, perhaps of *One Shilling* only, or even possibly of *Four Pence!* The impolicy of the measure is felt, in the loss to the publick of the debtor's services; in his discharge from prison a worse member of society than he went in; and in the loss to his creditor of the debt: So that it seems to possess no one obvious or incidental good; and the only end at all answerable by it, will be found in the gratification of one of the worst passions of our nature;—the vindictive resentment of a creditor!

Whilst the Law allows a confinement of the *person* for the debts here spoken of, it is submitted, as a desirable regulation, First, that all Publicans' scores should be precluded from recovery; and, Secondly, that a limitation of time, to the period of one year, should be fixed, for the recovery of all debts under the amount of Forty Shillings. These two regulations alone, it is conceived, would

produce much good, and materially diminish the number of imprisonments for Small Debts.

But, the restoring of *Courts Baron,* The *Hundred Courts,* and The *County Courts* would, it is believed, be productive of so many commercial advantages, that the arrest of the debtor's *Person* might very safely be laid aside, (without the smallest hazard of injury to his Creditor,) to the benefit of the Country at 'large; the lessening of the Poors' Rates in particular districts; and the great relief of a class, the most laborious and useful in the community.

The truth, and the application of the Observations which have here been made, roust be known to many persons: But, to that honourable and most 'respectable class of Gentlemen, who, with such distinguished credit to themselves, and satisfaction to the Country, discharge the important duties of Magistracy, they must be particularly known: And it is, therefore, with the most profound respect that they are more immediately addressed to *them;* in the earnest hope that some amongst them will deem the subject deserving of their attention, and as such, exert the weight of their talents and influence to call it to the consideration of Parliament, as a measure of internal regulation, that highly merits their deliberative wisdom; and from which abundant benefit will be derived to the Country, and to those humble individuals, who stand so much in need of every indulgent exertion for their relief.

Of the ruinous effects of the system here decried, enough is said to convince the greatest sceptic, that its tendency has been to degrade the human character; to corrupt and vitiate the minds of the labouring people; and thus to increase and establish a general profligacy of manners.

OBSERVATIONS ON CRIMES AND PUNISHMENTS.

When the mind contemplates the vast variety of offences by the Laws of England made punishable with death, surprize must naturally follow the reflection, mingled with sympathy and regret at the degraded state of society; but when, to this dark series of crimes, is added the almost incalculable number of offences, serving as it were like feeders to a reservoir, which are made punishable by transportation, fine, and imprisonment, how greatly will that surprize be increased, and the mind of the philanthropist be stimulated to inquire into the cause of this increasing load of human misery; forming so complex and numerous a catalogue, that an eminent and learned barrister deemed the making a list of them a task of almost impracticable difficulty; but which, (from the work of a late worthy magistrate, who long discharged the arduous duties of the Bench at a public office, with distinguished credit to himself, and service to the community,) we may conclude not to be of less enormous magnitude, than six thousand seven hundred and eighty-nine; for to this extent has the author observed upon the penal statutes, under numbered heads. And although more than one number may, and in fact does, in many cases, relate to the same offence, yet new crimes have arisen and been made punishable since the appearance of that publication. Offences at the Common Law, and declared as such by local and private acts of parliament, did not fall within the scope of the work; but will, it is expected, be found to supply sufficient substitutes for all those crimes, which are referred to under more heads than one; sufficient, at least, to maintain the original number, as so many distinct heads of Crimes and Punishments.

It would be at the same time both instructive and interesting, if we could look back into the early ages of society, and trace with any tolerable degree of correctness, the history and progress of crimes and punishments. But, unfortunately, the materials for such a view of the subject are scanty, and not easily attainable: Sir William Addington's " Abridgement of the Penal Statutes." fbr, upon inquiry, the page of history will be found principally occupied with matters of state, and historians busy in recording the actions of princes and their nobles. Thus, in handing down to posterity the wars, negotiations, and treaties of empires, they have suffered the moral characters of the people, and the natural history of countries (subjects infinitely more interesting to the general welfare of mankind), to pass unnoticed, and be lost in the obscurity of time.

The English Statute-Book, however, as relating to this country, and during the age it embraces, may be considered to supply, in some degree, the defect of history; and be referred to as a standard, from which conclusions on the moral state of the people, at different periods, may, with tolerable safety, be drawn. Although in a work of this nature it cannot be expected that every statute inflicting the pain of death, or subordinate punishment, should be expressly noticed; yet a reference to a few of them, it is conceived, will not only render the subject more familiar to such persons as are not accustomed to think upon it; but at the same time throw somegeneral and useful light upon the inquiry. And truly grateful will it prove to the feelings of the Author, if at any future time, some able pen, desirous of engaging in the cause of humanity, and with leisure and ability to do justice to the work, should be engaged in a general revision of the English Statute-Book, as regarding crimes and punishments, and indulge the publick with his remarks.

Before we enter on the proposed ref-

The Rev. *Daniel Williams* of Caermarthen was confined at the Suit of one *Broker Cvok,* 21st July 1807, for a Debt of *ll.* 18. *6d.* The Costs amounted to *6s. bd.* This Gentleman paid into Court *11. 10s.* He then went into Wales; and upon his return was arrested for the remaining *lis.* lid. on the 5th of May 1809, and confined twenty days in the Borough Compter.—*John Bird,* at the Suit of *Lawrence Newman,* a Publican, for a Debt of *Four pence,* and Costs *7s. Gd.,* had a Warrant of Execution granted against him, dated 9th July 1808, and was committed to Giltspur Street Compter, 14th May 1310, nearly two years after. For the latter of these Cases, see my Statement in page 232.

erence to the Statute-Book, it will not be amiss if we first consider, What is understood by the Common Law of England, or, at least, so far as it regards our subject.

The unwritten or common Law, as it now stands, may be considered as a remnant of the jurisprudence of our Saxon Ancestors; who, ignorant of the art of communicating ideas by characters, were of necessity obliged to commit to memory their Laws, as well as the portion of learning they had acquired, and by the force of tradition to hand them down to posterity. And although our haughty Conquerors (proud of a knowledge they scarcely possessed, as being confined to their priests at an early period after the Conquest), adopted the written or Statute Law for the government of the people; yet it is by no means a clear deduction, that in those early times it was of any advantage to the nation: for, so long did the bulk of the people continue in a state of ignorance, as to reading and writing, that even at so late a period in our own history as the year 1547, considerably short of three centuries ago, an act of parliament was passed , to give the benefit of clergy to *peers of the realm,* and to save them from the ignominy of being burnt in the hand, notwithstanding they were *unable to read.* And these written laws not always carrying with them that perfection of reason, which is considered one of the attributes of the Common law, became as it were a drag-net to catch the people in j. for l.Edw. VI. Cap. 12.
e
the justness of the apophthegm was lost, and the multitude were unable to read the written substitute. And it must be presumed, that a government ruling a nation by oral laws, will be more particular in promulgating its decrees by oral proclamations to the people, than the government which relies on its *lex scripta,* and the legal maxim that " Ignorance is no excuse."

In these times, when reading and writing are so generally understood, and practised by all classes of the people, the observations here made lose much of their force; but it is conceived they will serve to elucidate some remarks that may arise in the progress of the inquiry.

Notwithstanding what has been here said, the Common Law, as it now stands, cannot be considered as being purely oral, or traditional; for it may now be found in our ancient Law-Books, in our reporters, and in our records of judicial proceedings.

A short account of the origin of what is termed "Benefit of Clergy," and a few strictures on the absurd continuation of it to this day, when scarce a remnant of the principle remains, of describing offences of the greatest magnitude as felonies with, or without benefit of clergy, it is expected will not be uninteresting to some persons, whom humanity may incite to the perusal of a work like the present; whose author has no other aim in view than the hope of contributing his feeble efforts to rescue such of his fellow-creatures as unfortunately fall into the way of temptation from greater evil; to reclaim such as do fall, and generally to ameliorate the lowest condition of human wretchedness: and the informed reader, and those who are better acquainted with the subject than the author himself, will, it is hoped, in the gentleness of their natures, excuse this digression: a digression, into which he is led from the general ignorance he has found to prevail through large classes of the people; and even in those circles of society, where better information might be expected to exist, of the important distinction in the natures and consequences of crimes so designated by the legislature.

The Saxon Kings of England, remarkable for their devotedness and submission to the see of Rome, were ready on all occasions to enlarge the privileges, and augment the revenues of the church; but, when the Norman race ascended the throne, the affairs of the church assumed a new aspect. Accustomed to arbitrary sway, these hardy chieftains were not disposed to possess a divided power; and they equally struggled for absolute authority over both the church and the people.

William the Conqueror carried his endeavours so far, that he openly denied doing homage to the pope, seized on the consecrated vessels of the church, and interdicted the British clergy from receiving orders without his permission.

The reigns of William Rufus, and of Henry the First, were not less remarkable than the Conqueror's, for the steady opposition of those princes to the influence of the see of Rome; nor was the policy of that church less conspicuous for the wisdom, with which she gave way to the resolute steadiness of these determined Kings, rather than, by fruitless struggles, afford them a pretence for shaking off the small influence she was allowed to retain; and which afterwards so completely extended itself, as in future reigns to effect the entire subjugation of the kingdom.

The publick troubles during the reign of Stephen, and the obligations he owed to the church, for seating him on the throne, which he had seized against the rightful heir of his uncle, fitted this period for the policy of the see of Rome to act upon: and although we find him, within a few months after he ascended the throne, violating his coronation oath, by seizing upon the revenues of the archbishop of Canterbury, and acting in other respects like his Norman predecessors; yet he suffered the court of Rome to appoint a legate to his kingdom; and thus laid the foundation of afterwards humbling the English bishops, and other ecclesiastics, as well as the monarchs of the empire at large .

The influence of the Church of England, during the four succeeding reigns, was gradually on the increase, and at times most prodigiously advanced; though subject to those occasional fluctuations, which naturally resulted from the turbulence of the times, and the fickle disposition of the reigning monarch; who, too frequently regardless of every solemn pledge, however formally made, governed the country according to existing circumstances, and as opportunities arose favourable to the indulgence of his appetites, or calculated to subserve the capricious pursuits of his mind. Thus we find, in the Great Charter, or what is more emphatically termed "the Charter of Liberties," obtained from king John by his hardy barons, on that memorable plain called Runnimead, and which retains its name to this day, the first article is, "That the Church of England shall be free, and enjoy her whole rights and liberties inviolable:" But what those rights and those liberties were, we are not informed; the holy fathers most probably considering it more for the advantage of the church to rest themselves on a reference to the unwritten maxims and customs of their Saxon ancestors, than to have them defined by any written law, even though it should be framed under circumstances most favourable to their own desires.

The primitive doctrine, "that the Church of Christ should be treated with the tenderness of an infant, and have all the privileges of a person under age," by a confounding of times was readily extended to the clergy, in their individual characters; and they personally claimed the exemptions and indulgences of a figurative expression, originally used to describe the perfect state of the infant church, in its Alberic was the Pope's Legate. Rapin says, " that the troubles in Stephen's reign *exalted the Mitre* above the *Crown;* and instances also the penance of Henry II. and the excommunication of the Primate of York, and Bishops of London, Durham, and Exeter.

collective character, *u* without spot or wrinkle ." The affectionate regard that subsisted between the early Saxon Christians and their teachers, and the devout and submissive character of these people in matters of religion, induced them not to be over tenacious, in regard to the privileges they allowed to persons so much within their affections; and who taught a doctrine, by which they were to be considered as the peculiar lot and inheritance of God, and as separated from the noise and bustle of the world, that they might possess leisure to spend their time in meditation and prayer. Hence, viewing their church in the favourable light of persons neither addicted, nor scarcely liable to the temptation of immoralities, they readily suffered them to declare themselves independent of the civil power: and whenever it so happened, that the frailties of human nature prevailed against these presumptions, the guilty churchman was handed over to the ordinary, to be dealt with according to the rules of the Canon Law.

The privileges thus acquired by the Clergy from the pious Saxons, were frequently trampled upon by the Norman princes, during the long continued struggles for absolute sway, which subsisted between them and the church of Rome. This may be gathered from the passage already noticed in the Great Charter; but which, it seems, did not, as must have been expected, secure them from the hand of the Civil Power: For, in the subsequent reign of Edward the First, anno 1275, we find it declared by the Statute of Westminster, "That a clerk taken for guilty of felony shall be delivered to his ordinary, according to the privilege of the holy church, after the custom aforetime used;" or, in other words, That the Civil power should not proceed to convict a clerk in holy orders.

One of the most distinguished features of the Saxon criminal law, which prevailed in England before the Conquest, was its mildness, the infrequency of capital punishment, and the allowance for notorious offenders to commute even that punishment for a fine; But it is from the time of the Norman Conquest, we are to trace the origin and progress of that extreme severity, which now so materially disfigures the criminal code of England: for, notwithstanding the conquest of William has been treated as a conquest or overthrow of a monarch, who had usurped the throne, and not of the people, yet it was such a conquest of power, that the people were in no condition to resist. And as the Conqueror, on all occasions, endeavoured to introduce a community of language between his newly-acquired and his Norman subjects, by ordering schools to be established throughout the kingdom, for teaching, and bringing the *language* of the latter people into general use, and by causing the pleadings in the courts of judicature to be carried on in the same language; it may, with the aid of the many authorities on that head, be naturally.concluded, that the same motives of policy and partiality, which induced the King See Epistle to Ephesians, chap. v. ver. *17* to endeavour at establishing his native tongue, extended also their influence to occasion his introduction of the *Laws of Normandy;*— such, in particular, as seemed best calculated to support his newly-acquired power, or to contribute to his favourite diversion of hunting; no punishment or privation being deemed too severe, for the subject who infringed on either. Hence we find , that he put great numbers of his English Subjects to death; caused the eyes of many others to be put out, or their hands and feet to be cut off, and condemned abundance of them to perpetual imprisonment, for very small offences. We also learn that he caused another violent infringement of the English Constitution, bv dispeopling whole Countries-f-, for the purpose of his Royal diversion of the Chase; and subjecting both those Districts, and all the ancient forests of the kingdom, to the unreasonable severities of the " Forest Laws," imported from the Continent.

"From this Root," as a learned and elegant Commentator *%* expresses himself, "although the Forest Laws have been mitigated, and are almost grown obsolete, has sprung a bastard Slip, known by the name of the *Game Law,* now arrived to, and wantoning in its highest vigour."

With the Norman Conquest, the more homely, but more intelligible and less cruel Maxims of distributive Justice amongst the Saxons, gave way to the deeper chicanery of Norman Jurisprudence. That Monarch, who could introduce a Trial by Combat, for the decision of Civil and Criminal Questions of fact, was not likely to be scrupulous about inflicting death, or other punishment, disproportioned to the nature of the Crime committed. And yet, notwithstanding its general application in the present day, it was not until the reign of Henry the First, who succeeded his brother Rums, that the crime of Theft was made punishable as a capital offence §.

The small portion of Learning which existed in that Age of Ignorance and Superstition, was confined to the Clergy, and to those who were designed for Holy Orders; for scarcely to any others were the arts of reading or writing known. The Benefit of Clergy, which perhaps originated in the assumed infallibility of Churchmen, as being members of an infallible church, and which, under the mild administration of the Saxons, was little more than a mark of distinction; yet, when the Normans introduced their Forest Laws, with new-fangled Cruelties as punishments, was no longer considered as a mere privilege of distinction; but it became a matter of solid Advantage to the Clergy, to be entitled to claim their exemption from liability to the secular power; or otherwise, to be delivered over to their Ordinary, when accused of a Crime.

Rapin, vol. I. p. 181. t Blackstone'j Commentaries, vol. IV. p. 415. Ibid. p. 415.

§ Ibid. p. 420.

Cruelty in Punishments universally defeats its own end, and never fails-to raise a general desire of disappointing its operations. Even a sanguinary Monarch, who introduces a cruel law, must, at the last moment, feel a natural repugnance to its execution; and a readiness to catch at any excuse, under which mercy may be extended to the delinquent, without forfeiting his own consistency.

The Privilege or Benefit of Clergy was, in'its Origin, confined to the Members of the Church; and as Learning was peculiarly their own, so the being able to read was considered and taken as Evidence of the party accused being a Clergyman, op, as it was then termed, a Clerk: And although,, in the course of time, other persons, neither in the Church, nor designed for Holy Orders, became capable of reading, the natural reluctance against giving effect to cruel punishments suffered the same Evidence to prevail. If the party accused were but found able to read, he was allowed the Benefit of Clergy, and delivered over to the Ordinary. Thus originated that distinction, which, notwithstanding its obsoleteness, and its having been limited, and even abolished, under modern Acts of Parliament, as to its original operation, is still allowed to disfigure the Criminal Law of England, by the division of Felony, under the heads of " *Felony with,*" or " *Felony without the Benefit of Clergy:*" Terms, not understood by one tenth part of the people, who may forfeit their lives under the distinction.

A modern learned Writer, (not more distinguishable for his learning than his humanity; and to whom the publick are largely indebted for his late arduous exertions, to produce reform in part of the Criminal Law, although unattended with the success they merited,) describes the astonishment which was expressed in the language, and painted in the countenance of a wretch, who was convicted of stealing his master's wine, at finding that the Sentence pronounced upon him was that of Death; or, to use the language of Paley, "at finding himself inextricably entangled in the fatal net." Fatal, indeed, it was to him! for the Judge left him for Execution. Here is an instance of the ruinous effect of Ignorance, in a man, who, in all probability, would not have committed the Offence for which he suffered, if he had known the awful punishment that awaited his Crime. He might have heard of *Felony;* but the word, in its abstract meaning, implies nothing like loss of Life: and he probably knew of some amongst his associates, who had been convicted of felony, and only suffered transportation, or some less punishment; and most likely the distinction of *Benefit of Clergy* was wholly unknown to him.

In a late publication we are told, That a memorial, addressed to the Sheriff of Middlesex from the Prisoners in Newgate, signed by 152 of the Criminals, had 25 names written in a fair hand; 26 in a bad and partly-illegible hand; and that the Sir Samuel RomUly, on Criminal Law, p. 44.

remaining 101 were signed with a cross. On another occasion it appeared that but few of the prisoners could read with facility; that more than half of them could not read at all; and that a large majority were totally unacquainted with the nature, object, and end of Religion itself. Happy, indeed, was it for this mass of ignorance, that the humane Act of the 5th of Queen Anne existed as Law; by which it is provided, "That a Convicted Felon shall not be required to read, but only be punished as a *Clerk Convict,* the same as if he had read as a Clerk;" or otherwise, they would have found themselves entangled in Dr. Paley's inextricable net, and have been hurried into the presence of their Maker, to seek that mercy for their ignorance of the Divine Law, which was denied them on Earth by their persecuting brethren.

The above remarks may by some persons be considered as a cavil about words: but let them who entertain such an opinion consider, what is the sad effect of those words; and whether it is within the reach of human language, with the fairest intentions, to describe, in terms too distinct, and clear, and void of all possibility of misapprehension, the awful consequence of being convicted of Felony, without Benefit of Clergy: and then, let them determine, whether the words " Felony, without Benefit of Clergy," are best calculated to convey their intended meaning to an unlettered Offender.

It is foreign to our purpose, to institute a particular inquiry into the motives that first induced man to quit his state of nature, and become a social animal. It may be sufficient, if we consider him in his gregarious character, as we now find him; and generally conclude, that it was the attraction of the sexes, the helpless state of infancy, mutual wants, and mutual preservation, but, above all, the Law of God imprinted on his breast, which placed him there.

What portion of his natural rights he surrendered, in exchange for the protection of society, or what in particular he retained, it will be equally unnecessary for us to inquire into; as we shall prefer drawing our conclusions from the known axiom, that "Law is the absolute perfection of Reason; and that nothing which is contrary to Reason can be consonant to Law." But, in regard to the punishment of Death, it may deserve to be remarked, that man, not having the right to take away his own life, could not by possibility have surrendered that right to others; and that those who support the infliction of capital punishments, must seek the right from some other authority than a supposed surrender of *Man* on his becoming a *Member of Society*. "And in making the Inquiry it will be well, (as a humane and elegant writer on the Penal Law expresses himself,) for lawgivers to remember, that they are, virtually, and in effect, the executioners of every fellow Citizen, who suffers death in consequence of any penal statute." Principles of Penal Law, p. 28.

Happy indeed must we picture that State of Society, in which the passions of man occasion no disorder, nor the clashings of private interest any difference of opinion, or disturbance of the public weal. But alas! such a view of mankind must be purely imaginary; for the practical experience of life, and the history of all ages, deny the possible existence of such a state of society. They prove the melancholy contrast; and that, while the passions of individuals range without controul, tlie private interests of all will too frequently be suffered to obscure every idea of natural Justice. Hence, Laws must be made, to restrain the one, and regulate the other; or the end of society will be destroyed: For infinitely better would it be, for a man to remain in a state of Nature, and inhabit the desert, with all his wants and all his fears upon his head, than to be the member of a Society, in which the Laws afford him no protection.

Laws, thus considered, appear to be the legitimate offspring of necessity; and so far as they are confined within the principle of being necessary for preserving the existence of the State, they certainly fall within the natural and implied compact, (whatever it may be called or considered), under which Society was first formed. But, when the Laws exceed this bound, the right of making them becomes more doubtful; and the doubt encreases in the same proportion, as the urgency of the necessity decreases.

The prevention of crimes, then, appears to be the only true object of human punishments. This, it is believed, may be effected by the adoption of laws, calculated by their mildness, and certainty of execution, to produce a reform in the habits of the Culprit, and fit him again for the duties of Society: And this should at all times be attempted, as deserving the highest consideration of the Legislature, by the infliction of Fines, Corporal Inflictions, the Pillory, or other public mark of ignominy, temporary imprisonment, or transportation; instead of those cruel and sanguinary laws, which, as long and sad experience has taught us, defeat their own ends, and stand without even the excuse of necessity for their continuance, or any apology for their original adoption; unless it can be found in their hasty creation. But this is an excuse which a Legislator, professing to be the friend of mankind, would scarcely be pleased to accept. There may, however, be crimes, of a deeper magnitude than those which the preceding punishments are calculated to prevent, such as offences which are immediately destructive of the existence of Society. These it may be necessary to put it out of the power of the delinquent to repeat; and an end so important may be effected, either by perpetual imprisonment or transportation for life. In some extreme cases, the ultimate punishment of death may perhaps be resorted to; but this, like sacred ground, should only be converted to the ordinary purposes of Man, under circumstances of the greatest possible urgency..

How far the British Legislature has, for a succession of ages, been governed by these principles in its Law-giving capacity, will be best discovered by the proposed reference to the Statute-Book; preparatory to which it may be proper to remark, that the Great Charter, and the Charter of Forests, are not to be read as original Laws, or as containing all the then existing Laws of England: But the first rather as a declaration of the ancient Rights of the Subject, which had been infringed upon by the Norman Monarchs; and the latter as a reform of the excesses and encroach ments which had been made on the milder laws of Saxon government, in respect to the Royal Forests.

In the Great Charter it is provided and declared, That no Man shall be amerced for a small fault, but *after the manner of the fault;* and for a great fault, *after the-greatness thereof;* thus equalizing and adapting the punishment to the magnitude or smallness of the Crime: principles of justice, upon which the Saxon Laws were founded, and which have preserved their character through all ages; but which, ill suiting the turbulent and haughty spirit of the imperious Normans were trampled upon in their excess of pride; and Cruelty, in all its wantonness of power, created inventive punishments for small offences, disgraceful to Barbarians, and shocking to humanity. This is manifested by the 10th Chapter of the Charter of Forests, declaring That " no man should suffer castration, loss of eyes, or cutting off his hands or feet, for destroying or disturbing any fowl of the air, or any beast of the field, reserved for the royal amusement of the Sovereign."

Surely, in the punishments here meant to be restrained, there was no Analogy between the smallness of the offence, and the penalty to be inflicted. It must have been the arbitrary will of man, acted upon by a heated imagination, that could alone have given them birth. And yet, horrid as they are in their natures, it must not be supposed that they were unfrequently inflicted; for, had that been the fact, the declaration of equality of punishments to the extent of crimes, contained in the Great Charter, might have satisfied a single Case, and operated as a restraint upon the cruelty of the Laws in future. But the state of Society, at that period of the History of the Kingdom, naturally made men eager in the pursuits of the Chase, from the absence of many employments of industry, which have since presented themselves; and the frequency of the crime, and consequent punishment, notwithstanding its enormity, influenced the Baronage; who, being able to demand these declarations of the rights of the people from their Royal Master, were but little disposed to leave any point open to the chicane and subtile refinements of the Norman Lawyers.

In the reign of Edward I. the Benefit of Clergy originally appears upon the Statute-Book; but it was in the succeeding reign of Edward II. that it became more fully provided for, and a certain history was given of that seeming absurdity, f which has been so long suffered to disfigure the criminal laws of England, by the distinction of felony with, or without Benefit of Clergy.

The 4th of Edward the Third provides, That " Sheriffs and Gaolers shall receive, and safely keep in prison, thieves and felons, without taking any thing for their receipt." Where, then, is the origin of *Gaol fees* to be found? Before this earlv reign they may be supposed to have existed in abuse, and this statute made to correct and restrain their being taken in future: and yet, to this day, they are permitted to exist, as will hereafter be justly observed upon.

The Reign of Edward III. is also remarkable for the Statute of Treasons, which is valuable to the Subject, not only as defining what shall be deemed Treason in future; but for the restraint it puts upon constructive Treasons, by leaving it to the King and his Parliament to declare, what other cases, not therein specified, ought to be adjudged Treason, or other felony: and also, for its declaring certain offences not to be Treason, but only felony, or trespass, according to the laws of the Land, of old time used, and as the case required.

With these Statutes before us, and in the recollection of the amiable and manly virtues of the Prince under whose reign they passed, it will be scarcely possible to refer to the Statute in the 25th year of his reign, (inflicting the punishment of loss of life and limb, with forfeiture of estate and effects, for engrossing or forestalling Gascony Wine,) without lamenting the imbecillity of our nature, and remarking on the great caution which men should use, to divest themselves of their prejudices and their appetites, when they assume the characters of Legislators: or otherwise they will for ever incur the hazard of assigning excessive and unjust penalties to the commission of small and unequal faults, in which their passions or interests may be engaged.

In this Law we find the Great Charter of the Land expressly violated; all the principles of Humanity and Justice, and the bond by which man is united to society most wantonly outraged, for the riot of a Feast! and yet, in that early age, as in the still earlier time of Richard the First, the effect of sanguinary laws defeating their own end was discovered, and acknowledged, by a repeal of the horrid amputations inflicted on transgressors against the Forest Laws, (which had been then so recently grafted on English jurisprudence), by reason of their extreme severity; even in that age of rudeness, preventing prosecutions against the offenders: whilst in the 37th of Edward theThird, the cruel and impolitic law to prevent the engrossing and forestalling of Wine, was for the same reason repealed, and more equal and natural restraints were imposed on the offence. This milder law may be considered to have proved itself the better remedy, from its being suffered to continue through a long succession of years, until grown obsolete by a change of circumstances.

The like remarks will equally apply to another statute of this reign (Edw. IIL) making the transportation of wool out of the kingdom a capital offence; which wa afterwards repealed, as to the loss of life and member: And fortunate was it for the people of that day, that so long and venerable a reign afforded sufficient opportunities to determine by experience, (the best touchstone by which to evince the wisdom or folly of all human actions,) whether sanguinary or milder Laws were most clearly calculated to restrain the commission of offences.

In the reign of Henry the Fourth, it was forbidden to use "the Craft of multiplication of Gold or Silver," under the pains of felony; and in the third year of the succeeding King's Reign, it was declared Treason, to clip, wash, or file the Money of the Land; both of them severities of punishment, that would require considerable ingenuity to justify their application; whilst the long continuance of the latter offence proves, by the practical experience of ages, that the severest laws in the power of man to inflict, are not effectual remedies against the perpetration of Crimes.:

In a subsequent reign, that of Henry VIII. remarkable for the Vices of the Prince, (who, by an elegant and not uncourtly Historian is described as violent, cruel, profuse, rapacious, unjust, obstinate, arrogant, bigotted, presumptive and capricious, a catalogue of crimes scarcely to be found in the same person,) and for the almost incredible number of 72,000 persons, who are stated to have died by the hands of the executioner; we shall not be surprized to find the Benefit of Clergy, that screen to the lettered man, taken away, by one general act: and then, as it were with a drag-net, drawing in and subjecting a class of persons to the ultimate punishment of death, who were not in the contemplation of the Law-makers, when the laws themselves were framed. This reign is also remarkable for a law, wantoning in cruelty, which declares That wilful poisoning shall be adjudged High Treason, "and the perpetrator be boiled to death:" a punishment, that bespeaks as much ferocity in the Law-maker, as wickedness in the offender.

In this reign Servants, guilty of embezzling their Master's goods to the value of *40s.* were deprived of the privilege of Clergy and Sanctuary, and thereby subjected, without distinction, to the pains of death: surely, a punishment highly disproportioned to the comparative smallness of the offence; and such a one as naturally leads the mind to inquire, in what possible view of just or political Legislation, the mere act of embezzlement to the value of 40. unaccompanied with other circumstances of aggravation, can be considered as a crime of magnitude sufficient to merit the infliction of death. But, a Monarch, who was himself the slave of passions, with Parliaments abject in submission to his will, was not likely to make Justice in Mercy the basis of his laws. From such reigns we can only expect to find those monstrous inconsistencies, described by Hume in the following manner. "By one Statute, for instance, it was declared Treason, to assert the validity of Hume's History of England, vol. IV. pp, 2GG, 275.

the King's marriage either with Catherine of Arragon, or Anne Boleyn. By another, it was Treason to say any thing to the disparagement or slander of the Princesses Mary and Elizabeth, (the Issue of those Queens;) and to call them spurious, would no doubt have been construed to their slander. Nor would even a profound silence, with regard to these delicate points, be able to save a person from such penalties: for, by the former statute, whoever refused to answer upon Oath to any point contained in that Act, was subjected to the pains of Treason. The King, therefore, needed only propose to any one a question, with regard to the legality.of either of his first marriages: If the person were silent, he was a Traitor by Law; if he answered, either in the negative or the affirmative, he was no less a Traitor."

This Reign, towards its close, affords also another striking instance of the little attention which was at that time paid to the inflicting of punishments, *after the manner of the fault,* in an Act, which makes it felony to take the Eggs of a Falcon, Goshawk, or Lanard, or the Birds out of their nests. Is it possible that the Egg of a Bird can be worth the life of a Man? and yet the Legislature of that day must have so considered it.

It has already been noticed, that in the reign of Henry the Eighth, the Benefit of Clergy was wholly taken away, without distinction of persons. But this, in the following Reign, was qualified, in favour of Peers of the Realm; the first of Edward the Sixth, anno 1547, granting the Benefit of Clergy to such Peers as had place and voice in parliament, although they should be unable to read: a Statute, that distinctly marks the state of learning in those days; and presents an apology in the ignorance of the people, which better times are not entitled to. Robbing in any dwelling-house, the owner being therein, and whether waking or sleeping, by an Act in the same reign, forfeits the Benefit of Clergy.

The reign of queen Elizabeth, glorious in many respects, is greatly chequered by a variety of Laws, which appear to have passed upon the spur and temper of the moment; and to proceed on the abominable principle, that it is better to extirpate offenders, than to be at the trouble of attempting their reformation: for how, otherwise, could it be made felony, and subject to the pains of death, for persons, calling themselves *Egyptians,* to remain one month in the realm?

By the 8th of Elizabeth, Cap. 3. persons sending live rams, sheep, or lambs, on shipboard, to be carried out of the kingdom, are, for the first offence, to forfeit all their goods for ever; to suffer imprisonment for one year; and at the year's end, in some open market-town, in the fulness the market, on the market-day, to have their left-hand cut off, and nailed up in the market-place; and for repeating the offence, to be adjudged felons, and suffer death. What a detestable ingenuity of cruelty is displayed in this statute! and surely, for a comparative and trifling offence; and that without any reserve, in favour of vessels going to sea on long voyages! The next Act following the above, and passed by the same Legislature, is introduced under a formal preamble, that would equally suit a similar act, if introduced in the present day; while, by the undiminished prevalence of the crime, it is clearly shewn, that severity of laws doth not prevent the crimes they are avowedly intended to restrain. The preamble to the Act recites, "That cut-purses, or pick-purses, confederated together, making as it were a brotherhood, or fraternity, of an art or mystery to live idly, by secret spoil; and, at sermons and preachings of the word of God, and in times of service and common prayer, in churches, chapels, closets, and oratories, and in the prince's palace, house and presence, and at courts of justice, and in fairs, markets, and other assemblies of the people, and at the time of execution of persons attainted of murder, felony, or other criminal cause, ordained chiefly for terror and example of evil-doers, &c." The Act then declares, That " persons feloniously taking money, goods, or chattels, from the person of any other, privily, without his knowledge, shall lose the benefit of their clergy; and suffer death, as if they were no clerks." There is a studied formality in the recital of this act, which leads to the opinion, that the very legislators who passed it, were conscious at the time of its want of humanity and justice.

The same spirit of cruelty and deadness of feeling prevailed throughout the whole reign of Elizabeth; for, so late as in her 39th year, we find persons feloniously taking to the value of five shillings, in any dwelling-house, or outhouse belonging to the same, although no person should be therein, are declared to lose their Benefit of Clergy. And thus, while in her father's time the life of a man was not considered equal to a hawk's egg, the trifling sum of five shillings, in the reign of the daughter, was supposed to be of still greater consideration.

In the third year of the reign of William and Mary, the Benefit of Clergy was taken away from persons robbing any other; or feloniously taking any goods or chattels in a dwelling-house, the owner or other person being therein, and put in fear; or robbing, or aiding or assisting to rob, any dwelling-house in the day-time, any person being therein; or breaking any dwelling-house, shop, or warehouse used therewith, in the day-time, and feloniously taking money or goods, to the value of five shillings, although no person should be therein. Here is a catalogue of offences, which upon the first reading are not very intelligible; and, to the discredit of English Jurisprudence, the object and operation of this act will be better understood from the judicial determinations upon it, than from the language it adopts. There is, however, one controuling feature in it, which neither the learning nor.humanity of the judges who are called upon to decide on it can effectually remove, whatever latitude they may recommend our juries to use, in the valuation of stolen property; namely, that the life of man is again put into such a scale of estimation, as not to exceed the value of five shillings.

Before this time, women-felons suffered death, whilst men were allowed Benefit of Clergy for the like offences: so miserably defective was the criminal law as to just principles of legislation.

Benefit of Clergy is by the 10th and 11th William III. cap. 23. taken away from persons privately stealing, by night or day, in any shop, warehouse, coachhouse, or stable, to the value of five shillings; although such places be not broke open, and whether the owner, or other person, be or be not therein. Is it possible, that a human being can be found, to offer any thing in justification of such a law? Its sanguinary effects are too manifest to require a remark: every line is an acme" of cruelty, and every word written in letters of blood: and yet, the subject was brought before the consideration of Parliament, by a member eminently distinguished for his humanity and splendid abilities; and, after deliberate consideration, is allowed to continue, as the law of the land.

We come now to a period, than which no time has afforded men more eminent for wisdom and abilities, living under one of the best and most unblemished sovereigns that ever sat upon the throne of England: But, unfortunately, a deliberate revisal of objects is not the general character of persons at the height of power; and this evil we find exemplified by a Statute, in the 12th of queen Anne, subjecting persons stealing to the value of forty shillings, in any dwelling-house, or out-house, although not broke open, and whether inhabited or not, to the penalty of death; and extending the like punishment to certain explained doubts, whether the entering into the mansion-house of another, without breaking the same, with an intent to commit some felony, and breaking the house in the night-time to get out, was burglary? However, injustice to this reign, we ought not to omit referring to the Statute passed in the 5th year of its continuance, in part repealing the Statute of 10th and 11th William and Mary, before referred to, so far as it inflicted on persons convicted of theft, and entitled to the Benefit of Clergy,, that most impolitic punishment of burning, in the most visible part of the left cheek, nearest the nose: and also for extending the Benefit of Clergy to convicted felons, who are unable to read, in like manner as if they had read as a clerk.

The 9th George I. cap. 22. presents a string of offences to be deemed felony, and punished with death, many of which it is difficult to consider as crimes endangering the existence of the state, or for which the life of man ought to be taken away; such as, "appearing armed, with blacked faces, or otherwise disguised, in any forest, or grounds enclosed, wherein deer are usually kept; or in any warren or place where hares or conies are usually kept; or in any high road, open heath, common, or down; or robbing any warren, or place where conies or hares are usually kept; or stealing or taking away any fish out of any river or pond; or 3 William and Mary, c. 9. §. 6. breaking down the head or mound of any fish-pond, whereby the fish shall be lost or destroyed; or cutting down or destroying any trees planted in any avenue, or growing in any garden, orchard, or plantation, for ornament, shelter, or profit; or knowingly sending any letter, without a name, or signed with a fictitious name, demanding money, venison, or other valuable thing."

Can it be possible, that the mere stealing of a rabbit in a warren, or fish out of a pond, merits the penalty of death? or that such legal cruelty is excusable, under the erroneous opinion, that lesser punishments will not restrain the crimes?

The above are only a few of the many statutes that might be referred to, in support of the observations here submitted: and, although the references have purposely stopped short with the reign, of George the First, it must not from thence be concluded that the Statutes of the present, or of the preceding reign, will be found free from the like defects,, of inflicting punishments too highly disproportioned to the quantity of moral wrong committed by the punishable delinquents.

How" far these wide-spreading statutes of death agree with the principle, that "nothing but the result of the most absolute necessity can authorize the destruction of mankind by the hand of man," is left to the determination of the Reader; who, it is conceived, will be under little difficulty in forming his conclusion: For, if the infliction of death is not to be considered as a punishment, bat as the last resource in the extermination of such persons from society, whose continuance therein is no longer consistent with the public safety; how can this sentiment of morality and truth agree with those inconsiderable offences, which are so inconsiderately made punishable with death? or will it be pretended, that a person who steals to the value of five shillings in a stable, although not broke open, nor any person being therein; or who steals a fish or a rabbit out of a pond or warren, is on that account to be considered as a member of society, whose continuance in it is become inconsistent with public safety 5

The same inattention that has prevailed in framing those numerous Statutes, the breach of which is made punishable with *death,* equally displays itself in certain Laws, which inflict the punishment of *transportation;* although in the latter respect it is true, that an error or indifference is the less culpable in the Law-makers, inasmuch as the consequences are less destructive of the human species. The punishment of transportation, perhaps, only removes the offender to a new Country, with a better Climate; civilized, and capable of maintaining the social intercourse of. Life, and leaving his parent country the principal sufferer by his banishment, from the considerable expence incurred in the transportation of a convict, and the loss of the future labours of himself and progeny for the benefit of the state. This species of punishment ought solely to be inflicted on the incorrigible, and such as by other means are incapable of being reclaimed from their viciouspursuits; as death ought alone to be inflicted on those, the continuance of whose existence is absolutely incompatible with the safety of the State.

So early as the reign of Edward the Second, prisoners breaking prison were declared not to be subject to the judgment of life or member, unless the cause for which they were taken required such judgment. In this law there appears much good sense and judicial reasoning; for what is there in an escape from prison, that can increase the moral enormity of the crime committed? and it seems attended with considerable difficulty in this age, to reconcile the punishing with death a return from transportation, before the expiration of the period of punishment, more particularly when the original offence was not liable to that awful penalty. The transportation of the criminal again, for the whole of the original term, as though none of it had run out, or for a lengthened period (if that should be considered necessary), appears better calculated to meet the humanity and justice of the case.; and, it is presumed, would be found equally sufficient to deter persons from making the attempt.

Transportation, when considered as a punishment, must be supposed to carry with it the anxieties of separation from kindred and friends, and all the best affections of the human heart; and if a convict, transported for one of the many inadequate offences, no way implying incorrigibility, to which that punishment is affixed, should embrace an opportunity to effect his escape, and return to a destitute wife and family, deprived of every means of support by his absence; how justly may the heart, agonized with the feelings of sensibility, complain of that law, which subjects a man thus unfortunately circumstanced to the punishment of death; and to be hunted down by the unfeeling Runners of some public office of Criminal Justice!

To conclude the Remarks here submitted on the Criminal Law, and which have already exceeded the length at first intended them, or which, indeed, a work of this nature admits; It may be observed, in the words of an ingenious writer, well acquainted with the principles of human action, that "the degree of punishment and consequences of a crime, ought to be so contrived, as to have the greatest possible effect on *others,* with the least possible pain to the *delinquent.*" This sentiment of truth and humanity will stand the test of time, and remain to the remotest ages of the world, however broken in upon by man, in the practical course of life, under the influence of his passions and his prejudices.

To the above humane reflection may be added another position of the same author, as also of several other writers of eminence, who have treated on the subject; That "crimes are more effectually prevented by the *certainty,* than by the *severity* of *punishment."* This maxim of sound jurisprudence is very warmly Beccaria, c. 19. pp. 75, 76. adopted by a most sagacious Commentator on the Laws of England, who has amply expressed himself with so much force and elegance, that it is considered the following extracts from his writings will be highly acceptable. They contain sentiments which cannot be too often revived, nor too deeply impressed on the mind of the Legislator, the Philanthropist, or the Man of the World; and as such, deserve to be engraved on Tablets of Gold.

In treating on the measure and effect of human Inflictions for offence, he says, "We may observe that punishments of unreasonable severity, especially when indiscriminately inflicted, have less effect in preventing crimes, and amending the manners of a people, than such as are more merciful in general, yet properly intermixed with due distinctions of severity. The excessive severity of Laws, (says Montesquieu,) hinders their execution: When the punishment surpasses all measure, the publick, out of humanity, will frequently prefer impunity to it. We may farther observe, that sanguinary laws are a bad symptom of the distemper of any State, or at least, of its weak constitution."

"It is moreover absurd and impolitick to apply the same punishment to crimes of different malignity. A multitude of sanguinary laws (besides the doubt that may be entertained concerning the right of making them,) do likewise prove a manifest defect, either in the wisdom of the legislative, or the strength of the executive power. It is a kind of Quackery in Government, and argues a want of solid skill, to apply the same universal remedy, the *ultimum supplicium,* to every case of difficulty. It is, it must be owned, much easier to extirpate than to amend mankind: Yet that Magistrate must be esteemed both a weak and a cruel Surgeon, who cuts off every limb, which, through ignorance or indolence, he will not attempt to cure."

"Though we may glory in the wisdom of the English Law, we shall find it difficult to justify the frequency of capital punishment to be found therein; inflicted (perhaps inattentively,) by a multitude of successive, independent Statutes, upon Crimes very different in their natures. So dreadful a list, instead of diminishing, increases the number of offenders. The injured, through compassion, will often forbear to prosecute: Juries, through compassion, will sometimes forget their oaths; and either acquit the guilty, or mitigate the nature of the offence: and Judges, through compassion, will respite one half of the Convicts, and recommend them to the Royal Mercy. Among so many chances of escaping, the needy and hardened offender overlooks the Multitude that suffer: he boldly engages in some desperate attempt, to relieve his wants, or supply his vices: and, if unexpectedly the hand of Justice overtakes him, he deems himself peculiarly unfortunate, in falling at last a Sacrifice to those laws, which long impunity has taught him to contemn." Judge Blackstonb, vol. IV. p. 16—19.
g

The practical effects here described, are accurately and distinctly shewn by a learned modern writer, eminently distinguished by his zeal for the cause of humanity, in his Observations on the Criminal law of England; and to which the reader is again referred, as containing lessons and maxims of Philanthropy highly meriting his adoption and cultivation.

That great and excellent Man, Sir Matthew Hale, observes, that more offenders escape, by the over easy ear given to exceptions in Indictments, than by their own Innocence; and many times gross murders, burglaries, robberies, and other heinous and crying offences remain unpunished, by these unseemly niceties, to the reproach of the law, to the shame of the government, to the encouragement of villainy, and to the dishonour of God." And may it not be inquired, if these unseemly niceties owe not their origin to the too sanguinary character of our criminal laws, and to the desire of Judges, as they advance in learning and the practice of humanity, to catch at any pretence to blunt their severity? To a man of plain understanding, not versed as a professor in the Law, it seems difficult to account, from any other principle, why a more technical accuracy should be required in Indictments, than is sufficient to describe, in distinct and unequivocal terms, the nature of the offence committed, with its attendant explanatory circumstances: and why Common Sense should be outraged, by the many unseemly niceties which are allowed to prevail, in the form of exceptions to indictments, from the too easy Ear of Justice having lent itself, in the first instance, to a case of hardship; and, having established the precedent, unable, on account of that necessary consistency which must follow the administration of tbe Law, to refuse it even to the most heinous criminal; who thus escapes punishment, and puts to shame the offended laws of his country. Moderate Laws, firmly executed, would better answer the ends of Justice; and the subtile refinements of cavilling Lawyers would then give way to more substantial forms, and the intelligible voice of reason.

"Imprisonment," says the humane Beccaria, " is a punishment, which differs from all others in this particular; that it necessarily precedes conviction, but should never be inflicted, except when ordained by the Law. When punishments shall become less severe, and prisons less horrible; when compassion and humanity shall penetrate the iron-gates of dungeons, and direct the obdurate and inexorable ministers of Justice, the Laws may then be satisfied with weaker evidence for imprisonment."

The first end of imprisonment is the security of the party accused of injuries to Society, until he can be tried, and either condemned or acquitted, according to due course of Law. But, the innocent as well as the guilty may be accused, and put upon his trial; and as no person, according to the mild and equitable Spirit of pur Jaw, should be considered as guilty, until he is actually tried and convicted; ina Sir Samuel Romilly. Observ. p. H, *et passim.* prisonment, for safe custody under such circumstances, should be attended with the utmost lenity to the prisoner, consistent with his custody, and the necessary regulations for orderly management in the prison; and also of as short duration as circumstances may by possibility admit: And whether he is affluent or poor, he should on no account whatever be obliged to associate with those prisoners, on whom the Law has pronounced its Sentence.

The next end of imprisonment is the safe Detention of the party who has been found guilty by his country of the injuries done to society with which he stood charged, and is remanded to prison, to abide the execution of his Sentence. But, as Imprisonment forms no part of this Sentence, it should never be accompanied with further duress, or restraint, than what the necessity of safe Detention absolutely requires.

The third and last end of criminal imprisonment may be considered, as it relates to the punishment of the offender, in those cases where imprisonment forms part of the sentence. But, even in such cases, no greater or other severity ought to be exercised, than what the express direction of the Sentence requires: for whatever exceeds such direction must be absolute tyranny, by whomsoever it may be practised or allowed.

It has been too much the practice for Ages past, to consider prisoners (and particularly those confined for Offences against the criminal Law) as the outcasts of Society; no longer meriting protection, nor entitled to the common claims of suffering humanity. For how, otherwise, can we reconcile the horrible prisons and frightful *Cells,* dangerous to existence, and destructive of the health and lives of their pitiable inhabitants, which have been suffered to increase in wretchedness, and remain a disgrace to Society for such immeasurable lengths of time; and, in many places, even to the present day, without the poor apology of inadvertence for an excuse! Who in these Kingdoms, after the labours of that great and good Man, Mr. Howard, can venture to sanction so absurd a pretence?

It is a truth in which the Author rejoices, (with the deepest gratitude to the great disposer of all human Events, for having allowed him to pass, and protracted his advanced Age,) to witness that his humble endeavours have been attended with the most promising success. Much has been done in many places, and some of them the most remote from the Capital, to render those habitations of misery less unfit to maintain life: to comfort the existence of their unwilling inhabitants; and to restore the prisoner, at the end of his confinement, if not a reformed, at least not a more depraved member of Society, than at his first incarceration. But much, still, and very much remains to be done, before abuses and neglects so long accumulated can be effectually removed.

The unwarrantable cruelties practised on prisoners, (by loading them with Irons, or fastening them one to another with heavy Chains; by bolting them to the walls or floors of the prison; and by shutting them up, at the discretion of a Gaoler, in dark and loathsome Cells, void of almost every necessary to support life; all of which *illegal severities,* to a very aggravated degree, the Author has repeatedly witnessed,) may, it is conceived, have derived their origin from the improper places set apart for confinement: many, at first, insufficient for the purpose; and all of them, by the decays of time and neglect, become insecure for the safe-keeping of prisoners.

The Gaoler thus circumstanced, and made responsible for the custody and forthcoming of his prisoners, naturally resorted to those artificial means of security which his situation in life enabled him to provide, as substitutes for his defective prison: and hence fetters, chains and bolts were introduced, according as he considered his responsibility involved, or as the torpor of an unfeeling heart for the sufferings of others induced him to adopt them, rather than incur the hazard of an escape: For, as Blackstone (Vol. IV. ch. 22.) remarks, "Gaolers are, frequently, a merciless race of Men; and, by being conversant in scenes of misery, steeled against any tender sensation." But here, while allowing the general truth of this remark, it is but Justice to except, with Applause and Honour, those Keepers of prisons, whom the Author, in his extended journies to the different parts of the Kingdom, has found treating their prisoners with exemplary humanity; and kindly administering to the wants of the most forlorn and wretched, without the exaction of Fees for their improved condition. I refer my Reader's attention to the several instances related in the body of this work; and which, as proceeding from a class of men wherein they are least expected, do the Authors of them the greater credit, and well deserve the warm approbation of the Publick.

Necessity is a plea too frequently urged, as an apology for every species of narrow policy and indolence; and (having been once allowed to prevail in excuse for the fettering of prisoners, and otherwise securing them, at the unfeeling discretion of their Gaolers,) no surprize ought to be expressed, that such a class of men, grown unmindful, by the indolent permission of judges and the magistrates, of that humane Maxim of the common law, which forbids the fettering a prisoner, "unless he is unruly, or attempts an escape," should convert so terrible an instrument of power to. their own advantage. For what mortal, can it be supposed, would not part with his last shilling, to avoid being bolted by his neck, or his leg, to the floor of a prison, or to convert a massy chain, or ponderous fetter, into a flimsy wire? or to be wholly excused, at the discretion of his Tyrant Master, from so odious an addition to the many other grievances, which must rend the heart of Man, in so fallen a condition? Whatever be the external appearances, which pride or obstinacy may induce him to assume, the Nature within him cannot but revolt at such Degradation.

Few men, or, perhaps, it will be better expressed, no Man is fit to be entrusted with uncontrouled power. And yet by Common Gaolers, (so truly described by Blackstone as a merciless race of Men, and remarkable for a general want of hu manity,) is this mighty trust permitted to be exercised. If the law itself do not in terms authorize the tyranny and coercion which they practise upon their prisoners, yet, if Judges and other Magistrates wink at the abuse, may it not be likened to *a power withaut controul?* For what prisoner, upon his trial, could expect favour or redress, who began by a complaint of his Gaoler's having wantonly, illegally, and without necessity, confined him in fetters and chains, or otherwse treated him with hardship and cruelty?—No: Prudence admonishes him, that he had better endure in silence, than provoke the consequences of such a challenge, against power deputed, and subordinate insinuation.

The gradation to wrong is considered as more uniform in its course, than the progress of that which is right. A wrong, once admitted and established, is almost certain to be followed by another: and thus *Gaol-Fees,* with other despotick extortions, have crept in; and, by long usage, are become hardly distinguishable from matters of right. The progress of iniquity, steady in its course, has proceeded: until at length, the denial or supply of *prison conveniencies,* even to the article of *Water,* so essentially connected with the support of life, has been frequently, and is still, in some instances, made a source of corrupt income to Gaolers; to the disgrace of the Laws of our Country, and of every humane feeling.

Amidst the multiplied occurrences of life, there will be found no condition in which man can be placed, however exalted his rank, or extensive his power and wealth, so as wholly to secure him from the possibility of becoming an inhabitant of one of these dreary abodes of misery. See the *Notes,* in page lix.

The impetuous Man may be brought thither by the unbridled impulse of Ins passions: the good man may equally become paralysed, from the false testimony of the wicked: And thus, a denned restraint on the power of Gaolers, together with healthy and well-regulated prisons, may be of more personal consideration to every man, than in the day of joy, and in the pride of his heart, he is apt to imagine. But, whether this probability be remote or at hand, it is equally the duty of every one, from the highest to the lowest in Society, to contribute his best endeavours, according to his rank and means, to alleviate the sufferings of wretchedness, whereever they may present themselves; and even in the case of criminal imprisonment, (but especially where the voice of suffering is confined within dungeon-walls) to be watchful that the unhappy, repenting, or even hardened prisoner, may endure no other or worse punishment than what the Law assigns him.

Self-preservation is a common law of nature, implanted in the breast of every Animal. But, there are other sentiments in the human heart, that justly predominate in our Estimation. Which of us can hesitate to decide, betwixt the generous *Youth,* who, forgetful of his own security, and regardless of impending danger, hazards his existence to rescue a fellow creature from destruction; and the more cautious *'Man,* who, governed by this first Law of Nature, the equal motive of every brute, alone consults his own personal safety, avoids the hazard, and allows the victim to perish, without an attempt to save him? And yet, however the feelings of refinement may revolt at the comparison, such seems to be the condition of those in Society, who, relying on their own security, when persons in their station of life become inhabitants of a dreary prison, consider the abuses which prevail there as no way affecting themselves, and suffer them to be continued. But let such persons, in the fullness of their confidence, call to recollection the dreadful ravages which the pestilence engendered in crowded prisons, has scattered in all directions; and that, from the Judge who tries the Prisoners, through the gradation of Witnesses, (from which no rank can excuse a man,) down to the lowest officers of the prison, and the associates of the culprit, the dreadful contagion may be induced to spread abroad, and visit the house of the very man, who feels most confident of personal safety, from the little probability, as he conceives, of his having any thing to do with the prisons of his country. Such considerations ought to have their weight with those persons, who are solely influenced by the narrowest principles of self-preservation; whilst the more generous sentiments of a feeling heart will lead it to sympathize with the sufferer in misfortunes, however they may have been occasioned; and to advocate the cause of that languishing distress, which cannot so raise its voice as to be heard from the dreary depths of a dungeon!

Whatever may be a man's offence, the Laws will be found to assign its appropriate punishment, or it must go unpunished. Nothing ought to be inflicted on any Criminal, beyond the legal visitation annexed to his crime; no more than punishment ought to be hurled upon the Innocent. Beyond the extent of the crime, and the punishment to be inflicted on the Guilty, both are alike innocent in the eye oP the Law. But the limitation or measure of punishment appears a folly, if a (iaoler be suffered to add what load of severity he thinks fit to the condemnation of the law, on a pretence of the insecurity of his prison. Ought he not rather to be told, "Raise your Walls; Strengthen your Gates. Make your Gaol a place of security; and no longer oppress your prisoners with unlawful chains, for the worst purposes of corruption, under the miserable subterfuge of a pretended County-GDconomy?"

Solitary Confinement, as affording an opportunity to the reflective powers, aided by religious advisers to discriminate with truth between the extremes of right and wrong, (an advantage which the hurrying scenes of vice are calculated to deny) presents a scheme of reform to the victim of crime, secluded from the exercise of his bad habits, and communication with his worse associates, that at first sight warmly recommends itself for adoption. But, when the description of those persons is considered, to whom this peculiar trust is likely to be devolved, every thinking mind must naturally hesitate; and look with anxiety for some 'controuling power, to check the apprehended evils of Total Seclusion'.

The recent management of a prison of this description, in the near vicinity of the Metropolis, has created serious doubts in the minds of some of the best of men, as to the propriety of entrusting so great a power with any individual; And, indeed, establishes beyond contradiction, that if, and wherever it is entrusted, it ought to be guaranteed by the wholesome interference of an immediate, constant, and certain visitation.

The County Magistrates, from the honourable class of Society out of which they are chosen, and from their intimate acquaintance with the Criminal Laws they are appointed to administer, seem the fittest persons to be invested with this visitatorial and conteouling power. And, indeed, if all of them possessed the same talents, zeal, and unabating energy as that worthy Baronet , who, with distinguished credit to himself, and benefit to the community, has wrought such excellent effects in the prisons of the County where he resides; (establishing a model, to which needless severities are unknown, and by which the reformation of the Culprit is secured) no further inquiry need be made, as to where the law might repose so truly important a trust. But alas! in what branch of society is perfection to be found? The pursuits of pleasure, the attraction of gain, the negligence of many, and the ill-placed confidence of others, lead astray from those duties, which, being equally the business of every body, are but too frequently neglected-; and the artful Gaoler, with words of submissive cant, finds no great difficulty in persuading a Bench of Magistrates, so circumstanced, to wave the trouble of visiting his prison. Thus, a house designed for reform, may be converted into a chamber of lasciviousness and debauchery; denied only to those, who are not objects of pleasure, or without the means of payment for indulgences. But how will the feeling heart exclaim, when it apprehends such scenes may be forced upon the virtuous, yet unfortunate inhabitant of these secluded houses; shut out from an.appeal, to friends; debarred every means of complaint; and neglected by those, whom the Law considers as their guardians against injury and oppression!

When a principle is intrinsically good, it ought not to be relinquished, merely on the ground of difficulty to carry it into effect: And even should every attempt hitherto made of putting prisons for Solitary Confinement on an eligible footing be found to have failed, it would not follow from thence, that Solitary Confinement ought to be abandoned, as unequal to the beneficial ends proposed from it: But, so long as its possible utility is acknowledged, new attempts should be made to adopt such checks, as may effectually prevent the abuses apprehended, or complained of.

Grand Juries, from their respectability and numbers, and fronV-the frequency of their being changed, present a desirable medium of controul, in aid of the magistrates, and to supply any casual defect in their attention.

Sir George Onesiphorus Paul

For this purpose, the walls of the rooms in which Grand Juries assemble, might be furnished with the Sections of all the Prisons in their respective Counties: the dimensions of every room and cell might be stated; the manner of its ventilation, and how warmed, and protected from damps and cold; with the nature and quantity of its furniture, the name and offence of its inhabitant, his time of commitment, the period fixed for his enlargement; and an account also of his general demeanour. The Rules and Regulations made for the orderly government of the Prison might, in like manner, be hung up in some conspicuous situation, together with the names of its religious and other officers, their salaries, and their duties.

In possession of such materials, it might not be left to the discretion of Grand Juries to visit, or omit the visitation of the prisons of their Counties; But it might very honourably be required of them, as a part of their duty; and that they should report, not only upon the abuses, if they found any, but upon the general conduct and management of each prison, as they found it, whether good or bad. One part of such report might be presented to the Judge, from whom the Grand Jury received their charge; and another be entered in a book, called "the *Prison Booh*" to be preserved and laid upon the table of their successors; and in like manner continued by them in succession. The Foreman of every Grand Jury also might be intrusted with the power, by virtue of his office, to inspect the Prisons of his County at any time, until another Grand Jury was sworn in.

With such controuling checks as here pointed out, Corruption would veil its hydra head; the good order and better regulation of prisons would be the result; or else, a removal of Gaolers would follow the continuation of evil practices. Had some such regulation been adopted only a short time back, we may confidently believe it would not have remained to be told that in the year 1810, to the disgrace of Society, the shame of the great City of London, and even' in the Gaol of Newgate, surrounded by the splendour and opulence of the kingdom, Women Felons lay upon the bare boards, in crowded wards, with a space of less than twenty inches in breadth for each to sleep on .

It cannot be expected that in General Observations, like the present, any regular plan should be laid before the public, for the internal regulation of our various Prisons at large. Such an attempt to meet all the prejudices of time, and long habits of error, would require a work of no inconsiderable magnitude. It may however be justly premised, as an invariable maxim, that not only should nothing be allowed, which can tend to destroy or injure the health of prisoners; but that *every possible attention*, consistent with their situation, ought to be paid to its preservation: and that an equal consideration should be shewn to their moral principles also, together with an earnest endeavour to regulate and improve them.

See my description of Newgate, in p. 425.

To effect the first of these ends, all the apartments of the building should be properly ventilated: sufficient beds and covering should be provided for all the prisoners: means should be taken to exclude the cold air and damps of the night; and sufficient firing should be allowed during the inclement season. All the internal walls of the building should be lime-whited once, if not twice a year: coarse, yet wholesome food should be supplied, in sufficient, but at the same time in moderate quantities, and not more than enough to maintain healthy life. Water should be the only article that might be supplied with profusion, for of this invaluable blessing it is scarcely possible to allow too liberal a supply. Temperance should not only be encouraged, but enforced, in every prison, during every stage of confinement, before, as well as after the trial of a prisoner; and even the humane and just principle of our Law, that no man ought to be considered as guilty, until he is tried and convicted, should not be allowed to have any effect in regard to the internal regulation of a prison, as affecting the health and morals of the prisoners. It is a serious affliction for an innocent man to endure confinement, till he is acquitted by his peers; but the being obliged to subscribe to regulations of temperance and morality, ought, and must be considered by every good man, as a very small portion indeed of his sufferings.

No prisoner, however wealthy, or whatever his rank in life, or cause of confinement, should be permitted to break in upon the Rules laid down for the orderly and good government of his prison. They should in all cases be impartial, and invariably alike to all. Wine, beer, spirits, and other strong liquors, of whatever description, as tending to disqualify the mind for the humiliation consonant to the place, should be expelled as poisons, baneful to morality; confined exclusively to the stores of a medical attendant, and allowed by him only in cases of absolute necessity. Should it be urged on the behalf of persons in confinement, that there may be those, whose former habits of life require the continued use of wines, or other liquors, to maintain their health, the answer is plain and ready; that the Medical Attendant of the prison will be the proper person to decide on such cases; and that his certificate to the Gaoler, stating the grounds on which it is granted, must be the only sanction for obtaining the required indulgence.

Universal Cleanliness, through all parts of a prison, is an equal essential with Temperance, to preserve the health of its inhabitants, and should on no account be omitted.

As Temperance is the basis of health, so is it the sure foundation of morals. The one without the other is little better than good maxims, which are repeated, but not followed; and privations patiently endured, are the certain forerunners of reform. In fact, it seems essential, in such a school, (where almost every thing is to be *unlearnt,* if such an expression may be allowed) that the habits and customs of the prisoners should be wholly changed, and religious and moral duties substituted h in their place, by daily admonitions: And upon every return of the Sabbath, Church-service should on no account be omitted, but the attendance of all the prisoners should be insisted on, enforced, and encouraged. As idleness is the bane of morals, so the means of labour should be provided for every prisoner; and proper encouragement, I am fully persuaded, would render their being compelled to work unnecessary.

The duty of the Medical Attendant should not be, as it has hitherto frequently been, merely a form, to entitle him to claim his salary; but a strict attention to the health of every inhabitant of the prison.

A very important point still remains for consideration; namely, the providing for a prisoner, whose time of confinement has run out the means of supporting himself, until he can get into employment. Released from confinement in a gaol, few are willing to receive him; and in the state in which his mind has been placed by the discipline of a prison, it would be doubly cruel, from necessity, to drive him again to the haunts of his evil associates. A County Fund might be easily j-aised for this special purpose, and prudently advanced to the prisoners on their discharge; under the directions of the Grand Jury, according to their well-informed discretion, and founded on the Gaoler's stated reports of the prisoner's demeanour.

Fees, or entrance money, under whatever pretence they are taken from the prisoner, ought to be abolished; and, if possible, a still stronger restraint should be laid against the taking any kind of fees from him at his discharge.

The health and the morals of prisoners are, as it were, first principles, which ought never to be lost sight of; and, rightly considered, they will readily point out what should be done, better than a thousand essays on the regulations and management of prisons.

Vice in its course is gradual: no man was ever perfectly vicious at once; but step by step he graduates to his height in villainy. Small crimes should therefore be considered as the forerunners of greater evils; and be punished with more promptness, and perhaps with greater comparative severity, than in other respects may seem actually to belong to them. Restoration of property purloined, and a certainty of immediate but moderate punishment, would deter more from the commission of offences, than heavier punishments at a distant period; when vicious habit has combined with the chance of escape, and the power of retaining or making away with a booty thus infamously acquired.

To repress inferior Crimes on their first appearance greatly deserves the closest consideration of the Magistrates.

A vigorous and active police particularly claims the attention of such of them as reside in great cities, or crowded neighbourhoods; it being far better to repress than punish crimes. But much care is requisite, that subordinate officers of the Police be not suffered to mingle themselves too closely with the Criminals, and thus become traffickers in their blood. The humane Beccaria (chap, xxxvi.) considers a Legislature's offers of reward for the apprehension of Criminals, as preventing one crime, but giving birth *to* a thousand: and too much reason is there to fear that this truth is often realized, in the practical career of some of our own laws.

The Observations here submitted have considerably exceeded the space originally allotted them; but, imperfect as they are, the Author, relying on the indulgence of his Reader, must of necessity conclude them: first begging to refer his attention to the admirable hint thrown out by Mr. Justice Blackstone,- in his learned Commentaries, for the appointment of a Committee to revise the Criminal Law: emphatically expressing himself, that " if such a Committee were appointed but once in an hundred years, many of the Acta in the Statute-Book already referred to, could not have continued to the present hour." Happy, indeed, would it at this time be for the Country, if the Legislature of that day had taken the hint of the learned Judge: and happy will it be in ages to come, if such a Committee should now be appointed, to revise the criminal Law; to direct the regulation and management of prisons; and assiduously to reform the Police by salutar' provisions.

Vol. IV. p. 4. ,,.. f£f= Notes, on the preceding Page liii. line 22.

An Author, whose name I do not now recollect, has very pointedly expressed himself on the subject referred to in the above page. "Let no one," saith he, "thus reason. I scorn the commission of a crime: A prison cannot be my lot: It is provided for the Miscreant, and for the Miscreant alone: who, having opposed the *ordinances,* has abandoned *the protection of the Laws.* Leave him to his doom of misery: Let him rot in the yapours of a dungeon; and drag his unwieldy chain, at the mercy of his Keeper."

But how far more nobly generous and true, is the following sentiment of that excellent Judge, Sir Michael Foster!" No rank of life; no uprightness of heart; no prudence or circumspection of conduct, should tempt any man to conclude, that he may not, at some time or other, be *deeply interested in these researches.*
" GENERAL LIST OP THE VARIOUS PRISONS IN ENGLAND, SCOTLAND, And WALES, MENTIONED IN THE COURSE OF THIS VOLUME; *Distinguishing each Prison in Alphabetical Order.*

Page *ABERDEEN,* Scotland, Tolbooth, or Town

Gaol 1 *r&berdeen,* New County and City Bridewell.. 4 *Abergavenny,* South Wales, Town Gaol.... 5 *t/Abingdon,* Berkshire, County Bridewell... 6
———-Town Gaol 7 *isAldborough,* Suffolk, Town Gaol 8 *Alnwick,* Northumberland, House of Correction 9 *'Andover,* Hampshire, Borough Gaol 10 *Annan,* Scotland, Town Gaol 11 */Appleby,* Westmoreland, County Gaol 12

County Bridewell 13 *Ashbourne,* Derbyshire, House of Correction 14 / *Aylesbury,* Buckinghamshire, County Gaol, and Bridewell 15 *Aylesham,* Norfolk, Bridewell 20 *Ayr,* Scotland, Town and County Gaol.... 21

Bala, Merionethshire, North-Wales, Bridewell 23

Banbury, Oxfordshire, Town-Gaol and Bridewell 23

Banff, Scotland', Town-Gaol 24 *Barking,* Essex, Gaol, and House of Correction 26

"*Barnstaple,* Devonshire, Borough Gaol, and

/ Bridewell 27 *Basingstoke,* Hampshire, Bridewell 25 *Bath,* Somersetshire, City Gaol 28 *'Battel,* Sussex, Town Gaol 32 *i/Beaumaris,* Isle of Anglesea, County Gaol.. 30

Town Gaol 32 *Beccles,* Suffolk, House of Correction 33 *Bedford,* County Gaol, and House of Correction 35 /. Town Gaol 38 *Jterkhamstead,* Hertfordshire, Bridewell... 41 *Berteick-upon-Tweed,* Town and County Gaol 39 *Beverley, Hall-Garth,* Yorkshire, for

Debtors 41
 Town and Liberty Gaol 42
 House of Correction 43
 New Sessions House, and House of Correction 44 *Birmingham*, Warwickshire, Town Gaol... 46
 Court Prison, for Debtors only 47 *y* Aston Gaol 48 *Blandford*, Dorsetshire, Town Gaol 60 Page Page *Bodmin*, Cornwall, County Gaol and Bridewell 51
y Borough Compter, Southwark, in Surrey.. 57 *Boston*, Lincolnshire, Town Gaol and Bride well 66
—— House of Correction 67 *Bottesdale*, Suffolk, House of Correction.. 68 *Bradford*, Yorkshire, Town Gaol 45 *Brecon*, South Wales, County Gaol, and *"Chichester*, Sussex, City Gaol and Bridewell 134 *cUrkenwell*, London, New Prison 135 *tsCeckermouth*, Cumberland, County Bridewell 139
Colchester, Essex, the Castle Bridewell. ... 139
Borough Gaol and Bridewell... 140
Cold Bath Fields, Middlesex, County House
of Correction 142 , *Coventry*, Warwickshire/City and CountyGaol 147 City Bridewell 149
 Bridewell , Town Gaol 72 *Bridewell*, London, House of Correction.. 73
Bridgewater, Somersetshire, Town Gaol.. 50
Bristol, City and County Gaol 77
 City Bridewell 80 . Law ford's Gate, the County Bridewell 81
Buckingham, Town Gaol 72 *Buntingford*, Hertfordshire, Bridewell.... 83
'Bury St. Edmund's, Suffolk, County Gaol, and
 House of Correction 8,3
 Town Bridewell 89 *Caermarthen*, South Wales, County Gaol and Bridewell 90
—————— Borough Gaol 91 *Caernarvon*, North Wales, County Gaol... 92 *Cambridge*, Town Bridewell 93 *(Cambridge Castle*, County Gaol and Bridewell 95
 Town Gaol 100 t *Canterbury*, Gaol, and House of Correction 101
 City Bridewell 104
 City Gaol 105 *Cardiff*, Glamorganshire, South Wales, County Gaol 107

Town Gaol 108 *Cardigan*, South Wales, County Gaol and
Bridewell 108 *L Carlisle*, Cumberland, City and County Gaol 110
City Gaol Ill *Castle-Town*, Isle of Man, Castle-Rushen
Gaol 112 *uChelmsford*, Essex, CountyGaol 117
County Bridewell 122 u *Chester Castle*, County Gaol 124
"*Chester*, New City Gaol and Bridewell 129 u *Chesterfield*, Derbyshire, Town Gaol 132 69 *wCowbridge*, Glamorganshire, South Wales, Bridewell 133
County Bridewell 123 *Croydon*, Surrey, Town Gaol 116 *Dartford*, Kent, the Bridewell 150 *Deal*, Kent, Town Gaol 151 *LDean*, (see Little Dean), Gloucestershire,
House of Correction 151 *Denbigh*, North Wales. Town Gaol 153 */-Derby*, County Gaol, and House of Correction 153
Town or Borough Gaol 157 *Devizes*, Wiltshire, Town Gaol, and County
Bridewell 158 *Dolgelly*, Merionethshire, North Wales.
Town Gaol 161
Bridewell 161 *JDoncaster*, Yorkshire, Town-Gaol 162 *t-Dorchester*, Dorsetshire, CountyGaol 163 *t-Dover Castle*, Kent, for the Cinque-Port
Debtors only 169
Town Gaol and Bridewell 172 *Dumfries*, Scotland, County Gaol 173 *Dunbar*, Scotland, Town Gaol 175 *Dundee*, Scotland, Town Gaol 175 *Durham*, County Gaol and Bridewell 177 the County Bridewell 185 *-Dymchurch*, Kent, Town Gaol and Bridewell 162 *-Edinburgh*, the City Tolbooth 187
Canon-gate Tolbooth 197
Holy-rood House 199
County and City Bridewell 200 *Elgin*, Scotland, the Tolbooth 202 *-Ely*, Cambridgeshire, City Gaol 203
Bridewell 205 *LEvesham*, Worcestershire, Borough Gaol.. 217 *-Exeter*, Devonshire, County High Gaol for
Felons 206
South Gate, City and County Gaol 209
Sheriff's Ward, County Prison for Debtors 212 *Exeter*, the County

House of Correction.. 214 / *Falmouth*, Cornwall, Town Gaol 217 . *ij Fleet Prison*, London, for Debtors, and Contempt of Court 218 *Flint*, North Wales, County Gaol and House of Correction 223 ; *Folkingham*, Lincolnshire, House of Correction 225 *Forres*, Scotland, the Tolbooth 227 v *Gilt-Spur-Street Compter*, London 228 *Glasgow*, Scotland, the Tolbooth 238 . the Bridewell 242 *Gloucester*, County Gaol, and Penitentiary
House annexed 244 1 City Gaol and Bridewell 250 *Gosport*, Hampshire, Bridewell 251 *r Grantham*, Lincolnshire, Gaol, and House of
Correction 252 *Greenlaw*, Berwickshire, Scotland, County
Gaol 253
V *Greenwich*, Kent 227 v/ *Guildford*, Surrey, Bridewell 254 *Haddington*, East Lothian, Scotland, County
Gaol 256 *Halifax*, Yorkshire/ Low, or Town Gaol, for Debtors only 257
Town Gaol 260 *J Halsted*, Essex, Bridewell 261 *Harwich*, Essex, Town Gaol 261
Bridewell 262 *Haverford-West*, Pembrokeshire, South Wales,
County Gaol 263 : Town Gaol and Bridewell. 264 *-Helston*, Cornwall, Town Gaol 265 w *Henley*, Oxfordshire, Town Gaol 265 *Hereford*, County Gaol and House of Correction 266
City Gaol and Bridewell 269 *Hertford*, County Gaol and Bridewell 270
V *High Wijcomb*, Buckinghamshire, Bridewell 274 v *Hinckley*, Leicestershire, Bridewell 274
— *Hit chin*, Hertfordshire, Bridewell 255 *Hithe*, Kent, Town Gaol 265 *Horseley*, Gloucestershire, House of Correction... 275
-Horsham, Sussex, County Gaol and Bridewell 277
Hulks 627, 630, 632
MulL, Yorkshire, Town and County Gaol.. 279
Page "*Hull*, Bridewell 282 *Huntingdon*, the County Gaol. 283 the County Bridewell 286 *Ichester*, Somersetshire, County Gaol, and
Bridewell 287 *Inverness*, Scotland, the Tolbooth 291 *oLpswich*, Suffolk, Town and Borough Bridewell 292

Town and Borough Gaol 293
County Gaol 295
House of Correction 298' *Irven,* Scotland, Town Gaol 299 *Jedburgh,* Roxburghshire, Scotland, County Gaol 300
County Bridewell 300 *Y Kendal,* Westmoreland, Town Gaol and
Bridewell 301 *Kidderminster,* Worcestershire, Town Gaol 303 *Kilmarnock,* Scotland, Town Gaol 303 *King's Bench Prison,* Southwark 304 *Kingston-upon-Thames,* Surrey, Town Gaol 312 ; House of Correction. 315 *Kirkcudbright,* Scotland, Town Gaol.... . 318 *Kirton,* Lincolnshire 318 *JSnaresborough,* Yorkshire, Castle Gaol, for
Debtors 320 : Prison for Town Debtors.. 321
Town Gaol for Felons 321 *Lancaster Castle,* County Gaol and Bridewell 322
Town Gaol 330 *Llsangston Harbour* Hulks 630 *t-Xaunceston,* Cornwall, County Gaol for Felons 330
Town Gaol 332
Bridewell 332 *Leeds,* Yorkshire, Town Gaol 333 *Leicester,* County Gaol 333
County Bridewell 33G
Town Gaol 338 *Leith,* Scotland, the Town Gaol 340 -*Lenton,* late *Basford,* Nottinghamshire... 341 k *Leominster,* Herefordshire, Town Gaol.... 3-12 ji *Lewes,* Sussex, House of Correction, for the
East Division 342 *Lichfield,* Staffordshire, City and County
Gaol, and Bridewell 344 /*Lincoln Castle,* County Gaol 345
City Gaol, and House of Correction 351 /*Liverpool,* Lancashire, Borough Gaol 352 *Liverpool,* New Borough Gaol, and House of Correction 355
Bridewell 358
House of Correction 359 *Lostwithyell, or Lestwithiel,* Cornwall, Gaol lor Debtors 360 *I, Louth,* Lincolnshire, House of Correction 361
« *Ludgate,* London 363 t-*Ludlow,* Shropshire, Town Gaol 343 *Lydd,* Kent, Town Gaol 362 *S Lynn Regis,* Norfolk, Town Gaol, and House of Correction 369 "*Macclesfield,* Cheshire, Town Gaol 371
— *Maidstone,* Kent, County Gaol 374
—i—; House of Correction 378 *Malton,* Yorkshire, Town Gaol 380 *Manchester,* Lancashire, the New Bailey.. 381 *Marlborough,* Wiltshire, County Bridewell and Town Gaol 385 *i-Marshalsea,* Southwark, London 386
New Prison 393 *Melton Mowbray,* Leicestershire, Bridewell. 393 ' *Middlewich,* Cheshire, County House of Correction 394 *i-Monmouth,* Town Gaol 396
County Gaol, and House of Correction 397 _ *Montgomery,* North Wales, County Gaol... 400
House of Correction 402 *Montrose,* Scotland, the Town Gaol 399 u *Morpeth,* Northumberland, County Gaol.. 403
'Bridewell 404 *Musselburgh,* Scotland, Town Gaol 384 *Nairne,* Scotland, County Gaol 405
L *Nantwich,* Cheshire, Prison for Debtors.,. 40G
Town Gaol 406
£ *Newark-upon-Trent,* Nottinghamshire, Town
Gaol and Bridewell 407 *L Newbury,* Berkshire, the Corporation Gaol 408
Bridewell 408 j, *Newcastle-upon-Tyne,* Northumberland,
County Gaol 409 the Castle Garth.. 412 ; Sessions Prison... 413
Bridewell 414 *f.* Page *Northallerton,* Yorkshire, Bridewell 431 "*Northampton,* County Gaol and Bridewell.. 433
——————— Town Gaol and Bridewell. .. 436 -*Northlech,* Gloucestersliire, House of Correction 438 *Norwich Castle,* Norfolk, County Gaol.... 440
City Gaol 445
City Bridewell 449 for Precincts of the Close 460 *Nottingham,* County Gaol 451
Town Gaol 457
House of Correction 459 '*Oakham,* Rutlandshire, County Bridewell, and Town Gaol 461 *Odiham,* Hampshire, Bridewell 462 *Okehampton,* Devonshire, Town Gaol.... 462.J' *Orford,* Suffolk, Borough Gaol and Bridewell 462 *UOxford,* Castle Gaol, and County Bridewell. 463
City Gaol 467
L *Paisley,* Renfrewshire, Scotland,
Town Gaol 470 *Pembroke,* South Wales 472 *Y Penrhyn,* Cornwall, Borough Gaol 473 *Penzance,* Cornwall, Borough Gaol 473 *Perth,* Scotland, Town Gaol 474 *Peterborough,* Northamptonshire, Soke liberty Gaol 476
Bridewell 477 '-*Pelworth,* Sussex, County Bridewell, for the
Western Division 477 *Plymouth,* Devonshire, Town Gaol 478
Dock Gaol 479 *Pontefract,* Yorkshire, Town Gaol 480 *Poole,* Dorsetshire, Town Gaol 481
Bridewell 481 .*Portsmouth,* Hampshire, Town Gaol 481 *Harbour,* Hulks 627 *f-Poultry Compter,* London 484 +*Presteign,* Radnorshire, South Wales, County
Gaol 490
County Bridewell 491 *Preston,* Lancashire, House of Correction.. 491 *Reading,* Berkshire, County Gaol 495
Town Bridewell 500
Town Gaol, or Compter 50O *Renfrew,* Scotland, Town Gaol 501 u *Richmond,* Yorkshire, Liberty Gaol, for
Debtors only 501 -Corporation or Borough Gaol.. 502 *iJtipon,* Yorkshire, the Liberty Gaol 503
Page i, Canon-Fee Court Gaol, and House of Correction 504 *Rochester,* Kent, City Gaol and Bridewell.. 505 *y Romney,* Kent, Town Gaol 506 *Rothwell,* Yorkshire, Prison for Debtors only 507
Ruthin, Denbighshire, North Wales, County
Gaol, and Bridewell 508 . House of Correction 510 *Rye,* Sussex, Town Gaol 510 *affron-Walden,* Essex, Town Gaol and
Bridewell...-511 *Saint Albaris,* Hertfordshire, Borough Gaol 511
Liberty Gaol 512
House of Correction 513 *Saint Briavel's,* Gloucestershire, for Debtors only 514 *Salisbury,* Wiltshire, County Gaol and
Bridewell 515 *Sandwich,* Kent, Town Gaol and Bridewell 519
Savoy, Strand, London, Military exclusively 520
Scarborough, Yorkshire, Town Gaol 522 *Selkirk,* Roxburghshire, Scotland, Town

Gaol 523 *Sheffield,* Yorkshire, Town Gaol 524

Eccleshall Gaol 524

Debtors' Gaol 525 *Shepton-Mallet,* Somersetshire, Bridewell.. 526 *Shrewsbury,* Shropshire, County Gaol 529 *Southampton,* Hampshire, Town Gaol, for

Debtors only 531

Felons Gaol 531

Bridewell 532 *Southwell,* Nottinghamshire, County House of Correction 532 *Spalding,* Lincolnshire, Bridewell, for Holland Division 536 *Stafford,* County Gaol and House of Correction 537 *Stamford,* Lincolnshire, Town Gaol 543 *Stirling,* Scotland, Town Gaol 544 *Stockport,* Cheshire, Town Gaol 545 L *Sudbury,* Suffolk, Borough Gaol and Bridewell 546 *(Surrey,* County Gaol and Bridewell, Horsemonger Lane 547 Page i*Swaffham,* Norfolk, Bridewell 554 *Swansea,* South-Wales, Town Gaol 54S *Taunton,* Somersetshire, County Bridewell. 555 *Jhames,* Hulks 632 J*Thetford,* Norfolk, Town Gaol 556 *Lttdeswell,* Derbyshire, House of Correction 557 *Tiverton,* Devonshire, Town Gaol 558

Town Bridewell 558 *(-Tothill-Fields,* Westminster, Bridewell 560 u*The Tower,* London 563 *V Tower Hamlets,* Wellclose Square Gaol 564 iJ*Truro,* Cornwall, Town Gaol 564 r'*Tynemouth,* Northumberland, House of

Correction 565 i*Wakefield,* Yorkshire, House of Correction 566

Town Gaol 569 i*Walsall,* Staffordshire, Town Gaol 570 1 *Watsingham,* Norfolk, Town Gaol 570 *Warrington,* Lancashire, Town Bridewell.. 571 - *Warwick,* County Bridewell 572

County Gaol 575 i *Wellington,* Shropshire 578 *Wells,* Somersetshire, Town Gaol 572 L*Whitechapel,* London, for Debtors 578 *Whitehaven,* Cumberland, House of Correc 579 tion. (*Winchester,* Hampshire, County Gaol 580

City Gaol and Bridewell 585

County Bridewell 586 *Wirksworth,* Derbyshire, Bridewell 588 *Wisbeach,* Cambridgeshire, Town Gaol and

Bridewell 589 *Wolverhampton,* Staffordshire, Bridewell.. 590 *Woodbridge,* Suffolk, Bridewell'. 591 '*Worcester,* City Gaol 593

Castle Gaol and Bridewell 594 *Wrexham,* Denbighshire, NorthWales, House of Correction 599 L*Wymondham* (Windham), Norfolk, County

Bridewell 600 i*Yarmouth,* Norfolk, Town Bridewell 602

Town Gaol 603 C*York,* City Bridewell 605

St. Peter's Gaol 606

City and Ainsty Gaol 608

Bridewell, St. George s Fields 551 i*York Castle,* County Gaol 6H STATE OF PRISONS, IN ENGLAND, SCOTLAND, AND WALES.

IT IS OF LITTLE ADVANTAGE TO RESTRAIN THE BAD BY PUNISHMENT,

UNLESS YOU RENDER THEM GOOD BY DISCIPLINE.

ABERDEEN. *Scotland.*

The *Tolbooth,* or *Town Gaol.*

Gaoler, *Alexander Brown.*

Salary, from the Magistrates--55 from the County--*1ol.* 10$.

Fees, for *Felons,* none. For *Debtors,* fourpence a night.

Chaplain, Rev. *Alexander Thorn.* Salary, 50/.

Duty; on Tuesday, Thursday, and Sunday.

Surgeon, Mr. *Ogilvie*; who makes a Bill.

Number of Prisoners, Debtors. Felon. Petty Offendeif.

1809. Sept. 30th-----5----8----7

Total---20

Allowance, *Debtors,* as they are alimented, on Application to the Magistrates. Felons, fourpence a day in Bread, and a pint of Milk.

A REMARKS.

This Gaol adjoins to the Town-Hal), and the ascent to it is by a flight of stone steps; at the top of which is a corporal's guard, night and day. The outer gate of entrance is of wood, strongly cramped with iron, and the inner gate is iron-grated.

On the left of the entrance is a miserable hole of a room, 15 feet by eight; with an arched roof, and a small iron grating for light and ventilation, which it can hardly ever enjoy. It has two wooden bedsteads, with two dirty blankets and coverlets, and a fire-place.

In this wretched place were *three Women',* one of whom *had been under the sentence of transportation for Jive years!* And these women all ate, drank, and slept in this sink-hole of human privation, a focus of disease; pent up and surrounded by an atmosphere of pestilence, from which they have no power to escape, whilst yet alive!

Whoever visits the Gaols in Scotland will,.generally speaking, be forcibly struck with that "Destitution", which Hooker declares to be "such an impediment to virtue, as, till it be removed, suffereth not the mind of man to admit of any other care." How happy is it for human society, that the evil is *not unremovable* by wholesome and vigorous exertion!

The filthy tubs are emptied into a well, or uncovered receptacle, to which a door opens, close to the *Women Felons'* room.

The second story of this Gaol has one room for Criminals, somewhat larger than the foregoing; with two wooden bedsteads, and the same scanty kind of dirty bedding, but without a fire-place. Here are also two rooms for *Debtors,* with fireplaces in them, but neither coals nor any kind of bedding allowed: And, adjoining to these apartments, is a third for Debtors, called "The *Long Room,"* which has a large iron-grated but unglazed window. This is the Debtor's general Day-room; and in it *divine service is performed!*

There is no *Chapel* here: But, a place set apart for the worship of God, should seem to carry some respect with it,-even 'to the most unfeeling eye and indurated heart. In the above *Long-Room,* 'however, let me avow, it is hardly possible to be devout. What a close and motley assemblage is here exhibited! Clergyman, Gaoler, Criminals, Debtors, Men and Women, all huddled together in one small room; to which Joseph's dungeon must seem to him and his Egyptian associates a calm and tranquil retreat, if compared with this-memorable wilderness of human comfort. There is no need of adding, that a *House of Prayer* like the above, can not but, in the spirit of contrast, remind every one at the same moment, how it resembles the constant abode of an avowed *Den of Thieves*. In short, this is one of the worst constructed and constituted Gaols in Scotland.

The *Third Story* has what is termed the *Stock-Room* for criminals. Within this is a strong iron bar, sixteen inches in circumference, laid across the floor, garnished with rings for receiving the prisoners' legs, who are chained to it night and day, without the possibility of moving a step. The woman who lighted me along, and who had been here five years, said she remembered five prisoners at one time in this unhappy situation. Those, as I understand, who escape being chained to this formidable bar, are only fastened to a ponderous chain, rooted within the wall, of about four feet in length, which is padlocked to their fetters. In this room, and in this manner, the *wearied* and *heavy laden* are tantalized with the unenjoyed sight of a wooden *bedstead,* that has a little loose dirty straw scattered upon it: None of the prisoners, thus accoutred and secured, could make use of so desirable an indulgence.

Near to the above *Stock-Room,* a small door opens into another horrid place, called "The *Black-Hole* and most justly so, for it is buried in total darkness. The keeper, however, told me it was now become obsolete; and coals only, for the use of the prisoners, were here deposited, as there was no other place to lodge them.

I visited this Gaol at mid-day, but it was necessary to have lighted candles for inspecting it in every part. The turret staircases, of stone, are so very narrow, that two persons cannot pass each other except at the landing-place; and, to prevent falling down, you must have firm hold of the iron rail.

Debtors, Felons, and Petty Offenders here mix indiscriminately in the daytime; nor can it be otherwise whilst there are no court-yards for separation.

No sewers are provided; and the tubs substituted to supply their use are tnost extremely offensive. Water, none, except what is fetched by the Keeper from the town-well.

The whole Prison is filthy to a degree, that cannot be described but by an eyewitness. In a word, it is hardly possible to form an idea of this dreary recess of human wretchedness, or to conceive how it should be tolerated in a civilized country.

It is in contemplation to build a new Gaol.

The reader will please to observe, that under the words *sewers* and *drains* are comprehended those conveniences which delicacy forbids enlarging upon, though absolutely necessary to all houses, and the situation and construction of which are of the greatest importance in prisons. The want of carft respecting them is a principal cause of unhenlthiness in many of our Gaols and as such has always engaged my peculiar attention. ABERDEEN. *Scotland.*

The ATeu? *County and City Bridewell.*

Keeper, *James Watson.* Salary *l6ol.* out of which h« has to pay his Assistants, Fees, none.

Chaplain, not yet appointed.

Duty, once every Sunday.

Surgeon, Mr. *Moir*; who makes a Bill.

Number of Prisoners, 1809, Oct. 3, One.

Allowance, contracted for by the Keeper, from. 2. *id.* to 2. *9d.* per week each, according to a Dietary established by the Magistrates.

REMARKS.

This handsome Gaol stands about a mile from the centre of the town and was first opened for the reception of prisoners on the 2d of October, 1809; at the ceremony upon which occasion I was present. It commenced with an excellent and very appropriate prayer by Dr. Shirriff, surrounded by the Provost, Magistrates and Council, and attended by a number of other respectable Gentlemen.

The boundary wall encloses two acres of ground, and affords an ample space for the growth of vegetables, as well as court-yards for the prisoners.

At the entrance in front is a noble Arch, having on one side a Turnkey's Lodge, 'and a Guard-house on the other.

The Prison, in the centre of the area, has a 'very conspicuous and beautifully castellated appearance. The Keeper resides in 'the middle of the Prison.

On the ground-floor are fourteen sleeping-cells, and eleven work-cells, eight "feet by seven, and eight feet high each, to the crown of the arch; which open into a well-ventilated lobby, four feet wide. Every sleeping-cell has an iron bedstead, a straw-in-ticking bed, two blankets, a sheet, coverlet and bolster; a wooden stool to sit on, and, in one corner, a covered chamber conveniency. These cells have a glazed window in each, four feet long, and twelve inches wide, turning on a pivot, as at Edinburgh Bridewell. The work-cells have each two similar windows: every door has a circular grated aperture for ventilation; and there are two water-closets in the lobby adjacent.

The first story is similar to the ground-floor already described; and, besides apartments for the Keeper, contains the Visiting Magistrates' Room, which Jhas-six handsome sash-windows, tables, chairs, law-books, &c.

The second story is exactly the same as the first, with the Chapel, over the Magistrates' Room: The Prisoners are seated on forms in the area, and the sexes are separated by a curtain thrown across the centre.

The third story, which is like the other two, has a Store Room, over the Chapel, where bedding and the materials for work are deposited.

The fourth story, of similar dimensions, has the Large Room divided into three; two of which are for the Surgeon's accommodation, and the other for the nurse.

The attick story has two sleeping cells in the centre, and eight small cells, lighted from the roof; which therefore must be too hot in summer, and equally cold in winter to sleep in. The whole number of cells is 115. In the four first stories, each has *26*; the attick story has 11; and in each story, there is a dark cell.

A forcing pump throws up water into the cisterns, to supply the Prison, and cleanse the sewers, &c.

The employment here is picking of oakum, spinning, &c. And the Prisoners, after defraying their maintenance, have the whole net profit of their earnings; viz. half upon their discharge, and the remainder six months afterwards. Their uniform clothing, on admission, becomes their own at being discharged.

Here are no fire-places provided: But it is intended to introduce warmth into several rooms, by stoves placed in the several lobbies.

ABERGAVENNY. *South Woks.*

Keeper, *William Thomas:* Salary none. Consists of two Rooms; that fbi Prisoners, ten feet by four, with arched roof, wooden bedstead, and straw; lighted by an aperture in the wall; a grating of eight inches square in the door, through which they receive their provisions.

Prisoners, Nov. 16, 1802, none. Sept. 6, 1803, none. Sept. 12, 1806, none. Dimensions. To many of my Readers, the descriptions which I have given in this work, with respect to admeasurement, and other circumstances in the construction of Prisons, may possibly appear tedious, and too minute: But variety of description may also suggest something very useful, in the plana of such Prisons as shall be erected in future; and whatever can shew itself to be worthy of imitation, may thus be extracted from the best specimens. Let it moreover be considered, that in the construction of Building, as well as in the formation of New Establishments, it is important to be acquainted with many things, which, though apparently trivial, are often of material consequence for the purposes intended to be answered by them: And Magistrates, from being better informed as to the real state of Gaols, will be enabled to judge, whether the Prisons over which they preside, and to which they commit Offenders,, are judiciously adapted to effectuate the object of the design,

B ABINGDON. *Berkshire.*
The County Bridewell.

Keeper, *John Walker.* Salary, 100/. No Fees.

Chaplain; none yet appointed.

Surgeon, Mr. *Grinley,* who makes a Bill.

Number of Prisoners, August 22d 1811, Six.

Allowance, one pound and half of household bread, sent from the Baker, in loaves of that size. On weighing them singly, I found some nearly two ounces deficient; but on weighing four loaves together, the whole deficiency was about one ounce and a half.

REMARKS.

This New Prison, not yet quite finished, was first inhabited the 17th March 1811. It is situate near the Bridge, and part of its boundary-wall skirts the River *Ock.* The Sessions House, which forms the front, gives it a handsome appearance; and for the Prisoners here are four court-yards, of an irregular octagon shape, about 67 feet long by 64. Each court has a day or mess-room opening into it, of about 25 feet by 17, furnished with a table and forms, and warmed by a German stove. Here are likewise arcades, to work under, or for walking in wet weather.

The building consists of three wings, two stories high, branching in an angular direction. The Keeper's apartments, with the Sessions House and Offices, form the centre of it; and the windows of this structure command the several court-yards. On the first Prison story are sixteen sleeping-cells, of 8 feet *9* each by 7 feet 10, and,9 feet 6 inches high, to the crown of the arch. The upper story has the same number of cells; each furnished with a perforated cast-iron bedstead, on stonebearers, a straw-in-sacking bed, one blanket, a coarse hempen sheet, and a rug; lighted and ventilated by an iron-grated window, 4 feet by. 2 feet 3, with blinds to open, or shut close up, at the Prisoner's pleasure: the outer door is iron-grated, and the inner of wood.

The *Chapel* is on the second story of the central building, with doors of entrance for the several classes: Above it, in the attic-story, are two spacious Infirmaries, two foul wards, or rooms for infectious disorders, with two others for convalescents; and at the top of the building is an alarm-bell.

The excellent Rules and Regulations established in the Bridewell of *Reading* (See page 4Q7,) are ordered to be here also observed by the Keeper. All Prisoners wear the County Uniform, and their own clothes are purified, numbered, and deposited in the Wardrobe assigned, until the time of their trial, or discharge. The 42d article ordains clean straw, or chaff, for matresses, to be allowed as often as needful, and clean linen once a week. The 57th enjoins, that all Prisoners who receive the County Allowance, shall be kept to work: Those sentenced to hard labour are entitled to receive 20 *per cent,* of their nett Earnings; those not so sentenced are to have 50 *per cent,* agreeably to the Act 22 Geo. III. Cap. *64*; and the remainder to be equally divided between the County and the Keeper. The Prisoners' share is to be given them, in clothes or money, at their discharge; after deducting the cost of any wearing apparel issued, or any *extra allowance* of provisions, that may have been given them during confinement.

The 63d Article directs, "That if any Offender, during his confinement, has been industrious and obedient, the Chaplain and the Keeper shall give him, on his dismission, a certificate of such good behaviour; and no Offender is to be dismissed at the end of his term, (unless at his own request,) if he shall labour under any acute and dangerous distemper; nor until (in the opinion of the Surgeon) he can be discharged with safety: And when discharged, his own, or other decent clothing, shall be delivered to every Offender; together with such sum of money, as shall, by the Visiting Justice or Justices, in every Quarter Sessions, be deemed necessary for subsistence to the place of his legal settlement, not exceeding ten shillings."

ABINGDON. *The Town Gaol.*

Gaoler, *James Goldby,* Sergeant at Mace. Salary, 1*J I.* 16*s. Fees,* 6*s. Sd.* . Surgeon, when wanted, sent by the Mayor.

Number of Prisoners, 18th Aug. 1803, Two Criminals. 31st Aug. 18 *06,* One. 22d Aug. 1811, Two. I have not found one *Debtor* here at my several visits.

Allowance, sixpence per day, except

when committed to hard labour: They have then their Earnings only to subsist on.

REMARKS.

This Prison is the Old Gate-way. The ground-floor, about 14 feet square, with a fire-place, is chiefly used for Deserters: Its iron-grated window looks toward the street. Up stairs is a room for Debtors, who are committed by a Borough Process, and become entitled to their Sixpences in about six weeks.

For Felons, and other Criminal Prisoners, here are three small sleeping-rooms. A tub serves for a sewer; which, when emptied, on being nearly full, a Man receives one shilling. No court-yard: No water, but as brought in by the Gaoler; who appears to be a humane Man, and keeps the Prison as clean as its dilapidated state will permit.

ALDBOROUGH. *Suffolk.*

Town Gaol.

Gaoler. *Francis Osborne,* the town coal-meter.

Salary, none. 1805, Sept. 16. No Prisoners.

Two rooms on the ground-flour under the Town-hall; one of nine feet by four feet nine inches; lighted and ventilated by two apertures in the wall, 22 inches by seven: The other 15 feet six inches by eight feet four; lighted and ventilated by two apertures like the former, 18 inches wide by seven; mud floors, with loose straw. No court; no water. Prisoners are seldom confined here more than one night.

ALNWICK. *Northumberland.*

Town Gaol.

Gaoler, *John Thirlwal.* Salary none; but he lives at the Castle. This Prison is seldom used except for Deserters.

1802, Sept. 10th, and lSoj), Sept. 19th, no Prisoners.

The Town Gaol is under the Bond-Gate Tower, at the entrance of the town, and is the property of the Duke of Northumberland. It consists of one room 16 feet by 8, dark and damp, but lighted and ventilated by an aperture in the wall. Straw laid upon a barrack-bedstead.

At ALNWICK CASTLE are the remains of an ancient prison, which is kept in good preservation by his Grace of Northumberland. It is in the Inner Ward, or Tower, and is called The Dungeon, or Castle Keep. The entrance to it is through a passage 16 feet long, and 3 feet wide, leading to a room of 11 feet 4 inches by 10 feet 4. In the centre of this room is an iron-grated trap-door, nearly a yard square, which covers an aperture 2 feet 4 inches by 1 foot 10. The descent through this aperture is by a ladder into a dark and damp dungeon, 8 feet 6 inches square, and 11 feet high. The Arch appears to be of Saxon architecture. It was certainly built in the feudal times, when the *security* of prisoners, or captives, was *alone* considered. The servant who accompanied me said, there was formerly a dungeon in every tower of the Castle, but that this was the only one preserved.

ALNWICK. *Northumberland.*

The House of Correction.

Gaoler, *David Cousins.* Salary 25/.

Fees, for Felons, 13. *4d.* paid by the County; and 13. *4d.* for Assaults, and Bastardy, paid by themselves.

No religious attentions.

Surgeon, Mr. *Haswell;* who makes a Bill.

Number of Prisoners, 19th Sept. 1809, Two.

Allowance, *4d.* a day, paid to the Keeper for their support.

REMARKS.

This Prison, first inhabited in October, 1807, has, on the ground-floor, two of the Keeper's rooms in front. These are divided by a passage 4 feet 6 inches wide, leading to the Gaol door, and entrance into a lobby 24 feet long, and 4 feet 6 inches wide; with an iron-grated and glazed casement at the end of it, 19 inches by 16; and into this lobby five sleeping-cells open.

The smallest cell is 9 feet 5 by 7 feet 8, and 8 feet 4 inches high to the crown of the arch; the whole of stone, fitted up with wooden bedsteads for two persons, loose straw, two blankets, and a coverlet: a small uncovered tub for a sewer, emptied every morning; and a wooden stool to sit on. Every cell-door has an inspecting wicket 84-inches square.

On the North side is a court-yard for *Men,* who are allowed to be out for one hour in the day, accompanied by the Keeper: It is 42 feet square, and, in the centre, has a sewer, and a *pig-stye;* and part of it is planted with cabbages.

The Women's court is on the Southside, 63 feet by 36, with a detached sewer in it. The area forms the Keeper's garden, and is planted with vegetables. Females have the use of this garden one hour in the day.

Above stairs are three sleeping-cells for Women, of the same size with those below, and opening into a lobby of like dimensions. Their cells contain two wooden bedsteads for two persons each, and are fitted up like those assigned for the men.

There is also a large work-room on this floor, of 22 feet by 12, with two large grated and glazed lift-up sash windows, and a large fire-place; for which coals are allowed during the six winter months. For the rest of the year the prisoners work in their sleeping-cells, which, having no grate, are frequently very cold.

c

The Magistrates hold their Petty Sessions every fortnight in a convenient room above stairs. No rules, however, or regulations are printed and stuck up. Here are no rooms set apart for the sick: No day-room allotted: No bath or oven to purify foul or infected clothes: No water accessible: even the Keeper, for his own use, fetches it from a pump 300 yards distant! The Act for preserving the Health of Prisoners, and Clauses against Spirituous Liquors, are not hung up.

The employment of the Prisoners consists in beating hemp, picking oakum, winding cotton, cutting candle-wicks, spinning and knotting of rope. The average of earnings is *3d.* per day, which the Keeper has, in aid of maintenance. The Prisoners have no share; neither do they receive any money on being discharged, to carry them home, or prevent those necessities, which may impel them to predatory acts, when happily liberated from a gaol. ANDOVER. *Hampshire.*

Gaoler, *Thomas Cowley*; No Salary:

A Shoemaker by trade: but he is likewise Town-Crier, and Keeper of the Town-Hall, as also Collector of the Market-Tolls; from each of which appointments he derives some casual Fee.

Fees, Debtors and Felons, 3. *4d.*

Surgeons, Messrs. *Poore* and *Pitman*; they make a Bill.

Number of Prisoners, Debtors. Felons, &c.

l8oi, Jan. 10th,--------0-----0 1802, Dec. 28th,--------1 0 1807, Sept. 25th,-o 0

Allowance, to those who are unable to maintain themselves, *6d.* per day; and, in extremely cold weather, a fire.

REMARKS.

This Gaol, for the Borough of Andover, consists of two rooms, with boarded floors, one over the other. That for Men is about 16 feet by 14, and 8 feet high: the upper room, for the Women, 14 feet by 12, and of the same height as the former. Here is a small court-yard, about 16 feet square.

The Debtors sent here, are only those committed by process issuing out of Andover Town-court.

The Borough allows straw only on bedsteads.

Prisoners for felony, after final examination, are committed to the County Gaol at Winchester. The two rooms set apart for them look toward the river, through small iron-grated windows. The court is in front of the house, and the passage, or road through it, is separated from the main-street by a very low paling; so that the Prisoners can have no use of it....

When I was here in 1807, the Women's Gaol was filled up with tanner's bark, made into balls for fuel.

The Gaoler's house, being under the same roof as the Prison, a bed-chamber in it is appropriated to Prisoners, in case they are more than the Gaol can conveniently accommodate.

ANNAN. *Scotland.*

The Town Gaol.

Gaoler, *William Roxburgh,* who is a Shoemaker, and lives near the Prison. Salary, *lol.*

Fees, for Debtors, who are Burgesses, *2d.* a night: If not Burgesses, *4d.* a night.

No religious attentions; nor Surgeon.

Number of Prisoners, Debtor. Criminals.

2d Nov. 1809,---5------0

Allowance, Criminals, *4d.* a day in bread. Debtors, as alimented.

REMARKS

This Gaol is built at one end of the Court-House, in the centre of the High-street, and has, on the right-hand, a place called *The Black-Hole,* with an iron-grating toward the street, and straw on the floor; which is used for temporary confinement, till the Prisoners are sent to Dumfries.

On the left hand is a room for Debtors, with a grated and glazed window, fireplace, and wooden bedstead.

Up stairs are three other sizeable rooms for Debtors, the windows of which are large, and so made to open, that a cheerful view of the town, as well as light and ventilation are afforded; which ranks this amongst the very best Prisons in Scotland.

No bedding whatever is here allowed: No court-yard; no coals; nor water, except as brought in by the Keeper: and the place of a sewer is supplied by a tub.

APPLEBY. *Westmoreland.*

The County Gaol.

Gaoler, *James Bewsker;* a Blacksmith: His shop is at the foot of the Bridge nearly opposite the Gaol. Salary, *20l.* Conveyance of Transports to Whitehaven, *Is.* per mile. Fees for Debtors and Felons, (see Table.) But the Under-Sheriff demands *6s. 8d* from every Debtor for his *Liberate t* Garnish, not yet abolished, *Is.*

Chaplain, Rev. *James Metcalfe.* Salary 15/.

Duty, Sunday afternoon, Prayers and Sermon.

Surgeon, Mr. *Bushby;* makes a Bill.

Number of Prisoners, Debtors. Felons, &c.

1800, March 31st,-6 3 lS0«, Sept. 24th,--4 0 1809, Nov. 4th, 9 4

Allowance, to Debtors, none whatever: to Felons, and other Criminal Prisoners, fourpence a-day.

REMARKS.

This Gaol was built by the County. The Earl of *Tfianet* is Hereditary Sheriff, and pays the Gaoler his Salary. The Prison itself is out of the reach of the floods, but the river sometimes overflows part of the Court-yard.

In the lower part of the Gaol are four vaulted Wards for Felons, 144. feet by 13; with straw on the floor, and two blankets to sleep on; a small grated window in each, but no chimney: and over them are three good rooms with fireplaces for Debtors. There being no chapel, Divine Service is performed in the Debtor's Day-room. Here is only one court-yard, 96 feet by 66; so that debtors and felons, men and women of all descriptions, associate promiscuously together during the day-time. They have *no Kitchen,* and are therefore obliged to *dress their victuals under the open arch of the landing-place of the flight of stone steps, leading to the Debtors' apartments!* A pump in the court-yard supplies the prison with water.

Table Of Fees,

To be taken by the Keeper of *Appleby Gaol,* as agreed to by the Bench of Justices, at the Midsummer General Quarter Sessions, 14th July 1/97 *£. s. d.*

"For the discharge of a Debtor-0134

For every person committed by warrant of a Justice of the Peace 0 6 8

For a Copy of Commitment, when demanded------010

For a Certificate of Commitment, in order to obtain a Writ of *Habeas Corpus* ------026

For signing a Certificate, in order to obtain a Supersedeas, or a

Rule or Order of Court-----------026

For the Discharge of a Prisoner by Proclamation at the Assizes, or General Quarter Sessions----------013 4

Here is a Gaol Delivery *once* a year. No Employment is provided, and prisoners who are of handicraft trades, can seldom procure it from the town.

The Act for Preservation of Health, and Clauses against the use of Spirituous Liquors, are both properly hung up; as is also the foregoing Table of Fees, of which I took a copy.

i APPLEBY. *County Bridewell.*

Keeper, *John Atkinson.* Salary, 12/. No

Fees.

Prisoners, 24th September, 1802, Two Lunaticks. Allowance, none.

REMARKS.

This comfortless Prison, as appears by the date in front, was built in 1639, and consists of two cells, 13 feet each by 8, with vaulted roofs. Straw laid on the floor. No light or air, but what is admitted through an aperture of 12 inches by 4. These cells are subject to floods. There is one large room above stairs, but considered as insecure. No court-yard; no water accessible.

But how is a Debtor, on his entrance into Prison, to acquire money as fees for his discharge, when his credit has been crushed; the exertions of his 'industry precluded; and unusual expences have accumulated against him, in consequence of his dreary situation! Here is no allowance, either from his Plaintiff or from the County, for the sustenance of a poor confined Debtor. Here is neither provision, nor clothing, be the weather's extremity what it may i nor even bedding, except of straw, but what the destitute starveling must hire..Let us now shift the scene, and be astonished at the contrast. He wretch charged with crimes the most atrocious, and under the strongest presumptions of guilt, is perfectly attended to in the various respects of comfort above-mentioned. And what is the fatal consequence? All those notions of comparative turpitude, which it is so much the interest of society to keep clear and prominent in the mind of man, are thus utterly confounded and over-thrown. ASHBOURNE. *Derbyshire.*
The House of Correction.
Gaoler, *Thomas Lytton.*

Salary 25/. out of which he furnishes straw for the Prisoners.

Fees, none.

Surgeon, when wanted, is ordered by the Magistrate.

Prisoners,

1802, Oct. 12th. Criminal, 1. Deserters, 2.

Allowance, to each four-pence a-day; but if work is procured, they have the produce of their labour only.

REMARKS.

This structure was erected in 1784, and stands in *Back-Lane*. It is a neat square building, and consists of a room on the ground-floor for the Keeper, about 16 feet square, with a fire-place in it, and two glazed windows. These command the two court-yards, which are 30 feet each by *16,* and have sewers at the farther ends. The wall being only 14 feet high, the court-yards are rather insecure.

Men-prisoners hve a day-room, of 17 feet by 9 feet *6* inches, and seven feet high, which opens into their court-yard, and has a fire-place, and an iron-grated and glazed window. Into this room open two sleeping-cells, each feet long by feet, and 64-feet high.

No bedding is here provided; and the straw in lieu of it is furnished by the Keeper: But I observed in the sleeping-cells, not only some loose straw, but two old blankets and a rug.

Above stairs are two rooms for Women-prisoners, with sleeping-cells attached, like those for the men. In one of them was a bedstead, intended for the Keeper: but, as he lives in the town, the more orderly prisoners have the use of it; and either furnish their own bedding, or pay the Keeper for the use of his.

A trap-door in the flooring opens into a *loathsome dungeon,* nine steps down, which is about six feet square, and as many in height; dark and damp, with a bricked floor, but without even straw for bedding. I hope it is never used, and wish it were entirely bricked up.

No water: The Keeper told me he carried it to the Prisoners twice a-day. The whole Prison very dirty. No Rules and Orders. The Act for Preserving Health, and Clauses against Spirituous Liquors, are not hung up.

AYLESBURY. *Buckinghamshire.*
The County Gaol, and Bridewell.
Gaoler, *Henry Sherriff.*

Salary, for the Gaol, *140l.* for the Bridewell, 30/.

Fees and Garnish abolished: But the Under-Sheriff takes from each Debtor 2a-. *6d.* for his *Liberate.*

For Transports, the expenceof conveying them.

Chaplain, Rev. Mr. *Hopkins.* Salary 50/.

Duty, Prayers and a Sermon every Sunday: and daily attendance on those Prisoners who are left for execution.

Allowance, to Debtors and Prisoners of every description, one pound and half of best wheaten bread per day, and a pint of soup twice a week. *Convicts* under sentence of *transportation* have the *King's Allowance* of 2s. *6d.* per week.

The Allowance made to the Sheriff of Buckinghamshire, upon passing his accounts annually iu the Court of Exchequer, of 2s. *6d.* per week (for the maintenance of capital convicts, and convicts at the assizes for transportable offences, detained in the Gaol) is issued under an order from the Chancellor of the Exchequer. The Under-Sheriff makes out an account, containing the name of the convict, the time when convicted, and the number of weeks from that period till the convict is sent off, or till the end of the Sheriffalty, in case the convict so long remains in his custody. And, as the County supports the convict with bread and clothing, the Under-Sheriff from lime to time pays to the County Treasurer the sums so allowed in his bill of cravings, in aid of that expenditure. As there arc many Counties, who do not know how to apply for the transport's money, 2s. *6d.* a week, I insert this note to instruct them in the mode of application for it. REMARKS.

This Gaol adjoins to the back part of the magnificent *Shire-Hall.* The original construction of the building was faulty in the extreme; but the Marquis of *Buckingham,* ever attentive to the interests of the County, having humanely interfered in its Prison concerns, the *loathsome dungeon* is now inaccessibly bricked up, and the Gaol has received many other and great improvements.

Here is but one court-yard for *Debtors,* 54 feet by *26,* paved with flag-stones, and a sewer in one corner: two day-rooms, with fire-places, and glazed windows; the largest room 20 feet by 14.

Above stairs are seven good bedrooms, all *Free Wards*; furnished with wooden bedsteads, flock beds, a blanket, and coverlet, at the County's expence. One of the smallest rooms is set apart for Women Debtors.

Men Felons have a court-yard, of 32 feet by 24, paved with flag-stones, and the sewer is in one corner. They have three day-rooms, whose average size is 16 feet by 14; with cupboards for provisions, and benches to sit on, opening into the courtyard.

Their sleeping-cells, sixteen in number, are over the well-room and straw-room, and open into lobbies seven feet wide. Each cell is *6* feet 6 by 5 feet, furnished with a wooden bedstead, straw mattress, and one blanket; and ventilated by an iron grating in the door, 9 inches square, and another in the roof, 42 inches by 18. Here is one *solitary cell,* of *6* feet 6 by 1 foot 9 inches, totally dark, and without ventilation; where the refractory prisoner sleeps on the floor upon loose straw, with a blanket.

There being no stated *Chapel,* divine service is performed in the *Shire-Hall.* The Felons ascend to it from the lobby, into which their cells open, by a ladder of 25 steps, and three inches broad, to a trap-door made in the floor of the SessionsHouse, 2 feet 6 inches long, by 2 feet 3 broad, opening into the Prisoners' bar, which is about 10 feet by 9; and here they sit to hear divine service.

The Bridewell Prisoners are seated on benches within the bar: Debtors, on a row of benches, called The *Attornies' Seats*; and the women are placed in a pew, on the left hand of the chair.

When I attended divine service on the l›th January, 1805, thirteen criminals and four debtors received the sacrament, which is administered four times a year. Many persons also from the town are accustomed to attend upon this occasion; and the money collected is distributed amongst the criminals. All prisoners are required to attend divine service.

A Chapel *within the Prison,* properly partitioned *off,* so as to exclude the classes from the sight of each other, is an accommodation much wanted. It would afford their exemplary Chaplain an opportunity of selecting occasionally, and of applying particular passages from scripture, the most appropriate to each description of the prisoners.

The *Well-Room,* which is assigned for Prisoners under sentence of death, is 28 feet long by 13 feet 3, and 9 feet 5 inches high; with a brick floor, and small fire place. There are in it five well-ventilated cells, of *6* feet 7 by 5 feet and an inch; fitted up with a wooden bedstead, a straw-in-sacking bed, and two blankets each.

The *Straw Room* for deserters, of 20 feet *6* inches by 15 feet 4, has a barrack-bed, the whole length of the room, and raised two feet from the floor, with loose straw, and a blanket for bedding. It opens into a lobby, 20 feet by ll; in which there is a cell for one Prisoner, of feet by 5 feet; and adjoins to the Weil-Room.

Female Felons are confined in the Women's Bridewell, and have a court-yard, of 28 feet by 24; in which there is a sewer; a day-room, 20 feet by 10; a washhouse, 17 feet by 12, with a cistern, copper, and fire-place; and a sleeping-room, 13 feet by 12; all which have boarded floors. There are also five sleeping cells, of 7 feet by *6* feet 6, with a wooden bedstead, straw, and one blanket each.

The *Men's Bridewell* has a court-yard, 47 feet by 29, with a sewer; a large work-room, on the ground-floor, of 43 feet by 12; and a day-room, of 19 feet 9 inches by 15 feet *6*. On the first floor are five sleeping cells, each 7 feet by 6 feet 6; with iron-grated windows, and inside shutters; a bedstead for two persons, loose straw and a blanket. The second story has eleven cells, of the same dimensions, and furnished in the same manner as the former; also one dark cell for the refractory, of 7 feet by 3 feet 6 inches, ventilated by an aperture of 6 inches by 5.

The *Infirmary* is a neat building, detached from the Gaol, and consists of two large rooms on the ground floor, 24 feet by 18, and paved with brick. In one of them is an excellent mill, with a pair of mill-stones for grinding corn, and the apparatus for dressing the flour. Above are two rooms for the sick, of the same size as the former, with boarded floors and large glazed windows: A kitchen, 16 feet by 12 feet 9; a room for the nurse, nearly of the same size, with suitable conveniences for invalids.

A liberal supply of coals is allowed to the day-rooms, from the l6th of October to the lfith of April: But if the weather be very severe, the time is extended by the considerate Magistrates.

For Prisoners *under sentence of death,—*the mournful inhabitants of the " *WellRoom?* already described,—time, and the just reflections of reason, have at length given their lot a favourable turn: They are not, as heretofore, exposed to pitiless curiosity. There was a time, when the people of Aylesbury were greatly averse to having the place of execution fixed at the *Gaol, "*because it was *within the town."* During my sheriffalty, I represented to the Marquis of Buckingham what an excel

D lent place we had for the purpose; and, after getting several models made in London, the one fixed upon is, I think, the completest piece of mechanism in this kingdom, and was used, for the first time, this year, 1810. Tis an incident that 6eems to interest humanity; and I therefore wish some notice to be taken of it, that other counties may "do likewise." In this particular, my endeavours to that end have been very successful; and I hope that the remaining towns (few in comparison), will join to root out the old custom upon such distressful occasions. Here, now, in Aylesbury, the poor condemned wretch no longer passes his dreariest days in a loathsome dungeon, to be thence dragged *through the town* in a *cart* to execution, at some distance, to gratify the cruel insensibility of the multitude, and disgrace the character of civilized society: But an occasional platform, for the awful business, is fixed in front of the County-Hall; and the last comforts are calmly administered *to* the sufferer, previous to his public exposure and punishment.

Some years ago the Prisoners were employed by the Gaoler, (and shops were erected by him for the purpose) in sawing stone and timber, sifting of sand, &c. But this has been discontinued; and now a trifling quantity of hemp, beat once or twice in a month, is the only employment.

At the Summer Assize, Prisoners are removed from hence to Buckingham.

The following Memorial *of a Legacy,* is hung up in Aylesbury Church, and the donation is regularly paid.

"William Findall, in the year 1604, gave *Six pounds thirteen shillings and fourpence,* to be paid on Midlent-Sunday annually, into the bands of the Church-Wardens of the Parish of Aylesbury, for the time being, for ever, out of Summer-Leys, in the Parish of *Weston-TurviUe,* for the following purposes; viz.

£. s. d.
To the Poor of Weston-Turville--------- 068

To the Prisoners in Aylesbury Gaol- 013 4

To a Scavenger, to keep the Church-ways clean-----0134

The Remainder (after deducting 15s. 6d, for the Land-Tax) is distributed to the Widows and distressed Poor of the Parish of Aylesbury."

There are likewise other donations, which ought to be recorded; viz.

The Earl of Chesterfield has, for several years, given at every Christmas, two pounds of beef, and one shilling in money, to each Prisoner. It is distributed by Mr. Curry, his Lordship's Steward, at Eythorp, in the County of Bucks.

The Rev. Mr. *Hopkins,* for the thirty years of his officiating as Chaplain to the County Gaol, has given to the Prisoners every Christmas, One Guinea; which is equally distributed amongst them by the Gaoler.

Frequently have I attended Divine service at Aylesbury Gaol, and witnessed the pious and energetic spirit with which the above exemplary Chaplain has addressed the Prisoners; but, particularly, on Sunday the 5th of August, 1810, (the day previous to their removal to Buckingham for trial;) when he admonished the profligate, aroused the thoughtless, and comforted the afflicted, in a manner so pointedly impressive, that it not only drew tears from the Criminals, but visibly affected the numerous and silent congregation that usually attends the service with them in the Shire-Hall.

It is a circumstance peculiarly fortunate, when a Prison, ill-constructed for every humane purpose, attracts the notice of Power, and the warm attentions of BenevoLence, as is really the case with the one which I have here described. Not only *Fees* and *Garnish* are abolished, but a well-behaved Debtor is indulged with "the *Rules"* (or range of space for air and exercise) which extend along the Pavement in front of the County-Hall. Comfortable bedding also is here *gratuitously* furnished. No one is discharged from hence, without receiving the price of a day's labour, to convey him home: And thus, that punishment which the law ordains equally to vice, to folly or misfortune, is *here* meted out in mercy: an example worthy of imitation throughout the kingdom.

The Gaol is supplied with religious books; and poor Prisoners, when discharged, have money given them, according to their distance from home; not merely for immediate sustenance, but to remove the great temptation of committing a crime for that purpose.

Books are kept in the Prison, in which the Visiting Magistrates, Chaplain and Surgeon, enter their several Reports.

Water is well supplied from a rivulet at the bottom of the Keeper's Garden, by means of a forcing pump worked by the Prisoners.

The Act for Preservation of Health, and Clauses against the Use of Spirituous Liquors, are here conspicuously hung up.

AYLESHAM. *Norfolk.*
The Bridewell.
Keeper, *William Howes.*
Salary 40 now 55/. Also one-fourth of the Prisoners' earnings, and coals, mops, brooms, and pails for the use of the Prison.
Chaplain, Rev. Mr. *Addison.* Salary 30/.
Duty, Sermon on Sundays; Prayers on Wednesdays and Fridays.
. 1
Surgeon, Mr. *Taylor.* Salary, none; but makes a Bill.
Number of Prisoners, 1805, Sept. 3d. 14 1810, Sept 6th,--------g

Allowance, sixpence a-day in money, or in bread, pease, and potatoes.
REMARKS.
On the front of the Keeper's house, is the following venerable *Inscription,* cut or carved in wood.

"GOD save oure suprem Hed Kyng Henry the Eyght. Pray for the Good Prosperyte and Asstate' of *Robert Mersham* and lane his Wyfe, the wiche this Howse they cawsed to be made, To the Honor of the Towne be their Owyck Lyfe. FINES.

"This Howse was made in the Yer of our Lorde, 1543.
R. M. I. B."

At the back of the Keeper's house is a court-yard *60* feet square, with a pump in it, and two sewers. The Prisoners have one hour in the morning to wash and clean themselves, which the *Rules* require them to do, before they receive their bread; and likewise half an hour in the evening for the same purpose. Soap and towels are allowed them by the County, a clean shirt every week, and clean sheets once a month.

On the ground-flour 'are five cells, which open into a well-ventilated lobby, 40 feet long, and 4 feet wide; at the end of which is the *Chapel,* 18 feet by 10, and 8 feet *6* inches high; with a fire-place.

Above stairs are five other cells, and an *Infirmary* over the Chapel, and of the same size, which open into a lobby of the like dimensions. Each cell is 12 feet by 7, and 8 feet 6 inches high, with arched roofs, and fitted up with a crib bedstead, straw-in-sacking, bed, one sheet, two blankets, and a rug: In each door is a wicket, or pot-hole, of 6 inches by 4.

There are also four cells, adjoining to the Keeper's wash-house, for the women; and these have glazed windows.

Yellow and brown striped clothing is provided for the Prisoners by the County. Hemp blocks were heretofore used; but as there is no hemp supplied, a mill is now substituted for the grinding of corn, &c.

The Rules and Orders are hung up; but not the Act for Preserving Health, nor the Clauses against Spirituous Liquors. The Prison is white-washed once a year.

AYR. *Scotland.*
The Town and County Gaol.
Gaoler. *William Paul.* Salary 35/.
Fees, none, either for Debtors or Felons.

Chaplain, none; nor any religious attentions whatever: Not even to those under sentence of death, unless gratuitously and voluntarily attended.

Surgeon. When one is wanted, sent in, on application to the Magistrates.

Number of Prisoners, Debtors. Felons, &«.
2Sth Oct. 1 809.-----4.------10.

Allowance to *Felons,* &c. *4d.* a-day in bread. *Debtors* as alimented. One Man had only *6d.* the others *8d.* per day.

REMARKS.
This Prison adjoins to the Justiciary Court. The ascent to it is by a fine flight of 20 steps, and the entrance forms the Guard-House, a door from which opens into a room under the Court, and is called "The *L010 Prison*:" And this is the only place for the confinement of Debtors, male or female. It is 19 feet long by 12 feet wide; has double iron-grated and glazed windows, 4 feet square; a fire-place; two small tables, and benches to sit upon; a turn-up bed-stead, two wooden bedsteads on the floor, and two others at the top of them, ascended by a small ladder: But no bedding whatever, nor coals allowed.

Here are also two cells for criminals, each 14 feet by 9 feet 6; with an aperture, about 3 feet long and 8 inches wide, made through the wall; but both light and air are almost totally excluded by the iron stancheons and perforated iron plates which extend the whole length of the aperture. The floors of the cells are stone, and spread over with a little loose straw only to sleep on; no fire-places, nor water, save what is brought in by the Keeper; and a tub uncovered serves the purpose of a sewer.

The floor above is in the Steeple, and therefore, perhaps called "The HighPrison." It contains two cells, of 12 feet by 8, with light and ventilation equally obstructed, and, in other respects, similar to those before described.

The upper or attick story has two rooms, about *16* feet each by 11, with floors, for Criminals. The windows of the Women's-Room are iron-grated, and about 3 feet square: That for the Men has an aperture in the wall, about four inches wide, with an iron stancheon up the middle: No bedding but some loose straw: No fire-place in either of the rooms, nor any furniture whatever; a tub in place of a sewer: And no water, but what is brought by the Gaoler, who lives distant.

Some of the doors here are of iron, others strongly clouted with it; and all, excepting those on the upper-story, open into dark passages, so that I found a candle necessary, though both my visits were made in the day-time.

James Fisher, committed hither for stealing apples out of an orchard, had a pair of leg-bolts on him, made something like handcuffs, but the iron five times thicker; the stiff iron bar attached to which, must require uncommon and painful exertion for the Prisoner to rise on his feet; and even then he could not walk or move either foot more than two or three inches at a step before the other. At the time of my visit he had been thus shackled for sixty days. The Keeper told me the Prisoner had been very unruly; and his having discovered marks of insanity, was the cause of his being thus cruelly ironed. The Magistrates were desirous to release him, but neither his son, nor any other would take charge of him. Before I left Ayr, his irons were taken off; the Magistrates, however, could get no person to receive him. As the circuit is only twice a-year, April and September, a Prisoner may be here confined six months without coming out of his cell, or tasting the fresh air; and the Gaoler informed me that he has had 23 Prisoners at one time.

30th Oct. 1809. The Magistrates and Council of Ayr assembled, were pleased to honour me with the freedom of the Burgh, which was greatly enhaneed by the speech delivered by the Chief Magistrate on presenting it. BANBURY. *Oxfordshire.*
The Town Gaol and Bridewell.
Gaoler, *Joseph Wise.* Salary, 15/.

Fees, for Debtors and Felons, 13. *4d.* 1
for Bridewell Prisoners, 6. *8d.* J
Surgeon, when wanted, from the Town.

Prisoners, 1803, August 20th. Debtors, none. One Woman Felon. Allowance, to Debtors, none. Criminal Prisoners have sixpence per day.

REMARKS.
This Prison appears to have been built in 1706. It has two dark and offensive rooms below; one of them called The *Gaol,* the other The *Bridewell;* with straw upon the floors to sleep on.

The Debtors confined here are by process issuing out of the Borough Court; and in the Keeper's house there is a room above stairs, for such as can pay *2s. 6d.* per week. Here is no court-yard, but one might be made out of the Gaoler's garden, into which the iron-grated windows of the Prison look, and of which the back part of his house commands a view. No water accessible to the Prisoners; nor any employment provided for them. Neither the Act for Preserving Health, nor the Clauses against Spirituous Liquors, hung up.

BALA. *Merionethshire, North Wales.*
The Bridewell.
Keeper, *William Jones.* Salary, *6I.* 1803, Dec. 27th. No Prisoners. Surgeon from the town, if wanted. Allowance, three shillings per week for each, which is paid to the Keeper.

REMARKS.
This Bridewell consists of two rooms adjoining to the Town-Hall, of about eleven feet square. Here is a small court-yard. No water, but what is brought by the Keeper.' BANFF. *Scotland.*
The Town Gaol.
Gaolers, The four Town Officers, in weekly rotation.

Salary, none, except from the Town. See *Remarks.*

Fees, for *Felons,* none. *Debtors, 4d.* a night. No religious attentions.

Surgeon, Mr. *James Smith,* who makes a Bill.

Number of Prisoners, Debtor. Felons. Luna tick.
6th Oct. 1809,----1.--3. 1.

Allowance, Felons, *3d.* a day. Debtors, as alimented.

REMARKS.

This Gaol is built adjoining the Town-Hall; and has on the second floor two spacious rooms for Debtors, with flagged floors, lift-up sash-windows, and fire-places, but no coals allowed. Two wooden bedsteads enclosed by a dwarf partition, have a little loose straw as the only bedding afforded; and a sewer is enclosed in one corner. The doors of these rooms open into a flagged lobby, five feet wide, with a large grated window at the end, for light and ventilation. Two strong cells for Felons communicate with this lobby, and are about eleven feet square, with vaulted roofs; but no fire-places, nor bedsteads, or bedding, except a little loose straw on the floor. They are lighted and ventilated by a narrow aperture, with a strong iron stancheon run up the middle.

No court-yard. No water accessible: but there is a very convenient place at the top of the building for a cistern to supply the Prison; which, it is to be hoped, will not be forgotten, when the plan for furnishing the Town and County Hall with so necessary an article, is carried into effect. A forcing pump for so good a purpose might be worked by the Prisoners.

The following is a Copy of the Report made to the Court of Session in 1808, by the Town Clerk, in pursuance of an order to that effect.

"The Gaol of Banff, which was built a few years ago, is one of the most commodious, secure, and airy, it is believed, in Scotland.

"It contains, on the second story, two strong cells for delinquents, and two spacious rooms for civil debtors.

"Besides these there are two very large apartments, on the ground-floor also, intended for a House of Correction, and employment for many Prisoners; but not being finished, they have not yet been used.

The Town Officers, four in number, act as Gaolers by weekly rotation; for which, besides the perquisites specified below, they receive a small salary from the revenue of the town. The Gaoler, for the week, is obliged to attend the Prison, and clean the same; to procure the Prisoners what necessaries they may want, and carry any communications which they may have occasion to send out of the Gaol.

The Gaol Fees, exacted according to immemorial custom and practice, are, "From the Incarcerator of any Civil Debtor, under letters of caption, £. s. d.

"To the Town Clerk, for booking 0 5 0
To the Gaoler, for receiving the Prisoner------010

"From the Incarcerator, or person interested in the imprisonment of any person incarcerated under a Warrant *de meditatione fugce,* Laborrow, or any other Warrant of an inferior Judge, £. . d.

"To the Town Clerk-0 2 6
To the Gaoler--0 1 0

Every Prisoner possessed of Funds, except those who are committed for trial, and Convicts, pay for every night of confinement to the Gaoler, as follows, viz. £. . d.

"If a Burgess of Banff, 6 3 4
If not a Burgess--------------068

"No Fees are exacted on the liberation of Prisoners..

"There is no instance of a Prisoner having been confined here for Gaol-Fees, after his Incarcerator consented to his liberation: But the Gaolers frequently detain what effects the Prisoner may have had in Gaol, until they are paid their fees; and, for want of payment, sometimes obtain warrant, and sell the effects by auction. The rate of aliment allowed to poor Debtors, who apply for the benefit of the act, commonly called the Act of Grace, varies from *6d.* to 1. *per diem*; generally *8d.* or *gd.*

John Smith.' BASINGSTOKE. *Hampshire. Bridewell.* The Head Constable is the Keeper. No Salary.

Allowance, sixpence a-day.

Here are two close offensive rooms, adjoining the court-house, each 13 feet by 4, with a small iron-grating over the doors. Straw upon the floor. No court-yard, nor water. A very narrow passage to the sewer.

1802, March 20th,')-.1. 1803, October, jN-Pnsoners. i.' ....;. ; r BARKING. *Essex.*

,, 7%e Gao/, a«£ *House of Correction.* Keeper, *Thomas Miller,* a shoemaker. Salary 38/.

Fees, none. Conveyance of each Prisoner to Chelmsford for trial, 30.

Chaplain, *Rev. Ebert Jefferys.* Salary *20l.*

Duty, Sermon on Sundays. There being no Chapel, Divine Service is performed in the Keeper's house.

Surgeon, Mr. *Ireland.* Salary 15/.

Number of Prisoners, 1S06, June 21st,----------14 1808, Aug. 26th,---------5

Allowance, one pound and a half of bread, furnished by the *Gaoler;* and a quart of table beer sent from the Brewer's, at *20s.* per barrel. Women, for their children, have bread, milk, and sugar, to the amount of about seven farthings per day. Five chaldrons of coals also are yearly allowed to the Prison.

REMARKS.

This Prison, situate in the North Street, stands in the middle of a garden, containing about an acre.

From the Gaoler's house is a descent by a flight of eighteen steps, to a court-yard, paved with flag-stones, 64 feet by 11; which is divided by an iron-palisaded gate, and contains six well-ventilated sleeping cells, of 10 feet by 8, and 9 feet high. There is an iron-grating over every door, with a shutter to put up at night. The floors are of oak-plank, and the rooms are furnished with wooden cradle-bedsteads, strawin-sacking bed, one blanket, or two, as the season may require, and a rug.

One of the cells has a fire-place; and there is a pump of excellent water.

On the other side of the Keeper's house is the Men's working room, 14 feet by 13, with a fire-place, and glazed window. The employment of the Prisoners is to pick oakum; and they have the half of their earnings.

The Women's Court-yard is 28 feet by 8 feet 9 inches; and their work-room 15 feet by 14, and 10 feet high; with a fire-place and glazed window. They have also a *Lying-in Room,* 9 feet by 8, with bedsteads and bedding, like those for the Men.

Above stairs is a room for the sick, 17

feet square, with fire-place, and opposite windows. But this room, at my visit in 1806, was filled with breeding cages, and a variety of birds; and in 1808, was used as a cutting shop, and filled up with leather.

The Prisoners have County clothes, and a bathing tub supplied them: Clean linen once a week; and when discharged, which is always *in the morning,* they have money given them, according to their respective distances from home.

BARNSTAPLE. *Devonshire.*
The Borough Gaol, and Bridewell.
Gaoler, *Nathaniel Blackwill.* Salary, 5/. Fees, 4s. *4d.*
Chaplain, none: nor any religious attentions.
Surgeon, when wanted, is sent in by the Parish.

Prisoners, 4th Dec. 1810, Debtor, 1. Petty Offender, *I.* Foreigners, 2. Allowance to Debtors, none; to Criminals, *twopence half-penny per day,* from the Parish..... i.....:.
REMARKS.,.
Here is only one court-yard for Debtors, Felons, and all descriptions of Male Prisoners, which is 26 feet square, with a pump to supply it with water.

The *Debtors Prison* consists of one room on the ground-floor, 12 feet by 11, and 7 feet high, with a boarded floor, and an iron-grated window., No fire-place. Their sleeping room above is 15 feet by 14, and 8 feet high, with barrack bedstead, and straw only allowed. It has a glazed-window, and a fire-place; but no coals are supplied. Debtors committed hither are by process issuing out of the Borough Court, which is held once a fortnight, on Mondays; and the number confined within the last four years and a half has been only *seven.*

The part called the *Felons' Prison* is one room, 14 feet by 8, and 7 feet 6 inches high, on the ground-floor; with a barrack bedstead, to which straw only is furnished for bedding. Here is a fire-place, but incapable of being used: No fuel allowed; and the iron-grating looks to the street.

The *Bridewell Part* consists of one room below, 14 feet by 12, and 6 feet high; with boarded floor, an unglazed grated window, but no fire-place: And one room above, of the same size, with barrack bedsteads, and straw only allowed.

Females are kept separate from Male Prisoners, both day and night; but they have no court-yard.

Here is a Gaol-Delivery twice a-year, at the Session, which is held before the Mayor, Aldermen, and Recorder, who is a Barrister of this Borough. They have a Power of Charter, of trying all offences committed within it, except capital felonies: for which Prisoners are confined here only for a-day or two, till fully committed to the County Gaol. The Prison is dry, airy, and well ventilated.

I have heretofore been at Barnstaple, but never had an idea that a Prison existed there, no such having been mentioned by Mr. Howard. A petition, by letter, from Mr. Roberts, a worthy resident of the town, in favour of a poor debtor under very pitiable circumstances, caused me to institute an inquiry, and produced the above information.

BASINGSTOKE; *see page* 25. BATH. *Somersetshire.*
The City Gaol.
Gaoler, *George Griffin,* who is also a Sheriff's Officer; which no Keeper of a Prison should be. He must frequently be from home; and his business is incompatible with the Duty of a Gaoler.
Salary 30/. Fees 7. 8rf. No Table. Conveyance of Prisoners to the County Gaol at Ilchester, one shilling per mile.
Chaplain, Rev. Mr. *Marshall,* lately appointed.
Salary 20/.
Duty, no stated time of attendance, or arrangement of service. At my visit here, in Sept. 1806, it was *more than two months* since divine service had been last performed.
Surgeon, Mr. *Kitson,* also lately appointed.
Salary 207.
Number of Prisoners, Debtors. Felons. Petty Oflenders. Deserters. 1800, March 30th,--1--2---4---0 1801, Dec. 22d,---2--3---10--0 1803, Oct. 5th,---l--0---4--_ 1 1806, Sept. 19th,--2- -1 .-6---2
Allowance to Debtors, none whatever. *(See Remarks).*
Felons and Criminal Prisoners, sixpence, or fourpence per day in bread, as it is dear or cheap; it is sent from the Baker in two-penny loaves: Weight in Sept. 1806, eleven ounces each.
REMARKS.
This Prison, situate in Grove-street, is unfortunately built on very low groundThe ascent to it is by a fine flight of stone steps. On the entrance-floor are the Keeper's parlour, kitchen, and two bed-rooms. Above are three stories, and on each, five good-sized rooms; two of which are used by the Keeper: the rest are for Debtors; one bed in a room, for which the Prisoner pays 3, *6d.* per week.

Two rooms on the second-story are*' free-wards;* one for.Men, the other foe Women; to which the Corporation allows straw laid on the floor.

No employment is furnished by the city. Coals are sometimes allowed to the Prison: But here is no Chapel. Divine service (when *performed at all),* is in a front-room, of 17 feet by 14; one half of which is taken up by a large barrack bedstead . Previous to my visit in 1801, there had been little or no religious duty for many years; and yet, at one of my visits, there were 31 Prisoners in the Gaol.

The police of this splendid and matchless city appears to be well-regulated in every respect, except as to its Prison. The Act for the Preservation of Health is not hung up; but on a painted board is inscribed, "No strong Liquors admitted, "under the Penalty of Ten Pounds, or three Months Imprisonment. "

For Petty Offenders, here is, *seventeen* steps down, a dark damp day-room, about 14 feet square, with a fire-place; and three damp sleeping-cells, one of which is 14 feet square, and 9 feet high; the two others 9 feet square: One of them has no light nor ventilation, but what it receives from an aperture in the door, 9 inches by *6:* The floors are boarded, and have loose straw to sleep on.

These cells are frequently crammed

with *vagrants*; and there is a flagged courty 52 feet long and 16 feet wide, used in common, both for Prisoners of the latter description, and for debtors, through which lies the passage to the court-yard, where felons are confined. This court was formerly overflowed by water, the marks of which, at least, till lately, were visible on the walls; but siuce the canal has been cut, the ground is dry.

In the centre there are 12 cells, which the Corporation have very properly built upon arches: They consist of a double range, six in each, of about 8 feet square, and as many high; light, well-ventilated, and to every one there is a fire-place, and a small stone-sink as an urinal in one corner. The floors are of boards, with loose straw to sleep on. The doors of the cells open into stone galleries, 42 feet long, and 3 feet 9 inches wide, guarded by an iron railing, and with a sewer at each end. No room set apart for an Infirmary. No Bath, nor County clothing. No mops, brooms, pails, soap or towels, for personal or prison cleanliness. No Rules and Orders. Mrs. Dickenson, who resides at Bath, has sent annually, for the last seven years, at Christmas, Easter and Whitsuntide, one pound and a half of mutton or beef, a half-quartern loaf and potatoes, to every Prisoner in this Gaol.

Debtors are sent hither from the Court of Requests for the City of Bath, and Liberties thereof; the parish of *Walcot;* the several parishes and places in the Hundreds of *Bath-forum* and *Wellow,* the Liberties of Hampton, Claverton, Easton and Amrill, all in the County of Somerset: which Court takes cognizance of all debts not exceeding ten pounds. The imprisonment for debts exceeding five pounds is 200 days.

As I shall, in the course of this Work, have frequent occasion to mention barrack-beds, or bedsteads, I wish my reader to understand they are low stages of boards, raised from the floor; and sloping from the wall towards the middle of the room; as in the barracks for soldiers.

BATTEL; *see page* 32. BEAUMARIS. *Isle of Anglesea.*
The County Gaol.

Gaoler, *William Hopson;* now *Thomas As hurst.*

Salary, in 1802, was *Ten Pounds*; but in 1803, *Five Pounds from the Sheriff;* and for tbe Bridewell 30/. ",,,i

Fees, Debtors, *Js.* Felons, &c. 13. 4d. No Table. Conveyance of Transports, the expence..,

Chaplain, Rev. Mr. *Thomas,* now Rev. Mr. *Williams.*
Salary, heretofore 10/. now 20/.

Duty, At my visit in 1803, DivineService *had heen discontinued for two years:* But the Salary having since been increased, as above, here are Prayers and a Sermon once a-week.

Surgeon, till lately, Mr. *Sparrow:* But since his death none has been regularly appointed. When wanted, sent by the town, and makes a Bill..:

Number of Prisoners, Debtors. Felons, &c. Bridewell.
1800, April 24th,-4----0----0 1802, Jan. 26th,----5----0----0 1803, Sept. 15th,---3----o----1 1806, Nov. 13th,----1----0----5 1809, Feb. 21st,----5--1 and Bastardy, 3

Allowance, *4d.* a-day to all.
, REMARKS.
This Gaol is also die *County Bridewell.* It stands on the strait or narrow channel, called *the Menai,* and near the old castle fortified by Edward I.

For Debtors here is a court-yard, an oblong square, of about 16 yards by 13; and on the second story they have six good-sized sleeping rooms, with fire-places and glazed-windows; for which, if the Debtor brings his own bed, he pays nothing; otherwise straw, in lieu of bedding, is furnished by the County: But if the Keeper furnishes a bed, the charge is 2. per week.

On the ground-floor there is a common kitchen, with a fire-place, and a pantry. There being no Chapel, divine service is performed in the Keeper's parlour. The window of this room commands the debtors' part of the Prison; but of the felons' part there is no view whatever, except through the iron palisaded gate hereafter mentioned.

Felons have a court-yard of about the same size as that for the debtors; a day-room, with a fire-place; and five sleeping cells on the ground-floor, each 8 feet 4 inches by 7 feet two, and 7 feet 9 inches high. These have arched roofs, with brick floors, and are dark, damp, and insecure; supplied with plank bed-steads, chaff-in-ticking beds, two blankets, and a rug.

A wall intended as a separation divides the *Debtors'* court-yard from that of the *Felons,* which is of the same size; but a constant communication is kept up, by means of two iron-palisaded gates, through one of which you must pass to the felons' part of the Gaol. This, however, is insecure, a felon having made his escape about three weeks before my visit in 1803. At that period the court-yards, dayrooms, pantry, and common kitchen, had all of them mud-floors, which have since been paved with flag-stone. For Bridewell Prisoners here is one roonl.

I remember the Gaoler told me, that the whole of his Fees, amounted'only to 12/. 13. *lod.* So that, his Salary included, he had no more than 47/. 13. lorf. to maintain himself, and support his wife and seven children: adding, that Lord Bulkeley humanely employed him at times amongst his labourers, or he must be in a state bordering on starvation.

It is but an act of humanity and common justice to observe, That every where in *Wales,* in *Cornwall,* and some nearer parts of England, the Salaries of Gaolers are very small, and inadequate to the faithful discharge of so important a trust.

This Prison is said to be whitewashed once in two or three years; but the good effects of that salutary process are destroyed, as every chimney in the place is smoky.

Here is no water, but what the Gaoler fetches from a fine spring, ninety-six yards distant, and then pours into a square box, lined with lead, which holds about 22 gallons. This task, however, might easily be prevented, and the water laid on at a small expence.

No Fuel is allowed the Prisoners. No separate court-yard, day-room, or kitchen for *Women Debtors,* who therefore must mix with the Bridewell

Prisoners. No mops, brooms, pails, towels or soap, to keep the Prisoners or their Prison clean: So that I was not surprised at finding the Gaol dirty.

Neither the Act for preserving Health, nor the Clauses against Spirituous Liquors hung up. The Keeper informed me, that *no Magistrate had been within side the Gaol for seven years. . ,;,*

Mr. *Ashurst* also told me in 1803, that the *Under-Sheriff* had reduced his Salary as Gaoler to *Five Pounds.* Now by the Statute, 24 Geo. Ill it is clearly expressed, "That the Justices of the Peace are to order and direct the Salaries to be paid out of the County-Rate, by the *Treasurer* of such County." BEAUMARIS. *The Town Gaol.*

Keeper, *Richard Ellis,* the Town Sergeant. Salary, as Keeper, none.
Fees, 13. *Ad.*

Number of Prisoners, 1803, Sept. 15th. Deserters, 3.
Allowance, as in the County Gaol, fourpence a-day.

Here is one room for the Keeper; and for the Prisoners, two small ones, of about 10 feet by 6, under the Town-Hall, with loose straw thrown upon a wooden bedstead. No court-yard. No water.

BATtEL. *Sussex,*
Gaoler, *William Croft,* a Sheriff's Officer, who lives at a distance.
Salary 10/. Fees, *3s. d.*

Surgeon, from the town, when wanted.
1802, Sept. 20th, One Prisoner.

Allowance, *Ad.* or *6d.* per day, according as bread is cheap or dear.

This Gaol consists of two rooms on the ground-floor, 14 feet by 124-, in one of which is a chimney, and the fire-place was filled with rubbish; the other has a strong staple, to which felons are chained. There is straw laid upon the floors, with a blanket and rug to sleep on; and an offensive sewer in each room. The irongrated windows look into a small court; but of which, as being insecure, the Prisoners have not the use. No water accessible to the Prisoners, although it might be laid on from the little garden belonging to the Keeper. The Prison very filthy.

BECCLES. *Suffolk.*
The House of Correction.
Gaoler, *William Cadmore,* Salary 35/. now *Samuel Drewell,* Salary 42/.; with Coals for his own use, and 14s. per week for a Turnkey; paid by the Beccles Division of the County.
Fees, for Felons, 13. *4d.* No Table.
Conveyance of Transports to Ipswich, one shilling per mile.
Chaplain, Rev. *John Penn.* Salary 10/. 10.
Duty, Prayers on Tuesday and Friday.
Surgeon, Mr. *Crowfoot.* Salary, none; makes a Bill.
N of Prisoners, 1805, Sept. 10th, 7. 1807, Dec. 17th, 5. 1810, Sept. 15th, *6.*
Allowance, one pound and a half of household bread per day, sent from the Bakers, which I found to be of full weight.
Dietary, *Breakfast,* each day, oatmeal gruel.
Dinners, on *Sunday,* half a pound of meat, and one pound of potatoes. *Monday,* three-fourths of a pint of pease, or rice in stead, when pease are dear; with broth from meat of the preceding day. *Tuesday,* rice, or oatmeal, made into porridge, with leek or onions. *Wednesday,* two pounds of potatoes. *Thursday,* as Sunday: *Friday,* as' Monday. *Saturday,* as Tuesday. When a Prisoner is sick, extra food, or bedding, supplied at the Surgeon's discretion.
REMARKS.

Great part of this Prison has been lately built: But the brick-work is not substantial: The mortar appears to be badly made; and the wood, not having been well seasoned, has shrunk, so as to leave considerable interstices. The Gaol, therefore,-is not secure.

The boundary-wall, seventeen feet high, incloses an area of 180 feet by 108. It fronts to the South; and over the gate the following motto is very suitably inscribed on stone, "PROHIBERE OUAM PUNIRE." "Tis better to *prevent* than *punish* crime."

On the right-hand,' at the entrance, is a room called *The Cage,* for the temporary confinement of what are termed *assaults,* or *night-charges.* On the left is the Turnkey's sitting-room; and over both of these is his chamber. A foot-path of 42 feet long leads to the Prison; and the residence of the Keeper being in the

F centre, the windows of his two rooms command a view of the Men's two court-yards, which are nearly 70 feet each by 30, and in one of them a pump and stone-trough, inclosed by a wooden paling, not more than five feet six inches high; upon which, as the Keeper justly observed, he could lay his hands and jump over. Here is also a small court-yard for the Women, of 24 feet by 12 feet 6, of which the Keeper has no view. They have all gravel bottoms.

On the ground-floor are two day-rootns for Men, about 10 feet by 9, with fireplaces and glazed windows; and six sleeping-cells, about 12 feet by 7, with glazed and grated casement windows, and 9 feet 6 inches high, to the crown of the arch. Also two other cells for Women, of nearly the same size; the doors opening into a well ventilated lobby, 4 feet wide, in which are two iron palisaded gates, to separate convicts from those who are not yet tried j and a wooden door excludes the Women from both.

On the first story, in the centre, is the Chapel, which is very small, where the Prisoners are seated in full view, and almost close to each other. The two prison lobbies open into it, each containing five sleeping-cells, similar to those before described; and in one of them is a fire-place.

The attick-story of each wing has two spacious rooms, with glazed and grated windows; which have fire-places, and may serve occasionally for Infirmaries or Store-Rooms.

Every cell that is occupied has a crib bedstead, with straw-in-sacking bed, two sheets, cleaned monthly, and two blankets. The Men Prisoners are clean shirted and shaved every Sunday morning; and cloth is ready provided for twenty suits of County clothing.

A forcing-pump throws water to the top of the building, and cleanses also the sewers and drains, which the Keeper informed me were not offensive.

The circumjacent ground, betwixt the court-yards and the boundary-wall in front, affords the Keeper a convenient garden for the growth of vegetables: The backpart consists of a *hog-cote*, with about half a dozen pigs in it. Ducks also range about at large. The Keeper, who is a cabinet-maker, assured me, that if he did not procure work at his trade, his salary was not adequate to support his family.

The total amount of Prisoners confined in, and discharged from, this House of Correction, between the 12th of July, 1802, and the 15th of September, 1810, was 372. £m s, d.

The Expence for their Maintenance--------394 12 8i

And the Value of their Earnings----------97 lfi 8£

Leaving a Nett Charge 011 the County...-.-296 16 0

Here is no bath, but an oven in the Keeper's house is provided to purify foul or infected clothes. The Prison is kept clean. No alarm-bell. No Rules and Orders; and neither Act nor Clauses are hung up.

BEDFORD. *The County Gaol, and House of Correction.*
Gaoler, *John Moore Howard.*

Salary, for the Gaol, 10oV. and for the House of Correction, *Q0l.*
Fees, Debtors and Felons, 17. *4d.* each, as per Table hung up: Besides which the Under-Sheriff demands of each Debtor 6s. 8d. for his *Liberate!* For the removal of Transports to Woolwich, 5/. each; and if to Portsmouth,, the expence of conveyance. Garnish, abolished.

Chaplain, Rev. *Thomas Cave.* Salary 40/.

Duty, Prayers and Sermon on Sunday, and Prayers on Thursday.

Surgeon, Mr. *Campion.* Salary, for Debtors, Felons, and House of Correction, 40/.

Number of Prisoners, Debtors. Felons. House of Correction.
1801, Aug. 19th,---5-__ 12-_ 4 1802, Jan. 26th,---4---6 ----9 1806, July 14th---11---3 9 1807, Sept. 1st---4---2----*Q* 1808, Feb. 18th---11---6 ----4

Allowance, *Debtors,* two quartern loaves each per week.
Felons, two half-peck loaves per week each.

I weighed the loaves at my several visits, and they were all just.
REMARKS.
This Gaol was first inhabited 17th June, l8o1, and stands in a good situation, being just out of the town.

The entrance to the Prison is the Turnkey's lodge, a handsome stone-building, with a sitting-room on one side; and on the other, a warm and cold bath, with an oven to purify infected or offensive clothes. Up-stairs is the Turnkey's sleeping-room, and another in which the County clothing is put on, and that of the Prisoner! ticketed and hung by till discharged. Here is likewise a reception-cell for the newly arrived Prisoner, till he is examined as to his health, previous to admission into the interior. At the top of the building is the flat-roof,—the place of execution.

After passing the lodge, the way to the Keeper's house is through a small garden, of 32 feet in length. The Keeper resides in the centre of the Prison.

On the ground-floor is his parlour, kitchen, and pantry; and behind them an open space, called *The Hall,* in which I *now* found both the Act for Preservation of Health, and the Clauses against Spirituous Liquors, conspicuously painted on sr board, and hung up; with weights and scales likewise for the use of the Prison. Into this hall three lobbies open, of five feet wide. Over the entrance-gate of one, is inscribed in stone, "Men-Felons and Convicts of a second, "Women-Felons, and Debtors;" and of the third, " House of Correction."

The above three lobbies contain two day-rooms each, which open into a courtyard, for the use of the several classes; one day-room for Men, the other for Women; having glazed windows and fire-places, to which coals are allowed during the six winter months: They are fitted up with benches and cupboards for provisions; and cooking utensils, towels, &c. are very considerately provided by the Magistrates. In each lobby there are four working-cells.

Criminals are employed in beating hemp, but receive no part of their earnings. Debtors sometimes procure employment from without, and have whatever they can earn. Transports *here* have not the King's allowance of 2. 6d. per week.

Over the Hall is a room, of the same size, in which the articles of County clothing are deposited: Also three lobbies like those below: Two of these contain eight sleeping cells, for felons and House of Correction prisoners; and the third has six sleeping-rooms for poor debtors, two of which are of 13 feet by 8, and the other four 10 feet by 8, having fire-places and glazed windows, and fitted up with iron bedsteads, sacking bottoms, a straw-in-canvas bed, blanket, and rug, furnished *gratis,* at the County's expence.

For those who can pay, here are rooms of better accommodation, which are supplied by the Keeper at 2. 6d. a single bed, per week; or if two sleep together, at 2s. weekly each. If the debtor finds his own bedding and sheets, he pays 1. *6J.* per week.

The Chapel is in the centre, on the second or attick-story, where the Prisoners are properly seated according to their respective classes; and all are required, not only to attend divine service, unless prevented by illness, but to deport themselves reverently there.

There are three other lobbies, like the former, that open into the Chapel: The first for Felons and Convicts, with eight sleeping-cells; the second for House of Correction Prisoners, and the same number of sleeping-cells: the third lobby has two store-rooms; and two others are set apart for Infirmaries, with boarded floors, 14 feet 8 inches by 10 feet *6,* and 9 feet 8 inches high; also with fire-places and glazed windows.

At the top of the building is an alarm-bell.

The Criminal Prisoners have thirty-two sleeping-cells, each 9 feet 4 inches by feet 9, and 10 feet high: These are all light, airy, and clean, fitted up with iron bedsteads, straw beds, two blankets and a coverlet: the iron-grated window has an inside shutter. Each cell has a double door;.the outer, iron-grated, the inner of wood. The Prisoners are shaved, and have clean linen every week. For the different classes here are six airy court-yards; their average size 54 feet by 30, with open wood palisades, about 17 feet distant from the boundary wall.

There is a pump in every court-yard, and the whole Prison is well supplied with water, and kept very clean.

Table.of Fees.

"County Of Bedford. At a General Quarter Session for the Town and County of *Bedford,* held on Wednesday, 3d October, 1781, before Sir *Philip Monoux,* Bart. *William Geary, John Nesbit,* and *John Miller,* jun. Esqrs.; and the Rev. *Hadley Cox, Henry Hinde, Peter Lepipre, W. Smith,* and *John Hawkins,* Justices of the Peace in the said County, and assigned to determine Felonies, Trespasses, and other Misdemeanours there. The following *Table of Fees* was perused, settled, and approved to be taken by the County Gaoler of Bedfordshire; but first sub mitted to the Judges of Assize for their approbation.

Debtors' Fees:

To the Gaoler, and his Turnkeys. i£. *s. d.*

For each Debtor discharged----------- 0 17 +

For the second, and every other Action--------0100

To the Turnkey, at the Discharge of every Debtor----0 2 O

Ditto, for a second, and every other Action-------010

For every Debtor for a Week's Lodging, on the Chapel Side, the

Gaoler finding bedding, sheets, and blankets------026

If two sleep together, to take of each---------020

Of every Debtor, for Chamber-Rent, finding his own bedding and sheets, per week--------------016

For a Copy of every Warrant of Detaiuer-------020

For Certificate, for want of a Declaration, in order to take out a *Supersedeas* -------------02 6

For Certificate, to sue for *Habeas Corpus* -------026

For entering every Declaration delivered to the Debtor in Custody 0 1 0

To the Under-sheriff, *for his Liberatur to the Gaoler, for the Discharge ofa Debtor, for each Action!* --------0 68

Felons' Fees:

To the Gaoler, and his Turnkeys, £. *t. d.* To the Gaoler, for every Prisoner sentenced to be burned in the hand, fined, or imprisoned, when discharged------ 0174

To the *Turnkey,* for each such person- 020

To the Gaoler, for the Discharge of every Person committed for want of Sureties of the Peace, Misdemeanor, or any other Crime,

not being felonious-----------0 17 +

And to the Turnkey for each Person-- ------020

For Copy of each Commitment, if demanded------020

For a Certificate of Commitment, to sue out a *Habeas Corpus* --0 2 6

For attending in the Town of Bedford, with every Prisoner, to give *s. tt.* bail, or be otherwise discharged--------- 0 2 0'

For the Discharge of every Prisoner, committed for Felony, or on suspicion thereof, and no Bill of Indictment found, or discharged on his or her trial; or delivered by proclamation; to be paid out of the County Rates 0 13

John Nesbitt. Approved, James Eyre, Wm. Smith. 7th March, 1782.

A correct Abridgement from a true copy, examined with the original, upon the File of Easter Session, 1782.

By Jeremy-fish Palmer,

Clerk of the Peace, of the County of Bedford."

Judging from my own feelings, I cannot but think that the foregoing account of an excellent Gaol will be pleasing also to others. There is one important article, however, in Prison-polity, to which I do not here find that attention paid, which, in my opinion, the subject deserves. A small sum of money given to each Prisoner on being discharged, according to the distance from friends and home, might prevent necessity from an immediate recurrence to those misdoings, which brought him to a Gaol.

The practice here earnestly recommended, has the sanction of very good success in many other Prisons of this Kingdom.

BEDFORD. *Town-Gaol*

Gaoler, *James Castleman,* the Macebearer, Salary, none. Fees, none.

Surgeon, from the town, if wanted.

Prisoners, 1st Sept. 1807, and 8th Feb. 1808, none.

Allowance, a half-quartern loaf of bread per day; and from Michaelmas to Lady-day, a half-bushel of coals is allowed weekly to both the day-rooms.

REMARKS.

This Prison is situate near the County-Gaol. Here is a house for the Keeper, and two court-yards adjoin to it; one for the use of Men, the other of Women, and each 38 feet by 14.

A day-room, with a fire-place, opens into each court; which has likewise two sleeping-cells, of 10 feet by 6 feet 4 inches, and 11 feet high, to the crown of the arch. Each wooden bedstead is made to hold three persons, and to each are allowed loose straw and a blanket. Over the door of the sleeping-cells is an iron-grated aperture, 18 inches by 10;

Here is no employment. Neither the Act nor Clauses hung up.

BERKHAMSTEAD; *see page $3.* BERWICK UPON TWEED, *The Town and County Gaol.*

Gaoler, *George Richardson;* now *William Brown,* who keeps the Berwick-Arfns, a public-house just by. Salary 40/. Two Men, as his assistants, have 15/. each *per annum,* with room-rent paid, and a coat and hat, from the Corporation, to attend in rotation, clean the Gaol, and go upon errands for the Prisoners.

Fees, none for Debtors who are Freemen, nor for Felons; but for Debtors, not free, 2s. *6d.* each. Garnish abolished.

No Chaplain, nor Surgeon. If *p.* Prisoner be ill, the Parish-Surgeon attends, upon application to the Magistrates; and is paid by the Treasurer of the Corporation.

Number of Prisoners, Debtors. Petty Offenders.

1800, April 7th,-----3-----5 1801, Nov. oth,-----1-----7 1802, Sept. llth,-----3 _

___ 2 run-away Appren 1809, Sept. 20th -----4 _-__ -1 tices.

Allowance, to *Debtors*. At a Guild, held 18th January, 800, it was agreed, on account of the dearness of provisions, "That every such Prisoner, being a *Freeman,* should have &d. and every *Non-Freeman,* 6d. per day. To *Felons,* and other Offenders, the allowance is at the Magistrates' discretion; but not to exceed 6d. a day for each.

REMARKS.

This Gaol, which was finished m 1754, stands over the Grand Town Hall, and has a fine steeple, the only one in the Town of Berwick. On each side of the Gaol are four windows, about four feet square, with a lifting-sash, for the benefit of fresh air.

The four damp-cells, on the ground-floor, and under the piazzas, where Prisoners formerly were confined, are now very properly discontinued as a Prison, and used as shops, &c. for the country butchers.

The long rooms extend the whole length of the building, which is judiciously partitioned off in the middle, to separate Felons, and other offenders, from the Debtors. The former have also five other rooms, of 14 feet by 12, and 8 feet high, which have grated and glazed sash-windows, with casements: They are supplied with straw on wooden bedsteads; and in each is placed a covered tub, to serve as sewers, which are emptied by the Town Beadle, when he thinks proper; and, consequently, are offensive,

For *Debtors* here are three rooms, with fire-places, two benches in each to sit on, a table, cupboard for provisions, and cooking utensils. These are all *free* wards, and the Corporation furnishes a bed to one of them. Their sewer also is a covered tub, inclosed at one corner of the adjacent gallery, and, like the others, emptied by the Beadle at his leisure.

The Debtors have no court-yard; but in their hall, or day-room, is a pump, which supplies the whole Prison with water; and for air and exercise, they are permitted to walk on the leaden roof of the building. They have a large fire-place in the hall above mentioned, with a sink, to carry off foul water. But the Corporation do not allow coals.

The bedsteads here are all of wood, with straw-in-ticking beds, two blankets, a bolster, and coverlet, both for Debtors and Felons.

This Prison is well lighted and ventilated by the long-room sash-windows. No employment is here provided; but handicraft trades may be followed by those who can procure themselves the means of working: And the Women sometimes get articles of spinning, for which they are paid the same prices as are given in the town.

There were no *Felons* here, at either of my four visits.

The Gaol is seldom visited or white-washed.

No water generally accessible, but as it is daily carried up by the Beadle, and put into a common cistern from the pump, to the several Prisoners. No Rules and Orders. Neither the Act for Preserving Health, nor the Clauses against Spirituous Liquors, are hung up. fpf" It is a matter so obvious in itself, that I need hardly remark, How very inconsistent is the *non-residence,* or distance, of any Gaoler from his important charge! If *he* is inattentive, or much absent, who else will be alert and active? The security of Prisons is their bounden duty; and if this be treated as a slight affair, who can wonder, that the great objects of cleanliness, good order, and personal comfort of the confined, are also glaringly neglected?

The above observation, I am sorry to say, may be extended to several inferior Gaols, South of the Tweed.

BERKHAMSTEAD. *Hertfordshire.*
The Bridewell.

Keeper, *William Rogers,* a Shoemaker. Salary, 20l. Fees 3s. Ad. and half profit of the Prisoners' work. At my visit in 1804, they were employed in cutting pegs; and the Keeper told me he allowed them three half-pence per thousand, and sold them at three-pence.

Surgeon, Mr. *Steele,* who makes a Bill.

Number of Prisoners, 1802, July 12th, 2. 1803, July 15th, 2. 1804, Sept. 3d, 1. 1805, July 25th, 2. 1807, May 10th, 1. 1810, Aug.4th, 0.

Allowance, one pound and a half of bread per day, cut from the Keeper's loaf. It would be better if the bread were sent, in loaves from the Baker, that the Prisoners might know their quantity.

Here is a room for Men, 12 feet by 10, and for Women, 14 feet by 10, with boarded floors. Straw and two blankets to sleep on. Each room has an iron-grated window, looking into a small court, 6 yards by 4, with a sewer in it, where they are allowed to walk one hour in the day. For Felons, a dungeon, nine steps down, of 13 feet by *Q* and *6* feet 3 inches high: Earth floor, very damp; totally dark, and without ventilation. No bedstead. Straw on the floor, and a blanket. At my visit, 1810, the Gaoler told me the Magistrates had determined to brick up the dungeon. Neither the Act nor Clauses hung up.

BEVERLEY HALL-GARTH. *Yorkshire.*
For Debtors.

Gaoler, *William Lundie;* now *Stephen Aclam.* Salary, none. Fees, 4. id. No Table. Allowance, none. It is a *Publick House,* and he pays Rent 25/. a year. Lord Yarborough holds a Court in it twice a year.

Prisoners, 1S02, Aug. 25th, and 1809, Sept. 8th, None.

The *Hall-Garth,* in the Liberty of St. John of Beverley, is a Manor-Gaol, or Court-Baron, belonging to Lord Yarborough.

Over the Hall it has five rooms, 16 feet by 10; of which two have fire-places. Some of them have brick, and the rest boarded floors. The custom has been for Debtors to pay 1. 3d. each per week, for a bed furnished by the Keeper. There are said to be 113 towns, or parts of towns, that lie within the Liberty of St. John, or *Beverley Hall Garth.* Its iron-grated windows give this building somewhat of the appearance of a prison; but I was informed that no Debtors have been confined here for these twelve years.

G BEVERLEY. *Town and Liberty Oaol.*

Gaoler, *Timothy Lundie,* Serjeant at Mace. Salary, 14/. 4.

Fees, for Debtors, 4. 4d. Felons, none.

Garnish, 1$.

Surgeon; when one is wanted, he is sent by the Mayor.

Number of Prisoners, Debtors. Felons, &c. Deserter.
1802, Aug. 25th,----0----3----0. 1809, Sept. 8th,-.--2----0----1.

Allowance, none to Debtors, unless certificated as Paupers; and then they have the same as Felons, *6d.* a-day.

REMARKS.

For Debtors here are three rooms; one below, well furnished, for which the Gaoler charges *2s. 6d.* per week; and a small one, where, if the Prisoner finds his own bed, he pays *6d.* a week. The third room is above stairs, where, at is. *3d.* per week, the Keeper provides a bed. Here is one small court-yard for Prisoners of all descriptions; with a work-shed in it, but no water. The Gaoler fetches it from over the way.

A Table of Fees payable to the Attornies and Clerk of Court, and signed by the Mayor, Recorder, and Aldermen, is hung up; and likewise a *Table of the antient Customs.*

Debtors are committed to this Prison by the Court of Requests, as well as those prosecuted by actions in the Court of King's Bench, and in the Town Court.

The Men and Women Felons have each a separate day-room up stairs. The Women's sleeping-room adjoins to it: and they are all rendered very offensive, for want of sewers; a half-tub only being substituted for the purpose.

Men Criminals sleep in two dirty cells below, of about four yards square; having in each a privy badly ventilated, and only a small iron-grated window to each cell.

The town allows straw-in-ticking beds, with two blankets, and a rug. The Felons' employment is to pound tilesherds, for which they receive *6d.* per bushej.

Neither the Act for preservation of Health, nor the Clauses against Spirituous Liquors are hung up.

About ten years since, the Gaol was white-washed.

BEVERLEY. *House of Correction.*
Keeper, *George Plummer,* now *Samuel Shepherd.* Salary, 84/.
Fees, two shillings from each Prisoner.
Chaplain, Rev. *Robert Right/,* lately appointed. Salary, 20/.
Duty, Prayers and Sermon every Friday, in the Old Court-House.
Surgeon, Mr. *Gill.* No Salary; but makes a Bill.
Number of Prisoners, Felon.-Petty Offenders.
1802, Aug. 25th,-----1 5.
1809, Sept. 8th,--0------31.
Allowance, *6d.* a-day to each, in money.
REMARKS.

This Prison, which adjoins to the Town-Hall, has, on the ground-floor, four sleeping-cells, of about 9 feet by 6, and a dark room used by the military for the confinement of Deserters, &c. On the first story, four sleeping-cells, and on the second story, three ditto, and a day-room, all of about the same size with those first mentioned. Here is also a lobby, 28 feet long, and 7 feet wide, for the Prisoners occasionally to walk in.

Below are three cells for Vagrants, and a small court-yard with a sewer in it. Also two work-rooms, one for Men, and the other for Women; with two small rooms set apart for Infirmaries.

The East-Riding allows straw, on plank bedsteads, and five chaldrons of coals yearly. No water accessible to the Prisoners.

Their employment consists in spinning, picking oakum, and pounding of tilesherds: but, *although so near Hull,* it being difficult, or deemed so, to procure the two last articles, I saw only one Woman at work, and she was spinning.

The Prisoners have half their earnings, if they exceed 1. per week.

It were to be wished that the Magistrates would not suffer a half-tub, or uncovered pail, to be in each room, as it keeps them continually offensive; and little occasion can be alledged, as a sewer is provided in the court-yard.

The Clauses against Spirituous Liquors were properly hung up; but not the Act for preserving the *Health of Prisoners,*—so liable to injury in neglected places of confinement.

BEVERLEY. *Yorkshire.*
New Sessions House and House of Correction.
REMARKS.

This Prison, for the East-Riding of the County of York, which was not inhabited at my visit in Sept. 1809, stands a little way from the town, without the North Bar. The ground, inclosed for the Court-House and Prison, is about two acres: a handsome iron palisade extends in front, with a gate of entrance at each end; and the approach is by a curved carriage gravel-walk.

The portico in front is supported by four Ionic columns, 25 feet high, and the ascent, by a flight of four steps, presents a noble appearance to the turnpike-road. The right-wing in front, which is detached from the Court-House, has on the ground-floor two rooms, each 17 feet by 11 feet 6; together with a bath for Men, 7 feet by 4, and another for Women, of the same size, with glazed windows to each.

Above are two infirmary rooms, of the like dimensions, with separate staircases; and behind are two courts, *16* feet by *13* each: These have iron-grates over them, and there is a sewer in each.

The ground-floor of the left-wing is the Turnkey's lodge; with sleeping rooms above: and a stable, cowhouse, and other offices, occupy the remainder.

The Prison itself is at the back of the front buildings; having the Keeper's house in the centre, and a wing on each side for the Prisoners. The ground-floor of the *right-wing* contains two day-rooms, each 16 feet 10 inches by 14 feet 10; a fireplace in both, with two grated and glazed windows, 3 feet square: Five sleepingcells 10 feet by 8, with arched roofs, grated windows, and an inside shutter with a pane of glass in each of them; a cast-iron bedstead, with sides of wood, and a covered sewer to each cell in one comer. The doors of the cells open into well ventilated and flagged lobbies 4 feet wide; and at the end of each is a washing-stand, and water closet. The chamber-story is in all respects exactly similar; and the Prisoners' day-rooms belonging to this wing, open into two spacious flagged courts, which have sewers at the upper-end.

The *left-icing* is appropriated to Females: It has seven sleeping-cells and one day-room on the ground-floor, with the like number above; and in other respects corresponds exactly with the right-wing.

The Keeper's house is separated from the Prison by a flagged walk of 9 feet wide; but his windows very judiciously command a view of the several court-yards.

At the back of the building there is a neat *Chapel;* to which the Prisoners ascend by a stone stair-case on each side. A dwarf partition runs through the centre of the area; and separates the sexes, who are seated on forms, and out of sight of each other.

Under the Chapel is a cooking kitchen, 18 feet by 15, with an oven and boilers, &c.; a pantry; a store-room, 13 feet by 10 feet 8. A room for uniform clothing of the Prisoners, of the same dimensions; and another room, with a stove in it to purify their own clothes against infection. Also a yard 26 feet by 12, to dry linen.

Here is likewise another yard, which has a forcing pump, to throw water into a large reservoir, which thus supplies the whole Prison with excellent spring water and another reservoir receives rain.from the roof, for washing, &c.

The Keeper has a convenient garden for his own family use; and another plot of ground (at present a corn-field), is set apart and intended as a garden for the Prisoners, of above an acre and a half.

BRADFORD. *Yorkshire.*
Gaoler, *William Lee.* Salary, 20/.
Surgeon, if wanted, sent for from the town.
Number of Debtors, Oct. 19th, 1805, Two.
Allowance, *Ad.* a day, if petitioned for, at the discretion of the Commissioners.
REMARKS.
This Prison receives debtors from the Court of Requests for Halifax, Bradford, &c. It is situate on an eminence, called the North Wing, and was first inhabited in the year 1797. The Gaol stands on the left of the Keeper's house, and consists of a court-yard for men, of about 34 feet by *16,* which has a sewer in it.

On the ground-floor are two rooms, about 20 feet square, with fire-places and glazed-windows; and above them is a room set apart for the sick, about 14 feet square, accommodated in the same manner.

The women have a separate court-yaid, 23 feet by 17, with a sewer; also a sleeping-room, 14 feet square, with fire-place and glazed window.

To all these rooms the Keeper furnishes beds, at is. per week each; but if the Prisoner finds his own bed, he pays nothing. No fuel nor bedding is allowed by the town; nor any employment furnished. The Act for preservation of Health, and the Clauses against Spirituous Liquors, are not hung up.

BIRMINGHAM. *JVarioickshire. . ,: The Town Gaol.*
Gaoler, *William Payne.* Salary 42/.
Fees, 2. for serving a Warrant, 1. for each Summons, and *2s.* on Discharge.
For *Prisoners,* see *Remarks.*
Allowance, Twopenny-worths of Bread, with a slice of Cheese, to each.
REMARKS.
This New Gaol was first inhabited in September, 1S06, and is situated in *MoorStreet,* at the back of the Publick Office.

Here is only one court-yard for all descriptions of Prisoners, 59 feet by 30, enclosed by a wall *26* feet high, on the top of which is a *chevaux de /rise,* for better security against escape. Attached to it are two day-rooms, or kitchens, fourteen feet square, which open into it; one for Men, the other for Women, with a pump of excellent water.

On the ground-floor are eight sleeping-cells, paved with flag stones; and on the upper-story, eight others, strongly planked with oak. Each cell is 8 feet by 6, well ventilated, and fitted up with an iron bedstead, a straw mattress, and three rugs.

The Prisoners have fire in their day-rooms all through the year, and are provided with every requisite for culinary purposes. Coals, bread, &c. paid for by the town. The number of Prisoners must be very uncertain from the nature of the Gaol: There are frequently twenty or more detained here at one time: To-day, perhaps, fourteen or fifteen; and to-morrow, not one. It is not a place of punishment, but a recess only for safe custody, till the Prisoners can be disposed of by a Magistrate. There are no commitments to it of any description: It is no more, in fact, than a lock-up house, provided and appropriated by the parish for the Constable's use and accommodation. The Magistrates have their Sittings three days in the week, and, consequently, except in cases remanded for farther discussion, they may be considered as so many Gaol-deliveries. Of course no Employment is provided, as in such a state of fluctuation no work can be regularly done.

No bath or oven is furnished, for the purifying of infected clothes; but every thing necessary for personal or prison cleanliness is allowed; as mops, brooms, pails, &c. &c.

There is no particular weight here specified of the bread and cheese allowed; but twice a day the custom is, to send a slice of cheese with the sixth-part of a sixpennyloaf, to as many Prisoners as happen to be in the Gaol. This, however, as the size of the loaf vanes with the price of wheat, is a very irregular standard and ought to be adjusted accordingly. It is not found, indeed, that any one suffers; but, on the contrary, much of the bread issued is generally left. Few, in fact, choose to take the above allotment for their subsistence, but have meat and other things brought in by their friends.

The Keeper of this Gaol is not permitted to sell ale, like his predecessor in the old one; nor to furnish any article of provisions for the Prisoners, as was the case at that period. My full description of the " *Old Dungeon"* was given in the Gentleman's Magazine for February, 1807, p. 107, and is now happily rendered Useless for ever.

BIRMINGHAM. *Warwickshire.*
The Court Prison, for Debtors only.
Gaoler, *John Downes.* No Salary; except what may arise from Fees, paid on serving Warrants of Execution, or for the furnishing of Beds. See Remarks.
Surgeon, as wanted, is sent from the Work-house.

xf *u Ctu.* J 1808, Nov. 5th, l. 1803, Aug. 23d, 2. Number of Debtors, . . xt,.. D, „..
"
'*I* 1805, Nov. 1st, 2. 1810, Aug. 6th, 5.

Allowance, none whatever was granted at the time of my two first visits: But in Nov. 1805, I was informed that poor Prisoners had a scanty dole of *threepence per day* from their respective parishes!

REMARKS.

This wretched receptacle for Debtors, in *Birmingham,* is situate in Philip-street; and consists of a damp, dirty *dungeon* (of about 10 or 11 feet square) with a descent by seven steps to receive Men and Women; which has one sleeping-room above it, about 12 feet square, with straw laid on the floor. These stand in a little back court-yard, not quite 14 feet square, belonging to the Keeper's house; where are three other rooms, furnished with beds for those who can pay him two shillings per week. The dungeon is occasionally used as a day-room, on account of its vicinity to the court-yard; and I have been informed that frequently it has had four, and at one time *fifteen Prisoners* in it.

In the year 1809, a large building, (formerly *The Publick Office,)* was converted into a Court of Requests in this town, and adapted also as a better Prison for the confinement of Debtors. Whoever suggested such an improvement was wise and merciful: Yet still the Men and Women Prisoners continue to associate together in the day-time.

Above stairs are six sleeping-rooms, to which the town supplies straw-inticking beds and a rug *gratis;* or, if required, the Keeper furnishes bedsteads and bedding, as before mentioned, at two shillings weekly.

No coals are here allowed; nor is water accessible, but as it is brought by the Keeper, together with other necessaries, when wanted by the Prisoners, for which purpose there is a Bell, to inform him of it.

A Plaintiff, it seems, has here the option of taking out execution either against the body or goods of his Debtor, but not against both.

I Strange as it may appear, Debtors, in the Old Prison, were *not allowed to work!* This almost singular circumstance is not let down to my comprehension; but it seems.cruel, inasmuch as their confinement may last *forty days.*

The Keeper told me, that were he to permit a Debtor to work, he should make himself liable to pay both debt and costs. This reminds me of Mr. Howard's remark, "That, when he visited this Court-Prison, in the year 1782, the Keeper informed him he had been obliged to pay a Shoemaker's debt, of fifteen or sixteen shillings, and costs, for permitting him to*Jinish* a piece of work, which the Man had *begun* before his confinement."

It was well said by a Biographer of my revered Predecessor, that we may hope his plans will terminate in such *General Regulations,* as to make judicial confine-: ment the means of *amelioration in morals,* and of *acquiring habits of industry;* whilst the few criminals, who may be too depraved for amendment, shall be *compelled to become beneficial by their labours*; and suflei nothing more, than that *restraint,* which is so needful for society, and that *exertion,* which they ought never to have abandoned." ordered for the maintenance of every Prisoner, by the Overseers of the Poor.

This Gaol which is also called *Bordesley Prison,* stands *within the back-yard of an ale-house.* Perhaps it is not in the power of language to convey an idea of grosser obscurity for a place of human confinement!

REMABKS.

It consists of two dark and damp *dungeons,* sunk ten steps under-ground; to which the descent is by a trap-door, level with the court-yard; and each of them is about 12 feet by 7; supplied with wooden bedsteads, straw, and a rug.

The only light or ventilation which the above gloomy dens can receive, is through an iron-grated aperture, about 12 inches square, made in the doors, which open into a narrow dark passage. Their brick floors, when I was here in 180-2, were an inch deep in water; but, luckily for humanity, at that time there were no Prisoners. In truth, these dungeons, which might be numbered amongst the very worst in the kingdom, were so unfit for the incarceration of any being that had life or sensibility, that it astonishes and humbles mankind, to think they could ever have been assigned to any fellow creature.

Over the dungeons are two rooms, which open into the court-yard, and are each about 12 feet square; one used as a day-room, the other as a sleeping-room, furnished with a wooden bedstead, straw and rugs, for petty offenders.

"At length," (says a worthy and much-valued friend), "about the end of the year 1808, one of the Church-wardens of the parish of *Aston, juxta Birmingham,* called a parochial meeting, for the purpose of taking into consideration the propriety of closing up the detestable dungeons of this Gaol, and of erecting suitable buildings in their stead: Previous to which he addressed a circular letter to the principal Inhabitants, containing a representation of the lamentable state of the Prison.

"This preparatory step had the desired effect: Several Gentlemen examined the dungeons, and were unanimous in declaring *themunjit even for the confinement of a dog* .

At the parish-meeting an order was made; and in the summer of 1809, the entrance to the dungeons was filled up; a new day-room built, and three cells, or bed-rooms, added in the upper-story.

"The above improvements took place in the old court-yard; in addition to which another court has been enclosed, and a convenient day-room assigned for the reception of runaway apprentices, and other offenders of a minor class. Iron bedsteads, with straw mattresses and rugs are provided: and some very heavy irons, which were formerly used, are now nailed up against the front of the day-room, in the old eonrt-yard, *in terrorem* only, as they are too securely fixed to be taken down, and are strictly prohibited for the future.

"This done, the renovated Prison was opened in the week preceding the *Royal Jubilee,.* 25th Oetober, 1$0$; on which festival, the workmen, together with the prisoners, were regaled by the aforesaid

Church-warden; who promises to make This general sentiment had a pointed meaning, and seems to have arisen in consequence of the following fact. A Collector of Taxes having seized two *pointers,* under a Distress-Warrant, brought them for security to this Prison of Aston, and desired *Brovmeti* to lodge them in one of the dungeons: but, on seeing the doors opened, the Tax Gatherer actually started back with horror, and begged, " that "some other place might be provided far the dogs, as they certainly should aot be confined there." frequent visits to the Gaol, and, as far as he is able, to contribute to promoting the proper comfort of its unfortunate inhabitants."

Soft water was heretofore brought hither at a half-penny per pail, and hard water at twelve shilhngs a year.

BLANDFORD. *Dorsetshire. Town Gaol.* Keeper, the Sergeant at Mace. Salary, none. Allowance 6d. a-day. 1803, Oct. 22d, no Prisoners.

This Prison consists of two rooms, called the *Outer* and the *Inner Gaol.* Prisoners are confined in the Outer Gaol during the day-time, when they beg charity, see and converse with people in the street; and at night are shut up in the Inner Gaol. Straw on the floor. Both rooms dirty and offensive. No court; no water. Formerly Debtors were sent hither by the Court of Requests.

BRIDGEWATER. *Somersetshire.*
The Town Gaol.
Gaoler, *Samuel Brevitt,* now *Samuel Slocomb:* He is a Sergeant at Mace. Salary, none. Fees, both Debtors and Felons, 3. 4d.

N of Prisoners, 1803, Oct. 5th, Debtors, none. Felons and Petty Offenders, One.
1806, Sept. 2d,--none.--------One.

Allowance to Debtors, none. Felons and other Criminal Prisoners, *Jburpence half-penny,* or *sixpence* per day, as bread is cheap or dear.

This Gaol is within the Cross-Keys Publick-House, situate near the bridge: The entrance down a long passage, over which are the Council-Chamber and SessionsHouse. It consists of one room for Men, about 15 feet square, with two iron-grated windows, and straw for sleeping on the floor. Here is also another room for Women, nearly of the same size, with a fire-place and boarded floor; and a third, with a fireplace, is used as a workshop.

Up-stairs are three rooms; in one of which there are five beds, furnished by the Keeper, at 1. or 1. *6d.* per week, if two sleep together; or at 2. per week for each single bed.

No Debtors are sent hither, but by process issuing out of the Borough Court, and then commitable for sums to any amount.

Here is one very small court-yard, with a sewer in it, a pump, and a *pigsty.* Water is brought to the Prisoners as they want it. The straw for bedding is changed ©nee a fortnight. No *Rules* and *Orders.* BODMIN. *Cornwall.*
The County Gaol, and Bridewell.
Gaoler, *James Chappie.*

Salary, 30/. with Fees as per Table; and if both together do not amount to 100/. the County makes good the deficiency. Also Coals for his own use.

The two Turnkeys under him have 25/. each *per annum,* paid them by the County, and Fuel likewise is allowed them. Fees, see Table. The Under-Sheriff does not claim any Fee for his *Liberate.* Garnish, abolished.

Chaplain, Rev. Mr. *Morgan,* now Rev. Mr. *Plummer.* Duty, Prayers and Sermon every Sunday. Salary, 50/.

Surgeon, Mr. *Hamley.* Salary, 30/. for Debtors, Felons, and Bridewell Prisoners.

Allowance. To poor *Debtors,* who petition the Magistrates, one pound eleven ounces of bread per day each, made of wheat and barley meal, in equal proportions; and when employed, they have the whole of their earnings.

Men Felons, who are not permitted to work, for fear of escapes, have sixpence a day. Those for *smaller offences,* and the *Bridewell Prisoners* receive half their earnings, in addition to the County allowance of bread. *Convicts* under sentence of *Transportation,* have the County allowance of bread, and one shilling in money. Every Prisoner, on Sunday, has half a pound of beef; and coals are furnished for the whole Prison. Debtors on the Master's side have no Allowance. REMARKS.

This County Gaol, which is also the Bridewell, stands on a fine eminence, at a small distance from the town of Bodmin. It fronts the South; and the steepness of the ground appears to be of peculiar advantage in many points, by placing the several buildings one above another, and thereby giving to each a full sun, and fresh air. A copious stream of excellent water is brought in above the Gaoler's house, and distributed through every ward, for supplying the baths, with other useful purposes; and is then, ultimately, and with great propriety, carried off through the sewers; which, being thus judiciously placed and circumstanced, are never offensive.

The Prison was first inhabited in June, 1779. Its boundary-wall encloses an area of 180 feet by 145. The Turnkey's lodge is in front; and has two rooms below, and two above stairs.

The court-yard of entrance is 30 feet by 15. In the approach to the Gaoler's house the several court-yards are on different levels.

On the right, is the *Men Bridewell Court,* 62 feef. by 47; on the left, that for the *Men Felons,* of the same size; and to each of them belongs a day-room 47 feet by 14, under arcades, with a bath, and a boiler for warm water to each.

Ascending up four steps is another court-yard, 50 feet by 30, with a workshop in it for vagrants, and a day-room of 40 feet by l6 From this court, the next ascent is by fifteen steps, to the court in front of the Gaoler's house, which is 30 feet square, with doors opening into four other court-yards. Of these, that on the righthand is for *Bridewell Women*; that on the left, for *Female Felons;* both are 62 feet by 20, with day-rooms 47 feet by 14, and arches for shelter and exercise in wet weather.

Higher up still, on the right-hand, is the *Infirmary Court,* of 54 feet by 20; adjoining to which is a passage 3 feet 6 inches wide, with three iron-grated windows. Into this passage open the three *Condemned Cells,* each of them 10 feet by 8, and 9 feet high to the crown of the arch: The floors are of brick, and they have each loose straw, two blankets, and a rug to sleep on. Close to the Infirmary Court, and near the Condemned Cells, there are in all four infirmary rooms, with the Surgeon's shop, or examining room, adjacent.

Opposite to the Infirmary court-yard is another of the same size, for poor, or *Common-side Debtors,* with arcades, 24 feet by 14, and two day-rooms, one of them 30 feet by 14, the other, 20 feet by 12. Each having a fire-place, with an oven, benches and stools to sit on, cupboards, and other conveniencies for frugal cookery. Here are also six sleeping-rooms, 10 feet by 7, and 8 feet 9 inches high; each calculated to accommodate two *debtors,* and for which, those on the Common Side pay i)d. per week, or 1. 6d. for a single bed.

In short, the Magistrates have here established a lasting monument of their humanity, by displaying a very liberal attention, both to the health and morals of the Prisoners.

The Gaoler's house, placed in the centre of the Prison, has a turret, with an alarmbell and clock. For the *Master's Side Debtors* are set apart four good rooms, well furnished, at *2s. 6d.* each single bed per week, or if two sleep together, 1. *3d.* each; but if a Debtor brings his own bed, 1. 3rf. per week for the room. They have likewise the indulgence of a very neat semicircular garden, lGofeetby 80, lying on the North side of the house; in which, not only they, but the convalescent criminals also, occasionally take the air at proper times

The Chapel, 30 feet by 20, is within the centre building. The Criminal Prisoners are seated below, the Women are placed out of sight of the Men, and a pew is appropriated to Convicts under sentence of death. The Debtors, and the Gaoler's family severally occupy the galleries. All are required to attend Divine service: Their behaviour, at my several visits, was orderly and devout, so as to answer the idea of a House of Prayer, and the duty was impressively performed by the worthy Chaplain.

I well remember, that in October, 1803, the Psalm read for the day happened singularly to be the LXXIXth. The three poor Men-convicts, then under sentence of death, were present, and appeared very sensibly affected by that pathetick ejaculation in the concluding part of the 12th verse; "*Preserve thou those that are appointed to die !*" It was not a Psalm specially selected for the solemn occasion; but it was rendered, therefore, the more striking. By the way, it might be exceedingly useful to have *selections,* for times like the above; and many of the Psalms, are peculiarly suitable and appropriate.

In this Gaol, the humane, active, and intelligent Keeper furnishes employment for all those Prisoners who are *willing to work:* And, indeed, all criminals here, who receive the County Allowance, as well as those committed for hard labour, *must work,* in order to have it, if well in health, and able so to do. The Women card and spin wool, or make, mend, and wash the other prisoners' clothes and bedding. The Men are chiefly employed in sawing timber, for which a double saw-pit is provided; or in sawing and polishing head-stones for church-yards; or else in weaving at the looms, which are also ready prepared. This the Gaoler takes charge of, and lays in the materials for labour, at his own risk of sale, when the work is done. By these means many, under his care, have been enabled to send a comfortable relief to their families; and others, from the exercise of talent, and acquiring habits of activity, have, *in a prison,* created to themselves a new resource for their industry, when *discharged from it.* In proof of this, and to the honour of the Keeper, I was informed, that one Prisoner, sometime after being discharged from hence, declared, "that the day of his commitment was the most fortunate of his life, as he had learnt here the trade of a sawyer, by which he could earn two guineas a-week." Such *may be* the happy effect of diligence in a Gaol: and, sensible of such effects, the Magistrates very judiciously allow to Mr. Cftapple that portion (a fourth-part) of nett earnings from the labour of the Prisoners, which formerly was paid to the County.

If a *Debtor* works here, he has the whole of what he earns to himself. Those Criminals that are employed in preparing timber and stone, have one-half of their earnings, beside the County Allowance: and the Women have the same, who are occupied in spinning and carding of wool.

The various rooms and court-yards of this Gaol, are (with some exceptions, which I shall presently notice,) kept distinct and separate for each class and sex of offenders. Every such Prisoner has a separate lodging-room, of about 8 feet 4 inches by 5 feet 4, and 9 feet S inches high; furnished with a wooden bedstead, strawbed, two blankets, and a coverlet. In each court-yard there is a stone-trough, with a pipe and cock, to supply each ward constantly with water.

Closely adjoining to three of the day-rooms, are baths and boilers, with ovens for purifying the clothes of those who are newly admitted. When a Prisoner is brought into custody, the Surgeon is sent for to examine him. If found unwell, medicines are sent him; if ragged and dirty, he is stripped, washed in the bath, and the County clothing substituted for his own.

The Men's Gaol is two stories high, and contains eight cells on each floor, divided from the court by a passage of 4 feet *6* inches wide. Their Bridewell is the same. The Women's Gaol and Bridewell are one story high, each of them containing seven cells, divided by a lobby, or passage, the same as for the Men. Here is also a large work-room, with several looms for weaving; and a court-yard to work in, of 138 feet by *96.*

A Table of Fees and Rates,

Approved by the Justices, and confirmed by the Judges of Assize, the 25th of March 1789, is printed, and stuck up in various parts of the Prison.

From Debtors. First Class. *£. s. d.*

Every Debtor voluntarily going into the Master's Ward, to pay the

    Keeper at entrance--------------034

    To the Turnkeys--------016

    To the Keeper at Discharge------------068

To the Turnkeys----------026

Every Debtor lodging in the Master's House, a Bed to himself, per Week 0 2 6

Two such Debtors in a Bed, each----------013

Every Debtor in the Master's house bringing his own bed, for lodging-room----------------018 SECOND CLASS.

Every Debtor, lodged over the Arcades, to the Keeper at entrance-0 2 6

To Turnkeys----------------010

To Keeper at discharge-------------050

To Turnkeys----------------020

Every such Debtor over the Arcades lodged in the Keeper's bed and room to himself, per week------------016

Two such Debtors in a bed, each per week--------009

Common Debtors having only straw, mattress, or their own bed, to £. s. d. Keeper at discharge------------06O i

To Turnkeys-----020

Debtors in general.

For signing every Certificate to obtain a Supersedeas, or Rule or

Order of Court-------------016

For Copy of Sheriff's Warrant, if demanded-------010

For registering any Declaration against a Prisoner------01O

For Discharge of every Debtor, on Composition, or by an Act of Insolvency, or for want of Prosecution (of which *two shillings and Jive-pence* is to be the Turnkey's Fee) except where it is otherwise directed by Statute--------------0 12 5-

Fee from every such Debtor, charged with more Actions than one, not exceeding five, of which *ten-pence* is to be the Turnkey's Fee on each 0 6 0

From Felons.

For every Felon acquitted and discharged--------o 15 4

For every Person bailed out or discharged, for which the Fee is not paid by the County---------------0134

For every Convict discharged----------0134

From Persons committed to Bridewell.

For every Person discharged from Bridewell-------0184

Epiphany Sessions, held at *Lostwithiel* the 15th January, 1789, for the County of *Cornwall,* the above List of Fees was produced, examined, and approved of by us, his Majesty's Justices of the Peace for the said County,

We, the Judges of Assize on the Western Circuit,

have perused and examined the above List of Fees,

and do approve and confirm the same. Dated 25th

March, 1789. W. H. Ashhurst.

F. Bl/LLER.

In the important discharge of his duty, the Surgeon is very attentive and humane. The Prison is frequently visited by the Magistrates, and kept very clean. All the apartments are white-washed twice a-year, and the sleeping-cells four times a year. The floors of the day-rooms and cells are washed once a-week ill winter, twice in summer, and swept out every day.

$33 It is worthy of especial remark, that out of 3877 Prisoners, there happened but *Jifteen deaths* in the space of twenty-seven years:—strong proofs not only of the healthy situation of this Gaol, but of that good government also, which assiduously keeps it such.

Thomas Graham,

John Coryton.

H. Hawkins Tremayne,

And yet, like so many others, it has, m some instances, its inconveniences, or defects. There is still wanting *a distinct court-yard for Convicts;* who, too often, remain a long time here after sentence, and should certainly be separated from such Prisoners as are *committed for trial.* Another court-yard also is essentially desirable, in order to preserve a proper separation betwixt young beginners in vice, and such old offenders,, as are both hackneyed and hardened in the practice of every enormity. But—I speak not to deaf ears.

From the 4th of Oct. 1802, to the 5th of Oct. 1803, the number of Prisoners committed to the Bridewell was 85. Their earnings during that period amounted to 117/. 8. 0d. of which sum the working Prisoners received one-half; the Keeper one-quarter; and the remainder was paid into the County stock.

Statement of *Prisoners* in general, from January, 1780, to February 17th, 1807, received here during the course of 27 years, from the Gaol and Bridewell's being first inhabited:

Gaol. Bridewell. Debtors. Totals.

Commitments,---125.8--1846---773.---.-3877 Deaths-----2--5---8---15

Prisoners are always discharged from hence *in a morning;* and, if necessitous, money is given them, according to their respective distance from home.

(£3 Whenever, to benefit the living, we honour the dead, it becomes no less a pleasing than a bounden duty. I cannot here omit this last opportunity of paying a tribute of great respect to the memory of my learned friend, Dr. Hall, the much lamented Physician of *Bodmin.* At my first visit to the Prison, I found this excellent Man visiting, and gratuitously prescribing for the sick, which I was informed had been his constant practice. Its singularity inspired me with the highest veneration. I had seldom, nay hardly ever, seen an instance of the kind during my walk through our Gaols, in any place, except the Metropolis: It was exemplary, and worthy of a more extensive imitation; and with Dr. *Hall* it continued until: September, 1806, when a fatal accident deprived society of one of its most useful members.,. i '., THE BOROUGH COMPTER. *Southwark in Surrey..*

Keeper, Sir *PVatkin Lewes,* Knight, Bailiff of the Borough; appointed by the Lord Mayor of London, and Court of Aldermen.

Deputy, *John Frost;* afterwards, *John Bullevant;* now *John Law..*

Salary, none. Fees, for Felons, see the Table.

c Garnish, two Shillings," painted on the Prison-Doors..

Surgeon, none; nor medical assistance in case of sickness.

Number of *Debtors;* and also of their *Wives* and *Infant Children,* humanely, and necessarily in the Prison with them. .;

Allowance, To each Debtor; a twopenny loaf per day , from the City; and every eight weeks, sixty-five penny loaves, from Mrs, Margaret Symcott's

Gift; more properly known as-" *Eleanor Gwynns* Legacya memorial whereof is fixed up in this Prison. Also twenty Shillings at every Christmas, fronv the Archbishop of Canterbury.

REMARKS.

The *Borough Compter,* vulgarly called " *The Clink"* is under the Jurisdiction of the Bailiff of Southwark, controulable, however, by the City of London; and extends its influence over five Parishes. But, in August, 1806, the powers of theCourt were still farther-extended:to *Norwood,* about seven miles distant; thenum The weight of this loaf, on the 10th of March, 1801, was *six ounces.* In August, 1783, the twopenny loaf weighed *twenty-one ounces.* The allowance of bread, every where, and at all times, should be in *weight,* and never according to its casual *value* in money; because of the frequent variation *of. frice* in an article of such important consequence.- ber of commitments thereby increased in more than a triple degree. For the six years preceding, the annual average had been 152; but no sooner was the Jurisdiction enlarged, than the number of the committed in the first year increased to 549. The following is an exact List of Commitments hither, from 1801 to 1806, inclusive: In 180U— ISO. In 1802,—160. In 1803,-170. In 1804,—125-In 1805,— 131. And in 1806,—147

Debtors have here one small court-yard, about 19 feet square. On the groundfloor, on the right-hand, is the Women's day and sleeping-room, of 24 feet by 9 feet 6 inches. On the left hand is another, intended for Men, 41 feet by 10:, But the floor of this room being only of *earth,* or *mud,* and unfit to sleep on, no use has been made of it for *many years;* so that the Men and Women associate promiscuously together in the Women's apartments, during the day-time.

Above stairs are two rooms, of the same size as the former, and in pretty good repair. All these rooms have fire-places; but *no coals are allowed;* no kettles or saucepans to cook provisions; no mops, brooms or pails to keep the Gaol clean; no bedsteads, bedding, *nor even straw to lie upon!* Hence, the Debtors are obliged every night to sleep in their clothes upon the boards, than which the very streets can hardly be more filthily dirty.

Alt who are arrested by process issuing out of the *Borough Court,* are sent to this miserable Prison; and in the house there are rooms, of about S feet square, for such as can pay sixpence per night for a bed.

The extreme distress and wretchedness which I had often witnessed in this place, 'particularly in the years 1801, 1802, 1803, and 1804, induced me, at length, to address the Lord Mayor by letter, of which the subjoined is a transcript:

"-MY LORD, Chelsea, 11th December, 1S04.

"I Beg pardon for the liberty I take in addressing myself to your Lordship; but, when the importance of the subject, and the object it has in view, are considered, they will, I trust, plead excuse. It is now more than three years since I made my *Urst* report to the Lord Mayor and Court of Aldermen, on the state of the Borough Compter. A Committee was appointed to inspect it. The windows were repaired and glazed: it was white-washed, and swept. This being all the improvement it has received, permit me to trespass on your Lordship's patience, and that of the Honourable Court, whilst I describe its present state.

"Sir Watkin Lewes, as Bailiff of the Borough, is, I presume the Keeper. His Deputy, John Bullevant, has Bo salary. This Prison, extends its jurisdiction over fjye. parishes. Men and Women Dfcbtors have one small court-yard, about 19 feet square, and they appear to me at all times to associate together. They have nothing but the dirty boards to sleep upon. No bedding, nor even straw allowed. No fire, even in this cold and damp season. No medical assistance in sickness. No religious attentions whatever. The few remaining boards in the Men-Debtors', room, (mentioned in my former report) are now taken away, as are the joists on which they were laid. The room is useless; the floor is earth. Neither mop's, brooms, or pails are allowed to keep the Prison clean. Soap and towels are not afforded to the Prisoner; so that a man may, for a debt of one guinea, remain in this wretched place *forty days,* without once taking off his clothes, or washing his hands and face.

"Permit me now, my Lord, to submit to your consideration the Allowance to this Prison. It is a two-penny loaf per day; weight 10th March, 1801, *six ounces!* and 7th December, 1804, *eight ounces.* This scanty provision, without any nutritions liquor, only water, is not sufficient to support the cravings of nature; and the Prisoner at his discharge may be fit for an hospital, but he cannot be fit for labour. The County of Middlesex allows to Prisoners of this description, in Cold Bath Fields, a loaf of bread of one pound weight every day, a pint of gruel every morning, a quart of broth made of rice and oatmeal for dinner, and every other day six ounces of meat for dinner, instead of broth. They have a common room, with a fire-place, and a peck of coals per day; a sleeping-cell 7 feet by 54., with plank bedsteads, straw-in-ticking beds, a blanket, and a rug. What a contrast T what shall I say to a system still continued, though respectfully submitted to the Court more than three years ago? I am informed there has been no *resident* Alderman in this ward for many years, which may in some measure account for the total neglect of this miserable place. The £5 penny loaves every eight weeks (from Mrs. Symcott's gift) might, if distributed at proper periods, according to the number of debtors, be of real service; but they are sent all at one time; and the late Keeper informed me, when there was only one debtor, he had the whole, and sold them.

"No inquiry ever appears to be made about the state of this prison, and there being no *resident* Magistrate, the cries of the miserable never reach that Court, here distress seldom supplicates in vain. The annual donation of 20. by the Archbishop of Canterbury, is distributed in the same inconsiderate manner as the bread. Liberality, Benevolence, and Humanity, are the characteristics of the City, and on all public occasions she extends them in a manner worthy the first city in the. world. The Gaols of Newgate, Ludgate, Giltspur-street, and Poultry, are ample partakers of its bounty, whilst the miserable one I have been describing, situate in Surrey, has no claim to the provision made by that liberal County. Forgot by the City; out of reach of being heard; it seems a wretched *cast-off'*, and may be numbered among the worst prisons in the Kingdom. At my visits the 7th and 8th of this month (Dec. 1804) the number of Prisoners, eight; *viz.* six' Men, two Women; their condition ragged and dirty, starving, and (except one) without employ. In this extremity *2s. garnish* is exacted from every new comer. That this picture is not over-charged, I am ready to prove; and will attend the Court of Aldermen any time they please to appoint, to interrogate the Keeper as to *facts..* Mr. Alderman Combe,, when Lord Mayor, honoured my remarks on the Poultry Compter with the most prompt and effectual relief; and I humbly hope, my Lord, for a like exertion *of* your high authority, and Tor the exercise of a like compassion towards the unhappy objects of it. I have the honour to be, with great respect, my Lord, your Lordship's most obedient and faithful humble servant,

"*To the Right Honourable* James Neild." Peter Perchard, Esq. Lord Mayor"

To the above letter I had not the honour of receiving any answer.

Benevolence, however, occasionally, though very rarely, has sometimes found its way to these dreary walls. At Easter, 1804, two legs and two shins of beef were sent. On the 15th of March, 1805, there were three Men and one Woman Prisoners: the Woman was extremely ill of a bloody flux, and the poor Men bad raised eighteen pence amongst them, and bought a truss of straw, of which they had given their sick associate a large portion. This act of sympathy pleased me much: The DeputyKeeper too had lent her an old blanket, and humanely permitted her to come into hk house, during the day; by which means, and with some other charitable assistance, she recovered.

. On the 9th December, 1805, two legs and two shins of beef were sent, the number of Prisoners beingwr; and also, the same year, two pair of blankets, and two rugs. On the 25th March, 1806, were sent three legs of beef, the number of Prisoners at time *eleven.* At my visit on the 28th, I found here five Men-Debtors, who had with them in the Prison three wives and nine children: some humane gentleman had sent them eight small flock beds, and he likewise in the same year liberated eight Prisoners. On the 2Sth May, lS06, there were seven Debtors, who had with them in prison five infant children.

For Felons and other criminal Prisoners here is a court-yard, of 16 feet by 11, with a sewer and pump in it, separated from that of the Debtors by a brick-wall. Their day-apartment, called the *Stone Room,* is 17 feet by 12, and has a fire-place, but no coals are allowed them. Vagrants sleep below, in two cells; one of them 10 feet by 7, the other 9 feet 6 inches by 7 feet

Felons, &c. have also four sleeping-cells above stairs, the average size of which is 10 feet by 7. They all sleep on the bare boarded floors: No bedding, nor even straw is allowed. Prisoners of this description are now sent hither for a night or two only, until fully committed for trial. I have not met with any here at my different visits.

Within the house is hung up the following ... "Table Of Fees

"To be taken by the Keeper of the Borough Compter. For the admission of every Prisoner, for felony, trespass, or other £. *s. d.* misdemeanor---------------- 0 1 1 4

Fo» every night's lodging------------ -0 0 6 £. *t. d. r*-To the Turnkey, for the admission of every guch Prisoner- --0 i O, For every person brought by any Peace Officer for safe custody, until hearing can be had before a Magistrate- -----O 2 O j

"And, for the better information of such Prisoners, the Court doth further order and direct, That a Table of the said Fees be fixed up in the most conspicuous part of the said Prison, for the perusal and inspection of the said Prisoners, and others resorting to the said Gaol.

, "By the Court, Man."

I cannot speak with precision as to the number of those Plaintiffs who have received debt and costs, in consequence of the imprisonment of their Debtors in this Borough Compter; because the late Deputy-Keeper died before I had finished my extracts, and Sir Watkin had sent for the books: But *Jeremiah Beavis,* a former Deputy-Keeper, in his evidence before a Committee of the Lords, in 1791, says, "that where one pays the debt, twenty are discharged after staying out their time." And I have no reason to believe it is otherwise now.

The Act and Clauses are here conspicuously hung up.

--*ft* .. SHORT ACCOUNT OF THE. '.'. `i , i Ancient Institution or Courts Of Conscience,..... Within the Metropolis and its Vicinity; and of their much improved Condition as effected by the Society for Relief of Small Debtobs-..

Courts Of Conscience, anciently denominated *Courts of Request,* had their origin in 151.8 (theoth of Henry VIII); when the Commdn Council of the City of London issued an Act for the Recovery of Debts under Forty Shillings due to Citizens, by a Court to be called a Court of Conscience, and to be held in Guildhall: and those debtors who failed to obey the award of that Court were to be imprisoned in one of the City Compters, until they complied with such award; even though it were *durante vitd.* In 1605 (the 3d year of James I.) the powers of the Court so formed in 151S by the Common Council of London, were established by Act of of Parliament.

In 1750, Alderman Dickenson brought in a Bill for extending similar powers to the whole County of Middlesex; but with this difference, that all persons refusing to submit to the decision or award of the Court, were rendered liable to imprison ment, in Newgate, for *three calendar months,* which cancelled the debt.

Thus it seems evident, that different

degrees of punishment were inflicted for one and the same offence, contrary to true policy, justice, and common sense; as will appear by stating the various expences and fees that were incurred to recover a debt from one shilling up to forty shillings: and which were nearly the same in all the Courts of Conscience: . rf.. :i

    For three Summonses--2 0
    The Order 2 2
    The Hearing-----1 3
The Execution--, ,, St 6
The Officer.-.--10
8 n.

On this original document are formed the following statements.; *vbu*

    At the City Compters, io *Wood St rat* and the *Poultry.*

Debt of one shilling-,-»-t 0
Expences to recover it as above--8 11
Fees exacted by the Gaoler when cleared-15 8 £. s. d. 1 5 7.
which the debtor must pay, or be imprisoned for *life,* with felons. At the *Borough Compter,* Southwark.
Debt, as above---10.
Expences, ditto-----8 LI
Fees exacted by the Gaoler when cleared-7 0
— 0 16 11 which the Debtor must discharge, or incur imprisonment for life, with felons.

    At *Newgate,* the *County GaoL*

Debt-'10
Expences------8li
Fees exacted by the Gaoler when cleared-8 10 0 IS *0* which the debtor must pay, or be imprisoned with felons, for *three calendar months*

    At *Cterkenwell.*

Debt.--,---10
Expences------811 . Fees exacted by the Gaoler when cleared-3 0
—0 14 11 which the debtor must pay, or be imprisoned with felons*forty duys.*

    At *Tothill Fields.*

Debt,--io
Expences ----8ii
Fees exacted by the Gaoler when cleared-5 0 0 14 11 which the debtor must pay, or *be forty days* imprisoned with felons.
f?cc my Remark on "Thomas Dobson," under the article Newgate. f£f Such once Was the legally-sanctioned, the severe, and miserable lot of these poor, unthinking, and unfortunate classes of mankind, at the time of the institution of our Society: Nor was it till near fourteen years after its auspicious establishment, that their repeated applications were so attended to, as to effect a total change in the horrid system. At length, however, Truth and Humanity prevailed. The exactions before specified were published by order of the Society in February 1785; and in the same year an Act of the legislature passed "for reducing the Time for Im"prisOnment of Debtor committed to Prison upon Prosecutions in Courts of Con"science in *London, Middlesex,* and the *Borough of Southward,* to the same' "Periods in each Court; and for abolishing Pees paid by those Debtors to Gaolers, "or others, on account of such Imprisonment." The happy result has been, that all Fees to Gaolers on these petty and injurious prosecutions are every where abolished; expences are reduced; the term of imprisonment is restricted (as hereafter mentioned); and in most of our County Gaols, throughout the kingdom, a due separation is observed betwixt unhappy debtors and the most flagitious offenders.

The perfect completion of so salutary a reform cannot fail to excite the just hope and warm expectation of every feeling heart. Particular care ought to be taken, that *Debtors* of the kind here specified, should *netieY* be suffered *to mix with Criminals-:* but in my various tours of visitation to the Houses of Correction, and Bridewells, in places remote from the metropolis, I have but too Often' fdurid fftettt associated with Felons, and other offenders of the worst description; who, both by instruction and example, frequently make them is abandoned as themselves; nay, and even extinguish *every* spark of modesty in the females, by daily habits of intimacy with the lewdest of their sex.

Another consideration, of much importance, demands also the peculiar attention of every conscientious Magistrate. Whilst the law ordaitis imprisonment, there ought to be a County *Allowance of food,* and of *Bedding* for every indigent and friendless Prisoner: instead of which, I have sometimes found *debtors,* Who have in prison become indebted to *felons* for their food; and, in some instances, have painfully witnessed, that when liberated from a gaol, they were fitter for an hospital than for labour.

In August 1806, an Act passed, extending the limits of jurisdiction beyond the *parishes* to which I there alluded, and enlarging, the powers of the Commissioners, by the style and title of " The Court of Requests for the Towft and *Borough of Southwarh,* and *Eastern Half* of' the Hundred of *Brixton,* in the County of Surry:" Three Commissioners to have jurisdiction over debts not exceeding Forty shillings and five over debts not exceeding Five pounds.

By the above Statute it was enacted, That the several Fees and sums of money following, and no other, should be taken by the *Bailiff'*, *Clerks,* and *Officers* of the said Court of Requests, for their respective services in the execution of the Statutes 22d and 32d of King George II. instead of the fees limited and expressed in the former of those two Acts; *viz..* ....

To the Bailiff.
For every Summons------------
For every Summons for the Attendance of not more than two) Witnesses--------------j
For every Hearing on Trial---------
For every Order, Decree, or Judgment, on Hearing---
Fbr paying Money into Court--------
-
For every Attachment----------'
For every Execution----. _.----
For every Nonsuit-----------'-
For receiving Money out of Court, in part------
Ffar receiving Money out of Court, hi full------
For every Search in the Books---. --.---
For swearing every Witness----------
For calling the Defendant before the Court------
To the Clerks.
For every Summons--------.j «

For every Summons for the Attendance of not more than two)
Witnesses------------.--,-f
   Fbr every Hearing on Trial----------
   For every Order, Decree, or Judgment, on Hearing r--.
For paying Money into Court----------
   For every Attachment------------
   For every Execution------------
   For every Nonsuit--------------
For receiving Money out of Court, in part------
For receiving Money out of Court, in full------
For every Search in the Books--------
-
   For swearing every Witness---------
For calling the Defendant before the Court------ :.. To the Officers.
For serving every Summons on Defendant, or Witness
For serving Notice of Attachment on Defendant--
For giving Nouce of such Service to the Plaintiff-
For levying Executions on Debts not exceeding 15*s.*
Above 15. and not exceeding *20s.* -----
Above *20s.* and not exceeding 40j.-----
Above 40s. and not exceeding 60j.-----
Above *60s.* and not exceeding *80s.*-----
Above *80s.* ....

The foregoing Tables of Fees were ordered to be conspicuously hung up in the Court-house, or where the Commissioners meet, that all concerned may see and peruse them at all times.
In consequence of the said Act, the term of imprisonment was ordained to be thenceforth limited as follows; and accordingly it now is, upon each action,
For all sums under, and up to 20.... Twenty days.
Above twenty, and not exceeding *40s.* - Forty days.
Above forty shillings, and not exceeding 3/.--Sixty days.
Above 3/. and not exceeding *Si.* ---One hundred days.

The following observations of Mr. Justice Blackstone demand a peculiar attention. He tells us that "divers trading towns, and other districts, had obtained Acts of Parliament for establishing in them Courts of Conscience, upon nearly "the same plan as that in the City of London. The anxious desire that has been *fi* shewn to obtain these several Acts, proves clearly, that the nation in general "is truly sensible of the great inconvenience arising from the disuse of the antient "*County* and *Hundred Courts;* wherein causes of this small value were always "formerly decided, with very little trouble and expence to the parties. But, it is "to be feared, that the general remedy which of late hath been principally applied "to this inconvenience (the erecting these new jurisdictions) may itself be attended, "in time, with very ill consequences: as the method of proceeding therein is en"tirely in derogation of the common law; as their large discretionary powers create *u* a petty tyranny in a set of standing Commissioners; and as the disuse of the "trial by jury may tend to estrange the minds of the people from that valuable pre"rogative of Englishmen, which has already been more than sufficiently excluded "in many instances. How much rather is it to be wished, that the proceedings in "the County and Hundred Courts could again be revived, without burthening the "freeholders with too frequent and tedious attendances; and at the same time "removing the delays that have insensibly crept into their proceedings, and the "power that either party have, of transferring at pleasure their suits to the Courts "at Westminster! And we may with satisfaction observe, that this experiment "has been actually tried, and has succeeded, in the populous County of Middlesex; "which might serve as an example for others. For, by Statute 23 George II. c. 33. "it is enacted, 1. That a special County-court shall be held, at least once a month, "in every hundred of the county of Middlesex, by the county clerk. 2. That twelve ' freeholders of that hundred, qualified to serve on juries, and struck by the sheriff, "shall be summoned to appear at such court by rotation, so as none shall be sum"mooed oftner than once a year. 3. That in all causes not exceeding the value of "forty shillings, the county clerk and twelve *suitors* shall proceed in a summary Sic Orig. Q. *Jurors,* or *Jurats?*
K
"way, examining the parties and witnesses on oath, without the formal process "antiently used; and shall make such order therein, as they shall judge agreeable "to conscience. 4-That no plaints shall be removed out of this court by any "process whatsoever; but the determination herein shall be final. 5. That if any "action be brought in any of the superior courts against a person resident in Mid"dlesex, for a debt or contract, upon the trial whereof the jury shall find less than "40. damages, the plaintiff shall recover no costs, but shall pay the defendant "double costs; unless upon some special circumstances, to be certified by the Judge "who tried it. 6. Lastly, a Table of. very moderate Fees is prescribed and set "down in the Act; which are not to be exceeded upon any account whatsoever. "This is a plan entirely agreeable to the Constitution and genius of the Nation: "calculated to prevent a multitude vexatious actions in the superior Courts; "and at the same time to give honest creditors an opportunity of recovering small "sums; which now they are frequently deterred from by the expence of a suit at "law: a plan, which, in short, wants only to be generally known, in order to its "universal reception" ?i BOSTON. *Lincolnshire..* y-
The Town Gaol and Bridewell.

Gaoler, *William Vaux;* a Gunsmith by trade, and his workshop adjoins the Felons' Gaol.

Salary, for both, 31/. Fees, on discharge, 2. *6d.*

Surgeon, when wanted, is ordered by the Mayor.

Number of Prisoners, Debtor. Criminals, Men. Woman.
1802, Aug. 25th,----1----. 8 -r.--. '.
Allowance, to Debtors, none. To Criminal Prisoners, four-pence per day.

. REMARKS.

This wretched Gaol seems to have been made under the arches of some old monastery.

For Felons here are, on the groundfloor, two damp offensive rooms, 14 feet square, with iron-grated windows, the bars of which are sufficiently set apart for a prisoner to put his head through, and they were conversing with their friends in the street. The Keeper told me they had liquors brought to them at all hours in the night, so that his life was in danger from their frequent intoxication. Their two rooms have wooden bedsteads, two blankets, and a rug each, and an offensive sewer in one corner. Over these are two other rooms, for Female Criminals, one of which in a bed-room of o feet 3 by 6 feet 4, dark, and without ventilation, the aperture, which was formerly in the door, having been stopped up: the other has an iron-grated window, through which the Woman Prisoner, young and dressy, was nodding to and conversing with her admirers in the street.

Close adjoining to the above are two rooms for Debtors, who are sent hither from the Court of Requests for the Borough of Boston, Skirbeek-£)uarter, and the parishes of Boston and Skirbeck. Here is no clear ventilation. The Debtor whom I met with in August 1802, complained of excessive heat: he appeared as in the last stage of a consumption; and, being a medical man, said it was owing to the want of air. Hard-fated captive! His debt was one guinea: his commitment, for forty days', which were nearly expired when I came hither.

Here is no court-yard; no water accessible: The Keeper fetches it as wanted, for his own use, from the street adjoining. The Gaol did not look as if it had ever been white-washed; nor could its filthy state be a matter of surprise, when its communication with the street was considered.

The irons here used are excessively heavy, owing, as the Gaoler informed me, to the insecurity of his prison. Neither the Act nor the Clauses hung up.

BOSTON. *Lincolnshire. The House of Correction.*
Gaoler, *William Appleby.* Salary, 30/.
Surgeon, Mr. *Davis.* Makes a Bill.
Prisoners, 1810, August 6th, none.
Allowance, sixpence a day.
REMARKS.
This New House of Correction was built in 1S09, in Skirbeck-Cjuarter, near Boston, for the division of Holland. The Keeper's house, which fronts the road, forms the centre building; and on each side is a day or work-room, 17 feet by 14, one for men, and the other for women; and above each is a sleeping-room of the same size, the ascent to which is by a step-ladder from the lower room. The doors and windows of these rooms open into their respective court-yards, which are 17 feet by 14, with a boundary wall, only 14 feet high. Water is supplied from a pump in the Gaoler's court-yard.

BOTTESDALE. *Suffolk.*
The House of Correction.
Gaoler, *John Bond.* Salary, 52/. 10.
Chaplain, none; nor any religious attentions. See Remarks.
Surgeon, Mr. *Thomas Reeve.* Salary, none; but makes a Bill.
Number of Prisoners, 1805, Aug. 30th, 4. 1810, Sept. lfith, 3.
Allowance: The following Dietary is painted on a board, and hung up.
One pound and a half of bread daily.
Breakfast each day, oatmeal gruel.
Dinners, Sunday, half a pound of meat, and one pound of potatoes.
Monday, three-quarters of a pint of pease, with broth of the preceding day.
Tuesday, rice or oatmeal porridge, with leeks or onions.
Wednesday, two pounds of potatoes, if in season, or gruel.
Thursday, as on Sunday,
Friday, as on Monday.
Saturday, as on Tuesday.
Salt for the week.
This diet costs *Is. 6d.* per week, besides the one pound and a half of bread daily.
REMARKS.
This Prison, first inhabited in April 1801, stands in a healthy situation, about a quarter of a mile from the town. It is a new building, and surrounded by a boundary-wall, 13 feet high, 64± yards long, and 294-yards wide, having the house in the centre. The approach is through a handsome stone entrance, along a flag pavement, skirted on either hand with a neat grass-plat and small garden. Behind the building is an excellent kitchen-garden for vegetables. On the righthand of the entrance are the Keeper's apartments; on the left is a kitchen, fitted up with fire-place, an oven, copper, and other utensils for frugal cookery; and adjoining to it is also a small room for prison-utensils. Through the centre of the building is a passage 37 feet 6 inches in length, 5 feet 6 inches wide; and in the middle of the passage an iron-grated door divides the Prison from the Keeper's apartments. On the ground-floor are four cells, two on each side of the passage 14 feet 6 by 8 feet, with arched roofs 8 feet 6 inches high, and iron-grated and glazed windows, with casements 2 feet square. Up one pair of stairs there are also four other cells, of equal size; and on the same floor is a room in front of the Keeper's house, 21 feet by 12, and 9 feet 6 inches high; which has a fire-place, and is used occasionally as a dayroom or infirmary. Here is likewise a court-yard 40 feet by 37, surrounded by a wall 14 feet high, and paved with flag stones. In this yard is a pump and sewer, and each prisoner has access to it, for about one hour in the day. Every cell is furnished with an iron-frame bedstead, wooden bottoms, a sacking bed filled with straw, one blanket and a rug; and a bell is fixed in each cell for the use of the prisoners, in case of being taken ill, or wanting assistance. The Keeper informed me at my visit in 1810, that a Chaplain was to be appointed to the Prisons

The Schedule of Laws for governing Houses of Correction (22d G. III. c. 64.) and the Clause against Spirituous Liquors, are painted on boards and hung up; but not the Act for preserving the Health of Prisoners.

Their employment is the spinning of wool; half their earnings from which are paid them at the time of their discharge. All of them are allowed clean linen once a week; and coals, mops, brushes, brooms, soap, towels, and vinegar, are here considerately allowed, for personal comfort and prison cleanliness.
BRADFORD, *Yorkshire. See page* 45.
BRECON. *South Wales.*
Tlie County Gaol, and Bridewell.
Gaoler, *Walter Wathins;* Salary, 52/. 10.
: Now *Thomas Gittins*; Salary, 105/. and half of the Prisoners' earnings; out

of which he provides a Turnkey.
Fees, Debtors, as per Table. Felons, when discharged in Court by proclamation, 11. 4d. which is paid by the County Treasurer. For Conveyance of Transports, the expence attending it, Garnish, abolished.

Chaplain, Rev. *John Jones.* Salary, 20l.

Duty, Prayers on Sunday and Thursday; and Sermon once a month.

Surgeon, Mr. *Williams.* Salary, for *Felons only, 26l. 5s.*

Number of Prisoners, Debtors. Felons, &c. Bridewell.
1803, Sept. 7th,----3----4 2
1806, Sept. 12th,---0----6 -4
Allowance, to Debtors and Felons, one pound and a half of bread per day. Transports have not the King's Allowance of *2s. 6d.* per week.

REMARKS.

This Gaol and Bridewell was finished for the reception of Prisoners in 1782; and, since my visit in 1803, has been benefited by many improvements.

The Prisoners, at that time, complained to me of being cruelly treated, and half starved. They were literally half naked; and two Women, without shoes or stockings, heavily loaded with double irons . At my earnest request the then Gaoler promised to take them oft', but added, "he would not do it to oblige any Magistrate in the town." Conversant in scenes of misery, this Man seemed to be steeled against every tender sensation. He told me that a Felon and a Deserter had made their escape a short time before my visit. My answer was, that I should not be surprised at any act of desperation, under circumstances of such severity. The said Keeper, who was a weaver, and dyer of worsteds, also informed me, " that he had to support the Prisoners committed to the House of Correction, in return for which he received the whole of their earnings." The countenances of all the Prisoners, at the period alluded to, bespoke neglect and oppression. The learned Judge, to whom I sent my Remarks, was pleased to mention them in his Charge to the Grand Jury at the next Assize; adding, that the Keeper was an incorrigible drunkard; and the Magistrates humanely interfered.

Here is, now, a boundary-wall, of 51 yards by 37, and the Gaol is in the centre of the area. The ascent to the Keeper's house is by a flight of steps, and he has apartments on the ground-floor. On the right of his kitchen is the infirmary-room, and on the left a room for Female Debtors. Men Debtors have a court-yard, with a pump and sewer in it; a large day-room, with a fire-place and glazed windows; and on each side a large.sleeping-room, termed a *free-ward,* with fire-place and windows like the former. Up stairs are four other sleeping-rooms, with similar windows, and in two of them a fire-place. If the Debtor brings his own bed, he pays nothing; if the Keeper furnishes one, *2s. 6d.* per week.

Men Felons have a court, about 35 feet by 25, into which opens one sleeping-cell; and a day-room, of 26 feet 6 inches by *lgfeet,* into which two cells open. Adjoining to the day-room is a passage *16* feet long, and 4 wide, called "*the Iron Gate*" into which four cells open. These latter are assigned for Prisoners of the worst class.

The court, day-room, and sleeping-cells for Women Felons, are similar to those for the Men, but on the opposite side of the Gaol. The Bridewell House of Correction is under the same roof, but separated from the Gaol by the Chapel. The At the Lent Assizes for *Thetford,* in 1782, Lord Loughborough laid a fine of twenty pounds on the Gaoler of Norwich Castle, "for putting irons on a *Woman."* The lesson is exemplary, and it is hoped may ever be felt as a caution.

t A Welch Writer has volunteered in the cause, and attempted to vindicate this very unworthy Man, by saving, that "One of the Women thus ironed was young, and stout, and refused tamely to submit to be double-ironed; in consequence whereof, the Gaoler was obliged to get assistance to effect it." He ridicules the idea of giving money to a Prisoner on discharge, and he even compliments the Gaoler for his humanity! *Noscitur d sociis I* Who has not heard of the famous *Owen Glendower?* He, too, was a Gentleman of Wales, and very apt to assert what few could easily believe: And to him, it is said, th« gallant *Hotspur* addressed that never-to-be-forgotten precept of sound morality, "Oh! while you live, *Tell Truth,* and *shame the Devil."* Hen. IV. Part I. Act 3. Sc. 1.

day-room has a fire-place, with iron-grated windows; and two sleeping-cells open into it.

In the court-yard is a double cell, for those under sentence of death. The outer cell has an iron-grating over the door, and is of 15 feet by 10 feet 6 inches. The inner one, which opens into it, and where the Prisoner sleeps, is *6* feet *6* by 5 feet *6* inches, and almost totally dark.

There are also two reception-cells for Prisoners when first brought in; each of 6 feet by 4 feet 10, and 8 feet high; fitted up with a wooden bedstead, straw-in-sackmg bed, fresh straw every month, two blankets and a rug: The door-way only 3 feet 10 inches high.

Mops, brooms, and soap are supplied for cleansing the Prison,—which is kept very clean,—but neither pails nor towels are allowed. The employment of weaving has lately been introduced; and the Prisoners are to have one-third of their earnings,the Gaoler and County the other two.

Here are books provided for the Visiting Magistrates, the Chaplain, and the Surgeon, to enter their Reports. The two former are very regular; from the latter, none since the 14th August (l8o6) No money is here given to Prisoners, when discharged, to prevent a recurrence to former sufferings.

No Rules and Orders. No County clothing. The Act for Preserving Health not hung up, nor the Clauses against Spirituous Liquors.

"At an adjournment of General Quarter Sessions, held at Brecon, 13th March, 1805, for settling the Fees, to be taken by the Gaoler for commitment or discharge of Debtors; it *was ordered,* That the following, and no more should be taken, viz.

"For entering every fresh Action or Process, whereon a Prisoner may be charged----------------036

For the Turnkey, or Under Turnkey, on each fresh Action-0 10

For entering the discharge, or for the discharge of every Prisoner-0 7 0

To the Turnkey, for the discharge of every Prisoner-----01Q

For the receiving and entering every Declaration against a Prisoner in custody----------------02 0

To the Turnkey on every Declaration---------006

For a Certificate, for want of a Declaration, in order to take out a

Writ of Supersedeas-------------036

For a Copy of the Warrant of Commitment against each Prisoner-0 10

Edward Morgan, Esq. Chairman. Walter Jeffreys, Esq. Penry Williams, Esq. Approved by George Hardinge and Abel Moysey, Esqrs. Justices of the Great Sessions of the several Counties of *Glamorgan, Brecon,* and *Radnor."*
BRECON. *Town Gaol,*

Gaoler, *David Morgan,* Sergeant at Mace, a Shoemaker. Salary, 5/. Fees, 3s. 6d.

Prisoners at my Visits, 7th Sept. 1803, and 12th Sept. 1806, None.

Allowance, two-pence a day in bread.
REMARKS.

A dark dungeon, about 12 feet square, down ten steps. Straw on a mud-floor. No court! No water! The only light it receives is from a small iron-grating, level with the street. Up stairs were heretofore four rooms for Debtors, who furnished their own beds, or paid the Keeper for each bed 1. per week.

The Keeper told me that the Allowance was now one pound and a half of bread per day; and that his Salary had been discontinued for two years.

There are only two rooms now for Debtors, who are committed by process issuing out of the Borough Court, *from one shilling to any amount.* BUCKINGHAM. *Town Gaol.*

Gaoler, *Samuel Danby;* a Collarmaker, who works at the opposite side of the street. Salary, *$l.* 5. Fees, none. Allowance, *Is.* per week.

Debtors, 1802, Nov. 25th, One. 1804, July l6th, Two. 1805, Sept. 16th, One.
REMARKS.

Behind the Keeper's apartments is a court-yard, about 30 feet square, and two rooms which open into it, about 16 feet by 12 each, with barrack bedsteads and straw: one is the Bridewell, the other for Felons. Over these are two rooms for Debtors. No water: The Gaoler fetches it from over the way. The Prison clean: The floors had been rotten and full of holes; but at my visit in 1810, they were in good repair. Debtors for small sums are committed by process issuing out of the Borough Court. There are seldom any Criminals confined here except for one or two nights at the Assizes. It is chiefly used as a place of confinement for vagrants, night-charges, and deserters.

Over the Gate is the following Inscription.
"The Right Honourable
Richard Grenville Temple,
Lord Viscount Cobham,
caused this Edifice to be erected at his own Expence,
For the Use of this Town and County,
the Summer Assizes being restored to this Place,
and fixed here by Act of Parliament,
in the year 1748."
BRIDEWELL. *London.*
The House of Correction.
Steward, Mr. *Bolton Hudson.*
Chaplain, Rev. *Henry Budd.*
Duty, Prayers and a Sermon every Sunday morning, and Prayers in the afternoon, in a Chapel appropriated to the Governors, Officers, &c. and a Sermon every Sunday, and Prayers twice a week, in the Prison. See Remarks. Salary, *2Q0l.* and apartments in the house.
Surgeon, Mr. *Bryan Crowther.* Salary, 50/. ASee *Remarks.*
Apothecary, Mr. *John Haslam.* Salary, 33 5I, and medicines provided. See Remarks.
Matron, *Mary Rundle.* Salary, 60/. See Remarks.
Porter, Mr. *Richard Weaver.* Salary, 70/. Porter's Man, *Richard Allen.*
Number of Prisoners for nearly sixteen years, beginning in 1794, and continued up to my last visit, in 1809, inclusive.

Allowance, one quartern loaf per day for six Prisoners, provided by the Hospital; independent of the contract made with Mr. Hudson, the Steward; who is allowed one shilling per day for the maintenance of each Prisoner, and furnishes the following diet for each, as settled in the Special Committee, 19th January, l8oi.

Monday, Wednesday, Friday, One pound of beef without bone, boiled down to a consistency of ten ounces; and three pints of eighteen shilling table-beer.

Tuesday, Thursday, Saturday, The broth of the meat of the preceding day, with three ounces of rice, which, when properly boiled, produces 15 ounces at least. The quantity of soup for each Prisoner to be three pints; and one. quart of table-beer.

Sunday, One pound of beef without bone, boiled down to the above consistency, together with the broth of the meat; and three pints of table-beer.
REMARKS.

This Edifice was rebuilt by King Henry the Eighth, near to a remarkable well, called " Bride's Well," upon the scite of a tower or castle, which had belonged to the Kings of England from before the conquest; and where those Prihcte lodged, and sometimes removed to it their Courts of Record from Westminster, They herealso occasionally held their Parliaments.

By Henry the Eighth it was prepared for the reception of the Emperor' Charles the Fifth, who came there in-15#2; but having.at length fallen to decay, it was for some time disused. King Edward the Sixth, in the seventh year of his reign, gave it to the Mayor, Commonalty, and Citizens of London, to be used as a harbour or asylum for poor destitutepeopte; but Echtard--dying'-soon after, the City did; not take possession of it till-the-Royal Granty two years afterwards, had been confirmed by his sister Queen Mary; when Sir William Gerard the Mayor entered, and, having taken possession, an Act of Common Council was made, of which the following is an extract.

"Inasmuch as King Edward" Sixth

has given' his-House of Bridewell unto the "City, partly for the setting of idle and lewd people to work, and partly for the lodging "and harbouring of the poor, sick, and sOre people of this City, and of poor way"faring people repairing to the same; and hath for this purpose given the bedding "and furniture of the Savoy; therefore, in consideration that very great charges "will be required for the fitting up of the said house, and the buying of tools and "bedding, It is ordered, &c. &c."

In the Reign of Queen Elizabeth, mills were invented to grind corn, and to be worked, some of them by the hand, and others by the foot; so that even the lame (if they possessed but one sound limb) might find employment: and we are told, that the mills were so constructed, that two men could grind as much corn, in any given time, as could be ground by ten men with the other mills then in use. In the year lfiit), twelve public granaries were here erected, large enough to contain six thousand quarters of corn; which1,' iri case of1 scarcity, or' of combination among other dealers, was to be sold to the" poor at prime cost.

(&3r' A noble example surely, in the *rude times* of our forefathers $ and, perhaps, not unworthy the public consideration of those, who would wish to add true dignity to the spirit of modern refinement.

In the yearl66f5, the old building of Bridewell was'almost wholly destroyed by the dreadful fire of London; but afterwards again rebuilt in the style and manner of its present appearance; the front only excepted, which has lately been' taken down, and a handsome row of houses erected, in a line with the rest in Bridge Street.

The Hall of this venerable structure is a noble room; in which is a fine painting of 'Ring Edward VI. delivering his Charter to Sir George Barnes, the then Lord Mayor. Several other good portraits are also hung up, to decorate the wall.

The-©hit Chapel has been: taken down, and a New one erected on the North-side of the: present front.

That part of Bridewell, which peculiarly relates to the subject of my investigation, ihas wards assigned for Men and-Women Prisoners, separated very properly by the Porter's house, placed in the centre of those divisions.

The *Men's Ward,* which occupies the ground-floor, on the left of the entrance,. has a Jarge day-room, in which they pick oakum; and adjoining to it is another room, wherein to deposit the raw materials for work; with a small apartment, called "the *Iron Room,"* from the irons which are kept there.

;From the large day-room a stain-case leads oa to the first story, or gallery; 'which contains nine sleeping-cells, of about 10 feet square, supplied with iron-grated and glazed windows, well contrived for the benefits of light and ventilation. These cells are fitted up with wooden bedsteads, straw beds in Russia duck, one 'blanket and a rug to each, and a shelf for the placing of provisions. Here are also two cells for the refractory; and all the cells open into a well-ventilated lobby,.7.feet 6 inches wide.

The second gallery is of the same width, and contains 12 cells of the like dimensions. Of these, six are set apart for petty offenders, and fitted-up'as those already described. A door of partition across the lobby separates them from the other six cells; over the doors of which is painted " *Apprentice'*. " These latter cells are furnished with flock beds, a pillow to each, two sheets, two blankets and a rug.

The third, or attick story, contains three rooms, of about 19 feet square, for'Men-Vagrants, who sleep upon the floor; which, to separate each Prisoner, is partitioned. to the height of about four inches, 'and has long wheaten straw, with one blanket and a rug to each compartment.

Here is also a large room,-occasionally used as an Infirmary, with a fireplace in it, and four opposite windows for fresh air; adjoining to which is another apartment, called The Dispensary.

'YkteWomen's Ward, on the right-hand of the entrance, has three sleeping-cells upon the ground-floor, fitted up in the same manner as those appropriated to the Men. Their first gallery contains three dther sleeping-cells, and a large day or messroom, which opens into a wide and well-ventilated lobby. The second gallery is similar to it; and the attick story contains three sleeping-cells; together with a Targe room, the floor of which is partitioned in the manner before described, to receive 21 Women Vagrants,, furnished with loose straw, a blanket, and a rug for each compartment.

The Chapel, already noticed, is on the ground-floor of the Women's side of the Prison, and the sexes are so duly separated, as to be placed out of sight of each other. The Chaplain's duty is particularly to admonish and instruct the Prisoners from time to time, to read the Liturgy and the exhortation already provided for the Institution *1* or to preach on Sundays once, and read Prayers on two other days of the week in the Prison. On all which occasions he is to wear his usual officiating dress, and to see that such Prisoners as are able and proper do always attend divine service. And here it is but just to remark, as far as has come under my observation, that the duty has been impressively performed; and that short religious tracts are printed, which the Chaplain delivers out to the more orderly Prisoners who can read.

The Surgeon's duty here is to attend the Prisoners, and surgical cases, both at this and at Bethlehem Hospital, as well as the resident officers and servants. Mr. Haslam, the apothecary, has apartments in this building, where constant residence is required. He is to give all necessary attendance upon the Prisoners and other inhabitants of the Hospital, and to sign the Matron's bills for sick messes to the Prisoners, &c. To her is consigned the charge of all Women Prisoners, and to attend upon the sick, both male and female, with care and humanity, in all manner of disorders. She is allowed three-pence for each mess of gruel, and fifteen pence per day for the maintenance of all prisoners on the sick list. The Porter's man is required to serve out the prisoner's diet: He is allowed three-pence for each mess of gruel supplied to the Men, and must assist, as directed in all matters respecting the Prison aud the Prisoners.

The Prisoners here are served with their respective allowance of provisions daily-at twelve o'clock.

The care devolved upon Mr. Weaver, the Porter of Bridewell, is to receive all prisoners into his custody, and enter their names and other circumstances in a book provided for the purpose: to see that the Men's Prison be well washed once a week with vinegar, fumigated weekly with tar, and white-washed regularly, conformable to Act of Parliament; to treat the prisoners with humanity and kindness, and keep them safe and clean, till they are duly discharged; to visit them frequently; to see that they are kept to labour, humanely treated, &c. and to sign the Steward's Diet-Book, as a voucher for the same.

Formerly the prisoners were employed by a hemp-dresser, who had an apartment in the Prison, with a Salary of 20l. per annum, and the profit arising from the labour of the prisoners. But the chief employment now is, and for some years past has been, picking of oakum. The junk for this purpose is provided by the Porter of Bridewell, and when picked is sold at from three to five shillings *per Cwt.*

The earnings of the prisoner appear to have been as follow; s. d. «£. s. d. *1799* ----21 18 9 1805----14 5 *6* 800----23 4 4 1806----15 18 5 1801----35 5 11 1807----115 9 1802----28 0 3 1808----956 1803----29 6 8 1809----9 9 0. 1804----15 13 4

Their hours of labour, deducting meal times, are from eight till four in winter, and in summer from six to six.

The bath, placed here in the basement story, is well supplied with water. Firing is allowed in severe weather. Here is no court-yard; but in extreme hot weather the prisoners are sometimes taken out for air in the adjacent burying ground.

BRIDGEWATER, *Somersetshire. Seepage* 50. BRISTOL. *City and County Gaol.* Gaoler, *William Humphries.* Salary, *200l.* and *2l.* a year gown-money. *s. d.*

Fees, for *Debtors,* first Action,-------- ---68 second, and every subsequent Action--'-3 4 a *London* Action----------9 0 for *Felons* --------13 4

Transports, 5/. each when delivered at Portsmouth. Garnish abolished.

Chaplain, Rev. Mr. *Walcam;* now Rev. Mr. *Day.*

Duty, Sermon on every Sunday, and Prayers on Wednesday and Friday. Salary, 35/.

Surgeon, Mr. *SaffbrcL* Salary, none; makes a Bill.

Number of Prisoners, Debtors. Felons, Ike. Deserters, 1801, Dec. 16th,---18---*26* ----0.. 1803, Oct. 4th,---34---26----*2.* 1806, Sept. 20th,---33 u._ 27----0.

Allowance, to Debtors, none.

to Felons, a threepenny loaf of standard wheaten bread. Its weight on the 16th Dec. 1801, was lib. 5oz. 20th Sept. 1806,--------1 lb. 3 oz. REMARKS.

This Gaol, called *Newgate,* is built on a declivity, and stands in the middle of the City. It is very antique, and by much too small for the general number of its inhabitants. The lower rooms are dark. For Debtors there are about fifteen large and airy rooms'; two of which are termed *free wards,* for poor Debtors, who find their own beds.

Those rooms, which are oji.tbe Master's Siderpay tfrf.(per week.each; andtwo Prisoners sleep in a bed. Here is not a proper separation.,qf,Men And Women..Only one courtyard,. (called,the *T-enmsrcour)* .that jg snfficiently.brge for air and exercise. Its. dimensions re yartk by *fi,* jnte which debtors jand.felone ape separately admitted, a»d in different hours of theday. When J;was4ber.e,-lineo Was hanging out to dry. In this court-yard there is a pump with good water; and also a convenient bath, but seldom used.

The Men-Felons have two day-rooms. Adjoining to the first, 15 feet by 13, and 7 feet 8 inches high, *is* a sleeping-room of about-the same size;-which has no air but what is admitted through an iron-grated window in the day-room. There is a small but very close court adjacent, about 20 feet long and *12* feet wide. On one side of this court, is an ascent by twelve steps, to a sick room for felons, 18 feet by 124-, and 7 feet 6 inches high; pth;ich.hastiwn-gratqd and glazed windows, a fireplace, a small aperture in the door, 14 inches by 11, and a ventilator.

The second day-room is.24-feet by 18, and 8 feet high; with a fire-place, and two treble iron-grated windows, which, in consequence, nearly exclude the light.' This room has two sleeping-cells, of 11 feet'by *"J,* With arched roofs; and a very small court, with a sewer in it.

The " Condemned-room," as they term it," is 18 feet'by 13, and 9 feethigh, which has a double iron-grated window, that looks into the felons' yard. Their dungeon, (the *Pit)* to which you descend by eighteen: steps, is 17 feet in diameter,:and Sfeet *6* inches high. It has barrack bedsteads,.with.beds of straw in canvass; and *some benevolent Gentlemen ofthe City occasionally send a few rugs.* This dreary place is close and offensive; with only a very small window,.whose light is merely sufficient to make darkness visible. In the year 1801 I remember it was chiefly appropriated to convicts under sentence of transportation. Seventeen *'Prisoirers are said to have slept here every night!* The Turnkey himself told me,."'that in a. morning, when he unloeked the door,-he-was so affected by the putrid" steam issuing from.the dungeon, that it was enough to strike him down." Atiiny-next visit,. 4th Oct. 1803, it so happened, that only one Man slept there...

When Turnkeys are thus affected, by only opening the. doors, what must the pitiable wretches suffer, confined, through the whole night, in such fetit) hot-beds of disease! There are many narrow passages about this. Prison, so that the utmost attention seems requisite to keep it healthy; and yet, at my several visits, I It has very judiciously been remarked, that a Gaol, considered as.a place for.safecustody of the disturbers of peace and property, nirely attracts our attention-as an object of pity and benevolence. Gratified with the first idea, of its powe to tefei/iadaring murderer, how often dp »e overtook that'most huncntablc groupe, which it so di'cadjfully *oppresses!—rl* ,uiean the victims of. mere-misfortune;_-th« feeble and unresist less sacrifices to false and, giqu&dss accusafym!. Yuhuues might Aw crowded, orw this head of *legal suffering.* found it comparatively clean, considering that, the. fbn-Side was so close and crowded. It is scraped and white-washed once a year. i";

The Female Felons'ward is a large room, 42 feet by 24, and 6± feet high, at'the top of the house, which serves the purposes of a day-room and sleeping-room-It-overlooks the Men-Felons' court, and had once four windows) but two of th«m afe now stopped 'up. There is in it a sink, but no water' supplied, except what is ordered by the Keeper from below. Near this ward are two rooms set apart for infirmaries.

Some time since Mr. John Heydon-lert1oh'ff hundred pounds to be lent to two nrcrclrfinfrts; eatymg atrtraalty to ttfe" Corporation, for the benefit of the debtors, lj. *4it.'* as the interest *o+lfti* moiety. This is paid to the Treasurer of the Sbciety for1 StrfaU fiebtS'iitstidtlted here:

Mr! Freemiiw fefFoftT Pounds' Nine S&ilings to be laid out in bread and beef, and! distributed oil Christmas-Eve to the Prisoners of air descriptions. To this legacy' Mrs.-Freeman liberally makes ah ahnual addition of eleven Shillings.

The'Chwchwardens 'rrave, for'many years past, paid four Pounds two Shi Flings for the use of th'e'ptisowerS'; twotfArds of which' are given to the debtors, and onethird tohe'elon'S. IFtns *I* apprehend to be the Legacy of Mrs. *Aldsworth,* who is, memorfled'ljy'MT. HoWARTb'. But no memorial appears in the Gaol of any legacy.

The'Act'f6r preservation of Health' is hung up in the Chapel, which, though large, is nof properly partitioned'to's separate the'classes. The attendance of Debtors on Divine-worship' is optional,' and T was sOrry to observe only nine present, in lS06 out of thirty-three. Neitherwefe' the Criminal Prisoners so attentive as one might have expected from the devout and'serious manner in which the duty was performed by their pious' Chaplairt." So" little regard, indeed,' was paid to the Chapel, as a place of worship, that I'have repeatedly seen the prisoners drinking, smoking, and chewing tobacco in the gallery.

The'Clauses against strong-Liquors' are hung up at the entrance of the Gaol. No employment: and such is the' confined situation of the Prison, as to preclude the possibility of work! No Table of Gaoler's Fees.

Besides the clerical duty before noted, here are thirteen Sermons in a year; for wfrrch tle Rector of the parish receives four pounds from a legacy.

I'tfhderstattd that a person arrested by an action from the Tolsey Court here, may, at the next Court; confess the debt; and at the first Court after (which occurs monthly) may be charged in execution, and become immediately entitled to his sixpences, or a supersedeas.

Several years since, an Act passed for the building of a new Gaol. That it has not been carried' into execution by this rich commercial City, is much to be regretted; for; really the present Gaol is disgraceful.

How long shall young beginners and old offenders, both here and elsewhere, be suffered to associate promiscuously together!

i BRISTOL. *City Bridewell.*
Keeper, *John Parsons*; now *Thomas Evans.* Salary, 50/. Fees, *3s. 6d.*
Chaplain, none; nor any religious attention paid to the Prisoners.
Surgeon, Mr. *Saffbrd,* who makes a Bill. """'
N of Prisoners, 1801, Dec. 17th, 8. l803,Oct. 4th, 16. 1806, Sept. 20th, 5.
Allowance, a threepenny loaf of household bread, which I weighed,—1 lb. 5 oz.
REMARKS.

This Prison was built in 17SI. Part of it is in the Keeper's house, on one side of the street, and part on the other side. In the Keepers house, the Master's-Side criminals have a day-room on the ground-floor, 15 feet square, 10 feet high; and up-stairs, two rooms supplied with beds by the Keeper, at 1. per night. In these three rooms the following notice is painted: "Whoever shall write against, or daub the walls in any manner, will be punished as the Magistrates shall think proper.

The Common-Side, (the Bridewell) over the way, consists of two parts, separated by a court 50 feet by 15, in which there are a pump and cistern for hard and soft water, which is laid on by a pipe from the quay. The first part has, on the right hand, two cells for Vagrants on the ground-floor, each l6i feet by feet, an irongrated window facing the court, and a most offensive sewer in one corner: The sleeping-room above is large and airy, but the straw upon the floor was short, dirty, and almost worn to dust. On the left hand is a room for *Jines,* 22 feet by 17, and 10 feet high, with an iron-grated window to the court; and the room is not rendered offensive. Above stairs is an apartment of the same size.

The second part of the Common-Side has upon the ground-floor, on the right-hand, two cells, 16-1-feet by 6, and 9 feet high to the crown of the arch; with an aperture 12 inches square, to admit light and ventilation, and an iron-grating over each door. The sewers, being near the river, are not very offensive; but on my visit in 1803, they were so terribly infested by rats, that a cat was kept in each cell, to prevent their gnawing the prisoners' feet. On my next call, however, in 1806, and the appointment of a new Keeper, I found the rats prevented from such annoyance. The floors were mended, cells white-washed, and the whole Prison very clean.

Over the cells is the Infirmary, 22 feet by 17, and 10 feet high, with a fire-place and glazed window. On the left-hand is the Female Vagrants' day-room, 18 feet by *16,* and 10 feet high, with an iron-grated window toward the court; aqd over this a sleeping-room of the same size. The court itself being quite out of sight from the Keeper's house, he does not permit prisoners to use it, nor the pump there, except three times a week, in the middle of the day; yet some offenders are confined here for three years together, and, during that time, kept in irons.

No employment here. Neither the Act

for preserving Health, nor the Clauses against Spirituous Liquors, hung up. No fuel allowed. Those who are imprisoned for a term have a rug allowed them by the Mayor.

BRISTOL. *Gloucestershire.*
Lawfords Gate; the County-Bridewell.
Keeper, *Joseph Hallam.* Salary, 50/. Fees, none.

Chaplain, Rev. Mr. *Page;* now Rev. Mr. *Eden.* Salary, 20/.

Duty, Sunday, Prayers and a Sermon; also on Christmas-Day, and GoodFriday; and Prayers on every Wednesday and Friday.

Surgeon, Mr. *Baynton.* Salary, 15/. 15s.

Number of Prisoners, 1801, Dec. 17th, Nine. 1803, Oct. 4th, Two. 1806, Sept. 20th, Three.

Allowance, one pound and a half of good household bread per day for each Man; and one pound three ounces each Woman.

REMARKS.

This Prison was finished in 1791. The boundary-wall encloses about an acre of ground, and being at the distance of 16 feet from the court-yards of the Prisoners, affords the Keeper a convenient garden for the growth of vegetables. The Gaol does credit to those who superintended the work, being every way substantially strong.

On the right of the Gate of entrance is a room, where the Magistrates hold their Petty Session every Thursday, except in the Assize and Quarter Sessions week. The approach to the Prison is through a small garden, separated from the courtyards by close wooden palisades. The Keeper's house is in front; and in the centre stands the hall, which is nearly circular, with a j)assage or lobby on each side, 4 feet 6 inches wide, which open into it. The lobby on the right has seven work-cells; that on the left has eight ditto, and of the whole number eight have glazed-windows.

Here are four airy courts, of 28 yards by 15, with a pump and a sewer in each; and three day-rooms, 13 feet by 11 feet 6, with fire-places, stone seats and shelves. The Women's court has a grass-plat, to bleach and dry the linen.

The Chapel is on the first story, and over the hall here are two lobbies or passages, of the same width as those below; one containing nine sleeping-cells for Women, the other ten such for Men; which all open into the Chapel.

On the upper-story is the like number of cells, divided in the same manner; the lobbies of which open into the gallery of the Chapel, and at the top of them there is a large sky-light. Each sleepingell is 7 feet 4 inches by six feet 1, and 10 feet high, with an arched roof, to prevent danger and confusion in case of fire. Every one is fitted up with a cast-iron bedstead, straw-mat, hair-mattress, a blanket, sheet, and double rug. Every cell has two doors, one of them iron-latticed; and is lighted by an iron-grated window with sliding shutter, and a ventilator of 12 inches diameter on the opposite side. There are two cells set apart for Vagrants, and they have straw only, which, when worn, is taken out and burnt.

On this upper-story are also two infirmary rooms, with fire-places and waterclosets; and three small rooms used as foul-wards, *from which iron-gratings communicate with the Chapel, to accommodate the sick Prisoners for hearing Divine service.* Here is likewise a Dispensary for the Surgeon; and all these latter apartments have glazed windows.

For the refractory two dark cells on the upper-story are allotted, each 9 feet 6 inches by *6* feet *6,* and 9 feet high, ventilated by apertures in the wall. There are forty sleeping-cells in this Prison, and the greatest number of Prisoners confined at one time, has been twenty-four.

In chapel, the prisoners are separated according to their classes; and all are required to attend Divine service, and placed alike under immediate inspection, either from the Keeper's or the Turnkey's pew.

An alarm-bell at the top of the building: A warm and cold bath: an oven to purify the prisoners' clothes, and County clothing is put on in their stead.

Here are also four *stoves, from the flues of which warmth is communicated,* *in Winter, to every part of the Prison;* and a peck of coals per day allowed for each stove.

Prisoners, when employed, receive a proportion of their earnings, according to their classes, sufficient to purchase an addition to the Gaol allowance of food: but the Keeper told me that frequently they had nothing to do. The remainder of what they earn is paid them at their discharge.

From the quantities of old cables and junk that I saw at Bristol,—to which city this Prison very nearly adjoins,—I should think that oakum might always be prepared, as a ready and useful article. If any of the Prisoners refuse to be employed, when' the means of working are presented to them, they are punished by *solitary confinement.*

The Surgeon's charge is to attend and see every Prisoner, at least once a week, and always when sent for. He has the power, either to suspend punishment, or to vary the diet, according to his discretion; and a book is kept wherein to enter his observations and directions, ready to be laid before the Visiting Justices at their next meeting.

Books of moral and religious instruction are provided, to be distributed by the Chaplain, as he thinks proper.

Proper cisterns, with soap and towels, are supplied to each court-yard, near the pump, for the daily use of the Prisoners, on opening the cells. *Weights* and *measures* also are kept for their use; and they have clean linen once a week. Copies of the excellent Rules and Orders are pasted up in various parts of the Prison; the whole of which is kept very clean.

BUCKINGHAM *Town Gaol. See page* 72.
BUNTINGFORD. *Hertfordshire.*
Bridewell. Keeper, *Bullen.* Salary, 12/. Consists of two rooms, for *Men,* of about 19 feet by 8, and one for *Women,* 13 feet, by 10; having straw for bedding, but no fire-place. They both look into the Keeper's large garden, out of which a court-yard (which is now wanting) might conveniently be made. Allowance, one pound of bread per day. No water, but what is brought in by the Gaoler. An offensive sewer. Neither

Act nor Clauses hung up; and the whole Prison dirty.
1802, Feb. 4th, and 1803, July 15th, no Prisoners. BURY St. EDMUND'S. *Suffolk. The County Gaol, and House of Correction.*
Gaoler, *John Orridge.*

Salary, for both, 300/. He has also coals and candles; together with other perquisites specified in the Rules and Regulations, as approved by the Magistrates, and confirmed by the Judges of Assize.

Fees, as per Table. Garnish prohibited.

For conveyance of Transports, one shilling a mile each.

Chaplain, Rev. *Simon Pryke.* Duty, Prayers three times a week, and a Sermon on Sundays, Christmas-Day, and Good-Friday. Salary, for Gaol and Bridewell, *60l.*

Surgeon, Mr. *Hubbard.* Salary *60l.* for Debtors and Felons in both Prisons.

Number of Prisoners, Debtors. Felons, &c. House of Correction 1801, Oct. 15th,-----6 ----13-- i8 1802, Aug. 25th, 9----17---21 1805, Aug. 20th, 10----23---20 1810, Sept. 17th, 10----11---24'

Allowance, one pound and a half of bread per day, and one pound of cheese per week, both to *Debtors* and *Felons:* But Prisoners and Convicts, employed in work by the County, have the addition of a quart of small beer per day, and three-quarters of a pound of meat for their *Sunday's dinner.* REMARKS.

This new Gaol is situate at the East-end of the South gate, near a mile from the centre of the town; and the prisoners were removed into it on the 8th of December, 1805. The buildings are enclosed by a boundary-wall, 20 feet high, built in an irregular octagon form, the diameter of which is 292 feet.

Four sides of this Gaol are 192 feet each, and the other four are 70 feet *6* inches each. The entrance to the Prison is the Turnkey's lodge, a handsome stone-building, which consists of the entrance-room, sitting-room, and bed-room for the Turnkey. On the right-hand is a room, with a fire-place, 12 feet by 7, and 9 feet *6* inches high, used as a reception-room; into which all prisoners are brought and confined, till they have been examined, properly cleaned, and found to be free from any infectious disorder, before they are admitted into the interior of the Gaol; and there is a water-closet adjoining, for the use of this room.

There are also two cells up one pair of stairs in the lodge, fitted up with iron bedsteads on stone bearers, into which all prisoners are put when brought in at night. The size of each cell, 9 feet *6* inches by *6* feet, with arched roofs, and 7 feet *6* inches high. The Turnkey's sleeping-room and a large store-room are also on this floor.

On the left of the entrance, within the lodge, there is a convenient wash-house, fitted up with an oven, copper, warm and cold bath, for the use of the Prison; and adjoining to it is the brew-house.

The lead-flat over the Turnkey's lodge, which extends sixteen feet in length, is assigned for the awful execution of criminals.

After passing through the lodge, you proceed down an avenue, paved with flagstone, with posts and chains, enclosing on each side a beautiful shrubbery border, which leads to the Keeper's house: This is also an irregular octagon building, situate in the centre of the Prison, and from which the several court-yards are completely inspected.

The Prison consists of four wings, 69 feet long, and 32 feet wide, detached from the Keeper's house by an area of 15 feet, which, with the different court-yards, completely surround it. In all the wings there is a partition-wall, 14 inches thick, running along the centre; so that each wing contains two Prisons.

The wing, numbered 1 and 2, is the Prison for *Male Debtors;* in which there are two kitchens, fitted up with every convenience for frugal cookery: the size of each 18 feet by 14, with arched roofs, 10 feet high. There are also two passages 44 feet long, and 3 feet *6* inches wide, communicating with their different rooms, of which there are twenty. Of these, eighteen are 9 feet by 8 feet *6* inches, with arched roofs 10 feet high; fitted up with iron bedsteads on stone bearers; gashwindows and a fire-place in each room.

Every Debtor has one of these rooms to himself. Eight are on the ground-floor; the rest on the upper-story to which you ascend by a stone staircase at the end of the passage, or lobby. On this upper-story are two rooms assigned for the sick, each of them 18 feet by 8 feet *6* inches, with two bedsteads and a fire-place in each. There are also two courts attached to this wing (N 1 and 2.) which are an irregular polygon; the one *64* feet by 42,-the other 64 feet by 34.

Every court-yard has a pump, with shy-boards in the centre of it, to which all the prisoners have access in the day-time.

The second wing, numbered 3 and 4, contains also two Prisons; in each of which there is a day-room 20 feet by 14, with arched roofs 10 feet high. From these are passages or lobbies 42 feet long, 3 feet *6* inches wide, leading to the cells: and adjoining to each day-room there is a work-room 14 feet by 9, with a fire-place in each.

This wing contains 18 cells, six on the ground-floor, with glazed windows, and 12 on the upper-story, all of 9 feet by 6; with iron bedsteads, and iron-grated windows with shutters, which have a square pane of nobbed glass in the centre. Here are likewise two rooms for the sick, 13 feet by 9, with a fire-place and two beds in each. The two courts for the use of this second wing are *64* feet each by 34.

The third wing, numbered 5 and *6,* is exactly the same as the second.

The fourth wing, numbered 7, 8, and 9, is in three divisions, *viz.* N 7 contains a day-room, 20 feet long by 14, with an arched roof, 10 feet high; an adjoining work-room, 14 feet by 9; three cells on the ground-floor, 9 feet by 6; and six cells on the upper-story, of the same size: also another room 14 feet by 9, with two iron bedsteads and a fire-place, used as a sick-room for the class confined in this wing. The court adjoining is *64* feet by 34.

N 8, the Prison for *Female Debtors,* has a day-room, 14 feet by 13, with a fire-place; and one cell, 9 feet by *6,* on the ground-floor; and on the upper-story, one cell of the same size. Also a room, 13 feet by 9, with two bedsteads and a fireplace, for the use of the sick in this division. The court adjoining is 40 feet by 22.

N 9, has a day-room likewise, of 14 feet by 13, and two cells on the ground-floor, 9 feet by *6*; two other cells of the same size, on the upper-story; and a room for the sick, of 13 feet by 9. The court adjoining to this wing is 40 feet by 36.

Every court-yard has a bench for seating the prisoners; and there are waterclosets at the end of each wing, which are so contrived, that the water runs all the time that the closet is opened.

These wings, being detached 15 feet from the Keeper's house, and the open fences that enclose the court-yards being at the same distance from the house, they form a court round it; by which means the whole Gaol, and all the prisoners, are conveniently attended to, or visited by friends, without going into any of the rooms or court-yards.

The ground-floor of the Keeper's house is raised six steps above the level of the other buildings; and the windows of the house are so placed, that all the prisoners in the different court-yards are under constant inspection, as well as all persons coming into the Gaol.

The Chapel is in the centre of the Keeper's house, up one pair of stairs. The prisoners go to it by means of stone galleries, which lead from each wing to the Ghapel; and it is so partitioned off, that each class is separated in the same manner as in the Prison.

By the late regulations, this Gaol, and the nearly ad joining *House of Correction,* are, in a manner, consolidated. The latter is bounded by a separate wall, which incloses about an acre of ground; and the Prison stands in the centre, having a garden round it. It is a square building, the Keeper's house being in front. It consists of two divisions: One has a day-room, *16* feet by 9 feet *6* inches, and *16* feet high, with a fire-place and sink; and seven cells, 10 feet by 7,

and 12 feet *6* inches high, all on the ground floor; together with a court-yard, 62 feet by 24.

The other division has also a day-room, of 18 feet by 10, and 16 feet high; with fourteen cells, 10 feet by 7, and 12 feet *6* inches high, all on the ground-floor; and a court-yard, *66* feet by 32. Each of the yards has a pump, to which the Prisoners have access during the day; and a sewer in the corner.

There are two infirmary rooms up one pair of stairs, each of about 17 feet by 12. On the top of the Keeper's house are five cells; two of which are 12 feet by 8, end the other three, 10 feet by *6.*

The Chapel *here* is a room in the Keeper's house; in size, 13 feet by *9* feet 6.

All *poor Debtors* in Bury *Gaol* have the County Allowance; and, from the fifth of November to Lady-Day, the Debtors receive four bushels of coals per week, and forty Shillings at every Christmas, from a Feoffment, or Deed of Gift.

Here is also a most excellent charitable Fund, called "*Pembertori's Charity,n* (being left by a gentleman of that name): Which Fund is directed by the Donor's Will, "To be applied by the Trustees towards the relief of such poor distressed "*Insolvent Debtors, as shall be imprisoned within any of the Gaols of the County "of Suffolk; either for delivering them out of Prison, or relieving their necessi"ties whilst there,* as the Trustees shall think fit; *provided such Debtors be per"sons born in Suffolk, and no way indebted to any of the Trustees."*

TheGentlemen, engaged in the trust under this very exemplary Charity,frequently allot three or four, and sometimes five Pounds to poor deserving Debtors, towards obtaining their discharge: They also allow to each Debtor two pounds of beef, a pint of porter, and a twopenny loaf every Sunday; under this condition, however, "that every Debtor, receiving the bounty, *shall regularly attend Chapel,* unless prevented by sickness." But no *Crown-Debtors* partake of this charity.

The Rules, Orders and Regulations

for the Government of both the above Prisons are truly excellent. They are printed for the use of the Gaol and its Guardians; and I here subjoin with pleasure a few of the most essential Articles:

I. As principally affecting *Debtors.*

Art. 16. "The Gaoler shall, at his own expeuce, provide proper bedding for the Debtors; which, for each room, shall consist of a feather-bed, mattress, pair of blankets, coverlet, and sheets; the latter to be changed once a month. The charge to be paid for the use of the room, including the above, with the expence of cleaning, shall be painted over each door." ,

Art. 42. "A Table Of Fees And Rates, To be paid by Debtors: being regulated as directed by the Act of the 32d Geo. II. and 31st Geo. 111.

To the Gaoler, for Commitment Fee, and Discharge of every Debtor, *s. d.* on each Action,----------------8 8

To the Sheriff, for Discharge on each Action--------20

To the Gaoler, for a Certificate, in order to sue for a Supersedeas »-3 6

To the Gaoler, for each Copy of Warrant---------20

"The following *Rates* to be paid to the Gaoler for Room-rent, Lodging, &c. Every Debtor occupying one of the Rooms No. 1, 2, 3, and 4, shall pay each week-----------------20

Every Debtor, occupying one of the Rooms, No. 5, 6, 7, 8, or 9, shall pay each week----------------I 6

Every Debtor, occupying one of the other Rooms, appropriated for the use of Debtors, shall pay each week---------10

Every Debtor finding his own Bedding, shall pay for his room each week 1 0." II. As respecting *Criminals.*

Art. 25. "There shall be provided proper bedding for the use of the Prisoner! committed on charge, or convicted of Felonies and Misdemeanors, and all necessary utensils for keeping the Gaol in a state of health and cleanliness."

Art. 29. "Every Prisoner, committed for trial, may hire bed and bedding, upon paying one shilling and sixpence per week." III. Comfort and Accommodation.

Art. 31. "A quantity of coals, not exceeding *two bushels* a week, from Michaelmas to Lady-Day; and not exceeding *one bushel*, from Lady-Day to Michaelmas, shall be allowed to each division. Should the number of Prisoners, in any division, be materially reduced, the Allowance of Coals shall be regulated at the discretion of the Gaoler."

Art. 34. "Thereshall be provided proper scales, weights, and measures, duly stamped, for the use of the Prisoners, to weigh and measure their allowances, whenever it shall be required by them: Notice of which, and likewise their different allowances, shall be painted on a Board, and hung up in the courts of each Division.

Art. 35. Convenient places being made where the Prisoners are to wash themselves, clean towels shall be provided in each Division, twice a week; and the Men shaved every *Saturday.*

The *Employment* of the respective Prisoners consists in the grinding of corn, &c. (for which there are two mills) and in spinning of wool. Each class to be kept separate, according to the following arrangement, Art. 21.

"No. 1. and 2. *Male* Debtors.
3. King's Evidence; and, occasionally, other prisoners. 4. Convicted of Misdemeanors. 5. Transports, and convicted atrocious Felons. 6. For Trial, for such Felonies. 7. Do. for small offences. 8. Female Debtors. 9. Female Felons for Trial. 10. Females convicted of Misdemeanors. 11. Do. convicted of Felonies."

A mill has been erected here, upon a very large scale, for the employment of Convict-Prisoners: It is worked by a wheel, 20 feet in diameter, and about 7 feet wide in the rim; so as to admit of five Men walking abreast in it: And there has always been sufficient employ here, in grinding barley for fattening pigs, at one shilling the coomb; so that it answers very well. I am informed that the mill itself cost 300/. and the building that contains it 300/. more.

f£F' Before an expence, therefore, of this magnitude is incurred, it would be well to consider, First, whether there is good employment for it: and, secondly, Whether the aVerage number of Convict-Prisoners be *ten;* which it will constantly require, so as to relieve each other, or to work it in succession. N. B. The Prisoners here are chiefly labourers in husbandry; and for men of their vocation it seems peculiarly calculated.

The *earnings* of the Prisoners employed by the County, are divided in the following manner:

Two fifths to the County.

One fifth to the Gaoler, or Governor of the House of Correction; and

Two fifths to the Prisoners, *viz.* one fifth of what becomes due to them, is to be paid them weekly; and the remaining fifth on their being discharged.

All Prisoners, *before trial,* have *the whole* of their earnings. What an idea does not this convey of British discernment, justice, and the truest philanthropy! Let Britons ever bear so short a lesson in their minds and hearts.

Every Prisoner here is required to put on clean linen once a week. If they have it not of their own, it is provided for them, and supplied by the County.

It is not a compliment, but a verdict, to say, That these Prisons do honour to the County of *Suffolk,* and are superior to most in this Kingdom, whether we consider their construction, for answering the three great purposes of *security, health,* and *morals;* or the singular liberality of the Magistrates, in providing every comfort, that can tend to alleviate the unspeakable sorrows of *Imprisonment.*

The Keeper, Mr. *Orridge,* is well qualified for the discharge of his important trust, being active, intelligent, and humane.

BURY St. EDMUNDS. *Suffolk.*
The Town Bridewell.
Keeper, *Thomas Bass;* now *William Neal,* Beadle and Town Crier.
Salary, 67. and a Chaldron of Coals.
Fees, One Shilling on every Commitment.
Surgeon, when wanted, sent by the Town.
Number of Prisoners, 1801, Oct. 15th,----1, A Boy, then knitting Garters. 1805, Aug. 20th,----2. 1810, Sept. 17th,----0.

Allowance, One pound and a half of bread per day, sent from the Baker's.
REMARKS.

This very curious old building, "majestick, though in rain," exhibits a noble Saxon mansion, consisting of two stories. The second, being the principal one, has, at the South end, a double-arched window, supported by columns. Three of the same double windows occur also on the East side, divided each from the other by pilasters, or projecting piers. It is built of flint and free-stone; and was long since converted into a Jewish Synagogue, by a singularity, which it is now needless to account for. In the old writings it is named *"Moses' Hall."*

The walls, faced with stone, manifest, at this day, their great solidity; and the style of the windows bespeaks its venerable age,—not less, perhaps, than the aera of the Norman Conquest; soon after which period the *Jews* settled at Bury in great numbers.

In the reign of Henry II. they made this town one of their chief places of residence, and thus, certainly paid no ill compliment both to their taste and judgement, for it is situated in a spot so healthy, as on that account to have been called *"The Montpelier of England."* It is said, that in the year 1179, they murdered here a boy, by crucifying him, in derision of the manner of our Saviour's death. His name, it seems, was Robert. The story, having been gravely narrated by one *Joscelyn,* a monk of the Abby of Bury, was so gravely credited, that from this catastrophe, we are told, the lad was canonized, and afterwards reverenced, if not worshiped, as *St. Robert the Martyr.*

So many assertions, of the like kind, have, from time to time, appeared against the Jews, (but especially in the days of the Grand Crusade) as almost to quash that credence, which they might be intended to establish. Upon some similar occasion, good *Sir Richard Baker,* (who was not "an Unbeliever,") has very judiciously remarked, that " Writers, perhaps, had been more complete, if they had left this story out of their writings." Possibly it may be esteemed a circumstance more

N worthy of notice, that when all the Synagogues of the Jews were ordered to be destroyed, in the 11th year of Edward III. (1338) the present structure, though falling accidentally under that description, happened to escape the general devastation.

The ascent to this Prison was formerly by XIX steps, rising from the street, whence it was vulgarly called "*The Nineteener.*" The entrance to it is now made through a lobby, of 13 feet by 10, and leads up a stair-case, which, singularly enough, has as many steps to it, so that it still retains the name of *Nineteener.* On this floor is the Keeper's residence. The first room communicating with his apartments, is of 37 feet by 26; and from it a day-room has been partitioned off by open wood palisades, for the use of the Prisoners, 21 feet by 18, and 20 feet high; brick-floored, and fitted up with a fire-place, three benches, and a table fixed: a leaden cistern also and sink for prisoners' washing; and in pne corner a sewer.

In a passage from this room are two sleeping-cells, of 11 feet each by 7 feet 6; and up a ladder stair-case are two other cells, of 11 feet by 9. All these are furnished with a crib bedstead, a bed, two blankets and a rug, provided by the town.

Water, for the Keeper's family, and for the use of the prisoners, is brought from a publick-house close by; for which the Corporation pay Five Shillings a year.

As the *County Gaol* and House of Correction receive the Prisoners properly belonging to the Town, persons committed to this Bridewell are for small offences only; and Travelling Vagrants are also here lodged for the night, to whom the Town furnishes straw.

Beneath this Prison are a Guard-House for the Military, the Town-Cage, and a room for the Fire-Engine. A Town-clock has been lately placed on the top.

CAERMARTHEN CASTLE. *South-Wales.*
The County Gaol and Bridewell.

Gaoler, *John Thomas,* afterwards *Thomas Calkin;* now (1810) *Benjamin Waugh.*
Salary, 31/. 10$. from the County, and 6/. 6. from the Borough.
Fees, Debtors and Felons, 13. *4d.* each: Petty Offenders, 3s. *4d.* No Table.
For the Conveyance of Transports a Bill is made. Garnish, 2. *6d.*
Chaplain, Rev. *Thomas Price.*
Duty every Sunday and Holiday. Salary, 12/.
Surgeon, Mr. *William Price.* Salary, 20l. for *Felons* only.
Number of Prisoners, 1803, Sept. 29th, Debtors, Six. Felons, &c. Sixteen.
Allowance, to Debtors, none; except very poor, on application to the Parish: to *Felons* and other *Criminal* Prisoners, Two Shillings each per week.
REMARKS.
This Gaol, finished in 1792, is also the County Bridewell. Here is a spacious court, 38 yards by 22, for Men and Women Debtors. A well is sunk in it, and a reservoir prepared to supply the Prison with water; but, having been out of repair four months, at my visit in 1803, the Prisoners had been without that necessary article all the time, except what they bought at a *halfpenny for a jug-full!*

For Debtors here are five rooms below, and five above stairs, each about 12 feet by 9, with fire-places; but the windows were much broken and out of repair. They are all free-wards. The County allows iron bedsteads, with straw-in-sacking beds; and Five Pounds in *coals* yearly, to be distributed amongst all the Prisoners.

Formerly there were Rules, or Bounds to this Gaol, as at the Fleet and King's Bench Prisons, which extended half a mile; but for 10 or 12 years past no Debtor has been permitted to enjoy this privilege.

The *Felons* have two courts; one 29 yards by 8, the other 18 yards by 11. Also eight sleeping cells on the ground-floor, and seven above; with vaulted roofs, dark, damp, and ill-ventilated. Those below have floors of flag-stone; the upper paved with brick: Each has an iron bedstead, and straw-in-sacking only to sleep on.

For Bridewell Prisoners are also two spacious courts, 36 yards by 14 each, and twenty-four sleeping-cells, 10 feet each by 7, with arched roofs.

The Chapel is in the centre of the Prison; and three lobbies or passages, 4 feet wide, open into it, for the different classes of Prisoners.

In one of the courts is *a long range of work-rooms,* but *no employment* furnished.

Transports have not here the King's allowance of 2. *6d.* per week; and, from sickness, want of water, and filth, were in a state bordering on desperation, and begging to be sent any where, to get out of so miserable a place. One of them, a Woman, who had been two years under sentence of transportation, had a young Child at her breast, of which she said the late Gaoler was the father. A similar instance I met with at Dover Town-Gaol, in September 1801.

Several of the Prisoners I found here ill; and one in particular could not turn herself in bed: yet, they told me, the Surgeon had not, for two months, either seen any of them himself, nor sent his Assistant, though frequently applied to.

The several court-yards had loads of ashes and rubbish in them: The Gaoler wa» ill in bed, and the Prison in every part appeared totally neglected. Neither the Act for preserving Health, nor Clauses against Spirituous Liquors were hung up. No Rules and Orders.

CAERMARTHEN, *Borough Gaol.* Formerly consisted of four rooms in the Old Gate-way. It is now pulled down, and shops are built on the Scite. The Prisoners are sent to the Castle; and for this privilege the Borough allows Six Guineas a year to the Keeper.

CAERNARVON. *North-Wales.*
The County Gaol.
Gaoler, *William Griffiths.* Salary, 15/.
Fees, *Debtors, Js.* besides which the Under-Sheriff demands 3.y. *6d.* for his *Liberate I* Felons, 13. *4d.* No Table. For the Conveyance of Transports he makes a Bill.

Chaplain, none; but a Clergyman is desired by the Magistrates to attend a Prisoner under sentence of death.

Sursreon, Mr. *Currie* attends when one is wanted, and makes a Bill.

Number of Prisoners, Debtors. Felons. Bridewell. Deserters.
1800, April 3d,--2---I---3---O 1801, Nov. 7th,--'--3---2---4---0 1803, Sept. 20th,---3---3---S---4

Amongst the Bridewell Prisoners were *two Lunatichs.*

Allowance, to Debtors who are very poor, 2. per week from the County, to Felons and other Criminals, 2. 4d. a week.

REMARKS.

The Gaoler is a Shoemaker: his workshop and apartments occupy the front of the Gaol towards the street, and a passage in the centre, 12 feet long, leads to the iron-grated door of entrance.

The Debtors' day-room is on the right-hand; the Felons' on the left; each 27 feet by 15; and both have fire-places. Here is also, farther on, and in the centre of the Prison, an inspection-room, 18 feet by 13; and over it another room of the same size. The Gaoler's family ought properly to live here, because both rooms command the several court-yards; one of which is for Men and Women Debtors; the second for Male Criminals; and a third for Females of the same description. Each court-yard is 72 feet by 31. They are none of them paved; and a pump is in one of them only, which being out of repair, when I happened to visit the Gaol, the Prisoners were without that needful article, except as supplied elsewhere. Poultry were very improperly kept in the courts.

The Female Criminals' day-room is 15 feet by 13; and adjoining to it are their two sleeping-cells, containing two wooden bedsteads, straw-in-ticking bed, a pillow, two blankets and a rug.

From the Men-Criminals' day-room a passage, 3 feet wide, leads to their three condemned cells, each 8 feet by 6, and 7 feet high, with arched roofs. To these cells there is attached a small court-yard, for Prisoners under sentence of death. Above the condemned cells are three others, of the same size, for Felons.

Debtors have six sleeping-rooms above stairs, which are all free-wards, and have iron bedsteads, with sacking bottoms, stravv-in-ticking bed, pillow, two blankets and a rug, furnished at the County expence.

The Chapel is over the Debtors' day-room, and of the same size, (27 feet by 14.) There are three pews in it; and benches also for the Prisoners, who are *seated promiscuously,* and *mfull view oj each other.* The Infirmary room is about *26* feet by 11, and stands over the Women Felons' day-room. All the sleeping cells are nearly of a size, and fitted up in the same manner.

Neither the Act for preservation of Health, nor the Clauses against Spirituous Liquors were hung up. No fuel supplied. No mops, brooms, soap, or towels allowed, to keep the Gaol clean. The lunatick and felon were confined together; a painful circumstance for both, and which I have been sorry to notice in *many County Gaols.*

The *Jour Deserters* before mentioned were in double-irons. And here, (as at *Brecon,)* I found that even a Woman did not escape this savage treatment. Tis but charity to the inflictors of such tyrannick and unmanly severity to inform them, that at the Lent Azzize at Thetford, in 1782, Lord Loughborough fined the Gaoler of Norwich Castle *twenty pounds, for putting a Woman in irons.*

CAMBRIDGE.

The Town Bridewell.

Keeper, *Samuel Barker,* a *Wool-Comber;* whose Salary was 30/. from Mr.

Hobson's Charity, and 5/. from the University. (See Remarks.) Now *Thomas*

Leach, who keeps a Chandler's shop in front of the Prison, and is the billeting Constable of the Town.

Salary, 50/. from Mr. Hobson's Charity, and 5/. 5. from the University. No Fees.

Surgeon, for University Prisoners, Mr. *Tinney;* for Town ditto, Mr. *Bond.* Salary none: They make a Bill.

Number of Prisoners, 1802, Aug. 7th,-1.
1805, Aug. 25th, *6.* 1807, Aug. 30th-- ---3, one a Vice Chancellor's Prisoner. 1810, Sept. 2d,------2, one of them ditto.

Allowance, now, is eight-pence a day to all.

REMARKS.

This Prison is a square building, surrounded by a boundary-wall, fifteen feet high, and about five feet distant from the Bridewell. It stands in the back yard of the Keepers house, which was originally bought and endowed for the encouragement of wool-combers and spinners of this town.

The basis of the institution was a Legacy of the famous and justly celebrated "University Carrier," Thomas Hobson of the Town . His will is dated on Christmas-Eve, 1630,0. S. and on New-Year's Day, 1st January 1630, (the very day on which he died,) he added to it the following codicil:

"Item, I give unto the Mayor, Bayliffs, and Burgesses of the Town of Cambridge, ' the sum of One Hundred Pounds; to the intent, that they shall, within as con"venient time as they may, purchase lands or tenements therewith; and the rents "thereof yearly arising to be employed and bestowed towards the maintenance of "the *House of Correction* and *Work-house* within the town of *Cambridge,* and of "the poor which shall be set on work there for ever."

To answer, as far as might be, the liberal intention of the Testator, the Keeper of this House of Correction and Work-house was required to be a *Wool-Comber;* who should employ, not only several hands upon the foundation of the Charity, but many others; and amongst them the Prisoners under his charge. At my visit, however, in 1807, I found the old Keeper almost superannuated, and very little work done; which is now totally discontinued, and the pious intentions of the Donor frustrated.

The Men Prisoners here have three cells at the entrance of the building, of 9 feet each by 7 feet 6, and nearly 8 feet high, with straw laid on the floor; and each also supplied with a mattress, two blankets, and a rug for bedding.. For the Women Prisoners there are ten cells of the same size as the former, and four court-yards, rendered offensive by the sewer in each. Within the cells a tub is made to serve the purpose; and for ventilation they have an iron-grating over each door, through which is an aperture of six inches square. The floors have all, except one, been repaired since my visit in 1807.

Soap and coals are allowed, yet the whole Prison is very dirty. There is indeed but one pump in it; and those confined have not the option, given by good Hobson to his customers, of "*that or none*"

The only employment here is spinning; and those who work at it have the whole of their earnings. Neither the Act for preserving Health, nor the Clauses, are hung up.

This excellent Man, whose name is celebrated by Milton, and his beneficence recorded in many parts Of Cambridge, was used to let horses out to hire i and, being willing that each should have hii portion of rest, resolutely refused a choice being made; but every one was to take the beast that stood next in rotation. Little did he think, that the phrase, "*Hobson's choice, That, or none,*" would in time become proverbial. CAMBRIDGE CASTLE. *The County Gaol and Bridewell.*

Gaoler, *William Gregory;* now *Robert Orridge.* Salary, 200/.

Fees, both for Debtors and Felons, are laudably abolished. The Under-Sheriff makes no demand for his Liberate. Conveyance of Transports Is. per mile.

Chaplain, Rev. Mr. *Holmes;* now Rev. Mr. *Pearce.*

Duty, Prayers and Sermon every Sunday, Good Friday, and Christmas Day.

Salary, was formerly 25 /. from the County, and 20/. from the Earl of Hardwicke, Lord Lieutenant: But the County having increased the Salary for Mr. Pearce to 50/. his Lordship has ever since discontinued his donation.

Surgeon, Mr. *Oakes.* Salary, *26I. 5s.* for Debtors and Criminal's'.

Allowance, to every Prisoner 7 lbs. of good bread per week; to be at least one day old.—To every Felon Convict two ounces of salt per week, and 12 lbs. of potatoes, except in the months of June and July; when, in lieu of potatoes, each Prisoner is supplied with 34-lbs. of rice, or pulse, weekly.

REMARKS.

This New Gaol, built in the centre of the Old Castle-Yard, was completely finished, and began to be inhabited in the year 1810.

The boundary-wall, 20 feet high, encloses an acre and quarter of ground; and being, upon an average admeasurement of the circuit, about 30 feet from the Prison, it affords the Keeper a convenient garden for the growth of vegetables.

The Turnkey's lodge is in front of the building, and occupies a space of about eighteen feet; so that executions, which are to be performed on the flat-roof of the whole (about 38 feet by 15), may be rendered more public.

On the right-hand, at the entrance, are two reception-rooms, for the examination of the Prisoners, in point of health, previous to their being admitted to the interior:.

It may be proper here to remark, that *Debtors* from the Isle of Ely are generally sent to this *Castle Gaol* of Cambridge.

Also two sleeping-cells above, 8 feet by 6 each, lighted and ventilated by iron-grated windows, and an aperture of six inches in the opposite walls near the door. These cells, (like all the others in this Gaol) are supplied with iron-bedsteads on stone bearers, straw-in-sacking beds, two blankets, and a rug; and to each of them is a small semicircular court-yard, of 18 feet diameter, with a water-closet.

On the left-hand of the entrance is a room, of 14 feet by 12 feet *g,* with glazed windows; where Prisoners, upon their admission, are stripped, washed, and the County clothing is put on: also an oven, for purifying any thing offensive in their own apparel, together with a warm and cold bath. Over this are the Turnkey's sleepingroom, and another, in which locks, irons, &c. are deposited. The Prisoners' clothes are then ticketed and hung up, to be given back to them at their discharge.

The Turnkey's sitting and sleeping-room windows command a view of four court-yards. The Gaoler's house stands in the middle of the area; and the approach to it is by a narrow slip, enclosed by posts and chains, extending 55 feet by *16,* and bordered with flowers and shrubs.

On the ground-floor, which is elevated three feet above ground, are the Keeper's hall, parlour, and kitchen, together with the Visiting Magistrates' Committee Room, the windows of which also command all the court-yards of the Prison, except those appropriated to the Women-Debtors, and Women-Felons, which are under the eye of the Turnkey.

In the Gaoler's house, and on the same floor with the Chapel, are two rooms, furnished, for Master's Side Debtors, at 10. *6d.* per week; and both these rooms were inhabited at my visit in 1807. But their respective tenants were absent from Divine service.

In the centre of the building is a circular stair-case, made of oak, leading up to the *Chapel,* which is on the first story, and has a door opening into it from each of the wings. The Prisoners are there seated, in eight divisions, appropriated to their several classes, and all in full view both of the Minister and the Gaoler.

Above the Chapel are three rooms, originally intended for *the sick,* about 15 feet square, and 9 feet high, with an apartment for a nurse; and to each is assigned a leaden sink and water-closet. I twice visited the Gaol in 1807, and plainly saw that these rooms, so designed, and so fitted up for the purpose of *Infirmaries,* would soon be the Gaoler's rooms only; because, in each of the wings, I found (in August) that two cells were making into one, for the purpose now laid aside. My conjectures appear to have been just; for, in September 1810, Mr. Orridge told me they were then used as sleeping-rooms for his servants. To *Him* there could be no objection, whilst not wanted for the Prisoners. They certainly have many conveniencies, which the cells cannot afford to Invalids.

Here is also a reservoir, with a warning-pipe, that supplies the whole Prison with water, and holds 36 barrels: and at the top of the building is a lead-flat, about 40 feet square, with a parapet wall, for convalescents to take air and exercise.

The Gaol itself consists of four wings, detached from the Keeper's house by an area of sixteen feet, and encircled by the ten different court-yards, whose average size is 55 feet by 40, with open fences at each end, so that a thorough air is transmitted. Each court-yard has in the centre a brass cock and stone sink, and is provided with a water-closet.

One wing is solely appropriated to the Debtors, and has two court-yards; the one of them (N 8 and Q,) for Men, the other (N 10,) for Women.

Master's-Side Debtors have a Day-room, *16* feet by 14, and 9 feet *6* inches high, with a fire-place and two sleeping-rooms, 9 feet each by 7 feet *6,* and of the same height. Over these are four other sleeping-rooms of the like dimensions; all of which have sashed glazed windows, with iron bedsteads on stone bearers, and are furnished with beds at *is. 6d.* per week, for such as can afford it. They are all single beds, and the rooms are arch-roofed.

Common-Side Debtors have a day or mess-room, 23 feet by 14, 9 feet *6* high; and ten sleeping-cells, of the same size as those on the Master's-Side; to which the County furnishes a straw-in-sacking bed, two blankets and a coverlet each.

Women-Debtors have their day-room on the ground-floor, 14 feet by 13 feet 6; and two sleeping-rooms above, fitted up in the same manner as the Men's. All the day-rooms have benches to sit upon, and fire-places.

The Male-Convicts' day-room is also 14 feet by 13 feet 6, with a work-room of the same size; and two sleeping-cells, each 9 feet *6 by* 6 feet 2, and 9 feet *6* inches high. Above these are six other sleeping-cells, of like dimensions, with wooden shutters to keep out the weather, and a square of knobbed glass in one shutter; opposite to which is a grated aperture, of 9 inches, for ventilation. The passage to these is about 50 feet long, 3 feet 6 inches wide, with a window at each end; and three circular gratings opening into the roof for air. Each of the above cells is fitted up with a cast-iron bedstead, *6* feet long, by 2 feet 3 inches wide; a straw mattress, straw-in-sacking bed, two blankets, and a coverlet.

Men Felons, *before trial,* (Class I.) have a lobby, or passage, the same as that above noticed; which leads to their day-room, work-room, and eight sleeping-cells, all of the like size, and fitted up in the same manner as those for the Men-Convicts.

Men Felons, of Class II. have their day and working-room in one, of 20 feet by 14; with five sleeping-cells the same as already described. And above are three condemned-cells for Convicts under sentence of death, with a day-room, 14 feet square, which has a fire-place, benches to sit on, and a water-closet.

The Women-Felons have, on the ground-floor, a day-room, 14 feet by 13 feet 6; and three sleeping-cells above it, exactly like those assigned for the Male-Felons.
o
The Men-Prisoners of the House of Correction, or Bridewell, (Class I.) have both' a day and work-room, each of the same size as the last-mentioned; also two cells on the ground-floor, and six above, with a passage, and fitted up like the preceding. Those of Class II. have the same number of cells, and the like accommodations.

Women Bridewell Prisoners have their day-room and work-room below, and over them six sleeping-cells, the same as the Men.

All the sleeping-cells throughout this Gaol and Bridewell are alike in size; but those of the Debtors have glazed windows. Every door has a small wicket in it, about six inches square, through which the Keeper inspects the cell, without going into it.

The communication from the different wings to the Chapel is by four stone bridges, with iron-rails over the area, of 16 feet, round the Keepers house. These bridges serve, not only for a passage-way in different directions to the Chapel, but likewise for the Keeper to visit the various districts at night, as he may find occasion.

In his garden is an engine-house, where the pump, worked by two Men-Prisoners, one at each handle, fills the reservoir, before noticed, in about two hours. When full, the warning-pipe, which is in the cistern, or reservoir, at the Keepers house, gives notice to leave off. The well, from whence the water is thus drawn, must be a happy resource. I was assured it is no less than 140 feet deep, and 8 feet in diameter; and that the water, with which nature supplies it, constantly rises, after pumping, to within *6* feet of the surface.

Debtors in this Prison have occasional relief, though very scantily, from legacies and donations, paid by several Colleges in the University of Cambridge.

From *Sidney-Sussex* College, four pounds are annually given at Christmas to poor Debtors. In 1801, that sum was distributed and applied as follows, *viz.* —To six poor Debtors a shirt each, and the rest in coals and bread;—in 1806, to five poor Debtors a shirt each, and the rest in coals:—in 1809, the four pounds were distributed to four poor Debtors, in coals, meat, and bread.

From *Saint John's College,* sixteen-penny worth of bread every Saturday morning.

At Christmas, in each year, a Collection is sometimes suffered to be publicly made in the Town of Cambridge; which now and then has amounted to one guinea for each poor Debtor: but, as to sanction this Application the Signature of the ViceChancellor is held necessary, (which cannot always be obtained,) I understand that a new Collection was not made till Christmas in the year 1804; and the last in 1806, which to nine poor Debtors produced *Ss.9d.* a piece.

About sixteen shillings, as a *Donation,* or *Legacy,* are also made payable, in some sort, from an Estate at *Croxton,* in the County of Cambridge; but *no memorial of it is recorded in the Gaol.* fph The payment of this Donation, Legacy, or Rent-charge, was, at one time, *two years* in arrear. My applications respecting it, for some time, proved ineffectual; but I am informed it is *now* regularly and justly paid.

Prisoners belonging to this Gaol are tried at the Town Hall, which is half a mile distant; and they walk thither,— *digito praetereuntium monstrari, et dicier flic est!*

The *Contents,* or various departments of this Prison, may best be shewn by the following enumeration of the different *rooms,* and how they are applied.

Rooms.
Reception Cells, 2. Men-Debtors, Master's-Side, 6.------8
Men-Debtors, Common-Side, 10. Women-Debtors, 2.-----12
Men-Convicts, 8. Convicts under Sentence of Death, 3.-----11
Men-Felons, (Class I.) 8. Ditto, (Class II.) 5. 13
House of Correction, Men, (Class I.)------------8
Ditto, (Class II.) 8
Women-Felons, 3. House of Correction, Women, 6.------9
Total, 69.

Here is *no employment* yet furnished by the County. The Visiting-Magistrates, Chaplain, and Surgeon, regularly enter their Reports in books kept for that purpose: But neither the Act for preserving the Health of Prisoners, nor the Clauses against their use of Spirituous Liquors, are hung up.

The Rules and Orders for the Government of the Gaol, were confirmed by the Judges at the Summer-Assizes in 1808.

On my visit to the old Gaol, in August 1802, the Prisoners stated, that Divine service had not been performed there for some months, nor any religious attention paid to them. For this suspension of duty, the reason, afterwards assigned, turned out to be, "That a *Felon* had made his escape on the way to Chapel, in going across the Old Castle Yard." It was, indeed, not only spacious, but insecure; and, in consequence, no Prisoners thenceforward were indulged the use of it; such only excepted, as were confined for small sums, and in whom the Keeper (then *Gregory*) could place confidence.

The complaint above-mentioned, however, was at length removed. On the 25th of August, 1805, I found twelve out of the fourteen Debtors, and all the Criminal Prisoners, attending Divine service as formerly. On the 30th of August, 1807, only five Debtors out of the eleven were present; but, on the 2d of September, 1810, all the Debtors, except one, and all but one of the Criminals, attended Chapel both morning and afternoon; when their behaviour was orderly, and attentive to a very appropriate discourse.

, An allowance of coals is made to Felons, and House of Correction Prisoners, yearly, from Michaelmas to Lady-Day; but Debtors are obliged to provide fuel for themselves. Mops, brooms, pails, soap, and other articles for cleanliness, are granted by the County. The Gaoler appears to be humane and attentive to his charge, and the Prison is very cleaiu CAMBRIDGE.

. *The Town GaoL*

Gaoler, *Thomas Adams,* Bell-man of the Town. Salary, 20/.

Fees, for Debtors and Criminals, 13. *4d.* each. No Table. Garnish abolished

Chaplain, none; nor Divine Service ever performed here.

Surgeon, if wanted, sent from the Town.

Number of Prisoners, Debtors. Criminals, 1800, May 16th,--___ 1--2 1801, Aug. 20th, 1-------3 1802, Aug. Jth,------0-------2 1807, Aug. 30th,-----0-------5 1810, Sept. 2d,------0-------3

Allowance, to *Debtors,* none statedly: But see Remarks.
to *Criminals,* sixpence a day in bread and cheese. REMARKS.

Formerly here was a room below, for *Criminals,* 21 feet by 7, called *The Hole;* and above it another, termed *The Cage.* On a visit, in August 1800, I had the pleasure to find that *The Cage* had fallen into *The Hole,* and both formed a heap of ruins. The Prisoners were destitute of court-yard, water, and allowance.

The present Gaol, erected in 1788, has a small court-yard, about 18 feet square, with a pump and sewer in it, for Prisoners of every description. There are five cells below for Criminals, each about 9 feet by *6,* and 7 feet 6 inches high. Above are two rooms for Men and Women Debtors, and a day-room, 24 feet by 15. They pay weekly two shillings for a single bed each; and if two sleep together, each pays one shilling and three-pence. The Town allows straw and blankets to Criminals. a

The cells are ventilated by an iron-grating over each door, in which is made an nperture, about 6 inches square. There is one dark, solitary cell, with a double door; the inner one of wood; the outer, iron-grated, and ventilated by an irongrating above it: also one cell in the garden, of 9 feet by 5.

No employment is furnished by the Town; but Prisoners are allowed to work, on their own account, if they can procure the means.

Debtors receive broken bread from several of the Colleges every Friday, which a Woman is paid fourpence a time for collecting. The Mayor of Cambridge sends yearly three sacks of coals for both Debtors and Criminals, which are occasionally used, either to cook their victuals in the bjouse, or to warm themselves by, there being no common room for them accommodated with a fire-place.

Water is *now* accessible to all the Prisoners, I found the Gaol clean, though more than two years since its having been white-washed: But it appears to be insecure; for, about a month previous to my visit in 1S02, a house-breaker had made his escape through a breach in the brick-work.

Neither the Act for preserving Health, nor the Clauses against Spirituous Liquors, were hung up..

Canterbury; *The Gaol, and House oj Corredtion.*

Gaoler, *Samuel Aris.* Salary, 200/. with coals, candles, and soap:
Fees, none. Garnish prohibited.

Chaplain, Rev. Mr. *Chafey.* Salary, 50/.

Duty, Prayers and Sermon every Sunday; and Prayers on Wednesday and Friday.

Surgeon, Mr. *Chandler.* Salary, *20l".*

Number of Prisoners, / 189 *Jn* 10th' Felom and Pettr ffenders 1 1810, July

9th, Ditto,-----15.

Allowance, one pound of bread per day, and a pint of gruel, with salt. To those who work in the outer ground, half a pound of meat, with vegetables, for Dinner; and the next day broth, from the meat that has been boiled: also a pint of 20. table beer at dinner, and half a pint of strong beer in the afternoon.

REMARKS.

This *New Gaol*, for the Eastern division of Kent, (substituted instead of the Old Prison, called St. Dunstan's,) is erected on thescite of St. Augustin's Monastery, a little way out of Town; and the Prisoners were removed hither on the 14th of December 1808.

The boundary-wall is an octagon, enclosing about two acres of land: the entrance to it is through the Turnkey's lodge; and on the ground-floor are his sitting-room, a wash-house with a boiler, warm and cold baths, and an oven to purify foul or infected clothes.

Here is a *reception-room* also, of 12 feet 7 inches by 6 feet 4; in which Prisoners are examined, properly cleaned, and must be found clear from any infectious disorder, previous to their admission into the interior of the Gaol. For the use of this room a court-yard, 144-feet square, and a water-closet, are provided.

Above stairs are the Turnkey's sleeping-room, and another apartment, for the New Prisoners' clothes to be ticketed and hung up, till he is discharged, in case the County clothing was put on at his admission. Also two sleeping-cells, of 9 feet each by 6, with arched roofs, and iron-grated windows; which have inside shutters, with a pane of knobglass in them, to put up at night.

After passing through the lodge, an avenue, 40 feet long, and enclosed with posts and chains, leads into the Prison; which is a handsome stone-fronted building, with the Gaoler's house in the centre. This, likewise, is of an octagon construction; and from it the several court-yards are very judiciously and completely inspected. On the ground-floor is also the Magistrates' Committee-Room, of 14 feet, and in the same form.

The Prison consists of three wings: That for Felons is 53 feet long, and 32 feet wide; the other two are 46 feet by 32, detached from the Keepers house by an area 12 feet square, which, with the different court-yards, completely surround it. In all the wings there is a partition-wall, 14 inches thick, running along the centre; so that each compartment, in a manner, contains two Prisons.

The North-wing is for *Male Felons, before and after conviction;* and of these two descriptions each has a separate court, 40 feet by 35, with a day-room 14 feet square. It is most humanely fitted up, with a fire-place; and a fixed grate, shovel, tongs, poker, and coal-box, are provided; for to each day-room a peck of coals is daily allowed, and even more, in case the weather should be particularly severe. Cooking vessels also are assigned, together with trenchers and spoons: tin pots, or basons, with handles, to breakfast out of: a roller and towel are supplied to every room, and mops, brooms, pails, and soap, for personal and prison cleanliness. The iron-grated windows are glazed, the floors are of brick; and adjoining to each day-room is a working-room, of 14 feet square, with a fire-place.

The lobbies, or passages, leading to *the cells,* are 3 feet 6 inches wide, with bricked floors. This wing contains seventeen sleeping-cells; five, on the ground-floor, have grated and glazed windows, and the other twelve above are secured with iron gratings, and have each an inside shutter, with a pane of knobbed glass in them, to be put up at night.

The attick compartment of this wing, which is one story higher than the other two, contains four infirmary rooms; two of them are 21 feet by 14, and the rest 16 feet by 10, and 10 feet high: with iron bedsteads on casters, having a screw so constructed, as *to raise the head of the sick Prisoner;* and furnished with flock beds, a pair of sheets, two blankets, and a rug. To these comforts also are added a stone sink, lined with lead, the water for which is laid on with a cock; and in each room are two or three chairs, with fire-places, grates, and large sash-windows. Even over the door of each room is a sash window, about a yard square, which turns on a pivot for ventilation. Such attentions surely demand notice.

Between the Infirmary rooms are a lobby, with a water-closet, and a neat surgery apartment, of 14 feet by 7, fitted up for medicines, &c.

The flat leaden roof, defended by a parapet-wall, is very conveniently appropriated to convalescents, for taking the air; and upon it is placed a large reservoir, replenished, as needful, by a forcing pump, which supplies the whole Prison with excellent water.

The East and West wings have court-yards, day-rooms, and working-rooms, similar to those already described; and twentyfour sleeping-cells, making, in the whole, forty-one: each of them 9 feet by 6, and 9 feet high.

The apartments below have glass-casement windows; those above are furnished with inside shutters; and in every door there is a wicket, with iron-gratings, each @ inches square; a cast-iron bedstead on stone-bearers, supplied with a straw mattress, straw-in-ticking bed, two blankets, and a rug.

The court-yards, (seven in number) have each a bench for the Prisoners to sit on; and water-closets are judiciously placed in them

The three wings are detached twelve feet distant from the Keeper's house; and the open fences, which enclose the court-yards, being at the same distance from the house, form an ample area round it: by which means the whole Gaol is conveniently attended to, and the Prisoners are visited by their friends, without the necessity of going into any of the rooms, or court-yards.

The ground-floor of the Keepers house is raised three feet above the level of the other buildings; and the windows are so placed, that all the Prisoners, in the several court-yards, are under constant inspection, as well as every other person coming into the Gaol.

The *Chapel* is placed in the centre of the Keeper's house, up one pair of stairs. The Prisoners go into it by means of stone galleries, leading from each wing to the Chapel; which is so partitioned off, that each class is kept separate, in the same manner as in the Gaol. The Keeper has an alarm-bell at the top.

From the boundary-wall a space of *24* feet encircles the whole Prison, and its court-yards: and thus affords the Keeper an excellent garden for the growth of vegetables. The Sessions-house adjoins the boundary-wall, and Prisoners are brought into court for trial by a subterraneous passage.

The Visiting-Magistrates, Chaplain, and Surgeon, make their Remarks every time they inspect or visit the Gaol; which are entered into the proper books by a Clerk, in the same manner of *peculiar weakness,* as are all the accounts of this Prison.

T-he following voluntary DONATIONS, which for several years were sent to the Prisoners in St. Dunstan's Gaol, are now transferred to that of St. Augustin; viz.

Ten shillings a year, by the County at large, for Religious Books. They were sent to the Old Gaol when I was there in September 1804. Two guineas % by the Dean and Chapter, and two guineas by the Denn for the time being; which afford the Prisoners a dinner on the three great festivals-of Christmas, Easter, and Whitsuntide. And also other occasional aid.

These Donations have been usually made in the month of *December.*

Prisoners committed hither by the Magistrates, or sentenced at Sessions to hard labour, are employed in ground belonging to the Gaol, but without the walls; and a Man is paid eighteen pence a day by the County for *guarding tltem.*

CANTERBURY, *Kent.*
The City Bridewell.

Keeper, *Humphrey Crouch;* who is also Master of the Workhouse.

Salary, Two Shillings on each Commitment; one of which the Beadle receive.

Surgeon, Mr. *Trimnel.* Salary, 75/. for Workhouse and Bridewell.

1803, Sept. 25th,----One Woman.
1808, Aug.. 14th,----One Man.
1810, July 9th,----One Woman.

Allowance, to Men, seven ounces of bread, at three times a day: To Women, five ounces, ditto. And water is brought iu thrice a day by the Keeper.

REMARKS,

This Bridewell is situate in *Stour-Street;* and consists of a room about 12 feet square, in the front court of the Workhouse, furnished with wooden bedsteads, straw-in-hop bagging, and two blankets to each. And in it are fixed the whippingstocks, and a block for beating hemp.

Here is no court-yard; but a small one might be taken from that assigned to the Workhouse, which is finely situated, as the *Stour* rivulet runs between the two courts. The Workhouse has two well-ventilated cells, of 10 feet by 7, with sewers, which empty themselves into the stream. These cells are intended for the refractory poor; and very convenient, if a Man and Woman should at one time be committed to the Bridewell.

CANTERBURY. *Kent.*
The City Gaol.

Gaoler, *Evan Jones.* Salary, 15/. Fees, Debtors and Felons, 13. *4d.* No Table.

Chaplain, none: but the Rev. Mr. *Chafey* attends, if any Prisoner is under sentence of death.

Surgeon, Mr. *Trimnel,* who makes a Bill.

Number of Prisoners, Debtors. Felons, &c.
1800, March 26th,---1.--o. 1801, Sept. 20th,---2----3-
1803, Sept. 24th,---*2*----3-
1806, Aug. 12th,---2----1.
1808, Aug. 15th, 2--.--ffor Bastardy.
1809, July 9th,--3----8. (One of whom was under Sentence 1810, July 9th,----0----*6* of Death; andoneforBastardy.

Allowance, the half of a half-gallon loaf per day; the weight of which, at my visits, was 2 lbs. 2 oz. 12 drs.

REMARKS.

This Gaol is over the West Gate. Here is only one common day-room, which, till within these few years was about 27 feet square; but, having recently had five sleeping-cells for Criminals taken out of it, it is now a mere slip of a room, with a fire-place at one end, a pump with a stone-sink at the other end; and, in the corner, an uninclosed, uncovered, and filthy sewer. The pump is luckily supplied with water by a forcing syphon from below; otherwise it must be unbearably offensive.

In this wretched place, Debtors and Felons, male and female, with those committed for assaults or bastardy, mix indiscriminately throughout the day! The nasty state of the walls, cielings, and floors, shews how very little attention is paid to that Clause of the Statute, which enjoins, "That *once in the year,* at *least,* the. Gaols shall be *white-washedT*

In each of the two Towers there is a sleeping-room, 11 feet 6 inches diameter, and well-ventilated; but a bucket here supplies the place of a sewer,, and no water is accessible.

The Gaoler told me that he sometimes permitted a Prisoner to walk on the leads; but as I never found any to whom this indulgence was granted, at my several visits, I believe it to be only when he had leisure or inclination to attend them.

p r

Escapes, it seems, have been effected; and this, he told me, was the reason why Criminals, for comparatively trivial offences, were heavily double-ironed.

The stated bedding here is a rush-mat, laid on the floor, with two blankets and a rug: but I never saw more than one old rush-mat in each cell; and in three of them was only one old rag of a rug, and a bit of tattered blanket in the other two, which I learned had been furnished by the City. Whatever addition there was to this scanty supply, the Prisoners' friends had sent in. A stranger, who visited the Gaol in July 1809, sent them twelve rugs. There were at that time *three Debtors,* (but one of them, an Officer, being able to pay for a bed, was accommodated in the Keeper's house, which nearly adjoins the Gaol;) and also eight Criminal Prisoners. These rugs had been well taken care of by the Gaoler, who told me, in July l810, that they had been of the greatest service to poor Prisoners, particularly in the cold inclement weather preceding.

An old Man, to whom the Corporation give yearly a great-coat and laced hat, goes about the City with a basket every Saturday, to collect from the green-stalls and butchers, meat and vegetables: For his trouble he receives one-third of the Collection, and the remainder is divided equally among all the Prisoners.

No court-yard; no Rules and Orders. The Act for preservation of Health, and Clauses against the use of Spirituous Liquors, are not hung up. A begging-box is fixed, indeed, in the wall of the gate; but so obscured now, by rust and dirt, as not easily to be seen.

The state in which this miserable Prison is suffereoVto remain, is certainly a discredit to this highly respectable City,—" a Metropolitan See!" But I would humbly submit, That whilst it is continued as a place of long confinement, *the walls and cells be frequently washed with unslacked lime during its effervescence;* the *floors* sprinkled, and the *cells* fumigated *with vinegar.* This would greatly freshen and relieve the air, tending to counteract the effects of so many pitiable creatures being congregated in so small a space. A dwarf partition also, placed before the detestable sewer, would separate the sexes when decency most requires it. There were two Women-Prisoners in this room at my visit in 1809.

The pitiable Man whom I found here under sentence of death in July 1810, was a Roman Catholick, and wished to be attended by one of his persuasion, rather than by Mr. *Chafey,* who offered his spiritual services. He seemed truly penitent, and burst into tears when I addressed him.

It were needless, surely, to add, that this opprobrious Gaol is seldom, if ever, visited by the Magistrates. It cannot be:—Having remarked on the wretched bedding, or rather *no-bedding,* at my previous visits, without any suitable effect, (for the *rugs* then found, as a Wanderer's Gift, had not produced a single blanket of comfort,) it is evident that very little attention is paid to the hapless Prison, or its concerns; and I can even doubt, whether the Mayor, or his Brethren, either know, or remember if they have known, any thing about them.

CARDIFF. *Glamorganshire, South-Wales.*
The County Gaol.
Gaoler, *Thomas Morgan.* Salary, 1 *OOl.*
Fees, Debtors, *6s. Sd.* Felons, 13. *4d.* No Table. For Conveyance of Transports a Bill is made.

Chaplain, Rev. *John Evans*; now Rev. *John Jones.* Duty, Prayers and Sermon on Sunday. Salary was *30l.*; now *40L*

Surgeon, Mr. *Williams;* now Mr. *Griffiths.* Salary, heretofore, *20l.* now *30l.* for Debtors and Felons.

Number of Prisoners, Debtors. Felons, &c. Deserter.
1801, Nov. 21st,---5----3 0. 1803, Oct. 2d,----6----4-----1. 1810, May 9th,---10----7-._-_0.

Allowance, to all descriptions of Prisoners, *2s. 6d.* each per week, bytheCounty.
REMARKS.
This Gaol has three large airy court-yards, one of which is 54 feet by 45; the second, 48 feet square; and the third, 36 feet by 27; paved with flag-stone, and supplied with a pump and sewer.

One court-yard is appropriated to the Debtors; who have *ajree-ward,* or common sleeping-room, capable of holding four beds, for such Men-Debtors as cannot supply their own, and to whom the County allows straw: Also six rooms, 16 feet by 14, for those who can pay 2. per week for bed and bedding. *Debtors are no longer confined in the Town-Gaol now.*

The Chapel is in the centre of the building, neat and commodious, where Debtors and Felons are placed separately to hear Divine service.

Two rooms, about 16 feet square, and a bath, are assigned for the sick; but the latter, I understood, had not been used for two years.

The Felons have the other two court-yards, with a day-room to each, having fire-places, for which fuel is supplied by the County. They have, likewise, seven sleeping-cells on the ground-floor; eight others above them; and two more, set apart for Prisoners under sentence of death, which are very near the Chapel. The cells are all 7 feet 5 by 6 feet 9, and 10 feet high, with arched roofs, well-ventilated; and separated by lobbies, or passages, 4 feet wide, which respectively lead to the Chapel.

One of the above cells had an iron bedstead; the others, straw on the floors, with a rug to each. Here is a cast-iron stove, with pipes to convey warmth to the cells; but more particularly to those, in which Prisoners are consigned to solitude.

I found the Prison very clean: but, in 1803, the pumps in the court-yards had all been out of order for above four months, owing to the dry weather, and the wells not being sunk sufficiently deep. The Surgeon, I was told, never visits the Gaol, but when sent for.

Here is no employment furnished to the Prisoners. Transports have not the King's allowance of 2. *6d.* per week. The Act for preserving Health, and Clauses against Spirituous Liquors, both hung up.

The Great Sessions are removed from Cowbridge hither.

CARDIFF, *Town Gaol.*
Keeper, The Town Constable.
It consists of two rooms, arched with brick, under the Town-Hall. Debtors not being now sent hither, the Prisoners here are only confined for a night. At my visit, 2d October, 1803, there were none.

CARDIGAN. *South-Wales.*
The County Gaol and Bridewell.
Gaoler, *William Langdon.* Salary, *30l.*
Fees, for Debtors and Bridewell Prisoners, *6v. Sd.* For Felons, tried at the Great Sessions, 13. *Sd.* and for the Conveyance of Transports, 1. per mile.

Chaplain, Rev. *John Evans.* Salary, *20l.* Duty, on Sundays; and at other times, if required.

Surgeon, Mr. *Williams.* Salary, for Debtors and Felons, *lol.*

Number of Prisoners, Debtors. Felons. Bridewell.
1801, Nov. 30th,----6 ----5----2.
1803, Sept. 26th, .-, --3----1----0.

Allowance, to Debtors, none whatever. If the Debtor be poor, he must apply to his parish for relief. To the Gaoler, for the maintenance of Felons and other Criminal Prisoners, 4. *8d.* each per week.

REMARKS.

This Gaol, which is also the *Bridewell,* was finished and inhabited in 1797i and stands at the North-eud of the Town; having in front a paved court, 42 feet by 27, with cast-iron palisades, which give it a very handsome appearance.

On one side of the entrance is the Gaoler's kitchen, and, on the other side, his office; beyond which, and in the centre of the building, is the *Great-Hall,* or *Inspection-Room,* 38 feet by 30, of a circular shape: It has a flag-stone floor, *with two fire-places,* and four windows, commanding a view of the four different courts, each of which is 20 yards by 16.

Were the Gaoler to live in the Great-Hall, he would then have a full and complete view of the whole Prison, from a point the most eligible for effectual inspection: But, at my last visit, in September 1803, *I found it filled with corn, and two Men were absolutely threshing it out!* The six passages, which lead to the Criminals' sleeping-cells, open into this room.

For Debtors here are four rooms on the ground-floor, and four above stairs, each 13 feet by 11, and *furnished with fire-places;* but *nofuel allowed,* which had rather a tantalizing appearance. Straw is the only bedding supplied by the County for Prisoners of every description.'

The entrance to the Felons' ward is at the lower end of the Great-Hall, and forms a detached wing of the Gaol. They have four sleeping-cells below, and four above stairs, each 10 feet 6 inches by 9 feet, and 10 feet 6 inches high. To this wing are attached two small courts, 15 feet each by 11; but, as *being out of the Gaoler's view, the Prisoners seldom have the use of them.*

The Bridewell part of the Prison comprizes twelve rooms and sleeping-cells, about 10 feet each by 8, with loose straw in them to sleep on.

The Chapel is properly partitioned off, so that the sexes do not see each other; their respective lobbies leading distinctly to their seats. Over the Chapel are two rooms for the sick, each 38 feet by 30, the size of the Great Hall below. They are both light and airy, and furnished with fire-places.

There is no water laid on to the premises of this *County-Prison:* The Keeper must therefore fetch it from a well, a quarter of a mile distant: Even the inhabitants purchase water for their own use. No bath: The whole Prison is, and must be, very dirty, till some improvement takes place, to supply the means of ablution and cleanliness. Geese, ducks, and poultry inhabited the court-yards. The Prison is a new structure, of little more than ten years standing. A *Lunatich xr&s here* confined with a *Felon!* No particular care seemed to be taken of the maniac; although, probably, by medicines, and a proper regimen, some, at least, of this melancholy description, might be restored both to reason and usefulness in life.

No Table of Fees. No fuel allowed to any part of the Prison. Seldom visited by Magistrates. No Rules and Orders: Neither the Act hung. up,, for preserving the Health of Prisoners, nor the Clauses against their use of Spirituous Liquors.

CARLISLE. *Cumberland.*
The City and County Gaol.
Gaoler, *Joseph Mullender;* afterwards *Robert Nichole;* now *Richard Jackson.*
Salary, *40L* and to a Blacksmith Two Guineas for his attendance.
Fees, Debtors, 11. Felons, *13s: 4d.* No Table. Transports, *Is.* a mile to Whitehaven. Garnish, l v. *6d.*

Chaplain, Rev. Mr. *Mark.* Salary, 30/. Duty, Prayers and Sermon every Sunday.

Surgeon, Mr. *Hodgin;* now Mr. *Blamire.*

Salary, Two Guineas for making his Report, and paid for medicines.

Number of Prisoners, Debtors. Felons, &c.
1800, April 1st,-------28------5 1802, Sept. 20th,------16-7. 1809, Nov. 3d,------- 3-------16.

Also for Bastardy, Four. Assaults, Three. Deserters, Two.

Allowance, to *Debtors,* on application to the Magistrates, nine-pence a week until the first Session after Commitment; and thenceforward 1. *3d.* is allowed: So that a poor Debtor may remain here twelve weeks, upon the scanty pittance of *nine-pence a week,* which is then increased to little more than *two-pence per day J* To *Felons, 2s.* a week, before Conviction, and 2. *6d.* afterwards.

REMARKS.

The court or area of this Gaol is spacious, (85 yards by 36",) and has a pump in it, with fine water. Formerly it was common to all Prisoners, but now one part, 15 yards by 8, is appropriated to the *Felons,* and separated by iron palisades; through which they can converse with the Debtors, or any Persons who visit there. The Gaoler's house is at one end of the court, and adjoining to it is the *Chapel,* built in 1734; where the Prisoners are indiscriminately mixed to hear Divine service.

The *Master's-Side Debtors* have five rooms in the Gaoler's house, for which they pay *2s. 6d.* per week, and two sleep in a bed. *Common-Side Debtors* have four *free wards,* (so called,) 23 feet each by 18, and another small room. Here they must furnish their own bedding; but the rooms have a very dirty and ruinous appearance, with windows opening into the court-yard: formerly they looked into the street. The sexes are separated at night, but assemble together all the day.

The wards for *Felons* are two rooms going down a step or two, dark, damp, and dirty. One of them, 21 feet by 15, is their day-room, but serves likewise as a night-room. It once had a window opening towards the street, through which spirituous liquors, and tools, capable of great mischief, might easily be conveyed. But it is now bricked up. The *condemned-room* is only 11 feet by 9; which, should there be more than one or two Convicts, must be very close.

There are two rooms over these Felon-wards, called *The Home of Correction,* in which Women are lodged. Heretofore, straw only was allowed to those Prisoners who could not pay for a bed; but now (in 1809) both Felons and

House of Correction Prisoners are supplied with a rug, in addition to the straw.

At this, my third visit, I found a wooden paling raised at ten feet distance from the iron-palisades of the Felons' court-yard, which prevents their intercourse with the Debtors.

The five rooms in the Keeper's House are occupied in this manner. Those Masters-Side Debtors, who sleep on chaflf beds without curtains, have three blankets and a quilt; for the use of which each Debtor pays three shillings per week, though sometimes three sleep in one bed. Those who have feather-beds, with sheets, blankets, a quilt, and cotton furniture, pay each five shillings per week, and sleep two in a bed.

Here is no infirmary, nor bath: No Rules and Orders. The Act for preserving Health, and Clauses against the use of Spirituous Liquors, are not hung up.

In short, this Prison is in a very ruinous, dilapidated condition; seldom visited by the Magistrates, and extremely dirty. But a *new Gaol,* with Courts of Justice adjoining to it, are now building, in an elevated and airy situation.

CARLISLE.
The City Gaol.
It stands over the Scotch-Gate; and is only one ruinous room, about 20 feet square, with a fire-place, and a window of 4 feet by 18 inches.

Prisoners from the City are kept in the County-Gaol, by agreement between the Corporation and the Gaoler. No *Town-Debtor* can now be imprisoned for less than ten pounds. They have seldom exceeded two or three in a year, and those were only detained for a short time.

The Gaol room was filled with lumber when I was there, and no Prisoner had been confined in it for several years. No allowance: No court-yard: No water.

CASTLE-TOWN. *Isle of Man.* -; i *'Castle Rushen Gaol.*
Governor of the Isle, His Grace the Duke Of Athol.

Lieutenant Governor, and Keeper of the Castle, *Cornelius Smelt,* Lieut. Colonel in the Anny.

Gaoler, *John Fitzsimmons,* Headborough of Castle-Town.

Salary, 50/. British, besides Perquisites.

Turnkey, *William Quayle.* Salary, 20*7*.

Constables, Fifteen, at l0/. each *per annum;* one of whom is in daily attendance on the Gaol. Also five Centinels, on guard night and day.

Number of Prisoners, Nov. 10, 1810, Debtors, 9. Felons, &c. none.

Allowance, none, nor any medical assistance in case of sickness. *Water inaccessible,* but as brought in by the Constable, or other attendant of the day.

REMARKS.
Castle-Town, in the Isle of Man, is divided into two districts, by a small creek, which opens into a rocky and dangerous bay. In the centre of the town stands Castle Rushen; which overlooks the country for many miles, and was built in the year 960, by Guttred, a Prince of the Danish line, who lies buried within its walls. Founded on a rock, it presents the appearance of much strength; and, previous to the introduction of artillery, must have been impregnable by any force that could assail it. In figure it is irregular, and thought to resemble Elsineur. A stone glacis surrounds it on all sides. It still continues to brave the rude injuries of time, and arrests attention, as a majestic and formidable object. The early Kings of this Island are said to have resided' here/ 111 that barbarous pomp, which alone could distinguish them at so remote a period.

That there should have existed, and perhaps for centuries, a *Prison for Debtors,* in so distant a part of his Majesty's British dominions, I had no intelligence whatever, till it was communicated to me by two very interesting letters, dated Aug. 20, and Nov. 10, 1810, from a gentleman, formerly a Lieutenant-colonel of Dragoons; and, at the time of writing, an imprisoned Debtor in Castle Rushen.

Whilst I regret the want of knowledge that has hitherto prevented my visiting this lonesome Prison, (of which I have been favoured with a drawing,) I cannot convey to my Readers a better idea of it, than must arise from transcribing a part of the letters in question.

"Castje Rushen," says my unknown Correspondent, "was built upwards of 9oo years ago, and (contains only three inhabitable rooms, in which Felons and Debtors' are promiscuously confined. Here *no Insolvent Act* hath ever reached; neither have the laws of this Island ever provided any mode of relief for the honest, though unfortunate Debtor.

"After a Debtor has given up all his effects, there is not any public provision of food, beds, fuel, or medicine, for persons confined in this place. Many of them, therefore, suffer the severest consequences of want and wretchedness; and, as there is *no parochial support* afforded to their *wives* and *families,* they are reduced to the greatest distress, although formerly enjoying comfort and respectability. Strange also as it may appear, *no subscription* was ever known to have been entered into, throughout any part of this Island, for the relief of the unfortunate. For, as the indigenous Manx are not *liable to imprisonment for debt,* their feelings seldom are 'tremblingly alive' to the miseries of an incarcerated Stranger."

My mournful Correspondent mentions, as his fellow-prisoners, the descendant of a celebrated Antiquary, and formerly M. P. for H, who has been confined there for four years; the Rev. Mr. M——:—, a vicar in Queen's County, 18 months; and Major H. formerly M. P. for B——:. "This gentleman," he adds, " was released, in.consequence of the non-payment to him of the *p/anx-groat* per day; and yet, after a lapse of eight months, was put into prison again for *the same debt!"*

The writer thus concludes his first melancholy letter: "The darkness of the room I sit in, must apologize for the badness of my writing; the state of my mind, for the incoherence of my letter; and my poverty, for *this paper."*

The court-yard.of this prison is a part of the old fosse (the ditch or moat round it) which formerly was filled by the tide; and the water kept in, or let out, as might be necessary for the defence or accommodation of the inner Castle. It is, of course, exceedingly damp; surrounded also by high walls; find seldom does the sun shine upon any part of it. The privy attached to it is pot sunk, as propriety might have suggested; it is dirty beyond belief; and, in the summer months (for some Prisoners have spent all the seasons here) it emcts such, almost pestilential effluvia, as to render the court-yard intolerable. The *pump* also, ordained to supply the essential beverage of life, is out of order; and, though long ago the Prisoners have prayed to have it mended, this grand desideratum of comfort is still left in the same useless state. Many unpleasant instances, both of want and vexation, have occurred, from the negligence of furnishing the Prisoners with a regular supply of *water.* Complaints have frequently been made on this head, which, it is hoped, may never again be rendered necessary.

It has been doubted by Manx gentlemen of the Law, whether, and how far, English Acts of Parliament can bind this Island, except in matters of *revenue.* Is a it thus, then, that *.pecuniae omnia obediunt!* or can it be suffered that *imperium in imperio* shall thus prevail? Such a decision it is the interest of no one to desire; for to all it must prove injurious in some degree, and could benefit no honest man. We are told, that such laws of innovation, even if originating from England, ought to be first promulged on the *Tynwald Hill,* a consecrated spot, in the centre and heart of the Isle of Man, where all new Laws are necessarily proclaimed. It may be so, locally; but, surely, this reasoning cannot reach so far as to militate against the Common Law of humanity.

The apartments for confinement in this Gaol consist of three principal rooms. One of them is about 20 feet by 14, with a single window in it; which does not open, but has two wooden panes made occasionally to be taken out, and thus let in air. It was not long since occupied by *fourteen,* but now by *three* Prisoners only.

The second room is 14 feet by 12, having two Gothick windows, 8 inches each in breadth, with an iron bar through the centre. Here, recently, were nine inhabitants; but now only *two.*

The third room is of the same dimensions; and lighted (if *light* it may be called) by two windows, like those above. It lately held, of Prisoners, 13 in number: but now, only *three;* besides an infant boy, son of *a man and his wife,* who (so strangely is the Law here constructed) are both of them confined in this Gaol *for the same debt!*

On the walls is a small apartment, about 8 feet square, said to be a Danish watchturret, and in which *one* gentleman is detained.

Of the above four rooms, it may seem almost difficult to believe, though true, that not one has been white-washed in the last three years; and when they were so refreshed, for the most obvious reasons, it was done at the expence of the Prisoners themselves, who inhabited them at the time.

At present, they are obliged to contribute to the expence of having a woman to clean out their respective rooms daily; to pay 2. *6d.* per week for the hire of a bed and bedstead 5 sixpence a week also for the use of a little table and a chair; and coals cost them each about 2. per week. These articles, together with the charge for their female attendant, stand every individual (if he has it to command) about 26. per month, exclusive of the expence for candles; and " by the badness of this writing," my Correspondent observes, "you will readily perceive that the darkness of our regions requires them."

"The apartments here, or rather dungeons, are very damp and cold. Mr. S——, who lately occupied the room in which I am now confined, has declared to me, that, had he remained another Winter in it, he must have entirely lost the use of bis limbs" *u* The *iron bedsteads,* &c. which you mention, would answer the best. If thebeneficence of the donor should extend the number to *six* (or *two for each room)* it would be *impartially* benefiting the whole: and in that case I would advise that some impression, or stamp, should be made upon the iron; such, for instance, as ' The Donation of to the Prison (or the Prisoners) of Castle Rushen Gaol.' The kind gift would thus become exclusively secured, and perpetuated to the use of the Prisoners."

So very singular and unsystematic do the proceedings of this secluded Island appear, that certain arbitrary and lawless events in it may occasion less surprize. The venerable Bishop WILSON, (whose name here is only not adored; and by whose exemplary life and writings, the world has received, and will long continue to receive, unspeakable edification,) was, on the 29th of June, 1722, together with his two Vicars-general, committed to this destructive Prison of Castle Rushen, for the non-payment of a fine, which he had just reason to oppose, and which afterwards appeared to be unjust. They were kept closely immured within these dreary walls, and no persons admitted to see or converse with them.

The horrors of a Prison were aggravated by the unexampled severity of the then Governor, in not permitting the Bishop's house-keeper (who was the daughter of a former Governor) to see him, or any of his servants to attend upon him during his whole confinement; nor was any friend admitted to either his Lordship, or his Vicars-general. They were not treated as common Prisoners, but with all the strictness of Prisoners confined for High Treason. Their sole attendants were Common Gaolers; and even these, we are told, were instructed to *use their Prisoners ill!* In this wretched Gaol, the good Bishop and his innocently suffering friends were confined for two months; and, at the end of that time, released, upon his Lordship's Petition to the King and Council, before whom his cause was afterwards heard and determined. On the 4th of July, 1724, his Majesty in Council reversed all the proceedings of the Officers in the Island, declaring them to be oppressive, arbitrary, and unjust.

From the dampness of his Prison in Castle Rushen, even in a *Summer season* of the year, this excellent Prelate contracted a disorder in his right hand, which disabled him, through life, from the free use of his fingers. He ever after wrote backwards, slanting towards the left, with his whole hand grasping the pen. A friend has just laid before me some autographs of Bishop Wilson (from his excellent Tract in Manuscript, on *the Visitation of the Siclt)*; and but too clearly do they evince the injury he must have sustained by so vile and cruel an incarceration. The following lines upon the occasion are cited from Feltham's " Tour" of the Island in 1798 , p. 109; and cannot but gratify the lovers of Religion and Virtue: An elegant Octavo, printed by Cruttwell of Bath, and sold by the late Mr. Charles Dilly.

' But, oh! the sad reverse of fate,
That neither spares the good nor great,
Not e'en can cherubs paint.
Lo, Envy, brooding o'er the scene,
Dash'd with a cloud the bright serene;
  And bore to Rush En's walls the persecuted Saint!
,(There, as immur'd the good man lay,
Awhile to Tyranny a prey,
Sate Patience, with calm eye;
And there too, Faith, who gives to flow,
O Innocence, thy robe of woe,
Oped, through the vale of tears, a vista to the sky."

My best apology for giving this long description, is from the hope of its attracting the attention of some member of the British Legislature.

CROYDON. *Surry.*
Town Gaol.
Keeper, a Turnkey, who has charge of the Prisoners in Assize Time.
Prisoners, l6thJune, 1806, and 23d June, 1810, none.

Allowance, none to the Debtors from the Court of Requests: But to other Prisoners, one pound and a half of bread per day.

REMARKS.
The ground, on which the stable of the Three Tuns Inn once stood, is now occupied by a room for the confinement of Prisoners, during the time the Assizes are held here. It is a large apartment, 36 feet by 27, and 9 feet high, with six opposite iron-grated windows, and a boarded floor; with iron staples, to which the Prisoners are chained all night, and have straw to sleep on.

Adjoining to this apartment are four cells; one for Debtors, sent from the Court of Requests, of 13 feet by 10, in which there is a wooden bedstead, spread with straw, and a rug. The next is about the same size, which is appropriated to the use of the *Turnkey,* and has a fire-place and glazed-window: the two other cells 13 feet by *6* feet 4, and 9 feet high, are for male and female King's Evidence..

In all the rooms there is a sewer.

CHELMSFORD. *Essex.*
The County Gaol.
Gaoler. *Robert Pnrnell:* now *Thomas Archer.*

Salary, 345-and for the conveyance of Convicts to the Hulks, *Is.* per mile.
Fees, for Debtors, See Table. Besides which the Under Sheriff demands 5. *6d.* for his *Liberate!* It would be an act worthy the humanity of a
County so opulent and respectable, if *Debtor's* Fees were wholly done away.
For *Felons,* no Fees but for Lodging. Garnish abolished.

Chaplain, Rev. Mr. *Morgan,* who, on common occasions, attends twice a week; and every day on Prisoners under sentence of death.

Salary, 50/. the Act of Parliament not having granted more. But to this sum the Magistrates, about the year 1802, added twenty pounds, as a remuneration of Mr. Morgan's attentions to the *House of Correction,* which, for many preceding years, he had visited gratuitously.

Medical Attendants, Dr. *William Bird,* Mr. *John Gilson,* and Mr. *George Asser Gepp,* who attend alternately every third year. These Gentlemen consider themselves, *now,* as equally engaged: They attend all descriptions of *Debtors,* midwifery not excepted; and, at every Session and Assize, report the State of Health of *them,* as well as of the *Felons,* &c... Salary, 50/. to each, in the course of his attendance.

Allowance, one pound and a half of bread each , and a quart of small beer daily. Also ten bushels of coals per week for the prison, from 1st November to 25th March; equally distributed to Debtors and Felons. Convicts under sentence of transportation have only 2. *6d.* per week allowed themby Government, and paid in money.

The bread is made within the Prison, of the best wheatTM flour. Weights, scales, aad measuresare provided at the County expence, and fixed in the several Courts of the Gaol, in wooden cases made for. the purposeso that each Prisoner may see the allowance fairly delivered out.
REMARKS.

This new and elegant County Gaol, erected upon a very liberal plan, at the ex» pence of the County, was finished and inhabited in the year 1777, Its handsome appearance cannot fail to excite the admiration of every passenger. But the original design, as to some of the internal parts of the building, was found to be rather incommodious. It was deemed to be too much crowded, not only with a large Chapel, but with a needless *Tap-room,* a spacious kitchen, and several domestic offices, which were thought to impede that free circulation of air, so necessary for the Preservation of Health in all Places of Confinement.

These defects, or redundancies, however, have been since very judiciously remedied, by the removal of the Chapel to a more eligible situation, &c. and many *single cells* have also been added to the plan, without the least interruption to a free currency of air.

Debtors and *Felons* are here happily and entirely separated from each other; their Prisons being divided by a spacious gravel walk, with a flagged foot path.

The Debtors have a common court-yard for men and women, of 99 feet by 19, containing eight sleeping-rooms, 18 feet each by 14; four at bottom, and four above, with boarded floors, fire-places, a table, seats, and sash windows in each; for which they pay, as per ensuing Table. Those who furnish their own beds are not charged for room-rent, and when they work, receive all their earnings. But the cast-iron sewers, injuciciously placed near the Debtors' rooms, are at times extremely offensive.

At the upper end of the court-yard is a large day-room, 43 feet by 16, with three sash windows, boarded floor, a fire-place, large oak table, with benches to sit on, and cupboards to secure provisions: And here the *Gaol Rules* and *Regulations* are conspicuously hung up.

The last-mentioned room is moreover appropriated to such handicraft tradesmen, as can procure work from without the Prison; and likewise as the sleeping-apartment of those poorer Debtors, who, being unable to pay for, or provide themselves with bedding, rest here, upon straw laid on the floor. T-ke sloping blinds before the windows of this spacious room greatly obstruct both light and ventilation.

No room is yet set apart as *an Infirmary* for Debtors.

Here is also a large apartment, to which the approach is through the Keeper's dwelling house. It was formerly called *The Smuggler's Room,* and is *42* feet long, by lo wide. It is not used at present; but with little expence might be converted into lodging apartments for such Debtors, as may wish to be accommodated in a superior manner, within the dwelling house.

Table Of Fees,

To be taken by the Keeper of the Gaol at *Chelmsford,* for the County of Essex, as varied and altered (pursuant to the Act 32 Geo. II. chap. 28, Sect. 5), from that which was originally settled and established, under, and by virtue of an Act of Parliament, passed in the second year of his said late Majesty, King George the Second.

sB. s. d.

"For the chamber-rent, bed, and bedding of each *Prisoner upon*
Criminal Process, per week, provided that not more than two be put into one bed, nor more than two beds in one room-0 3 6

For the chamber-rent, bed and bedding of each *Debtor,* per night, provided that not more than two be put into one bed, nor more than two beds in the same room-----00 4

For the Turnkey's Fee, into Gaol, for every Debtor---0 1 0

For the Turnkey's Fee, out of Gaol, for every Debtor--0 1 O

For the Gaoler's Fee upon each Debtor's Discharge---0 13 4

Essex. Michaelmas Session, 4th Oct. 1796.

Signed by us, Justices of the Peace for the said County,
T. B. Bhamston. 23d January, 1797.
T. Kynaston. We have reviewed, and do confirm the
John Conyeks. above Table of Fees.
Ken Yon.
W. Bullock, B. Hotham.
Clerk of the Peace for the said County.

The *Felons* have twenty-seven cells, ten feet each by five, and seven feet highr (of which eight are *solitary*;) and two large *condemned rooms,* containing seven, sleeping-cells, each of which is seven feet by six and a half, and eleven feet high. Every common and solitary cell has a crib bedstead, furnished with a straw mat, flock bed, bolster, blanket, and rug; but the condemned cells have their crib bedsteads supplied with straw and blankets only.

Attached to these cells is a small flag-paved court, into which the Convicts are admitted for two or three hours in the day.

Every cell in this Prison is flagged and well ventilated; the court-yards airy; and all, except the solitary and condemned cells, have a day-room attached to them respectively, with a fire-place, to which fuel is allowed, at the County's expence, during the Winterly half year. For those criminals who choose to pay as per Table, extra bedding is provided by the Keeper.

In several of the Felons' sleeping-cells are placed cast-iron sewers, without cover to them, which must render them very offensive.

With respect to the Women-Felon an excellent alteration has taken place; a large and useless room having been converted into a comfortable ward, with boarded floor, fire-place, large sash window, table, benches to sit upon; and containing eight crib bedsteads, furnished in the same manner as for the Men Felons. To this room are likewise attached a cooking and washing kitchen for their use, and a small court-yard for air and exercise.

§3=-I have always observed the Prisoners in this Gaol to be *very heavily ironed.* In four of the Felons' wards, which contain barrack-beds for 36 Prisoners of this class, a ponderous chain is eyery night passed through the main link of their fetters, and made fast at each end, so that the Prisoner cannot turn himself on the bed. Of this description there were eight Felons in one ward, six in another, and two in a third. The fourth ward was unoccupied. It is but justice to add, that the present Gaoler, upon my representing the cruelty of this addition to the daily misery of a Prisoner, ordered this chain to be taken away, and promised to discontinue the practice of his predecessor; so that it is to be hoped Prisoners are no longer threaded together by a heavy chain, during those hours Which are destined by Nature to repose.

"If the Gaoler keep the Prisoner more strictly than he ought of right, whereof the Prisoner dietli, this is Felony in the Gaoler by the Common Law." 3 Inst. 91. Fost. 321, 322.

Here are two separate *Infirmaries,* for men and women: the former is flagged, and the latter has a boarded floor. That assigned for the men is 20 feet by 15. The women's somewhat smaller, with glazed windows, fire-places, crib bedsteads, and forms. Both, however, of these apartments *for the Sick,* are at present placed on the *ground Jloor;* which I humbly presume to be wrong; and would respectfully recommend some other apartments, in a higher situation, to be adopted as Infirmaries. They certainly would be:less subject to damps, and have better ventilation, from a larger quantity of fresh air.

At the North end of this Gaol there is exhibited a very humane and excellent idea, for the execution of capital convicts. Hooks and eyes of iron are firmly fixed in the wall: the scaffolding is thus easily adjusted; and, by a simple contrivance, the platform falls back, and the wretched criminals cease to mourn their hopeless existence among the living!

On the North side of the Gaol, is The Chapel, upon an amended construction, and to which the apartments called." *Condemned Cells"* closely adjoin. Its area is occupied by the Keeper's own family, the Debtors, and Women

Felons. At the end/.opposite the Communion Table, are seated the Men Felons, classed according to the nature of their offences, and separated by a wainscot partition, and an iron railing placed before their seats. The respectable Chaplain, Mr. *Morgan,* is emplary in his whole deportment and the Prisoners, at my several visits, evinced their esteem for him, by being very attentive to their duty. Those of every description are required to attend the sacred duties of the place: and here I cannot help expressing the pleasure I received from the worthy Minister's selecting in his discourse those passages of Scripture, which struck me as most suitable to the class he was immediately addressing. He firmly admonished the profligate, exhorted with gentleness the unthinking, and comforted the afflicted hearer: In a word, as if not content with a formal and stipendiary discharge of prescribed duty, he appeared to be, in heart and principle, A Christian.

In the County Gaol of *Chelmsford,* every criminal, at his entrance, is stripped and washed. His own clothes are taken from him; and, being purified in a bath or oven, the County cloathing is put on, which has either a sleeve or collar so coloured, as to discriminate the nature of his offence. Caps, also, like the forage caps of soldiers, are worn by them.

The Felons here are employed in a manufactory of ropes, and other cordage. Old junk, from the King's Yards, is purchased and plucked in pieces. The best of it is knotted together by them, and made into what is called *twice-laid rope;* the refuse of the junk is then sent to the several Houses of Correction, and picked into oakum. New rope is also spun and made up; and the articles so fabricated are disposed of at reduced prices, for various purposes in the shipping and farming lines, &c. I am informed that the nett profit of this work to the County Stock, from 1st April, l800, to 1st January, 1803, was *228l. 8s. gd.* and has produced, upon an average of the years *l8o')-6-J-8,* 130/. *per annum.*

Some years since, Mrs. *Herris* gave certain lands in trust to the Incumbent of the parish of Chelmsford; out of the rents whereof five pounds are distributed annually, at Christmas Eve, in equal proportions to the Debtors here confined. A Memorial of this Donation is hung up in the Gaol.

In the *Rules* and *Orders* of Chelmsford County Prison is the following article, expressive of the truest humanity: "No Person shall be dismissed, (unless at his or her own request,) if he or she labour under any acute or dangerous distemper, "until, in the opinion of the surgeon, he or she can be discharged with safety. "And at the time of his or her discharge, his or her own, or other decent clothes, "shall be delivered to him or her, together with such sums of money as the visiting "Justice shall judge necessary for subsistence to the place of his or her legal set"tlement."

Every part of this Gaol is well supplied with excellent water. It is whitewashed.once a year. The Act for Preservation of Health, and Clauses against Spirituous Liquors are hung up in it: And the very judicious Rules and Orders established for its good government, confer grt honour upon their authors.

CHELMSFORD. *Essex.*
The County Bridewell.
Gaoler, *Richard Brooke,* now *William Couthorn.* Salary, 100/. and for coals and other contingencies, Go/, or more, if necessary.

Chaplain, Rev. Mr. *Morgan.* Salary, *iol.*

Duty, Prayers and Sermon every Sunday morning.

Medical Attendants; the same Gentlemen as at the *County Gaol;* with a Salary, for both, of 50/. per annum.

Number of Prisoners, Men. Women. 1808, Nov. 12th, 34------10 1809, Aug, 4th,-30------6 1810, Sept. 26th, 54------14

Allowance, the same to each Prisoner here as in the County Gaol.

REMARKS.
This new House of Correction, first inhabited at Michaelmas 1806, adjoins to the County Gaol; and being fronted with Portland-stone, has a very handsome appearance. The house appointed for the Keeper immediately occupies the front; and in it is a room entirely appropriated to the Magistrates, with every convenience of books, &c. necessary for the duties of their office.

Behind this building, and in the centre of the large area, is the *Bridewell;* on the right and left of which are two large court-yards, with a day-room attached to each.

The *Men's court* is 144 feet by 32, and has on each side separate cells, amounting in all, to *thirty-eight.*

Over the cells, on the right hand, is a workshop, 152 feet by 14; and at the end next the street are two rooms for Overseers, and two others, set apart for a deposit of various articles necessary to the situation. At the farther end is an *Infirmary,* 38 feet six inches by 14 feet, which, on the *Mens side,* has seven crib bedsteads, with each a straw bed, blanket and rug; also a cast iron grate, and pegs for clothes. Annexed to it is a foul or infectious wa-d, containing four crib beds, and furnished in all respects as the Infirmary.

The *IVomen's court-yard* has twenty-six cells, a work-room of 72 feet by 14, and at the lower part of the court-yard, an Infirmary for Women, of 12 feet by 9 feet seven, fitted up in the same manner as the men's. Here are likewise a room for temporary confinement, 48 feet ten inches by 14 feet, and a sleeping-room above it, of the same dimensions.

The *Chapel,* 65 feet by 21 feet six, is built partly over the cells; and has a wall running through the centre of it, to the length of 42 feet six inches, so as effectually to prevent all communication between the men and women, who have each their separate doors of entrance. At the end of the Chapel is a spacious room, assigned for stores of every kind that may be wanted for the employment of the Prisoners.

The men have two rooms, one for a working and day room; and the other, for lodging, has seven beds in it. Over which the women also have two rooms, of the same size and descripcion; to which latter the ascent is by a stair-case from their court-yard.

The size of each cell here is ten feet by six feet 6, and eight feet high, all archroofed, and fitted up with a bed, mattress, blanket, and coverlet. Over each door is an aperture for light and ventilation, with a shutter on the inside.

The employment of the Prisoners is picking of oakum. They have no portion of the earnings; but, if they have behaved well, receive money at their discharge, according to their distance from home.

The *bread* here distributed is made, and the beer brewed, in the house. The *commitments* to it, from 1st January, 1807, to 1st January, 1808, were *one hundred and Jifty-eight.* Persons confined for Bastard), or for petty offences, as servants, are not permitted to have any intercourse with the other Prisoners, but have a separate court-yard, rooms, &c.

Firing is humanely allowed here, the same as at the County Gaol; and all the court-yards are well supplied with excellent water.

The Rules and Regulations of this House of Correction are properly and very conspicuously hung up in the different wards.

The loathsome old Bridewell, now pulled down, I have fully described in the Gentleman's Magazine for August 1S04, p. 704.

COWBRIDGE. *Glamorganshire.*
The County Bridewell.
Keeper, *Evan Deer.* Salary, 50/. Fees, None.
Prisoners, 2d Oct. 1803. Four.
Allowance, four-pence halfpenny each per day.
REMARKS.

The Keeper's house fronts the street. In the back court-yard are two rooms 15 feet square, and one above. They are supplied with straw and two blankets each. There is a pump in the court-yard. No employment provided.

CHESTER CASTLE. *The County Gaol.*
Gaoler and Constable, *Matthew Hudson.*
Salary, 500i. as Keeper, out of which he pays three Turnkeys: From the Crown he receives 18/. 5. as Constable. Fees, which are accounted for by the Keeper; See Table. Debtors pay *4s.* 1 *d.* to the stock for Coals. For conveyance of transports he is allowed the expence.

Chaplain, Rev. *Rowland Hill,* who officiates by his Deputy, the Rev. Mr. *Fish.*
Duty, Sunday, Prayers and Sermon, (See *Remarks,)* and Prayers on Wednesday and Friday,
Salary, 30/.
A Debtor officiates as Cleric, for which the County allows 2/. a year.
Surgeon, Mr. *Hughes.*
Salary. The County pays to the Infirmary *60I.* for attendance and medicines; out of which the Surgeon receives *ten pounds* for his attendance.
Number of Prisoners, Debtors. Felons, &c.
1801, Nov. 7th, 26 12 1802, Oct. 16th,------31------26 1803, Dec. 28th,------28------14 1805, Oct. 26th, 38------25 1809, Nov. 16th,------25-33

Allowance, to Debtors, weekly, seven pounds of good wholesome bread, which is to be at least one day old; viz. 3lbs. and a half on every Tuesday and Friday. Felons have the same quantity of bread, together with two ounces of salt per week; and likewise 12 pounds of potatoes each week, viz. four pounds on every Monday, Wednesday, and Saturday. See also the *Remarks,* on the Ladies' and Gentlemen's Christmas Subscription, in behalf of *very poor Debtors.* REMARKS.

This Castle, which by its magnificence does honour to the County, is, I am informed, one of the finest specimens of Grecian Architecture in this Kingdom. The Architect, Mr. *Harrison;* of whose professional abilities the Bridge and Castle at Lancaster will stand as lasting records to posterity.

The grandeur of the design, the elegance of its appearance, (being all of white stone,) and the convenience with which every part of Chester Castle is constructed, render it equal, at least, to any Gaol in England.

Its front.extends about 100 yards, and in the centre of it stands the County Hall; before which is a colonnade, projecting about 15 feet, composed of twelve solid pillars, six in a row, and each in length 21 feet, without a joint.

The Court itself describes a semi-circle; round which there are twelve other solid pillars, 18 feet long. On these rest the stone beams which support the roof. The Court of Justice is well calculated for seeing and hearing; the audience being raised one above another, upon steps 18 inches broad, in the manner of the Greek and Roman Theatres.

From the Prisoners' Bar there is a private passage into the Gaol, for bringing them into Court. On the left hand of the Hall are the entrance to the Gaol, and the Turnkey's Lodge. After passing the vestibule is the Debtors' Yard, which is both spacious and airy, 72 feet by 63, exclusive of the Terrace, 6"3 feet by 17; and overlooks a large tract of Country.

Above the Turnkey's Lodge, and a small arcade of *9* feet, is a day-room, of 24 feet 6 by 18 feet *6,* and 13 feet high; with a cistern of water, a stone sink, and stone shelves to set the provisions upon. Also a sleeping-room adjoining, *26* feet by 18, and 13 feet high, well lighted and ventilated. Under the stairs is a small cellar for coals.

On the *right side* of the Yard is another day-room, 24 feet by 20, and 12 feet 6 inches high; which likewise has a water-cistern, stone sink, a pantry, with stone shelves for provisions; and above this is a sleeping-room, 32 feet by 20, 13 feet six inches high, well ventilated. The four rooms here noticed are for *Common-Side Debtors,* who are allowed by the County a straw bed, two blankets, and a coverlet lined with flannel. At the top of the stairs is a large cistern of water, used for cleansing the sewers in this part of the Prison.

On the *left side* of the Yard are two stories of small sleeping-rooms, twelve in number; ten of which are 13 feet 6 by 7 feet 6", and 12 feet high; the end room on each landing-place is 19 feet by 8, and 12 feet high, with fire-places. Two pleasant day-rooms also adjoin to each, 19 feet *6* by 15 feet, and 13 feet high, with two windows in each room. These are for the *Master's-Side Debtons.* They have no water-cisterns in these apartments, but are accommodated by a pump, well supplied with spring-water, which stands in the centre of the yard. Each sleepingroom contains one bed; for which, if provided by the Keeper, the Prisoner pays *2s.* per week; if, by the Prisoner, he is charged per week one shilling, which is accounted for to the County by the Keeper. Debtors have no access to their sleepingrooms during the day: their bedsteads consist of two iron tressels, with boards painted and varnished.

At the extremity of the yard, on the right-hand, is a passage, of 81 feet by *6,* leading into another yard, 63 feet square, exclusive of the *Terrace,* (as before,) 63 feet by 17: On the farther side of which is the *Infirmary,* 42 feet by 18, with *convalescent-rooms* adjoining, 13 feet high, airy, and well-ventilated. At the end of the yard is a large cistern of water, supplied from the River *Deva,* or *Dee.*

Opposite to these are the apartments for the *ff omen-Debtors,* of which description, at present, there are but two; — a sitting-room, 20 feet by 17, and a sleepingroom, 23 feet by 20, both airy and well-ventilated. Here also is a large cistern, with water to cleanse the sewer; and, in the middle of the court-yard, a pump, well supplied with spring water.

In the centre of the lobby, or principal passage, is the great stair-case; down which, by a descent of *fifty steps,* (the ground being on different levels,) are the *Felons' court-yards.*

Round the stair-case are the Constable's apartments, consisting of two elegant parlours, and a kitohen 011 the first-floor, with five handsome bedrooms above. The front parlour projects about four yards beyond the lower parts of the house; and is surrounded by a stone terrace, *6* feet 10 inches broad, with open iron palisades, from which the Keeper has a full view of the Felons' yards, inclosed by a boundary-wall, 25 feet high. They are respectively numbered 1, 2, 3, 4, 5, and divided by partition-walls, 10 feet 9 inches high, each of which is furnished with its own distinct apartments.

Yards, N 2, 3, 4, consist each of a spacious court, 75 feet by 57, and a pump, well supplied with good spring-water, in the centre of each, having an arcade of of 20 feet by 15, and two day-rooms to each yard, 14 feet *6* by 13 feet 6': Above which are two stories of sleeping-cells, six cells in each story, and all of them 8 feet *6* by *6* feet 4.

The end-yards, N 1, and 5, are 56 feet by 2,0, with a day-room to each, of 14 feet 10 by 11 feet; and arcades lg feet by 15. These have only six sleeping-rooms, three in each story. Each cell is provided with a cast-iron bedstead, 27 inches wide, perforated with small round holes, on which is a straw-mattress, bed stuffed with straw, two blankets, and a coverlet lined with flannel.

The Felons' apartments are all of stone and iron; and the roofs also, which are on the same level with the Debtors' yard, are of stone, painted, to prevent the weather from making the cells damp.

The Female-Felons are separated from the Males. Round the apartments and court-yards of both is an area of 12 feet broad, flagged with stone, 4 feet wide, and the other part gravelled; which the Prisoners cross in going to Chapel.

The Chapel, which stands directly under the front-room and terrace of the Keeper's house, is a very neat little building, ornamented with seven solid pillars, 18 feet long. There is a gallery erected for the *Del/tors,* under which the Felons are placed in five seats, or boxes, each *I t* feet by 6 feet 8 inches, corresponding with their respective court-yards. The Keeper's pew is behind the Clergyman, and the Communion Table below, *where the Sacrament is administeredJour times a year.*

Oil each side of the Chapel, in a straight line, are 13 *solitary cells,* 7 feet 8 inches hy *6* feet 4. Each has a small anti-room, of 8 feet 2 by 7 feet 8, and 8 feet *6* inches high; three of which anti-rooms are now made into work-shops, and, of the rest, seven may be heated by a stove for that purpose. Over these cells, on each side, are work-rooms for Debtors, the roofs of which being of nagged stone, form the terraces in the Debtors' and Infirmary-courts: and in front of them are two rows of iron-railing, placed a little distant from each other, in order to prevent the Debtors or their friends from seeing or conversing with the Felons below.

Here is a warm and cold bath, with a stove to purify the Prisoners' offensive or infected clothes; which are taken from them on coming into Prison, and the Gaol uniform put on.

Such Debtors as work, have two-thirds of their earnings; but, as *C/iester* is not a manufacturing city, there are few of them, except taylors and shoe-makers, that can get employed.

Felons have half their earnings, from which, when working, they receive three shillings per week, besides the Gaol-allowance: The remainder is paid to them, or remitted for the assistance of their families, if any, or, on producing a certificate of their good behaviour, *at the end of three months after their being discharged.*

The earnings of the Prisoners are accounted for at each Easter Sessions.

There is a book kept in the Prison for Visiting-Magistrates to enter their Remarks. And here I cannot help expressing my sincere regret, for the loss, to this City, of that able and upright Magistrate, the Rev. Doctor *Pcploe Ward,* who, by virtue of the late Statute, is now obliged to reside nine months in the year at Ely. By the active energy and unremitted attentions of this truly excellent Divine, industry and morality were inculcated and encouraged; and, possessing temporal authority to make his spiritual advice respected, its influence was felt through every department of this very interesting Gaol.

Table Of Fees. s. d.

Commitment-Fee for every Prisoner,--------82

For Copy of each Commitment-----------10

Discharging Fee---------------10

To the Turnkey on Discharge----------06

Chamber-rent, Prisoner finding bedding, per week,-----10

Bedding, if found by the Constable, for each, not exceeding per week, 3 0

Ditto, in a room, with a fire-place, ditto,--------4 0

For attendance into Court, with every Prisoner brought there by
Rule of Court,---------------10

The only Legacies which I find on record are the two following: "Mr. *John Norney,* Citizen and Merchant-taylor of London, by his Will, dated "10th October, 1615, left six shillings and eight-pence to be distributed on Candle*f*mas, yearly, for ever, by the Mayor, to the poor Prisoners, in money or bread."

"*Valentine Broughton* of *Chester,* Alderman, by his Will, 16th June, *1608,* left "thirteen shillings and four-pence, to be distributed at Michaelmas and Lady-day, "yearly, for ever, by the Mayor, to the Prisoners in the Castle, by equal portions, "or twenty days after."

The above-written List of Gifts a true Copy.

Tho. Tagg. *Cl. Pads.* N. B. 1805 These are regularly paid by the Mayor.

Of the *Debtors,* when I was here in 1805, thirteen were at work, and one of them, Shoe-maker, had saved upwards of *ten pounds.* Of the *Felons* I found seven at work. Every one of the Prisoners attended Chapel the next day, where their appearance was clean, and their behaviour orderly, and attentive to a serious and appropriate discourse. The worthy Chaplain has a discretionary power of distributing to them moral and religious books, as he thinks necessary.

Every Christmas, the Ladies and Gentlemen of Chester are waited upon by the Turnkey, and their Subscriptions for Relief of the Criminal-Prisoners are generally from 14 to 18 pounds; part of which is distributed in money and coals, as the Visiting Magistrates direct. Out of this Fund the worthy Gaoler is humanely authorized to allow any very poor Debtor the same quantity of potatoes and salt weekly, as the Felons receive. From the same Annual Donations also he assists many poor Debtors in obtaining their *six-pences;* and, frequently, to effectuate their discharge, by a small addition to the sums voted by the Society for Small Debtors in London.

A book is here kept for the purpose of entering all donations, and the manner of their application, which is under the constant inspection of the Visiting Magistrates.

In the method of treating Prisoners left for execution, there is a singularity which merits attention. They are delivered by the Constable, or his Deputy, at a stone called " Glover Stone, a little way distant from the Gaol, into the hands of the Sheriffs of the City; who receive them at that stone, (as being the extreme limit of the Castle-Precincts,) and from thence convey them to the place of execution, of which, also, they have the charge.

This Prison is kept remarkably clean. The County Magistrates have evinced great liberality, in providing every comfort which can attend the privation of Liberty, and in shewing pity to the misery of even the most guilty. In the choice of a Gaoler, the qualities of the MAN-secm to have been particularly attended to. Mild of temper, patient in manners, humane and firm in conduct, he is much respected by all, and satisfaction is visibly displayed in the countenance of every Prisoner.

The following Notice is entered in the Magistrates' Book, and struck my attention; perhaps the more forcibly, as being both singular, and worthy of general imitation.

"By order of the Visiting Magistrates, loth April, 1805. "We, the Publicans *permitted to serve* the Prisoners confined within the "Castle of Chester, with Ale, &c. Do hereby publickly declare, That from the "date hereof, we will exonerate every Prisoner, on his discharge, from all debts' "whatever, which we may have permitted him to contract with us, either for Ale, "Porter, or Wine. Witness our Hands, "Rob. Oldham,

"Rob. Goff."

There is an elegant Armoury building at the extremity of the Castle Yard, where the Towers formerly stood, of 120 feet by 25, for storing 30,000 stands of arms. The front and each end of it are of white stone, and built by the County; the remainder to be done by Government. A handsome stone gateway, of about 12 feet, leads to the lodgings assigned for the use of the Judges. But what surprised me extremely was, an immense *Powder-Magazine, placed within ten yards of these elegant buildings!* It is surely an ill neighbour. A more convenient structure of the kind, and very safe in case of explosion, might easily be built near the Banks of the Dee, at a proper distance from the City.

CHESTER. *The New City Gaol, and Bridewell.*

Gaoler, *Samuel Hughes.* Salary, 80/.

Fees, the same as at Chester Castle, which are his perquisites. For the Conveyance of Transports he is allowed the expence.

Keeper of the Bridewell, *Jonathan Taylor.* Salary, 60/. No Fees.

Chaplain, Rev. *William Fish.* Salary included in that of Little St. John's Chapel, to which this Gaol is an appendage. Duty, Prayers and Sermon on Sundays.

Surgeon, Mr. *George Harrison,* who makes a Bill.

Debtors. Felons. Bridewell.

Number of Prisoners, 1809, Nov. 16th,-.-6---4--»9.

Allowance, to Debtors, none, except on petition to the Sheriffs; and then, one pound of bread per day. To Felons, and other Criminals, in Gaol and Bridewell, seven pounds of bread weekly, sent from the Baker's, in loaves of 3-i. lbs. each.

s REMARKS.

The horrid Gaol at the North-Gate, which so long disgraced this very ancient and respectable City, having been pulled down, and the New one I am about to describe being got ready, Prisoners were removed to it on the 15th of February 1807.

These two Prisons are situate in a field betwixt the Infirmary and Stanley-Place. The boundary-wall, 17 feet 6 inches high, is of an oblong square, running from West to East, and incloses three quarters of an acre of ground.

The entrance to the City Gaol is West of the City walls: The front commands an extensive.prospect of the Cambrian hills, and likewise enjoys the salutary breezes of the River Dee, which runs about 300 yards distant from the Prison.

There are four pilasters, two on each

side of the door of entrance, projecting about two feet; and at the top of the building, on a stone tablet, is inscribed, *xc* City Gaol." This part of the structure is of stone; the remainder of brick. An inspecting walk, 9 feet wide, runs close to the boundary-wall, and encircles the court-yards., A passage, or lobby, five feet wide, and 89 feet long, leads through the whole building; on each side of which are cells and rooms, both for the Prisoners, and to accommodate their respective Keepers, whose apartments are judiciously placed in the centre, commanding a view of the several court-yards.....

In the part appropriated for the City Gaol, there are, on the ground-floor, four sleeping-cells for *Criminals,* 12 feet by 7 feet *6* each, and 10 feet high, with a glazed and grated window, 3 feet square; and furnished with an iron bedstead, a straw-mattress, straw-bed, two blankets and a coverlet, as at Chester Castle. Here are also two day-rooms, one for Male, the other for Female-Felons; each 19 feet by 12 feet *6,* and 10 feet high, furnished with tables, shelves, and seats, and opening into their respective court-yards, of 43 feet long by 34: at the extremity of which is a wooden paling, 6 feet 6 inches high, inclining inwards, so as to prevent any access to the boundary-wall.

For *Debtors* in common, male and female, here is one large day-room, 18 feet by 14, with a fire-place, tables, shelves, &c. and opening into their court-yard, of 43 feet long by 34; in which there is a pump of good spring-water, and a workroom, 19 feet by 12, supplied with fire-places, shelves, &c.

On the chamber-story are two airy bed-rooms, 16 feet by 12, with boarded floors, glazed-windows, and fire-places. Each has three iron-bedsteads; and a strawmattress, straw-in-sacking bed, two blankets, and a coverlet, are allowed by the City. But, if a Debtor furnish his own bed, the Gaoler charges him one shilling per week for this indulgence!

Here are two well-furnished rooms for Debtors, who can afford to pay four (billings per week for a single bed, or two. shillings each, if two sleep together. Also four small rooms of the same dimensions as those of the cells below: One of them, having a fire-place and grate in it, is set apart for the Infirmary, and the other three are assigned to Female Felons.

In the centre, and between the two Prisons, is the *Chapel;* to which the ascent is by two flights of steps, one leading out of the City Gaol, and the other out of the Bridewell: It is a large room, 36 feet long by 24, and 18 feet *6* inches high. On the Gaol-Side of it are two ranges of seats, one for Male, the other for Female-Felons, having the entrance-door betwixt them: the like seats also are on the BridewellSide, with the door of entrance; and the Debtors, placed between, are opposite the pulpit.

In the middle of the before-mentioned long passage, on the ground-floor, is a door that communicates with the *Bridewell,* which forms the East end of the Building; and in the number and size of rooms, cells, and court-yards, both on the ground-floor and above stairs, it is exactly similar to the City Gaol. Over the Bridewell door of entrance is a flat space, for the execution of Criminals under Capital sentence from the County or City Gaols. i

The sewers in the different court-yards are judiciously placed, and not offensive. Soft water is laid on to the Prison by Pipes from the City, and spring-water from the pump in the Debtors' Court. The Visiting Magistrates allow such extra nourishment for the sick as the Surgeon judges proper.

In the outset of my present description, I have alluded to the Old North-Gate Prison, as horrid, and a disgrace to the distinguished City in which it stood at my former visits, in 1801, 2, 3, and 1805. Injustice, however, let tne add, that, in the wretched Gaol referred to, one alteration had taken place, which, until my visit in 1805, I had almost despaired of. I then found that the veteran *dungeon,* that slough of despond, was made *dry,* for the only time I had heard of its being so, during a series of at least thirty years sinoe my first remembrance of it. It seems that a daring Man, who had been committed thither for felony, and was lodged in this famous *night-room,* had formed the selfish resolution to drain it, if possible. I found him here; and he told me that he had, singly, emptied above twenty buckets of water and filth out of it; a laborious task, surely, when the narrow ascent of eighteen steps every time from *his dormitory* is considered. The City being informed of such singular exertions, humanely ordered the dungeon to be so secured against the land-springs beneath, that I was given to understand it had continued to be comparatively dry ever after; though damp it must have been, from close confinement at so great a depth. The Man in question afterwards attempted.to escape, but was severely punished for it; having, in addition to his heavy doublefetters, a strong iron belt passed round his waist, together with a collar of the same about his neck, and a prong also, that went down his back. These, engines of *correction* I recollect him to have said he had had upon him for *three months;* but *his Keeper* assured me *it was only for two months /"* In the same old Gaol of North-Gate, I likewise recollect were the only *iron gloves* I had ever seen, as the accompaniments of a British Prison. This was too striking an incident not to awaken my curiosity; which the Gaoler candidly gratified, by telling me "That he had lived for some years in the Leeward Islands, *where these things were frequently usedfor the Negroes;* and that upon his return to Chester, and being appointed to the office of Gaoler, he had got a pair made." If these iron gauntlets are not yet annihilated, I sincerely hope, for the credit of humanity, that they will soon quit the New-Gaol for ever.

From past circumstances let me now revert to some, that actually tend to disparage and deform this modern Prison; in which, with regret, I find neither the Act of Parliament for preserving the Health of Prisoners, nor the Clauses against their use of Spirituous Liquors, are as yet hung up. No bath provided, nor oven to purify foul or infected clothes. Neither Debtors nor Criminals, in Gaol or Bridewell, have coals allowed, or any Fuel whatever. No soap, or towels, for personal comfort and cleanliness. No employment furnished, to prevent the bane of idleness; and even if the Debtor can procure it from without the Prison, he must pay one shilling per week to the Gaoler, *for his permission* to work:—a hard tax upon industry! But, in January 1809, it was exacted from five Debtors; *viz,* a Hatter, a Limner, a Wireworker, a Tailor, and a Cabinet-maker.

Here are no books for a Visiting Magistrate to enter his Remarks, or to specify the attendances of Chaplain, Surgeon, &c. The court-yards want paving with flagstones, (of which there are plenty in the neighbourhood;) and having only mudbottoms, it is difficult to keep the Prison clean.

I was sorry to be informed, that the indecent, immoral, and unmanly practice of *whipping the Women* in the Bridewell is still continued, in defiance of the Act 32 Geo. III. which expressly prohibits it.

CHESTERFIELD. *Derbyshire.*
The Town Gaol.
Gaoler, *Thomas Shepherd,* who lives in the House; and is Deputy to Mr. George Gosling, as Bailiff".
Salary, none. Fees, one shilling on the Discharge of each Prisoner.
1805, Oct. 11th, Debtor, One.
Allowance, none whatever.
REMARKS.
This Gaol, for Debtors within the Hundred of Scarsdale, is the property of the *Duke of Devonshire,* who lets it to Mr. Gosling, together with the Tolls of the Market, at 18/. *12s.* per annum. It stands under the Town Hall, and consists of two rooms on the ground-floor, which open into a close passage, 25 feet long and 5 feet wide, lighted and ventilated by two iron-grated semicircular windows. The Men's room is 18 feet by IS; the Women's 25 feet by 14, which last has a copper in it; and both have iron-grated windows opening to the Street.

If the Debtor find his own bed and bedding, he pays nothing: but there are some rooms in the House, to which the Deputy Keeper furnishes bedding at 1. *6d.* and 2. per week, for those who are able to pay.

CHESTERFIELD. *Bridewell.*
Keeper, *Daniel Glossop,* a Cabinet-Maker. Salary, 30/.
Fees, 2. Garnish, 1. for *Coals.*
Chaplain, none; nor any religious attentions.
Surgeon, Mr. *John Cartledge.*
Number of Prisoners, 1805, Oct. 11th, Four. The average number annually confined here is *Twelve.*
Allowance, a four-penny loaf per day each; except when they work, so as to supply themselves from their earnings.
REMARKS.
This *Bridewell,* by the date in front, appears to have been built in 1614. It has three court-yards, one for the Men, and one for Women, of 45 feet by 15 each: the third a small one for the Women also, of 10 yards by 5, with a room in it about 12 feet square, in which I found a woman employed in stocking-weaving.

Here are likewise two day-rooms with fire-places, 15 feet square.

The Men Prisoners have one sleeping-cell upon the ground-floor, and two others above, each about 12 feet square; also a dark cell, of 9 feet square, set apart for *Solitary Confinement.* Half a guinea per annum is allowed for coals, to *heat Jlues for warming the cells.*

The Women-Prisoners both sleep and work in their day-room, where spinning wheels are provided for them by the County; and whatever they earn is their own. They have wooden bedsteads, with loose straw, two blankets, and a rug each.

The Gaol is well supplied with water, to which all the Prisoners have access.

A room in the Keepers House was appropriated to *two French Prisoners* in October 1805. Its size, 14 feet by 12, with fire-place, furniture, *feather-bed,* &c.

The Act for Preservation of Health, and Clauses against the use of Spirituous Liquors, not hung up.
I. ...: . " ".
CHICHESTER. *Sussex.*
The City Gaol, and Bridewell,
Gaoler, *John Humphreys,* Sergeant at Mace. Salary 20/. No Fees.
Surgeon, from the Parish, when wanted.

Number of Prisoners, 1804, Sept. 17, One.
Allowance. A *Quart Loaf* of bread per day; each of which, when I was here, weighed 2 lbs. 3 oz.
REMARKS.
Here is a small court-yard, of 25 feet by 13, with a sewer. A pump and bathing tub in the wash-house adjoining.

On the first floor is a good-sized room for Women. On the second floor are four rooms for Men, which open into a lobby, or passage, four feet wide. They have all glazed windows, with sloping blinds, to prevent communication with the street; and each has a straw bed in canvas on the boarded flooring, with three blankets in Winter, and two in Summer. They are well ventilated and lighted. The City furnishes straw.

None of the rooms have fire-pldces.

Bibles, Testaments, the Whole Duty of Man, and small devotional and other tracts, are furnished to the Prisoners, and religious Poor, by the Society in this City for Promoting Christian Knowledge, established 25th May, 1799.

The Rules and Orders are written on paper, and stuck up in the Gaol; but not being signed, I omit transcribing them.

No employment for the Prisoners. The Act for Preserving Health hung up; but not the Clauses against Spirituous Liquors.

The whole Prison is very clean.

There appears to have been formerly a Court held in a part of the Cathedral; to which adjoins a dungeon, 15 feet by 12, totally dark, except the borrowed light which it receives from an aperture over the Cloisters.

CLERKENWELL. *London.*
Gaoler, *Samuel Newport.* . #
Salary,-------" 400 0 0
Clerk, *William Beeby,* 2/. 2. per week----109-4 0'
Turnkeys, six, at *ll. Is.* per week each- 327 12 0 : Total 836 16 0.
Fees, as per Table. See Remarks. r Garnish, two pots of Beer.
Chaplain, Rev. Mr. *Evans.* Salary, 56/.
Duty, Prayers and Sermon on Sundays.
Surgeon, Mr. *Webb.* Salary, 300/. for

this Prison, and the House of Correction in Cold Bath Fields.

Allowance, one pound of bread per day, sent from the Baker's, in loaves of 2lbs. weight, every other day.

REMARKS.

This Prison, built in 1775, has, over the gate-way, two rooms, called " Between Gates,'' and "Bed-Prison;" each containing three beds. These are occasionally occupied by Prisoners brought in at night, who can pay one shilling the first night, and six-pence every night succeeding; and two sleep in a bed. Others, who cannot pay for this reception, are put into the *Strong Room,* which is about 16 feet square: On the Women's side of the Prison it has barrack-beds, but no bedding; and is lighted by two iron-grated windows.

Over the Turnkey's Lodge is a bed-chamber, furnished, and called the " Guinea Room," because the Prisoners who occupy it pay one guinea each per week.

From the outer gate is a passage to the gate of the Men's court, on the right hand, and to that of the Women on the left: to each of these, the descent is by six steps.

In the Men's court are two sheds, one 18 feet by 12, the other about 12 feet square, partly enclosed, and without windows. In each there is a table, with shelves for provisions, benches to sit upon, and a fire-place; to which a peck of coals per day is allowed in Summer, and half a bushel during the Winter.

The *Gates-Man* has a double allowance of bread, half a pound of meat, with the broth in which it is boiled, and a pint of porter daily. He likewise sleeps in the *Bed Ward,* hereafter noticed. His duty is to attend at the Inner Gate, and assist in cleansing the courts and sleeping wards.

Here are also two *Sheds-Men,* one of whom acts as Clerk in the Chapel, and the other as a Barber, to shave the Prisoners. They are likewise employed to keep the Prison clean, and receive the same allowance as the Gates-Man. N. B. The Prisoners thus occupied are what they here call *Fines,* or persons imprisoned for a certain limited time.

The *Night Ward,* (into which Prisoners are not permitted to go in the day-time, that the air in it may be fresh and cool,) is a building on the side of the court-yard, divided into two apartments. The ground floor of it, on the right, is called "Newgate Ward which has barrack-beds, without bedding; and above it is a room with nine wooden bedsteads flock-beds, two blankets to each, two sheets, and a rug; for the use of which each Prisoner pays one shilling the first night, six-pence every night after, and two sleep together. This room is called the " Bed Ward;" and over it, on the attic story, is the Men's sick ward, which has five iron bedsteads, and bedding for single persons; a fire-place also, with iron-grated and glazed windows.

The ground floor, on the left hand, is denominated "the Lower Ward," and has barrack bedsteads, without bedding. The chamber above this is called the " Middle Ward," and set apart for Felons: the attic story is of the same size, and appropriated to *Fines.* These rooms are of an irregular shape, measuring in the widest parts 32 feet by 28; nearly 10 feet high, and strongly planked all over, but without chimneys. For the free circulation of air, every room has in front, toward the courtyard, two windows, and three or four backward; all enclosed with iron bars, but, very properly, not glazed. In this court there is a dark cell, of 11 feet by 8 feet 7 inches, and 8 feet 8 inches high; with a barrack bed, for the refractory.

The Women's court has two sheds, or day-rooms, similar to those for the Men, and without windows; one 15 feet by 9, the other 12 feet by 10, with fire-places, coppers, benches, and table. A Gates-Woman is here stationed, who has a double allowance of bread for attending the Gate; and also two Sheds-Women, whose office is to clean the court-yard and sleeping-wards; for which they also have the same allowance of bread, and half a pound of meat daily, but no strong beer. The Prisoners thus employed are likewise called *Fines,*

On one side of the Women's court-yard, upon the ground floor, is the "Strong "Room" before-mentioned; and

over it, in a passage, or gallery, are five cabins, called *Pigeon Holes,* each of 9 feet 4 inches, by 4 feet 2; with a barrack bedstead for two Prisoners, feather beds, and bedding. In the passage room is a wooden turn-up bedstead, with bedding; and every Prisoner sleeping in any of these beds pays one shilling the first night, six-pence every night after, and two sleep in a bed.

Adjoining to the last-mentioned room is another, for Women *Fines,* 21 feet by 16 feet 9, with barrack-beds, and three windows looking to the court-yard.

Adjoining the Strong Room, and on the ground-floor, is the Lower Ward for women, who cannot pay for beds, but sleep on barrack bedsteads: this is 21 feet long by 16 feet 9, and has three iron-grated windows.

The Women's Infirmary is above stairs, and has five iron bedsteads, with bedding for single persons; it is 25 feet by 15, fitted up with fire-place, glazed windows, cupboard, and other conveniencies. The patients, at the discretion of the Surgeon, are supplied with better diet, &c. and a Woman Prisoner attends as Nurse, who is allowed a double dole of bread, with half a pound of meat, and a pint of porter per day.

The windows of both the men's and women's ward, are, as they should ever be, too high for the occupiers to look out at. All the staircases are of stone; the ground floors and courts are paved. In each court-yard is a pump, with cisterns, and New River water is laid in from the Main.

In the Chapel, the Men Prisoners are seated below, and the Women in the gallery above. Divine Service was well attended, when I was there on Sunday 19th July 1808, and the Prisoners appeared clean.

Witnesses for the Crown are carefully detained between-gates, in order to secure them from the mal-practice of other Prisoners. Here is no oven to purify infected cloathing, nor a bath for personal cleanliness; an essential accommodation, peculiarly needful in so crowded a Prison, especially during the Summer months, and where two thirds of the Prisoners constantly sleep in their wretched habiliments on the bare boards, without even straw afforded them for bedding.

Within the gate-way of entrance is affixed a board, on which, very properly, is painted as follows:

"A Table Of The Fees

"To be taken by the Keeper of *New Prison,* at Clerkenwell, in the Count' of Middlesex.

£. s. d.

M For keeping and discharging every person committed by a
  Warrant of Commitment------046
  For turning the Key at every such Person's Discharge---0 10
  T *ag. s.* fc
  For going with any Person before a Justice---«.--0 10
  For a Copy of Commitment---------01
  Prisoners brought in by Constables of the Night, and carried before Justices of the Peace, and discharged------020
  "By the Court,
  "Selby:
  "N.B. No Spirituous Liquors allowed to be brought in here."

Prisoners are discharged from hence at all hours, after payment of the Fees; but for failure in which they continue to be detained, unless the Magistrate writes " Poor" on the back of their Discharge.

The court-yards here are by much too small for the number of Prisoners: But both might be enlarged, and a salutary separation of the young beginner from the veteran in offence secured, by taking in a part either of the Keeper's Garden, or of the adjacent Field.

No money is given to the Prisoner at the time of discharge, so as to prevent an immediate recurrence to those predatory acts which brought him or her hither.

The Act for preservation of Health is not hung up, but the prohibitory Clauses against Spirituous Liquors are duly exposed for inspection; and the Gaol is kept very clean.

There are Rules and Orders, printed; but, being signed only by the Gaoler, I do not transcribe them.

Formerly, Mr. Wildman, a Salesman in Smithfield, and afterwards, his Widow, sent the Prisoners beef and beer twice a week; but this kind bounty has been discontinued many years, and I have constantly been told that no donations are sent hither now.

The allowance of bread is too scanty, in a place where there is no opportunity afforded of earning any thing by labour; and the want of bedding must at times be most severely felt, as not even straw is allowed to the poor and destitute Prisoners, who must sleep in their rags on the boarded floor.

gd3 I do not recollect having ever visited The New Prison, without seeing *Lunatics* confined in a place so very ill-adapted for them: And, whilst Persons committed for Fines, and lesser offences, are unavoidably associated with the daring and desperate Criminal, that Confinement which was intended for wholesome Correction, can prove no other than a Seminary of Vice; a sure introduction to the most infamous practices. COCKERMOUTH.

The County Bridewell.

Keeper, *Joseph Bowman.* Salary, 20/. Surgeon, Mr. *Bell,* who makes a Bill. It has a small court-yard, 21 feet by 12, and two sleeping-cells, one 18 feet by 10, the other 10 feet by 5: one of these is called *The Strong Room.* No bedding allowed, but loose straw upon the floor. No water accessible. Allowance, *2s.* per week. At my visits in 1802 and 1809, no Prisoners.

COLCHESTER. *Essex.*

The Castle Bridewell.

Gaoler, *John Smith.*

Salary, 30/. He is also allowed 3/. *per annum,* to furnish straw, and other 3/. *per annum,* to provide firing for the Prisoners. Fees, none.

Surgeon, Mr. *Newell,* who makes a Bill for Medicines; and has also Two Guineas a year, for reporting, quarterly, the state of the Prison.

Prisoners, 1801, Oct. 12th, One Man for Bastardy.

1805, Sept. 18th, Three disorderly Women. 1810, Sept. 24th, Three Men; one of them for Bastardy; the other two sick in bed.

Allowance, one pound and half of bread daily, and a quart of small beer.

REMARKS.

The *Castle* of Colchester was formerly the County Gaol. That part of it which is now the *Bridewell,* has one-large room, 20 feet by 14, and 12 feet high, with a fire-place. On one side of this room is another, with a window; and on the other side are two more rooms, at a right-angle with the former, and in the farthermost of them a window. These last three are lofty, and about 13 feet square: the partitions to them are iron gratings, to admit light and air from the grated window at each end. Here are also glazed windows, ready prepared to be put up in cold weather.

In the court-yard, about 17 feet square, excellent water is introduced by a pipe and cock: But of this area the Prisoners never have the use, though it is immediately under command of the Keeper's window.

In the chamber-story are two rooms appropriated to the *Women-Prisoners:* one of them, about 28 feet square, and 10 feet high, has a fire-place, and is used as a day-room; the other, which is over it, is 90 feet by 10, and 10 feet high. This is employed as their sleeping-room, and, as well as the rooms below, supplied with crib-bedsteads, straw-in-sacking beds, and two blankets each.

At my visit in October 1801, the only Prisoner was a Man for bastardy. It "was very cold weather; but he had no fire, neither were the glass windows put up. He was not permitted to come into the court-yard for exercise; water was brought to him by the Keeper; and of both these objects he had a confined and tantalizing view, through the gratings of his window. As he had no soul to converse with, employment might have beguiled the hours of captivity, and must have proved an evidence of humane attention. The-Keeper was from home; but at my subsequent visits he appeared rough, rude, and ignorant. He kept a Fox in the court, just under the Prisoner's window, the smell of which could not be very grateful.

A Gaoler should never be permitted to furnish his Prisoners with either food, fuel, or bedding. The Prison had just been white-washed, and I found it clean: But here was no religious attention: no employment. Neither the Act nor Clauses hung up.

COLCHESTER.
The Borough Gaol and Bridewell.
Gaoler, *John Hardy.* Salary, 12/. Fees, see Table.
Chaplain, none.
Surgeon, Mr. *Gritton.* Salary, none. He makes a Bill.
Number of Prisoners, Debtors. Felons, &c. Disorderly Women.
1801, Oct. 12th, ---0----1----10 1805, Sept. 18th,---1-4--8 1810, Sept. 24th,---0----6 ----6
Allowance, to *Debtors,* unable to maintain themselves, one pound and half of good wholesome bread, and a quart of small beer, daily. To *Felons,* and other criminal Prisoners, sixpence a day, and the like quantity of small beer.

REMARKS.
This once-despicable Gaol, of which I gave an ample description in the Gentleman's Magazine for August 1804, page 705, has lately received great improvements.

Debtors are *now* separated from Criminal-Prisoners; and have a spacious courtyard assigned them, of about 60 feet by 50, with a water-closet very conveniently placed. Also a day-room, about 14 feet square, with a flagged floor, two large sash windows, and a fire-place; to which two bushels of coals per week are allowed, from Michaelmas to Lady-Day, and one bushel weekly, from Lady-Day to Michaelmas.

In the chamber-story are three rooms; two of which have one bed each, and the third will contain two or more beds, if needed: They have boarded floors, fire-places, and glazed sash-windows, which command a very extensive view. They are liberally furnished by the Town with bedsteads, chamber utensils, water pitchers, and brooms; but the Prisoners must provide their own beds and bedding, or pay to the Gaoler, as per Table.

"table Of Fees,
"To be taken by the Keepers of the Debtors' Gaol of the Borough of Colchester. *s. d.* "For the Turnkey's Fee on admitting every Debtor------10
For the bed and bedding of each Debtor per night, provided that not more than two be put into one bed------------04
For the Turnkey's Fee on the going forth of every Debtor----1 o
For the Gaoler's Fee upon every Debtor's Discharge------134
"*Moot-Hall,* Colchester. The foregoing Fees were, at the General Quarter Session of the Peace, holden in and for the said Borough, on Monday the 10th day of July 1809, seen, examined, and allowed.
"By the Court.
"W. Mason, Town-Clerk." *tgw'* A Woman, in this Gaol, attends the Female Debtors, and they have the exclusive use of the court-yard daily, from twelve till two.

That part of the Gaol which is appropriated to *Felons,* and other criminal Prisoners, continues in much the same state as at my former visits; and consists of a room, about 15 feet square, with two iron-grated windows, straw-insacking beds, three blankets, and a rug, laid on the boarded floor. I found it occupied by six disorderly Women. Another room, 16 feet by 11, with one iron-grated window, had four *Men-Felons* in it; and a third room, 15 feet by *9,* with a very small irongrated window, held two other Felons. The bedding in these two last rooms is similar to that for the Females. In each apartment a covered tub was made to serve as a sewer; and it is needless to add that all were shamefully offensive.

I had the pleasure to learn that the two dark *strong-rooms* below, of 16 feet each by 11, were at length deemed unfit for human confinement, and I found them far better filled with lumber.

The whole of this *Felon's-part* of the Gaol is to be taken down, and likewise some old buildings adjacent; which, from the plans I have seen, will afford space for a convenient Felons' Prison, with a court-yard adjoining, which cannot fail of doing credit to the respectable Borough of Colchester.

The Surgeon here has a discretionary power, with respect to the diet and bedding of sick Prisoners under his care.

COLD BATH FIELDS. *Middlesex.*
The County House of Correction.
Gaoler, *Thomas Arts:* now *William Adkins.*
Salary, 400/. Fees, see Table.
£. *s. d.*
Task-Master and Store-Keeper, Salary, 2*l*. 2*s*. per week--109 4 0
Clerk, Salary per week, 2*l*. 2*s*.----109 4 0
Turnkeys, Ten, at one guinea per week each-----546 0 0
Watchmen, Two, at one guinea per week each----109 40
Chaplain, Rev. Mr. *Evans.*
Duty, Prayers and Sermon on Sunday; and Prayers twice a week. Salary, 20/. and also an allowance of 30/. per annum for superintending the education of those children in the House of Correction, who are properly kept separate and apart from their parents. For *Clerkenwell Prison,* likewise, the same emolument of 50/.
Surgeon, Mr. *Webbe.*
Salary, 300/. for this Prison, and Clerkenwell Bridewell.
Number of Prisoners, See the *Remarks.*

Allowance, to each a loaf of one pound weight every day. A pint of gruel for breakfast every morning. For dinner each other day, a quart of broth, made from beef, with oatmeal, celery, onions, leeks, pepper, and salt: and on the alternate days, six ounces of meat for dinner, instead of broth.

tC The total expence of their Prison diet is estimated at *seven pence three farthings* each per day: And, in addition to this County allowance, their friends are permitted to bring them any proper kinds of provision. REMARKS.
This extensive Gaol, which comprises also the County Bridewell, or House of Correction, is encircled by a boundary wall, enclosing nearly four acres of land; and to it are committed *Debtors* from the Court of Conscience for the Tower Hamlets.

From the best accounts I could collect out of the books, it appears, that in the course of eleven years, from the nth of June 1800, to the 21st of May 1810, the whole number of *Debtors* sent hither has been *seven hundred and fifty; viz.* Detained their full term of Imprisonment------332

Discharged by small Compositions--------353

And, the whole Number who paid Debt and Costs----65 Number of *Criminal Prisoners* received within the same period, viz.

By Commitments----------93421 g

Upon Conviction----------2216 J

To which add the *Debtors* (P. 142)---------750

Making the total of Prisoners to be---12308.

The Prison of *Cold Bath Fields,,* now under consideration, stands in front of Bayne's Row. The entrance to it is the main gate, with the First Turnkey's room adjoining; from whence a court-yard, of about 35 feet, leads on to the Inner Turnkey's Lodge.

From the iron rails next the Gaoler's house, to those nearest the Prisoner's workyard, is another court, 48 feet in length, paved with stone, which forms a carriage way into the Prison.

At the end of the court-yard next the main gate, stands the Inner Turnkey's lodge, which.has two rooms above it. The gateway below, leading on to a courtyard in front of the office, of about 28 feet by 12 feet 9 inches wide, is paved with broad Purbeck stone, and has an iron gate, with a wooden one also across it.

The former gate is where the friends of Prisoners are admitted who come to visit them, and stands about four feet distant from the wooden gate, at which the Prisoners are allowed to receive their friends; both gates being under cover, and having between them a door belonging to the Inner Turnkey's lodge.

Another court-yard, of 45 feet by 42, leads from the last-mentioned lodge, and extends to the front of the Turnkey's office. The office itself, 15 feet by 14 feet 6, has two rooms above it: one of them is for the Gaol Committee; and over it is the Store-keeper's apartment, 17 feet by 16.

A passage of 5 feet 9 inches wide, reaches from the court-yard just noticed, to the kitchen. The *Chapel,* which is above the passage, and in the centre of the whole building, is so constructed as to receive all the six classes of Prisoners, male and female; and contains, also, a pew for the Magistrates, the Communion Table, and seats for the Keeper and Turnkeys. On the 19th of June, 1808, I attended Divine Service here, when all the Prisoners were cleanly in their persons, and decently attentive to a very suitable discourse.

The kitchen, 33 feet by 32, is furnished with two cast-iron boilers, for the use of the Prisoners.

In the interior of the Gaol are eight other court-yards, extending each about 66' feet from the doors to the water-closets in them, and from the front of the cells to the back-wall of the Colonnades, 32 feet 6 inches wide. These courts contain each from seven to nine cells, and a water-closet. The 'staircases to the different apartments are about five feet wide, and the several passages to the galleries and cells, about 4 feet 6 inches.

Next the garden grounds also are eight smaller court-yards, about 41 feet by 23, surrounded by iron rails; arid a ninth, *16* feet *6* by 13 feet 10. These are all appropriated to the Prisdners for taking air and exercise.

A spacious garden is thrown round the whole Prison, and extends to the boundarywall on all sides. On the right-hand from the Main-Gate is the *Gaoler's House,* which I am given to understand was *built by the Prisoners* here confined, and contains two cellars, and as many kitchens, a water closet, two parlours, and the Keepers office. On the first-floor are a drawing-room, dining ditto, and a bedchamber; on the second-floor, three bed-rooms. The house is enclosed within a small iron palisade, and a gate (said also to have been made by the Prisoners): And on the right of the Inner Turnkey's lodge is the Keepers wash-house, with coppers, and other Utensils.

On the left of the Main-Gate is the working-yard, containing sheds for coals, and a large one for the drying of oakum; under which last is sunk a capacious saw-pit, and nearly adjoining, on the left of the Inner Turnkey's lodge, are placed an oven for fumigating clothes, with various shops for shoe-rtiakers, taylors, blacksmiths, and other handicraft Prisoners.

The garden is cultivated, sown, and planted with different kinds of vegetables for the use of the Prisoners, and the labour of it is done by themselves, under the Gaoler's direction. The Gaol is white-washed at least twice a year, which is also performed by the Prisoners; and it is supplied with water plentifully from a well on the East-side, which is carried to different parts of the building, by means of an engine occasionally set to work by two of the Prisoners. Here is also a large workrobin at the top over the well, of 27 feet 10 inches by 2Q feet 3 inches wide.

The Debtors here have, on the Eastern-side of the Prison, a court-yard, 35 feet by 20; a day-room about 12 feet square; and two sleeping-cells, 7 feet by 5 feet ' inches on the first story, furnished with wooden bedsteads, a straw-in-ticking bed, one blanket in Summer, two in Winter, and a rug each. The County humanely allows them a peck of coals per day.

On the South-west Side, being the department of the Females, is a small well, 'supplied from the one before-mentioned, to serve this part of the Prison; which is done by an engine set to work by the disorderly Females. Over this well, likewise, there is a large work-room of the same dimensions as the former; and also a courtyard, of 37 feet 9 inches by 28 feet, in which are the Turnkey's apartments.

At the South-comer is the general laundry, or wash-house, with copper, washingtroughs, &c. in which the *Female Criminals* are employed to wash and get up the linen of' the Prisoners at large. Here is also a drying-yard next the garden, of 41 feet by 23, and another for the like purpose, of I3 feet 10. Over the wash-house is a work-room for the Females, 25 feet by 15; and above this, at the top of the building, is the *Female Infirmary,* of the same dimensions.

At the East-corner is a day-room, for

the first class of *Male-Felons,* about 23 feet square; over which, on the first floor, is another day-room, set apart for the aged and infirm Prisoners, of like dimensions; and above all these, on the top of the

Prison, is the Male Infirmary.

Statement Of The Number Of Rooms.

Infirmaries for the Male and Female Sick-------2

Work-Rooms-5

Ditto for Pass-Vagrants------------2

Ditto for disorderly Females----------2

Ditto for the Aged and Infirm---------2

Ditto for *Debtors*-------------1

Ditto for Female Misdemeanours---------2

Ditto for Male ditto------------2

Best Rooms, furnished by the County, at 10. *6d.* per week--5

Total-------23.

The number of *cells* was 366, each 6 feet 3 inches wide by 8 feet 3 inches long, and 11 feet high. Of these, ten are *solitary* cells; and four of the others have been laid into two: so that the original number of sleeping-cells is at present reduced to 354

The *distribution of employment* into its various branches is as follows, and deserves to be recorded; viz.

1. White-washing and painting the Prison. 2. Washing and mending the Prisoners' linen. 3. Making and mending their clothes and shoes. 4. Carpenters' and Smiths' work for the Gaol. 5. Making rope and spun-yarn, and spinning tow. *6.* Knotting yarn, and picking oakum. 7. Working in the garden, and at the water-engines.

S. Sweeping and cleaning the Prison; and

0. Attending as Nurses to the Infirm and Sick.

The Prisoners (except such only as stand on the Surgeon's List,) are constantly engaged at their several occupations; and, during the hours of labour, are kept as much separated as the nature of their respective employments will admit. Of their earnings they are allowed one sixth part, or two-pence in every shilling; which they receive at the expiration of their Term of Imprisonment, and are then discharged without paying Fees. N. B. No Prisoner who appears to be distressed, is sent forth, without first receiving some relief, either in money or clothes; and sometimes they have both.

"Table Of Fees,

"To be taken by the Keeper of Cold-Bath-Fields Prison, or House of Correction, at Clerkenwell, in the County of Middlesex.

s. d.

"For keeping and discharging every Prisoner committed by Warrant-4 6 For turning the Key at every such Prisoner's Discharge-----*1* o

For a Copy of every Commitment-------------i 4

For going with every Prisoner before a Justice-------10

Prisoners brought in by Constables of the Night, and carried before a

Justice----------20

"By the Court,

"Butler."

At the South-west front of this Prison are two store-rooms, for depositing the different articles of provision, clothing, bedding, &c. for the use of the Prisoners; and also for laying by the clothes of such as are convicted, from Session to Session, either at *Justice-Hall,* in the Old Bailey, or from other of His Majesty's Courts belonging to the County of Middlesex: which clothes, upon the Prisoners' coming in, are examined; and, if found in an offensive state, are fumigated, washed, and carefully kept separate, till the time of their discharge. Frequently, however, they enter the Prison so wretchedly equipped, that their apparel is obliged to be destroyed.

Since writing the above account some alterations have taken place; *viz.*

A room, heretofore used as a store-room, has been turned into a day-room for Male-Prisoners detained for misdemeanours, which was much wanted. The number of day-rooms is thus increased to *seventeen,* and there is a fire-place in each.

The Old Infirmary-rooms have been converted into foul-wards; and two new Infirmaries, (large and airy apartments,) are built over the *tanks,* or wells.

All the sewers have been turned into water-closets, and cisterns very properly constructed for their supply.

A new stove has been put up in the *Chapel,* which is thus rendered warm and comfortable.

There are still some other improvements which this Prison is very capable of receiving; and after being specified in detail by the judicious Commissioners appointed to examine into the state of it, they will, no doubt, be readily adopted by the considerate Magistrates of the County of Middlesex. COVENTRY. *fFaruHckshire.*

The City and County Gaol.

Gaoler, *Basil Goode.* Salary, 120/.

Fees, Felons, none. Debtors, See Table. Transports, the expence of conveying them. Garnish, now abolished.

Chaplain, none; except to attend on Convicts under Sentence of Death.

Surgeon, Mr. *Whitwell;* who makes a Bill.,

Number of Prisoners, Debtors. Felons, &c.

1800, March 26th,------2-------9. 1802, Jan. 26th, 7 8. 1803, Aug. 22d,------3-15. 1805, Nov. 1st, 2--7. 1807, July 27th, 2-------4. 1808, July 31st,------5 9. 1809, Aug. 21st,------3

And Three for Bastardy.

Allowance, to Prisoners of all descriptions, a sixpenny loaf every other day, sent in from the Baker's. Weight, at my last visit, 2 lbs. 2oz.

REMARKS.

This Gaol, built in the year 1772, stands in a very close part of the City. Here is one court-yard only, of about 60 feet by 40, which is common to Debtors, Felons, and every description of Prisoners; and a day-room, called "The *Den"* from its being the place of general and promiscuous association. To this room the Corporation allows lcwt. of coals in Summer, and 2cwt. in Winter, the price of which, at my visit in 1809, was *8% d.* per cwt. This, surely, is but a scanty allowance, where coals are so abundant, and so cheap.

Seven lodging-rooms are provided

for Master's-Side Debtors, to which the Gaoler furnishes beds, at 3$. per week; or, if two sleep together, at 2. weekly each.

Here is a common ward for poor Debtors, to whom the City allows a *bed*stead, with loose straw, (which is said to be changed every three weeks,) a blanket, and a rug, for which they pay *six-pence* a week. Women Felons have only one room.

There are two other rooms, which open into the court-yard, and were intended for Prisoners; But one of these I found filled with straw, and the other with the Gaoler's coals, although he has a good coal-cellar in the house.

To their *horrid dungeons,* (which still remain a disgrace to the City,) there is a descent by twelve steps, to a narrow passage, 4 feet wide. The dungeons, four in number, are about 9 feet by 6, and at the top have a little grated aperture, 11 inches by 7, which admits a glimmering light from the court-yard above, just sufficient to make" darkness visible." All of them are damp, and offensive.

A *Boultin* of straw (long wheaten straw, about 24lbs. weight, so called) is said to be allowed to each Felon, every three weeks. The bedding consists of two rhgs and two blankets; which, as well as the straw, I have always found nearly worn out, and very dirty. I was told that torches of pitch, or tar, were Occasionally burnt in these dungeons, to dry and purify them; and that, now and then, they were fumigated with vinegar. When I went down to them, we always had lighted candles, to behold, what?—the discredit of a large Manufacturing Town, thus manifesting its natural apprehensions of disease, and probable infection!

The Gaoler seems to have overlooked that Clause of the 14th Geo. III. which prohibits Prisoners from being kept underground: for, of the three men committed for bastardy, one of them, Jonathan Hobley, not having money to pay for a bed, was thrust down into a dungeon every night: while two *convicted Felons,* being able to pay, were indulged with the Debtors' room to sleep in.

A private passage from the Gaol conducts Prisoners into Court for trial.

This Prison might be much improved, by enclosing a small piece of ground adjacent, and turning it into a separate court for the Women Prisoners; in consequence of which the opprobrious caverns before-noticed might be happily annihilated. And, if a few old houses in *Pope's-Head Alley,* were pulled down and added, a new Gaol might be built, or the present rendered sufficiently large for the City.

"Table of Fees,
"Settled at the General Quarter Session for CbvlEttrttY, ath Jan. 1797.
"Every Prisoner on the Keeper's side, if he has a bed! to-him-*Jt. s. d.* self, pays by the week-----------030
Those Prisoners on the Keeper's siile, who have a bed between two,, pay by the week each,----------0 2 d
If on the Common side, each Prisoner, weekly,----0 0 6
To the Gaoler for discharging every Prisoner, or detained in custody 0 13' 4
To the Turnkey-on every such Discharge---.-----0 2 0
To the Under Sheriff for every Discharge------0 4 0
For receiving and entering every Declaration------010
For a Copy of each Warrant against a Prisoner----0 1 0 *Pot* every Certificate of the cause of a Prisoner's being detained in Prison, in order to his being discharged------030
Approved 27 Mar. 1797. B. Butterwortu, Mayor. I. Carter.
N Grose. John Clarke. N. Norman.
G. Howlette. I. Williamson.

The Act for preserving Health is conspicuously hung up in the Gaol, but not the Clauses against Spirituous Liquors. The whole Prison is very dirty.

COVENTRY *btty Bridewell.*
Keeper, *John Hussdl,* a Shoe-Clicker. Salary, 20/. Fees, 1.
Chaplain, none.' Surgeon, Mr. *iPhitweil;* makes a Bill.
Number of Prisoners, ISO0, March 26th,----*2 f* 1807, July 27th,---12 1803, Aug. 22d,----5 1805, Nov. 1st,----6 1S08, July 31st,--4 1809, Aug. 21st,---3

Allowance, The same as for the City Gaol.
REMARKS.
This Prison was formerly the old Town Hall: It wa6 afterwards used as a Riding School; but at length converted into a large work-room, with two other very dark lodging-rooms for men. Here is no court-yard for their use. The workroom,' now paved with flag-stone, has a fire-place, and fuel allowed. Of the two lodgingrooms, one is now converted into a cell for the refractory; the other is called, very suitably, " *The Dungeon:*" and in lieu of them, four new cells, each *9 feet by 7,* are built in part of the large work-room, which have boarded floors, straw for sleeping on, a blanket, and two rugs each. Up stairs is a room for vagrants, and one in another part, for faulty apprentice boys.

The Women's ward has a small court-yard, with a sewer in it; and one room above stairs, with three beds, and bedding, like those in the City Gaol.

The Women were winding silk, procured them by theKeeper, who receives one third of their earnings. The City allows coals for the Bridewell. Neither the Act nor Clauses hung up. The Prison very clean.

COWBRIDGE, *Glamorganshire.* See *P. 123.*—CROYDON, *Surrey.* See *P. 116.*
DARTPORD. *Kent.*
The Bridewell.
i
Gaoler, *Thomas Okill;* now *Robert Okill.* Salary, 55/.
Fees; Felons, 13s. *4d.* Misdemeanors, *6s. 8d.* No Table.
No religious attentions. Surgeon, Mr. *Peet;* makes a Bill.
Number of Prisoners, 1801, Sept, 24th,----7 1808, July 13th,----36 1804, Sept. 26th,----6 1810, July 8th,----17. 1807, Sept. 8th,----14

Allowance, three half-quartern loaves per week. Those Prisoners, who are committed for more than one month, have the fourth-part of a quartern loaf more per week; and the whole of their earnings, when employed.
REMARKS.
The Men's court-yard here is 40 feet long by 22 feet, and has a fire-place for

cooking their provision in dry weather; but in wet weather it is dressed in the infirmary-room, which is at the upper end of the Court. The latter is 14 feet 7 inches by 11 feet 6, with glazed windows, and a fire-place, barrack bedsteads, straw-in-sacking bed, one blanket, and a rug; to which an addition is made in case of sickness, if ordered by the Surgeon. Their common-ward, or day-room, is 26 feet by 17; and they have likewise two sleeping-cells; one of which, 12 feet by 11, with two iron-grated windows, has only loose straw on the boarded floor to sleep upon: the other, 11 feet by 7, and totally dark, is to confine the refractory.

Here is also another ward, 22 feet by 11 feet 6 inches, for faulty Apprentices, and other servants.

The Women have a court-yard, of 25 feet by 18; adjoining to which is their first ward, or day-room, 13 feet 8 inches square, with wooden bedsteads, straw-insacking beds, one blanket to each, and a rug. The second ward is 14 feet 6 inches square, and 9 feet 6 inches high, with straw-in-sacking laid on the floor. All the sleeping-rooms are on the ground-flpor.

I have seldom met with any of the Prisoners here in irons, the Keeper very justly observing, "that he finds mildness to do better than harsh severity of treatment." Their employment is generally to pick oakum. They have a pump and sewer in «ach court-yard..
DEAL. *Kent.*
Gaoler, *Thomas Langley,* Sergeant at Mace. Fees, 2a
Prisoners, 24th Sept. 1804, One Woman, for shop-lifting; the first who had been 10th Aug. 1806, None. committed here.

Allowance, Sixpence a day.
REMARKS.
This Gaol is a new building, at the back of the market-place. Adjoining to it is a small court-yard; but, as being insecure, the Prisoners have not the use of it. Here is one large room, 24 feet by 12, very lofty, light, and well-ventilated, with double doors, a pump, stone sink, and a sewer. Also two sleeping-cells, 7 feet by 4, which have dwarf partitions, and wood-grated roofs; straw, on crib-bedsteads, with two blankets: and one dark room, 17 feet by 8, with an iron-grated window.

The only Debtors sent hither are from the Court of Conscience.
DEAN, (called LITTLE-DEAN.) *Gloucestershire.*
The House of Correction.
Keeper, *Robert Gunn.*
Salary, 40/.; with a ton of coals to keep the Prison well aired, and 20.y. for hi attendance at each Quarter Session. Fees, none.
Chaplain, Rev. Mr. *Jones.* Salary, 20l. Duty, Prayers twice a week.
Surgeon, *Mr. Phillips.* He makes a Bill.
Number of Prisoners, 5th of Sept. 1806, Three.
Allowance, one pound and a half of good wheaten bread, from the Baker's, in loaves; several of which I saw weighed, and they were of full weight.
..' REMARKS.
This Prison was first inhabited on the 18th of Nov. 1791. The boundary-wall encloses about an acre and three quarters of ground. The Turnkey's lodge is at the entrance-gate on the left, and over it his sleeping-room. On the right, a warm and cold bath, and a fumigating-room, where the Prisoners, on coming in, are washed; and if ragged, or offensively clad, County clothing is put on before they are admitted to the interior of the Prison, which stands in the centre of the area.

The approach to the Keeper's house is through a small garden, with a close wooden fence on each side. On the ground-floor, in front, are the Gaoler's office, and the Sessions-room; the latter opening into a neat Chapel, in the centre of the building, and separating the Gaoler's kitchen and wash-house, which command a view of the two court-yards behind.

The Prisoners are divided into classes, and have four courts, about 42 feet square, a pump and sewer in each, with open wood palisades; which being *16* feet distant from the boundary-wall, the Keeper has within it a convenient kitchen garden for vegetables.

In front of the building, on each side of the Keeper's house, is a work-room, 18 feet by 7 feet 7, with stone seats in each, and a fire-place: also two day-cells,, of 7 feet *6* by 5 feet *6,* and 10 feet high, on one side; and three similar cells on the other. Above stairs are eleven sleeping-cells, and one for *solitary confinement.* These lead into a stone gallery, with open railing towards the front court-yards.

On each side of the Chapel, a passage on the ground-floor, 5 feet wide, separates the back work-rooms and five day-cells from those in front of the building; the same, likewise, on the *upper-story,* where the twelve back cells open into the passage. On this story are also two sleeping-rooms for the Keeper, two Infirmaries with glazed windows, and two bedsteads in each; a store-room for the Prisoners' apparel, and a small dispensary-room, with a fire-place, for the use of the Surgeon.

Every sleeping-cell has an iron-grating, with inside shutters, and is 8 feet long by *6,* and 10 feet high to the crown of the arch; fitted up with a perforated cast-iron bedstead each, straw-mattress, a hair-stuffed bed, two blankets, two sheets, changed monthly; a coverlet lined with flannel, and a woollen nightcap.

An excellent reservoir in the garden affords a constant supply of water. Here is but little employment for the Prisoners; but if those of handicraft trades, taylors, shoemakers, &c. can procure it from without, and maintain themselves, they have the *whole of their earnings*; but if otherwise, one half only. Soap, towels, mops, pails, and brooms are allowed by the considerate Magistrates, to keep the Prisonersand Bridewell clean.

The number of Commitments, from the first opening of the Prison to the 9th August, 1806, was *one hundred and sixty.*

Here are cells for lodging twenty-four Prisoners, and the greatest number confined at one time is *six.* Books are kept here, in which the Visiting-Magistrates, Chaplain, and Surgeon enter their respective Remarks. Prayer Books are allowed to the Prisoners, who in all respects are well attended to. The whole building is clean and well-ventilated, and the same excellent Rules and Regulations are here established and observed, as in all the other Gaols of this exemplary County of *Gloucester* DENBIGH. *North Wales.*

Gaoler, *Thomas Williams.* Salary, 6*l.* No Fees.

Allowance, sixpence a day. Prisoners, 29 Oct. 1802, None.

The Gaol, built in 1790, stands in the middle of the High Street, and consists of three rooms, about 9 feet by *6* feet each, lighted by an aperture in the wall 3' inches by 8. Straw, on brick floors.

No Court, no water: The Prison very dirty: The Keeper lives at a distance.

The Prison called The *Black Hole,* under the Town Hall, is now converted into a shop.

DERBY. *The County Gaol, and House of Correction.*

Gaoler, *William Eaton.*

Salary, 170*l.* and 30*l.* for the House of Correction; also 8*l.* 8. for straw, and 2*l.* 12. 6*d.* for Coals. Fees, Debtors, and Felons, each 17. 4*d.* besides which the Under Sheriff claims of every Debtor 6*s.* 8*d.* for his *liberate*. Transports, *jl.* each to Woolwich, and 10/. to Portsmouth.

Garnish, abolished.

Chaplain, Rev. *Ellis Henry,* now Rev. *Nicholas-Bailey.*

Duty, Prayers on Monday and Wednesday; Prayers and Sermon on *Saturday;* and daily attends Convicts while under Sentence of Death. Salary, 35 /.

Surgeon, Mr. *Francis Fox.*

Allowance, two twelve-penny loaves per week, sent in from the Baker's, weight 16th Nov. 1801, 5lbs. 7oz. and 9th Oct. 1805, 4lbs. each. When a Debtor obtains his sixpences, he ceases to have the County Bread, REMARKS.

This Gaol is situated on *Nun's Green:* the front of it is occupied by the Keeper, and extends 126 feet, including the passage leading to the Garden, of 5 feet wide; the depth is 121 feet; so that when the width of the passage is taken off, it forms a complete square. It was finished and inhabited in 1757, and the situation is airy and healthy.

The Keeper's back rooms command all the court-yards, except that assigned for the Vagrants.

Here is one large court-yard, 82 feet by 43, well supplied with both hard and soft water, common to the Debtors, and Men Prisoners in the House of Correction. But Debtors have the exclusive privilege of walking on the flat roof, which is 90 feet by *26*. They have also a large day-room, 20 feet by 15, and 10 feet *6* inches high, with an oven and utensils for frugal cookery: to which add eight sleeping and work rooms above stairs, of the average size of about 17 feet 6 by 11 feet, and 9 feet 3 inches high; with fire-places, glazed windows, and wooden bedsteads. Chaff beds, two blankets, two sheets, a bolster and a rug, are furnished by the Keeper, at six pence each per week; but if the Debtor finds his own bed he pays nothing. Convenient water-closets are placed at the end of the lobbies or passages, to which they have access in the night time; they have also an exceeding good cold bath, and a copper for warm water.

There are no work-rooms either in the Gaol or House of Correction, nor any employment furnished by the County; but the humane Gaoler frequently procures them employment in weaving of Calicoes. They are furnished with looms from the Town, at *four-pence* per week, and receive all they earn.

The Women Debtors have a separate court-yard, 23 feet 9 inches by 12 feet 6, supplied with hard and soft water, and a sewer in it. Their four lodging-rooms are up a flight of 18 steps; the ayerage size about 12 feet square, and 9 feet high: They have each a fire-place and glazed window, and are fitted up with bed and bedding, the same as the Men's. Two of the lower of these rooms, are occasionally assigned to Women Felons, and misdemeanours.

Men Felons have a court-yard 93 feet by 43, supplied with water and a sewer, like the last-mentioned; also a day-room 25 feet by 18, and 10 feet high, with an oven, and proper utensils for simple-cooking. A door opens from it into a lobby of 24 feet by 3 feet 4 inches; in which there are four sleeping-cells on the groundfloor, 7 feet by 7 feet 4 inches, and 8 feet 3 inches high, with boarded floors, sacking filled with straw, two blankets, and a rug. To these cells warm air can be introduced, by means of flues under the floors, which keep them perfectly dry. The only light, however, that these cells enjoy, (and that borrowed,) is from an aperture over the doors, each 12 inches by *6*; so that when the door is shut, they are almost totally dark, and ventilation is very much obstructed.

Near to these is another door, that opens into the court-yard. The lobby here is 25 feet *6* inches long, and 3 feet wide, and contains three cells on the ground-floor, of about the same dimensions as those above described: two of them equally dark and ill ventilated: the third has an iron grating, which looks into the Debtors' Court, and is much preferable to any of the others. Into this cell a Convict is put when left for execution; and there is a slip or day-room near, of 12 feet *6* by *6* feet, with glazed window, a fire-place, table, chairs, and religious books, where the Chaplain daily attends him.

The humanity of the considerate Magistrates likewise allows to Criminals in this unhappy situation, a hot dinner every day, and tea, morning and afternoon.

"Table Of Fees.

"Derbyshire, to wit

"At the General Quarter Sessions held at *Bakewell,* on Tuesday the 10th July, 4th year of George III, 1764; before the Rev. Sir *John Every,* Bart, the Rev. *John Simpson,* Clerk; *Philip Gell, John Twigg, Henry Thornhill,* and *Joseph Briggs,* Esquires, Justices, &c. Leonard Fosbrooke, Esq. Sheriff.

"It is Ordered that the following Fees be taken by the Keeper, and no other.

For the lodging of every Prisoner in his house per week-.--0 2 6

For the Discharge of each Prisoner out of Custody----0 13 4

To the Turnkey-020

For the Copy of every Warrant----------010

For signing a certificate, in order to obtain a Supersedeas--0 2 0

For registering each Declaration-----------010

For attending with every Prisoner, in order to give bail, or be otherwise discharged------------020

"And it is further ordered, that the Clerk of the Peace do cause this order to be printed, and the Keeper of the Gaol do observe the same, upon pain of being prosecuted according to Law. By the Court, Heathcote, Clerk of the Peace.

"We, the Judges of Assize for the County of Derby, have reviewed, and do hereby confirm, the above-written Table of Fees. Given under our hands, at Derby, the 11th day of August, 1764. T. Parker. E. Clive."

The House-of-Correction Prisoners here have one common court-yard with the Debtors. Their day-room is 17 feet 6 inches by *16* feet 6, and 11 feet 3 inches high; with a fire-place, and glazed window. There is also a room on the groundfloor, of 7 feet 6 by 7 feet, for Deserters; supplied with wooden bedsteads and bedding, the same as to the other Prisoners. Above-stairs are two sleeping-rooms, 17 feet *6* inches by 16 feet *6,* and 11 feet three inches high; and also a small room, similar to that for Deserters. These have all convenient water-closets, to which, there is access in the night time

Vagrants have a separate court, out of sight, at the farther end of the Gaol, 39 feet by 20, with a sewer in it; but no water laid on, which is carried or sent to them by the Keeper four times a day.

On the ground-floor are two rooms, 12 feet 6 by 10 feet, and 7 feet 6 inches high, with a fire-place and glazed window; to which beds and bedding are furnished, as for the other Prisoners: and above these are two others, of the same dimensions.

The Chapel is *26* feet by 25, and 10 feet high; with four sash windows, and pewed off in such a manner, that the women and men are unseen by each other: the Clergyman has a way into it through the Keeper's house. All the Prisoners, (Roman Catholicks excepted,) are required to attend it; and Bibles, Prayer-Books, and Religious Tracts, are furnished to them by the County.

Over the Chapel are two Infirmary Rooms, each 35 feet by 11, and 9 feet 3 inches high, with fire-places and glazed windows. The wall, which has *eleven courses of loose bricks on the stone coping,* is 21 feet high.

Here is a man, *Thomas Jenney,* who goes round the Country at Christmas-time, with a Book soliciting relief for the Debtors, in which the donors enter their names and subscriptions. The amount of his collection at Christmas 1802, was thirty-one Pounds, and the number of Debtors, twenty-three: at Christmas 1804 it was about thirty-two Pounds; for the trouble of collecting which, he receives one fourth. For the Felons, also, there is a Woman who calls in at Gentlemen's houses three Sundays in the month, for the like purpose, and has a quarter part of the sum collected: it is said to amount generally to three or four shillings a Sunday. She carries with her a tin box, which has an aperture for receiving these casual donations; but, at my visit in 1809, I found the custom had been discontinued.

All descriptions of Prisoners have a hot dinner on Christmas and New-Year's Day, with bread and cheese at supper, and each a pint of ale.

An exceedingly good cold bath is here provided, and a copper for warm water. No oven, however, for purifying the offensive apparel of Prisoners, nor is Countyclothing statedly allowed; but, if a Prisoner be very ragged, he is put into better garb at the County's expence. All are humanely discharged in the morning, and have money given to them, according to their distance from home.

The Act for Preservation of Health, and Clauses against the use of Spirituous Liquors are both hung up. The whole Prison is very clean, and frequently visited by the Magistrates.

DERBY. *Town or Borough Gaol.*
Gaoler, *Charles Smith.*
Salary, 50/. for Gaol and Bridewell.
Fees, Debtors, and Felons, 12. *Sd.* No Table. For Transports, the ex pence of conveyance.
Garnish, (not abolished,) 1.
Chaplain, none, nor any religious attentions whatever.

Surgeon, Mr. *Haden;* who makes a Bill.
Number of Prisoners, Debtors. Felons, &c. Deserters.
1800, Nov. 16th,---1-7..---o. 1802, Jan. 29th,-3---*6* --.--0. 1803, Aug. 24th,---2-8-----1.
1805, Oct. 9th,----1 _-. 2-----1.
1809, Aug. 24th,---1-1 _-Vagrants, 4.
Allowance, for all descriptions, three twelve-penny loaves per week, sent from the Baker's: weight, October 9, 1805, four pounds each. Two tons of coals are given yearly, for the use of the whole Gaol.

REMARKS.

This Prison, which is also the *Town-Bridewell,* is situated in Willow Row. The Gaoler's house fronts the Street, and his back room has a full command of the court-yard, which is 33 feet by 24; and has a pump and two sewers in it, with a leaden cistern for a cold bath: Hard and soft water are accessible at all times. The above court is the only one for Prisoners of every description.

Debtors have a day-room on the ground-floor, 12 feet by 11, which has a fireplace, and an iron-grated window, looking towards the Court. Above-stairs, they have four sleeping-rooms, of about the same size, with glazed windows and fireplaces; and to each room the Corporation allows wooden bedsteads, loose straw, two blankets, and a rug. i

Debtors from the Court of Requests are seut here, and have the same allowance as paupers, from their respective parishes.

The Felons' day-room is about 10 feet square, with a fire-place, and iron-grated window. Their sleeping-cell, called *The Dungeon,* is 12 feet by 8, lighted and ventilated by a small iron-grated window, of 11 inches only by 10; with a barrack bedstead, straw, three blankets, and a rug.

The Women's day-room, 10 feet square, has a fire-place, and iron-grated window towards the court. Their room to sleep in is above-stairs, and of the same size as that below; but the window is glazed. Closely adjoining are two rooms for petty offenders.

All are allowed to work who can procure employment, and they receive the whole of their earnings. When I was last here, in 1805, the single Debtor was cutting Butchers' skewers, at *three 'pence* a thousand.

No room set apart for an Infirmary. The Act for Preservation of Health is hung up, but not the Clauses against Spirituous Liquors. The Prison is whitewashed and visited once a year.

» DEVIZES. *Wiltshire*.
The Town Gaol, and County Bridewell.
Gaoler, *Joseph Draper*. Salary, 100/. Fees, none.
Chaplain, Rev. Mr. *Leddiard*. Salary, 20/. Duty, every Sunday.
Surgeon, Mr. *Gibbs*. Salary, 15/.
Number of Prisoners, Debtors. Felons, &c. Lunatic.
1801, Dec. 15th,---3----41-1.
1804, July 27th,.--0----29.
I80G, Oct. 15th,---2----22.
Allowance, to Debtors, none; unless certificated as Paupers. To Felons, &c. one pound twelve ounces of best wheaten bread, in loaves to that amount from the Baker s and which I have always found of full weight.

REMARKS.

The Debtors sent to this Prison are committed by the Court of Requests for the adjacent Hundreds of *Bradford, Melksham,* and *Whorlsdown*. The expence attending their commitment sometimes becomes highly aggravated; frequently it exceeds the original debt, and is such as almost to preclude the possibility of a compromise.

One of the commitments, which I copied in 180I, was as follows: Debt, 10.s *Gd.* Costs, 1. *9d.* additional Costs, *lid.* Further Costs, if the Defendant is carried to Prison, are 10. *Cd.* Now, as *Debtors of this description* are never enabled to pay the original debt, and costs, and charges, they must suffer confinement for 20 or 40 days, as prescribed by the Act;—to the injury of health, or the destruction of morals, or both.

They are not here, as in many County Gaols, confined amongst other Debtors; they ought not therefore to be sent to *Bridewells;* but, so long as this system of Imprisonment for Driblets of Debt, is cruelly permitted, they should be sent either to the County Gaols, or to one purposely built, with an allowance of proper society, food, and bedding. But here, there is no separate ward, nor a court-yard for Debtors; who therefore must associate (if at all) with Felons, and other criminal Offenders.

At my visit in October 1806, several, in the Women's ward, appeared to be of the most lewd, profligate, and abandoned sort: yet, confined to such association, I found a poor hard-working *Woman-Debtor,* and a Man who had been committed hither from the Court of Requests, both living in common with the Criminals .

In this Prison are six court-yards. The principal, or Felons', is 38 feet by 30: Their day-room, 18 feet by 17, and 7 feet high, lighted by one iron-grated window. Over this their sleeping-room, of the same size, 7 feet *6* inches high, with a chimney and ventilator; and good beds and bedding are furnished by the Keeper, at 2. and 1. *6d.* each per week.

On a level with the Felons' day-room is a work-room, *26* feet by 14, and 7 feet high, with three iron-grated windows: The floor is excavated, and contains two hemp-blocks. Over this is their night-room, of equal size, *6* feet 9 inches high; supplied also with three iron-grated windows, inside shutters, and two ventilators, and containing fourteen beds.

From this court-yard you enter into a lobby, 21 feet by 10, and 9 feet 6' inches high; leading to twelve cells, six on each side of a passage five feet wide. The cells are 10 feet by 7; lighted by an iron-grated window, and each fitted up with two ventilators, a crib bedstead, straw-in-canvas bed, and one blanket. These cells are encircled by a narrow court-yard.

Adjoining the Women-Felon's ward is a court-yard, of 50 feet by 20, with a dayroom, 21 feet by 16 feet 9 inches, and 7 feet 2 inches high. In this ward were nine Women and two Children confined. Above it is their sleeping-room, of the same size, with two iron-grated windows, five beds, and a chimney-piece.

The *Infirmary,* 22 feet 6 inches by 16 feet, and 7 feet 4 inches high, consists of two rooms above each other; the higher one, with a boarded floor, appropriated to the Women, the other stone-floored, assigned for the Men: They have each a fire-place, with two iron-grated glazed windows, and are well-ventilated. In the Men's Infirmary was one poor *Lunatick*. The Infirmary court-yard is 23 feet by 27, The court-yard belonging to those committed for misdemeanors is 38 feet by 32, and has two hemp blocks, placed under the arcades. Their day-room, 38 feet Bridewells and Houses of Correction, being the general receptacles of the idle, the vicious, and the profligate, the confinement of a Debtor there constitutes a principal source of those mischiefs, which give an unfavourable turn to the manners of the labouring classes. It is here the mind receives the first impressions of vice; and the force of evil example *U* powerful.
by *16,* is-7 feet *6* inches high: sleeping-room, 25 feet by *16,* and of the same height as the former; each having three iron-grated windows, and two ventilators.

The *Chapel* is small and neat. The Women have a separate gallery to themselves, opposite the pulpit.

There is a day-room in every court-yard, with a fire-place in each; but *no fuel allowed*. The sleeping-cells are well-ventilated, and fitted up with a wooden bedstead, straw-in-sacking case, and a blanket each, for every Prisoner, all laid on the boarded floors.

Notwithstanding the work-rooms and hemp-blocks above enumerated, *decipimur specie recti:* Appearance is the order of the place. There is seldom any employment in this *County Prison* of *Wiltshire:* and yet, the Keeper told me, that he had had, at one time, sixty-four Prisoners under his care. If they can procure work, they receive half of their earnings; and the County has the other half, deducting only one penny in every shilling, which is allotted to the Keeper for his trouble.

§3-The Corporation provides no bedding for Debtors, nor is there any fuel allowed, even in winter.

Of the six court-yards, that only

which is for the Felons can be viewed by the Keeper from his windows; the area of one of them is nearly occupied by sleepingcells. Each court-yard has a sewer, and water.

The Prison is white-washed once a year. Here is a bath of stone, with a boiler for supplying water warm and cold. An oven also is provided, for purifying the Prisoners' clothes; but, according to the Keeper's account, it has never been used.

No Rules and Orders. The Act for preserving the Health of Prisoners is *printed,* not hung up; but the Clauses against their use of Spirituous Liquors are properly exhibited.

A *palisaded fence* was wanted before the back door of the Keeper's house. If a latticed partition and door were made in the Criminals' court, about six feet from the Keeper's door, it would prevent Prisoners from rushing out, of which, as he told me, he was sometimes apprehensive.

This ill-constructed Prison, however, is expected to be soon taken down; and as a new one is building, in a better situation, a more ample description of every particular is needless..

DOLGELLY. *Merionethshire, North Wales.*
Gaoler, *Rice Edwards,* now *Edmund Jones.* Salary, 40/.
Fees, for Debtors and Felons, &c. *6s. 8d.* No Table.
Chaplain, Rev. *William Williams;* Salary, 17/.

Duty, Prayers every Saturday, and sometimes a Sermon.
Surgeon, Mr. *Evans,* now Mr. *Owen.* Salary, for Debtors and Criminals, *lol.*
Number of Prisoners, Debtors, Felons, &c. Deserters.
1800, April 2d,---5--4--0 1802, Jan. 30th,---5-3 0 1S03, Sept. 23d,---2----2----3

Allowance, Poor *Debtors, Is. 6d.* or 2. per week, from the Parish to which they belong. *Felons, 2s.* a week.
REMARKS.
This miserable Gaol has one small court-yard for all descriptions of Prisoners, with a mud bottom, and a sewer in it: likewise a pump, with a stone trough under it, to serve for a bath. Nine steps down, are four loathsome cells, or dungeons for Felons, 12 feet *6,* by *6* feet *6;* two of which have vaulted roofs, 5 feet 10 inches high. Each is supplied with a wooden bedstead and straw, a blanket, and a rug.

Above-stairs are five dirty rooms for *Debtors,* one of whom private benevolence enabled me to release. Poor *Hugh Robert Evans* had been in confinement near twenty years, for a debt of 27/. 5. 5rf. He was eighty years of age, and his wife, older than himself, was with him. They were carding and spinning, and earned about three pence a day each; and this, with two shillings weekly allowed him by the Parish, was what they had to subsist upon!

Here is no distinction of Debtors, and they must find their own beds. The Passage, where Prayers are read, is the common entrance into the Gaol; I cannot suppose the Service ever to consist of more than a short Prayer; but the Gaoler told me there was sometimes a Sermon: Possibly it may be so once a month. There are fire-places in all the rooms, but no coals allowed. No room for an Infirmary. The Gaoler has only two for his own use. Neither the Act for Preserving Health, nor the Clauses against Spirituous Liquors, are hung up. A new Gaol was begun several years since, but is not nearly finished yet.
DOLGELLY. *Bridewell.* Gaoler, *Robert Owen.* Salary, *4I.* Two rooms under the Town Hall. No court. No water. Prisoners, 23d Sept. 1S03, none. DONCASTER. *Yorkshire.*
The Town Gaol.
Gaoler, *Joseph Farrington,* Sergeant at Mace. Salary, *lOl. 1Os.* Clothes and a laced hat yearly. Fees, Debtors, *2s. 6d.* ; Felons, *Is. Ad.* Conveyance of Transports, 1. per mile. No Chaplain or religious attentions. Surgeon, from the Dispensary, when wanted. Prisoners, 14th August 1802, one *Debtor,* one *Felon, both together!* Allowance, fourpence, or sixpence per day, as bread is cheap or dear.
REMARKS.
This Gaol is a detached building in St. Sepulchre's, Gate-street. The Keeper's house overlooks the court. Inscribed on its front, in stone, is, "John Whitaker, Esq. Mayor, 1779." For all kinds of Prisoners, one small flagged court, with a pump. Felons have two good-sized rooms below; one totally dark, except a small aperture in the door: the other has an iron-grated window, not glazed. Above etairs are two rooms with iron-grated and glazed windows, for Debtors. The rooms have fire-places. The Borough allows fuel in winter, straw on wooden bedsteads, two blankets, and a rug. Debtors are brought here by process on Borough Writs, to any amount; likewise for smaller sums, from the Court of Requests. No sewer, nor means for decent cleanliness! The Prison most intolerably offensive. The Gaoler told me "it was usually so. It had been white-washed but twice in ten "years by the *Corporation;* but the Prisoners had sometimes bought white-wash, "and done it themselves. " DYMCHURCH. *Kent.*

Gaoler, *Thomas Bourne,* Sergeant at Mace, and lives distant from the Prison. Salary, none. Fees, *6s. 8d.* Surgeon, Mr. *Walter;* who makes a Bill. September 10th, 1807, One Prisoner. Allowance to Prisoners, sixpence a day.

This Gaol adjoins to the New-Hall, and was built in 1797. It consists of two rooms; one of which, called "*The Gaol*" is 15 feet by 10, and 8 feet high, with a boarded floor; a table and shelf for provisions. No fire-place. The sewer is in one corner.

The other room is named " *The Bridewell*" of 11 feet by 10, and 6 feet 3 inches high. Both these have an iron double-grated window, looking into a small court paved with flag-stone, of *16* feet 4 inches by 10 feet *6.* The rooms have double wooden doors, strongly clamped with iron. Straw and blankets on the floors to sleep on. No water, but what is sent in by the Keeper.
DORCHESTER. *Dorsetshire.*
The County Gaol.
Gaoler, *George Andrews.*
Salary, 218/. for himself and two Turnkeys.
Fees, Debtors, 13 *Ad.* which are paid to the Treasurer of the *County Stoch.*

The Under Sheriff demands also 2. for his *Liberate!* Felons pay no Fees. Conveyance of Transports, 1. per mile each. Garnish abolished.

Chaplain, Rev. Mr. *Bryer.*

Duty, Twice every Sunday, and once on Wednesday. Salary, 50/.

Surgeon, Mr. *Arden.*

Salary, AOl. for both Debtors and Felons.

A Task-Master, 60l. per annum.

Number of Prisoners. Debtors. Felons, &c.

1800, Mar. 31st,------7------65 1801, Dec. 29th, 3------SO

1803. Oct. 21st, 9 55.

Allowance, to Debtors, none, except they work for the County; in which case they receive half of their earnings, and a pound and half of wheaten bread, made with the whole of the bran in it, and a quart of broth per day. Master's-Side Debtors, who do not work, maintain themselves. All Prisoners committed for trial have the same allowance as the working Debtors, and on the same conditions. After conviction, every Prisoner, whose earnings amount to 5. per week, has, in addition to the above allowance, three pounds of meat per week, with a proportionate quantity of potatoes, and one sixth of his earnings. If they do not amount to 5s. a week, he has the same allowance, and only one sixth of the profit. The County finds employment for all who chuse to work, and all must work, or maintain themselves. The last Prisoner committed, (of whatever description,) takes the broom, and sweeps the Court; or else gives seven-pence halfpenny to another Prisoner to do it for him. Criminal Prisoners, during the six Winter months, are allowed a peck of coals per day for their common-room, and half a peck daily during the six Summer months.

. REMARKS.

In the building now under consideration, are united the *County Gaol, Penitentiary House,* and *House of Correction.* The situation of this Gaol is most judiciously chosen, on the North side of the Town of Dorchester, on a piece of ground still called "The Castle;" where formerly was the site of a structure of that description, and at the foot of which flows the river *Frome.* It is bounded by a wall 20 feet high, which, from the Turnkey's Lodge, situate at the North side of it, completely encircles the whole of the buildings. Around ihe outside wall is a spacious esplanade, laid down in grass; and on the North side, in front of the Lodge, a handsome slope inclines to the River, with trees planted on its banks.

The ground on which the Prison is erected, was, in the handsomest manner, given by *Francis John Browne,* esq. late one of the Members for the County.

The entrance building consists of a room for the Turnkey and Task-Master to sleep in; a room containing a mill for grinding corn, with every other requisite for dressing the flour, and where all the corn used to supply the Prison with bread is ground; a Committee-Room, for the Magistrates to transact business; an office for the Gaoler; a bake-house and brew-house, with oven, iron boilers, and other conveniences in cooking for the Prisoners. Also a warm and cold bath.

Above-stairs, in the Lodge, are six *Reception Cells,* about 9 feet by 4, and 8 feet 6 inches high. In these Prisoners are placed immediately on their entrance, till they can be examined by the Surgeon, and thoroughly cleansed by means of the baths above-mentioned. If in a foul or infectious state, they remain here, until the Surgeon pronounces them fit for removal into the interior of the Gaol; and then they are sent to join their proper classes.

Felons are apparelled in the Gaol uniform; their own clothes, if worthy of being preserved, are fumigated in a kiln; and then, either laid by in the wardrobe, till their liberation, or delivered to the care of their friends.

There are likewise three work-rooms in this building; and, on the top of the Lodge is a flat roof, covered with copper, on which Executions take place, in view of all criminal Prisoners, who are brought out of their cells for that purpose, into the different galleries; the Church bell tolling solemnly during the awful transaction!

From the Turnkey's lodge is a passage through the Gaoler's court to the central buildings. On the ground-floor are the Gaoler's parlour, kitchen, and scullery; and another passage, which leads to two spacious day-rooms for *Men Debtors,* 6' yards long by 13 feet 6 inches, and 12 feet high. The Men Debtors have also two airy court-yards, 70 feet each by 30; and over the South front of the SouthWest wing are their ten sleeping-cells, five on either side of the upper stories; and each cell 8 feet 6 inches by 6 feet 6, and 9 feet high, to the crown of the arch.

When the friend of a Debtor comes to see him, he is introduced into a narrow space, or slip, the inner door of which is kept constantly locked, the outer one left open. There are two windows opening from it, one into each Debtor's day-room. These windows are iron grated, but a table goes through each of them, one half being in the Debtor's room, the other half in the narrow slip, where the visiting friend is. Thus, though Debtors are not excluded from the society of their friends and relations, the visitors are not in general allowed to come into their rooms; by which means irregularities are prevented. In particular cases, the Gaoler, where he finds it proper, unlocks the inner door, and suffers the Debtor to take his friend with him into his cell, or court. The friends of *Debtors* are permitted to stay with them, if they please, from ten o'clock in the morning till four in the afternoon; after which hour no stranger whatever is allowed to remain within the walls.

In the centre building are also two store-rooms, and a large pair of scales. There are nine airy court-yards, of the average size from 70 to 80 feet long, and 30 to 40 feet wide: five of them communicate with the centre building; viz. one for Male Debtors, and four for Criminal Prisoners, into which open eight single workingcells.

The first floor contains the *Chapel,* to which Prisoners have access by different doors, to their respective divisions. They are seated in classes; and all are required to attend Divine Service, unless prevented by sickness.

At each corner of the Chapel is a cell for Prisoners under sentence of Death, which are light and airy; and over these are four cells for refractory Prisoners, perfectly dark, but well ventilated.

On this floor are two spacious sleeping-rooms for Men Debtors, each containing four beds, to be used in case the number should be greater than can be well accommodated in what is called " *The Debtors Wing*"

Any Debtor, male or female, who is content to sleep in the County-beds, has them free of expence: otherwise, they must provide their own beds and bedding, which they are allowed to do; or else pay the Gaoler *2s. 6d.* a week for those articles, with one sheet, or 3. *6d.* for bedding, with a pair of sheets.

Over the last-mentioned rooms are two others; one for Female Debtors, the other for Female *Fines*: these have no communication with the floors above or below; they are furnished with beds, &c. the same as the men; and above them are the two *Infirmaries,* each 18 feet by 13, and 8 feet *6* inches high, light and airy, with washing-troughs and water-closets; and also a communication to a separate flat, on the different sides of the roof, one for each sex of convalescents, for the benefit of the air. Between the Infirmaries, here is a Dispensary for the convenience of the Surgeon; and a pew, from each opening into the Chapel, for the use of such sick Prisoners as may be able to attend Divine Service.

Those who are imprisoned until they pay a certain fine, and those for Felony, have each, as the Debtors, but in a different mode of treatment, a small slip or space for their friends to converse with them, *in the presence of the Gaoler.* The three gates of the slips or small avenues being all locked, the Gaoler, on application, lets the friend into the space between the first and second gates, and stands himself between the second and third, the Prisoner remaining in the court-yard. The Keeper can thus effectually prevent the introduction of weapons, liquor, or other articles, *(the use of which is forbidden in this Gaol,)* as well as be a check upon any improper conversation. In the case, however, of some known relation of the party, or other person having real private business with the Prisoner, the Gaoler, after previously searching the friend, admits him or her into the space between the second and third gates, and then himself retires. The friends of Felons, and of those imprisoned for Fines, are allowed to remain but a short time only with them, except in cases of real business, when the Keeper is authorized to indulge them at his discretion.

The other part of this excellent Prison consists of *Four Wings,* detached from, but communicating with, the centre building on each story, by means of cast-iron bridges leading to it from the several galleries; each Wing containing eighteen sleeping-cells. The exemplary distribution of persons here established is such, that not only the Male Prisoners are separated from the Female, and the Felons from the Debtors, Fines, &c. but those of each description are subdivided into classes. For each class also, by means of distinct staircases, separate subdivisions of the building are very accurately appropriated, with court-yards, working-rooms, and other suitable accommodations.

The two classes of Female Debtors, and Females detained for Fines, have each a commodious day-room, with every possible convenience, over the Male Debtors' sleeping-rooms, and under the two Infirmaries; separate and detached from every other part of the building, except the Keeper's house and court-yard, to which they have access through the Chapel.

The subdivisions of the Prison, for the accommodation of the respective classes, are distributed as follows:

Male Debtors.
Male Felons.
Male Convicts, classes I, II, and III.
Male Prisoners for Fines.
Male Bridewell Prisoners.
Female Debtors.
Female Felons, and Bridewell Prisoners for Trial.
Female Felons, and Bridewell Prisoners Convict.'
Female Felons.
Reception Cells.
Condemned Cells; or for King's Evidence, when not used for the Condemned.
Refractory Cells.
Infirmary for Males.
Infirmary for Females.

In the several departments of this comprehensive building, there are eighty-eight *single sleeping-cells,* each of 8 feet *6* inches, by *6* feet *6,* and Q feet high, to. the crown of the arch; to which the County allows a cast-iron bedstead, a *paillasse,* (or ticking filled with straw,) a pair of blankets, and a coverlet.

To every ward there are arcades, 16 feet *6* by 10 feet *6,* as day-rooms for the several classes, and water-closets on every stair-case. *Net towells,* on rollers, are provided for the Prisoners: and, besides the water-cocks and troughs in the different court-yards, here is an engine that throws up water to the several cisterns on the top of each building; from whence every part is plentifully supplied with that essential element; including also the several water-closets, allotted for the use of each subdivision of cells.,'

There are no sleeping-cells on the ground-floor; by which arrangement the custody of the Prisoners is rendered more secure, and their health not liable to injury from the rising of damps. By means of air-holes, so constructed at the back of. each cell, (except in the upper stories, where they are placed in the arches of the cells.) and so managed as to preclude conversation, whilst they transmit air, a thorough circulation is preserved.

The County provides an iron bedstead, a paillasse, two blankets, and a coverlet or rug for each Prisoner.

Here is no allowance of coals to *Debtors,* male or female, except in very severe Winter weather, or unless an especial order is made for that purpose by the visiting Magistrates. The coals so ordered are not paid for from the *County Stock,* but out of the *Gaol Charity Fund.*

In the different day-rooms is stuck up the following notice. "If any Prisoner "does any wilful damage to his or her

Paillasse, Blankets, or Rugs, he or she shall "be immediately punished by close confinement in one of the refractory cells; and "there fed on bread and water only, for a space of time, in proportion to the da"mage done."

There are several work-rooms in each division of the Gaol; some, for single persons to labour in solitude; others appropriated to two, three, or more Prisoners, for the purpose of employing them in such particular kinds of work as they may best be capable of executing: and these are accompanied with store rooms, and every other convenience to render the apartments complete.

Prisoners of all descriptions, Debtors as well as Felons, work together in the manufactory: and, although *Dorsetshire* is not a manufacturing County, yet,, through the laudable exertions of its Magistrates, who alternately superintend the concerns of the Prison, employment is found for all.

A considerable edifice for the manufacture of *Hats* was built here, at the expence of *William Morton Pitt,* esq. one of the Members for the County, as a testimony of his gratitude for the confidence reposed in him, and for the repeated favours conferred upon him by his Constituents. This manufacture was tried for several years, with great success. In 1803, I saw numbers engaged in it; but was sorry to find it discontinued at my last visit, in 1805 . Many Prisoners are now employed in Owing, I was informed, to a combination amongst the Hatters to undersell, and make it unproductive.

shoe-making, tayloring, carding, spinning, &c. and these branches go on very successfully.

Prisoners who work in privacy, or solitude, are employed in the first stages of their respective branch; and such parts of the works as require the joint labour of several, are performed by those, who, consistent with the Prison Rules, are subject to a less degree of restriction. The produce of the work done is divided into shares: of which each Prisoner has one half; the Keeper a sixth part, to excite his attention to the object; and the remaining *third part* is accounted for to the County, and *defrays a considerable proportion of the Prison expenccs.*

Upon enquiry made into the characters of all the Dorsetshire Prisoners, on charges of Felony, during a period of fourteen years, it has appeared, that out of 393 persons of both sexes, no less than 242 have been so well reclaimed, as to maintain themselves by honest industry: A striking example this, of the beneficial efficacy of *Employment in Prison;* and which, it is hoped, will be seriously considered by every County, but more especially by those where manufactories have been introduced, and then discontinued on account of their being unproductive of profit in an infant state! Surely an expectation of County emolument from the labours of a Prisoner ought never to weigh so forcibly, as the Patriotic credit of restoring to Society a reformed, a worthy, and an useful member.

It always gives me pleasure, from various considerations, to find Prisoners employed; because, in the first place, they are then more healthy. It also diverts them amidst the dreariness of confinement: it is an honest and laudable means of procuring them clean linen, or stockings, or a little milk or meat to their bread, or other articles, to which they are very properly limited by the Magistrates, and of which an account should be hung up in every Prison; 'such as tea, coffee, butter, cheese, vegetables, &c. And, lastly, it has this further and political advantage over idleness, that it prevents the Prisoners from combining together, to foment disturbance, or effect escapes.

The kind Donation of *Edward Morton Pleydell,* Esq. who, for many years, sent each Prisoner, at Christmas, sixpence in money, and two pounds of beef, has been discontinued since his death in 1799. Lord *Digby* formerly sent at Christmas two guineas to this Gaol, and one guinea to the Bridewell, which I was sorry to find has also ceased.

The Legacy of Mr. *John Derby,* of twenty shillings a year for bread, to be distributed amongst the Debtors on the four quarter days, is still regularly paid, and applied to the *Gaol-Charity* Fund; which is placed in the hands of the Chaplain, but under the direction of the Visiting-Magistrates. It arises from the humane contributions of Individuals; and from it. an additional quantity of coals is purchased in extreme hard weather, for the different classes of Prisoners. The Debts also of such as, upon enquiry, appear to be truly objects of compassion, are occasionally compounded and liquidated out of the same Fund.

This County, with a liberality that reflects upon it the highest honour, rewards those former Prisoners, who, twelve months after their discharge, can produce Certificates, properly attested, of their having faithfully, honestly, soberly, and industriously served those who kindly afforded them employment.

A perusal of these Remarks will amply manifest the great good whieh may be produced by constant employment, and salutary regulations; and it is hoped that the example of the Visiting Magistrates of the County of *Dorset,* in restoring so many Prisoners to usefulness in society, will raise a spirit of emulation throughout the whole Kingdom.

DOVER-CASTLE. Kent.
For the Cinque-Port Debtors only.
Gaoler, and Bodar , *James Hawker;* now *William Collison.* Salary, 307;
Fees; see the Table. Garnish, (not yet abolished) *Is. 6d.*

Chaplain, None. Surgeon, None.

Number of Debtors, 1800, May 20th, ----6. 1802, Jan. 27th,----2.
1804, Sept. 24th,----4. 1806, Aug. 4th,----6.
Allowance; none whatever. See the Remarks.
1808, Aug. 14th,----8. 1809, July 13th,----9. 1810, July 11th,----14. 1811, Feb. 22d,----13. REMARKS.
This Gaol is for Debtors within the Cinque-Ports; viz. Hastings, Dover, Hythe, Romney, and Sandwich. The late Constable was the Right Honourable William Pitt; upon whose decease succeeded Lord Hawkesbury, the present *Earl of Liverpool.*

Here are three rooms for Debtors; one 18 feet by 12, another 13 feet by 11;

and the third, a new room, 15 feet by 12 feet 6. Each Prisoner pays 2. 4d. per week for a bed; two sleeping together. The court-yard is 50 feet by 20, and the wall 28 feet high; so that the sun and air are almost excluded. A very small part only of the court is paved: The ground is consequently damp, and the place unhealthy. It is bounded on one side by the Gaoler's house; on another, by the rock, or cliff; and on a third, by the Military stabling.

It would be a considerable improvement, if a grated window were opened on the fourth side, which looks toward the South, and the public path; by which means both *Bodar,* vulgarly termed "Boarder," means the Messenger and Bailiff of the Cinque-Ports.

sun and air would be freely admitted, and the Prisoners might see their friends, and passengers, or other visitors of the hill, and occasionally solicit charity. The courtyard also should be wholly paved, both for exercise and comfort ; and some retired place provided, to deposit the putrid vegetables, dirt, and ashes, which I have constantly seen thrown there into an offensive dunghill.

The *Gaoler* told me that he sent a boy across to Dover daily, to fetch what was wanted for the Prisoners; but, as he himself is the acting Bailitf of the Cinque-Ports, and sometimes necessitated to be absent on business, for days together, Debtors are frequently obliged to pay a Man for bringing them the common necessaries of life; which, in consequence, stand them in *c20l. per cent,* above their value: nay, sometimes, even a *pail-J'ull of water* costs a *penny.* They are also obliged to pay a Woman for washing out their rooms, as neither mops, pails, brooms, fire, or candle are allowed. It would be an essential mercy to those confined in this very singular kind of Gaol, if the Fees were abolished, or at least, reduced; for, besides those specified in the following Table, there is one guinea charged for the *Latitat-Writ;* and, in case the Prisoner is brought from Margate, the expence of a guinea and half is added; making together, on the first commitment, *four pounds nineteen shillings and ten-pence.* "Table Of Fees, hung up in Dover-castle Gaol. £. s. d,
Arrest-----------------110
Commitment---------------0134
Guard-Money, and Bed for a Night--------004
Discharge----------------068
Yeoman Porter--------------0 26
Clerk of Dover Castle 036 £. 2 7 4

Let it be considered, that all this is to be paid, over and above the weekly room-rent, by every Prisoner, on gaining a release from Gaol; and that not one in ten of them can discharge the sum sued for;—that the *sixpences* are not allowed to any Debtor till after the third term from his commitment;—that regular Sessions of *Oyer % Terminer,* or Gaol-Delivery, are held in all Gaols (except such as, like the present, are termed *privileged)* twice in every year; but that here no regular or settled times are fixed for such deliveries. Let all these circumstances be considered, and pity and Ienjty might surely urge a very powerful argument for Relief!

Since the drawing up of this Narrative, in 1808, the Writer has been enabled, by the beneficence of one of the Society of Friends, or people called Quakers, to *pave the whole court-yard,* and likewise to make a permanent provision for the poor Debtors here confined, by a transfer, on the 24th of May, 1810, of sooi. 3 per cent, consolidated annuities, into the names of ' The Mayor, Jurats, and CommonCouncil Men of the Town and Port of Dover." The Dividends whereof are to be for ever applied to their support and relief. A Memorial of this singular instance of Liberality has been recently put up to record it, both in the Castle and in the Church of St. Mary's, Dover. At the suit of the Crown, a Prisoner may lay eleven months in the Town Gao of *Dover,* and from ten to twenty months in the Castle Gaol, without a trial, or being brought before a Court of Justice; and perhaps be discharged, at length, on *a petition.* Here I could find no instance of any Debtors having received the *benefit of the Lords Act.*

Yet *this* I did find, and it not a little painfully surprized me; That" Prisoners of this privileged and distinguished Gaol, though ever so much aggrieved by prosecution, are many of them absolutely incapable of sueing for their *Habeas Corpus!"* How, indeed, can that Man be supposed equal to the expence of procuring so great a blessing, who, after many months', nay, or even weeks' confinement, cannot find himself in daily bread? A Remedy provided, is no Remedy to him, who fails to obtain the use of it through invincible penury.

From a Jurisdiction thus irregularly privileged, neither dignity nor emolument can accrue to the Crown. Would it not, therefore, be a worthy exertion of liberality, if some independent Member of the British Parliament would propose a Bill, for fixing, in such cases as the above, both a *time* for trial, and also, when found necessary, some *allowance to the Prisoner,* in order to give him, or her, the same certainty and facility in Gaols of this description, as is granted under the general administration of Justice elsewhere?

One hardly knows how to term that *a favour,* which seems supported by *so strong a claim.* Many evils in this life fail of redress, merely from the want of being duly reflected on. The Lord Warden, if clearly apprized of them, might, without doubt, greatly mitigate such evils as I have here humbly presumed to point out, from a sense of duty, in a very peculiar situation. But, when we consider with what important national affairs such minds must continually be engrossed, it is not to be wondered at, if a scene, and if circumstances of distress like the before-mentioned should be little or not at all known to him, although so immediately under his very respectable jurisdiction.

A great and good writer has observed, that "there should be an uniform Code "of Laws framed for the Police of all Gaols. The laws of a kingdom ought to be "general in a well-regulated state. " (Jd As very few Persons who visit Dover Castle can have any idea of there being within it a Prison for Debtors; in order to arrest attention, and to excite sympathy in the breasts of the opulent, who resort thither in summer, an iron begging-box has lately been affixed to a post, near the summit of the hill, where, as a *Siste, Viator!* a small flat space invites the pedestrian to stop awhile for rest: and above it, on a broad iron plate, are inscribed or painted the following lines.

Oh ye, whose hours exempt from sorrow flow,
Behold the seat of Pain, and Want, and Woe:
Think, while your hands th' entreated Alms extend,
That what to *Us* you give, to God you lend!

I am informed, that of the produce and distribution of this true charity, an account is kept by the Gaoler in a book; and that to the wretched Prisoners it has proved of much alleviation, amidst the miseries of dreary solitude.

Indeed I have been well assured of the great success which has attended the business in question. The Gaoler acquaints me that his number of Prisoners (in Feb. l811,) is no less than *thirteen;* that he has not had fewer than *ten* for many former months, and even *fifteen* at one period. "Seven of those," says he, "who were most in need, now receive one pound and a half of bread per day; and had it not been for the great goodness shown towards them, I am not able to say what would have become of these poor unfortunate Men, who, as being so many in distress, I could not have provided for them, and they must have wanted the common necessaries of life."

My Readers will participate the pleasure which it gives me, in being enabled to inform them, upon the most respectable authority, that Dover Castle Gaol and its repairs are considered as belonging to the department of the Board of Ordnance: and that orders have been issued for putting the rooms in repair, and furnishing them with grates, which were extremely needful in so very bleak a situation, and especially during a very severe winter season.

DOVER.
The Town Gaol and Bridewell.
Gaoler, *William Harris;* now *John Mitchell.* Salary, 40/. a chaldron of coals,

and a suit of apparel.
Fees, on Commitment, 8s. 2d. On Discharge, 1. 6d. No Table.
Garnish, (not yet abolished) one shilling.

Chaplain, none; nor any religious attentions.

Surgeon, Mr. *King,* who makes a Bill.
Number of Prisoners, Debtors. Felons, &c Debtors. Felons, &t.
1801, Sept. 19th,--I--3. 1804, Sept. 24th,--1--2. 180G, Aug. 6th,--0--5 1808, Aug. 12th,--0--0. 1809, July 12th,--0--1. 1810, July 11th,--0--8.

Allowance, to Debtors, none whatever. To Felons, and other Criminal Prisoners, sixpence a day.

REMARKS.

This Prison is in a close part of the Town, and has one room for the Bridewell. The Gaol consists of two rooms on the ground-floor, 12 feet by 6 feet 9 each. The iron-grated windows look into a small court-yard; but the Prisoners have not the use of it. Both the rooms are not only close, in point of situation, but rendered offensive also, by sewers placed in the corner.

Felons, &c. are supplied with wooden bedsteads, loose straw, two blankets,and a rug.

For Debtors and Misdemeanors here are three rooms above stairs; to-which, if the Gaoler furnishes bed and bedding, the charge to the Prisoner is 7. per week.

The Corporation allow yearly four gallons of vinegar, to fumigate the Gaol; 12 lbs. of whitening, and 6 lbs. of soap, together with mops, brooms, and pails for cleaning the Prison; and straw, whenever the Gaoler requires it. It gave me great pleasure to be informed that the Corporation are going to build a new Gaol.

At my visit in September 1801, *Isabella Mode,* a Woman who had been here *three years, under sentence of transportation,* had a young child born in the Prison, of which she asserted that Harris, the late Keeper, was the Father. He is since dead. This hapless Female had an allowance of ten-pence a day during her detention, and one shilling on a Sunday, for the maintenance of herself and Infant.

The Act for preservation of Health, and Clauses against Spirituous Liquors, not hung up. No Rules and Orders. No employment.

i "TM DUMFRIES. *Scotland.*
The County Gaol.
Gaoler, *John Dogherty.* Salary, 30./. with coals for his house, oil for the lamps, and allowed an assistant, at 10s. 6d. per week, paid by the County. See Remarks.' Fees, for Criminals, none. Debtors who are Burgesses, 2d. per night; those who are not Burgesses, 4d. a night; and for payment of which the Debtor's effects are detained till satisfied.

Chaplain, none, nor any religious attentions, unless voluntarily and gratuitously afforded to those under Sentence of Death.

Surgeon, for *Felons* only, sent from the Town when wanted.

Number of Prisoners, 1st Nov. 1809, Debtors, 4. Felons, 2.

Vagrant, 1. Deserter, 1.

Allowance, to Felons 6d. a day. Debtors, as alimented.

REMARKS.

The County Court-house is situate in Buccleugh-street, and the basement story of it forms-the Gaoler's house. The right-wing is the Police Guard-house; and under it are three cells, each a feet by 6. The middle cell is dark; the other two have each a glazed, and grated window, with straw on the stone-floor for bedding. No fire-places. The left-wing is the Military Guard-house, and has two small rooms for the Turnkey. In the basement story of this wing are three cells, similar to those already described, except that two of them are dark. On the flat-roof of this wing is the place of Execution.

The entrance to the Gaol is by a descent of 17 steps, from the street to the low ground on which the Prison is built; and the Gaol slands detached within a boundary-wall, which encloses about half an acre. It was first inhabited 23d February, 1807, and has, on the ground-floor, a day-room for Felons, of about 14 feet square, with a fire-place: also a cell, or room of communication, with iron-gratings, to receive provisions, or enable them to receive their friends: But at my visit in 1809, they had never been used.

Adjoining to the above is a large day-room, of 18 feet square, for the Debtors, with a fire-place and room of communication for their friends. These however I found were converted into a dwelling for the Turnkey's family.

On the first story is a double range of cells, four on each side of a lobby or passage, 4 feet 6 inches wide.. Each cell is 8 feet 4 by 6 feet 9, and 8 feet high; and four of them have boarded floors, grated and glazed windows to open, iron-bedsteads, with loose straw, two blankets and a rug, but no fire-places. The other four cells have stone floors, iron-grated windows, with sloping blinds, and two panes of glass in each. Beds and bedding the same as the others before described. The cells have double-doors, the outward iron-grated, and the inner one of wood.

The upper, or attic-story, has four sizeable rooms for Debtors, with two grated and glazed windows made to open, of about 3 feet square; boarded floors, and lireplaces; wooden bedsteads, with straw mattress and bolster; but no bedding or furniture whatever. No coals are allowed to any part of the Prison.

Here are separate stair-cases, for the Debtors and Felons-to go to their respective day-rooms, if permitted the use of them. In the court-yard for Debtors there is a pump and sewer; but the *Felons* not being suffered ever to come out of their cells, a glazed pan is made to serve them as a sewer, which is emptied daily; and water, as wanted, is brought to them by the Gaoler.

Of the Gaoler's Salary, *20I.* is paid by the County, and *lol.* by the Town of Dumfries. The plan of this Gaol had originally intended separate buildings for Men Felons, Women Criminals, and Debtors, with court-yards judiciously designed for the several classes. But at present the whole area remains in its rude state, and *Debtors only* have the liberty of walking in it. Several loads of ashes are laid in one part, and poultry are kept in it, which might better be removed.

The Keeper has a licence to sell ale, beer, and porter; and as the Prisoners receive their allowance in money, he supplies them likewise with other provisions. This is done also in Prisons elsewhere, but I cannot approve of a practice so justly unsatisfactory.

The Magistrates and Council will be;leased to accept my grateful acknowledgements lor the honour of their presenting me with the freedom of the Burgh.

DUNBAR. *Scotland.*
Gaoler, *John Carrs.* Salary, *6I. 10s.*

Fees, One Shilling; and four-pence per day during confinement.

Surgeon, from the Town, if wanted.

Prisoners, 1802, Sept. 10th, None. 1809, Sept. 21st, None.

Allowance, eight-pence a day for *Felons. Debtors,* as alimented by the Magistrates, which commences 14 days after commitment.

REMARKS.

This Prison is in the middle of the High Street. The ascent to it is by a flight of fourteen steps, which lead to two rooms about 21 feet square; one for Felons, and the other for Debtors who are *not Burgesses.* Both have flagged stone floors, and were found in the filthiest state imaginable. The Debtors' room was occupied by the Gaoler and his family. The iron-grated windows look to the street. A little short dirty straw upon the floor was the only bedding.

Above these is a large room for Debtors who are Burgesses, without furniture or bedding.

The dark room below is called *Thieves-Hole.* The Keeper, at my visit in 1802, told me it was not used; but in 1809, I found a window made in it, and the Gaoler himself lived there. No Prisoners were here at either of my visits. Here is no court-yard; no water accessible to the Prisoners; and no sewers. A tub supplies the purpose.

DUNDEE. *Scotland.*
The Town Gaol.
Gaoler, *Thomas Christie.* Salary, 25/. He is a Town Officer, and lives distant from the Gaol.

Fees, on the Commitment of *Debtors,* one shilling. Caption *Ss.*; and fourpence a night during confinement. *Felons,* &c. pay no fees.

Chaplain, none.

Surgeon, none.

Number of Prisoners, 28th Sept. 1809, Debtors, 4. Criminals, O.

Allowance, to Debtors, as generally alimented, one shilling a day: *Felons,* &c. three pence a day.

REMARKS.

This Gaol is over the Town Hall; and for Debtors there are three rooms, with grated and glazed casement windows, flagged floors, and fire-places, but *no Firing allowed:* wooden bedsteads but no bedding furnished. A sewer is in the passage, to which Debtors have access in the day-time.

On the same floor is one room, of 20 feet by 7, for Felons; in which are two wooden bedsteads, with short loose straw, for their whole bedding, and a large doublegrated and unglazed window. Into this room open the doors of three cells, each feet 2 inches by 3 feet 7; two of which have apertures into the room, about a foot square, for light and ventilation. The third is almost rendered totally dark, by the small apertures having a double iron-grating, and is used for those under sentence of death. Short straw is scantily and loosely scattered on the stone floors of all.

Adjoining to these apartments is one room with a cistern for water, now used by the Gaoler: But formerly it was a cell for Felons; in which the leg of the Prisoner was secured by a shackle of iron, three inches broad, and a quarter of an inch thick, connected with a strong chain, three feet in length, and fastened to an iron weight of jGlbs. For other Prisoners two bars of iron were fixed into the floor to fasten the feet, and a strong chain drawn across the breast, with another athwart the neck, padlocked to the floor; and thus they passed the night! This apparatus, however, I was assured had not been used for many years.

Below the Town-Hall, and by a descent of sixteen steps, are sunk three loathsome dungeons; one of which, called " The Thieves' Hole," is almost wholly dark, and measures 8 feet by 7, and 6 feet high, without ventilation, where a little dirty short straw is the only bedding. The Gaoler told me that sometimes four or five vagrants had been here confined for seven days together! The other two dungeons are 18 feet by 10, and 9 feet high. The town engine was deposited in one of them; the other had a little dunghill kind of straw on the stone floor. *The Thieves' Hole* is generally used for Prisoners.

The water brought to this Prison is introduced by a pipe to the cistern beforementioned, and would be very useful for the Debtors to wash their rooms, if they could have access to it: but water for drinking must be brought by their friends, or the Keeper, during admission hours. Here is no court-yard.

DURHAM.
The County Gaol and Bridewell.
Gaoler, *John Wolfe;* appointed by Patent from the Bishop, *durante beneplacito.*
In the Patent this Prison i« called "The Outer Gate."

Salary, 200/.; also for the Bridewell, 40/.; and *19I.* from the rents of four small houses adjoining. Out of this Salary of 259/. the Gaoler pays Thirty Pounds *per annum* to a Turnkey and Assistants, and likewise provides them a house to live in. For removing of Transports, he is allowed the expence attending it.

Fees and Garnish are abolished.
Chaplain, Rev. *James Deason;* now Rev. *William Baverstoch.*
Duty, Prayers and Sermon every Sunday. Salary, 40/.
Surgeon, Mr. *Green.* Salary, *6I. 6s.* and his Bill for Medicines.
Number of Prisoners, Debtors. Felons, &c. Bridewell.
1801, Nov. 8 th,---15---18---11. 1802, Sept. 5th, 18---8 "*i Lunaiick* 1809, Sept. 15th,---12---14---36.
Allowance; *see Remarks.* If certified as Paupers, the *Debtors* have four-pence a day. Felons three-pence a day. Those in the *Bridewell* have the same as the Felons.
REMARKS.
The High Gaol is the property of the Bishop of Durham. By patent from Bishop *Talbot* in 1723, Sir *Hedworth Williamson,* Bart, was appointed Sheriff, with a Salary of 10/. *per annum;* and it continued in the family till 18lo, when the present Bishop, Dr. Shute Barrington, appointed *Adam Askew,* Esquire.

There is a small room over the North front of the gateway, 12 feet 6 inches by 9 feet 10 inches, and 9 feet 9 inches high. This formerly was the Felons' day-room, but the active and intelligent Keeper has converted it into a *Soup-Kitchen;* the establishment and support of which arises as follows. There are twelve Prebendaries of the Diocese, and a Dean. Of the Prebendaries, three have dispensations, and do not keep any residence, nor contribute to the soup-establishment. The Prebendaries, who, for many years past, had sent an abundant dinner to the Prisoners in the Gaol, at the time they severally kept their residence, have, for the four or five last years, given in lieu of such dinners, five Guineas, which is paid to Mr. *Wolfe,* the Gaoler, who supplies both the Gaol and Bridewell with a good dinner, twice every week throughout the year.

The benevolent Bishop of Durham also gives ten Guineas yearly at Christmas, and the same at Lammas, for the like purpose; and the Dean of Durham, (Bishop of Lichfield,) ten Guineas annually. At the time of my last visit, in 1809, there was a surplus in Mr. Wolfe's hands of 28/. It gave me great pleasure to be informed that this admirable Fund has so increased, as to enable the Gaoler not only to furnish his Prisoners with dinners, as before mentioned, but occasionally *to release Persons imprisoned for Small Debts,* and assist them often in obtaining their sixpences.

Here is a court-yard, of *62* feet by 50, the only one for Prisoners of every description. It is open all day for the accommodation of Debtors, except whilst the Felons are in it; which is for an hour or two in the day, when thought fit: and then the door is locked, *to prevent any communication* between them.

The *Low-Gaol,* as it is called, consists of two rooms, 10 feet 4 inches square; by the gateway under which, out of a door, are now conveyed the dirt, ashes, &c. which formerly lay undisturbed for many months. Both these rooms are *FreeWards.* There are likewise three others at the top of the Gaol; the largest of which contains seven beds, the others one bed each; and to all of them the County furnishes *iron* bedsteads and straw matresses *gratis.* These rooms are now ceiled and limewhited: But the Debtors complained of a great nuisance from the bugs, which the straw matresses harbour, so as to preclude a possibility of riddance.

Two rooms, formerly set apart for Infirmaries, are now appropriated to Women Debtors. The Master's-Side Debtors have six separate rooms, furnished by the Keeper at *$s. 6d.* a week; or, if two sleep together, at 1. *6d.* each. Two of these rooms look towards the street, and open into the Chapel, which, formerly, was the Debtors' Hall.

The High-Gaol is supplied with water by a *double-barrelled pump,* which raises it about *seventy feet.* Half a crown per quarter is paid to a Woman, for supplying with water the Debtors in the Low-Gaol.

The County, hitherto, has provided no work for the Prisoners: but their humane Guardian, the Keeper, told me, " that he constantly procures employment for such as "are not of handicraft trades, in spinning, picking of oakum, beating flax, &c. And "that every Prisoner, however employed, *receives the whole* of his or her earnings." RULES and ORDERS, as settled in the year 1796.
"Chamber Rents,
To the Keeper of Durham Gaol, from the Prisoners for Debt, weekly.
s. d.
"In an entire Chamber in the High Gaol, without a bedfellow---3 0 Ditto, with a bedfellow---------------16

In the C omnion Chamber, without a bedfellow, the Gaoler providing bedding, bed-clothes, and sheets-----------26

In the Common Chamber, the Prisoner providing his own bedding, bed-clothes and sheets, and not admitting a bedfellow------00

In the Common Chamber, the Prisoner providing the bedding, &c to admit a bedfellow who shall pay the Gaoler--------13

The said Prisoner to pay, himself, to the Gaoler-------0 4.

"Visitors to Debtors shall be admitted on week or working-days, from nine in the morning till twelve at noon, when, on Bell-ringing, all Visitors and Strangers whatsoever shall leave the Prison.

"All Debtors shall retire to their respective rooms at nine o'clock in the evening, in the Winter, and at ten in Summer; when all lights shall be extinguished, and their wards secured-: and no visitors shall be admitted on Sundays.

"No description of Prisoners shall be permitted to go upon the leads. As far as the situation of the Prison will admit, Felons shall be classed, and separated. An-charity given to the Prisoners, shall be funded, and distributed to them, in addition to their earnings; and a regular account of such distribution kept by the Governor, which is to be produced when any Magistrate shall require the same. "Durham, to wit.

"We, his Majesty's Justices of the Peace, present in open Court, at the General
Quarter Sessions of the Peace, holden at the City of Durham, in and for the said County, the thirteenth day of July 179G, Do approve and allow of the foregoing Rents and Rules.

"John Eden. "Ra. Milbanke.

"C. Spearman. "Hen. Hopper.

"H. MlITHOLDE. "Cha. Eggerton. "Ralph Orde. "Henry Mills.

"R. Burdon. "Ron. Green."

"WE, his Majesty's Justices of Assize for the Northern Circuit, having inspected the above Account of Chamber-Rents and Rules, Do allow, approve, and confirm the same. Dated 23d July, 179G. "G. Rooke.

"S. Lawrence."

Debtors in the Low Gaol receive, from a Legacy, 1. 6d. a week in Winter, and 1. a week in Summer: but of this there is no memorial in the Gaol. From the Mayor of Durham's book, however, it appears, that he charged the Corporation of Newcastle with having paid the above sums; and it also appears, that the Corporation of Newcastle reimbursed him. By an entry in the Common-Council books of Newcastle-upon-Tyne, it is recorded as follows:

"December 23d, *1699.*—3/. *6s. Sd.* is paid out of the Revenues of the Corporation of Newcastle to the Mayor of Durham, for the use of the Prisoners, annually on St. Andrew's Day."—See Brand's History of Newcastle, Vol. II. pp. 193, 194. It is the donation of a Mr. *Franhland.*

How the distribution of this charitable Bequest became changed from St. Andrew's day to a weekly Dole, and that payable to Prisoners in the *Low Gaol solely,* does no where appear: But, if neither of the low rooms within the gateway is occupied, (as has frequently been the case,) the arrears havenever been paid: and, on this account, the Keeper takes care to have one Prisoner-at least there, to secure the regular payment.

There is another donation, of fifteen shillings *per annum;* viz. 5. at Christmas, 5. at Easter, and 5. at Whitsuntide. This is a charge on lands heretofore belonging to Mr. Jackson, of Witton-le-Wear, in this County. The Estate has been lately purchased by Mr. John Wood, of Bishop's-Auckland, subject to the said charge, which is regularly paid to the Gaoler as it becomes due. Of this Legacy there is a memorial very properly recorded in the Gaol.

The " Legacy of Bishop *Crewe,"* noticed by Mr. Howard, seems to be mistaken, with respect to the name. It is not in Bishop Crewe's Will, which I have perused. But a donation similar to that of Bishop *Wood,* hereafter mentioned, is left to the Debtors in Durham Gaol, by Dr. *Hartwell;* in the copy of whose Will, (dated March 9th, 1724, and now in the possession of Mr. Wolfe, the Keeper,) after several other Bequests, is the following. "Item, I give and bequeath to the "*Gaol of Durham* for the use and benefit of Insolvent Debtors there, *Twenty* "*pounds per annum,* to be disposed of *under the same restrictions and limitations* "*with the Charity of the like kind by Bishop Wood;* and that in the application "of it respect be first had to the Parishioners of *Stanhope."* This Bequest, with several others specified in Dr. Hartwell's Will, and amounting to eighty pounds *per annum,* are chargeable upon an Estate at Fishbourn in this County.

The Estate at Fishbourn, out of which this Legacy is paid, as well as several others, is somewhat more than sufficient for the discharge of the ordinary demands made on the Treasurer, according to the Will. The rents are regularly paid by the Tenant to the Treasurer; and hence there is a yearly surplus in hand. If the demands of the year do not equal in amount the *twenty pounds* given to Durham Gaol, the Will has not provided for the disposal of the residue; and of course, it remains in the hands of the Treasurer of the Charity.

Out of this accumulating surplus, the Trustees have occasionally relieved very great distress; as, particularly they did, a few years since, in the case of the Tenant of the very estate in question, whose corn-crops had been destroyed by that tremendous hail-storm in the year 1792, which did so much mischief in the neighbourhood of Sedgefield. They allowed him sixty pounds, at two different payments, towards repairing the loss of his corn-crop.

For the honour done me by the following account of Dr. Hartwell's Legacy, I beg to express my respectful acknowledgements to the Right Rev. Dr. 'I'. Burgess, Lord Bishop of St. David's, one of the immediate Trustees authorized to execute the Will of the benevolent Testator.

By this charity were released, in *1797, Jour Debtors;* in 1798, *one;* in 1800, *one;* in *1802,Jour;* in l805,and 1806,ve each; in 1807, *three;* in 1808, *eight;* and up to my visit in 1809, *Jour.* The persons to be released are nominated by the Mayor and Corporation. If none are released, it is because none are nominated. The Mayor and Corporation are not the Trustees; but they nominate objects, and recommend them to the Charity, as directed by the will; and their recommendation is always accepted.

The Trustees in Dr. Hartwell's Will are the Dean and Chapter of Durham, or any three of them. The acting Trustees have been, for many years, the Dean, and four of the Prebendaries. As vacancies happen in the trust by death, other Prebendaries are elected by the Surviving Trustees.

Besides the Bishop of Lichfield, who is Dean of Durham, the present elected Trustees (1809) are the Bishop of St. David's, the Rev. R. G. Bowyer, and the Rev. George Barrington.

It appears that Dr. Hartwell was Rector of Stanhope in this County; which accounts for that part of his Bequest, enjoining, "That respect be first had to the Parishioners of Stanhope."

Dr. William Hartwell was formerly Secretary to Lord Crewe, when Bishop of Oxford. In the year 1681, he held the Rectory of Wickham, in this County; in 1685 was removed to that of Stanhope; and in 1709 was made Prebendary of Durham. He died in June 1725, and was interred in the Cathedral Church here.

The accounts relative to *Bishop Wood's Legacy* appear very intricate and perplexed; but, from the highly respectable characters who are at present engaged in the business, there is no doubt of its being very soon investigated, and attended with ultimate success. By his will, made in KJ90, the Bishop charged his Estate or Manor of Ecclescliff, in the Bishoprick of Durham, with the payment of twenty pounds annually, for ever; "to be applied for the relief and discharge of poor Prisoners, who then were, or thereafter might be, in Gaol at Durham, for Debt; each poor person's Debt not exceeding five pounds." And, by the said Will, the Mayor and Aldermen of the City of Durham, for the time being, were appointed Trustees of the Charity in question.

From the books, now in possession of Mr. Wolfe, it appears, "That the Estate chargeable with this Legacy was, in the year 1750, purchased by Anthony Hall, of Flass, in the County of Durham, Esq. and subject to the above devise. That between the years 1750 and 1766, there appeared to be arrears due from Mr. Hall to the Charity, to the amount of 54*l*. *4s.* 1That a suit in Chancery was instituted by the Bishop's Attorney General against the said Anthony Hall for those arrears, together with a further sum of 165*l*. *15s.* which had been paid into the hands of the then Mayor and Aldermen of the City of Durham, as Trustees of the Charity, by the said Anthony Hall, according to the Will of the said Bishop Wood, but which had never been duly accounted for to the Charity, by the said Mayor and Aldermen; and that in the year 1776, it was decreed by the Court that the said Anthony Hall should pay the whole of the arrears due to the said Charity, together with the Costs. That in the Michaelmas Term following, Mr. Hall filed a Bill in the Court of Exchequer against the Mayor and Aldermen, charging them with an abuse of the said Charity; in consequence whereof it was decreed, That the said Mayor and Aldermen should account for the arrears before stated. In 1/68, the Corporation lost their Charter: other Trustees were then duly appointed by the Court of Chancery at Durham, to manage the said Charity: and the said Trustees, from time to time, as any of them died, or declined acting, have been replaced by others, according to the directions of the said Will."

The present acting Trustees are Sir Ralph Milbanke, Bart. Sir John Eden, Bart. Henry Mills, Ralph Orde, Rowland Burdon, Charles Spearman, Esqrs. Rev. John Hutton, Rev. W. Nesfield, Arthur Mowbray, F. Johnson, W. Russell, and R. J. Fenwick, Esqrs. The balance of the Account due to the Charity at Midsummer 1802, as appears by the books of the late Treasurer, was *Two hundred and Jive pounds;* at Midsummer 1804, it had increased to *Two hundred and forty-Jive pounds;* and at Midsummer 1809, it amounted to *Three hundred and forty Jive pounds.* Means, however, I understand, are taking, not only to recover these arrears, but to secure a punctuality in payment for the future; so that hopes are now entertained of seeing the benevolent intentions of the Donor put into a regular and secure channel.

Bishop Wood was Chaplain to King Charles I. and in 16.35, Rector of Wickham $ in *1660,* Prebendary of Durham; in 160"3, Dean of Lichfield; and in 1671, consecrated Bishop of Lichfield, with which he held *in commendam* the Prebendal Stall at Durham. He died April 18, *1692,* and was buried at Ufford in Suffolk. His Will, by which he bequeaths several other charities, as well as that to the Gaol at Durham, is dated Nov. 11, lfjo.0.

Having thus stated my Remarks on the Debtors' Side of this Gaol, I proceed to that of the *Felons.*

L The Men Felons' day-room, large and commodious, is situate at the top of the Prison, 28 feet in length, 18 in breadth, and 9 feet 7 inches high. It has two large windows fronting the Southeast, which look also on the River; and one smaller window on the South-west side, by which means a thorough air is admitted. No other place is assigned for all descriptions of Male Prisoners.

II. The Women Felons' day-room is immediately under that appropriated to the Men: It has the same aspect, from two large windows looking to the South-east, I understand thete two Trustees are dead (1809), and none since elected in their room. and is *26 feet 6 inches* long, 18 feet wide, and 8 feet 3 inches high. This, likewise, is the only day-room, both for the Women Felons, and all other Female Offenders. III. I come now to the five cells, in which the Felons sleep. They are surely to be *numbered amongst the very worst in the kingdom;* and the descent to them is by a flight of forty-one steps from the Men's day-room.

The lowest and largest of these five cells, called " *The Great Hole,"* is 15 feet 2 inches by n feet 8 inches, and 7 feet 9 inches high. It has a flagged stone-floor, with straw and rugs furnished by the County. In this dungeon five of the Felons slept every night, when I was here in l802; but none are kept there now (1809), being removed to the room where the Women Felons used to sleep in 1802.

The second cell, in which three

Felons sleep, adjoins to the former; it is 11 feet 3 inches by 7 feet 4, and 7 feet 9 inches high. This too has a flagged floor, the same as the Great Hole. Both of them are totally dark, and, I may say, without ventilation, although each cell has a wooden tube, 8 inches by 5, which communicates, in a zig-zag direction, with the top of the building. But, as it is impossible to clean them, while in that form, I imagine they must long ago have been stopped up; for, on applying my candle to the mouth of the tube, not a breath of air was discernible. Both were damp and offensive.

The great attention of Mr. *Wolfe* to his Prisoners is manifest here, as well as in the *Soup-Kitchen*, by his frequently having them white-washed, and the doors kept open during the day. They would otherwise be fatal to many.

The two other Dungeons, in which the Women Felons sleep, are equally dark with those of the Men; but rendered somewhat less uncomfortable, by having boarded floors. They are immediately over those which I have already described. The largest of them is 16 feet 9 inches by 12 feet, and 11 feet 9 inches high: the other 11 feet 9 inches by 7 feet 10, and of the same height. Straw and rugs are allowed, as before; and here is the same obstructed ventilation.

There is a part of this Prison, which seems to have either escaped the vigilance of our excellent Howard, or to have been cautiously concealed from his acute inspection. This is a *third Dungeon*, on the same level with, but, by a passage, divided from the *Great Hole*. Having heard of it, I expressed a desire to see it, and the Turnkey fetched his keys.

This Dungeon, totally dark, is 7 feet by *6* feet 7, and 7 feet 9 inches high. In the midje of the flooring is a large, massy, wooden-grated trap door, strongly clouted with iron, and perforated with apertures 4 inches square. The Reader may guess my surprize, when upon this door's being lifted up, another dungeon presented itself!

I went down four stone steps: To the bottom one I found a ladder fixed; but not liking to trust myself upon it, turned back, and desired the Turnkey, with his candle, to go first. I followed down the ladder, which consisted of eleven rounds, or staves, and brought me into a vaulted or arched landing-place. Here I was most See page 177.
miraculously preserved from instant death; for, retreating at the bottom of the ladder two paces, I fell backwards: my coat pocket caught hold of something, which, with my weight, tore through the strong tape binding, and during the momentary suspension, I fortunately caught hold of the Turnkey; otherwise I must have precipitated to the bottom, and been dashed in pieces.

When I had recovered from the fright, and lighted my candle, I descended, by eleven stone steps, into the lowest Dungeon of all, which is 10 feet by 9, and 7 feet high to the crown of the arch. There is in the stone wall a niche, or narrow passage, with a privy, and a round hole cut in the seat.

Though there was no ventilation whatever in this *dark Cimmerian* Cavern, I found it perfectly dry, and even less disagreeable than the arched landing-place above it. The air was warm, but not oppressively so, nor loaded with vapours. My candle, which I letdown the sewer several feet, to ascertain if there had been any Prisoners there lately, shewed no signs of a feculent, excrementitious, or corrupted atmosphere.

When the Prison was built, in times now long since past, this place of extreme durance must have been intended as an *Oubliette*. The ruins of some I have seen, in what is called a "Castle-Keep;" and there is one in excellent preservation at Alnwick Castle, which, by the roof, appeared to be of Saxon architecture. They are subterraneous caverns, in which such unhappy persons as had incurred the displeasure of a powerful Baron or Chieftain, in feudal times, were, to gratify his malice, let down, with a loaf of bread, and a bottle of wine; and the ladder being then drawn up, were never more heard of, or enquired after, but suffered to perish in solitude, famine, and darkness!

The Rev. Mr. *Nesfield,* an active Magistrate of this County, (See p. 182,) told me that he remembered a Man's being confined in this Dungeon; but no sooner did he receive the information, than repairing to the Prison, he ordered him to be immediately taken out. This, probably, was done by that unfeeling wretch, of whom Mr. Howard speaks, as torturing his Prisoners with *thumb screws* -f-!

That Oubliettes were constructed (says my inestimable friend, Dr. Lettsom) for the *final exclusion* of Man from light and society, is fully confirmed by History. There weye several of these in Europe, and particularly in France, in which persons were shut up, who had been condemned to perpetual imprisonment. Bonfons, in his *Antiquity de Paris,* speaking of Ungues Aubriot, Prevost of the City, who was assigned this punishment, says, "qu'il fut pr6ch£ et mitre publiquement au parvis Notre-Dame; et qu' apres cela, il fut condamne a (Stre en f *oubliette,* au painet l'eau." .j-Ol such a one, to be for ever forgotten is a benefit. It is a far more grateful task, for *me* especially, to make known the following Letter, which 1 find in the Gentleman's Magazine for 1806, p. 115. "Mr. Ukban. Jan. 11th, 1806.

"I shuddered at Mr. Neild's account of the *oubliette* in Durham Castle (Vol. Lxxv. p. 9S9); and earnestly hope that the worthy Bishop, whose property it is, will lose no time in having it filled up. The present Gaoler may be trusted; but such a horrible dungeon should not remain. Let it not be said that there is one *oubliette* in British ground. Melancthoh. "

It is a fortunate circumstance for humanity, where so much power is lodged, that the present Gaoler, Mr. *Wolfe* never treats his Prisoners with that rigorous severity, which so often hardens the Gaolers heart; and that the ear of the learned Prelate, who adorns the Diocese, is ever open to the cries of distress.

I have often wished that a new Gaol were built at this place. There is a plot of ground behind the Sessions House, seemingly but of little use; and not only well adapted for the purpose of both Prisons, but abundantly supplied by a spring of water, and with stone and lime almost upon the spot.

On my visit here in September 1802, I observed, that out of the 18 Debtors, 11 only were at Divine Service, but that of the 8 Felons, all attended, except one. Their general behaviour was orderly, and attentive to a very appropriate discourse from the Chaplain.

The County Bridewell at Durham was built, as appears by the date over the door, in 1634. It is situate on the side of a hill near the Bridge.

On the ground-floor next the street, which is the upper part of the Prison, is a convenient room for the Magistrates, who meet here to do business. The Turnkey's rooms are on the same level, and have a command of the whole Prison. The old Gaol consists of two good day-rooms, and several sleeping-apartments. The first day-room, now occupied by Women, is three stories from the ground; and has two windows, which look to the River, *26* feet by 12, and 7 feet high, with a boarded floor, and good fire-place.

Underneath are two rooms, which are used as sleeping-rooms for the Women. The first is 17 feet hy 12, and 8 feet *6* inches high; the other 12 feet 6 inches by 11 feet, and *6* feet *6* inches high. They have each a window, which has the same aspect as the day-room above. They have boarded floors, wooden bedsteads, with straw, and coverlets, and are dry good rooms. Immediately underneath these two rooms, *on* the ground-floor, are two others, exactly of the same dimensions; but which have not been in use/except for lumber, for some years, being very, damp and unhealthy.

The second day-room, also occupied by Women, is on the second storv, in the adjoining wing of the BridewelL It is 19 feet by 15, and 7 feet high, and has three windows, that look to the Northeast, with a boarded floor and a fireplace. Under this are two other rooms on the ground-floor. The first, 13 feet by *9,* and 7 feet high; the second, 9 feet by 7, and 8 feet high: Both of them very damp and unhealthy; but I was informed, that they had not been used since the building of the new apartments.

From the second day-room there is a passage communicating with an arch of the Bridge, which lies at the back or West side of the Old Prison. *Under this Arch*

B B was an access to two large cells, where, till lately, Prisoners convicted of capital offences were used to sleep. The first cell is 19 feet 5 inches by 13 feet 9, and 9 feet high; the other is 14 feet 3 inches by 13 feet 3, and 14 feet high, with flagged floors; both of them totally dark, and fitter for a deposit of coals, than the reception of any human being. I am now happy to add, that at my last visit, in 1809, the Keeper informed me that these detestable Cells, "under the Arch of a Bridge," had not been used for the preceding twelve months, as the bottom part of the straw upon which the *Prisoners slept,* was found to have rotted into dung!

The new building consists of seven rooms. The upper story, the third from the ground, is divided into three apartments: The first, 13 feet by 9, and 8 feet high; the second and third nearly of the same dimensions. Each has a good window fronting the North-east, with a fireplace, a wooden bedstead, with straw and coverlets, and is occupied generally by such Prisoners as can work at any business, Tailors, Shoemakers, Weavers, &c. These are all dry good rooms, and have no communication with each other.

The second story immediately underneath is the Men's day-room, in which the principal part of the Male Prisoners are kept. It is a very large and good room, 31 feet 3 inches by *16* feet 5, and 9 feet high; and has four large windows fronting the North-east, a good fireplace, a boarded floor, and ceiled roof, which make it a very comfortable apartment.

The story on the ground-floor is divided into three rooms, of the" same dimensions as the upper, or third story. One of them is appropriated to beating of hemp, for, which purpose blocks are fixed; and here the Prisoners from the day-room are alternately taken to their work.

This Prison is well supplied with water. Each Prisoner has not only the County, allowance of 3d. per day, but receives also the whole profit of his or her earnings. People of the Town attend daily with victuals, and each Prisoner purchases for himself what he thinks proper.

No Chaplain, nor any religious attentions.

There is an useless piece of ground adjoining the Bridewell, and desirably calculated for a court-yard and workshop, which, as being immediately in view of the Turnkey, would be perfectly secure. I was sorry to observe a very large dung-hill at one end of this ground, just under the Prison windows, so that it is worse than useless, by becoming a nuisance, which might easily be removed.

QZt A *New Gaol,* with Courts of Justice adjacent is now building in a good situation, and a little way out of the Town DYMCHURCH, *Kent; See page 162.* EDINBURGH. *The City Tolbooth.*

Gaoler or Captain, *James Welch;* now *Thomas Sibbald.*

Salary, 150J. in lieu of all Fees or Perquisites whatever, which are to be accounted for to the Magistrates. The Gaoler has a licence for selling porter and ale: He likewise furnishes the Prisoners with bread and small beer.

Garnish prohibited.

Chaplain, Rev. Mr. *Porteous.* Salary, 15/.

Duty, once on Sunday, to *Debtors only.* Criminals are *not permitted to attend Divine Service;* but are allowed a Bible each, or a Testament.

Surgeon; when wanted, application is made to the Deacon of the Surgeons' Company.

Number of Prisoners, Debtors., Felons, &c.

1S02, Sept. 13th, 17------26. 1809, Sept. 25th------30------15.

Allowance, to *Debtors,* according to the discretion of the Magistrates.

Felons have fourpence per day, till indicted: and afterwards (which is fifteen days before trial) they have sixpence a day. REMARKS.

The entrance into this Prison lies

through three doors, the innermost opening into what is named "*The Debtors' Hall.*" The first object that here struck my notice was the following Copy of Lines, enclosed in a gilt frame, and painted on a board conspicuously hung up. They have a mixture of wit and truth that merits some consideration: and I-therefore make no apology for inserting them.

"A Prison is a House of Care; A place where none can thrive:
A touch-stone sure to try a Friend;...
A grave for men alive.
Sometimes a House of Right;
Sometimes a House of Wrong:
Sometimes a House of Whores and Thieves,
  And honest Men among."

This Gaol, and a large mass of old buildings which adjoins to it (but since taken down) nearly block up one of the most spacious streets in the City, by being built in the centre. Here is no court-yard, and the Gaoler has no apartments within the Prison.

If a Prisoner for Debt declares, upon oath, that he has not wherewithal to maintain himself, his Creditor must *aliment* him, with at least threepence per day, within ten days after notice given for that purpose. By an Act of the first Parliament of King William, *1696,* Sixth Session, Chap. 32, Debtors are to be alimented by their Creditors, at the discretion of the Magistrates. The lowest order to this end, that I could find on record, was four pence a day, when the Debt was only one guinea': The highest order was eighteen pence. This principally, however, depends on the rank of life in which the Debtor has been accustomed to move. When I was here in the Prison, on the 13th of Sept. 1802, the Keeper received *Jive pounds* from the Creditor of Mrs-Stuart, being one hundred days' aliment, at one shilling per day. The Debt was three pounds; the Costs *three shilCtngs;* and the aliment was to commence from the first of September, the day of her commitment.

By the process of *Cessio bonorum,* a Debtor, after having lain one month in Prison, may obtain liberty, and be secured against execution for any previous Debts, upon making a surrender of all his effects, to be divided amongst his Creditors; though if afterward he come into better circumstances, his effects may be attached for the payment of those previous Debts. This truly-compassionate Law precludes a Creditor from putting his Debtor in Prison, unless there be good reason to think that he is acting fraudulently.

Perjury is not, I believe, frequent m Scotland. The Oath, and form of administering it there, are very solemn. The Witness, holding up his right-hand, epeatsthe following words after the Judge: "By God himself, and as I shall answer to ' God at the Great Day of Judgement, I shall declare the Truth, and nothing but "the Truth, in so far as I know, or 9hall be asked at me." The depositions are then read over by the Clerk, and signed by the Witnesses and Judge .

Male-Debtors in this Prison have two rooms with glazed windows, and WomenDebtors one, on the West-side of the building; in which they are furnished with wooden bedsteads, straw mattress, two pillows,, a blanket and a rug each, for which they pay as per Table.

Felons also have four rooms on the East-side of the Gaol; two of which have grated and glazed windows, and the rest are iron-barred. They are supplied with mattresses only on the floors, a blanket and a rug each.

In all the above rooms there are two tubs; the smaller one M filled every morning, with fresh water, and the other serves the purpose of a sewer.

From what I saw here, I cannot but think that very little attention is paid to reforming the Prisoners of the *Tolbooth*. In the first place, an attendance on Divine service is singularly made *optional with the Debtors,* and *not permitted to Felons*. Both descriptions, Men and Women, without distinction, mix promiscuously See "Principles of the Law of Scotland," 5th Edit. 8vo. Edinburgh, 1777, P-462, 463; and Louthian's "Form of Procces before the Court of Justiciary in Scotland." Edinb. 1753, p. 109.

together of a morning, when their tubs are filled with water; and in the same room were four Women-Felons, confined with as many Female-Debtors. Every Prisoner *may have as much beer as he can pay for!* The tap-room, in consequence, was full, and many persons from the Town were drinking indiscriminately with the Prisoners. The Gaol, indeed, had been white-washed about six months before my visit in 1802; but it was the only time, *t* was told, in the space of *twenty years.* No employment is permitted here; nor any firing allowed, except in the common-hall, or day-room, which is also used as the Chapel.

The following Tables xf Fees and Regulations for the Gaol and Gaoler are worthy of insertion.

ACT OF COUNCIL; *At Edinburgh, the fifth day of September, in the year Eighteen hundred and ten*;

Which day the Right Honourable The Loho Provost, Magistrate, and Council of the City of Edinburgh, in Council assembled, Rescinded the Regulations adopted on the l/th of July 1728 for the Government of theCJaol i and-ORDB-RBD the following Rules and Regulations to be substituted in their place, and to be strictly observed during the pleasure of the Council. PART I. Relating To The Office And Duties Of Gaoler, And Clerk To The Gaol.

Section I.—*Gaol Dues*.

The Gaol dues are to be exacted-by the Gaoler and Clerk, partly from the Incarcerator, or person interested in the imprisonment, and partly from the Prisoner, whether a Civil Debtor or Delinquent.

I. Dues Payaele To The Gaoler.

1.—*By the Incarcerator, or Person interested in the Imprisonment.*

For every person imprisoned, or arrested in prison, for any Civil Debt, there shall be g£. s. d.

paid at imprisonment, and when any Warrant on which he shall be arrested is booked, for each pound Sterling of the Debt for which he.is so imprisoned or arrested-------006

For every person imprisoned on any Warrant, as being in *meditatione fugte*, there shall be paid at his imprisonment, if the debt is under 10l.-.-. — -0 2 6 If above 10i.------.-.-----050

For every person imprisoned on a Warrant of Lawburrows, if granted by the Court of Justiciary------------050

If granted by any inferior Magistrate-------O 2 G

For every person imprisoned for exhibition of papers, or *ad factum prasiandum,* whether by Wan-ant of the Supreme or Inferior Court-----0 2 &

For every person imprisoned by any Warrant which does not pay Fees in terms of the foregoing regulations, except Criminal Warrants, there shall be paid--0 2 0 Q.—*By the Prisoner.*

The Prisoner, whether a Civil Debtor or Delinquent, shall pay for every night of his confinement, to the Gaoler, the following dues: If a Burgess of Edinburgh----'----0 0 S

If.not a Burgess--------'--004

Any person imprisoned for Civil Debt desiring to have a room by himself, shall pay for the same such sum as shall be agreed on with the Gaoler, and that in full of all fees; but such sum shall, in nocase, exceed 10. weekly.

II. Dues Payable To The Clerk Op Thb Gaol.

For every attestation of Commitment, signed by the Gaoler or the Clerk, the party £, *t. d.* requiring the same shall pay---------01$

For every Diligence, or Warrant, delivered up by the Gaoler or Clerk, the party requiring the same shall, if the requisition be made within eight days of the Prisoner's liberation, pay----------006

And if the requisition be made after that period------0 1. 0

Every person incarcerated upon Letters of Lawburrows, if granted by the Court of

Justiciary, shall pay at his liberation--------020

If granted by any inferior Magistrate--*r*-----010

Each person incarcerated by Warrant of the Magistrates of the City, shall, at his liberation, pay------------006

If by Warrant of the Sheriff, or a Justice of Peace of the County----O 1 O

For each Petition by a Prisoner for the act of grace, and for the Clerk's declaration thereto..-----------016

All Government Prisoners shall, at their liberation, pay-----034

Every person imprisoned for exhibition of papers, or *ad factum prastandum,* at their liberation-------------026

All persons imprisoned, or arrested in Prison, for any Civil Debt, if amounting to 5/.

and not exceeding 10/. shall, at their liberation, pay-----020

If 10/. and not exceeding 30/.---------026

If 30/. and not exceeding 50/.----»----034

If 50/. and upwards-----------050

And no Prisoner is to pay any thing to the Servants of the Gaol.

The Gaoler and Clerk are hereby strictly prohibited and discharged, under the penalty of dismission, or such other punishment as the Magistrates shall judge proper, from demanding or receiving, by himself or any of his servants, directly or indirectly, from any Incarcerator, or Prisoner, or from any person in his or her name, at entry during his or her confinement, or at liberation, any sum or sums of money, in name of entry money, or liberation money, or garnish money, or under any other name or pretext whatsoever, except the dues and fees above established.

Section II.—*Regulations regarding the Internal Management of the Gaol.*

I. Both in summer and winter, the Gaol shall be opened at nine o'clock in the morning, for the admission of visitants, and shall continue open till three o'clock in the afternoon. Between the hours of three and half past four o'clock afternoon, the Gaol shall be shut: at half past four the Gaol shall be again open, for the admission of visitants, and shall continue open till nine o'clock at night, but no longer.

II. No person is to have admission, for the purpose of visiting any of the Prisoners, before nine o'clock in the morning, between the hours of three and half past four o'clock in the afternoon, or after nine o'clock at night, excepting Physicians or Surgeons visiting any of the Prisoners as patients, and Lawyers or Agents engaged in the defence of any of the Prisoners accused of crimes 3 and excepting also any person who shall have received a written order of admission from any of the Magistrates: but no person to.be admitted to persons committed on Criminal Warrants for further examination, without an order frqm the Judge by whom such persons are commited. III. The Gaoler shall not, at his peril, admit into the Gaol, as a visitant, any person who there is reason to suspect has any illegal or improper object in view; and shall search the person of every one claiming admittance to Criminals, professional gentlemen excepted. IV. When the Gaol is shut, the whole keys are to be kept by the Gaoler in his own custody, and are not to be entrusted to his servants. When the Gaol is open, he is always to be at hand, to superintend the conduct of his servants.

V. Prisoners for debt, or any other civil cause, are to have the best rooms, and *be kept separate from delinquents and disorderly persons.* The Gaoler is to prevent civil Debtors from associating or conversing with Delinquents, as far as it is possible for him to do so, in the present confined and incommodious state of the Gaol.

VI. The Gaoler shall allow the friends and servants of Debtors, at all convenient times when the Gaol is open, to bring in victuals; but no spirituous liquors. VII. The present state of the Gaol makes it necessary for the Magistrates to order that all Prisoners accused or convicted of capital crimes, or condemned to transportation, banishment, pillory, or corporal punishment, be at all times locked up in their respective rooms, except when a Magistrate, on account of their health, shall permit any of them, not convicted of capital crimes, to get the liberty of a certain part of the Prison during the day. VIII. Prisoners accused or convicted of offences not capital, and not condemned to transportation-, banishment, pillory, or corporal punishment, that is, petty Delinquents, are to be separated as much as possible from Prisoners for civil debts, and prevented from associating with each other, as far as the present state of the Gaol will permit. Prisoners of this description are to be locked up every night before. nine o'clock in their respective apartments. IX. The Gaoler shall at all times *keep the Male and Female Prisoners separate,* and *shall preve ntall intercourse between ihem.*

X. If it shall happen that Prisoners are at any time imprisoned for delinquencies during the night, or by the verbal order of a Magistrate, the Gaoler shall at all times, on the morning after such imprisonment takes place, give in to the Sitting Magistrate a written report of the name of the Delinquent, the crime with which he is charged, and the name of the Magistrate by whose order he is committed. And if there is not lodged with the Gaoler, within four hours after he makes such report, a legal written Warrant against the offender, the Gaoler shall instantly liberate all such persons from Prison.

XI. The walls of the whole apartments in the Gaol are to be washed down twice every year with strong lime water.-The whole stairs are to be swept and scraped twice, and washed once every week. The different rooms and apartments are to be swept twice, and washed once every week; and the windows of each thrown open every morning, for the admission of free air. All dung, filth, and ashes, &c. is to be removed from every apartment before ten o'clock in the morning; by which hour a full supply of fresh water is to be carried up to each room. The Gaoler is to employ the persons necessary for all these operations 5 but for their regular performance he is himself to be responsible. XII. The Gaoler shall every morning after opening, and every evening before shutting the Gaol, personally visit every room and apartment therein, and make a minute inspection; in order to discover and prevent the accomplishment of any attempts to cut the iron bars, or break through the walls, roof, joists, or floors of the Prison: and he shall take particular care that no instruments of any kind be conveyed to, or be in the possession of the Prisoners, whereby they may effect their escape. XIII. When the Gaoler shall observe any of the Prisoners in a bad state of health, he shall give intimation to the Surgeon appointed by the Magistrates and Council, to lake charge of those confined in Gaol. XIV. The Gaoler shall prevent the Prisoners from doing each other bodily harm, or committing any riots. And for this purpose he is invested with the power of putting the offender in such cases, in the iron or strong room until next day, when he shall make a report to the Magistrates 3 but the Gaoler is. oa no occasion to exercise this power, without reporting to the Magistrates. XV. The Gaoler shall not, under the penalty of dismission, and such other punishment as the Magistrates shall think proper, furnish the Prisoners with any spirituous or other liquors -r and be shall, under the same penalty, use erery means in his power to prevent spirituous liquors from. being brought into the Gaol, and the Prisoners from being furnished therewith. XVJ. The Gaoler shall not, at his peril, allow any liquor or beverage to be furnished to the Prisoner except ale, beer, or porter; and he shall at his peril use every means in his power to prevent intoxication and gaming among the Prisoners. XVII. The Gaoler shaH not permit the Prisoners to make any exaction in money, or otherwise, on any. pretext whatever, from their'fellow Prisoners, whether recently incarcerated or not: and to enable hiin to enforce this rule, he shall have the power of confining the delinquent in the iron or strong room until next day; when lie sliall report the case to the sitting Magistrate. XVIII. As it sometimes happens that Delinquents are committed to Gaol in a state of great filth, without any change of clothes, the Gaoler is authorised to provide, and at all times, to keep a dozen of coarse linen shirts for the use of the Prisoners in this situation, to be taken from them beforethey are liberated i and he is authorized to adopt such other measures for ensuring the due attention of the Prisoners to the cleanliness of their persons, as particular circumstances *way* require. XIX. The clerk to the Gaol shall, under the superintendance of the Gaoler, keep a book or books, which shall be open and patent to all the licgea; and which shall be regularly produced to the Members of Council appointed to visit the Gaol, as after-mentioned; in which book the following)articulars shall he carefully inserted: 1st, The name and designation of the Prisoner, as expressed in the Warrant of Commitment or Diligence on which he is incarcerated. 2d, The name of the incarcerator, with the ground of commitment, as contained in the Warrant or Diligence, whether for crimes, payment of debt, or otherwise. 3d, The date of the Warrant or Diligence, and by what Judge it is issued. 4th, The date of Imprisonment, with the name of tlie officer who executed the Warrant or Diligence. 5th, The date of the Prisoner's liberation, and by whom, and on what account liberated. This book is also to contain an index, with an alphabetical list of the names of the Prisoners, distinguishing Criminals by the letter C after their names, and Debtors by the letter D. XX. The Gaoler is, at his peril, to beware of giving up the person of any Prisoner upon tlic *verbal order* of any Magistrate, or other Judge. He is at all times to require a written order, for whatever purpose, or for how short time soeer such Prisoner maybe wanted; and is to take a proper receipt from the person who receives him: a precaution the more uecessary to be observed, as accidents have happened, from the loose and vague way in which it has been the practice for Officers to require the delivery of Prisouers to be carried to the different offices for examination. XXI. Divine Service is to be performed in the Gaol every Sunday: but, as the present state of the Gaol is such, as to render it impossible to assemble all the Felons on this occasion, a discretionary power is lodged with the Gaoler, to permit such only as he shall think proper to attend.

PART II. Relating To The Superintendence or The Gaol, On Thb Part Of The Magistrates.

I. A standing Committee, consisting of the Lord Provost and Magistrates, and any other members of Council, shall be annually appointed, along with the other annual Committees, and shall be termed

"The Committee on the Gaol;" which Committee shall hold regular quarterly meetings, and shall likewise hold such occasional meetings as may be found requisite.

II. The duty of this Committee shall be, to take a general superintendence of every thing connected with the Gaol: to enforce a rigid observance of the Regulations; and to see that the Gaoler and Clerk KTfbrm their duty with fidelity and attention: to attend to the state of the Gaol in regard to the sufficiency of the building, and accommodation of the Prisoners; and to suggest such rej»irs as may appear necessary: to observe and correct any disputes or abuses in the management of the Gaol, and suggest improvements on the Regulations. III. If any Prisoner has reason to complain of the cause of his detention, or the duration of his confinement, ho is to apply to the Clerk of the Gaol, who is to state the case to the Gaol Committee, free of all expence to such Prisoner. IV. A copy of these Regulations is to be hung up in a conspicuous part of the Gaol, for the Information of all concerned.

Extracted from the records of Council,' By C. Cunningham, *Conj. Clk.*

In three of the Felons rooms, within the Tolbooth, are stocks fixed on the floors, the upper part of which lifts up, to receive the leg of the Prisoner, who must lie on his back until released; and in these stocks they have been confiued night and day.

After sentence of death a Criminal is taken to the *Gad,* as it is called, or *Condemned Cell.* Here a blacksmith fixes an iron strap to his leg, fastened again to a ring, which encircles a strong iron bar, running across the room; so that he cannot lift up that foot from the floor: In this situation the wretched sufferer has been sometimes detained during six weeks, until the execution of his awful sentence.

The horrid *Cage* likewise remains in the above *Gad-Room:* But the Gaoler told me it was no longer used.

My first visit to this Prison, in Sept. l8oo, was on a Saturday; but the Lord Provost being out of Town, the Gaoler would not permit me to enter the Prison rooms: therefore I did not gain admission till Monday, the 25th, when I found the place clean, as I expected, and the tubs all emptied: But it did not appear to have been White-washed since my former visit, in 1802.

The Clauses against Spirituous Liquors I found hung up, but not the Act for Preserving the Health of Prisoners.

A New *City Tolbooth* is now building, which will communicate with the Justiciary Courts. The spacious street will thus be freed from obstruction; Prisoners will then enjoy fresh air, that genuine cordial of life; and the present sad place of confinement, will be happily effaced from memory.

I here beg leave to make my respectful acknowledgements to the Right Hon. the Lord Provost, Magistrates, and Council, for the great Honour conferred upon me, by presenting me with the Freedom of the City.

James Chalmer, esq. formerly Practitioner of tire Court of Session, and a writer to the signet, in his evidence before a Committee of the House of Lords on the 27th of February, 1S09, states the following extract from " The Institute of the Laws of Scotland," by Mr. Erskine, (Book IV, Title III, Sect. *26, 27, 28,*) to be the present practice respecting the *Cessio Bonorum.* c c . "Our Law, from a consideration of compassion, has allowed Insolvent Debtor to apply for the liberty of their persons, upon *Cessio Bonorutn;* that is, on making a full surrender to their Creditors of their whole estate, real and personal. Before a Debtor has a right to make this demand, he must be *under actual Confinement;* for it is in itself incongruous, and might be of bad example, that any one should claim the privilege of personal Liberty, who is not truly deprived of it..

"The benefit of *Cessio* must be insisted in by way of action, in which the Prrj soner must make all his creditors parties to the suit; and it is cognizable only by the Session.

"The Pursuer must set forth in his libel the misfortune or accident by which he became insolvent, and bring proper evidence of it. He must produce, with the. process, a certificate, under the hand of one of the Magistrates of the Borough where he is imprisoned, bearing, that he hath been *a Month in Prison;* without which certificate the Process is not to be sustained.

"He must exhibit, upon oath, a particular *Inventory of his Estate*; and depose, that he has neither heritage nor moveables, other than what is contained in that inventory*I* and that he hath made no conveyance of any part thereof since his imprisonment, to the prejudice of his Creditors. He must also declare upon oath, whether he hath made any such conveyance *before his Imprisonment;* and point out the persons to whom, and the cause of granting it, that the Court may judge whether he has, by any fraudulent or collusive practice, forfeited his claim to liberty: And he must make over to his creditors the whole of his estate, absolutely,, and without the least reservation. The *Decree* ordaining the Prisoner to be set free, can have no effect as to future Debts contracted by him, nor even as to posterior corroborations of former Debts; neither can it affect Creditors who were not called as Defenders in the Action upon, which the Decree proceeded: And therefore, if the Debtor shall, after his release, be again imprisoned upon any such Debt, he caunot avail himself of his former Decree, but must raise a new Action of *Cessio.*

"The disposition which is granted by a Debtor to his Creditors upon a *Cessio Bonorum* is not in satisfaction, or *Solutum* of the Granter's Debts, but merely in *further Security.*

"If, therefore, the Debtor shall acquire any Estate after the Decree recovered by him upon the *Cessio,* such new acquisition may be affected by his Creditors, as if there had been no *Cessio;* but still he may retain as much of it as is necessary for his own maintenance.

"This is agreeable to *our ancient Law,* and likewise to the Roman.

"No Debtor, whose debt arises from a crime, or delict, is entitled to this privilege; which is also conformable both to the Roman Law, from whence we have borrowed it, and to the analogy of the "Act of Grace," to be immediately explained. Hence it is not competent to fraudulent Bankrupts, nor to Criminals liable in *Assythment,* (that is, in a sum in name of damages or indemnification to the party injured, though the crime itself should be extinguished by a pardon,) nor to those debts which have been contracted by fraud, or breach of trust."

The foregoing course of proceeding is stated to have been the constant and uniform practice in *Scotland,* and is also understood to be so stilt

As to its having ever been complained of, as of any material inconvenience to trade in that Country, the Judges of the Court of Session have been heard to complain, not of the *Principle of the Law,* (for that was universally approved of) but Of the *Practice under it.*

The Judges observed, that they ought not to grant the *Cessio,* but to persons whose Insolvency was owing to misfortune: They complained of the difficulty of discovering whether the Insolvency was really owing to misfortune, or to imprudence.

The Actions of *Cessio* were understood to be conducted by Gentlemen at the Bar, and Solicitors, *gratuitously,* out of compassion: The Creditors, again, *were obliged to pat/ their Counsel, and their Agents*: There was little to be got, generally, by opposing the *Cessio;* and therefore it was remarked, "that there was little opposition, and that the representation and evidence to the Court, was *all of one side."*

With respect to the nature of the "*Act of Grace'* the following passage from the above Work of Mr. Erskine is extracted, Section 28.

"Anciently there was no legal provison for the maintenance of those imprisoned for Debt; and, as they could not be allowed to starve, it frequently happened that Royal Boroughs, who had received them into their Prisons, were burthened with the expence of their maintenance.

It was therefore provided by *I6)6,* C. 32. usually called The *Act of Grace,* 'That where any Prisoner for a Civil Debt shall make oath before a Magistrate of the Jurisdiction, that he has not wherewith to maintain himself, the Magistrate may require the Creditor, upon whose Diligence he is imprisoned, to provide, and give security for an alimony to him, at a rate not under threepence a day; and if the Creditor refuse or delay, for ten days after, to exhibit the alimony ascertained, it shall be lawful for the Magistrate to set the Prisoner at Liberty."

"The Debt, and Diligence upon which the Debtor was imprisoned, are not discharged by the Magistrates' setting him free upon this Statute; and therefore the Creditor may again use personal execution against him upon the former Caption: But, if he abuse that power in an oppressive manner, he may be condemned in a Fine for that abuse, and the Debtor will have relief by a suspension. This obligation upon Creditors to support their indigent Debtors took its rise from the *Romans,* and was not altogether unknown in our *Ancient Jmu:*

"If the Magistrates themselves shall,, after the Creditor's refusal to exhibit aliment to the Prisoner, chuse to be at the expence of his subsistence, rather than dismiss him from Prison, they may continue his confinement.

"This *Statute* is expressly limited to the case of Prisoners for civil debts; and therefore, no person imprisoned either for not performing a fact which was in his power, or for the non-pavnient of a Fine, or of a sum awarded against him, in the name of damages upon a delict, or penal law, can claim any benefit of it."

It has been asked, whether the foregoing is an exact statement of the practice upon the Law in question; or whether, through accident or design, any modifications of that practice have taken place in later years. No material ones seem to have been introduced; and the practice, in substance, is said to be nearly the same. One circumstance, however, has been mentioned, with regard to the process of *Cessio Bonorum.* The Cessio is either refused or granted, according as it appears to the Court (from the proof which has been laid, or from the circumstances of the case) that the *Pursuer* of the *Cessio* has a right to it, as having acted honestly and fairly.

Thus, for instance, if it shall appear that he has not kept regular books, when be is a person in that situation of life who ought to keep regular books; and, if there be no good reason assigned for such books not having been kept, or not being exhibited to the Court; then the benefit of the Cessio has been often denied to such persons, even. although there be no. other evidence, direct or presumptive, of fraud. v

Whether this practice is fouud to answer publick convenience in Scotland, has been matter of enquiry; to which the following seems a satisfactory answer. *t* enables those who are confined for Debt, and who are conceived by the Courts not to have been guilty of any fraud, to get out of Prison: And, sometimes, it leads to this, That where proof of fraud cannot be obtained, Debtors, (who, it may be conceived, ought not to be protected from the Diligence of their Creditors, in so far *as* respects *Imprisonment,)* do, notwithstanding, obtain the benefit of the Process *Cessio.* But it does not appear that any great inconvenience or injury arises from such a process being allowed to exist in the practice of the Scotch Courts.

EDINBURGH.

Canongate Tolbooth.

Gaoler, *William Pursell;* now *John Goulan.* Salary, 25/. Fees, see Table.

Licence for porter and beer. Garnish, prohibited.

Chaplain, none; nor any religious attentions.

Surgeon, Mr. *Burt,* who makes a Bill.

Number of Prisoners, Debtors. Felons, &c.

Sept. 12th, 1802,------8-2.

Sept. 23 d, 1809,------4 0.

Allowance, to Debtors, as they are alimented. To Criminals, *4d.* a day.

REMARKS.

The Gaoler of this Prison lives on the opposite side of the street; but he has one room on the first floor for his own use; and to it adjoins his tap_room, and the day-room assigned for the *Debtors.*

The *second-jloor* has two rooms for Debtors, which have grated and glazed casement windows, table, benches to sit upon, and corner shelves for their provisions. There is also a fire-place in every room, but coals are not allowed. On this second floor is likewise a room, called "The Gad-Room," of 12 feet by 8, allotted for *Felons;* with a strong iron bar running across the middle of the floor, to which they are chained at night. It has a grated and glazed window, but no fire-place.

The *third-story* has one room for Debtors, similar, and fitted up in the same manner with those below. They are all on the South-side of the Prison; and furnished by the Keeper with wooden bedstead, straw-in-sacking beds, two blankets, and a coverlet, at *4d.* per night.

On the North-side are two small rooms upon the first-floor, for the better sort of Debtors, and furnished by the Keeper with bedding, &c. at 5. per week.

If the Incarcerator does not aliment his Debtor in twelve days after confinement, he is discharged; and one, under this circumstance, was liberated on the very day of my visit, in Sept. 1809.

No court-yard. Water is laid on by pipes. There is a sewer below. The whole Prison very dirty.

"Table Of Fees.

"ACT Of COUNCIL, anent the Fees and JiEGi'LATiONs of the Canongate Prison. At Canongate, the Seventeenth day of June, in the Year One Thousand Seven Hundred and Ninety-five,

The which day William Coulter, Esq. Baron Bailie, Messrs. Daniel Miller and Robert Scott, resident Bailies, and William Murray, Treasurer of Canongate, sitting in Council, Having taken into their conr sideration the many complaints and disputes anent the Prison-Fees of Canongate, owing to there being no public authorized copy of these Fees in use; And considering that the Right Honourable the Lord Provost, Magistrates, and Town Council of Edinburgh, as Proprietors of the said Prison, by their Act of Council, dated the 4th November, 1799, 'authorized the Gaoler of Canongate to exact the same Fees as are exacted by the Keeper of Edinburgh Prison, and contained in an Act of Council, dated the '17th July, 1728:' therefore the said Baron, resident Bailies, and Treasurer, hereby statute and ordain the Fees mentioned in the said Act of Council, of date the 17th July, 1723, and no other, to be exacted by the Keeper of the Tolbooth of Canongate; and which are as follows, *viz.*

Fees payable to the Gaoler of Canongate. *Scots.*

The Incarcerator of each Debtor shall pay at incarceration to the Gaoler two and *eg. s. d.* one half per cent, of the sum for which the Prisoner shall be booked.

Item, The Incarcerator of any person or persons by the Lords Letters of *Lawborrowt,* shall pay at incarceration---*t*--'-----300.

Item, The Incarcerator of any person or persons, upon Lawborrows by a Magistrate,
Sheriff, or Justice of the Peace, shall pay at incarceration,----1 10 0

Item, The Incarcerator of any person for exhibition of papers, or for implementing of writs (captions for re-production of processes before the inferior Courts excepted) shall pay at incarceration-------. 1 10 ft

Each person imprisoned for a civil debt, or otherwise, not being a Burgess, shall pay to the Gaoler of House-Dues each night--.----068

Item, Each Burgess of Canongate or Edinburgh, imprisoned for a civil debt, or otherwise, shall pay to the Gaoler of House-Dues each night----0 3 4

Item, Each Piisoner for Civil Debt shall pay at liberation, over and above the aforesaid House-Dues, two and one half per cent, of the sum for which he or she hath been booked, as relief-money, unless liberated by Decree of the Act of Grace, or Cessio Bonorum.

Creditors consigning Aliment-money for Prisoners, shall pay to the Gaoler five per cent, on the same.

All Deserters shall be free of Prison-dues to the Gaoler, in terms of the Act of Parliament, called the Mutiny Act, Sect. 51.

Any Prisoner, chusing a room for more conveniency. (if such can be spared at the time,) shall pay for the same, in place of Prison-Fees, according to agreement with the Gaoler, not exceeding ten shillings sterling per week.

Regulations for the Gaoler.

The said Tolbooth to be keeped clean, and opened at nine in the morning, and shut at ten at night; and furnished with sufficiency of water.

All malt liquors sold by the Gaoler shall be good of the kind, and of no higher price than what is commonly charged for the same in taverns. And he is hereby prohibited from exacting, or allowing to be exacted, what is called *Garnish-money* from Prisoners.

The Gaoler, by Act of Parliament, 24th Geo. II. Cap. 40, is prohibited from selling spirituous liquors, under the penalty of One Hundred Pounds sterling; and also from allowing spirits lo be brought into the Prison, except by way of medicine, ordered by a Physician, or Surgeon, and allowed by a Magistrate.

Fees payable to the Clerk for keeping the Prison Records. The names and designations of all Prisoners, with the diligences or warrants on which they are imprisoned, together with the acts and warrants of liberation, shall be regularly entered into a hook, to be kept by the Clerk, or Assistant Clerk of Court, and reported to the Sitting Magistrate each Court-day: and for which there shall be paid the Fees mentioned in the Clerk of Court's Table of Fees, *vix. Sterling.*

The Incarcerator of each person shall pay, at incarceration, for booking the dili-*£. s. d.* gence, Ac. along with the Gaoler's Fees-------010

Each Prisoner for a civil debt, or otherwise, shall pay, at liberation, for entering the order or warrant of liberation, &c.------*r* -010

For each Certificate of imprinment, to be signed by the Gaoler, or Clerk, in applications for the Acts of Grace, &c.-------,--010

For each Certificate, attested by the Magistrates, in processes of Cessio Bonorum, and for writing the same------—026

For Borrowings, and inspection of the Warrants of Record---'-006 Ordain this Act of Council to be extracted; and a printed copy thereof to be affixed on the wair of every room in the Prison, for the inspection of all concerned; and the Gaoler and Clerk to regulate themselves thereby, under the penalty of Ten Pounds Scots, *toties quoties,* payable to the Charity Workhouse of Canongate. All disputes, relative to the premises, to be determined by the Magistrates for the time being. Extracted by James Tait."

EDINBURGH.

Holyrood House.

Hereditary Keeper, His Grace the Duke of Hamilton.

Warden, *William Petrie,* Officer of the Abbey.---., Salary, half a merck, or sixpence three farthings a day, from each Debtor, paid during confinement. At my visits, l6th Sept. 1802, and 23d Sept. 1809, there were no Prisoners. Allowance. They are alimented, as in the Tolbooth at Edinburgh, at the discretion of the Magistrates.

REMARKS.

This Royal Palace was originally an Abbey, but converted by King James V. to the purpose of a Mansion-House; and contains within a *Prison,* and an *Asylum.*

Over the door of the Warden's house is painted on a board, "Protection, for the "benefit of the Sanctuary, given out by William Petrie, Shoemaker.",

The house has one room above stairs, about 15 feet square, with a fire-place in it, and a window that looks into the court; set apart for the imprisonment of those who contract debts within the Abbey J

This antient structure, and its adjacent domain, have also the privilege of exempting from arrest all persons who flee to them for protection from any part of the kingdom; upon application being made to the Recorder, and paying fifteen shillings each for the registry of their names. The boundaries of security, or *Verge* of Court, are, on the park side, of considerable extent; but if any person, thus privileged, *contracts a debt here,* he may be arrested for the same, and confined in the *Prison* above mentioned.

EDINBURGH.

The County and City Bridewell.

Governor, or Keeper, *David Murray;* whose Wife officiates as Governess, or Matron. Salary, 120/. with coals and candles.

Cashier and Clerk, *Alexander Cunningham.* Salary, 20/.

Accomptant, *David Murray,*jun. Salary, 20l.

Turnkey, has 12. per week, and apartments to live in. Fees, none.

Chaplain, Rev. *Duncan Forbes,* whose Salary was 20/.: now the Rev. *James Porteous.* Salary, 27l. 6s. Duty, once every Sunday.

Precentor, or Clerk; Salary, 5/. 5.

Surgeon, Mr. *James Law,* Salary, 35/.

Number of Prisoners, Men. Women. 1802, Sept. 13th, 5 46. 1809, Sept. 23d,- ----24 40.

Allowance; the diet in 1802 was estimated at 1. *6d.* per week, for each: In 1809, from 2. to 2. *4d.* See *Remarks.* REMARKS.

This building, which has a beautiful castellated appearance, was first inhabited in 1795. The boundary-wall encloses about two acres of ground; part of which lying round the Prison, is converted into a large garde% in whieh are grown vegetables, sufficient for the consumption of 100 Prisoners throughout the year. A small part is also laid down with grass, for the bleaching of clothes, and where the Prisoners walk in the Saturday afternoon, after bathing. ; There is no wood in the whole building, except the doors and roof; the cells and passages being all arched with stone. A general reservoir on the Castle-Hill supplies two large cisterns on the upper-story of the Prison, from whence water is conducted to the different parts.

At the entrance of the Bridewell, the Governor, or Keeper, has a convenient house, detached by a flag-paved court from the Prison, which is semicircular. The ground-floor has a washing-house and bathing-tub; where every Prisoner is washed, not ouly at entrance, but on every Saturday afterwards, previous to receiving their clean linen..

The clothes of each Prisoner on being first admitted, are taken off, cleansed, and laid by; and the house-clothing put on. Their hair is also cut off, and two flannel caps substituted for wear,......

Here is a kitchen, with boilers, on Count Rumford's plan, for cooking their soup and other provisions; and two small court-yards adjoin to the washhouse and kitchen, which are well supplied with water.

The *Chapel* is semicircular, and on the ground-floor, with benches for the Prisoners; and has in it a German stove which diffuses warmth through the whole Prison.

Withinside the building there are three observatories, or spy-rooms, whence the Keeper can see how the Prisoners are employed, without being seen himself.

The Prison consists of four stories, and in each story are thirteen workrooms; divided from which, by a well-ventilated passage, of about four feet wide, are thirtysix sleeping-cells, each furnished with an iron bedstead, a straw-mattress, a binder, two sheets, a blanket, and a rug. The window of each cell, for light and ventilation, is of castmetal, turning on a pivot; and over each door is a ventilator opposite the window.

At the top of the Prison is the Surgeon's room, or dispensary, where every Prisoner is examined. On the attic story are twenty-five rooms; two of which are spacious, and warmed by a large iron plate in the wall, from a stove fixed up in the passage.

The following is a statement of the different apartments principally constituting the whole building of the Bridewell:

On the attic-story, or sick-ward,---------25 *Single,* or *solitary* cells, (thirty-six on each flat, or floor) for one Prisoner to sleep or work in,--------144 *Workrooms,* or cells, in front; thirteen upon each flat or floor, 52

Total---------221.

To each room above specified a *Bible* is assigned; and those who *cannot read,* are *everi/ Sunday detained* with those who *can* read.

No Prisoners here are allowed to go to'their sleeping-cells, after rising in the morning, until bed-time.

The accounts of this Prison, both with

respect to diet and to work, are kept on a plan of singular correctness,' The *diet* of each Prisoner is estimated at 1. *fid.* per week; to which is added the expence of *clothes during confinement*: What the Prisoners' earnings exceed the above disbursements, is entered in a book for the purpose: one third is given to them on discharge; another third six months afterwards; and the remaining one third twelve months afterwards, upon their producing a certificate of good behaviour, under the hand of a Magistrate.

D D

Had so very prudential and' excellent an arrangement as this been adopted at Glasgow, I should not perhaps have found a recently-enlarged Female Prisoner so soon remanded to her old habitation. To characters indiscreet from ignorance, the exertion of strict ceconomy, at *their Liberation from a Gaol* is, in fact, the truest charity.

Justice requires me to observe, that as the construction and judicious accommodations of this Prison in particular, reflect a distinguished honour on the County, so do its cleanliness and good government establish the credit of the worthy Keeper.

ELGIN. *Scotland.*

The Tolbooth.

Gaolers; the three Town's Officers, who act in weekly rotation.

Fees; Felons and Criminals, none. Debtors, *4d.* a night. No religious attentions.

Surgeon, Mr. *Scott,* makes a Bill.

Number of Prisoners, 7th October, 1809, none.

Allowance, to Felons and Criminals, *6d.* a day. Debtors, as alimented; generally *is.* a day.

REMARKS.

This Tolbooth adjoins the court-house, and on the first story is a dismal, black, and smoky place, about 16 feet square, with a low arched roof; so low, that one can stand upright only in the middle of the room. The floor is of very rugged stone, without a bedstead, or even straw to sleep on, for common Debtors. The second story has a room of the same size, for Criminals, without fire-place, bedstead, or bedding.

The third story has a well-lighted and glazed window, with a fire-place, assigned for Debtors who are Burgesses of the Town; and would be comfortable, if there was a sewer in it: but this defect is supplied by filthy tubs.

At the back of the court-house, and three steps below the level of the street, is a dungeon, called *The Thieves' Hole,* about 15 feet square, without one ray of light, or any apparent ventilation whatever; in which Vagrants are confined, and it is sometimes used by the Military as a Black-Hole. No water, except what is brought in by the Gaolers.

IN ENGLAND, SCOTLAND, AND WALES.

ELY. *Cambridgeshire.*

The City Gaol.

Gaoler, *John Leaford;* now *Benjamin Barlow,* Sheriff's-Officer for the Isle of Ely.

Salary, *40l.* Also one guinea to furnish Straw: Twenty shillings for each Prisoner taken to the Assizes at Wisbeach; and for conveyance of Transports, *7/.* each.

Fees, Debtors, *16s. 8d.* No Table. Felons, no Fees. Garnish *abolished.*

Chaplain, Rev. *Charles Mules.*

Duty, once a week. Salary, 20/.

Surgeon, Mr. *George Muriel*; who makes a Bill.

Number of Prisoners, Debtors. Felons, &c.

1801, Aug. 20th,------*1* 7. 1802, Aug. 8th, 2-1. 1805, Aug. 25th,------0--2, 1810, Sept. 4th, 0 3.

Allowance, Debtors who are very poor, Felons, and other Prisoners, have each a loaf of wheaten bread, weighing two pounds and a half, every day; and scales and weights are provided to weigh it.

REMARKS.

This Gaol is the property of the Bishop, who is Lord of the Franchise of the Isle of Ely. It was partly rebuilt by Bishop Mawson in 1768, upon a complaint of the cruel method,'which, for want of a safe Gaol, the Keeper took to secure his Prisoners. "*This*" Mr. Howard informs us, " *was done, by chaining them down "on their backs upon a floor; across which were several iron bars, with an iron "collar with spikes about their necks, and a heavy iron bar across their legs,* "An excellent Magistrate, *James Collyer,* esq. presented an account of the case, ac"companied with a Drawing, to the King; with which his Majesty was much "affected, and gave immediate orders for a proper enquiry and remedy."

This Prison is much improved since my visit in 1802: nor can too much praise be given to the Visiting-Magistrates, for causing all unnecessary severity to be discontinued; for its better ventilation; County-clothing, and bath; for the regular entry of their visits in a book for that important purpose; and for the great cleanliness and good order in which every part is kept.

As here is no Chapel, Divine Service is performed in the Keeper's house.

For Debtors there are three good-sized rooms above-stairs; and another, called the *Nursery Room,* set apart for the sick, with a fire-place in it; one iron bedstead, (made a present of to the Gaol by the Bishop's Lady), and one wooden bedstead for the Nursery. If a Debtor has a bed furnished by the Keeper, he pays 2., 1. *6d.,* or I, per week, according to his circumstances. Some of the windows are glazed, and have sloping boards before the iron gratings, to prevent Prisoners from looking into the street, and conversing with passengers.

The *Condemned Room* is up stairs, 15 feet 6 by 13 feet 6, and 8 feet 10 inches high; ventilated by an iron-grated window, and an aperture in the door about 6 inches square. Across the floor of this room are spread twenty-six iron bars, and two staples fixed in the floor; to which, formerly, Prisoners were fastened by a strong iron chain, run through the main link of their fetters, which, passing through the side-post of the door, was locked on the outer side. No Prisoners now experience this severity.

Below stairs is the Felons' day-room, together with their cell, or night-room, of 18 feet 6 inches by 10 feet. The latter has a double door; the outer is iron-grated, the inner, of wood; lighted and ventilated by a window of 2 feet 4 inches by 2 feet 2, and improved by two air-pipes.

Mr. Leaford, the late Keeper, at one of my visits, told me, that in the year

1798 he had *twelve Prisoners,* in Assize-time, confined within the before-mentioned cell for four nights together; of whom, upon trial, *six were acquitted!*

The court-yard is about 45 feet by 39, with a sewer in it; and the whole Prison is well supplied with water, by a pipe judiciously laid on from the pump to the day-rooms.

Compared with how many Prisons, even in Great Britain, may not these Prisoners say, of such a resource,

"We thank our Friends, and call it Luxury!"

As there is but this one court-yard for all descriptions of Prisoners, the Debtor who conducts himself well, is indulged with the range of the Keeper's garden. The *two Debtors* were comfortably walking in it, at the time of my coming here in *August,* 1802.

The Gaol is *now rendered secure.* In some of our best regulated Prisons the Irons employed are but from 6 to 8 lbs. weight. Those now occasionally used here, are of 18 or 19lbs. One pair is still kept, *weighing forty three pounds,* which, in the year 1799, one *John Gothard,* a Transport, had on for three days successively: But, as his body became greatly swelled in consequence of such a pressure, they were taken ofIT, upon the Surgeon's representation. There was only one *iron collar with spikes* left at my visit in 1802: the last time it had been used was on *James Thompson,* in the year 1798. At my visit in 1805, I had the pleasure to find that not the shadow of one was remaining, to dishonour an English Gaol. Wooden bedsteads, with straw mattresses, are now (1810) allowed to each sleeping-room.

Every Sunday a begging-box is permitted to be carried about, through the two Parishes of Trinity and St. Mary, for the benefit of the Prisoners. The average collection is about three shillings each Sunday; and when I was here in 1802, it amounted to nine-pence for each Prisoner.

Those who find employment (for none is provided,) receive two-thirds of the net profit of their earnings.

Both the Act for Preserving the Health of Prisoners, and the Clauses against their use of Spirituous Liquors, are conspicuously hung up. Here are also Rules and Orders, but they are *not signed, to avouch their Establishment.*

The Assizes in this Isle are held twice a year, viz. in Lent, at Ely; in Summer, at Wisbeach.

$3" Debtors are sent hither from the Court of Requests, otherwise called of *Conscience:* And, painful to think of! the *Costs* of prosecution may be *six shillings and one penny,* to recover (if it be ever recoverable) a debt of *Half a Guinea.* If this be not hunting the flea upon the mountains, Heaven only knows what is. ELY. *Bridewell.*
Keeper, *Benjamin Richmond,* now *Benjamin Barlow.*
Salary, 10/. No Fees. Twenty shillings for each Prisoner taken to the Assizes at Wisbeach.
Surgeon, sent by the High Bailiff when wanted.
Number of Prisoners, 1802, Aug. 8th, one. 1805, Aug. 26th, two, and a *LunaticJc.* 1810, Sept. 4th, one.
Allowance, to Debtors, none. To Bridewell Prisoners it once was sixpence per day, as at the Gaol: But it has since been taken off from the Town Prisoners; and they have their earnings only to live upon; except on Sundays, when they receive four-pence.
REMARKS.
This ancient Prison, built in the year 1651, consists of four rooms; viz. one below, for men, 16 feet by 15 feet 4 inches, with a sewer: another above, called The *Strong-Room,* about the same size, which has 34 iron bars running across the floor, in like manner, and for the same cruel purpose, as those in the Gaol: a small room detached, with a sewer, for the men; and, adjoining to it, an apartment for the Women. These rooms have wooden bedsteads and straw mattresses, to which the Prisoner furnishes his own bed, or hires one from the Gaoler at three-pence a night.

The employment here is beating of hemp. Prisoners committed to hard labour have the whole of their earnings for their maintenance. The Prison is out of repair; and I do not find that it has been once white-washed these ten or twelve years. No water accessible to the Prisoners. No court-yard, although one might easily be made out of a part of the Keeper's ample garden. No Chaplain, nor religious attendance.

By an Act "for the more easy and speedy recovery of Small Debts, within the Isle of Ely, in the County of Cambridge," (1778,) *Debtors* are sent hither by the Court of Requests; and *they have no allowance whatever.* EXETER. Devonshire.
The County High Gaol, for Felons.
Gaoler, *James Brown.*
Salary, 200/. with two fields for his use, of about six acres of ground.
For conveyance of Transports, *Is.* per mile. Fees and Garnish abolished.
Chaplain, Rev. *William Bowness,* now Rev. *Edward Chave.*
Duty, at the *Gaol,* Prayers every morning: On Sunday, Prayers and Sermon. At the *House of Correction,* Prayers and Sermon on Sunday, and Prayers on Thursday.
Salary, for the *Gaol, House of Correction,* and Duty at the Quarter Sessions, 126/. 10. He is a Priest-Vicar of the Cathedral, and to hold no other Cure.
Surgeon, Mr. *Walker.* Salary, 50/. for the High Gaol and House of Correction.
Number of Prisoners, 1802, Feb. 1st, 28. 1803, Oct. 6th, 32. 1806, Sept. 26th, 31.

Allowance, twenty-two ounces of bread per day, in loaves from the baker. I think it but justice to mention, that I found many of the loaves weighing 23 ounces. Convicts under sentence of Transportation (see *Remarks,*) have not the County bread, but the King's allowance of . *6d.* per week for their support.
REMARKS.
This Gaol is very conspicuously placed in a fine situation, elevated and healthy. The boundary-wall encloses nearly two acres of land; and, being sixteen feet from the several court-yards, the Keeper has thrown round, within that limit, a convenient garden.

The Turnkey's lodge, which is in

front, has, on the right-hand, his sitting-room; and on the left-hand are two baths, and a copper. Above stairs is his sleeping-room, and four *reception-rooms,* for Prisoners, who are either unhealthy, uncleanly, or sent in by night; and likewise a room, in which some of the Prisoners' own clothes are deposited, and the Gaol-Uniform put on them instead.

Above the Turnkey's lodge is a leaded flat-roof, upon which Criminals are executed! The Gaoler's house is in the centre of the building; and the approach to it lies through a small garden.

On the ground-floor are *thirty sleeping-cells,* which open into a lobby, or passage, five feet wide; and also twelve other cells of the like description, that open into two court-yards, six cells in each. These last, however, being damp in winter, are prudentially unoccupied, except when the Gaol is crowded.

There are two day-rooms for men on the ground-floor, nearly octagon, and about 22 feet in diameter; with glazed windows and two fire-places in each; to which the County liberally allows coals, seats, and tables; with shelves for putting by provisions.

To this Prison there are no less than *fourteen court-yards.* Two of them, 84 feet by 60, are for Men-Felons, both before trial and after conviction; enclosed by a brickwall, and each having in it a pump, and arcades, for accommodation in wet weather.

One court, for the Women-Felons, has open wood palisades, surrounding a grass-plat. Several of the other court-yards, since their first laying out, have been temporarily converted into gardens; there being, at the time of their destination, no Prisoners of the class for which they were originally intended.

The *Jirst-story* has *forty-eight sleeping-cells,* which open into passages 5 feet wide, leading (24 feet on each side,) to the Chapel; and also two day-rooms, similar to those below.

The *second-story* has *fifty cells;* which, twentyfive on each side, are separated by a j assage, of the same width as the former, and opening toward the Chapel in the same manner as those below. Here are two day-rooms also, of similar construction with the foregoing.

The *third-story* has fifty sleeping-cells, and two day-rooms, like those on the second-story.

The Chapel, a very neat structure, is partitioned off, to separate the different classes of Prisoners; and in the gallery there are six cells, made occasionally to open. These are for Prisoners under sentence of death, and generally kept in utter darkness; but during Divine service, the inner door (a wooden one,) is thrown open, so that they can hear very well. They are each 8 feet *6* inches by 7 feet, and 10 feet high; and the Turnkey's sleeping-room is close adjoining.

The common sleeping-cells are 8 feet 6 by 6 feet *6,* and 10 feet high; with arched roofs and double doors: the outward iron-grated, the inner of wood; with glazed windows, well-ventilated; and fitted up, some with wooden crib-bedsteads, others with those of cast-iron, straw-in-sacking beds, two blankets, a coarse sheet, pillow, and rug...

On the attic-story of the Keeper's house are two neat rooms, with conveniences for the sick; and communicating Jo the Chapel by a lobby.

Every Prisoner is required to attend Divine Service, unless prevented by sickness: and only one Prisoner was absent when I was there. '.

Religious books are distributed amongst them, at the Chaplain's discretion. Forty Bibles, with the Common-Prayer and Psalms, were sent by an unknown Lady, just before my visit in September 1806..... "

Those Criminal-Prisoners, who wish to be better accommodated than the rest can afford to be, have feather beds and bedding furnished by the Keeper, at *2s. 6d.* per week.

The Act for preservation of Health, and Clauses against Spirituous Liquors, are conspicuously hung up; and excellent Rules and Regulations for the government of the Gaol, signed by the Justices in Session, and confirmed by the J udges of Assize, are duly printed and published.

Previous to the appointment of the present Keeper, a singular custom had prevailed, for a party of the Prisoners, doubly-ironed, to be escorted, and to beg charity everyChristmas throughout the City. The custom is, now, very judiciously discontinued.

The only permanent Donation to this Gaol, of which I could get information, is the sum of ten shillings *per annum,* from the Dean and Chapter of Exeter.

Here, as in many other County Gaols, *Lunaticks are received.* Of this description were four, when I was here; who failed not very much to disturb the quiet of the Prison, as well as to endanger the safety both of the Gaoler and his Turnkeys. It appears a very desirable object, that persons so peculiarly pitiable should be admitted to the blessings of an *Hospital;* where, by medical aid, tranquillity, and judicious treatment, they might be restored to usefulness in life, or rendered at least more comfortable both to themselves and others, than the circumstances of a *Gaol* can possibly afford.

This Prison is very frequently visited by the considerate Magistrates of the County, and every comfort supplied to its inhabitants, consistent with the privation of liberty.

Although the situation of the building is excellent, the original plan of it is extremely defective. The Gaoler's house is so placed, as to command the view of but a small part of the whole concern. The twelve cells which open into the courtyards are unfit for any human being to sleep in. It would be a great improvement, if most of those cells, built on the ground-floor, were converted into work-shops; the local situation of this City affording an inexhaustible supply of resources, in the picking of oakum, making of nets, mops, and various other articles for shipping; and in which the most flagrant Criminals might very usefully be employed, without availing themselves of any means to facilitate their escape.

Every Prisoner, on being discharged, receives money to carry him home; and thus prevents the danger of an immediate recurrence to those practices which brought him hither.

The Gaoler is active and intelligent, and the whole Prison very clean.

I cannot close this narrative without expressing my very grateful acknowledgements to the Magistrates of the highly respectable County of Devon, for the honour which they have done me, in so conspicuous a manner, by noticing the faithful Remarks I had presumed to make in my several visits to Exeter. The result is truly pleasing. Where the Prisoners heretofore had but loose straw to sleep on, they have now comfortable beds and bedding. Their day-rooms are supplied with every requisite for decency and cleanliness in a Prison. The impediments to health, and the consequent hazards of disease, have been removed.

EXETER. South-gate.

The City and County Gaol.

Gaoler, *Thomas Dodge,* now *Richard Tarbart.* Salary, 30/. 10.

Fees, for Debtors, *16s. Sd.* (No Table.) Besides which, the Under-Sheriff demands *$s.* for his *Liberate!* No Fees for Felons. For the conveyance of Transports, 1. per mile.

Garnish, for Debtors, not yet abolished; 2.

Chaplain, none.

Surgeon, Mr. *Walker,* for Felons only. Salary, none. Makes a Bill.

Number of Prisoners. Debtors. Felons, &c.

180a, Feb. 1st,-9 G 1803, Oct. 6th,------ 3 6 1806, Sept. 26th,------4------9.

Allowance, to Debtors, See the Remarks. To Felons, and Criminal Prisoners, one pound and half of bread per day, sent from the Bakers, and which I have always found of full weight.

REMARKS.

This Prison is within the *South Gate,* from which, popularly, it takes its name; and consists, amongst others, of two rooms in the Keeper's house, called the *Long*

E E *Room,* and the *Shoe.* The latter, it seems, was so first denominated, from a Shoe that was formerly suspended by a string from the iron-grated window towards the street, to solicit the charity of passengers; but the practice is now discontinued by order of the Magistrates. This room is set apart for such Debtors as bring their own beds, and pay sixpence per week.

The *Long Room* is for the Debtors to walk in, here being no court-yard. There are also nine other rooms, to which the Gaoler furnishes beds and bedding, at from 3. to *10s. 6d.* per week, according to the ability of his Prisoners.

It is a singular circumstance, but every week sixty *penny loaves,* (weighing, 6th Oct. 1803, nine ounces and a half each) are sent to the Debtors of this Gaol. If there be only one Debtor, he has the whole batch; if more, it is equally divided amongst them. From what source they come was not known in the Gaol, but the Keeper gave me the following account: "Mr. and Mrs. Seldon's legacy, *2s. 6d.* Mrs. "Pengelly, 1. Mrs. Reed, *6d.* and the Chamber of Exeter, *Is.* Total, 5."

On the side of the gateway opposite to the Gaoler's apartments, are the three wards appropriated to the Felons, dark, dirty, and offensive. We went into them with lighted candles. They have no chimney for ventilation. No court-yard belonging to them, nor water, except what was brought by the Keeper, at his pleasure or convenience. Nothing could exceed the squalid wretchedness of the Prisoners.

At my visit in 1803, I found the old Gaoler had been dismissed, a new one appointed, and windows were now made through the wall, which gave sufficient light, without the assistance of candles.

The cell for women (No. 1,) is 16 feet 9 inches by 9 feet 6, and only 6 feet high. It has barrack bedsteads, with two straw-in-sacking beds, and three rugs each; and is lighted by a window, of 3 feet and an inch by 2 feet 8 inches.

Cell No. 2, for men, is 9 feet 6 by 8 feet 9, and 12 feet *6* inches high; fitted up with two wooden bedsteads, straw-in-sacking beds, and rugs. The window of this cell is 2 feet 6 inches by 2 feet.

No. 3 is also a cell for men, 18 feet 6 by 11, and 12 feet high; fitted up as the former, and lighted by a window, of 3 feet by 2 feet an inch.

Over these miserable night-cells are two day-rooms; the one 17 feet 6 inches by 14 feet 9, and 13 feet *6* inches high, with a window, 2 feet 5 by 2 feet; the other 16 feet 3 by 9 feet, and only *6* feet 3 inches high, with a window of 3 feet 3 inches by 2 feet 10. Both these day-rooms have fire-places, and coals are allowed for them by the Chamber of Exeter, during the six Winter months. When Prisoners are indulged the use of these day-rooms, a trap door is opened in the floor, and they ascend through it by a ladder from the cell below.

Besides the foregoing weekly allowance of bread to the Debtors, the Taylors' Company give *Is. d.* on every Easter Eve. At the same time they also receive from the Chamber thirty-six penny loaves; and as many more at Christmas.

Two painted boards are here put up, containing Memorials of sundry Bequests. They are not dated; but one of them seems to be very antient; *viz.* "Legacies.

"A Memorial of certayne Guyftes, to the yeerlie value of Twenty Poundes, geeven by *Laurence Seldon,* and *Elizabeth* his Wife, to be distributed by the Maior and Bayliffes of the Citie of *Exon* for ever; as followeth: *s. d.*

"In bread, weeklie, to the poore Prisoners in the Kinge's Gaole, near the Castell of Exon-0 6

Not paid these many years.

"Prisoners in the Sherive's Warde Gaole, and Countie of the Citie of Exon 2 67'

The other Memorial, on the second board, is this:

"Exon, South-Gate. Mrs. *Hester Reed* gave six-pence a week for ever to this Prison; to be paid out of a tenement called *Ven,* in the Parish of *Cullumton,* and laid out in middling wheat bread, and distributed always to the Prisoners in the *Shew.* Shoe."

The following Memorial also is framed, and hung up:

"*Francis Pengelly,* of this City, Apothecary, by deed, dated the 1st of January 1700, gave two pounds twelve shillings a year to be laid out in bread, for the use of the Debtors in this Prison, for ever; issuing out of his estate called the Dolphin Inn, and premises adjoining, situate in the Parish of St. Mary Major, in the said City."

This estate was sold in 1805, and 1095*l*. 19. *6d.* three *percent,* consolidated annuities purchased with the produce, in the names of W. B. Kennaway, Thomas Smith, A. Tozer, and G. Giffbrd.

Debtors likewise receive ten shillings yearly from the Chamber of Exeter, on the Monday fortnight following St. Michael's day; ten shillings a year from the Church, at the disposal of the Keeper; and six-pence a year from the Lay-Vicars of the Church, on the day their Court is held at *fVoodberry.*

There is no memorial in the Prisons at *Exeter* of the following donations, mentioned in *Richard Izacke's Alphabetical Register,* &c. printed in 1736. Such valuable *registers* of persons' List wills, grants, &c. in other cities, would prevent the misapplication of many charities.

Reynold Hayne, in 1354, bequeathed all his lands and tenements lying in the suburbs of the said City to the Cathedral Church of St. Peter there, for the relief of those imprisoned in the common Gaol. This legacy appears to be lost. *William Paramore,* by will, 22d February, 1570, bequeathed to the needy Prisoners of the King's Gaol in Exeter, in the *South Gate* there, and in the Counters, to every of them ten shillings for ever, yearly, to be paid out of his lands in the *Cook Row,* in Exeter. This is regularly paid to the Prisoners in the South Gate. *Thomas Bridgman,* by will, 3d April 1641, gave to the said City the sum of sixty pounds, to be continued as a perpetual stock; whereof the interest of forty pounds to be bestowed upon the Prisoners in the upper Prison; and the interest of the other twenty pounds to be bestowed upon the Prisoners in the lower Prison; and this likewise to continue for ever. This legacy appears to be lost. *Edward Young,* D. D. 6th June, *1663,* by will gave twenty shillings a year to the prisoners of the Castle, to be distributed, by the *Dean* of Exeter for the time being, on the 29th of May.

Transports in this Gaol have not the King's allowance of 2. *6d.* per week.

Here is no bath nor oven: The Gaol is but seldom *visited*. The Act for Preservation of Health is not exhibited; but the prohibitory Clauses against Spirituous Liquors are written on paper, and stuck up. No Rules and Orders. It is not in the power of repairing to make this a good Prison; but it is to be hoped that so opulent a *City* will ere long follow the example of the *County,* and build a new one in its stead.

EXETER. Sheriff's Ward.
The County Prison for Debtors.
Gaoler, *Richard Rice,* now *William Birch.*

Salary, 25*l*. Fees, as per Table. Garnish, prohibited by the Prison Rules, yet generally exacted by the Prisoners.

Chaplain, none; nor any religious attentions whatever, notwithstanding the great number of persons here confined. No Surgeon.

Number of Debtors, 1800, April 1st,----33-I 1803, Oct. 6th,----32.
l802, Jan. 29th,---45-J 1806, Sept. 13th,---19.

Allowance, at my first visits, none: But now, two shillings per week, in cases of extreme poverty, upon application made to the Magistrates.

REMARKS.

This Prison, called the *Sheriff's Ward,* is in the parish of *Saint Thomas* the Apostle. The boundary wall is of mud, with a thatch coping, except a small part, "Visiting Prisons is trulv a Christian choice: the lot, in which is to be found the least of that which selfish nature covets, and most of what it shrinks from." of brick, which fronts the street. It encloses about an acre of ground; and¥rom the Turnkey's Lodge to the Prison is a walk of 60 yards, shaded by a double row of large elms, and well supplied with water..r At the left entrance of the Prison is a room, *ig* feet by 18, which still retains the name of Church: the reading desk remains, and on the walls are portions of scripture; but it is now the common day-room. On the right of the passage is a room called the Pin-hole with a fire-place and glazed window, where Debtors dress their provisions; and adjoining to it is the Strong-room, which has a fire-place and small glazed-window, a barrack-bedstead, but no bedding, nor even straw, to sleep upon. This is the only free ward in the Prison.

For Master's-Side Debtors there are seven rooms, with beds and bedding furnished by the Keeper, for which they pay as per following Table: one of the rooms has seven beds, and two slept in each bed. Common-Side Debtors have six rooms; each pays *6d.* a week; but they have neither bedding nor straw. Two were sick in bed; another had the jaundice; and a fourth was in the last stage of a consumption at my visit in 1803, *without any medical assistance.*

This Building is very old;.the rooms were dirty, and swarming with bugs. It is a fortunate circumstance, in so crowded a Prison, that the court is spacious and airy. Here are Rules and Orders, signed by the Under-Sheriff only, and no attention is paid to them: There were constant broils between the late Keeper and his Guests, and it was difficult to determine where the fault most lay. The Gaoler said, *no Magistrate,ever came there* without being sent for; but any one visiting this Prison must see the necessity of Rules and Orders, both for *Prisoners* and *Keepers,* being fixed by the Legislature. The Gaoler added, that his salary was small, so that his chief dependance rested on the hire of his beds, and Prison-Fees. It is difficult to conceive the extreme wretchedness and misery here exhibited. The Debtors, for the most part mechanics and labourers, seem to be more unfortunate than criminal, and have an abundant claim to pity and relief. No employment; nor rooms to work in, if it were procured. One Prisoner (Anne Fisher, committed for contempt, 13th Nov. 1791,) I saw here in 1803; but, at my last visit, she was discharged.

"Table Of Fees,
Settled and established at the General Quarter Sessions of the Peace,
held 14th April, 1801.
"For the Commitment-Fees of every Prisoner for Debt, Damages, £. *s. d.* and Contempt, though it be for several actions or processes only,-0 13 4

For every *Liberate,* ---------------020

For the Turnkey,-010

For the use of a bed in a single room, for one person per week,--0 3 0

For the use of a bed in a room wherein are two or more beds, and two.'; lodge in each bed; then, for each Prisoner,-------013

For the *vise* of a bed in a room wherein are two or more beds, and one £. s. d. only in each bed,--------------026

For the use of the Common-Room, if the Keeper finds bedding; each person per week,---------------010

If the Prisoner finds bedding,------------006

"Devon, Easter Sessions, 1801. We allow and approve of the above Table of Fees, to be taken at the Sheriff's Ward of the said County,

"J. B. Cholwick, Chairman.
"W. F. Hall.
"J. Newcombe."

"Lammas Assizes, 1801. We do allow and confirm the above Table of Fees,
S. Le Blanc.
Rob. Graham."

EXETER. *Devonshire.*
The County House of Correction.

Keeper, *William Ford.*

Salary, 150/. and a considerable portion of the Prisoners' earnings.

Chaplain, Rev. *Edward Chave;* who is also Chaplain to the Gaol, and to the Magistrates at their Quarter Sessions. Duty, on Thursday, Prayers: on Sunday, Prayers and a Sermon.

Salary, for the whole duty, *126l. 10s.*

Surgeon, Mr. *Benjamin Walker.*

Salary, for the Gaol and House of Correction, 50/.

Number of Prisoners, 1810, June 21st, 68. Every one of whom is employed in some kind of labour.

Allowance, to each, twenty-two ounces of good wheaten bread per day.

REMARKS.

This extensive and noble structure, now compleated, is equally admired for the solidity of its construction, the excellence of its masonry, and its handsome appearance, which will remain a lasting honour to the County of Devon. It stands on somewhat more than an acre and a half of ground, and is situate in a field on a fine eminence adjoining to the County Gaol.

Its foundation was laid near four years since, and underneath it is placed a tin plate, with the following Inscription:

"The Foundation-Stone of this House of Correction was laid hy Samuelfre"Derick Milford, esq. Chairman of a Committee of Magistrates of the County of "Devon, in the presence of the said Committee, on the 22d day of August, in the "year 1807.

"Geo. Moneypenny, *ArchxtectT* The Prison is encircled by a boundary wall, 22 feet high; in the front of which is the Turnkey's lodge, a handsome stone building, rendered very conspicuous by a noble gate of entrance, 16 feet high, and 8 feet wide, adorned with rustic cinctures, and arch-stones of uncommon grandeur; adopted from a design of the Earl of Burlington, as executed in the flanks of Burlington-House, Piccadilly. i Above the gate is a stone cornice, crowned with a tablet; on which is inscribed,

"The House Of Correction For The County Of Devon:
"Erected In The Year 1809."

On passing the Lodge, in which are the Turnkey's apartments, amply fitted up with every accommodation, a spacious flag-stone pavement leads through a neat shrubbery to the Keeper's house, an octagon building, situate in the centre of the Prison r on the ground-floor of which are a Committee-room for the Magistrates, a parlour for the Keeper, an office room, and a kitchen: and underneath, in the basement story, are large vaulted apartments for domestick purposes.

The *House of Correction* consists of three wings, detached from the Keeper's house by an area 12 feet wide; each wing containing two Prisons, totally distinct; so that there are six divisions, for as many classes of Prisoners, with a spacious court-yard appropriated to each, surrounded by wrought-iron railing, 6 feet high, which prevents access to the boundary wall, and preserves a free communication, of 12 feet in breadth, betwixt the wall and the court-yards.

The entrances to all the court-yards and Prison apartments open from the area round the Keeper's house, through wrought-iron grated gates, opposite the several windows of his apartments.

There are also iron-grated apertures in the arcades of the ground-floor, which open into the area; so that the whole Prison is completely inspected, and the different classes attended to, without the necessity of passing or entering the courtyards; the Keeper, from the windows of his own dwelling, having a view into the airing-grounds and work-shops of all the divisions.

In each court-yard, on the ground floor, are spacious vaulted arcades, fitted up as *work-shops for light employment,* and in which a number of Prisoners are occupied in weaving, picking and sorting wool, beating hemp, cutting bark, &c. Adjoining to the arcade in each division is a day-room, lighted by two large sash windows, and fitted up with a patent kitchen-stove, which answers every purpose of domestic cookery. Between the stone piers that support the vaulted ceiling of the day-rooms are wooden dressers, and benches of wood are placed round the rooms. The Prisoners have access to the day-rooms only during their meals, and previously to their being locked up.

On the first floor of each division, to which the ascent is by stone stair-cases, are six cells, and on the second floor six others, making in all, seventy-two; each 7 feet by 10, and 10 feet 6 inches high, to the crown of the arch; lighted and ventilated by iron-grated apertures over the doors, of 2 feet 6 inches by 1 foot, without glass. Each cell is fitted up with one, and some with two wooden bedsteads, formed like those in the Royal Hospital at Haslar, and to be used in case of necessity. All the cells open into spacious and lofty arcades, guarded by iron rails; and thus a free circulation of air is preserved, which cannot fail to render this Prison always more healthful than it could be with close confined passages, into which the cells and rooms of other Prisons too generally open. The floors of all the cells and arcades are paved with large flag-stones, and the cell-doors lined with iron plates.

On the upper floor, at the back of the right and left wing, are two rooms, each 13 feet 6 inches by 10 feet, and 10 feet 6 inches high, to the crown of the arch, set apart for faulty Apprentices. These rooms are lighted by sash windows, and have a fire-place in each: the floors are paved with flag-stones, and each room is fitted up with wooden bedsteads, in the same manner as the cells.

On the first floor of the Keeper's house is *the Chapel;* an irregular octagon, 38 feet in diameter, and 14 feet high, lighted by eight large sash windows, and neatly divided by framed partition-pews, which are so heightened by crimson blinds, as to prevent the classes seeing each other. The Prisoners have a communication with the Chapel, from the first floor of the arcades, into the different divisions set apart for each class of the Prisoners, which they enter and quit, without mixing with, or being in sight of each other.

This Prison is supplied with fine water from a reservoir, (placed on an arcade in the area, between the back wing of the Prison and the Keeper's house,) which is filled from a well underneath, by an hydraulic pump of excellent contrivance, that is worked by the Prisoners every morning. From the reservoir pipes are laid into all the day-rooms of the Prison, the Turnkey's lodge, and the kitchen of the Keeper's house; and in each of the rooms, eight in number, is fixed a stone trough, with a pipe and cock.

The sewers of this Prison are judiciously placed at the ends of the different wings: they are spacious, lofty, well ventilated, and the vaults are 30 feet deep.

All the areas and walks round the Prison, and the arcades and day-rooms, are paved with krge flag-stones, and the six court-yards with fine gravel. The roofs of the whole building are so constructed, as to shelter the walls and the foot-paths round the Prison in wet weather. They project 5 feet beyond the walls, and the Soffit of the projection is relieved by Cantilivers, in the manner of the Grecian Temples; of which the church of St. Paul Covent Garden, is an example.

At the back of the Prison, and communicating therewith, is a spacious workyard, in which are some extensive working-shops, for the purposes of more laborious employment than is carried on immediately within the Prison; such as hewing and polishing stone, sawing timber, cutting bark, &c. In this work-yard are two sewers, and a pump which affords a supply of very fine water.

It is in contemplation to erect a Hospital for the use of the Gaol and Bridewell; which will be a detached building, and contain airy wards for Male and Female Invalids, with hot and cold baths.

The Rules and Regulations for the Government of this Prison are excellent. Their principal tendency is to enforce cleanliness, morality, and habits of industry. The greatest stress is also laid on the constant separation of the Prisoners into distinct classes, arranged according to the respective nature of their offences; so that the more, criminal may no longer corrupt those who have been committed for slight offences, and thus render them far more depraved than before their Imprisonment; which was inevitably the case in the Old Bridewell, and of which I have given a full description-in the Gentleman's Magazine for May 1808, p. 414.

EVESHAM. *Worcestershire.*
The Borough Gaol.. --
Keeper, /. *Knowles,* Sergeant at Mace. Salary, none.
Prisoners, none, 27th August, 1803.
Allowance, one pound of bread per day.
REMARKS.

This Prison consists of two rooms under the Town-Hall; one on the ground-floor, and one above it, with straw on the floor.

No court-yard, nor water. The Recorder of Evesham acts as Judge.
FALMOUTH. *Cornwall.*
The Town Gaol.
Keeper, the Town Sergeant. Salary, none. Fees 6f. *Sd.* No Table.
Prisoners, 1803, Oct. 12th, One. 1806, Oct. 2d, None.
Allowance, sixpence per day.

Here are two rooms, under the back part of the Keeper's house; the largest is 10 feet 8 inches by 9 feet 8, with loose straw on an earthen floor, and each has a small iron-grated window. No Court. No water.

FLEET PRISON. *London. .... For Debtors, and Contempt of Court.-,-.*
Warden, *John Eyles,* Esq.
Deputy Warden, and Clerk of the Papers, Mr. *Nicholas Nixon.*
Fees, on Commitment, to the Warden, *1l. 6s. Sd.* to the Turnkey, 2. ' on Discharge, to the Warden, 7. *Ad.* and to the Clerk of the Papers, for every Discharge of1 every Action, 2. *6d.* " Garnish abolished. Licence for Beer and Wine to *Robert Richards,* who is Tapster to the Warden ' ' '
' '.'!:..'..' i.
Chaplain, Rev. *John Manley Wood,* M.A.-. ., ,?'.!
Duty, Prayers and Sermon on Sunday; and on Christmas Day and Good Friday the Sacrament is administered.
Salary, 30/. paid by the Warden.
Surgeon, none. No medical assistance in case of sickness.
Number of Debtors,
Within the Walls. In the Rules. Within the Walk In the Rules.
1800, June 14th,--192--60 1801, April 27th,--250--70 1802, Jan.11th,--230 -75 1803, Dec. 10th,--229--67 1804, Feb. 10th,--256--58 1805, April 22d,--171--50
Allowance. See Remarks.
1806, May 24th,--256--75 1807, March 22d,--178--53 1808, June 21st,--246--70 1809, June 16th,--309--83 1810, Oct. 17th,--221--48 1811, Feb. 20th,--305--100 REMARKS.

The Fleet became a Prison for Debtors, and for Persons charged with contempt of the Courts of Chancery, Exchequer, and Common Pleas, in the 16th of*Charles I.* after the abolition of the Star Chamber.

In 1729 an enquiry was made into the state of the public Gaols; and it appearing that great cruelties had been practised, particularly on Sir William Rich, Bart, who was found in the Fleet Prison loaded with irons, *Thomas Bambridge,* the then Warden, with *John Huggin,* his Predecessor, were committed close Prisoners to Newgate, and many useful regulations were enacted..,

In the front of this Prison is a narrow court-yard, and at each end of the building a small projection, or wing. There are four floors, called *Galleries;* besides which is the cellar-floor, called *Bartholomew Fair.*

Each gallery consists of a passage in the middle, the whole length of the Prison, 66 yards; and of rooms on each side of it, about 14-3-fe by 121 aQd 9 feet 6" inches high. A chimney and window in every room, except three, which are called *Slip Rooms,* and without a chimney. The passages are narrow, not 7 feet wide; and dark, having only one window at each end.....

On the first-floor, the *Hall Gallery,* to which the ascent is by eight steps, are a tap-room, a room called the Cellar _Head, another for one of the Turnkeys, and nineteen rooms for the Prisoners; at the North-end of which is the Chapel.

When I was there in March 1807, I was surprized to find eleven Debtors only attended Divine Service; the excuse being that the Chapel was damp and cold. A fire-place in it, with coals allowed, would be a very great improvement; and I have no doubt the Chapel would then be well filled, to hear the excellent Preacher.

The *Cellar-Floor* is sixteen steps below the Hall Gallery. It consists of the public kitchen, four large beer and wine cellars, sixteen rooms for Prisoners, and one for another of the Turnkeys. V,;..

In the *Coffee-Room Gallery,* which is the next above the Hall, are the CoflfeeRoom, made out of two; the Strong-Room, for confinement of the Refractory, and twenty-two more for other Prisoners.. '."

In the *third Gallery,* above the Cotifee-Room, are twenty-six others, and a room at. the North-end. Over the Chapel is an Infirmary.

In the *Top Gallery* are also twenty-seven rooms; some of which, being over the Chapel, are larger than the rest..

All the rooms I have here mentioned are for the *Masters-Side Debtors,* taken unfurnished, at the weekly rent of 1. *2d.* They fall to the Prisoners in succession, (except those called *Bartholomew Fair,* which are in the entire disposal of the Warden;) that is to say, when a room becomes vacant, the first Prisoner npon the list of such as have paid their Commitment-Fees, succeeds to it. When the Prison was built, the Warden gave each Prisoner his choice of a room, according to his seniority.

If all the rooms be occupied, a newcomer, upon the payment of his CommitmentFees, is *chumm'd,* as they term it, on the next room in rotation, beginning at No. I. in the Hall Gallery.

The apartments for *Common-Side Debtors* are only part of the right wing of the Prison. Besides the cellar, (which was once intended for the kitchen, but now occupied with lumber, and shut up,) there are four floors. On each floor is a room near twenty-five feet square, with a fire-place; and on the sides seven closets, or cabins, to sleep in.

Such of the Prisoners as swear in Court, or before a Commissioner, that they are not worth five pounds, and cannot subsist without charity, partake of the casual donations which are sent to the Prison, and the Begging-Grate. Of this description there are generally about eight or ten Prisoners.

In the Report of the Committee of the House of Commons, in 1728, there is a Table given of some Charities; and it was ordered by the Judges, *Eyre, Price, Page,* and *Denton,* that a Table of Gifts and Be&uests made for the Prisoners in the *Fleet,* expressing the particular purposes for which they were given, should be prepared by the *Warden,* and hung up *in the Hall* of the said Prison." (See Table of Fees, Trin. Term, 1727, in the Report of the *Gaol-Committee,* page 16.) It is hung up, indeed, but hung up in the *Begging-Grate,* instead of *the Hall,* which is the roper place prescribed by order of the Judges.

Here is plenty of water, both from the river and pumps; and a spacious yard behind the Prison, in which the Prisoners play at skittles, fives, and tennis, &c. And not only the Prisoners, but Strangers also are admitted here, as to any other public place of amusement!

On Monday and Thursday nights here is a *Wine and Beer Club,* which sometimes lasts till two or three o'clock in the morning; but those who frequent them, that *are not Prisoners,* must depart at eleven o'clock, or remain all night.

This *voluntary frequenting a Prison* seems but too likely to lessen the dread of being *confined* in one.

Seeing the Prison always crowded with *Women* and *Children,* I procured an accurate list of them; and found, that in February, 1801, there were 230 Prisoners. Their Wives (including Women of not so honourable an appellation,) and Children were about two hundred: And on the 10th of December, 1803, the number of Prisoners being 229, their Wives, &c. were 148, and Children, 391;—in all, *seven hundred and sixty-eight* Men, Women, and Children, living in the Prison. One poor Man had his Wife and Five Children with him there. On every visit to this place, I found the stair-cases and lobbies very dirty; and that every one preserved that degree of cleanliness in his own room which satisfied himself.

In the Office, (but not hung up in the Prison,) is the following *Table of Fees,* to be received by the Clerk of the Papers, and Clerk of Enquiries.

"Table Of Fees,

To be taken by the Clerk of the Papers, and Clerk of Enquiries of the Fleet Prison, pursuant to the Resolution of the Honourable Court of Common Pleas, in the Easter and Trinity Terms, 13 George I. 1727.

Resolution,

That there is due, and ought to be paid, to the Clerk of the Papers, for every *eS. . d.*

Discharge of every Action,--------.- 026

And for the Copy of every Cause, not exceeding three,-----010

And for each anil every Cause, exceeding three Causes, besides the one shilling a *s£. s. d.* piece for each of the said first three Causes,-------0 O 4

That there is due, and ought to be

paid, to the Clerk of the Papers, for his Certificate of the Prisoner's Discharge, delivered to the Prisoner himself, without any regard to the number of Causes he stood charged with,-----026

And for his Certificate to the Warden, of such Discharge,-----026

That there is due, and ought to be paid, to the Clerk of Enquiries, on the Discharge of a Prisoner by the Creditor, and not by Supersedeas,-----0 2 6

That there is a Fee of 5s. 4d. due to the Clerk of the Papers, for the allowance of every Writ of Habeas Corpus; and 4s. for the return of the first Cause, and 1s. for every other Cause, and no more."

The Warden's duty and that of his Officers are specified in the Rules and Orders of Hilary Term, 3 George II. 1729. They consist of twenty-nine Articles, signed *R. Eyre, Robert Price, Alexander Denton, J. Fortescue:* and are hung up in the coffee-room and tap-room of the Prison.

The Clauses against Spirituous Liquors are hung up on the large door, entering into the Prison.

The follow ing *Table of Fees* is correct, and hung up also in the Prison.

"Table Of Fees-,

"To be taken by the Warden of the Prison of the Fleet, for any Prisoner or Priners' Commitment, or coming into Gaol, or Chamber-rent there, or Discharge from thence, in any Civil Action; settled and established the 19th day of January, in the third year of the Reign of his Majesty King George the Second, A. D. 1729, pursuant to an Act lately made, intituled, 'An Act for the Relief of Debtors, in respect to the Imprisonment of their Persons.'

"Every Prisoner, charged with one or more Actions, who, at his own desire, shall *sS. s. d.* go on the Master's Side, to pay to the Warden, for a Commitment Fee--16 8 Every Prisoner, charged with one or more Actions, who shall go on the Common

Side, not being entitled to partake of the Poor's Box, to pay---0 1s 4

Every person entitled to partake of the Poor's Box------0O0

Every Prisoner to pay at his Discharge--------074

Every such Prisoner, on the Master's Side, who, at his own desire, shall have a bed to himself, to pay for a chamber-room, use of bed, bedding, and sheets, to the Warden per week----------026

If two in a bed, and no more, for chamber-room, use of bed, bedding, and sheets, each to pay to the Warden per week--------013.

If the Prisoner finds his own bed, bedding, and sheets, (which the Warden is in no sort to hinder him of,) then he shall pay, for his chamber-room, to the Warden per week-----------0 13 Of the three Fees here enclosed in , none are now taken; the Clerk of the Papers considering them as unreasonable and unnecessary. The rest in the above Table are taken.

If there be two Prisoners in one bed, finding their own bed, bedding, and sheets, £. s, d. then each of them to pay to the Warden per week....».".»:---0 0 7t Every Prisoner, not being entitled to partake of the Podr'sBox, to pay to the Porter and Gaoler, now called Turnkeys, on his appointment---., - 0 2 0 Every Prisoner, on a Commitment upon a Surrender, at a Judge's Chamber, to pay,t to the Tipstaff----...--....-- 068 Every Prisoner, on a Commitment upon a *Habeas Corpus,* at a Judge's Chamber, to pay to the Tipstaff--..--042

Every Prisoner, on a Commitment in Court, to pay to the Tipstaff---076

No other Fees for any Prisoner, for the use of chamber, bed, bedding, or sheets, or upon Commitment or Discharge of any Prisoner, in any Civil Action; nor any Commitment-Fee to be taken of any Prisoner intitled to partake of the Poor's Box; nor any chamber-rent to be taken of any Prisoner on the Common-Side.

"A List Of Donations, Paid to Prisoners on the Begging-Grate of the Common-Side of the Fleet Prison; as copied from the Board hung up.

"1. From the Court of Chancery, Hilary, Trinity, and Michaelmas Terms, *51. 5s. sS. . i.* each Term-lJ 15 O 2. From the Court of Common Pleas, *SI.* every Term---T 12 O 0 3. From the Court of Exchequer, 6. *8d.* every Term----,-16 8 4. From the Company of Drapers, annually at Christmas-----110 0 5. From the Company of Leather-sellers, at Lady-day, Midsummer, and Michael mas Quarters, 4. each, and at Christmas, *6s.* and bread, 2s. 6d. each.': 6. From the Company of Merchant Taylors, at Christmas-----lloO 7. From the Company of Saddlers, 2i. 6d. each Quarter----Oloo 8. From the Archbishop of Canterbury, at Christmas-----1 0 O 9. From St. Bartholomew's Hospital, at ditto----113 0 10. From St. Ethelburga's Parish, at ditto 090 11. From a Person unknown, every Easter Monday, from the Grange Inn, Caiy-Street f 2 0 0 12. The Gift of Mr. Thomas Stretchly, every three years 200 13. Executrix of Mrs. Misson, annually, about Christmas ----- 600 14. Warden of the Fleet, at Christmas---110 Two shillings and eightpence is received in bread. f This is paid in January.

X Mrs. Misson, by her Will, dated the 23d of May, 1770, and proved at London, 9th March, 1774, leaves the produce of *2001.* India Annuities to the Debtors of Ludgate Prison; likewise the produce of 200/. of the same Annuities, to the Debtors only of the Fleet Prison; and also of 200/. to the Debtors only of Newgate Prison.

'v ,, v FLINT. *North Wales.*

"'- *The County Gaol, and Home of Correction.*

Gaoler, *Robert Williams.* Salary, 45/. Fees, see Table. "Garnish abolished.

Chaplain, Rev. *George Davies.* Salary, 20/.

Duty, Prayers once only in every week!!

Surgeon, Mr. *Ingleby,* now Mr. *Jones.* Salary, *30L*

Number of Prisoners, Debtors. Felons. Bridewell.

1800, April 3d,---2---3---0. 1802,. Oct. 23d,----3-t 5---0. 1809, Nov. 17th,------4---7---1.

Allowance, to Debtors and Felons, *4s.* per week each; out of which *Is.* is paid for a bed. Now six-pence per day in bread.

:' REMARKS.

This County Gaol, which is also the Bridewell, stands on a fine spot, near the Old Castle. The Keeper's apartments are in front, on the ground-floor, and the entrance is through an iron-palisaded door. One Court, about 15 yards square, with a pump and sewer in it, is for Debtors. Those on the Common-Side have a *free-Ward* on the ground-floor, about 24 feet by 15, which is also their day-roomThe Master's-Side Debtors have five spacious rooms, light and airy, up-stairs, which are divided by a lobby 6 feet wide, and in four of them there are fireplaces. An Infirmary up stairs is set apart for the sick; and a warm and cold bath are provided.. 1.'

For Felons there are five sleeping-cells, divided by a passage 3 feet wide. One of them is totally dark; the others are lighted and ventilated by an iron-grated aperture in the wall, about 24 inches by *6*. Each cell is about 9 feet by *6,* with arched roof, and fitted up with a wooden bedstead, straw, two blankets, and a rug. They have likewise a day-room, with a fire-place, about 15 feet square; and a court with a pump in it, about 15 yards square.'

Men and Women Criminals associate promiscuously during the day. The Rules and Orders, settled by the Magistrates in 1787, are hung up, as also the Clauses against Spirituous Liquors; but not the Act for preserving Health. The Prison is clean.

"Table Of Fees.

"*Flintshire, to wit*. At the Court of Great Session held at *Flint* on the 22d of August, Fifth of Geo. III. 1765, before the Hon. *John Morton,* esq. Chief Justice of Chester, Flint, Denbigh, and Montgomery; and *Taylor White,* esq. his Majesty's other Justice there assigned, &c. It is ordered that the Gaoler, for the time being, do take no more than the Fees and Allowances hereafter mentioned, which the Court conceive to be sufficient and reasonable: that is to say,

A Table of Fees to be taken by the Gaoler of this County.

*s. i. "*For the receipt of every Prisoner for Debt--.-----26

For the use of bedstead and chamber by the week, the Prisoner finding his own bedding--------------10

If the bedding found by the Gaoler, per week, then------20

For a Copy of every Commitment----------16

Attending every Prisoner brought by rule of Court-----1 O

Fee on Prisoner's Discharge-----------26

Turnkey's Fee on Prisoner's Discharge---------10

"The above Table of Fees is ratified and confirmed by John Morton."

The House of Correction, which adjoins the Gaol, has two small rooms up stairs, one for Men, the other for Women; both dark, and ill ventilated, with low ceilings, about 6 feet high only. The bedstead in one is of iron, the other of wood. Each room had a small court in 1802; but at my visit in 1809, I found the walls taken down, in consequence of having facilitated escapes. No employment is here furnished.

In front of the Prison, on a black and white marble, is this Inscription:

"In the
Twenty-fifth year of his Majesty Geo. III.
in the Sheriffalty of
Sir Thomas Hanmer, bart.
this Prison was erected,
instead of the antient loathsome
Place of Confinement;
in Pity
to the Misery of even the most Guilty;
to alleviate the sufferings of lesser offenders;
or of the Innocent themselves,
whom the Chances of human Life may bring within these walls.
...' Done at the Expence of the County, aided by Subscriptions of several of the Gentry,
who,
in the midst of most distressful days, voluntarily took on themselves
Part of the Burthen;
in Compassion to such of their Countrymen,
on whom
. Fortune had been less bounteous of her Favours."

"Joseph Turner, Architect."

On the inside of the building appears a list, on white marble, of the names of the Subscribers to it, with the sums they gave, beginning with

"Sir Roger Mostyn, Bart.--------=£. 100." FOLKINGHAM. *Lincolnshire, The Home of Correction,*

Keeper, *John Speight.* Salary, 50/. Fees, none..

No Chaplain, nor any religious attentions.

Number of Prisoners, 1809, Sept. 4th, *16* Men. *6* Women.

Allowance. Two shillings and six pence per week in bread; one shilling in oatmeal and salt, and one shilling in meat, each...

REMARKS.

The Old Gaol, with its horrid Dungeon, now done away, are fully described in the Gentleman's Magazine for January l805 p. 5.

This *New Prison* was first inhabited on the 2d of June 1809. It is built on the site of the antient Castle, and the boundary wall forms an oblong octagon. The entrance gate opens into an area, that detaches the buildings and the court-yards from the boundary wall; close to which here is an inspecting walk, 5 feet wide, encircling the whole Prison.

A flagged foot-path, 8 feet in breadth, leads to the Keeper's house, which occupies the centre of the building, and has a wing on each side of it for the Prisoners; the whole, presenting a front 94 feet in length: and a lobby or passage, of 3 feet, divides the house in the middle.

G G.a

Here are four court-yards, distinctly and equally assigned for the Male and Female Prisoners; to each of which is allotted a day-room, about 12 feet square, and a workroom of *12* feet by *6* feet 6. The courts are well supplied with water; the sewers conveniently placed: open iron palisades transmit a thorough air; and a small garden adjacent furnishes the Keeper with vegetables.

On the chamber-story are seven sleeping-cells for Men, and six for Women Prisoners, with vaulted roofs. Some of them have two bedsteads, which are supplied with straw-in-ticking beds; and two blankets, a pair of sheets, a bolster, and a rug to each.

A circular room, 14 feet in diameter,

is appropriated for a *Chapel,* with two distinct pews for the Prisoners: Adjoining to it is a solitary cell, with a ventilator fixed in the crown of the arch; and the glimmering light which it enjoys is borrowed from the Chapel.

The iron-grated and glazed windows have each an inside shutter, and the cell doors an inspecting wicket, favourable also for the admission of fresh air.

No Turnkey's lodge is provided, nor any assistant for the Keeper: and as two of the court-yards have a view of the entrance-door, it not only seems to render the Prison insecure, but hazardous also to the Keeper.

Here is a good bath; but neither the Act for Preserving Health, nor the Clauses against Spirituous Liquors, are hung up.

FORRES. *Scotland.*
The Tolbooth.
Gaolers, the three Town's Officers, in weekly rotation.

Fees, for Felons and other Criminals, none. Debtors pay *4d.* per night.

No Religious attentions.

Surgeon, from the Town, when wanted.

Prisoners, Oct. *J,* 1809, None.

Allowance; Felons, &c. *6d.* a day. Debtors, as alimented.

REMARKS.
This Prison adjoins to the Council-room, and has on the first story a room for Debtors, with a fire-place and boarded floor; but no coals, no bedstead, bedding, or even straw are allowed.

The second story has one room for Criminals, of the same size, with a clay-floor, but neither bedstead, bedding, nor straw. No water, but as brought in by the Keepers. No sewer; but a half tub supplies its place.

Ten steps down, here is a Dungeon called the *Black Hole,* about 15 feet square; which has a small aperture to the street, and is occasionally used for Vagrants, and the refractory amongst the Military. It has a mud-floor; no bedding; no water accessible; with a filthy tub as a sewer.

SO3 Foures is the place, or town, to which *Macbeth* was travelling, when he met the Weird Sisters upon the Heath. It reminded me of what Dr. Johnson says, in his Tour to the Hebrides; "This, to an Englishman, is classick ground." On this road Macbeth heard the fatal prediction, which the magic pen of Shakspeare has immortalized. From hence I went to Nairne, near which stands the Castle of *Cawdor,* that gave Macbeth his second Title, previous to his usurpation of the Throne. GREENWICH. *Kent.*
Gaoler, *Robert Chantilope.*

Salary, *10I.* and has also Fees of office, as Beadle to the Court of Requests.

Allowance to Debtors, none.

REMARKS.
This Prison is behind the Court of Requests, and called the *Stone Kitchen,* from its being flagged with stone, and on the ground-floor. It has one small room, 16 feet 6' inches in length, by *9* feet wide, with a scanty fire-place; but the chimney's smoking renders it often useless, when Prisoners have a few coals given them, for none are allowed them by the Town.

The lower part of the Court of Requests is inhabited by the Gaoler. Women Debtors are confined in a small upper room, near the Court, of about 8 feet square, which has a fire-place, and an uncovered sewer in it.

When this Prison was first inhabited, there was no bed, bedding, nor even straw allowed; but in May 1810, I found two wooden bedsteads raised about 18 inches from the floor, in one corner, and fixed angle-wise, with loose straw to each, for one person to sleep on; but the head of one of the bedsteads is within about 18 inches of an uncovered sewer, which must be very offensive. I was told that *Jive Prisoners* have been confined here at one time, so that *three* must necessarily sleep upon the floor. The room cannot but be suffocatingly hot in Summer, and as piercingly cold in Winter.

A small court-yard might be made in the passage leading down to the above room, and a cistern also, filled with water for the use of the Prisoners. At present there is none supplied, but what is brought by the Gaoler, whose business, on captions must frequently take him from home.

GILTSPUR-STREET COMPTER. *London.*
Gaoler, *John Addison Newman;* now *John Teague.*

Salary, heretofore was 150/.; now 250/. are paid by the Court of Aldermen, and 30/. by the Common Council. Garnish abolished.

Fees, as per Table following, kept in the Prison; *viz.*

"Every Debtor, who, at his own request, shall go on the Master's-s. d. Side, to pay to the Keeper,-----------30

To the Turnkeys, ditto,-------------2 O

And for the use of bed, bedding, and sheets, each per week,--2 6

Every Debtor, on his Discharge, to pay to the Keeper----6 a

To the Turnkeys---------------2 O

To the Secondary---------------60

To the Clerk-sitter of the Poultry Compter-------10

To ditto, of the Giltspur-street Compter--------48

To the Secondary, for every other Action, "if more than one"-3 4

To the Messenger------------10

Masters'-Side Debtor to pay extra on his Discharge-----0 10

"Every Night-Charge, or other Criminal, upon criminal process,
who, at his own desire, shall be accommodated with bed and
bedding, to pay, for the first night------- --20

And for every other night----------10

If formally admitted on the Master's-Side, to pay on entrance--10 6

And for the use of bed, bedding, and sheets, per week-3 6

For every Night-charge, who shall be discharged before a Magistrate 3 6

For every Commitment after the first examination discharged, or bailed 14 8

To the Turnkey, for the Copy of every Commitment, or Detainer-2 0."
$3= If there be more actions than one, the expence varies, according to the number and nature of the Writs; which, if in execution, entitle the Secondaries to one shilling for every pound under the sum of loo/, and to sixpence for every pound above that sum: and this is called "*Sheriffs Poundage* ." -Chaplain, Rev. Mr. *Edmands;* now Rev. Mr.

Davis.

Duty, Prayers and Sermon on Sunday.

Salary, *§01.* and a Freedom of the City, voted annually by the Court of Aldermen, and valued at 25/.

An instance of ninety-seven pounds ten shillings being paid for poundage is in my possession

Surgeon, Mr. *Hodgson,* for the two Compters, and Ludgate.

Salary, 100/. and for medicines, 20/. a complete chest for which has been placed in the Infirmary, by the Committee for City Lands.

Number of Prisoners,

Allowance, a loaf of wheaten bread every other day, weight twenty ounces, to Prisoners of all descriptions, and 1 lb. of rice, 3 lbs. of beef, and 5 lbs. of potatoes, to each weekly. But see the *Remarks.* REMARKS.

The origin of this Prison is somewhat enveloped in obscurity: but, (according to Stow's Survey of London, wherein the following record, made in the reign of Edward the First, is recited, *viz.* "Rex vie. London, salutem: ex gravi quereld B. capt. "et detent, inprisond nostra de Criplesgate pro xl. quas coram Radulpho de Sand"wicq, time custod. Ciuitatis nostra London, et I. de Blachwell civis recognit. debit. &c") it appears that Cripplegate, which was one of the four original gates of this city, was then a Prison, as the Compter now is, for citizens and others, for debt. of trespass; and was rebuilt in the year 1244, and again in 1491; and was last repaired in the year 1663. In the mean time, and in the 13th century, a Prison was built for the reception of nightwalkers, and other suspicious persons; which, from its shape, was called the Tun, and was situated upon Cornhill. Afterwards there was a Prison in Breadstreet, pertaining to the Sheriffs which was called "The Compter;" and, in the year 1518, seems to have been recognized by the Act for establishing the Court of Conscience, which empowered its Commissioners to commit to one of the Compters, for Debts not exceeding forty shillings; but now, by subsequent acts, extended to five pounds. In this Compter Prisoners were received until the year 1552; when, by reason of the Keeper's misconduct, they were removed to a new Compter in Wood-street, provided by the City, and built for that purpose. This was burned in the general conflagration of *1666,* and being rebuilt N. B. The Poultry Compter having been deemed unfit to receive Debtors, forty-five were sent to' this Prison in 1808, thirty-three in 1809, thirty-eight in 1810, and twenty-four in 1811, who must otherwise have been confined in the Poultry Compter.

more commodiously than before, continued to receive Prisoners until April 2d, 1791, when they were transferred to the present Compter in Giltspur-street.

It appears necessary here to remark, that the Sheriffs of London have each a Court of Record, as well as a Compter, where each Sheriff, in his respective Court, presides. These Courts are now held at Guildhall, every Wednesday and Friday, for actions, &c. entered at this Compter; and on every Thursday and Saturday, for actions entered at the Poultry, excepting holidays, and a vacation in the month of August; and each Sheriff has his office at his respective Compter, where his Clerk-sitter attends for entering actions, &c. and also to discharge such Debtors as become entitled to their release.

This Compter is now appropriated for the reception of Debtors; of Felons, and other Offenders; and also of Vagrants and night-charges (the watch-houses in this city not being permitted to retain Prisoners there): But the Constable of the night must forthwith commit them to the Compter in his district; from whence a list of the night-charges so committed, is, the next morning, returned to the Lord Mayor, or one of the Aldermen; in order that they may be examined touching the cause of their commitment, and be either discharged, bailed, or re-committed, to answer for their respective offences, according to due course of law.

The Prisoners are divided into four classes: *viz.* Debtors, Felons, Misdemeanors and Assaults, and Vagrants; and the Prison into nine separate and distinct yards: that is to say, The Master's Side, South-yard, 28 feet by 20, containing a pump, affording soft water from the river Thames, and from whence a staircase leads to two galleries, having each a sink and a cock supplying Thames-water; which is thrown by a forcing-pump from a reservoir in the main yard to a large cistern on the top 'of that part of the Prison, and descends from thence to the galleries: But here a difficulty sometimes occurs, from the forcing-pump being out of the reach of the persons to be benefited thereby. These galleries lead to six rooms (exclusive of the Turnkey's-room on the ground-floor,) having fire-places, capable of conveniently accommodating two persons in each, male or female, as it may happen, provided that a Man-prisoner is not lodged in the same apartment with a Woman-prisoner: and these apartments are at present occupied by Master-Side Debtors, who pay for the same according to the Table of Fees before mentioned.

2d. The Master's-Side, North-yard, 30 feet by 18, is similar to the South in its construction and accommodations, but contains only five rooms with fire-places, (exclusive of another Turnkey's room on the ground-floor;) and is at present occupied by persons under commitment for assaults, or trivial offences; as also, occasionally, by the better sort of night-charges. 3d. The Common-Side, Men-Debtors' Yardj 75 feet by 18, contains two pumps, the one supplying spring-water from a well in this yard, and the other affording soft water from the river Thames. It has a room at each end; one of them occupied by a Turnkey, for the better security of the Prison, and the other by the Steward of the Charity-wards. The wards appertaining to this yard are built upon arches, and divide the sume into two parts; having communication by arcades under one part, and a room, in which is a large table fixed, whereon the Prisoners belonging to these wards divide such provisions as they receive by charitable donation. From this yard is a stone staircase, closed with doors at the bottom, and leading to four wards; two on the first story, and two on the second. The two upper wards are used as bed-rooms, and are fitted up with 16 low stump-bedsteads in each, (which lay upon barrack-forms, easily removed for the purpose of cleanliness,) and a supply of rugs for the use of the Prisoners. The other two wards are used as sittin-grooms, from eight in the morning until ten at night; when strangers are excluded,, and the Prisoners are locked up for the night. The Sleeping-wards would be much improved, if all the beds were separated by dwarf partitions, having a door to each, but not reaching to the ceiling. Thus a free circulation of air would not be impeded, and the quiet Prisoners would be protected from the insults of the disorderly, in the night-time; an evil which has sometimes occurred, but the offenders are seldom discovered. The Sitting-wards are fitted up with tables and benches.

These wards, together with that of the Women-Debtors, are denominated the Charity-wards; to which each Prisoner, at his or her entrance, pays five shillings, to be applied to the common stock, eight-pence to the Steward, and six-pence to the Scavenger; after which the Prisoner partakes of all the benefits appertaining to. the Charity-wards _ ($3" From the best account I could extract from the books of this Compter, it is evident, that, during a period of eleven years,bwr *hundred and ninety-Jive Debtorswere* committed hither from the "Court of Requests," (or, as it is now better known, the *Court of Conscience;)* and that out of this large number, the several creditors, or plaintiffs, who actually received their Debt and Costs, in consequence of such incarceration, were absolutely no more than *sixty-seven!* that is to say, not one Creditor in seven, of all the number, gained the object of his animosity. The fact is very striking; and, so far as human liberty is concerned in it, must produce an electrical effect upon every ingenuous heart. My own feelings on this head have been often agitated: I have sometimes expressed them: and now (very probably for the *last time,)* I sincerely wish to give them their proper influence..

The very small sums, for which many of these poor miserable creatures,—these outcasts, as it were, of British freedom,—are imprisoned, seem to preclude the distant possibility of the payment of, perhaps,, even a just Debt, more especially when loaded by an enormous aggravation of *legal Costs*. I remember, that on the 27th April, 1805, I found, here one *William Grant* detained for so trivial a Debt Those *Debtors* who cannot pay their feet, sleep in rooms assigned for the reception of *Night-Charges;*. and their allowance of beef is sold, until the deficiency is made up..
as *ls.9d.*—The Costs then amounted to five shillings; and on the l8th of December, of the same year, *John Lancaster* was imprisoned for a Debt of *twenty pence,* the Costs in pursuit of which arose to *seven shillings and sixpence I* " These, surely, I thought, were bad enough:" But it was nor so. The following extraordinary case, therefore, I recite at large; and hope it will, at length, produce some salutary effect, to appease the manes of injured humanity.
The following Warrant of Commitment is copied *verbatim* from its original in the proper office.
' Court of Requests, London.
To the Officers of this Court, or any customary Serjeant at Mace of London.

By Order Of The Commissioners Of The Court Of Requests In £. s. d. London, you are to commit to Prison, in one of the Compters of the Debt, 0 0 4. same City, John Bird, for *twenty days,* unless the full sum of *four-pence* Costs. 0 7 P. *flebt,* and *seven shillings and sixpence Costs,* due to Lawrence Newman, £. 0 7 10. be all paid, according to an order set down by the Commissioners of the Levy the whole. same Court, the ninth day of July, one thousand eight hundred and eight.

Hereof fail not. Dated at the Guildhall the ninth day of July, one thousand eight hundred and eight. Holmes."

The Defendant was arrested on the 11th day of May, l810, and discharged on the 14th May, 1 810, by a subscription of the Prisoners. The Plaintiff was a publican, and the Defendant a porter in the market.

Now, if this be not the crushing of a moth with a sledge-hammer, it is hard to say what is. What a pity, that the worst passions of mankind should thus, by the solemn sanction of *Law,* be countenanced in their exertions, equally against common sense and the decorum of Christian urbanity!

4th. The Main Yard, 35 feet square, leads to all the rest, except the Master'sSide, and Women Debtors, into which all persons in the adjoining yards (except Debtors) are occasionally admitted in the day-time, at their own request; and upon' behaving themselves orderly, but not otherwise. This yard contains two pumps, one of spring-water, the other from the Thames; also two forcing pumps, for the service of the Master's-Side, and a cock supplied with Thames-water upon the *Main;* to which, by means of a screw, can be applied a long leathern hose, and thereby plenty of water is conveyed to all the yards, to wash both them and the cells. For this purpose mops and brooms are regularly allowed by the benevolence of the Committee of City Lands, &c. On the North and South sides are two large rooms facing each other, and having communication with the arched passage before mentioned; which rooms are occupied in the day-time by those who desire it, and at night are the common receptacles for night-charges. They are fitted up with These two rooms are now (1810) appropriated to Debtors; and Night-charges and Female Criminals sent to the Poultry, till a new Prison is built. v,;,, j;, j. ' /.: benches all round, and a large German stove in both. They have detached privies, and are capable of containing about twenty persons each, for one night only; such night-charges being afterwards classed as aforesaid, having first undergone their examination before a magistrate. These rooms have stone floors; they are spacious, and very airy; and have a number of rugs laid on the benches, for the use of such persons as unfortunately may become inhabitants in the night-time. Under another arched passage leading from this yard, is the Inner Turnkey's Lodge, and a staircase leading to a very convenient

Chapel; over which are four good rooms, for the use of the sick Prisoners, fitted up with iron bedsteads, good tickings, blankets, rugs, and also canvass cases, ready to be stuffed for making beds, as occasion may require.

From this yard are two other staircases; each leading to three small bed-rooms, fitted up at the Keeper's expence, for the use of such night-charges, or others, as may desire to occupy them; having one bed in each room.

The above passage communicates with five other yards, separate and distinct from each other: one being a small yard, with a pump of Thames-water, and containing three scanty rooms, or cells, capable of lodging six persons. Another small yard, equally supplied from the Thames, contains five rooms or cells of the same dimensions. At the back of four of these rooms is a passage, with a fire-place at the end; which, communicating by means of an iron-grating to each cell, thereby renders them dry and warm.

The next yard, furnished in like manner with water, has a room with a fire-place, and four cells of the same dimensions; and near to this are two larger yards, having six cells of the like size, together with similar passages, and fire-places to keep them comfortably warm. The cells are all fitted up with barrack bedsteads, raised about three feet from the ground; each provided with a canvass case stuffed with straw, and two or three rugs, or blankets, allowed by the City.

These last five yards are for the reception of all Prisoners, except Debtors. Here are also very convenient cold and hot baths, to which all Prisoners have free access, as-necessity requires, and at convenient seasons. There are two rooms set apart for the sick, one 18 feet by 14, the other 14 feet by 12, and 12 feet high; and two other rooms of the same size, which can easily be converted into Sick wards, if, necessary.

The following Gifts from the City Companies, &c. are specifically appropriated to the discharge, or relief, of *Debtors,* in this and other Prisons of London; *viz.*

The *Merchant-Taylors'* Company give annually 35/. to each of the four following Prisons, fewgate, Ludgate, and the Poultry and Giltspur-street Compters, to assist in theMscharge of poor Debtors, at 3/. each.

H H

The *Drapers'* Company give annually, in December, 100/. to release poor Debtors from the before-mentioned Prisons, in aid of Sir John Kendrick's Legacy.

The *Grocers'* Company give annually 8/. to each of the following Prisons, Ludgate, the Poultry, and Giltspur-street Compter, for the discharge of Debtors, whose petitions are recommended by two housekeepers.

The *Cloth-workers'* Company give annually the same sum, at *ll. 19s. 6d.* for each Debtor, on petition..

Christ's Hospital allows *9l.* to each of the four first-mentioned Prisons to discharge poor Debtors, by payment of their *Fees:* Those in Ludgate are to be recommended by an Alderman, and those in the other three Prisons by their respective Keepers.

The *Mercers'* Company allow 12/. annually for the discharge of four Prisoners, at 3/. each.

Mr. *Ralph Carter* by Deed, dated 22d October, 1576, conveyed a house and garden, then called the Half-Moon, in East Smithfield, near the Tower of London, to Trustees for the parishes of St. Andrew Undershaft, and St. Allhallows, Lombardstreet, to the end that the rent thereof should be equally divided between the said parishes, and disposed of as follows:—To the Poor in bread every Sunday one shilling. In coals, to be delivered yearly, between the feasts of All Saints and Christmas, for ever, 30. The overplus of the moiety received by the parish of St. Andrew Undershaft to be given, if the Tenement shall not need it for repairs, amongst the poor Prisoners in the two Compters and Newgate, the King's Bench, Marshalsea, and White Lion in Southwark. These Premises now let for 207. *per annum,* of which the Parish of St. Andrew Undershaft receives half; and it is usually given in meat about Christmas.

Beside the above instances of liberality, coals, and other gifts are bestowed every year, by the Right Honourable the Lord Mayor, and Sheriffs; and broken victuals are often received from the great London Taverns.

Paupers, brought to this Compter as such, (in order to be removed to their parishes, or otherwise relieved,) are especially subsisted, and frequently clothed.

The gifts by the Lord Mayor and Sheriffs, at Christmas, New-year's day, Easter, and some uncertain day after, are the same as mentioned in my subsequent description of " *Ludgate.*"

Here are also some permanent Donations of bread and meat at stated periods; which, together with the Sheriffs' seven stone of meat weekly, belong to the Charitywards only; and are distributed among such Prisoners in the said wards as have attended, and properly demeaned themselves in the Chapel, during Divine Service on the preceding Sunday. These, in the way of ridicule, are called *Beef-eaters,* by the profligate few who absent themselves: But-nearly the whole attended Divine Service when I was here in March, 1807, and their behaviour was orderly, and attentive to a very appropriate discourse. The Chapel Clerk is Mr. Thomas Cooper, who receives half a crown every Sunday, for assisting the Chaplain, and setting the psalm, by order of the Court of Aldermen.

Money is paid by several of the City Companies, by the Common Council of Farringdon Within , and by others, towards the release of Debtors in this and other Prisons; and is applied as stated in the account of Ludgate.

Giltspur-street Compter Donations.

Annually, Nov. 5. Of Bread, Mrs. Margaret Dane. One quarter of Beef and five dozen Penny Loaves. Quarterly, Leathersellers Company, Ninety-one Penny Loaves.

Every eight weeks, Mrs. Margaret Symcott, Eleanor Gwynn's gift, Sixty Penny Loaves.

A Memorial, to the following effect, is hung up in the Vestry-room of Christ Church NewgateStreet; *viz. "*Mr. Edward Robinson, by his Will, dated 30th April 1712, left a yearly Rent-Charge of Four Pounds for ever, payable out of a house (No. 4.) Warwick-Lane, Newgate-street: and likewise the dividends on I99i. 5s. *7d.* 3 per cent. Consolidated Annuities, amounting to 5i. 19i. *6d.* per annum, for ever, to be applied in liberating poor Inhabitants of the parish of *Christ Church,* London, imprisoned for Small Debts." Both these legacies are vested in the Four Common Council Men of that parish. f Taylor, Grosvenor, Firebras, &c.

§ Mr. Chrke's Legacy is now paid by Messrs. Bleasdaile and Alexander, Attornies in Lyon's Inn, as Agents to Mr. Rhodes of Chichester.

All the Donations belonging to the Charity-wards are delivered to one of the Prisoners, who acts as Steward; in whose name, witnessed by the Keeper, all the receipts are signed, and given under the common seal of the Prison. This Steward Taylor, Grosvenor, Firebras, &c. f Of Carey-street, Chancery-lane.

§ Of Gloucester-street, Hoxton i and all arising from the ground-rent of houses there.

receives also the Subscriptions beforementioned: He advances money upon the credit of the donations, out of which he reimburses himself as they become due; pays five per cent, to a collector; furnishes the Charity-wards with a constant supply of coals, wood, salt, candles, &c. besides paying a weekly allowance to a basketwoman, to collect broken victuals at the taverns; and for other messages, on account of the wards. He likewise contributes to the support of such Common-side Debtors, as may, by the Surgeon's order, be placed in the Sick-ward: pays also a weekly allowance to the scavenger, and his assistant, called " the Twelverand is of real use to the Prison at large. This plan for the application of the donations was first adopted by Mr. Kirby, when Keeper of Wood-street Compter; and appears to be most beneficial to the unfortunate, as every comfort to be procured by the donations is thereby equally and impartially afforded. No disputes can arise from the Quarterly division of money; nor can the Prison be defrauded, as the Steward is obliged to submit his accounts to be audited by four of the senior Prisoners: and, though elected by the general suffrages of the Charity-wards, cannot be dispossessed, so long as he shall act soberly and honestly, for the general advantage, and not be guilty of breach of the trust reposed in him by the Keeper.

The Rules and Orders for the Government of this Prison were signed the 27th of November, 1792, by Lords Kenyon apd Loughborough, and by Aldermen Crosby, Anderson, and Combe. They relate principally to Debtors; the execution thereof is vested in the Keeper and his Turnkeys; and they are as follows, that is to say: Directions concerning the payment of six-pence to the Scavenger, or to assist him six days, and eight pence to the Steward: directions for dividing provisions; for persons under judgment of fine and imprisonment to partake, in certain cases, with the Debtors; to promote cleanliness; for due attendance on Divine Service; for cleanliness of Prisoners' persons; against opprobrious language; against profaneness and drunkenness; against molesting visitors, and to prevent visitors from molesting Prisoners; to prevent women from lodging in men's apartments, and *vice versd:* against keeping dogs; to determine who shall not partake of donations; to prevent tippling; time of retiring to rest, and rising in the morning; against striking the Steward, or defacing orders: more concerning performance of Divine Service; against disposal of Prison rugs; Master's-side Prisoners to clean their stairs, passages, and rooms; not to quarrel, or use opprobrious language; concerning the placing of Master's-side Prisoners in their rooms; to prohibit the admission of wine, or beer, after eight o'clock in the evening, &c.

The mode directed by the foregoing Rules and Orders to enforce obedience thereto, is by fining, or by confinement in a cell for any time not more than twelve hours, nor less than three, for one offence, at the discretion of the Keeper.

GLASGOW. *Scotland.*
The Tolbooth.
Gaoler, *Robert Hamilton,* now *James Gardner.*

Salary, *6ol.* Fees, see Table. He has a licence to sell porter, ale, and beer; and *supplies the Prisoners with Bread.* Garnish. From Prisoners confined in the upper flat (or story) 5. each; and from those in the lower flat 2. which goes to the General Fund for purchasing coals, candles, &c. But see the *Remarks.*

No Chaplain; nor religious attentions, except to those under Sentence of Death.

Surgeon, Mr. *Burns.*

Salary, 70/. for the Town Hospital, Tolbooth, and Bridewell; and Medicines found.

Number of Prisoners, Debtors. Felons, &c.
1802, Sept. 18th,------28-27. 1809, Oct. 25th,-20-------43.

Allowance, to *Debtors,* according to the discretion of the Magistrates, from *lod.* to *2s. 6d.* per day, which is paid by the Creditor; and on failure of which the Debtor is discharged. To *Felons,* fourpence per day, in money.

REMARKS.

This loathsome Prison is nearly in the centre of a magnificent City, and the Gaoler's apartments communicate with the Court of Session. On the ground-floor are the Turnkey's lodge, and the Gaoler's office.

The first flat (or floor) contains nine sleeping-cells, the average size about 7 feet square; four of which are totally dark, and without ventilation, except what is admitted through a very small apertuie in the door, and a fire-place in one of them. The other four have each a small iron-grated window, and one of them has a fireplace. The ninth sleeping-cell is called the *Iron Room;* to which the Prisoner, after sentence of Death, is immediately conducted. There, a blacksmith fixes an iron strap round his leg, again fastened by a ring, which encircles a strong iron bar, called the *Goad;* and this, running across, is rivetted down to the stone floor, so that he cannot raise that foot one inch from it. In this situation I beheld two wretched criminals, who had been condemned at the Justiciary Court in September 1809, and were to suffer on the 8th of November, on a platform in front of the Prison, which has a door conveniently adapted for the decent performance of that awful ceremony. In many parts of England such poor wretches are dragged, through the Town, to a place a mile distant, to the preposterous gratification of unfeeling curiosity, and to the disgrace of civilized Society! These unhappy men of the *Tolbooth* had been attended by Ministers of the Established Kirk, and others devoutly disposed: The Magistrates, in addition to the fourpence a day paid in money, had humanely ordered them a hot dinner, to be sent from a tavern every day, and each had a wooden stool to sit upon. The Criminals appeared sensible of the kindness, and resigned to their tremendous doom.

The second flat (or story) has one room for *Criminals,* 13 feet by 11, with a fire-place; and three rooms for *Debtors,* two of which are 10 feet by 8, the other 18 feet by 11; with fire-places, and a window in each. To this flat there is a water-closet attached, in a room 13 feet by 6 feet 4; but having a sink in it, into which the Felons' tubs are emptied, the good effects are sadly defeated; for I found it almost unbearably offensive, although there is a window in the room 3 feet square.

On a level with this second flat is the *Tap-Room, 22* feet *6* by 13 feet 9, and 10 feet 3 inches high, having two windows, *6* feet by 3 each, and a fire-place. To supply this room with coals and candle, I apprehend it is, that the *Garnish money* is exacted. It is generally filled both with Prisoners and Towns-people; so that the Tap is constantly kept running, and proves, indeed, a main source of Prisonfinance, as will be demonstrated in the sequel.

Having mentioned the Gaoler's Salary to be only *Sixty Pounds,* to which the Fees can make but a trifling addition, I shall proceed to state his expences: viz.
s. d.

To a Clerk, per week, 7. *6d.* -----19 10 0

To the Inner Turnkey, ditto, *1Js. 6d.*----45 10 0 To the Outer Turnkey, ditto, *6d.*----19 10.0

To a Woman for cleaning the Gaol, and going on messages, ditto, 6s. 15 12 0

Total 100 2 0.

The Salary of a Gaoler should ever be proportioned to the trust and trouble incident to his important charge. He should draw no Emolument whatever from Misery, nor have any concern in, nor profit from the *sale of bread,* or other food: and what is a licensed Tap, but the certain means of introducing drunkenness and profligacy?

The third flat has six rooms for *Debtors,* the average size of which is 9 feet square: there are windows in each, and four of them have fire-places. Here is likewise a common kitchen, 17 feet by 9, with a fire-place.

On the 4th flat, or attic story, are four rooms for Women, 15 feet by 10, with windows and fire-places; but the ceilings are too scanty, being only 7 feet high. To this story there is a water-closet. „

Iron bedsteads are furnished to *Criminals;* and *Felons* are allowed a mattress, two blankets, and a rug. *Debtors* furnish their own bedding. No coals are allowed to any part of the Prison. Water is now laid on to the two flats, or stories, occupied by the Debtors.

"Fees and Regulations, To be exacted and observed in the *Tolbooth* at Glasgow; as appointed by Act of the Magistrates and Town Council of Glasgow, dated the 31st of August, 1769.
Sterling. £. s. d. 1. Every Burgess incarcerated, shall, during his confinement, pay for
Jaylor-fee, for each night, at the rate of------002

And every person not a Burgess, shall pay for Jaylor-fee, during his or her confinement, each night, at the rate of----004 2. Every person imprisoned by virtue of an act of warning, shall pay to the Jaylor, exclusive of the dues in 1st article----0 1 4- And every person incarcerated by virtue of a written warrant from a Magistrate, a Justice of Peace, or a Sheriff, shall pay--0 1 8 *3.* Every person incarcerated by virtue of a caption, or a justiciary or admiral warrant, shall, exclusive of the dues in 1st article, if a
Burgess, pay---------------0 2 91

If an unfreeman,--------------05 64 4. The Jaylor, on signing an attestation of a commitment, shall receive 0 10 And on the delivery up of diligence to persons neglecting to require the same, within eight days after the Prisoner's liberation, he shall receive-------------- 010

Rules to be observed by the Jaylor and his servants.
1. The Jaylor shall not, by himself or any of his servants, directly or indirectly, demand or receive from any Prisoner, or from any person in his or her name, at entry, or during his or ber confinement, any sums of money, under the name of entry-money, *garnishing,* or any other denomination, separate from, and over and above the fees stipulated as above. Further, *the Jaylor shall not suffer any of the Prisoners to make demands of money or drink from persons newly incarcerated, on any pretence whatsoever.* 2. The Jaylor shall, all the year, open each day, the Prison at nine, and shut it at three in the afternoon; then open at five, and shut it at nine for the night: only, on Sundays, the Prison shall be shut during public worship, any thing in this rule to the contrary. And the Jaylor is always to keep the whole keys of the Prison in his own custody, while it is shut up, and not entrust them with any of his servants. 3. The Jaylor, every morning and evening,-at the opening of, and before shutting up the Prison, shall personally visit every room and place therein, carefully inspect the windows, chimnies, and walls thereof, in order to prevent and discover all attempts to cut the iron stancbers, or to break through the stone walls, joists, and floors of the Prison; and he shall take particular care that no instruments be conveyed to, or be in the possession of, any of the Prisoners, whereby they may effectuate their escape, or hurt one another: And in case the Jaylor shall, through indisposition be prevented from the execution of his duty, he shall take care to employ some faithful person in his absence.

The Jaylor and his servants are expressly prohibited, on any account, to sell, or suffer to be brought in to any of the Prisoners, spirits or strong liquor, whereby they may be in danger of being intoxicated; and to use their utmost endeavours to promote sobriety amongst those under their charge.

5. The Jaylor shall keep the Prisoners for debt in the best rooms, and separate from criminals and disorderly persons; and prevent, as much as possible, their associating and conversing together: and the friends and servants of debtors shall be allowed, at all convenient times, to bring in *vivers* for their support. 6. In order to make the Prison more healthy and clean, the Jaylor shall, at his own expence, *cause pare and clean the stairs, sweep the rooms, and remove and carry away all filth and nastiness, at least three times in the week.* 7. The Jaylor, in the event of his exacting, by himself, or his servants, more fees than stipulated as above, or in the event of transgressing any of the Rules or Instructions foresaid, shall be dismissed from his office; or, otherwise punished, as the Magistrates, for the time being, and council shall judge proper.

It is recommended to the Magistrates, frequently to examine and enquire into the fidelity of the Jaylor and his servants; and the Council hereby ordains these dues and regulations to be printed and published, that none may pretend ignorance; and ordains John Rowan, Jaylor, and his successors in office, to affix a copy hereof in the most public part of the Tolbooth, under the penalty of ten pounds Scots."

There are no court-yards to the Gaols in Scotland where Debtors are confined. The original cause of this seems to have been the following very severe maxim in the *Scotch* law: "After a Debtor is imprisoned, *he ought not to be indulged with the benefit of the air, not even under a guard*: for Creditors have an interest, that their Debtors be kept under close confinement; that, by the *squalor carceris* they may be brought to pay their debt!" Act Sess. 14 June, 1671. See *The Principles of the Law of Scotland,* 5th edit. p. 461.

The humane and public-spirited gentlemen of this opulent and highly respectable City, are about to erect a new Prison, on apian which will embrace Security, Health, and Morals: and Nature herself, as it were, has designated the spot.

I cannot help taking this opportunity of paying my tribute of respect to the Right Honourable James Black, esq. Lord Provost, and James Cleland, esq. Convener of Trades, who personally have visited various Prisons of England, in order to furnish the most approved plans, and under whose auspices this monument of national liberality is soon to be erected.

Nor must I here omit to add my grateful acknowledgements to his Lordship, the rest of the Magistrates, and Council of Glasgow, for the Honour they have done me, in presenting me with the Freedom of their City; and likewise to the Trades House, for the highly gratifying manner in which they were pleased to vote and transmit me their Thanks. Provisions, victuals,

ll
GLASGOW.
The Bridewell.
Keeper, *George Andrews.* Salary, 80/. with coals and candles. Fees, none.

Chaplain, Rev. Mr. *Williamson,* whose present ill health obliges him to officiate by deputy. Salary, 25/. Duty, once a Sunday.

Mr. *Reid,* School-Master; who acts as Precentor, or Clerk, and attends three times a week, to instruct such Prisoners as cannot read. A bible and catechism are furnished to those who are religiously disposed.

Surgeon, heretofore Mr. *Cowan,* now Mr. *Burns.* Salary, 70/. for the TownHospital, Tolbooth, and Bridewell, with Medicines found him. f 1802, Sept. 17th,-----90.

Prisoners, g7

Of the latter, six were in the Infirmary.

Allowance. Lowest class, per week, 2s. id. Second 2. *4d.* weekly, and a halfpenny each on Sunday.

Third, 2. *Qd.* weekly, and a penny each on Sunday.

Fourth, ditto 3. *id'* a week, and a penny on Sunday.

The last-mentioned class are employed in working the mills, and their diet is regulated in proportion to the work done.

REMARKS.

This Bridewell, situated in Duke-street, on an eminence at the North end of the Town, was finished and first inhabited in May, 1798. It is surrounded by a boundary wall, within which is a small space, intended for a garden originally; but it is too much confined for the growth of vegetables.

The Prison consists of a centre building, and two wings. The centre is appropriated to Prisoners; the East wing is used as a warehouse; and the Keeper resides in the West wing, where also are the Kitchen and the Infirmary.

On the ground-floor are 20 cells, of 9 feet 6 inches each, by 7 feet, with arched roofs, and stone floors; lighted and ventilated by glazed and iron-grated casement windows, 46 inches by 12. The Prisoners sleep on boards raised four inches from the floor, supplied with loose straw, two blankets, and a rug. An uncovered tub in each cell serves the purpose of a sewer. The cells are divided, ten on each side, by a passage or lobby, 4 feet 2 inches wide; which is ventilated at each end by an iron-grated window.

These cells are used for Convicts under Sentence of Transportation, and are called « The *Legal Prison."*

The 1st, 2d, 3d, and 4th stories have each 21 cells, all of the same size; divided in the same manner as the preceding, and fitted up with raised boards for bedsteads, straw mattress, three blankets, and a rug.

At the top of the building is the *Chapel,* where Divine Service is performed every Sunday.

The Infirmary has a boarded floor, a fire-place, and glazed casement windows, with six wooden bedsteads; and adjoining to it are two small rooms for single persons, and a convenient apartment for the nurse, who is paid a yearly salary. The bedding here is the same as in the other parts of the Prison; but a discretionary power is lodged with the Surgeon, to order additional bedding, diet, or wine, as he judges proper.

Coals are furnished for this wing of the Prison: but it is ill-supplied with water; and there being no regular drain, and the receptacle for the foulest deposits of the Prison being injudiciously constructed near the windows of the Kitchen and Infirmary, sometimes causes both of them to be very offensive. '

Two Women-Prisoners generally work in each cell, and are employed in weaving, tambouring, picking of cotton, and the fabrication of sprig-muslin.

A book is kept, with a regular entry of the work and behaviour of the Prisoners; and whatever their earnings exceed the cost of clothes and maintenance, they receive it upon being discharged.

During my visit in 1802, an account was given me of one *Margaret Raymond,* who at her discharge received no less than *Jifteen pounds ten shillings and eleven pence:* Another Prisoner had eleven pounds five shillings; and a third, five pounds nine shillings. Poor Margaret, however, became too rich to be prudent: she unluckily took the whole of her money at one payment; and being ineffectually lectured by past trials, the consequence was, that want of sobriety, and riotous behaviour, soon sent her back to her old habitation.

At my second visit, in 1809, I was informed of one *James Blair,* a weaver's having been sentenced to twelve months imprisonment, who had received no less than twentyfour pounds, as the balance due to him for Prison-work: and *Mary Boyd,* sentenced also to two years confinement, had received fifteen pounds, after deducting the cost of her clothing and maintenance.

The Keeper carries on a manufactory of linen and cotton thread, on his own account; to which a poor person out of employ may be admitted on petition, and receive an allowance of sixpence per day. The Keeper told me that a poor girl so admitted, had received eight pounds four shillings and nine pence halfpenny on the day previous to my visit; being the overplus of her earnings, after payment for clothes, &c. during a period of about six months.

A Corporal's guard is kept in the court-yard every night, and a centinel during the day.

GLOUCESTER.
The County Gaol, and Penitentiary House annexed.
Gaoler, *Thomas Cunningham.*
Salary, 300/. for Gaol and Penitentiary House. Also allowed a Clerk, whose. Salary is 50/. paid by the County.

Fees, for *Debtors,* as per Table. The Under-Sheriff demands *6s. 8d.* for his *liberate;* which is paid by the Committee of Prison Charity in all cases of distress.

Fees for *Felons, Fines,* and *Criminals,* none. The expence of conveying Transports is paid by the County.

Garnish, abolished.
Chaplain, Rev. *Edward Jones.*
Duty, Prayers Wednesday and Friday morning; and a Sermon every Sunday, Christmas day, and Good Friday. Salary 50/.

Surgeon, Mr. *Wilton.* Salary, 47/. for all descriptions.

Number of Prisoners, Debtors. Felons, and Criminals.
l802, Nov. 29th,----20-------50 1806, Sept. 3d,----28-------47

And Two French Captives.

Allowance, to Debtors, Fines, and Felons, one pound and a half of good household bread, and one penny in money per day. The allowance of diet to Prisoners in the *Penitentiary House* is as follows:

Every morning a loaf of bread, of one pound and a half, to each; with an ounce and half of oatmeal, and a quarter of an ounce of salt, made into gruel.

Dinner, *Sunday* and *Thursday,* three quarters of a pound of beef, without bone, and one pound of potatoes. *Monday* and *Friday,* three quarters of a pint of pease, made into soup with the liquor of the preceding days. *Tuesday,* two pounds of potatoes, or one quarter of a pound of cheese. *Wednesday,* one ounce and a half of rice, and one ounce and a half of oatmeal. *Saturday,* a quarter of a pound of cheese.

The Women have one ounce of tea, and two ounces of sugar per week.

REMARKS.

The situation of this Prison is judiciously chosen, a little way out of the Town. The boundary wall encloses nearly three acres of ground; and the buildings consist of the Gaol, and the Penitentiary House, calculated for separate and distinct purposes.

In the front is the Turnkey's lodge; on the ground-floor of which is a fumigating room, a guard-room, porter s-room, and pantry; a bake-house, and warm and cold baths. Up-stairs, two rooms for flour and wheat, and four *Lazaretto cells,* each 7 feet *6* inches by *6* feet. Two rooms for Prisoners' clothes; one for irons, locks, bolts, &c. and a porter's sleeping-room.

On the flat roof above is the place of execution; and between the two chimnies is placed an alarm-bell, which is tolled during the awful ceremony.

In the outward gate are two boxes, to receive the donations of benefactors: One inscribed,

"To encourage Penitence and Orderly Behaviour in Criminal Prisoners." The other, "For the Relief of Poor Debtors."

A small court-yard leads to the Gaoler's house, in which, on the ground-floor, » the Magistrates' Committee Room, the kitchen, pantries, and brew-house, with cellars underneath.

Above stairs is a sitting-room, and two bed-rooms on the second story; a Dispensary, two Infirmaries, and a general Hospital-room, with a fire-place at each end. On the upper story is the Foul-Ward, containing three cells for Prisoners who have any infectious disorder; the leaden roof, serving for convalescents to take the air, is one story higher than the rest of the buildings.

The Prisons are surrounded by eleven separate courts, of an irregular polygon shape; and betwixt each is a small plat of garden-ground, to prevent conversation between the different classes. They have open wood palisades, by which a thorough air is admitted; and the ground, being an inclined plane, is constantly dry. The distance of about 15 feet from the boundary wall affords a convenient garden for the growth of vegetables.

The Debtors have a spacious airy court, of 70 yards in length, and 19 yard wide, with a colonnade at each end, 16 yards by 10 feet 6; and two smaller courts. A day-room, 15 yards by 12, with two fire-places, is fitted up with every accommodation for frugal cookery; and two large commodious work-rooms, wherein to carry on any trade for the *sole benefit* of those Prisoners who can procure employment from without: If not, they are supplied with work, on application to the Manufacturer, and receive two thirds of the estimated value of their daily earnings. The risk of sale for the articles so wrought up remains with the County.

Prisoners for Debt are here distributed into two *divisions,* or classes. The first is *under the Magistrates' protection:* to which all have admission on their commitment; but in which no one is suffered to remain, except on confonning to rules calculated for the preservation of health and morals, and to promote that decency and good order, which are so essential to the common benefit of all.

The *second division* is called " The *Slieriff's Ward;'* with Prisoners in which class the Magistrates no otherwise interfere, than to protect them against every possible means of extortion. The Debtors in this division are liable to all such claims and consequences as the Gaoler may, by Law or Usage, have authority to impose.

Each Debtor, desirous to live under the Magistrates' Protection, (or *First Class,)* has a separate bed-room, fire-proof, fitted up with an iron bedstead, hair mattress, blankets, sheets, and quilt, at the County cost: those confined in the Sheriffs Ward have the like accommodation, on paying the regulated room-rent.

Such Prisoners as are far removed from their friends, or totally destitute of any, and without the power to procure their sixpences; or who are not able to work; or, being able, cannot procure employment sufficient to provide themselves nece'ssary sustenance; *Such,* and such *only,* are relieved from the publick stock, "on producing a certificate from the Minister, and some other respectable inhabitants of the Debtor's place of residence, that he is not only destitute of friends, but a deserving object also of the publick bounty."

An unrestrained and unlimited construction of that Clause in the *Lords' Act,* which allows Debtors, at their will and pleasure, " to send for, or to have brought unto them, any ale, beer, &c." is what I have been ever taught to consider as the source of riot and disorder amongst Prisoners; and as, probably, a principal cause of their distress. Now, by the *Gloucester Bye-Laws,* the power to send for victuals and *small beer,* is not only unrestricted, but a messenger is paid by the publick to procure it for them *at all liours in the day-time.* With respect to *strong liquor,* however, no Prisoner is allowed to have, or receive, for his own use, more than a pint of wine, or a quart of *strong beer,* in any *one day.*

Here are thirtyfour single sleeping-cells, 8 feet by *6,* with arched roofs, furnished with iron bedsteads, hair mattress, blankets, sheets, and quilt, like the fire-proof bed-rooms before described, at the expence of the County; together with two large five bedded rooms, in case the number of Prisoners should exceed what the cells can accommodate.

The following is " The Table Of Fees to be paid by the Debtors, being revised and regulated as directed by the Acts of 32d Geo. II. and 25th Geo. III." *£. s. d.*

"For entering an Action, whereon each Prisoner is brought into

Custody, either on Process, Capias, Latitat, or Execution-10 0

For entering and discharging every second or other action, upon

Process, Capias, Latitat, or Execution-------0134

For the Certificate of the Want of a Declaration, in order to sue out a Writ of Supersedeas----------0 6 S

N. B. The above demandable of the Prisoner.

& s. d.

For receiving and entering every Declaration against a Prisoner in Custody----------020

For each Copy of a Warrant against a Prisoner-03 4

N. B. To be paid by Persons making the Declaration, or demanding the Warrant.

Attending upon every Prisoner, to give Bail, Special Bail, Habeas,
or other necessary attendance, out of the Gaol, as directed by
Statute, per mile--------------010

That all the above Fees (except for the Keeper's attendance out of Gaol,) when paid by any Prisoner to the Keeper, shall be accounted for by him to the public Fund, in aid of the Debtor's maintenance.

Every Debtor, who, during his confinement, has behaved orderly in Prison, and submitted to the regulations with decent respect and attention, on his discharge is entitled to a certificate of such good behaviour, from the Chaplain and a Visiting Justice, or Chaplain and Governor: And this certificate is a complete acquittal from all and every Fee payable to the Keeper."

§Cf By the Police of this Prison respecting Debtors, it is considered as the best expedient " to guide them to good deportment by the prospect of benefits; and no otherwise to punish their irregularities, than by removing them from a participation of those benefits. Had the exemption from Fees been *unconditionally* given, they would soon have claimed it as their right, and forgotten it as a benefaction; and this negative influence on their conduct would have been lost."

Besides the 34 sleeping-cells before-noticed, there are three sleeping-rooms for the Male Debtors, in the Keeper's house; for which they pay as per following Table:'

"Table Of Taxed Charges allowed for Lodging, Bedding, &c
£. s. d Every Person confined in the *Sheriff's Ward,* finding his own bedding, per week,-------------01O

Ditto, with bedding allowed by the County------0 3 &

The Certificate of Good Behaviour is a Discharge from all demands on account of the two preceding articles.

Every Person occupying a room *in the Keeper's house* shall pay per week---------------0 2 6

Furnished------Q 7

Women Debtors have a large room on the first story, with five beds; and Sheriff's Ward Debtors have two of the same size on the second story.

The sleeping-cells, of 8 feet by 6, with arched roofs, are well ventilated.

Here is a court where coals are deposited; in which is a large wheel for forcing water into 4 reservoirs; and from them every part of the Prison is well supplied wih water.

The goods manufactured here are stockings, girth-web, bottle-stands, boots, shoes, slippers, articles for weaving, &c.

The *Chapel* is a neat building. Each class of Prisoners enters by a separate door to the place assigned them; which is out of view of the others. Their names are called over before Divine Service begins; and none are permitted to absent themselves, except on some special occasion, or sickness. I was much pleased with the suitable discourse of the worthy Chaplain, which he very forcibly addressed to the several classes of his audience. Beside the service heretofore noted in its place, I learned that Prayers are read on *the other four week-days* by the Gaoler; who then distributes the daily allowance of bread and money to eveiy Prisoner that appears clean, and has behaved decently in Chapel.

The several court-yards for *Felons*, &c. in the interior of the Prison, are spacious and airy; with arcades, and day-rooms to each class, fitted up with every convenience for simple cookery. There is a wash-house and common cooking-room in the Penitentiary House. The washing of linen is done by the Female Convicts, who have a drying-ground, and three rooms also, to answer the purpose of drying in bad weather.

Here is a Task-Master, or Manufacturer, who has a Salary, and a share of the Prisoners' earnings, and acts likewise as assistant to Mr. *Cunning/tarn,* the Gaoler. A sale-shop is provided for the finished goods; a large room where the bedding is manufactured; another for weaving, and a third for picking the hair made use of in mattresses: a taylor's shop; and a store-room for pease, clothing, pots, paint, &c.

The *penitentiary Prisoners* have three courts, into which open *sixteen* work-cells. There are two passages, or lobbies, 5 feet wide, and communicating with these con ts, *each containing Jive* work-cells; in all twenty-six. These are heated by brick flues, and have a Thermometer to regulate the warmth.

The ground floor, and the first and second-story, have each of them a day-room for *State Prisoners,* about sixteen feet square, with fire-places and glazed windows. This Prison contains 178 sleeping-cells, and two others for the refractory; dark indeed, but, like the rest, well-ventilated.

Criminals sleep single. They have iron' bedsteads, a straw mattress, a hair ditto, with 16 lbs. of hair each; two blankets, a pair of sheets, a night-cap, and a coverlet lined with flannel. Sheets and night-caps clean every month.

At my visit in November 1802, 1 copied the following Remarks: "From the time the County Gaol was opened, in July 1791, until 1800, *Prisoners* committed, about *one thousand three hundred!* and constantly confined in it, on an average, one hundred. In the nine years *deaths* thirteen: of these, four sunk under the effects of disease, brought into Prison with them. The *nightcells,* built with brick, rest on an arch, and are arched over; so that no air can enter them, but through the opening near the crown of the arch provided for it; and by the sides of the wooden-shutter being imperfectly fitted, they are necessarily dry, as air is constantly passing immediately under and round them on every side. Fahrenheit's Thermometer, placed in the middle region of one of these cells, where a Prisoner was sleeping, has never, in the severest night, been observed to be below 33; and no complaint, of old or young, male or female, has been made, of suffering by cold in them."

The power delegated to the Magistrates, for public benefit in the police of Prisons, appears to have been exercised here with great care and discernment. The qualities of each Man concerned in the internal management of these conjoint Prisons, from the Head Gaoler to the lowest officer, seem to have fitted him for the situation in which he is placed. The excellent *Rules, Orders, and Regulations* are literally obeyed; and deservedly so, as they are worthy of the Magistrate who formed them, and whose zeal for public good is fully equalled by his powers of judgment in execution. Silence and obedience reign throughout the whole: Regu-' larity and decorum jjervade every department: Every comfort is secured which can attend the privation of liberty; and satisfaction is visibly demonstrated in the countenance of every Prisoner. In a word, these Prisons exhibit the highest pitch of perfection in polity I ever witnessed. To humane treatment, in the articles of food, lodging, &c. are joined strict provisions to prevent dissipation and riotous amusement. Confinement, sufficiently irksome to the idle and profligate, is here destructive neither to health nor morals.

It is much to be regretted that some *precise orders* are not, in every Prison; established for the conduct of Debtors; whose irregularities frequently embarrass their Keepers, merely from the want of knowing how to treat them.

Sir George Oncsiphorus Paul, Bart.

GLOUCESTER. *The City Gaol and Bridewell.*

Keeper, *William Dunn;* now *John Russell.* Salary, 31/. 10.

Fees, Debtors and Felons, 13s. 4f. Conveyance of Transports, 6/. «ach.

Garnish abolished. Chaplain, none.

Surgeon, Mr. *Wilton,* who makes a Bill.

Number of Prisoners, Debtors, Felons, &c.

1802, Nov. 20th, 3----0 1806, Sept. 3d,-----5----1 Woman Convict. Also a Boy, for leaving his work. Allowance, for Debtors in common, *three shillings* per week, paid by the City, and divided among them, be the number great or small. If only one Debtor, he has the whole. To certificated Paupers, sixpence a day each in bread. Felons, &c.

have sixpence daily. REMARKS.
This Gaol, which is likewise the City Bridewell, was first occupied 24th Nov. 1784, and is situate in South-gate Street.

The Keeper's apartments front the street, and his kitchen commands a view of the court-yard, which is flagged, and of an oval shape, 36 feet by 24 feet 6; supplied with two sewers and two pumps; and this is the only court-yard for Prisoners of all descriptions.

The Master's-Side Debtors have a day-room up stairs, and one bed-room, for which they pay 2s. per week each.

The Poor or Common-Side Debtors have what is called the *Straw-Room;* which is a *free-ward,* over the Felons' day-room, and of the same size, with a fireplace and glazed window.

The ground-floor contains a day-room, 12 feet square, for the Felons; and three sleeping-cells, furnished with barrack bedsteads, loose straw, and a rug to sleep on, lighted and ventilated by iron-gratings over the doors. Also a condemned cell, about 6 feet 3 inches square, totally dark, except what light can reach it through an iron-grated aperture in the door, 9 inches wide by 8. Deserters are sometimes confined here.

The *Bridewell-Room* is above stairs, 15 feet by 12; and has a fire-place, glass window, sky-light, a barrack-bed, and the whipping-post. The place of execution is at the end of the Gaol.

On the 13th of December annually, the Prisoners here have ten shillings worth of bread given them, arising from an estate in *Hemstead,* near the City of Gloucester. It is sent in twopenny loaves; but no Memorial of them is recorded in the Gaol.

A Table of the Chamber Rent, and Fees, belonging to the Gaol and Prison for the
City of Gloucester, and County of the same City.
Chamber Rents.
No. 2. The Debtors' Rooms, for each man, two shillings per week.
No. 3. The Straw Debtors' Rooms, nothing to be paid.
Fees. £. s. d.
For every Debtor discharged by *liberate* from the Sheriff,----0 13 4

Every Prisoner discharged by *liberate* from a Justice of the Peace,-0 13 4
Every certificate of Debtor, signed by the Gaoler, ---06 I
Every copy of Warrant,----------034
"City of Gloucester, and County of the same City, *to wit.* "At the General Quarter Sessions of the Peace, holden at the Tolsey for the said City of Gloucester, by adjournment, the 15th day of January, 1790.

"Whereas by an act maJe in the second year of the reign of his Majesty King George the Second, intituled, An Act for the Relief of Insolvent Debtors, with respect to the Imprisonment of their Persons,' amongst other things it is enacted, that no Fees shall be taken for Prisoners' commitment, chamber-rent, or discharge, except what are allowed by law, till such fees shall be settled by three or more Justices attending at the settling of. the Fees at the Quarter-Sessions, and shall be reviewed, confirmed, or moderated, and then signed by the Judge of the Assize, with three or more Justices. And whereas, upon the examination of the Gaoler of the Prison of this City, and County of the same City, it appearing to "us that the abovementioned Table of Fees are the ancient and accustomed Fees of the Gaoler of the said Prison; and we, having reviewed and moderated the said! Table of Fees in some articles, Do hereby allow and confirm the same, as they are now' settled. Signed by us, James Sadler, Mayor. Abraham Saunders. G. Greenaway.

Allowed and confirmed this 28th March, 1790, by us, J. Heath. J. Wilson.
" GOSPORT. *Hampshire. The Bridewell.*
Keeper, *Edward Hunt,* now *William Barber.* Salary, 52A 10. Fees, *6s. 8d.* No Chaplain, nor any religious attentions.
Surgeon, Mr. *Harper.* Salary, none; but makes a Bilk.. Number of Prisoners, 1802, March 3d,—14. 1807, Sept. l8th,—29Allowance, seventeen ounces and half of best wheaten bread per day; sent from the Baker's in loaves, and which I found to be of full weight.
REMARKS.
Here are two court-yards; one for the Men-Prisoners, 30 feet square; the other for the Women, about 12 feet square.

They are separated from each ether hy a single wooden palisade fence only, and thus exposed to continual intercourse, which might easily be prevented.

The Men's day-room opens into their court-yard, and is 20 feet by 13, with a fire-place; but, to go to their lodging-room, they must come into the other courtyard, assigned for the Females.

There are also two upper rooms, in one of which is included a single sleeping cell, and a inost offensive privy: the other room contain five sleeping-cells, about *g* feet by 4 each, and 9 feet high, supplied with loose straw on the boards, and a single blanket. The better sort of Prisoners, who sleep in the Keepers house, pay one shilling the first night, and sixpence every night after.

The Women's day-room below is likewise a sleeping-room, and; at my visit in 1807, had in it four crib bedsteads, with a flock bed and blanket eaeh, pestered by nauseous vermin; but, with the bed' clothesi, were then put out in the Gourt teair,—a severe reproof' to the inattentive for bestowing so lfrttle exertion to remove them. Such inconveniences as are voluntary, are culpable too.

Here is an oven to purify the clothes of Prisoners at coming in, and' a pump in the Women's court-yard. The Keeper's house, which commands a view of both court-yards, was in a very ruinous state, as well as the floors of the Prison; yet I found the whole very clean. Coals are allowed to poor Prisoners in case of sickness, upon application to. the Magistrates.

No *Employment* for the Prisoners in this House of *Correction.* How can we expect grapes from thorns, or figs, from thistles; or decency of manners from indolence and. sloth, amidst evil associations! A, new Bridewell is nearly finished.

GRANTHAM *Lincolnshire.*
Gaol and House of. Correction.
Gaoler, *William Cooper,* Keeper of the Town-Hall, who officiates by a Deputy, *Edward Elston,* Fees, 6y. 8 c?.

No Chaplain, nor any religious attentions.

Surgeon, when one is wanted) he is

sent by the Town.

Number of Prisoners, 3d. Sept, 1800 Two.

Allowance, to Felons, *%d'*. per day; to Petty Offenders, *4d*. REMARKS.

This-Prison is situated in Old Shop Lane, and has apartments in the chamber-story, for the Keeper, whose windows command.the. only courtyard. It. is for, all description of Prisoners, and about 30 feet square, with-a sewer and a dust-pen. No pump. The water is fetched from the court-house, which adjoins.

On the ground-floor here is a day-room, about 12 feet square, a glazed window, and a fire-place, to which the Town finds coals in the Winter: there is a hemp block in it, but no employment furnished. The seven sleeping-cells are all on the groundfloor, and open into the court-yard -r they have boarded floors with loose straw, and two rugs each for bedding.

There is a door in the wall of this court, which opens into the yard of the courthouse; in which, and under arcades, there are three sleeping-cells and a small dayroom: But the sight of the Prisoners being disagreeable to the-Gentlemen, they have not been used these eight years,, and at my visit were filled with lumber. Neither Act nor Clauses hung up. The whole-Prison very dirty. GREENLAW. *Berwickshire, Scotland.*

The Cotmtif Gael.

Gaoler, *Thomas Young*. Salary, 20/.

Fees, Felons, and Misdemeaners, none. Debtors; *2s. 6d*. on caption, paid, by the Messenger or Plaintiff.

No religious attentions. No Surgeon. s

Number of Prisoners, 20th Sept. l8oa, One Petty Offender.

Allowance, Felons, *8d*. per day. Debtors, as alimented by the Magistrates. The Prisoner here, at my visit, was alimented at *lod*. a day. REMARKS.

This Gaol, as appears by an inscription on the stone in front, was built by the first Earl of Marchmont, in 17121 He allowed to the Town the use of it, upon the condition of keeping it in repair. The Sheriff and the Baron Bailiff both hold their Courts here three times in the year.

The Prison stands within the church-yard; and the entrance door opehs into it, as do likewise the grated windows. In the front and centre of the building there are apartments intended for the Keeper; but, having damp mud-floors, they are not occupied. He lives, therefore, in a house near at hand.

To the left of the above apartments, and upon the ground-floor, is a rooirt for Debtors, of 16 feet by 14, with a glazed and grated lift-up sash window, two wooden bedsteads, a fire-place, two chairs, a table, and cupboard for their provisions; and a conveniently-placed sewer. No bedding, nor even straw is allowed. No coals.

On the right of the Keeper's intended house, and on the ground-floor, is a place called " *The Thieves' Hole,"* 9 feet square, and 6 feet 9 inches high,. to the crown of the arch; with a mud floor, and short loose straw laid upon it, two blankets, and a pillow. It is entirely dark, and without ventilation; but has two doors; the innerone of wood, the other iron-grated; and, to admit air and light, the wooden door is occasionally opened during part of the day: To prevent communication, however, from without, an iron palisaded gate is fixed at about 5 feet distant, which opens into the church-yard, and is constantly kept locked.

Above stairs, and immediately over Thieves' Hole, is another room for Debtors, 12 feet square, which has a small grated and glazed window, looking to the churchyard, but no useful fire-place. Both the Debtors' rooms have boarded floors; but in this last mentioned apartment there is no bedstead or other furniture.

Over the Debtors' small room just described, is the belfry staircase; which, by an ascent of 14 steps, leads on to a room for Men Felons, 12 feet square; with a' wooden bedstead, supplied with straw and two blankets, and a small iron-grated window on both sides.

Thirteen steps above the preceding room is one of equal dimensions, for *WomenFelons*; and 13 steps still higher, a smaller room for ringing the Church bell, and winding up the clock, which is done every day by the Keeper.

The single Prisoner I met with was a run-away apprentice, and had been for several months the only inhabitant of the Gaol. He was a decent-looking, wellbehaved young man, of about 18; but preferred remaining there in solitude, rather than return back to his Master.

GREENWICH, *Kent. See Page* 227.
GUILDFORD. *Surrey. The Bridewell.....* 1 Keeper, *John King*. Salary, 45/. Fees, 4. *2d*.

Chaplain, none; nor any religious attentions.

Surgeons, Messrs. *Merriman* and *Jackson*. Salary, 15/.

Number of Prisoners, 1805, June 30th, thirteen. 1807, Sept. 17th, nine.

Allowance, a one pound loaf of bread per day, and water: It formerly was one pound and a half. The Magistrates allow winter firing, when applied to by the Keeper. REMARKS.

The court-yard is 4© feet by 23, with a pump in it. The day-room for the Men Prisoners is 7 feet by 9 feet *6*, and has" a fire-place. The Women's ward opens into the Men's court, and is 14 feet by Q, and 8 feet high. The Infirmary room, likewise, communicating with the court, is 18 feet by *9* feet 6, and 8 feet high; and has a fire-place, with a glazed window of three lights, made to take out occasionally.

Here are two cells, with solid iron doors, and an iron-grated window to each. One of them, 14 feet by *9* feet *6,* and 10 feet high, has an iron-grated lattice, of about 3 feet by 2, and an open turret above. The other is 18 feet by *9* feet 6, with vaulted roof, an iron-grated lattice, 5 feet by 4; and, like the former, has an open turret above.

No sewer, but half tubs instead of them. The straw on the floor was bad, and,no other covering supplied.

Women's Side. The door of their court-yard opens into that assigned for the men. Their day-room is 10 feet by *9* feet *6,* and has a fire-place.

Up-stairs is a lumber-room, in which fuel is put; and two rooms with beds, furnished by the Keeper at six-pence each bed per week: One of them *16* feet by 10, and 7 feet high; the other 14 by 10, of the same height. No fire-places: the glass windows are made to take out in warm weather.

When the Assizes are held here, the Gaol is much crouded. The Summer Assize is alternately held here and at Croydon; the Lent Assize at Kingston. Prison white-washed once a year. Not visited by the Magistrates for two years previous to my being here in June 1805. No employment for the Prisoners.

The Act for preserving Health is hung up; but not the Clauses against Spirituous Liquors.

HITCHIN. *Hertfordshire.*
The Bridewell.
Keeper, *John Luck.* Salary, *24I.* No Fees.

Prisoners, 1803, July 15, None. 1S07, Sept. 2d, One.

Allowance, one pound of bread per day.; REMARKS.

In the Work-house yard, a large room on the ground floor for Men, 20£ feet by 10 feet 6, with two iron-grated windows, and loose straw upon the floor. Over it are two rooms for Women, who ascend to them by a ladder. No chimney in either of the rooms. No court-yard. No water, but as fetched in by the Keeper.

HADDINGTON. *East Lothian, Scotland.*
The County Gaol.
Gaoler, *Peter Coates;* now *John Lowrie*; a Town-Officer, or Bailiff, who *lives at a distance.*

Salary, heretofore six pounds; but now 20/.: viz. ten from the Town, and ten from the County. No Fees.

Surgeon, sent in, when needful, by order of the Provost.

Number of Prisoners, Debtors. Criminals.

1802, Sept. 12th, 0 1. 1809, Sept. 22d,'------0-3.

Allowance, to Criminals sixpence a day. Debtors, after fifteen days' commitment, are alimented at the discretion of the Magistrates.

REMARKS.

This Prison is partly built over the Assembly Hall. It has two dark rooms bejow, for Felons, called *Dungeons,* each 15 feet by 8; with vaulted roofs, and two small apertures in the wall, *16* inches by 7, for light and ventilation, which open towards the street. One of the rooms has a wooden bedstead, the other none; but both have loose straw, and a rug.

The lesser Criminals here have one miserable room above stairs, of 11 feet by 8, with an iron bedstead, and a small iron-grated aperture for ventilation, 18 inches by 12, looking to the street. The straw on the floors was short, dirty, and worn to dust.

Adjoining to the above room is one for common Debtors, Q feet by 8; which has a wooden bedstead, fireplace, and glazed window.

There are two other dark rooms below, in which Felons, till of late, have been occasionally confined: but they are now used by the military, as a *Black-Hole* for Deserters.

At the top of the building is a very good room, 19 feet by 13, for Debtors who »re Burgesses: it has a sash-window, but only straw provided for bedding. I found it dirty, and it seemed never to have been'white-washed.

Here is no court-yard for air and exercise. No coals are allowed to any part of the Prison. No water accessible, except as brought by the Keeper once a day. No sewers provided; and the nasty tubs substituted for them, are only emptied about once a week or fortnight.

The executioner, *Peter Carrs,* has a suit of clothes yearly, with a house to live in, and 4/. gratuity for clearing the tubs, and keeping the Prison clean. He became, however, so negligent of his duty, that upon repeated complaints made by the Gaoler, the Magistrates *committed him to Prison.* Little appears to have been the effect of so just a chastisement; for even now, the complainant says, he cannot get him to empty the tubs more frequently than once a week.

§CJ" The Gaolers of most Prisons in Scotland have no apartments there; which, added to the natural gloominess of Confinement, must surely aggravate the uncomfortable ideas of Neglect and Desertion.

HALIFAX. *Yorkshire, West-Riding.*
The Low, or Town Gaol: for Debtors only.
Gaoler, *Joseph Scott;* who keeps a Publick-House.

Salary, none. He pays a Rent to his Grace the Duke of Leeds, of 24?. *per annum;* and also Window Tax for the Gaol. Fees, on commitment, 6s. 4d. on discharge, 17. 4d. and 1. to the Turnkey. Garnish, (not yet abolished,) 3. 6d.

Chaplain, none. Surgeon, none.

Number of Debtors. 1800, March 31st,----13. I 1805, Oct. 20th,----7-. 1802, Feb. 4th,----17. 1 1807, May 12th,----14.

Allowance, a Legacy of forty shillings worth of bread *per annum,* be the number of Debtors great or small; one twelfth part of which is regularly sent in every month. (See the *Remarks.*) If a Debtor be very poor, and cannot support himself, the parish to which he belongs orders him a weekly pittance.

REMARKS.

This ancient Gaol, which seems to have been built in the year 1662, is for the Manor of Wakefield, and the property of the Duke of Leeds.

The Gaoler's house is the sign of the Ducal Arms; and under it is, singularly enough, inscribed,

"Neat Wines: *The Jail House."*

Master's-Side Debtors are assigned the use of four rooms in the Gaoler's house, for which they pay according to their respective accommodations: *viz.* If a single bed, 3. 6d. per week; or, if two sleep together, 2s. 7d. each Debtor.

Through the house lies a passage to the court-yard, which is 42 feet by 21; and at the farther end of it is a good-sized room, upon the ground-floor of the Prison for Common-side Debtors. This they call " *The Low Gaol"* and from it is an aperture to the street, of about a foot square, for the receiving of provisions.

Over that room is another, 28 feet by 19, and 8 feet high, named the " *Loiv Gaol Chamber;*" which has a fire-place, and an iron-grated glazed window: Also six sleeping-rooms, paid for at 2s. Ad. per week, each Common-Side Debtor sleeping singly in a bed provided by the

Gaoler; or, if two sleep together, at 1. 9d. each, weekly. Persons bringing their own bed and bedding, must pay half what they would have done, if they used the beds furnished by the Gaoler.

The distribution of legacy-bread before mentioned, to the Prisoners, is by 3s. and 4d. worth on the first Saturday in every month; and arises from the exemplary bounty of Mr. *Jonathan Turner* of Halifax/ a butcher; who, by his will, left *forty shillings* yearly to the poor Prisoners in the *Town Gaol,* to be given them in bread. This annuity is charged upon certain houses in *Cheapside,* Halifax, now in the possessi6n'of Miss" *Waterliouse,* who constantly pays the legacy .

On looking over;the Regulations for the' government of this Gaol, which follow the *Table* of Orders and Fees, allowed by the Justices at the Bradford Sessions, in July 1800, I could not help being struck with the singularity of the two following items:

"That every Person, who shall be *suspected* to break the Gaol, and make escape, and *all others* in the Gaol with such Prisoner, who shall be *suspected* to be aiding and assisting therein, shall be by the Gaoler *ironed,* to secure them from making their escapes."

"And, That if the Prisoners in the *Low Gaol* shall at any time mutiny against or upon the Gaoler, or his Deputies, or Servants, going amongst them to regulate abuses, or *any way disturb* him or them; he or they shall, for every such offence, be kept in close confinement, at the *discretion of the said Gaoler."*

Surely, every stranger that visits this Prison, and reads these Rules and Orders, must be astonished to find, that in the year 1800, such powers were delegated to a *Gaoler,* (and a *Publican,)* over the person of a *Debtor:* Powers, which, in a course of thirty years experience, I have never elsewhere seen so sanctioned or allowed; and which, if exercised any where about the Metropolis, or, indeed, in any Gaol much visited, might be productive of unpleasant consequences. I very much doubt the power, even of Magistrates, to order the trial of such expedients, unless the party *suspected* (or as a neighbouring State, in its *iron-age,* used to term it, *soupconn6 dtftre suspect,* " supposed to be of a suspicious character,") were taken in the actual attempt to break Prison; nor am I certain of its correctness even then. A *Debtor* is a *Sheriffs* Prisoner; and I am fully persuaded that *He* would not presume to do it.

See Watson's History of *Halifax.*

As heretofore, and under the Mosaic Law, *places of refuge were appointed* for certain offenders and others to *Jiee unto;* so in like manner, at *Halifax,* the following appears to have been established as a legal custom. It may seem a digression, but I trust its curiosity will be my apology for inserting it here.

"If a Felon, after his apprehension, or in his going to execution, happen to make his escape out of the *Forest of Hardwicke,* (which liberty, on the East end of the Town of Halifax, doth not extend above the breadth of a small river,—on the *North,* about 600 paces,—on the *South,* above a mile,—but on the *West,* above ten miles,) the Bailiff of Halifax hath no power to apprehend him out of his liberty: But, if ever the Felon come again into the liberty of Hardwicke, and be taken, he is certainly executed. An example whereof," says my author, "is continued in memory, of one *Ijicy,* who made his escape, and lived seven years out of the liberty: but, after that time, coming boldly within the liberty of Hardwicke, was taken, and executed upon his former verdict of condemnation."

In this Town, anciently, the Barons, and after them various other proprietors, had capital jurisdiction, or the power of life and death. The method of executing it was beheading the Offender by an axe in an engine, very similar to the *Guillotine* in France. Tlie last who suffered by it were Abraham Wilkinson, John Wilkinson, and Anthony Mitchell, in May 1650. I have seen the axe; and it is still preserved in the Gaol.

When any Felon was here found guilty, the Bailiff immediately returned him back to Prison, for about the space of a week. On every intervening market-day, of which there are three in a week, the Felon was set in the public stocks; and either on his back, if the thing stolen were portable, or, otherwise, before his face, the goods were so placed, that they might be noted by all passengers.

The manner of execution was thus: The Prisoner being brought to the scaffold by the Bailiffj and the axe being drawn up by a pulley, fastened by a pin to the side of the scaffold; if the article taken with the Prisoner were a horse, an ox, or cow, &c. it was brought along with him to the spot, and fastened with a cord to the pin that stayed the block; so that when the fatal moment came, (which was announced by one of the Juror's holding up one of their hands,) the Bailiff', or his servant, whipping the beast, the pin was plucked out, and execution done. But, if there were no beast in the Felon's case, then the Bailiff, or his servant, cut the rope. This engine continued in use at Halifax till the year 1650, and was then removed: but the basis, upon which it originally stood, is still remaining. See " *Halifax,* and its *Gibbet-Law;*" also *Camden's Britannia,* Gibson's edition, 1605, pp. 726, 727, where a print is exhibited of the instrument; which seems much like that called "*The Maiden,"* used heretofore in Scotland, for the same purpose. It is a broad plate of iron, about a foot square, very sharp on the lower side, and loaded above with a massy weight of lead. At the time of execution this was drawn up to the top of a narrow wooden frame, about 10 feet high, and as broad as the engine; with mouldings on each side, for the Maiden to slide in. A receptacle was constructed, about 4 feet from the ground, for the Prisoner to lay his neck, with a kind of bar so fastened as to prevent his moving. Thus secured, and the sign given, the engine was let loose, which, in a moment, closed his sufferings. See *Owen's* Dictionary of Arts and Sciences.

It is a singular circumstance, with regard to the instrument in question, that James Earl of Morton, and Regent of Scotland, having seen an execution performed by it, as he passed through Halifax on his way home, had a model of it taken, and carried it with him, for the intended removal of some who opposed his administration. After several years of inapplication and harmless privacy, during which it was called *The Maiden,* his Lordship's own head was the first cut off by it; and although after his, many others experienced the like, it still retained the name. "The Earl's government," says Mr. Granger, (Biographical Hist. Vol. I. p. 196,) "had been very justly censured, as oppressive and rapacious: while he held the Regency he was secure; but upon his resignation in 1578-9, he was abandoned to the fury of his enemies. Accordingly, in 1581, he was adjudged guilty of high-treason, for the murder of Lord Darnley; and on the 2d of June, executed at Edinburgh, for a matter, in which he is said to have been no otherwise concerned, than as being privy to the atrocious deed."

The " *Gibbet-Law* of *Halifax"* was originally ordained in the reign of Henry the Seventh, in order to put an effectual end to the then prevailing practice of stealing cloth in the night-time from the Tenter Grounds. "The value of the thing stolen," says Camden, "must amount to above *thirteen pence halfpenny,"* a Scotch *Merk i "*for, if only so much, and no more, by this custom he should not die for it."

The above Prison, like what it was in my great Predecessor Mr. Howard's time, *above* 30 *years ago,* is much out of repair: yet the rooms are clean. No firing is here allowed.

Circumstanced as Halifax Gaol is, it will occasion no surprise, that neither is the Act hung up for the preservation of the Health of the Prisoners, nor the Clauses against the use of Spirituous Liquors.

HALIFAX. *Town Gaol.* Is a building called the *Black Hole,* or Dungeon; which adjoins to the enginehouse, and consists of two dark sleeping-cells, about 7 feet 6 inches square, with loose straw laid on the floors, which open into a narrow passage. The Town Constable is the Keeper. Prisoners are never confined here for more than a night or two. There were none at my visit, October 20th, 1805. HALSTED. *Essex.*

The Bridewell.
Keeper, *Oglethorpe Wakelin;* now *Robert Whinyeates.* Salary, 40/. No Fees.
Chaplain, Rev. *John Houghton.* Duty, once a week. Salary, 20i,
Surgeon, Mr. *Gilson.* Salary, 10/.
Number of Prisoners, 1801, Oct. 17th, 17; 1810, Sept. 24th, 12.
Allowance, one pound and half of bread, and a quart of small beer per day.
REMARKS.

The court-yard of this Prison, 30 feet by 20, and paved with flag-stones, is used by the Men one part of the day, by the Women in the other; and has a pump in it, with a sewer in one corner.

Here is a day-room of 24 feet by 12, and an apartment, boarded, on the groundfloor, used as an Infirmary. The five sleeping rooms, which also have boarded floors, are 14 feet by 7 feet 6 inches, and contain each two barrack bedsteads, with straw-in-sacking beds, one blanket, and a rug. There is a cast-iron sewer in each room; and over every door an iron grating for light and ventilation, with an inside shutter to each grating.

The employment here is to pick oakum; but no Prisoner has any part of his earnings.

The Women's work-room (in which Prayers are read) is 24 feet by 12: Their sleeping-room, of the same size as those for the men, has three barrack-bedsteads, straw-in-sacking beds, a blanket, and a rug. There are four crib-bedsteads with bedding for sick Prisoners.

The Gaol is clean, and white-washed every year. The cells are well ventilated; and it was with pleasure I observed a religious book in each of them.
HARWICH. *Essex.*
The Town Gaol.
Gaoler, *Samuel Martin.* Salary, *2l. 8s.* Fees, Debtors, *6s.* 8. Surgeon, if wanted, sent from the Town. Number of Prisoners, 1805, Sept. 18th, None. 1810, Sept. 23d, One. Allowance, Debtors sixpence a day. Felons, four-pence; now (1810) one shilling per day to Prisoners of all descriptions. No Debtor had been confined here since my visit in 1805.
REMARKS. This Gaol is under the Town Hall.

Here are two Dungeons, to which the descent is down ten steps; the one 16 feet by 9, and *J* feet high; the other 16 feet by 10, and of the same height: They have an iron-grated window each, towards the street, but no fire-place: floors damp, with straw scantily laid on them; and tubs, instead of sewers.

On the ground floor are two rooms, with double iron-grated windows to the front; each of them 17 feet by 9, and 9 feet high, with a fire-place. They have also inner windows, nearly 4 feet square, and straw is laid on the floors.

Behind these rooms is a third, of 35 feet by 10 feet 8, and 8 feet high, with a wooden bedstead, and a large fire-place. Tubs, instead of sewers, are emptied when half full; for which the Keeper is allowed six-pence a time. Three Deserters, who were confined here for as many months, had been released about three weeks before I came; and to them the allowance given was nine-pence a day.

The Keeper's house has a large room, which he supplies with bedding, &c. at 8. per week, to such as can pay. In 1803, Capt. William Reid, committed for embezzling stores, was confined here two months, tried at Chelmsford, and transported. No water accessible: it is brought, when wanted, by the Keeper.
HARWICH. *Bridewell.*
Keeper, *Thomas Freeman,* the Bellman, or Town Crier.
Salary, none. Fees, 1. both at coming in, and going out.
Number of Prisoners, 1805, Sept. 18, One. 1810, Sept. 23, One.
Allowance, six-pence per day; and whatever they can earn.
REMARKS.

On the ground floor is a large room, 5 feet by 10, and 7 feet 4 inches high, with a double iron-barred and glazed window. Above stairs, two rooms, each holding two wooden bedsteads, with loose straw only to sleep on. No fireplace. No sewer, but tubs. No water accessible; but brought, when wanted, by the Keeper.

The employment is picking of oakum, and making nets; but the Prisoner being a Shoe-maker, was working at his own trade. The straw he had to sleep on was worn to dust.

HAVERFORD-WEST. *Pembrokeshire; South Wales.*
The County Gaol.
Gaoler, Samuel Howell. Salary, 30/.
Fees, for Debtors and Felons, 13. 4d.
No Table.

For the removal of Transports he is allowed the expence attending it.
Garnish, not yet abolished, 1.

Chaplain, Rev. *William Thomas.*
Duty, Prayers on Wednesday and Friday. Salary, *20l.*

Surgeon, Mr. *Thomas.* Salary, 15/. for Criminals only.

Number of Prisoners, Debtors. Felons, && 1S00, May 4th,--3 8 1803, Sept. 29th-------1------11.

And Three Lunatics.

Allowance, to Debtors, none whatever. To Felons, and other Criminals, 2 lbs. of bread per day each, sent by the Baker, on Mondays and Thursdays, in loaves of 7 lbs. each. Convicts under sentence of Transportation, have not the King's allowance of 2. *6d.* per week.
REMARKS.

This Gaol is built within the walls of the Old Castle, and has a spacious and airy court-yard, about 108 feet square, in which Men and Women, Debtors and Felons, are indiscriminately associated during the day time. It has a Chapel, but no Infirmary, nor a bath.

Here are five cells and a kitchen for Felons, with a Bridewell room for the men: and, above these, five rooms for Debtors, who are allowed straw, on wooden bedsteads: Also a room called the *Women's Bridewell,* and a store-room, where the straw for bedding is deposited.

The Felons' sleeping-cells, each 12 feet by *6* feet 9, open into a passage *4* feet wide. Their being sunk three steps under ground rendered it absolutely necessary they should have bedsteads: But at my visit in 1803, there was nothing but straw, laid on the brick floors; and the Gaoler told me, that, for a month together, *eight or ten Prisoners had been crowded every night into each cell!* $3 Formerly a *six-penny loaf* was given, weekly, to each *poor Debtor* confined here,—the produce, in part, of a pious and charitable donation; and the remainder of it was distributed, in *two-penny loaves,* to the poor in the Town of Haverford-West. It appears, (though not from any *Memorial* found here,) that "Mrs. *Martha Bowen* declared in her Will, that one hundred pounds had been deposited in her hands by an unknown person, about the year 1751, for the benefit of Insolvent Debtors, and the Poor; which said sum of 100/. was invested in New South-Sea Annuities, in Trust to the Rectors of St. Mary's, Haverford-West." I found the Rector, Mr. *Ayleway,* at the time of my visit, quite superannuated, so as to be incapable of giving me any account of its distribution; but, undoubtedly, his papers on the subject must be such, as to throw a beneficial light upon it, in favour of the humble Claimants. The Gaoler told me, that no *Debtor* had received the bread from the 16th of August, 1802, till the month of January, 1803, when *two six-penny loaves* were sent; and he afterwards informed me by letter, (for which I thank him,) that he had received the bread so lately as in December 1804. Matters of a nature so recent may easily be traced; or else the lapse of time may as easily obliterate them from the memory of others, and thus defeat the exemplary purpose of many a benevolent Donation.

The County allows a common fire for all the Prisoners in this Gaol, during the Winter months, from Michaelmas to Lady-Day. In the great dearth of provisions, (1800, 1801,) the sufferings of the Debtors induced Lord *Cawdor* to order the surplus of soup distributed on that occasion to be sent to the Prison; which proved a great relief.

There is a fine well of water in the centre of the court-yard. No employment furnished for the Prisoners. Neither the Act for Preservation of their Health, nor the Clauses against Spirituous Liquors, are hung up.

HAVERFORD-WEST. *The Town Gaol and Bridewell.*
Keeper, *Patrick Banner;* a Shoe-maker. Salary, *2l.* 10.
Allowance, to Prisoners, *two-pence* each, per day 1
REMARKS.

This miserable Gaol stands near the Court-House, and has one room below, for Felons, with two above it: one of which is for the use of Debtors; the other, about 13 feet square, is the Bridewell. These last, however, are occupied accordingly as the Keeper and his Prisoners determine their option.

Straw is allowed them, upon wooden bedsteads. No court-yard. No water accessible, fioth Sept. 1803, no Prisoners.

HELSTON. *Cornwall.*
The Town Gaol.
Keeper, the Town Sergeant. No Salary.
Prisoners' Allowance, sixpence a day.
REMARKS.

This Prison stands up a flight of steps, at the end of the *Old Cuinage Hall,* where, (as at other places in Cornwall, according to the ancient *Stannary* Laws,) tin is appointed to be stamped into pigs, or ingots. It consists of a narrow slip, or room, of 9 feet by 3 feet *6;* and another of about 12 feet square, opening into it, which has straw upon the floor. No court-yard. 1803, Oct. 12th, and 1806, Oct. 2d, no Prisoners.

HENLEY. *Oxfordshire.*
Keeper, *Charles Stokes,* the Town Sergeant. Salary, 5/.
Fees, 1. the first night, and *6d.* every night after.
Allowance, *eightpence* per day.
REMARKS.

Under the Town-Hall are two rooms, or *cages,* of 11 feet by 4 feet 10, with lofty arched roofs, and straw for sleeping on the boarded floors: a sewer in one corner. The rooms ventilated by iron gratings over the doors, which open to the cornmarket. No court-yard. August 18th, 1803, no Prisoners.

HITHE. *Kent.*
The Town Gaol.
Keeper, *Thomas Sampson;* now *James Higham.* Salary, *twenty shillings,* and half a chaldron of coals.

Prisoners, 1804, Sept. 23d, 2. 1806, Aug. 12th, 0. 1S09, July 10th, 1 Woman Felon.

Allowance, *threepence* a day each, in bread.
REMARKS.

To this Gaol there is a small court-yard, of *16* feet by 14 feet 4; and two rooms, about 9 feet 6 by 7 feet 5, and 7 feet 6 inches high. One of them has a fire-place; the other straw only on the floor, and two blankets; with iron-grated windows, about two feet two inches square. No pump. The Keeper fetches the water that is wanted from the town. A tub serves as a sewer, though one might be built in the court-yard. At my visit, in August 1808, I found that the former Keeper was dismissed, on account of a Prisoners having made his escape.

HEREFORD. *The County Gaol, and House of Correction.*

Gaoler, *James Gray;* now *John Preece.* Salary, 182/. out of which he provides a Turnkey.

Fees, *Debtors,* lSs. lod.; besides which the Under-Sheriff demands *4s. Sd.* for his *Liberate!* Felons, 13s. 4f. as per Table; and for the Conveyance of Transports, the expence. Garnish abolished.

Chaplain, Rev. Mr. *Underwood.*

Duty, Prayers and Sermon every Sunday, on Christmas Day, and Good Friday: and Prayers on Wednesdays and Fridays. Salary, 50/. of which twenty pounds are a Legacy, from William Bridges, Esq.
of Tiberton, in this County.

Surgeon, *Mr. Cam.* Salary, *42l.* for Debtors, Felons, &c.

Number of Prisoners, 1800, March 30th, 1802, Nov. 10th, 1803, Aug. 28th, 1806, Nov. 28th,

Debtors.

----10 ----8 ----6

Felons, and other Criminals.------27. -23.

------24-34.

Allowance, to Debtors, one pound of bread each per day. See Remarks.

To Felons, &c. and Bridewell Prisoners, the same, and some allotment from the Charity Box. Transports have the King's allowance of 2s. *6d.* per week.

REMARKS.

This Prison, which is also the House of Correction, or Bridewell, is built upon the site of the Old Priory. The Turnkey's lodge in front has, on each side, two reception-cells for the confinement of Prisoners, till examined by the Surgeon, previous to their being admitted into the interior of the Gaol; and two small courtyards for the Prisoners. Here are also a warm and cold bath; with an oven to fumigate and purify either infected or offensive clothing; and the flat roof above is the place for executions.

The principal court-yard is flagged, and in it are the engine-house, and a well, by which the whole Prison is supplied with excellent water. Adjoining is a house for the Manufacturer, or Task-Master, and a very neat shop for the articles manufactured in the Prison; consisting of shoes, slippers, gaiters, stockings, gloves, garters, flaxen-yarn, and nets of all sorts; the sale of which is promoted by advertisement, at the County expence . The Rules and Orders of the Gaol, which are painted on a board, and hung up in every lobby, recite, amongst other things, that "Any person wishing to work, may have raw materials from the Keeper; who will dispose of the work on the best terms he can; and, after deducting the prime cost, of the raw materials, pay the remainder to the Prisoner who has performed the work; except one fourth thereof, which is to be reserved for the County. Any person, to whom work is refused, or whose money is kept back, or has suffered any imposition from the Keeper, or his servants, is particularly enjoined to make complaint thereof to the Magistrate, at his next visitation."

At the upper end of the principal court is the Gaoler's house: on the ground-floor of which is the Magistrates' Committee-room; and a passage leading to the great Hall, or Inspection-room, which is nearly circular, and about 54 feet in diameter; with windows opening into every court-yard, so as to have a complete command of the whole Prison...::

Men and Women Debtors have each a separate and spacious court-yard, and a day-room. The Men have twenty sleeping-rooms, ten below, and ten above stairs, 12 feet each by Q, and furnished with beds and bedding by the Gaoler; for which they pay as per Table hereafter subjoined. The Women Debtors have eight rooms of equal size, four below, and as many above; and these are all *free-wards.* If a Debtor is too poor to provide his own bed, the County humanely furnishes him an iron bedstead, with sacking bottom, a straw bed, two blankets, and a coverlet *gratis.* There is a fire-place in every room, but no fuel allowed.

Of the six ample court-yards in this Prison, those for Men Debtors, and Men Bridewell Prisoners, are 114 feet by 78; those for Women Debtors, and Women Bridewell Prisoners, 108 feet by 102; and those for Male and Female Felons are 15 feet square. Each court has a sewer in it, and is well supplied with water.

In several of the court yards vegetables are raised for the use of the Prisoners, in addition to the Gaol allowance above stated.

Here are four excellent Infirmary-rooms, and the sick appear to be as well attended as in an hospital. The humane Surgeon having a discretionary power to order all things necessary, every page of the Prison books bears ample witness to his great attention.

The *Chapel* is a very neat building, in which the Prisonersare seated according to their different classes. All are required to attend Divine Service, which is most devoutly and impressively performed by the excellent and exemplary Chaplain: By whose serious discourses I was much edified at my several visits, and with pleasure remarked the number of Communicants when the Sacrament was administered.

A letter from the Keeper, just received, dated 14th February, 1808, has given mc equal surprize and concern; by informing me "that the *working system* is almost totally discontinued."

Every ward of this well-constructed Prison has a lobby, or passage, four feet wide; with an iron gate, that opens into the great Hall, or Inspection-room.

Men and Women Felons have each their day-room, with a fire-place, and twelve sleeping-cells, six below, and the rest above; all 8 feet by 7; and fitted up with wooden bedsteads, raised about two feet from the floor, straw bed, two blankets, and a coverlet. They have also the County clothing on admission, and their own apparel is returned to them when discharged.

The Male and Female Bridewell Prisoners have nine work-rooms below, and as many sleeping-rooms above; all of 9 feet 3 inches by 9 feet; and fitted up with beds and bedding, the same as the Felons. The Men Bridewell Prisoners have likewise a day-room, with a fire-place; but the Women of that class are obliged to be with the Female Felons in cold weather, having no day-room or fire-place allotted them. When the building was first constructed, stoves were placed to warm the several wards, but they did not answer.

"Table Of Fees,

To be taken by the Gaoler; as settled at the General Quarter Sessions for the County of *Hereford,* by the Justices, 15th January, 1799, pursuant to the Statute.

"It is ordered, that the several sum and sums hereinafter mentioned, and no more, shall from henceforth be taken: that is to say,

"For the entering of every Action or Process, whereon a Prisoner shall or *s. d.* may be charged-_ 3 6

To the Turnkey, or Under Turnkey, on each Action------10

For the entering of a Discharge, and for the Discharge of every Prisoner 1 3 4

To the Turnkey, on the Discharge of every Prisoner----10

I For the receiving and entering every Declaration, delivered against the
Prisoner in Custody--------------20

To the Turnkey, upon every Declaration--------06

For a Certificate, for want of a Declaration, in order to take out a Writ of *Supersedeas* ---------------36

For Copy of Warrant or Commitment against each Prisoner----2 6

Lodgings.

Every Prisoner, who lies in the Keeper's lodgings, in the Sheriff's Ward, on a single bed, per week-------------26 .

For two, in a single pair of sheets, per week, each-------16

Signed, Ja. Phillips. H. Morgan. W. Parry. March 21st, 1799. Approved by us, Justices of Assize and Gaol-Delivery for the said

County, G. Rooke. S. Lawrence." *William Bridges,* Esq. bequeathed eight pounds a year to poor Prisoners: and, on St. Thomas's day, one shilling is given to each poor Debtor, and one shilling to each Felon, by a Legacy of Sir *Thomas White.* But no Table of Bequests is kept in the Prison.

The Act of Parliament, for preserving the Health of Prisoners, with the Clauses against their use of Spirituous Liquors, are conspicuously hung up: And *in the lobby of every Ward,* the Rules and Orders for the government of the Gaol are painted on boards, and properly displayed to general view.

HEREFORD. *The City Gaol and Bridewell.*

Gaoler, *John Thomas.* Salary, 13/.

Fees, *6s. 8d.* No Table. Garnish, not abolished, 2. 6d.

Surgeon, none: when wanted, he is sent by the Mayor.

Number of Prisoners, Debtors. Felons, &c.

1802, Nov. 10th,---0-----4. 1803, Aug. 28th, _--1 2, and 1 Lunatick.

Allowance, formerly none: Now fourpence a day in bread, to the Prisoners of every description.

REMARKS.

This Gaol is the Bye-street Gate, in which one room is called the Bridewell. It has a small court, with a sewer in it, and the whipping-post.

For Common-Side Debtors here is a *free ward,* to which the Corporation allow straw. They have a little court, about 15 feet square, with a sewer; and it is well supplied with water.

Master's-Side Debtors have two rooms in the Keeper's house, for which they pay 2. 6d. per week each, single bed; or, if two sleep together, Is. 6d. each.

For Felons here are two small court-yards, about 15 feet square, with a sewer in each, and well supplied with water. In one of the courts, down eleven steps, are two horrid dungeons, totally dark. The keeper, indeed, says they are never used; yet, though they did not appear to have had any inhabitant in them for many years, I should have been better pleased at seeing them bricked up.

The Felons have also three close offensive sleeping-rooms, which I found scattered over with loose straw on the floor, dirty, and worn to dust. Here is likewise one room, justly denominated *The Black-Hole,* which, if not impenetrably dark, has no light nor ventilation, save what is faintly admitted through a small aperture in the door. It is supplied with a barrack bedstead and loose straw; and in this wretched sink-hole was found a poor deranged Man, in the most filthy and pitiable state that it is possible to conceive.

Upon my telling the Keeper, that in case he did not immediately remove the straw and filth out of the several courts, I would apply to the Magistrates, I had the pleasure of finding the old straw burnt, and the court-yards cleaned the next day.

Debtors committed to this Gaol are by process issuing out of the Mayor's Court. One shilling is given to each Prisoner at every Quarter Session by the Chamberlain. Neither the Act for preserving Health, nor Clauses against Spirituous Liquors, hung up. The whole Prison is very dirty. The commitments to it, in 180, were *one hundred and thirty-six.*

A letter from Hereford, dated l8th Feb. 1808, informed me that this Gaol was undergoing great alterations; and indeed it very much wanted improvement.

HERTFORD. *The County Gaol and Bridewell.*

Gaoler, *Charlotte Wilson,* widow of the late Keeper.

Salary, 180/. and for the Bridewell, 52/. 10.

Fees, Felons and Debtors, 15. *4d.* Besides which, the Under-Sheriff demands *6s.* 8rf. of each Debtor for his *Liberate!* For the conveyance of
Transports, 1. per mile.

Garnish, prohibited. On a painted board is affixed up "No Garnish to be taken." See Remarks.

Chaplain, Rev. *James Moore.*

Duty, Prayers and Sermon every Sunday. Salary, 40/.

Surgeon, Mr. *Bradley*. Salary, 20*l*.

Number of Prisoners. Debtors. Felons, and Bridewell.
1801, Aug. 14th,------7 *26* 1802, Jan. 31st,------2--22 1803, June 26th,------11-------19 1804, Sept. 9th,-12-*6* 1806, July 16th,------8 -------*26* 1807, July 31st,------11--29 1808, Sept. 20th,------9-------17 1810, April 9th, 7 15.

Allowance, to Debtors, none whatever. To Felons, and other Criminal Prisoners, one pound and half of bread daily, *cut from the Gaoler's loaf.* Convicts under Sentence of Transportation have the King's allowance for their support, 2*s.* 6*d.* per week.

REMARKS.

This Gaol, which is also the County Bridewell, is situated just out of the Town, and surrounded by a boundary wall, 15 feet high; which, being at a considerable distance from the building, admits a free circulation of air; and the Gaoler has within it a convenient garden.

For Men and Women Debtors here is only one court-yard, *60* feet by 36. Their Infirmary room is on the ground floor, spacious and lofty, but destitute of furniture; and they have no day-room.

For Common-Side Debtors there are ten sleeping-rooms, of 16 feet 8 inches by 11 feet 7, which are *Free Wards 1* but the County allows neither bedding nor straw; so that if a Debtor cannot provide himself with a bed, he must sleep on the bare boards.

The lobby which leads to these rooms is only *four feet wide;* and the pillars, being square, and of brick, make them both dark and close. The door-ways are but *twenty-two inches wide* t so that no crib bedsteads can be introduced into them. There are two other rooms, of 12 feet by 10, which are furnished for such as can pay seven shillings each per week, and two sleep together. No firing is allowed them.

The Men Felons have two court-yards, each of them about the same size as that for the Debtors. One of them, called " The Further Yard," has six cells, and a day-room about 15 feet square, on the ground-floor. The other, called " The Middle Yard," has eight sleeping-cells, built over those in the Further Yard; and on the ground-floor is a large day-room, and an Infirmary. The Felons' cells are about lo" feet 8 inches each by 11 feet 7, with straw on the floors, scantily supplied by the Gaoler out of her Salary.

In the Debtors' and Felons' courts are boards fixed up; on which, as I before remarked, is painted " No Garnish to be taken in this Gaol." But, at my visit in 1808, the word "No" was obliterated in the Felons'court-yard; and a gallon of beer is now exacted, as Garnish, from every new comer.

The court for Women Felons is 45 feet by 16, with a sewer in it, and two sleeping-cells, each 16 feet 6 inches by 12 feet; both of which have fire-places, and grated windows towards the court. Two sleep in a cell, upon the floor, which has a partition about 4 inches high, to keep the straw together; and that is the only bedding allowed them.

The Bridewell Men's court is 33 yards by 24, and has twelve sleeping-cells on the ground-floor, with as many above them, all opening to the court-yard. The aperture over each door has sloping boards before it, to prevent their view of the court; and at the farther end of each cell is a casement. Twelve of these cells have a fire-place.

The Bridewell Women's court is also 33 yards by 24, with a gravel-walk, surrounding a grass-plat. They have eight sleeping-cells, four at each end of the court, on the ground-floor, with a fire-place in each cell.

There is a pump in these, and in every other court-yard of this Gaol. The rooms for the Bridewell Prisoners have vaulted roofs, and are 12 feet each by 9.

The Men's Bridewell has a spacious and lofty room on the ground floor, paved, like the others, with flag-stones, and intended as an Infirmary, with a small room for the Surgeon; but it has never been used as such. It has no furniture, and is occupied by Vagrants, who sleep upon loose straw laid on the floor. The warm and cold baths adjoin to it; of which the former has never been used, and the latter only twice! Between the two baths is an oven, to purify infected clothes.

Here is also a small court-yard, and a convenient sewer, intended for the sick.

The Chapel of this Gaol has no cupola, and is very close. The Debtors appeared to me not only negligent in their attendance on Divine Service, but even frequently interrupted it by misbehaviour. At my visit in 1803, only three of them out of eleven were present; and in 1804, eight only attended Chapel, out of the twelve.

Of the twelve House-of-Correction Prisoners, at one of my visits (in 1804) four were sentenced to twelve months imprisonment, without any employment whatever, although they much wished for it; and bitterly did they complain, "at not being allowed more than one hour of enlargement out of the twenty-four, to get a little fresh air; at no firing being supplied to them in cold weather; and at being denied the indulgence of either soap or towels, for personal or prison cleanliness." At my visit also in 1808, I found four other Prisoners of the above description committed for a twelvemonth; and the whole number, as before, destitute of the blessings of that employment, which they earnestly desired to obtain. Their cells, however, are not now offensive, as heretofore; because they are permitted the use of a courtyard, and the loathsome pails, or buckets, seldom required. This indulgence, the Keeper's son informed me, was in consequence of my Remarks at former Visits.

It has been exceedingly painful for me to observe, though Truth and the Duty of Humanity call me to it, That those Prisoners committed to the Felons' Gaol, (and some of them even for comparatively trivial offences, and before a trial) are here immediately put in irons; and at night are fastened (two together) down to the flooring of their cells, by a chain passed through the main link of each man's fetter, and pad'ccked to a strong iron staple in the floor; and with this additional aggravation of their daily misery, are left to pass the hours destined by Nature to ease and refreshment, upon loose straw only, scattered on the floor. A man may thus suffer six months imprisonment under the bare suspicion of a crime, from which, at the end of that dreary term, his Country may, perhaps, honourably acquit him. Under circumstances of this kind I saw four Prisoners here, on the 20th of Sept. 1808.

The severities which *may be practised* under Imprisonment, are justly reckoned by Judge Blackstone as most dangerous, " because the least public, and the least striking engine of arbitrary Government: for" (to use that enlightened author's own words,) "it is there that the Prisoner's sufferings are *forgotten,* or *unknown."*

I saw no County furniture here, either in the Infirmaries, or in any part of the Prison, except one rug in the Felons' Gaol, one in the Men's Bridewell, and one in the Women's Bridewell: Neither is any County clothing allowed to the Prisoners.

Mr. Wilson, the widowed Keeper's son, who occasionally assists his mother in her arduous task, is a farmer in the neighbourhood of the Gaol: And he told me, that if a chaff-cutting machine were provided, and a shed erected over it, he could keep the Prisoners constantly employed.

But, no Employment is now regularly furnished. The County did heretofore attempt to establish a manufactory; but the expence having been found to exceed the Prisoners' earnings, it was soon discontinued. That Employment, however, (under due Regulations and a patient superintendence) may be rendered productive, has been already, and amply evinced at *Dorchestei; Gloucester,* &c. and it will be so evinced elsewhere, in various other Prisons, noticed in the course of this publication.

It has always struck me, that wherever the *Bread Allowance* to Prisoners is not judiciously distributed in distinct loaves, but cut off from the Gaoler's or Keepers loaf, (as is the case both here, and in other Prisons of this County of Hertford,) there ought to be scales and weights provided, and kept apart, not only for that purpose only, but for whatever relates to Provisions; in order that the Prisoners may always see that their respective doles ore fairly and fully dealt out to then). The complaints which have occurred upon this subject may thus be effectually prevented in future.

I found the Gaol, of late, much cleaner than at my former visits; and straw being cheaper, a more liberal supply has been issued, which is now changed once in six weeks.

There is still, however, a want of regularity and cleanliness in the management of the present Gaol. The Keeper's house commands but a very small part of it. Uncovered pails, buckets, &c. are most loathsomely made to serve the purpose of sewers. Here are no Rules and Orders. The Clauses against Spirituous Liquors are hung up; but the Act for Preserving the Health of Prisoners is omitted.
See *Dorchester,* p. 168, and *Gloucester,* p. 245, 8, 9. HIGH-WYCOMB. *Buckinghamshire.*
The Bridewell.
Keeper, *Thomas Snell.* Salary, *6I.* out of which he provides straw for the Prisoners.
Prisoners, 1805, Nov. 18th, 2. 1806, June 21st, 1. 1807, Aug. 28th, 0.
Allowance, sixpence a day to each, in money.
REMARKS.

This Bridewell, situate in St. Mary's-street, stands within the back court of the Keeper's house, and consists of two cells, 8 feet by 6, and *6* feet high; with an aperture of 8 inches square in each door; loose straw spread on the floor, and two blankets. Also a day-room, 12 feet by 8, with a fire-place, and two iron-grated windows. No fuel allowed.
HINCKLEY. *Leicestershire.*
The Bridewell.
Keeper, *Joseph Bolesworth,* now *Richard Nutt;* who keeps "The Chicken" Publick House. Salary, *4I.* Fees, one shilling.
Prisoners, 1803, Aug. 23d, 1. 1807, July 29th, 3. 1809, Aug. 21st, 0.
Allowance, fourpence per day, in bread.
REMARKS.

This Prison has a work-room, in which are fixed the whipping stocks. Two sleeping-eel Is, one for the Men, the other for Women; each 10 feet by 8, with two wooden bedsteads in each, loose straw, and a rug. The doors open into a narrow passage. Both these rooms are dark, close, and offensive, being ventilated only by a small iron-grated aperture: damp brick floors. No water accessible to the Prisoners.

The only Prisoner, at my visit in 1803, was a boy in irons, employed in weaving stockings; and the Keeper told me he could earn *18d.* a day. I found none of the three in 1807 employed.
IIITIIE, *Kent.* See *Page* 265. IIITCHIN, *Hertfordshire.* See *Page* 255. HORSELEY. *Gloucestershire.*
The House of Correction.
Keeper, *William Stokes.* Salary, 50/. and one third of the Prisoners' earnings.
Chaplain, Rev. *Anthony Keck.* Salary, 20/.
Duty, Sunday, Prayers and Sermon: also on Good Friday, and Christmas Day.
Surgeon, Mr. *William Fry.* Salary 10/.
Number of Prisoners, 1S0G, Sept. 18th, Eleven.

Allowance, one pound and half of best wheaten bread per day, sent in loaves of that weight from the Baker's. Also one ounce and half of oatmeal, and one quarter of an ounce of salt, made into a quart of gruel, for breakfast.

On Sunday, Dinner, one pound of meat, and a pound of potatoes. Weights and Scales are provided by the County; and every Prisoner weighs his own loaf, if he chooses.
REMARKS.

This Bridewell was erected in 178S; and its boundary-wall encloses about an acre of ground. The space between the open palisades is 16 yards in front, eighteen feet deep; and the remainder is judiciously converted into a convenient garden, for the growth of vegetables.

Debtors, from the Court of Requests for the Manor and Seven Hundreds of Cirencester, are sent hither for sums not exceeding forty shillings; and *the Creditor is bound to allow the Prisoner threepence a day during confinement.*

There are six court-yards to this house; two in front; at each end one smaller, and two behind. The entrance-gate to the Prison is the Turnkey's lodge. On the right hand is the *reception-room,* and above it a room for depositing the Prisoners' apparel, till their discharge; also a warm and a cold bath. Every Prisoner, on commitment, is undressed and washed: a complete suit of County clothing is then substituted for their own; with two caps added, of black worsted, for the day, and a woollen one for the night.

In the house are two *Infirmary rooms.* On the left-hand of the entrance is the Turnkey's sitting-room, and over it his sleeping apartment. The approach to the Prison is by a flight of steps, on each side of which is a little gardenplot. The Keeper's house is in the centre, and projects about two yards from each wing of the building.

On the ground-floor, in front, are the Magistrates' Committee-Room, and the Keeper's office; and behind them two kitchens, a pantry, and a store-room.

The *Chapel 1%* in the centre of the building; and here the several classes and sexes are very properly kept separate.';

There are two day-rooms also on the ground-floor, for the several classes of Male Prisoners, with a small stove in each, and stone seats: each room has a well, supplied with a hand-bason, and a cup of cast-iron, attached to the wall by a chain. Net-towels, soap, and combs are very decently provided for the use of the Prisoners.

Here are likewise, on the ground-floor, twelve *working-cells* in each wing, of 7 feet by *6,* and 9 feet high to the crown of the arch. On the first story, eight sleeping, and four *solitary, cells* to each wing; and on the second story, twelve sleepingcells, two solitary, and two for the refractory, in both wings. Each sleeping-cell is fitted up with a perforated cast-iron bedstead, straw mattress, a hair-in-sacking bed, a pair of sheets changed monthly, two blankets, a rug, a woollen night-cap, small shelf, and clothes-peg. The size of the cells, each 8 feet 5 inches by 6 teet, and 9 feet high.

Besides the cells before described, there are also, in each wing, four other sleepingcells, to which the ascent is by a ladder from a day-cell below. The day-room or hall for Males, is about 30 feet square, with a large sky-light at top. The sleeping-cells above open into a stone gallery, 2 feet 6 inches wide. All the cells have a double door; the inner, of wood, the outer one, iron-grated.

The number of lodging-cells for Prisoners is sixty; and the greatest nnmber confined at one time, thirty-seven.

Each class of Prisoners is allowed a peck of coals per day, in cold weather. Their chief employment is cutting of *logwood* and *fustick* across the grain, for the use of dyers; and they have one third of their earnings.

(£3 The sewers of this well-arranged Prison are judiciously placed. It is worthy of remark, that of *twelve hundred Prisoners,* committed within the course of *eighteen years,* no one has died here: nor has there been in it any specific or contagious disease. HORSHAM. *Sussex.*

The County Gaol and Bridewell.
Gaoler, *Samuel Smart;* now *John Smart.* Salary, 120*l.* Three Turnkeys also are assigned him, to whom the County pays 13s. per week.

Fees, of every kind, and Garnish, are very laudably abolished.

Chaplain, Rev. *William Jameson.*
Duty, Prayers every Day, and a weekly Sermon. Salary, 50*l.*

Surgeon, Mr. *Dubbins*: For the Felons, and other Criminal Prisoners. Salary, 20*l.* As medical assistance does not yet extend here to *poor Debtors,* this humane *practitioner* has hitherto attended them *gratuitously.*

Allowance, Debtors, none; except to Paupers, who, upon application, have one pound of bread per day, sent in loaves from the Baker's, and weighed by the Gaoler. Felons, and other Criminal Prisoners, two pounds of bread, in loaves, which I have always found to be of full weight. Transports have the King's allowance of *2s. 6d.* a week.

REMARKS.
The situation of this Prison, judiciously chosen, is a little way out of the town. In the door of the Keeper's house is placed a "Poor's Box," for obtaining small or other donations, in aid of the Prisoners' Sixpences. A small garden extends along the front of the building.

Here are two spacious court-yards, of about half an acre each, with gravel walks, surrounding a fine grass-plat: Both courts are well supplied with excellent water; and the wall which encircles them encloses the whole Prison.

It has two floors built over arcades; and the ascent to each is by a stone staircase, skirted with iron-rails. On each floor, both on the Debtors' and Felons' Side, are distributed ten rooms, five on each side; a passage 5 feet wide; a day room also to each, of 28 feet by 12 feet 3 inches; and a lodging-room for the Turnkey. Each Debtor and Felon has a separate room of 10 feet by 7, and 9 feet high to the crown of the arch. They are all arched over with brick, to prevent danger and confusion in case of fire; and each room has two doors, one of wood, the other iron-latticed; a shutter for the window, with a pane of knobbed glass in it, a wooden bedstead, a straw-in-canvas bed, and two blankets. The County, likewise, is so considerate as to allow each cornmon-room, of both descriptions, half a bushel of coals per day, during the six winter months, two tin kettles, and a wooden scuttle.

A Turnkey, paid by the County, goes twice a day to purchase provisions and liquors for the Debtors; and it is very properly fixed that none of them shall exceed a pint of wine, or a quart of strong beer per day. The Magistrates have supplied the Prison with scales and weights, for the use of its inhabitants; and I have always found the loaves of full weight as sent in from the Baker's.

Here is no regular Infirmary; but two apartments, with fire-places, are set apart distinctly for the respective sick.

The Chapel, which is in the Keeper's house, has a gallery for the Gaoler and his family. The pulpit is on the same level: The area below is 17 feet by 15, and has parallel benches for the Prisoners; so that Debtors and Felons of both sexes sit opposite each other, but almost close together. Every Prisoner, absent from Divine Service, without a proper cause, is punished either by close confinement, or short allowance. Religious books, at the County expence, are distributed by the worthy Chaplain; and when I was there in July 1806, not only all the Prisoners attended Chapel, but their deportment was orderly and attentive.

The Gaoler's house does not seem to command a proper view of the court-yards: This might be remedied, however, by a window made in his kitchen, towards the Debtor's court, and in his parlour, next to that of the Felons. Sitting-benches also in the day-rooms would be very convenient, and shelves for depositing the Debtors' plates and provisions; instead of which, at present, they have only the naked walls.

Felons, at their entrance, are washed with warm water, and each Man is clothed with the Gaol-uniform coat, waistcoat, and breeches; also two shirts, two pair of stockings, a pair of shoes, a hat, and a woollen cap. Here is likewise an oven to purify offensive clothes, and a place to hang them up, till the Prisoner is discharged.

At my two or three former visits the County allowed those Debtors to work, who could procure employment; by which many not only supported themselves comfortably, but gave some assistance to their poor families. I was sorry to be informed, in 1806, that this salutary indulgence was withheld, and the whole number (iS) in a state of idleness; no work whatever being permitted in the Gaol.

In many of our best-governed Prisons (such, for instance, as Gloucester. Dorchester, &c. &c. already noticed in this work,) it is a maxim, that every attention possible should be paid to the means and the encouragement of labour. Sir George Paul very justly observes, that " *Debtors,* and the *unconvicted* should, doubtless, be allowed to employ the wages of their own industry, to make life more comfortable; but, *under such restrictions as the good government of the Prison renders indispensable.* What is it less than a palpable absuidity, to commit a penniless offender, *till he fays a fine,* and deny him the exercise of his art and industry, to enable him to redeem his liberty?"

Since writing the above, however, candour obliges me to add, that I have been informed some Debtors in Horsham Gaol had heretofore attempted to escape; and that some others would not conform to the *Rules* and *Restrictions* of the house; which caused the above prohibition of work, as the most effectual mode of correction. Yet, might not some happier medium be adopted?

Every Christmas a Man goes about the County to collect donations for the relief of poor Debtors here confined. The money thus procured is distributed amongst them, at 2. each per week, till the whole net produce is expended. In 1805, the contribution amounted to 67/. 2.; and in 1S06, to 84/. 11. 11. out of which the Collector had one fourth allowed him for his expences, time, and trouble.

At my several visits here, I recollect to have seen one *Simon Southward,* a Debtor, who is said to have been committed to Horsham Gaol so long since as the 22d of February, *one thousand seven hundred and sixty-seven.* He styled himself *Simon, Earl of Derby, King* in *Man ſ* and was very orderly and inoffensive, though evidently deranged. He was allowed *6s.* a week by the parish of Boxgrove.

There are excellent Rules and Orders for the government of this Gaol, printed and hung up; as are the Clauses against Spirituous Liquors, but not the Act for Preservation of Health. The sewers throughout are very judiciously placed.

The *Lent* Assizes for Sussex are held at Horsham, and the *Summer* at Lewes.
HULL. *Yorkshire.*
The Town and County GaoL
Gaoler, *Francis Coates,* now *Robert Baines.*
Salary, 100/. out of which he provides a Turnkey.
Fees, for Debtors and Felons, 7. 6d. For conveying Transports, Is. per mile.: The Under-Sheriff demands 1. for his *liberate.* Garnish abolished.
Chaplain, none: but the Rev. Mr. Bromley, Vicar of Holy Trinity, frequently and gratuitously attends. Surgeon, Mr. *Clarke,* now Mr. *Hayes.* Salary, 8/. 8s. for Felons only.
Number of Prisoners, Debtors. Felons, &c.
1802, Aug. 25th,-----15-------17. 1805, Maytfth,.-----11-------16V 1809, Sept. 7th,-10-----20.

Allowance, Debtors certificated as Paupers, and Felons, have *4d.* a day each., This poor man died in Horsham Gaol the 20th June, 1810, aged 82, after an imprisonment of forty-three years, four months, and eight day.
REMARKS.
This Gaol is in a fine situation, just out of the Town, and refreshed by the Seabreezes. It would be a good one, if the Turnkey's lodge were rebuilt in front of the Prison, and if the boundary wall, which at present is only 13 feet 6 inches in elevation, were raised 5 feet higher.

Under the same roof with the Turnkey's apartments, are an oven, a bath, and a work-room for Debtors. These, however, are most injudiciously *built in the court-yard,* and near the Prison wall; thereby obstructing the Gaoler's command of view, and seeming, as it were, to invite escapes. Four, indeed, have been effected within these 14 or 15 years; and therefore Felons are forbidden the use of it.

The ground floor of the Gaol is occupied by the Keeper, except one room for the *Women Convicts,* of 21 feet by 14, which looks towards the garden. It is furnished with beds and bedding, and fitted up with tables, cupboards for provisions, benches to sit on, and a fire-place. The windows were heretofore too much exposed, but have now blinds, as I recommended in 1S05; which prevent the Prisoners here from seeing or conversing with the Debtors when walking in the garden.

Here is one spacious court, of *60* yards by 20, for *Debtors,* Male and Female.

In the second story these have a day-room, 22 feet 8 inches by 14 feet 4, with a fire-place, and three large grated and glazed sash windows, commanding an extensive view. It is fitted up with a settle, or screen seat, two benches to sit upon, a large table, cupboards to secure their provisions, and a place for coals. They have likewise three sleeping-rooms on the same story, of the average size of 14 feet 6 by 12 feet 6; each of which has a large grated and glazed window, and fire-place, with a table and chairs, cup-boards, and covered coal-box, bedstead, bed, and bedding; for which they pay *is. 6d.* per week for a single bed, or if two sleep together, *Is. 3d.* each.

The third story has three rooms, in every respect similar to those just described. Here is also a large room, 24 feet 6 by 16 feet 6, for poor op Common-side Debtors; with two large sash windows, and conveniences, the same as the others, for which they pay sixpence per week, and furnish their own bedding. Two Stocking-Frames, with many accommodations for working at their own trades, are provided by the County; and looms suited to the manufactory of garters, laces, &c. for those Debtors who are of no trade, but willing to work.

On the East side of the building is a court-yard, 42 feet by 17, with arcades; where the *Men Felons* are employed in pounding of Tile-sherds; and, on their discharge, if tlu-y have behaved well, they receive a proportion of their earnings, which is regularly entered in a book tor that purpose. The Women Felons spin, and receive the whole of what they can earn.

The *first floor* lias a day-room for Felons, 22 feet by 16', with a fire-place, and two large iron-grated and glazed sash windows, commanding a fine view of the river Humber; a table, and benches to sit on, and a place for coals. Their five sleepingcells, which are 14 feet by 6, have each a grated and glazed casement window, 22 inches by 14, with arched roofs, lofty, well ventilated, and warmed occasionally, by the tube of a German stove passing through each cell; and in every door is placed an inspecting-wicket.

In the *centre* of the building is a square room, with a reading-desk in one corner, which is used as a *Chapel:* but it is too small for the solemn purpose of Devotion; and all the Prisoners, of whatever class or description, are here promiscuously huddled, without distinction or order, when Divine Service is performed; which certainly cannot have a good effect..

The *second story,* on the East, has a day-room for *Male Felons before trial,* 14 feet and a half square, with five sleeping-cells, of the same size as those below. And in the centre is another day-room, of 17 feet 9 inches by 13 feet 6; where those committed for assaults are frequently confined, to prevent their mixing with common Felons. This story has also a room for *Women Felons before trial,* 14 feet by 12, with two large grated and glazed sash windows, commanding an extensive view; a fire-place, shelves, and cupboard. They sleep singly in cabins, as on board ship, which double doors conceal in the day-time.

Every Criminal is allowed a wooden bedstead, straw mattress, two blankets, and a rug. County clothing is not now provided, as heretofore, for Prisoners before trial: But if a Prisoner be ragged, he is clothed upon petition; and every such Prisoner is washed in the bath the day before trial comes on.

Water here, is at all times accessible to the Debtors. Felons have the tubs or buckets filled with fresh water twice or three times a day; not only for their drinking, but occasionally to cleanse the covered tubs, which serve the purpose of a sewer,

In the depth of Winter the Magistrates humanely order a bushel and half of coals per week, to every room that is occupied, and has a fire-place. I found the whole Prison clean in every part, well ventilated, and healthy. The Clauses against Spirituous Liquors, and the Act for Preserving the Health of Prisoners, were conspicuously hung up.

When a Prisoner is discharged, he has money given him for safe and comfortable accommodation, according to his distance from home.

A Bible and Testament are allowed to every room in the Prison.

($3 From the quantity of *Junk* I saw in this busy maritime town, it is evident that constant employment, in picking oakum, might be supplied to every Prisoner, if convenient work-rooms were built; which may easily be done. o
o HULL. *Yorkshire.*
The Bridewell.
Gaoler, *John Dunn.* Salary, 40/. a chaldron of coals, and a stone-weight, or 8 pounds of soap.

Chaplain, none; nor any religious attentions.

Surgeon, Mr. *Clarke,* now Mr. *Hayes.* He make6 a Bill.

Number of Prisoners. Debtors. Criminals.
1802, Aug. 25th,----0--------11 1809, Sept. 7 til,----2--------8.

Allowance. Fourpence per day each.
REMARKS.
To this Prison there is no court-yard; which, however, might easily be made from the adjoining waste ground.

By the Act 2 Geo. III. Cap. 38. Debtors, from the Court of Conscience are sent hither, or to the common Gaol, for three calendar months.

Here are three cells below ground. Two of them are dark, and ill-ventilated by a small iron grating, which looks into a narrow passage: the third has an iron-grated window toward the open air. In this last, at my visit in 1802, were four boys pounding tile-sherds, for which they received fourpence per bushel. Each cell is about 10 feet by 9; and the Corporation allows to each a wooden bedstead, straw mattress, two blankets, and a rug.

The first floor has three cells, of the same size as the former.

The upper story has one dark cell, with two beds in it: also a room for Women, 17 feet by 14, in which four Prisoners worked and slept; another, of the same size, with spinning-wheels; and a third room, for *Debtors,* 15 feet by 12. They have grated and glazed sash windows; and they might be healthy, were it not that the large tubs in each, made use of as sewers, were generally full before their being emptied. At my visit in iSOQ, upon enquiring into the cause of so cruel a neglect, the Gaoler told me "there was no drain to the building; so that they must remain in that nauseous state, until the scavenger came; and hence were sometimes so intolerably offensive to the neighbours during the operation of emptying, that they drove him away at times before he had finished." 1 felt myself almost suffocated.

The whole Prison is veiy dirty, and no water accessible to the Prisoners. But the Act for Preserving Health, and Clauses against Spirituous Liquors, are conspicuously hung up.

HUNTINGDON.
The County Gaol.
Gaoler, *James Drage;* now *William Aveling.*

Salary, 105/. from the County, and *4l.* from the Corporation. Also allowed *6l.* per annum, to supply the Criminals with straw for bedding.

Fees, Debtors, 12. *6d.* Felons, &c. 15. *lod.* See the Table. Besides which the Under-Sheriff demands of each Debtor four shillings for his *liberate!* For conveyance of Transports, if only one, twelve pounds; if more, nine pounds each. See *Remarks.*

Garnish, two shillings and sixpence each, by *Order of the Magistrates:* a most singular regulation.

Chaplain, Rev. *Isaac Nicholson;* now, Rev. *Daniel Williams.*
Duty, Prayers and Sermon every Wednesday.
Salary, *20l.* for the Gaol, and *1ol.* for the Bridewell.
Surgeon, Mr. *Desborough;* for Felons only.
Salary, 15/. 15. for Gaol and Bridewell.
Number of Prisoners, Debtors. Felons, &c.
1800, March 30th,------' 5 4 1801, Aug. 20th, 12-7 1802, Feb. 1st, 8-------6 1806, Aug. 2d, 3-2 1807, Aug. 31st, 4-*6* 1810, Aug. 30th,------5 2.
Allowance. To Debtors, nine pounds of bread weekly: To Felons, and other Criminal Prisoners, three quartern loaves, ditto.

REMARKS.
The Gaoler's house, which is situate in the High-street, has no appearance of an appendage to a Prison. The Gaol is behind it, to which the access is through a passage leading immediately to the *Felons' day-room.* This is about *16* feet square, and 10 feet high. It has a fire-place, with two iron-grated windows; and here, (as there is no Chapel) Divine Service is performed!

A place *set apart* for Divine Worship, should seem to carry some respect with it. I wish the present were not a glaring exception. The attendance of Debtors, I understand to be optional; and indeed it is scarce likely that a *serious* Debtor, who had his Prayer-Book, and could read, would come into a room where it is impossible he could be devout. What a close and motley mixture must it exhibit! Clergyman, Gaoler, Felons, Misdemeaners, — to say nothing of Debtors, (most of whom I suppose, never attend,) within a space of 16 square feet; all upon one floor. No reading desk, nor forms; to say nothing likewise of this House of Prayer's being made also the kitchen, day-room, and constant resort of an avowed Group of Thieves: In short, this is one of the worst constructed Prisons in the kingdom.

Adjoining to the Felons' day-room is another, about 14 feet square; in the flooring of which a trap-door is made, and through it a descent of eleven steps leads to their sleeping-room, of the same size as their day-room, having an arched roof, and two iron-grated windows. This last contains three bedsteads, for three persons each; to which straw-in-sacking only is allowed them to sleep on.

The *Dungeon,* or " Hole," formerly used for Convicts under Sentence of Death, adjoins to the sleeping-room before-mentioned; and is 10 feet by 4 only, 6 feet high, with an oak bedstead, and straw bedding as above. The Keeper, however, assured me that no Prisoners were ever put there *now;* yet, why continue its furniture, if never used? From what I thought, therefore, on seeing such a receptacle, I could not help wishing that it had been *inaccessibly bricked up.*

The court-yard to this part of the Gaol is about 21 feet square. In very severe weather the Prisoners are allowed two bushels ofjsoals per week. For Deserters there are assigned two sleeping-cells, which both together are 14 feet by 11, and 10 feet high, with straw only on the floortd sleep on: also a day-room of 11 feet by 4 feet *6.*

The sleeping room for the lesser Criminals is over the Felon's day-room, and of the same size. The common court-yard above-described is for the indiscriminate use of all.

The Women Felons have a court-yard 28 feet *6* inches by 17 feet 6, and a day-room and sleeping-room adjoining to it on the ground-floor; each about 13 feet by 10, with a bedstead.

The Hospital, or Infirmary-Room, has four good windows, and is 19 feet 6 inches by J 2 feet *6;* but the ceiling is too confined, being only 7 feet *6* inches high. Here is likewise a small room for the nurse. The bedsteads throughout the whole Prison are of strong oak, 6 feet long by 5 feet wide; with no other bedding upon them than straw, put into what they here call " Coarse Pickling."

Men Debtors have a court-yard also, 53 feet by *26,* and a day-room 30 feet by 14, with a fire-place. Their sjeeping-room above is about 26 feet by 14 feet 6, and has four bedsteads, for two persons each.

At my Summer visits, the Debtors complained to me of excessive heat, from a want of ventilation; the two small iron-grated apertures made to admit a thorough air being nearly stopped up on the outside. The County allows straw only, so that Debtors in general bring their own beds, or else the Keeper furnishes a single bed at 2. *4d.* per week; or, if two sleep together, at *Is. gd.* each: and for those who can afford it, there are two other rooms in the house, at 3s. *6d.* per week.

Women Debtors have a separate court-yard, 33 feet by 19; a day-room 21 feet by Iff, with a fire-place; and over it their sleeping-room, nearly of the same size, with four bedsteads, for two each, like those for the Men Debtors. They furnish their own bedding. The windows of this room formerly commanded a fine view of the Country, which made it both pleasant and healthy; but, at my last visit, the wall of the court-yard had been so raised as to intercept the scenery.

Mops, brooms, pails, &c. are allowed to keep the Prison clean. Convicts under Sentence of Transportation have not the King's allowance of *2s. 6d.* per week. For the conveyance of one Transport only to Woolwich, the Gaoler is paid 12/.; if more than one, *gl.* for each; and to Portsmouth, for each, 12/.

The following Table of Rates and Fees, approved by the Magistrates, is framed and hung up in the Prison.

"Huntingdonshire. A Table Of Fees, Demanded and Taken by the Gaoler, for the time being, of his Majesty's Gaol for the Town and County of Huntingdon; as well for Civil Prisoners as Criminal Prisoners. Established at an Adjourned Session, October 27th, 1785.

"As to Civil Prisoners, commonly called *Debtors. £. s. d.*

For the Dismission-Fee, for each Debtor; to the Keeper----0 10 0

For the like, to the Turnkey------------026

For the Debtor's bed per week-----------024

For the bed per week, if two Debtors lie together-----036

Garnish, at coming in, for the benefit of the other Debtors---0 2 G

If they find their own bed, &c.-----------000

For the Copy of a Warrant------------010

Filing a Declaration--------------010

Signing a Certificate for *Supersedeas* ----------010

As to *Criminal Prisoners.*

For the Dismission-Fee of each Criminal Prisoner out of Custody, & s. d. either by the Magistrates, or by the Courts of Assize, or Session 0 13 4

For the like, to the Turnkey------------026

For the bed, per week, to each Fine, Trespass, or Felon... 036

For the bed, per week, if two lie together--------048

For a Copy of a Warrant-------------01 0."

From the foregoing Table it appears, that the sum of 2. 6d. for *Garnish,* is absolutely *ordered by the Magistrates* to be taken of every Prisoner. It is to be hoped this respectable County will follow the general, and almost universal example of all others, and cause it to be abolished.

No allowance of money to Prisoners on discharge is ordered, unless the Gaoler sees it needful; but when so, he informed me, it is given by him, and charged to the County.

No firing is here allowed, except to Felons in very severe weather; Nor any employment furnished by the County. Such Debtors, however, as are of handicraft trades, and can procure it from without, are permitted to work, and receive all they earn.

There is a pump in every court-yard; but no bath, nor oven, which are much wanted. I found the whole of this ill-arranged Prison well supplied with water, and very clean. The Act for the Preservation of Health, and Clauses against the use of Spirituous Liquors, are conspicuously hung up.

HUNTINGDON. *The County Bridewell.*
Gaoler, *William Nichols.* Salary, 28/. from the County, and 2l. from the Borough.

Chaplain, (a new appointment since my visit in 1807,) the Rev. *Daniel Williams.* Duty, Prayers and Sermon every Wednesday. Salary, *lol.*

Surgeon, Mr. *Desbwough.*

Number of Prisoners, 31st Aug. 1807, Fourteen. 30th Aug. 1810, Twelve. Allowance, 1. 6d. per week; and half their earnings.

REMARKS.

This Prison would have been better situated on the rising ground at the back of it. The site on which it is built was the gift of his Grace the Duke of Manchester. At the edge of the Common its situation is low.

Here are four court-yards; two of them spacious and airy, and well supplied with water.

On the ground-floor are four work-rooms; two for men, the others for women. Also a day-room, or kitchen; and fire-places to each room.

Above stairs are eight sleeping-rooms, four of each for Men and Women, with straw-in-sacking to sleep on, which is furnished by the Keeper: and two dark rooms, set apart for the solitary confinement of two Prisoners in each.

No Infirmary, or other room appropriated to the sick.

The employment here consists in beating hemp, dressing flax, and spinning; and is furnished by the Keeper, who receives one half of the Prisoners' earnings.

No Rules and Orders. Neither the Act for Preserving Health, nor the Clauses against Spirituous Liquors, hung up. The Prison is clean.

ILCHESTER. *Somersetshire.*
The County Gaol and Bridewell.
Gaoler, *Edward Scadding*: now *William Bridle.* Salary, 125/.

Fees, for Debtors, Felons, and Bridewell, 14s. *4d.* Besides which the UnderSheriff demands from every Debtor, 6s. *8d.* for his *liberate!* Conveyance of Transports, one shilling each per mile. Garnish abolished.

Chaplain, Rev. *Thomas Rees.*

Duty, Prayers and Sermon every Sunday. Salary, 50/.

Surgeon, Mr. *Poole.* Salary, none. Makes a Bill.

Number of Prisoners, Debtors. Felons, &c.
1800, April;th,------28-------36. 1801, Dec. 27th,-----29-------34.

Allowance, Debtors and Felons, a sixpenny loaf each per day. Its weight, Dec. 1801, was two pounds seven ounces.

REMARKS.

The Gaol of *lvelchester,* now *Ilchester,* which is likewise the County Bridewell, stands near the river *Ivel,* whence the Town derives its name; and a great part of it is encircled by a boundary-wall, about 16 feet high, which, whilst it adds to its security, affords the Keeper a convenient garden for the growth of vegetables.

The Turnkey's lodge fronts the river, on the left-side of the gate of entrance; and on *the right* are a warm and cold bath. Over these and the gateway are three sleeping-rooms.

A small garden leads to the Gaoler's house; which, although placed in the centre of the building, commands but a very small part of the Prison. It has a cupola on the top, with a bell, which serves either for the Chapel, or for alarm, if needful.

The court-yards are five; of which the first, *on the right-hand,* is for those Prisoners who are committed for petty ofences, or until they pay a fine; and through which all who enter must pass to the Debtor's apartments. The pump, which stands in a small adjoining area, and supplies the whole Prison with excellent water, is another means of intercourse.

On the ground-floor are arcades, for the accommodation of Prisoners in wet weather. Over these rise two stories, to which the ascent is by a stone stair-case; each story containing five cells, 9 feet by *6,* and 8 feet *6* inches high, fitted up with perforated iron bedsteads, and straw, changed either monthly or oftener, as needful; a blanket, and a coverlet, or rug. Each cell has a double door; the outer iron-grated, the inner of wood, which opens into a passage 4 feet wide; the windows of it, which are four, looking into the court-yard. The cells have each a semicircular window, half glazed, half open, with sloping boards, and have a view into the Keeper's garden. Here is likewise an aperture in the wall, of 18 inches by 9, for light and ventilation in every cell, except two, which are dark, and destined for the refractory. In this part of the Prison Common-Side Debtors sleep, and pay as per Table: in the day-time they are allowed the use of the Master's-Side Debtors' court, as well as of the mess-room and fire.

Adjoining to the arcades before mentioned is the Keeper's cellar; and over it are two stories, containing six cells, fitted up with semicircular windows, &c. like those before described. These are appropriated to Prisoners for fines and petty offences.

The Master's-Side Debtors have a day-room and mess-room, of about 20 feet each by 12, with seventeen lodging-rooms above, capable of accommodating thirty persons, and for which they pay as per Table. Behind this part of the building is a spacious court-yard, where the Prisoners play at fives, skittles, tennis, &c.

On the *left entrance* from the Turnkey's lodge, is the *Male Felons' court-yard,* with iron palisades towards the small garden in front of the Keeper's house. On the ground-floor is a place for coals; and a large day-room, to which the County allows fuel in severe weather, having arcades to walk under when it is rainy. Over these are two stories, each containing eight cells, of the same size, and fitted up as counterparts, in the same manner as those on the *right entrance* already mentioned: and each cell is furnished with tq pounds of clean wheat-straw every week.

The *Women Debtors court* is l8 yards by *6,* and was originally intended for the use of sick Prisoners. It is separated from the *Men Felons' court* by a dwarf wall, and single iron palisade only, through which they can see and converse with each other. They have arcades also, under which they walk in wet weather; and over these are their two sleeping-rooms, and two Infirmaries.

On the upper-story are five cells, which, with six others over the Chapel, are appropriated to the most orderly of the Criminal Prisoners, and have boarded floors.

The Chapel, to which the access is through the Keeper's house, stands on the Felons'-Side of the Gaol, and the Women Convicts are placed out of sight of the other Prisoners. The Women Debtors, and Criminals, are seated in the gallery. The Men-Debtors sit underneath; and the rest of the ground-floor is occupied by Prisoners of all descriptions. On the whole, it seems not well partitioned off.

$3 The *Debtors,* 1 found, were not *obliged* to go to Chapel; and only eight out of the twenty-nine attended Divine Service, when I was there in December 1801. *Women Felons.* The court-yard appropriated for them is larger than that for the Men-Felons, and completely separated from it. There is a pump in it, but the water not being very good, it is seldom used. On the ground-floor are fourteen cells, of 10 feet by 7 feet 6, and 8 feet *6* inches high, together with a day-room.

On the upper-story is the same number of cells, and a lodge for a *Woman Turnkey,* who attends on the Female Felons, and is paid a weekly salary by the County. All the upper cells open into an iron-railed gallery, and have wooden bedsteads, with straw and blanketing, according to the season.

In the garden is the engine-house, from which reservoirs are filled, and the whole Prison supplied with *soft water,* through pipes conveyed into the several courts.

Men-Prisoners are washed regularly, and shaved, and have a clean dowlas shirt every week. The County clothing is provided for them, with brown and yellow stripes; but, not being compelled to wear it, they contrive by every means to do without; and very few of them had it on when I made my visits.

The sewers are judiciously placed, and not offensive. The whole Prison is white-washed once a year, or twice, according as occasion requires, or the cells are occupied.

Six only have died during the last seven years, out of seventy-eight, the average number of Prisoners here coufined. Convicts have the King's allowance of *2s. 6d.* per week.

The Act for the Preservation of Health is duly hung up, as well as the Clauses against Spirituous Liquors.

Here is no employment provided for by the County; but at my visit there were three Debtors at work, W!k were of handicraft trades.

The fifty shillings, formerly paid from a Legacypf Mr. *Kelson,* of Norton, to the poorest Debtors at Midsummer, has, from some unknown cause, been long discontinued. No Memorial of it being hung up in the Gaol, I could gain no better information concerning it.

"Somersetshire to wit.."At the General Quarter Sessions held the 31st day of March, at Ivelchester, 1761, before Edward Phelips, Esq. &c.

"A Table Of Rates and Fees,

Settled, established, and allowed to be taken by the Keeper of the Common

Gaol, in and for the said County, by virtue of an Act of 32d Geo. II.

£. s. d. "For the Discharge of every Debtor----0134

To the Turnkey---------------0 10

For every Debtor lodging singly, weekly, including the uie of bed and bedding-----------------016

But, if two Debtors lodge together, both weekly------009

The Gaoler is not to compel any Debtor to lodge single.

£. s. L

If a Debtor has a bed and bedding of his own, then-----0 10"

If he lodges in the outside ward, then weekly only-'-006

If a bed of his own, then nothing for it.

"Edward Phelips. William Rodbard. "Thomas Camplin. Giles Strangway. "Johh Brickdale.

"20th July 1761. We do hereby approve and ratify the Table of Fees above written, pursuant to the said Statute.

"Eardley Wflmot. "William Noel."

At my visit in December 1801, I paid the Fees of a poor Debtor, whose *Plaintiff' had forgiven him his debt*. But there was another demand, of six shillings and eight-pence, by the Under-sheriff of the County of Somerset, for his *liberate;* which I was obliged to discharge, before the Prisoner could be set at liberty'.

Sir Geo. Paul justly observes, that, "as no Man is the voluntary inhabitant of a Prison, and as Fees are no part of the sentence of the law, Fees, of all kinds, either from Debtors, or persons accused of crimes, are absurd in their institution, and oppressive in their practice."

Situate as Ilchester is, in a remote corner of the county, on the banks of the river *Ivel,* (anciently *Yeovil,)* this Prison subjects its inhabitants, and particularly *Debtors,* and those detained for-fines, to many and great inconveniencies.. Too far removed from their friends to receive occasional gratuities, and there being no manufactory in the town to af-fjtfd them regular employment, they offer an abundant claim to pity. Mr. *Gi/ e,* the humane printer of the Bath Paper, frequently represents their distressed situation, and receives casual benefactions for their relief.

The Assizes are never held at Ilchester. The Spring Assize is always at Taunton; the Summer Assize at Bridgewater and Wells alternately. At Taunton the Keepers lodge their Prisoners at separate inns. At Bridgewater the Prison is *only one room,* under the Town-Hall, with straw upon the floor; and where, as I was informed, *Jifty Prisoners* had been confined for six days together!

This County Gaol of Ilchester is the only Prison in the County of Somerset, except Bristol, in which there is *now* (lS0i,) a *Chaplain.* Formerly there was one both at Taunton and Shepton-Mallet; and the County had generously gone to the *limit of the Act,* by assigning a Salary of Fifty Pounds to each Chaplain. But the Chaplains having neglected their duty, the Justices, first, *re-limited* the Act, by reducing the Salaries, and afterwards took off the whole.

INVERNESS. *Scotland.*

The Tolbooth.

Gaolers; the four Town-Officers, in weekly rotation.

Salaries, to the Head-Gaoler, 15/. to the other three, 14/. each.

Fees; for Criminals, none. Debtors, *2s. 6d.* to the Gaoler, and 2. *6d.* to the Town-Clerk, for entering the Action; both which are *paid by the Creditor.*

No religious attentions, except to those under sentence of death; and then once a week .

Medical attendant, *James Robertson,* M. D. who makes a Bill.

Number of Prisoners, ath Oct. 1809, Debtors, Two. Felons, Four.

Allowance, *Debtors,* as alimented, from ten-pence to two shillings per day, according to their rank in life: but generally one shilling per day. Felons, &c. sixpence a day.

REMARKS.

This Tolbooth adjoins the Justiciary Court; and has, on the ground-floor, a dark cell for the temporary confinement of Vagrants, about 12 feet square. No fireplace, bedstead, or bedding, but a little loose straw, scattered on the stone floor.

On the *first story,* and on the same level with the Justiciary Court, are five sleeping-cells for Felons, of 10 feet by 8. One of them is dark, and assigned to the refractory: three have a gmted aperture, about a foot square, for ventilation; with loose straw upon the stone floors for bedding, and filthy uncovered tubs serve the purpose of sewers.

The fifth cell, for Women, which is somewhat larger, has a boarded floor, and a fire-place, but no fuel is allowed; also a grated and glazed sash-window, loose straw for bedding, and an uncovered substitute for a sewer.

The doors of all the above cells open into a stone lobby, about 4 feet wide, which has three very large grated windows looking to the street; and Prisoners have sometimes the liberty of walking in it in the day time.

The *second story* has two long rooms for Debtors, about 20 feet by 10, with flag-stone floors, grated and glazed lift-up sash windows, and fire-places, but no coals: a wooden bedstead, but no bedding. In each of these rooms a filthy uncovered tub as a sewer. The doors of these two apartments open into a lobby, like that above described; and Debtors have the privilege of walking there occasionally.

The upper, or *attich-story,* has one very spacious room for Debtors who are Burgesses, which has two large lift-up sash windows, with two fire-places; a boarded It is worthy of remark, that although the Assizes for *Eight Counties* are held at Inverness, only one Person has suffered death these sixteen years. floor, but no bedstead, bedding, or furniture whatever. The pipe of a German-stove introduces some warmth, during the meeting of the different courts below, which are held once or twice a week. No water is supplied, but what is brought by the Gaoler.

Wilham Taylor, the Executioner, cleans the cells and empties the tubs every two days; for which, and for executing the sentences of the Court, he receives a Salary of 6I. *per annum;* a house to live in, and other perquisites. I cannot say any thing in praise of his diligence: The Gaol throughout was very dirty, and had scarcely the appearance of having ever been white-washed.

Before I finish my account of Inverness, I must mention a *Dungeon,* or curious place of confinement, not lately used. It is buried betwixt two arches of the TownBridge over the river Ness. There is a trap-door in the pavement, 22 inches square, which being lifted up, exhibits a hole of the same size, square, and three feet deep. On one side of this narrow hole there is a grated iron door, 27 inches wide, and 30 inches high, whieh, upon being opened, can admit the Prisoner, by his erawling backwards, down three steps into the Dungeon below, which is 10 feet 4 inches long, 7 feet 6 inches wide, and 6 feet high, furnished with a sewer that communicates with the river. Here is also a stone seat all round it, which is covered with wood. The only light, or ventilation, which this miserable place can receive, is freman iron-grating toward the river, of lo' inches by 15; and it has a little loose straw for sleeping on. As this tremendous " Living Sepulchre" is rendered so very difficult of access, it should seem that the wretched inhabitant must dip for water, and have his provisions let down for him over the balustrade of the bridge, so as to receive them through the gratings of his window. This dungeon is said to have been-constructed in 1684, when the bridge was built. I was informed that several Highlanders were thrust down here, after the battle of Culloden; and that a very troublesome, deranged Man, called Hollow-Cheek, from a wound he received by, a musket ball, in the American war, had been occasionally confined here.

IPSWICH. *Suffolk.*
The Town and Borough Bridewell:
Keeper, *Edward Wade.* Salary, not fixed.
Allowance, a sixpenny loaf per day.
REMARKS.

The old Town and Borough Bridewell, (which I fully described in the Gentlemans Magazine for December 1808,) having been pulled down, this New Gaol wa ficst inhabited on the 30th of July 1810. It is situate near the Shire-Hall, and stands at the back of the Spinning-School, the Master of which is the present Keeper..

On the ground-floor are a day-room, of 15 feet by 12, having a fire-place, with a large grated and glazed sash window, looking toward the court-yard, (about 68 feet square) and made to open; and also five sleeping-cells, of 12 feet by 8, with similar windows, and an aperture over each door for better ventilation, furnished with iron bedsteads, straw-in-sacking beds, two blankets, and a coverlet. The doors of all these cells, like that of the day-room, open into a spacious lobby, 7 feet wide, which extends to the whole length of the building, and is separated from the court-yard of the Spinning-School by open wood palisades; thus affording an excellent space for air and exercise, when the weather will not permit the use of the Prison court-yard, into which the windows of the day-room and of the sleeping-cells open.

The chamber-story consists of a lobby, a day-room, and the same number of sleeping-cells, in every respect similar to those already described; except that two of them, having blinds fixed before their windows, are called solitary cells.

Sept. 21st, 1810, no Prisoners. The number of Commitments hither, from the first opening of the Bridewell to the time of my visit above mentioned, had amounted to *Seven.* The sewers are judiciously placed, and the Prison clean.

IPSWICH. *Suffolk*
The Town and Borough Gaol.
Gaoler, *Wilfiam Brame.* Salary, 50/. Also two chaldrons and a half of coals, and eight dozen pounds of candles.
Fees, Debtors, on discharge, *6s.* Sf-Felons pay no Fees. Garnish abolished.
Chaplain (a *recent* appointment,) Rev. *William Howorth.*
Duty, Sunday-, Prayers and Sermon. Salary, 30J.
Surgeon, Mr. *Sechamp.* Salary, none: makes a Bill-
Number of Prisoners. Dfcbtors. Felons, &e.
180 r, Oct. 13th,------3-------5
1805, Sept. 14th,------4---.-,. a . ii ',Q
1810, Sept. 21-st,-3-8

Allowance, to Debtors, poor and unable to support themselves, one pound and half of bread per day: And from *Pemberton's Charity* a twopenny loafy. one shilling's worth of meat, and a pint of strong beer on a Sunday, once in: three weeks. To Felons, &c. one pound and half of best wheaten bread, and one penay in money per day.

REMARKS.

This Gaol is situate in St. Matthew's-street, and since my visits in iSOl and 1805, is become so much improved, that I can *now* give some account of it with pleasure.

'The Gaoler's house fronts the street; and in it are rooms for Master's-Side Debtors, to which he furnishes beds at two shillings per week each. Behind the house is the Debtors' court-yard, 90 feet by 27, with a gravel walk; and at the end of it is a small area, in which to converse with their friends.

Women Debtors have separate apartments. The Infirmary-room is 17 feet by 12, and 7 feet 9 inches high, with a fire-place and glazed window.

Common-Side Debtors have a day-room, 16 feet square, with a fire-place; and also four rooms above stairs, to which the Corporation furnishes bedsteads and bedding.

Men and Women Felons have each their separate ward, distinct and apart one from the other, with an airy court-yard to each; in which the sewers are judiciously placed, and unoflfensive. Their sleeping-rooms are well ventilated, and furnished by the Corporation with bedsteads, a bed, two blankets, two sheets, clean once a month, and a coverlet each. They are obliged to make their beds, and sweep their wards every morning, before they receive their allowance of bread.

At the West-end of the Prison is a little neat Chapel, 22 feet by 18, where the Prisoners are properly seated in their respective classes, but in sight of each other during Divine Service.

At my visits some of them were employed in cutting skewers, at 2. a thousand; others spinning or making garters. They have all they earn; and the considerate Magistrates allow fire, soap, and towels for their use.

Debtors are confined here upon Writs of *Capias,* issuing out of the *Court of Small Pleas,* holden for the Town and Borough every fortnight, on a Monday. No Debtor in execution confined in this Gaol; had ever reaped the benefit of the *Lords' Act,* until the 30th of December, 1S05, when Mr. Pulham, a very worthy and respectable Solicitor, at Woodbridge, obtained the *Sixpences* for them at his own expence, after an application had been made by him to the Court of King's Bench, for a Mandamus to have them allowed.

Every Debtor here is permitted to purchase one quart of strong beer per day, but not more.

The Act for preserving Health, and Clauses against Spirituous Liquors, are hung tip in the Chapel. The Prison is well supplied with water, and kept very clean.

?" IPSWICH. *Suffolk.*
County Gaol.
Gaoler, *Samuel Johnson* .

Salary, 200/. and coals and candle for his own use.

Fees and Garnish, abolished. Conveyance of Transports, one shilling per mile.

Chaplain, Rev. Mr. *Lee,* now Rev. *IVilliam Aldrich.*

Duty, Prayers on Wednesday, and on Sunday, Prayers and Sermon. Salary, 50/.

Surgeon, Mr. *Stealing.*

Salary, 50/. for Prisoners of all descriptions, Gaol and Bridewell.

Number of Prisoners, Debtors. Felons, &c. State-Prisoners.
1800, Oct. 13th,----II----17----0. 1803, Sept. 14th----20----14----3. 1S08, Nov. 20th,----21----10----0. 1810, Sept. 21st,---. 8----8----0.

Allowance, Debtors, each 2lbs. of beef per week. And on Sundays a pint of porter and a two-penny loaf If very poor, and unable to support himself, he is allowed by the County, in addition, four loaves, each llb.; and half a pound of cheese per week.

Felons,, llb. of best bread per day, sent in from the Baker, in loaves of that weight; and three quarters of a pound of cheese weekly. I weighed the loaves; and found them both just in quantity, and of good wheaten bread.

N. B. Coals, mops, brooms, pails, and towels are allowed by the County for the use of the Prisoners.

REMARKS.

The boundary wall of this Prison encloses about an acre and half of ground, and is twenty feet high, with a sunk fence, about 5 feet deep, 10 feet wide, and 12 feet distant from the open palisade fences of the different court-yards.

The Turnkey's lodge is in front; and on the ground floor is the day-room, and another, in which the irons for Prisoners are deposited. In the lodge are a warm and cold bath, with an oven to purify their clothes, on being received.

He seems of weak intellect, and much under the controul of an ignorant and brutish Turnkey. See the account of "Pemberton's Charity," given under the Head *Bury St. Edmund's,* p. *36,* and. also noticed in p. 293.

Above stairs are two reception-cells, where the Prisoner is detained till examined by the Surgeon, previous to his admission into the interior. Also a room where the cleansed clothes are ticketed and hung up, and the County clothing put on; and close by is the Turnkey's sleeping-room.

The lead roof above the lodge is the place for execution of Criminate.

From the lodge extends »n avenue, of *gS* feet by 18, which leads to the *Keeper's house,* in the *eetftre* of die Prison, and from which the several court-yards are completely inspected.

The Prison consists of four wings, to which are attached eight spacious and airy courts, of 75 feet by 45; and three smaller ones, about 44 feet square, in one of which is the engine house, as a provision against fire.

The Men Debtors have the use of two of the larger court-yards, having water-closets in them; and both hard and soft water are laid on. Upon the ground floor is their day-room, 22 feet by 14, with a fire-place, and utensils for frugal cookery; a pantry, also, for their provisions, and four work-rooms.

To the refractory Debtors are appropriated one-of the smaller courts, and two work-cells, of 8 feet by 6, and 10 feet high on the ground floor.

The first and second story have each eleven sleeping-oells; which are severally divided, by lobbies-46 feet long, and. 5 feet wide.

The Women Debtors have a courtyard to themselves, of the larger size, and separated from the Men's by the avenue before-noticed, as leading from the Turnkey's lodge to the house of the Keeper. Their day-room, 14 feet by 8 feet 6 inches, is fitted up just like that for the Men Debtors. Above this, on the first story, is a lobby 46 feet by 5, leading to 10 sleeping-cells, five of them on one side, for Female Debtors, and the rest, on the other side, for Female Convicts.

On the second story are eleven other sleeping-cells, exactly similar to the former, and divided by a lobby in the same manner: And all communication betwixt Female Debtors and Female Felons is most judiciously prevented, by means of a grated door thrown across the lobby or passage.

Each cell has two doors; the outer iron-grated, and the inner of wood, opening into the lobby. They are all 8 feet 6 inches by 6 feet 6, and about *9* feet *6* inches high; lighted and ventilated by an iron-grated and glazed sash window, 3 feet *6* inches by 2 feet 4; and by an aperture also near the door, of 15 inches by 3,; all alike fitted up with a.wooden bedstead, flock mattress, two sheets, two blankets, a bolster, and coverlet, which are provided at the County expence.

Every Debtor has a single bed, and. all are supplied both with fuel, Winter and Summer, to cook their provisions; and with a cupboard, numbered like the sleepingroom, under lock and key, to secure them. Each Debtor has permission also to purchase one quart of strong beer per day, but no more.

Male Felons, before Trial, have a day-room 14 feet square, fitted up like those of the Debtors, for cookery, and every other accommodation. They, too, have acourt-yard, with excellent pump water laid on -y a sewer, which is a water-closet,, and seven work-cells. Above these, on the first story, are ten sleeping-cells, divided by a lobby 46 feet long, and 5 feet wide; and on the second story are eleven other cells, divided in the same manner.

The Female Felons, previous to trial, have a day-room 14 feet by S feet 6, fitted up for cookery in the same manner as the Men's. Their sleeping-cells also are exactly similar to the preceding; and they have a court-yard, like that appropriated to the Male Felons.

Convicts for Transportation have their day-room of the same dimensions with' that last-mentioned: and on the upper story are eleven sleeping-cells for their class, who have also the use of a separate court-yard.

Convicts sentenced to imprisonment have likewise a court-yard; a day-room of 14 feet square; on the ground floor seven work-cells; and on the first story eleven sleeping-cells, circumstanced and accommodated in all respects like those already described.

The Chapel of this excellent Prison is in the centre of the Gaoler's house, up one pair of stairs, and distinguishable by a turret-top, and an alarm-bell. The former was once somewhat open, for better ventilation; but being found to admit too much air, the sides have been nearly canvassed up. This very neat structure is well contrived, and easy of access from the several lobbies. The Prisoners, during Divine Service, are seated according to their respective classes: the sexes, by means of several partitions, are kept out of sight of each other, but all in full view both of their Minister and Keeper;

On this first story there are also three bed chambers for the Gaoler; and on the second story four neat Infirmary Rooms, 19 feet square, with fire-places, sash windows iron-grated, water-closets, &c. and above them is the lead flat of the building, appropriated to the use of convalescents, for the benefits of air and exercise. The Infirmaries have iron-framed and latticed wooden bedsteads, with a mattress to each, two blankets, two sheets, and a coverlet; and the sick are well supplied with suitable food,

and wine, if necessary, at the discretion of the Surgeon.

On the 17th of July, 1780, at a meeting of the Trustees of Mr. *John Pemberton's* Charity, it was Ordered,

"That the Treasurer should provide, as the Trustees shall see fit, for the Debtors imprisoned in any of the Gaols in the County of Suffolk, (either for *their relief* therein, by a proportion of bread, meat, and beer, as he shall think necessary, orfor the *delivering them* out of Prison,) until the Treasurer shall receive further orders. Nevertheless, such Debtors in *Ipswich* Gaol as do not regularly attend Divine Service,—unless prevented by sickness, or some reasonable cause, to be allowed of by the Chaplain, and behave decently and reverently,—shall not have any benefit or allowance from this Charity. Trustees / -EO' Drury. PH" B. Brooke.

'1 Lott Knight. Erw. Hasem," The visiting Magistrates frequently attend their important charge, and have their Committee Room in the Keeper's house; the windows of which room, and of the Keeper's kitchen and parlour, are so placed, as to command the several court-yards.

Recapitulation of the various departments of the Gaol.

Four wings: court-yards, 11; day-rooms, 7; work-cells, 27; sleepingcells, 86; solitary cells, 2. The County dresses, before Conviction, are red and grey striped duffell; and after Conviction, blue and yellow, for distinction.

The Act for preserving Health, and Clauses against Spirituous Liquors, are conspicuously hung up.

IPSWICH. *House of Correction.*
Keeper, *George dubbe.* Salary, 42l. and coals, candles, soap, mops, brooms, and pails, for the use of the Prison.
Fees, none.
Chaplain, Rev. Mr. *Tunney.* Salary, 20l. Duty, Sunday and Wednesday.
Surgeon, *Mr. Stehbing.* Salary, see *County-Gaol.*
Prisoners, 1805, 14th Sep. Three. 1808, 20th Nov. Five. 1810, 21st Sep. Nine.
Allowance, one pound and half of bread per day, sent in loaves of that weight

from the Baker's; whieh, upon weighing, I found to be just. They have also what they can earn by spinning.
REMARKS.

This Prison stands near the County Gaol, in an airy situation, and is surrounded by a boundary wall, 17 feet high, with an inside sunk fence, 2 feet 6 inches deep, and 7 feet wide.

On the ground-floor of the Keeper's house are the visiting Magistrates' room, the Keeper's parlour and kitchen, which command a view of the three different courtyards, each 60 feet by 30, and enclosed by open palisades. Here is a forcing pump, for supplying the Prison; and soft water also is laid on from the main to the Keeper's kitchen.

On the left side of the ground floor is a day-room, 18 feet by 10, with fire-place, and glazed windows; and five cells for the Women, which open into a lobby, 24 fee$ by 5, well ventilated.

Above these are five other cells, of the same size, with a lobby; and three Infirmary-rooms, 14 feet by 11, with glazed windows, fire-places, and boarded floors. Near the Infirmary-rooms is a lead flat, assigned to the convalescents, for the benefit of air and exercise.

On the right hand of the ground floor is another day-room for the Men, with cells and lobbies, sick-rooms, and other accommodations, of the same size and nature as those on the Women's side.

In the first floor of the Keeper's house is the Chapel, 20 feet by Id"; into which the respective lobbies open, and all the classes are seated on benches, in sight of each other.

The court-yards are all on art inclined plane, with brick gutters. Water is judiciously conveyed through the sewers, and the Courts are always clean.

Each cell in this Prison is 10 feet by f, and 9 feet 6 inches high, With arched roofs, and ventilated by art iron--grate'd arid glazed window, 3 feet 3 inches by 3 feet. They have iron bedsteads, straw beds in sacking, two blankets, and a coverlet; and are furnished with spinning-wheels.

The ventilation of the cells might be improved by a circular aperture over the door, of 6 inches diameter; or one in any other suitable situation, of 10 inches by 2. Each door has now an opening of 6 inches by 4.

Clean linen once a week is provided by the County. Here are no Rules and Orders hung up, nor the Act for Preserving Health, and Clauses against Spirituous Liquors. The Prison is kept Very clean.

IRVEN. *Scotland.*
The Toton Gaol.
Keepers, the Town's Officers, who have no Salary.
Fees, on Caption, 2. *6d.* paid by the Incarcerator to the Town-Clerk; and fourpence a night to the Gaoler. No religious attentions.
Surgeon, from the Town, when wanted.
Number of Prisoners, 30th Oct. 1809, Seven Debtors.
Allowance, Alimented as ordered, generally one shilling per day.
REMARKS.

This Gaol for Debtors is in the High Street, about the middle of the Town. A flight of about 20 steps leads to the Guard-room and Court-house; and adjoining are two rooms for Debtors. Each has a glazed window, boarded floor, and fireplace, with a wooden bedstead, but no bedding. Above, is a large room, with sash windows, a bedstead, and fire-place; set apart for such Debtors as can give security against escape. No coals allowed. A tub, in place of a sewer. No wateiy but what is brought in by the Gaoler.

JEDBURGH. *Roxburghshire, Scotland.*
The County Gaol.
Gaoler, *Andrew Henderson.* Salary, 5/.
Fees, for Debtors, on Caption, 2. *6d.*; none for Felons, &c. No religious duties; except that a Minister regularly attends those under Sentence of Death. No Surgeon. Number of Prisoners, 21st September 1809, Debtors, 2. Capital Convicts, 2.
Transport, 1.—Total, 5" Allowance. *Debtors,* as alimented by the Magistrates. *Felons, 8$c. 8d.* a day.
REMARKS.

This County Gaol was built in 1755-It fronts the Town, and the back part of the Church-yard; and on each side of the arched entrance is a vault: but these vaults are never used for imprisonment.

The first story consists of three rooms, which comprise the Gaol for *Felons.* Two of them are about 15 feet square; and the third 12 feet by 10, with grated and glazed casement windows, and fire-places in two. They have boarded floors, with straw-in-ticking for beds, two blankets, and a coverlet.

The next story has an apartment for the Gaoler, another room for Debtors, and a small room in what is called " *The Steeple,"* where the bells are rung.

The Debtors' room, 16 feet square, has grated and glazed casement windows, a boarded floor, a wooden bedstead, with bedding furnished by the Town. Also a fire-place; but no coals are allowed.

Here is no *water,* except what is brought in by the Keeper. No courtyard. In every room a covered close-stool instead of a sewer, for general use.

JEDBURGH. *County Bridewell.*
Keeper, *William Dunlop.* Salary, 20/.
Surgeon, *Mr. Watson,* who makes a Bill. Prisoners, 21st Sept. 1809, Offender, 1. Insane Persons, 2.
REMARKS.

This Bridewell, which was built about 20 years ago, is wholly on the ground floor. It has a court-yard, of about 30 feet square, for the Men; and a similar one for Women. In each court-yard are three apartments; one spacious, and two smaller ones, to work and sleep in.

The *Chamber Story* is occupied by the Keeper.

The glazed windows of the above rooms open toward the several court-yards. No fire-places; and, of course, no coals are allowed. Nor is any water supplied, except what is fetched in by the Keeper of this County Prison.

The employment of the Prisoners consists in pounding of sand for scouring.

KENDAL. *Westmoreland.*
The Town Gaol and Bridewell.
Gaoler, *Miles Hayton;* now *John Shepherd.* Salary, 8o/.
Fees, none. Conveyance of Transports, one shilling per mile.
Chaplain, Rev. Mr. *Briggs;* now Rev. Mr. *Sampson.* Salary, 15/.
Duty, on Sundays, in the afternoon.
Surgeon, when wanted, is sent from the Dispensary.
Number of Prisoners, Debtors. Felons. &c. Lunatieks.
1801, Nov. 3d,---2 7 _ 3. 1802, Sept. 25th,--3 7 1.
18OQ, Nov. 4th,---1 2 ____ 2.
Also Bastardy, 1. Vagrant, 1. Runaway Apprentice, 1.

Allowance, To *Debtors,* none: But every Debtor, arrested by process out of the Borough Court, was heretofore allowed sixpence per day, after three Courtdays; and a Court was then held every third week. That regularity, however, is nowdiscontinued; and a Debtor may be confined three months, without any allowance, except from casual earnings, in case he can procure work.

Felons, and other *Criminal* Prisoners, are allowed sixpence a day; but if they work, that allowance is discontinued. If the produce of labour amounts to *seven shillings* or more per week, the Gaoler receives one fifth of the whole of his or her earnings. $3" This may operate to discourage industry, by inducing Prisoners to limit their earnings to *6s. 6d.* per week; from which there could be no deduction. « REMARKS.

This Prison is judiciously situated on an eminence, a little way out of the Town. Debtors have a spacious airy court-yard, 69 feet by *36,* supplied with pump water; and six sizeable rooms, with boarded floors, sash windows, and fire-places in four of them. They are well ventilated and clean, and open into a lobby 3 feet *6* inches wide.

For the use of these rooms, with wooden bedsteads, the Debtor pays nothing; but he must supply his own bedding, or hire it from the Town.

The Men Felons' court-yard, which opens into that of the Debtors, is 30 feet by 21; and has in it a day and work-room, about 13 feet square, with two hemp blocks, a fire-place, and a large iron-grated and glazed window.

On the ground floor are two sleeping-cells, of H feet each by 10, with vaulted roofs, stone floors, wooden bedsteads, two blankets, and a rug to each. The only Jight or ventilation they receive, is from a wicket in the door, about 9 inches square.

The Women Felons have a separate court, in front of the building, 12 yards by 10; also four sleeping-rooms, about 8 feet stuare; Emd tvro work-rooms; in one of which was a Woman weaving, in the other a Woman spiwtling: and likewise a room, with a single loom in it, at which a Man was weaving. Looms for the use of the Prisoners, during their confinement, were heretofore sfent in from the Workhouse. They are allowed three fourths of their earnings for maintenance, and the remaining quarter goes to the Keeper.

Wheels and Swifts for the Prisoners are famished by the County *gratis;* and there is one loom, the prime cost of which having been made good, by hiring, it to Prisoners at *6d.* per week, I learned that it was intended to be allotted for their gratuitous use in future.

At my former visits, looms, as I just observed, were supplied from the Workhouse; first it was a charge of sixpence per week, and afterwards of fourpence. The two Men I saw weaving, at times, had their looms from the Manufacturers who employed them.

Some of the Prisoners have work from a quarry of grey marble, about four miles distant from Kendall; and others from one of black marble, about 12 miles off; while some also beat hemp, or are engaged in taylor's work, or shoetnaking.

Here was one Woman in *solitary confinement,* whose employment and support depended wholly on her friends.

An enclosed part of the Debtors' court afford another small yard for the use of Criminals; into which the doors of two sleeping-cells open; the one 11 feet by 10, the other 15 feet by *9*; supplied with such bedding as before described.

Here is a very neat *Chapel,* which has two distinct doors of entrance, and a folding screen in the middle; so that the Female Prisoners can neither see nor be seen tay the men. All of them, except one poor Lunatick, attended Divine Service, on Sunday, 5th of November, 1809, and their behaviour was orderly and attentive.

In the Keeper's house, there is one common day-room, about 14 feet square, with a fire-place: and here I found all the Prisoners congregated at my last visit, save the pitiable Maniac, as above, who had been confined seven years.

The Gaoler is allowed *10s. 6d.* weekly for the maintenance of each Lunatick: one shilling per mile for the conveyance of Prisoners to Appleby; and the same, if he brings them back.

It would be an act of kind humanity, if a Messenger were publickly employed and paid here, to procure for the Prisoners victuals and *small beer* from the Town; which they sometimes stand greatly in need of. The opening of the door of the Felons' court-yard into that of the Debtors requires attention, to prevent injurious intercourse.

Here is no bath, nor oven to wash the New-Comers, or parify their offensive or infected clothes. No County clothing is yet allowed.

The Act for preservation of Health, and Clauses against Spirituous Liquors, are conspicuously hung up. Eyery part of the Gaol is well supplied with water, and the whole is kept very clean.

KIDDERMINSTER. *Worcestershire.*
The Town Gaol.
For short occasional Confinement.
One of the greatest singularities met with in my various and wide excursions, occurred to me in a former visit to this Gaol.

From my notes, I recollect it was in August, (the 27th) J803. The *Town Crier* at that time was the *Keeper.* The Gaol itself stood in a very respectable and wellknown Town of England: It has long been, and long may it be, justly celebrated, from practical experience of the best judges, for Manufactures in the *Woollen and Mixed Line* of considerable importance. It once contained above a thousand houses; and the families, we are told, could amass near six thousand inhabitants.

How is it now? I saw, examined, and considered it; and I found, That the *ill accommodations* for Prisoners was a strong and pleasing proof, that, in this Town, *Prisons icere not considered as the absolute necessaries of life.*

I was shewn here *two Dungeons,* of about 10 feet long by 8 feet wide. But, to get at them, a *Criminal,* an *Offender,* and perhaps even a *Debtor,* must descend six steps below the World's eye; and be thus concealed from it, beneath the Market Place of the Town!

No court-yard could be provided here. No water. No sewer; and loose straw only scattered, in case harrassed and weary Nature should wish to rest from her labours, both of mind and body. It was a comfortable reflexion, however, to learn, that Prisoners are viever locked up here for above a night or two; and at my call itt 1803, not a single Prisoner was to be found.

KILMARNOCK. *Scotland..* Keepers, The Town's Officers. No Salary. Prisoners, 30th Oct. 1809, None. Allowance, to Criminals, Sixpence a day. REMARKS. This Gaol consists of one vaulted dark cell, for persons committed at night; and has dirty loose straw laid on the floor. Also a dark cell near the stairs of the Town Hall, and one very large vaulted cell adjoining, with a fire-place, and an aperture in the wall, about 3 feet long, and 8 inches wide. Straw only is allowed to sleep joo. A tab serves as a sewer, and water is brought in by the Keepers.

Criminals are confined here only a day or two before they are sent to Ayr. Debtors are sent to Irven, seven miles distant.

KING'S BENCH PRISON.
Marshal, *William Jones,* Esq. the Fees and Emoluments of whose office, from the Report made in July 1809, appear to be 2660/.

Deputy, Mr. *Hughes;* whose income is stated to be 210/. This office may be considered as a *sinecure;* for I am informed that the duties of it are executed by Mr. *Brooshoof,* as Clerk of the Day-Rules, as well as Clerk of the Papers.

Licence, Beer and Wine. Tap lett. (See Remarks.)

Allowance, none whatever.

Prisoners, within the walls, on an average of ten years, are from 5 00 to 700-"K

Prisoners in the Rules, on an average, 100 to 150.

Surgeon, none.

Chaplain, Rev. Mr. *Evans;* whose Salary arises from proceedings in suits against Prisoners, which are taken for, and paid to him, by the several Judges' clerks at their chambers. I am told the amount is about 100/. *per annum.*

Duty, Prayers and Sermon on Sunday; and Sacrament once a month.

N. B. Attendance at Chapel being *optional,* but few attended when I have been there; and devotion was extremely interrupted, by the continual noise of opening and shutting the Chapel-door during Divine Service.

The office of Marshal of this Prison was heretofore hereditary in a private family, by grant from the Crown: But in 27th George II. it was suggested as improper for a private family to hold such an office; and that it would be the means of more effectually preventing extortion and impositions on the Prisoners, if the appointment were vested in the Crown, subject to removal for *neglect of duty, non-residence,* or *improper conduct.* A Bill therefore passed, to enable his Majesty to purchase the future appointment of Marshal of the King's Bench Prison, and 10,500/. was voted for that purpose. By this Act the King appoints that officer to hold his place *quamdiu se bene gesserit.* Constant residence seems required, either *within the Walls, or within the Rules* If the account of Fees and Emoluments of the Marshal's Office, which has been sent to me, is correct, they appear to be upwards of 7900'. *per annum.* The Prison will not accommodate more than 220. They are generally chummed together, two, and sometimes three, upon a room.

% When sickness attacks poor Prisoners in this place, their sufferings must be extreme, from the want of medical aid; for sickness, accompanied with poverty, finds here neither pity nor relief.

The Marshal is to keep the Prison in repair, and pay his servants out of the fees and emoluments. The power of continuance and removal is vested in the Chief Justice, and the other three Judges of the Court of King's Bench.

By the Act 32 George II. the courts were required to meet, and to settle a Table of Fees, &c. to be taken of all prisoners for debt; and the prisoners were protected by that Act from the imposition and extortion of Gaolers. The Court of King's Bench settled the following Table Of Fees, to be taken of all prisoners for debt, &c.; and by the said Act they are directed to send, at certain times in the year, to see that this Table of Fees, as well as a List of all Bequests, are hung up in some conspicuous part of the Prison, and that the said Act is in every other respect complied with; and that eight days' public notice should be given of this visitation. Any violation of the Clauses in this Act subjects Gaolers and servants to a penalty of 50/. The limits and boundaries, or, as they are commonly called, "Rules" of the Prison, are very extensive, forming a circle of nearly three miles round the walls of the Prison. The purchase of these Rules appears to be seven guineas and a half, for the first fifty pounds every Prisoner i charged with, and ten guineas, if one hundred ; and such security is given to the Marshal as he approves of: But all taverns, ale-houses, and places of public amusement, are excluded.

Day Rules

Are allowed, to the number of *three* days in every term, unless the Prisoner can shew good cause, to the Court, why a greater number of days should be granted him. Those in the Rules, who have given to the Marshal two sufficient securities, pay for the first day-rule *4s. 2d.* and 3. *lod.* for every other day. The expence attending an application for a greater number is about a guinea and a half. Those who are within the walls, and are too poor to purchase the Rules, and unable, from the general desertion of their friends, to find security, cannot obtain this indulgence of the day-rules, without paying a Judge's tipstaff 10. *6d.* to attend them; and a further sum of *16s. Sd.* to induce the tipstaffto become security to the Marshal, in case of an escape. As the tipstaffs give to the Marshal security to the amount of 500/. only, those who are charged with demands, or debts, for more than that sum, can have no indulgence of this kind.

Of The Prison Itself.

It is situated at the top of Blackman-street, in the Borough of Southwark. The entrance to it, from St. George's Fields, is by a handsome court-yard, where there are three good houses. The largest of them is the proper residence of the Marshal; one for the Clerk of the papers, with his office on the ground-floor; and the third is generally let to persons of rank and fortune, who are committed by the Court for Bryant's evidence, 1791.

R R

challenges, libels, or other misdemeanors. From this court-yard the ascent is by a few stone steps into a lobby, which has a good room on the right-hand, and over it several good apartments, which, I was informed, usually let at five guineas a week; also two rooms, called *Strong Rooms,* to secure those who have attempted to escape. These Strong Rooms are about 12 feet by 8: one of them has a flagged floor, and is occasionally used as a coal-hole; the other has a boarded floor. No fire-place in either; no casements, or shutters, to keep out the weather.

From the lobby is a descent, by a few stone steps, into a small square yard, where there is a pair of great gates, and a small door, with a lodge for the Turnkeys, and a room over it, generally let at one guinea a week. On the right-hand of this gate, upon entering the inner part of the Prison, is a brick building, called "the State House," containing eight large handsome rooms, let at 2. *6d.* each per week to those who have interest to procure one. Opposite to the State House is the Tap-room, where from 12 to 24 butts of beer are drawn weekly. In this tap-room is a bar; and on one side is a very neat small parlour, belonging to the person who keeps the tap." On the other side is a room on a larger scale, called the Wine-room, where Prisoners and their friends occasionally resort. The residence of the Prisoners is in a large brick building, about 120 yards long, with a wing at each end, and a neat uniform Chapel in the centre. There is a space of ground in front of the building, of about forty yards, including a parade of about three yards, paved with broad flagstones. In the space between the building and the wall are three pumps, well supplied with spring and river water; also another pump, at the side of the further wing, with a spring of very fine water. Part of the ground next the wall is appropriated for playing at rackets and fives; and there are also, in different parts, frames of wood, with nine holes in each frame, called *Bumble-puppy grounds*; where the Prisoners amuse themselves with trying to bowl small iron balls into the holes marked with the highest numbers.

The building is divided into sixteen staircases, with stone steps and iron railings-. No. lr at the further wing, contains 21 rooms; and on each staircase the ranges of rooms are divided by a passage, or gallery, about two yards wide. In the staircases No. 2, 3, 4, and 5, there are four rooms on each floor, making 16 in each staircase; separated from each other by a passage, of about a yard wide. The staircase, No. *6,* contains 12 rooms, besides two small cabins. No. 7 8, and 9, contain eight rooms each. No. 10, contains 30 rooms, separated from each other by a passage, about 20 yards long and two wide. The staircases No. 11, 12, 13, 14, and 15, have eight rooms each, and are at the back of the building, but separated from the wall by a space of about eight yards. Each staircase has eight rooms, with a passage of about a yard wide. No. 16 is also in the further wing, at the back of the building; has a spacious wide staircase, with passages or galleries on each floor, four yards wide; and contains, in the whole, 20 rooms.

The whole number of rooms, including the eight state rooms, is 224; the size of them, in general, is 15 to 16 feet by 12 or 13 feet: some few are on a little larger scale. In each room is a strong iron range, and on each side a recess, either for a bed or cupboard. All the rooms that were destroyed by the fire, some years ago, are now arched with brick, to prevent in future any fire from extending beyond a *single* room. In the passage from the entrance to the back of the building is a Coffee House, where formerly there was an ordinary every day, at 2. per head, with a pint of porter included. The Marshal, I am told, receives an annual rent of 105/. from the person who keeps it.

Beyond the coffee-room is a Bakehouse, which pays also a rent of 36 guineas *per annum.* And on the opposite side of the way is the Public Kitchen, where the Prisoners may have their meat roasted and boiled *gratis,* before one o'clock. After that time the cook charges *2d.* or 3d. for each joint, according to the size of it. Between the coffee-house and the public kitchen, there are generally two or three butcher's stalls, a green-market, and persons selling fish: and in the further wing is a large taproom, called the *Brace,* from its having once been kept by two brothers, whose names were *Partridge.* Over this taproom is another room of the same size, occupied by a Prisoner; where the newspapers may be read, and tea, coffee, &c. maybe had: but the man having been detected in selling spirituous liquors, the Marshal turned him out, and gave the room to another Prisoner. The lower rooms on the parade are, many of them, converted into chandlers shops, kept by Prisoners-f-.

The superintendence and government of this Prison rest with the Marshal; who has under him a Deputy Marshal, a Clerk of the Papers, several other Clerks, three Turnkeys, and their Assistants. As the Marshal, Deputy Marshal, and Clerk of the Papers, I am informed, seldom come into the Prison, every complaint must be made by letter, or by a personal application at the office of the Clerk of the Papers. If it relates to any quarrel or disturbance, it is generally settled in a summary way. The Marshal is a Magistrate, and also armed with a Rule of Court, authorizing him to commit any person to the New Gaol for riotous or disorderly conduct; one month for the first offence, and three months for a second: But, the Prisoner may appeal either to the Court, or to a Judge out of term.

No spirituous liquors are allowed to be sold within the Prison: and, by a Rule of Court, no Women or Children ought to stay in the Prison after ten o'clock. At half past nine, therefore, a Man goes round, with a bell, and at certain places calls out, "*Strangers, Women, and Children, out!"* The number of Prisoners, before the Here a prisoner may be accommodated with a bed by the night, or week, (as he can agree,) till he gets *chummage,* or a room.

f I was informed by a prisoner, in January 1804, that there were fifteen *whistle-shops* in the prison, where debtors could buy gin, which was sold under various names*;* viz. Moonshine, Skyblue, Mexico, &g. and that *a hogsliead of gin* was consumed *weekly* in it!

Act of Insolvency in 1797, was upwards of 600; about 200 of whom were excluded, by the limitations of the sum, and time. After the Act of 1801, about 150 were left in Prison: many, of those who had been a great number of years confined, were excluded from the benefit, on account of the limitation of the sum; and others, who were not within the term specified by the Act. Not more than three or four were remanded under the Act, for fraud, &c. March 10th, 1802, the numbers within the walls were 315, and 57 within the Rules: Jan. 13th, 1804, within the walls and R'jles, 520.

When a Debtor is first committed to this Prison, he is entitled to have what is called a *Chummage,* as soon as he has paid his fees. This Chummage is a ticket given him by the Clerk of the Papers, to go to such a room; and whether it be to a *whole room,* the *half,* or the *third* of a *room,* must entirely depend on the number of Prisoners within the walls. But, as it is more convenient for persons, when they first come to this Prison, to hire a bed for a week or two, there are always great numbers of distressed persons willing to hire out their beds, on being paid two or three shillings per night. Others, who are distressed, *let their right to half a room at* 5. per week, and sleep in the tap-room, on the benches, in hammocks, or on nratresses. The Clerk of the Papers has the entire management and disposition of the rooms.

He is assisted by the eldest Turnkey, who goes round every Monday morning, and receives the weekly rent of one shilling.

The Poor Side of the Prison now consists of sixteen rooms, at the back of the building. The number of their Inhabitants seldom exceeds 30; and they are governed by a set of Rules of Court, made in the year 1720, as follows.

"Rules and Orders, For the better Government, &c. made and signed the 25th November, 1. The stocks to be kept up, for punishment of blasphemers, swearers, rioters, &c.
2. Against illegal methods of confinement. None to be confined in an unusual place, or manner, unless for attempting to escape. And such may appeal to the Court, or a Judge. 3. Marshal not to remove any to the Fleet by writ of *Habeas Corpus*. 4. Marshal not to remove any one from the Common-side, and its benefits, without three days notice; during which time the Prisoner may appeal to a Judge. 5. Coroner's Incp,est upon the dead. 0'. Against Garnish, and partial distribution of dividends. 7. Prisoners t» send out for necessaries; and to bring in their own bedding, &c. 9. Table of Fees, these Rules, and a List of Charities, to be hung up in a public room. *0*. Marshal and Servants to behave with the utmost tenderness. 10. Turnkey always to attend at the door. 11. No sen ants to partake of, or even distribute, the Charity. 12. Chapel to be kept in repair. Chaplain duly to perform. 13. The abusive to the stocks. 1 *i*. Dining-room to be kept in repair, for devotion, or conversation; with a fire. Two rooms for the i.ick. 15. Those who make oath before, &c. that they have not &2. &c. to be admitted to the charities, offices in the prison, &c. 16. No person committed for any criminal matter to vote for Steward, &c. or to partake of any charity, but the baskets. 17. Lodging in a cabin of any ward, gratis. 18. Any prisoner may be chosen Assistant, and enjoy the benefit of that station. 19. The seal of the Common-side to be kept by the Master of the King's Bench office; and not put to any deed, without the approbation of Marshal, Steward, and Assistants. 20. One supersedable action may be superseded with Common-side money: more than one, not without application to the Court, or a Judge. No Judge's Clerk to take a fee on the occasion. 21. The sick to be taken care of by the Steward and Assistants, who are to be reimbursed out of the first county-money. 22. Debts contracted by the Steward and Assistants, with the Marshal's and Master's consent, for support of the poor, to be paid out of the next dividend. 93. Steward and Assistants to have no pay for common business, or adjusting differences. 24. Prisoners entered after the first day of Easter-term, to have but one quarter of the Midsummer dividend. 25. All money brought in by the basket-men, or brought in at Christmas, Easter, and Whitsuntide, to be divided immediately, after paying the basket-men for their trouble. 26. If the Marshal advance money for a supersedeas, he is to be reimbursed out of the next countymoney. 27. Common-side prisoners may elect an annual Steward; who is not to be deposed, but on applica tion to the Court, or a Judge. No prisoner in the Rules may vote. 28. The Steward to enter in books the Table of Fees, these Rules, and a List of the Charities. All, together with his Accounts, for inspection of the Prisoners. 29. A Prisoner, wronged by the Steward and Assistants, on applying to the Court or a Judge, shall be paid his damages out of the next dividend of the Stewardand Assistants. If he complains unjustly, he shaH make satisfaction from his own next dividend. 30. If the Steward or Assistants embezzle the money, successors may call them to account*;* and stop their dividends of the grate-money, &c. for reparation of the injury. 31. These orders to be read publicly every third Monday. 32. Marshal, servants, and prisoners, to observe these Rules, under pain of the utmost punishment of law. 33. No clerk or servant of a Judge to take any fee, on occasion of apetition founded on these Orders, (Signed) R. Raymond. James Reynolds. E. Probyn. Further Rules and Orders for the Government, &c. made and signed the 10th day of May, 1J59 1. No person to bring any weapon.
2. Those on the Master's-side who demand Garnish, to be turned to Common-side for a time, not longer than a month. Those on the Common-side are, for the like offence, to be excluded, not longer than a fortnight, from all profits, except share of the baskets. 3. Doors of the great garden to be shut at dark: doors of the wards at nine. 4. The chambers at the disposal of the Marshal, &e. 5. If a Master's-side prisoner neglect for a month to pay his chamber-rent, he may be turned over to the Common-side till he pays. His goods to be delivered to him by a witnessed inventory. If discharged by the Plaintiff, he may yet be detained for fees, and a month's chamber-rent; 6. None to sell in the prison victuals or drink, without consent of Marshal. A prisoner thus offending may be turned over to the Common-side for a month. Marshal to take care that those who sell do keep good order, &c. 7. Confirms the 14th Rule preceding*; i.e.* the great room for exercise, and the two rooms for the sick. 8. Prisoners turned to Common-side, for offending, or non-payment, to have no profit, but share of the baskets: to bear no office; nor vote for officers. 9. These Rules to be fixed in the most public places, for inspection. (Signed) Mansfield. T. Dennison. M. Fohster. E. Wilmot.

A further Rule and Order, &c. made 19th May, 1760.

Those who attempt or assist an escape 5 who sell or promote the sale of victuals or liquors, without leave of the Marshal; who assault another; who blaspheme the name of God; swear, or make a riot; may be sent by the Marshal to any one of the following prisons in Southwark; *viz.* the County Gaol for Surrey, the Bridewell for that County, or to the Marshalsea*;* and there confined, for the first offence, not exceeding one month; for a second offence, not exceeding three months.

This Rule to be hung up. (Signed) Mansfield. M. Forster.

T. Dennison. E. Wilmot.

On the same sheet is, A Table of Fees, to be taken by the Marshal of the King's Bench Prison, in the County of

Surry, for any Prisoner or Prisoners' Commitment, or coming into Gaol, or Chamber-Rent there, or Discharge from thence in any Civil Action. Settled and established the 16th day of June, in the 33d year of the reign of his Majesty King George the Second, and in the year of our Lord 1760, pursuant to an Act for the relief of Debtors, with respect to the imprisonment of their persons; viz, £. s. 4.

I. To the Marshal, for every Prisoner committed on any Civil Action--0 4 8 9. To the Turnkey on the Master's-side. ...-.-016 3. To the Marshal, on the discharge of every such prisoner----0 7 4 4. To the Deputy Marshal, upon the discharge of one or more actions, executions, or other charge; and no further fee, though there be ever so many actions-0 4 O 5. To the Clerk of the Papers, for the first action, upon the discharge--0 3 0 S. To the Clerk of the Papers, for every action, execution, or other charge, to be paid on the discharge----------004 7. To the Deputy Marshal, upon a commitment of a Prisoner in Court, or at a Judge's Chambers, in any Civil Action, if carried to the King's Bench Prison 0 10 8. To the Clerk of the Papers for the same-Q 1 0 9. To the said Deputy Marshal, for a surrender in discharge of bail, be there ever so many actions....-.-----010 10. To the Clerk of the Papers, for each action, upon such surrender--0 0 6 II. To each of the four Tipstaffs, ft. 6d. for each Prisoner's commitment by the

Court, and earned to the King's Bench Prison, in the whole--0 10 0 IS. To the Tipstaff that carries any prisoner committed at a Judge's Chambers to the said Prison--..----» '-O 6 0 13. To the Marshal, for the use of chamber, bel, bedding, and sheets, for each Pri-a£. s. d. soner, if provided by the Gaoler at the Prisoner's request, for the first night, in the Common-side of the said Prison--------006 14. For the like use, every night the Prisoner remains in custody, after the first-0 01- 15. And if two lie in a bed, Id. each--------008 16. For the like use, of every Prisoner that goes on the Masters-side, for the first night O 0 6 17. For the like use, every night after the first,------0 0 3 IS. And if two lie in a bed, 2d each-------004 19. And if the prisoner finds his own bed, bedding, and sheets (which the Marshal is in no sort to hinder him of), then he shall pay for chamber-rent to the Marshal per week--_------010 *No other Fee for the use of Chamber, Bed, Bedding, and Sheets, or upon Commitment o r Discharge of any Prisoner on any Civil Action.*

Thomas Howard. Mansfield.
Anthony Thomas Abdy. T. Parker.
William Hammond.

I copied the following List of Benefactions, on the 6th of March, 1802, from the Book kept on the Common Side of the Prison. It is intituled, "An Account of "Gifts and Donations to the poor Prisoners, on the *Common* Side of the King's "Bench Prison."

County-money , paid quarterly by the Clerk to the Chief Justice of the Court of *sg. r. T.*

King's Bench, at 15/. per quarter--------60 0 0

The Gift of Sir Thomas Gresham, paid by the Chamberlain of London, at 2/. 10.

per quarter-----------lOOO
Lady Bertie, at Lady-day yearly, deducting Land-Tax-----200
Mr. John March, 1/. and interest of Old South Sea Annuities, *lis. 5d.* paid, at
Michaelmas by the Mercers' Company--------112 5
Mrs. Smith, at Christmas yearly, paid by Fishmongers' Company--0 3 4
Mrs. Hackett, ditto, by ditto------0 13 4
Arthur Mouse, Esq. by ditto----------034
Parish of St. Sepulchre, yearly---------OlOO
Sir John Peachy, Christmas, yearly, by Grocers' Company----050
Mr. Garrett, by Saltero'Company, ditto, annually------0G8
Mr. Home, ditto, by ditto-.--050
Robert Rampston, Esq. called Brass Money f, deduct Land Tax, 4.---10 0
Lady Osborne, quarterly, *19s.* ---------200
Lady Ramsey, every Christmas, 100lb. of beef, sent by AUhallows and St. Andrew's Undershaft, alternately.
Mrs. Margaret Dane, nine and a half stone of beef, and five dozen of bread yearly,
by Ironmongers' Company.
Mrs. Margaret Symcott, (Eleanor's Gwyn't) sixty-five penny loaves every eight weeks.
By the 43d Elizabeth, Chap. II. Sect. 15.
f So called, from a memorial engraved on a.brass plate, and fixed in the wall of the prison, by order of the donor, to perpetuate his gift: But since the wall has been rebuilt, it is taken away.

The LedthefsaUett' Company, in bread, St. *8d.* quarterly; in cash, at Lady-day, 6s.; *£. s. d.* at Midsummer, 4s.; at Michaelmas, 4.; and at Christmas, 8s.---12 0 St. Dunstan in the East, a fore quarter of beef, weight 27 stone, 6 lb. and a peck of oatmeal, yearly, at Midsummer. Legacy of Thomas Cottle, See Ludgate.

Company of Parish Clerks, yearly, on the 1st of November---I 1 0

The Company of Drapers, sixty penny loaves annually, in December--0 5 0

The Company of Cutlers, annually, in December, the Gift of Mr. Gaythorne-0 K 6

The Gift of Thomas Dawson, Esq. paid annually by the parish of St. Ethelburg-0 9 0

His Grace the Archbishop of Canterbury usually gives at Christmas---10 0

The Sadlers' Company, a free donation of 9. *6d.* per quarter---O 10 0 The City of Norwich, annually---------110

When once Prisoners are admitted on the Poor-side, they become entitled to their share of all charities, bequests, gifts, and donations: A list of them ought to be put up in some conspicuous part of the Prison; but, for some reasons, it is not complied with. Every person, as soon as he is admitted on this charity, must also take his turn to hold the begging-box at the door; which prevents many, who have lived in respectable situations, from applying for relief in this way. Nay, there are instances, of men that have held situations in the army and navy, respectable merchants, and tradesmen, who, (sunk in misfortune, and abandoned by their former friends,) rather than submit to this degradation, have shut themselves up for months in their rooms; and become so emaciated, from the want of wholesome and necessary food, as to lay the foundation of those disorders, which ended in their death!

The staircases and lobbies are in the most filthy state imaginable. With respect to the Prisoners' rooms, some are very dirty, others tolerably clean; but, *each preserving that degree of cleanliness which satisfies the individual himself!* KINGSTON UPON THAMES. *Surrey. The Town Gaol.*

Gaoler, *B. Sergeant;* now *William Walter..*

Salary, None. Fees,' for Debtors, or Eelons, 4. *%d.* No Table.

Surgeon, Mr. *Taylor,* who makes a Bill.

Number of Debtors, 1802, Jan. 19th, One. 1805, June 30th, One; a raving Lunatick, *Geo. Jiawson.* l&o£, May LUh, None. 1807, Sept. 16th One. 1810, June 23d, None. I have not met with one Criminal here at my several visits.

Allowance, None. The late Keeper informed me that he had frequently made application to the Bailiff of the Borough, for a *daily allowance,* but was.always told " there was none for them." REMARKS.

The *Hundred Court* of Ki Ngston is a Court of *Ancient Demesne,* holden before the Bailiffs and Suitors, on Saturday, once in three weeks. This, in the old Court Books, is called " Curia Cum Hundredo," to distinguish it from the Court of *Pleas,* which is holden every Saturday.

The *Town Hall stands* in the Market-Place, detached from all other buildings. The lower part is chiefly open, and used for the purpose of the Markets. The part at the *South end* is closed in at the time of the Assizes, and used by the Judge on the Crown Side. The room over it, up stairs, is appropriated to the Judge who sits at *Nisi Prius:* and the North end of this is the Grand-Jury Room; which, at other times, is used by the Corporation.

The Judges, who always hold the *Lent* Assizes here, have frequently complained of the badness and inconvenience of these Courts; and, it must be confessed, not without cause: for they make but a bad figure, when compared with the magnificent buildings «f this nature, which have been erected, both in this and some other Counties.

The present Town Gaol, belongs to the Bailiff and Corporation; and Debtor are committed by process issuing out of the Court of Record.

A Court is held here every Saturday; but application for the *Sixpences,* or a *Supersedeas,* can only be made at a Court in Term time, upon a fourteen days' notice. The Prisoner, on application, obtains a Rule for the Plaintiff-Creditor to appear at the next Court; who may then object to the Prisoners' *Schedule,* and will have till the next Court to make his objections, which if not satisfactory, the Prisoner will be ordered his sixpences, or superseded.

For poor Debtors here is one room on the gronnd-floor, 18 feet by 14, and *6* feet *6* inches high: adjoining to which is a narrow slip, or lobby passage, 14 feet long by 3 feet wide; with an iron-grated window looking towards the Street, where the *Prisoner solicits Relief from casual Charity.*

In this Town-Gaol I found in *January* 1802, one *Richard Holt,* confined for a debt of *six Guineas,* for rent: and the costs incurred against him had amounted to *three pounds, three shillings, and ninepence.* This poor man told me that "he had maintained a wife, and brought up *ten children,* without Parochial assistance; but, having been in confinement eleven weeks, his wife, and the three youngest children were then in the Work-house."

Is it not to be regretted, that where our Laws ordain a *loss of Liberty,* there should be no respect shewn to *Merit,* in the *conduct* of a *Debtor?* This victim to misfortune had surely an abundant claim to the attentions of pity; for here was *no Allowance* whatever, to provide him needful food, nor even water accessible to the Prisoner.

s s

In the narrow passage above-mentioned, (the " *Straits of Misery,"* as I might well term it,) was this Prisoner standing to beg; and, but for the casual interference of sympathy in others, could no longer have existed than human nature can do without food.

The Corporation of Kingston supplies neither sustenance nor bedding. The Keeper, however, had humanely supplied the solitary Debtor with a bedstead and mattress, a blanket, and a rug; in return for which the Prisoner did any such little jobs as the nature of his confinement would admit of.

Above-stairs here are four rooms; one of which is well furnished, for those Prisoners who can pay 7. *6d.* per week; another, with inferior accommodation, at *2s. 6d.* and a third for a Turnkey to lodge in, andt guard the Felons, who, during the County Assize, are lodged in the fourth room, and sleep on the floor. The Keeper informed me, that for two or three days together, four and twenty Felons had been crowded here, like sheep in a Market-pen, into a room of 19 feet long by *9* feet wide. It must have been judged needful to secure them there; and accordingly, they were fastened down to staples fixed in the.floor, by a ponderous iron chain, run through the main link of their fetters; one blanket being allowed to each Felon for his bedding.

The Gaoler at Kingston is a SherifTs Officer, and keeps a Publick House, the sign of *The Hand and Mace.* He told me he would gladly give up the Publick House, if the Corporation would allow him a fixed Salary. He appears to be a humane man, and sensible of the impropriety of a *Gaoler's* keeping a house of that description. Considering, however, that here is no allowance, it must operate to the advantage of the poor Debtor, by exciting commiseration from those who frequent it. A licenced Beerhouse should never be made a prudential article in any Prison-establishment, nor rendered an Ingredient of its Finance.

In the *Town-Hall* is the following ancient and very curious

"Table Of Fees.

It is dated the 10th of December, 1603, and confirmed by Charles, Lord

Howard, &c. High Steward of the said Town; Sir Edward Coke, AttorneyGeneral, and learned Steward of the Court of the said Town; the two Bailiffs; the Recorder, with the Assent of the Freemen.

"These are the several Fees of the Bailiffs, Town-Clerks, Attorneys, Sergeants, Gaolers, Cryers, Chamber-Fees; and, at last, Orders to be observed. £. s. d.

For every one arrested, wanting Sureties, and sent to Gaol--0 2 0

For every one sent to Ward, upon Commandment, or arrested for a

Trifle, or being very poor, not above- -------0 0 8 See under the head " Bath City Gaol," Page 28.

For the Fee of *the Irons* of every one Committed for Felony, or *£. s. d.*

Suspicion of Felony, or for any other heinous crime----020 For arresting any Freeman of this Town, inhabitant within the watch----------------0Q6

For the Attorney's Fee upon Evidence delivering to a Jury, when there is no other Counsel-----------026

Every Counsellor's Fee in this Court- --------06 8."

The above Items are now scarcely legible; and it was with some difficulty I transcribed them for this publication.

No court-yard. No water accessible. The whole Prison not white-washed, but out of repair, and dirty. The Clauses against Spirituous Liquors are hung up; but not the Act of Parliament for preserving the Health of Prisoners.

A *New Town Gaol* is building, and Sessions House to adjoin, which are in great forwardness at this time—1810.

KINGSTON UPON THAMES. *The House of' Correction.*

Keeper, *William Matthews,* now *Thomas Fricher.* Salary, 85/.

Fees, *Felons,* 3.V. *4d.* Misdemeuners, *6s. 8d.*

Chaplain, none, nor any religious attentions.

Surgeon, Mr. *Hemming,* now Mr. *William Roots.*

Salary, 10/. 10. and also *Gl. 6s.* for travelling charges, to make his Report at the Quarter Sessions, of the state of the Prisoners.

Number of Prisoners, 1802, June 19th,----22. 1807, Sept. 16th,----1 1805, June 30th,----14 1810, June 23d,----14

Allowance, by the County, *one Pound of Bread* each per day, sent in from the Baker's, in loaves of that weight.

The above seems too scanty a Prison Dole, where no nutritious liquid is allowed but water.

REMARKS.

Here is a house for the Keeper, and distinct Wards for Men and Women, with separate court-yards also, work-sheds, and pumps. Each Ward has two lower rooms, standing three steps above the ground, and two other rooms over them.

The *Men's court-yard* is 59 feet by 50. The *Women's* 46 feet by 36 -*T* with a bathing-tub in each.

The Men's room is 16 feet by 14, and 9 feet high; the Women's about 15 feet square. Every room planked round; one chimney in each, and two windows, with shutters, and iron bars; but no glass, except in two apartments assigned for the *Sick.*

Here is also a room (very properly separated from all the rest) for *faulty Apprentices* or *Servants;* which has afire-place, and is about 8 feet by 11, and 8 feet high.

The County allows straw only for the Prisoners to sleep on. The present Keeper furnishes beds at *2s.* each per week, for the first fortnight, and *is. 6d.* per week afterwards; and two sleep together.

The Act for Preservation of Health, and Clauses against Spirituous Liquors are conspicuously hung up. And tha Prison is clean.

Of the twenty-two Prisoners in the Kingston Bridewell, at my visit in 1802, eleven had been *committed to hard labour.* For this good purpose there is provided in every court-yard a convenient work-shed: yet, *not one of them was employed, nor any appearance of attention paid to the means of Industry!* "Thus it is," as Sir George Paul observes, "that the operation of the Law seems rather to *resent. the Injury,* than to *correct the Offender* There is little hope of amendment, where there is no

possibility of industry: The pennyless Offender, committed *till he pays a Fine,* is denied the exercise of his art and industry, to enable him to regain his Liberty. Of this Class are those for the smallest offences against the Crown, Excise, Ecclesiastical, or Game Laws." I have met with it even for *Angling in a River.*

By 14 Eliz. Cap. 5, and 12 Geo. II. it is enacted, That "Prisoners shall be provided by the *County Rate, '8lc* By 19 Cha. II.and 12 Geo. II. Cap. 29, "Justices, in their Sessions, may provide *a Stock of Materials* for setting the poor to work."

The Vagrant Act, 17 Geo. II. requires "That two Justices visit the Houses of Correction twice, or oftener, if need be, in every year; and examine into the estate and management thereof; and report, &e. And that the Justices, at Quarter Sessions, impose Fines and Penalties on the Governors or Masters who *do not keep their Prisoners to hard labaitr* and punish and correct them, according to the directions of the Warrants, &.c."

The work-shed in the Men's court-yard has been recently enclosed, and converted into a kitchen or day-room, with a fire-place, and proper cooking utensils.

Of the fourteen Prisoners iuJune 1810, twelve were sentenced to *hard labour* but *no employment jirovided* for any.

Of the four Women Prisoners, two, viz. *Elizabeth Smith,* aged *26,* and *Catheiherine Burke,* aged 25, were chained together, by a horse-lock round the leg of each, with three feet length of chain; and fastened by another chain, at night, ta two iron staples fixed in the floor, at *6 feet distance.* These Women, it seems, had been detected in an attempt to break through the Prison wall, for which their only implements were a knife and fork. One of their fellow Prisoners, however, gave notice of it by a letter to the Keeper, which I read; and they were thus prevented. They had been in this state of punishment a month, and begged hard to be released, or to be ironed singly. Their fetters were taken off; and I think their sufferings will prevent any cause for a like infliction.

It is scarcely necessary to add, that this House of Correction is seldom, if ever, visited by the Magistrates.

Before I dismiss the subject, let me observe, that the door which heretofore opened from the Men's court into that of the Women is now bricked up; and the Women's rooms have blinds, which effectually prevent their overlooking the Men's court, as formerly.

Withinside the gate is painted, and put up as follows:

"No Admittance in Church-time.

"No Garnish to be taken.

"If any Prisoner shall be guilty of profane cursing or swearing, or any indecent behaviour, complain to the Keeper.

"Whoever defaces this Board will be prosecuted.

"By Order of the Magistrates."

I found the Prison very clean; but no firing is allowed for the Winter.

The Corporation have lately purchased a large commodious well-built mansion, called *Clatton-House,* with spacious premises and garden-ground adjoining; on the site of which they are now erecting two convenient Courts for the Assize; which, communicating with the centre building, gives every prospect of accommodation and comfort to the Judges, the Gentlemen of the County on the Grand Jury, the Professional Advocates and Gentlemen of the Bar; the Witnesses, and all the attendants on such occasions.

The improvements, it is hoped, will be further extended to the building of a *Neiv Gaol* contiguous, in the room of the loathsome place of confinement now used by the Corporation.

KIRCUDBRIGHT. *Scotland.*

Gaoler, *Gurney Tuck.* Salary, *20l.*

Fees; for Felons, none. For Debtors, 5. on Caption, paid by the Incarcerator, and *2d.* a night from a Burgess. Non Burgess, *Ad.* a night.

No Chaplain, nor any religious attentions. No Surgeon.

Number of Prisoners, Debtors, Two. Felons, None.

Allowance, to Debtors, as alimented. Criminals, *6d.* a day.

REMARKS.

It is intended to convert part of the Old Castle into a Prison, and the walls of it still remain entire. The present Gaol has two rooms for Debtors, and as many for Criminals; to which there are fire-places, and coals are allowed. Wooden bedsteads, with chaff beds, two blankets and a rug, are supplied to Criminals; but Debtors find their own bedding.

Felons are confined here for a night or two only, till removed to Dumfries, 27 miles distant, for Trial.

No court-yard. A half-tub serves as a sewer. Water is daily brought in by the Keeper.

KIRTON. *Lincolnshire.*

The Bridewell.

Keeper, *John Parkin,* now *Samuel Lee.* Salary, 70/. Fees, none.

Chaplain, Rev. *Joseph Stockdale.*

Duty, Prayers once a week. Salary, *20l.*

Surgeon, Mr. *George Foster.* Salary, *20l.*

Number of Prisoners, 1809, Sept. 6th,—29; and 3 Children.

Allowance, formerly, was four-pence a day; but now 3. *lod.* per week each, in bread, meat, oatmeal, salt, and potatoes.

REMARKS.

The Keeper's house fronts the West; and on the right of the entrance is the visiting Magistrates' room, the windows of which command the Men's court, of 27 feet by 22, where there are two work-rooms, each *26* feet by 12, furnished with looms, twist-mills, and spinning-machines. On the left is a conrt-yard, and two work-rooms, of a similar description, which are inspected by the windows of the Keeper's kitchen; and adjoining is an oven and bake-house.

Here are eight solitary courts, *16* feet by 9, with a cell in each, about 8 feet square, and a hemp-block. The cells are lighted and ventilated by a grated window, 2 feet 6 inches square; and in every door there is one inspecting-wicket. Also three other court-yards, with day-rooms and fire-places, to which coals are allowed during the six Winter months; and furnished with benches to sit upon, and shelves for putting by provisions.

On the *Chamber Story* are twenty eight sleeping-cells, 8 feet *6* each by 7 feet 6, and 10 feet high, furnished with wood bedsteads, straw, a blanket, and a rug each. Two large rooms, with fire-places and glazed windows, are here set apart as *InJirmaries.*

The bath room is nearly 16 feet square, with a cistern for water, and a copper in it. There is no water laid on to any of the courts: it is brought daily to the Prisoners by the Keeper. The sewers are conveniently placed, and not offensive.

A flagged lobby, or passage, 53 yards long and 8 feet wide, runs from the Women's court-yard, the whole length of the Prison, and separates the work-rooms from the Solitary Courts, &c. A door likewise opens into it, through which Prisoners are brought to the bar for trial, without bustle or inconvenience.

Here is no *Chapel;* but the Sessions House, a very handsome building, under the same roof, is appropriated for Divine Service. Prisoners are supplied with religious books, and the Surgeon has a discretionary power to order them a change of diet, in case of sickness.

The Prisoners are employed in combing and spinning wool, and the portion which they receive of their earnings varies according to their deportment. In 1803, the amount of them was 26/. 0. *6d.* of which sum the Prisoners had one third, and the County the other two. An alteration in the working system then took place. In 1804, the earnings were 22/. 16s. *6d.* in 1805, 31/. 2. *6d.* in 1806, 46/. 18. 3«?. in 1807, 43/. 10. During this period, the Prisoners received no part of their earnings, except in clothes given them occasionally by the Magistrates.

At an adjourned Session, held 8th June, 1808, it was ordered, That every wellbehaved Prisoner should receive one half of his earnings on discharge; and the earnings up to Epiphany Sessions, 1809, amounted to 51/. *js. l%d.*

I could not help remarking, that though the large store-room was filled with wool, none of the Prisoners were at work upon it.

The present Keeper was to quit his situation at Lady Day 1810, and to be succeeded by *Samuel Lee.* The Act for Preservation of Health, and Clauses against Spirituous Liquors, both hung up; and the Prison clean.

KNARESBOROUGH. *Yorkshire.*
Castle Gaol for Debtors.
Gaoler, *William Ellison;* who officiates by a Deputy, *Edward Jeffery.* Salary, none. Fees, 6. *8d.* No Table.

Number of Debtors, 1800, May 17th, 1. 1S02, Jan. 28th, 2. 1802, Sept 2d, 0.

Allowance, none.

REMARKS.

This Gaol is in the honour or forest of Knaresborough; and the Liberty includes nineteen Townships, &c. It is the property of the Duke of *Devonshire,* lessee to his Majesty, and almost the only remains of a castle granted by King *Edward* III. to *John of Gaunt,* Duke of *Lancaster.* It formerly consisted of one room, 12 feet square, with a chimney, and glazed window; and an inner room 8 feet square, which had no window. A new gaol was built in 1794, wkhin the castle-yard.

This Prison now consists of two sleeping-rooms, each about 15 feet by 8, with lofty and arched cielings, in one of which there i9 a fire-place, and a sewer in one corner. The doors have each an iron cylinder, to admit the Debtors' provisions. The window, placed very high, is of a semi-circular shape, close glazed, and without a casement; so that I did not wonder to find the Prisoners had broken the glass, to prevent suffocation. The only place for the admission of air is an aperture in the wall, 9 inches by 2-, and even that is almost stopped up by an iron bar one inch thick, placed lengthwise. Ventilation might be introduced by an iron-grated window in the wall towards the castle; and it would have this farther convenience, that the Debtor might see his friends, and receive victuals, without the trouble of taking the Gaoler from his work-shop, and *passing through six doors* to gain admittance.

A begging-box, suspended from this iron-grated window, would in all probability compensate for *No Allowance';* by soliciting the notice of the numerous Gentry, who resort hither, to see the ruins of this once-famous Castle. At present it bears no appearance of a Prison, and thousands may go away, without knowing it to be a place of confinement. Here is a small flagged court, 17 feet by 8, and enclosed by a very high wall; but of which, the woman told me, the Prisoners had seldom the use, on account of its not being under the Keeper's view. No water, but what is fetched from the Town. When the Prison was built, a door opened into the Castle Yard; but this I found bricked up.

There is something so affecting in the following detail, that I cannot help transcribing it here, though published in the third edition of my " Account of Debtors:"

By a letter to me, dated 29th June, 1800, the only Prisoner here was William Elmsley, (committed for Debt 30th June, 1799); who says " Any person wishing to see him, upon the Gaoler's leave, must pass through *six doors.* He has only the yard above-described to walk in; the window and wall so high, that he has very little light or air. That, since he came in, he had a fellow Prisoner; but he only lived ten weeks. He himself had been ill for seven weeks; and the preservation of his life was owing to the gratuiteus attendance of Mr. Day, Surgeon at Harrowgate, and Mr. Dent, Surgeon at Knaresborough." Ehnsley's debt was 17/. 5. and the Costs amounted to *11l. js. ld.*

Neither the Act for Preservation of Health, nor the Clauses against Spirituous Liquors, were hung up in 1802; but I found the Gaol both light and clean.

KNARESBOROUGH.
The Prison for Town Debtors.
This Prison is vulgarly called *Nine Holes,* from as many spaces betwixt the qine bars in the window, which give it all the light it can receive. *t*

It stands under the Town Hall, and consists of one wretched room, 12 feet square, and *6* feet high; with the above-mentioned window, of 17 inches by (?.

Here is no court-yard. No allowance. No water! In so sad a place a» this, some years ago, two Debtors, named *Harrison* and *IVetherhftlly* were confined six months.

"Formerly," says Mr. Howard, "the common sewer of the Town ran through this Prison, uncovered; and an Officer, who was confined in it for a few days only, in the spirit of precaution, took with him a dog, to defend himself from the vermin. The dog was soon destroyed, and the Prisoner's face much disfigured by them. The floor, however, is now paved, and the drain is covered."

The Prison very dirty. At my visit, 2d of September, 1802, there were no Prisoners.

KNARESBOROUGH
Town Gaol, for Felons.
The Town-Constable is the Keeper of this Prison, which is also denominated *Small Ears"*

It stands under the landing-place of a flight of stone steps, leading up to the Town Hall; and is comprised in one room only, of 13 feet 8 inches by 5 feet, with a brick-arched roof, This, like the former Gaol, is nasty. No court-yard, no water.

I was informed, that at the Quarter Sessions there are sometimes five or six Prisoners, Men and Women, confined in this place for a night or two. There were po Prisoners, however, at my visit here on the 2d of Sept. 1802.

LANCASTER CASTLE. *The County Gaol and Bridewell.*
Gaoler, *John Higgin.*

Salary, 500/. and 250/. to the Turnkeys under him. For Conveyance of

Transports to Portsmouth, or Woolwich, one shilling per mile.

Fees and Garnish laudably abolished.

Chaplain, Rev. *John ffoodrow*; now Rev. *Joseph Rowley.*

Dutv, Sunday, Prayers and Sermon; Wednesday and Friday, Prayers. Salary, 50/. and in addition to it, 30/. *per annum,* as Auditor of Accounts. From the Dutchy, *4L* and also from the Sheriff, 15. for his attendance upon every Protestant Malefactor who suffers Death. Roman Catholicks are attended by a Priest of their own Persuasion, who receives the like sum from the Sheriff.

Surgeon, Mr. *Baxendale.*

Salary, 84/. and Medicines furnished by the County.

Number of Prisoners, Debtors. Felons, &c. Lunaticks.
1802, Sept. 22d,----76 90-----0 1805, Oct. 24th,----74 58-----4 1809, Nov. 7th,--.. 116-----97-----5.

Allowance, to Debtors, one shilling per week in bread, and ten pounds of potatoes. To Felons, &c. six pounds of good wheaten bread, ten pounds of potatoes, 2-J-pounds of oatmeal per week, and one pennyworth of butter daily. On Sunday, half a pound of boiled beef, and a quart of broth.

REMARKS.

This Castle, first built for a place of defence by the Romans, afterwards became the Palace, or feudal residence of the Dukes of *Lancaster;* and at an early period, was converted into a *County Gaol.*

The situation is elevated and healthy. The Gaoler s house, which is a handsome building, and well situate for commanding a view of the spacious court-yard, fills np the space between the gate-way and the Well-Tower to the right. The Female Debtors' Prison is a room within the gate-way, and their court-yard is occupied in common with the Men Debtors.

Its ancient British name was Caerwirdd, i. e. *Castra vxridia,* or " Green Fortress," from the verdure of the Hill on which the Castle stands. Its present appellation is from *Lon,* or *Loyn,* the name of the River adjacent, and *Castra,* from an encampment. Some have inclined to derive it from the British *Llan,* a Church, and *Castra;* the Church and Castle forming one groupe of buildings. The area of that part of the Castle-Yard which is appropriated to Debtors only, contains about 2792 square yards. On the West Side is a large arcade, for exercise in wet weather, or air in Summer; and over it are six day-rooms, each 14 feet 9 inches by 12 feet 3. In a wing adjoining are three rooms, each 40 feet by 14: that on the ground-floor is used as a workshop for Debtors.

In the Well-Tower are four rooms; one of which is 20 feet square, and the average size of the others, 23 feet by 11.

In the Gate-way Tower are eight rooms, and an apartment for the Turnkeys: over which is a room for Debtors, called the *Pigeon Box,* 33 feet 8 inches by 12 feet 10; and two very spacious Reception-Rooms, where diseased Prisoners are put, until examined by the Surgeon.

Above the entrance is the ancient *Court-Room,* now occupied by the Female Debtors, in size 25 feet 8 inches by 15 feet 3; also a narrow winding staircase to the attick story, on which are three ample rooms, of about 33 feet each by 16.

Every Debtor, on his Commitment, pays 7. *6d.* towards a stock of coals, and *2s.* for pots and pans. Formerly the Magistrates allowed a mop for each room; but from the insolence and extravagance of some of the Debtors, that indulgence is now discontinued. When a poor Debtor cannot pay for coals, he generally does the domestick work of the room instead of it; and if he cannot immediately pay for a bed, he obtains half a bed on credit, which is occasionally paid for by the Keeper, out of the Charity Fund.

When tire number of Debtors does not exceed seventy or eighty, many sleep in single beds; but when more, they are under the necessity of assigning a bed for two persons. At my visit there were only *three* single beds in the whole of the Debtors' apartments.

All the Wards are free; and poor Debtors, who hire beds from the Town, pay from six pence to eighteen pence a week for the use of one.

The Male Felons' part of the Prison consists of four airy and well-paved courts, each containing about 238 square yards, for different classes. Each of these has a shed, and a day-room about 21 feet by 12, with sixteen cells to each, in two noble towers, making in the whole, sixty-four; every cell S feet S by *6* feet 8, and 8 feet high.

The Prison department for Female Felons occupies the space from the gate-way to the Dungeon-Tower on the left; and corresponds with the Gaoler's house towards the Castle-Yard. It contains two night-rooms in the Dungeon Tower, each 23 feet 9 by 15 feet; a day-room under the Infirmary; a wash-house adjoining; three night-cells also, under the Infirmary, of 8 feet by *6* feet *6;* six smaller ditto, behind the new workshops; six working-rooms, 15 feet 9 by 11 feet; and, betwixt the gateway and the Dungeon Tower, two well-ventilated rooms for the sick, of 30 feet by 21.

Between the *outer* wall of the Prison, and day-wards, there is a solitary day-room for refractory Prisoners, of 21 feet by 12; and three solitary cells, which being rather damp, are seldom used. Also a warm and cold bath.

The boundary walls of the four court-yards converge to a point, where the Turnkey's lodge is very judiciously placed, so as to have a complete command of the whole. The Prisoners may thus converse with their Friends under full inspection, without being admitted into the interior of the Gaol; and strangers may likewise see the Prisoners without being incommoded.

Every Prisoner on the Criminal Side is allowed a straw mat, a straw or hair bed, three blankets, a quilt or coverlet, and receives also one third of his earnings: The profits on their labour are sometimes equal to the expence of their maintenance.

I cannot find a better place than the present, for the following *Statement of j &riwiial Earnings* of the Crown-Prisoners, clear of every expence attending the System of their Labour.
1795, 168/. 13. *4d.* 1800, 267/. 8. *6$d.* 1801, 238/. 14s. *0$d.*
1802, 287/. 1. *9d.* 1803, 343. 15. 11. 1804, 274/. *6s. 2d.*
1805, 184/. 10. *Ad.* 1806, 15 *ll.* 3-10§rf. 1807, 175/. 18. *id.*
1808, 229/. 1. *4$d.* 1809, 262/. 18. *3d.*
Total, Paid to the Treasurer of the County, 2583. 11. 10.

The Bridewell Prisoners, and some of the Felons, are kept in the Great Tower, which has a small open court adjoining. In this Tower there are two large apartments, used as day and sleeping-rooms; the first of them, 55 feet by 26, is over the Chapel; the other, 43 feet by 25, is called " the *Quaker's Room,"* because, as it is said, when these people were so cruelly persecuted in the Seventeenth Century, vast numbers of them were confined in it: Also three sleeping-cells, 10 feet each by 7. The work shops adjoining to this court are, the Old Shire-Hall, for carding and spinning, 43 feet by 25; three shops for weaving, 40 feet each by 14; seven small ones, about 9 feet square; and the Task-Master's day and ware-room.

That part of the Great Tower, or Citadel, formerly called the *Lungess,* is now the *Chapel,* 55 feet long by 26; in which there is a commodious gallery for the Debtors, with seven separate divisions in the area below, for Felons, &c. who are placed according to their classes, and out of sight of each other.

I remarked with pleasure, that the Men and Women *Felons* were particularly clean at Chapel, when I attended Divine Service on Wednesday 22d September 1802, and was informed that they were obliged to wash their hands and face every morning, before they can receive their allowance. The whole number *(ninety)* were present at Prayers, except two or three, employed on necessary business. Their behaviour wa9 silently attentive, and the countenances of all clearly shewed

I their love and reaped for *Mt. tliggin,* the Gadfef; *Whb;* to great humanity and firmness of character, adds those religious regards which do him honour.

Of the *Debtors,* on the above day, 1 was sorry to observe, that only *two* out of seventy-six attended Prayers; although the following Order is stuck up in various parts of the Prison. The republication of it in this manner, and in a work like this, may have its good effect in other Districts, which it would not be difficult to mention.

"At the General Quarter-Sessions of the Peace, held at *Lancaster,* in and for the County Palatine of Lancaster, the 15th day of July, 1777 in the 17 th, year of Geo. III.

"Whereas it appears to this Court, on the representation of the Keeper of the Gaol of the Castle of Lancaster, that several Prisoners in his Custody, being Members of the Church of England, and having no lawful excuse, make a common practice of absenting themselves from Divine Service, performed in the said Gaol, and misbehaving themselves during Service:

It is therefore Ordered by this Court, that if any Prisoner or Prisoners confined in the said Castle, (except Roman Catholicks and Quakers) and having no lawful excuse, shall absent him, her, or themselves from attending Divine Service within the said Castle, or shall in any way misbehave; such Prisoner or Prisoners shall immediately be deprived of the County Allowance, until further orders to the contrary.

AMD it is further Ordered, That the Treasurer of the said County Stock shall, immediately upon receiving a complaint from the said Keeper, against any Prisoner or Prisoners, strike his, her, or their name or names out of his book; and forbear to pay such Prisoner or Prisoners any more money, until further Order,

Kenyon, Clerk of the Peace.

N. B. Whereas, many of the *Debtor's,* of late, have absented themselves from attending Divine Service; This is therefore to give them Notice, that for the future, the above Rule of Court will be strictly put in execution." List Of Charitable Legacies

To the Debtors Imprisoned in *Lancaster Castle.*

"From Mrs. *Henrietta Rigby's* Executor, to twelve of the most ne-£. s. d. cessitous and well-behaved Prisoners, five shillings each; paid by the Mayor of *Lancaster,* on the first day of March every year,-300 From Mrs. *Langton,* paid by Lawrence Rawsthorn, Esq. at each

Assize------------------200

From Sir *Tlwmas Gerrard,* of Gartswood, paid by Mr. Pinsick,

Steward to the present Family; due about 1 st August--8 0 0

Paid, under a Decree of the Court of Chancery of this County, out of an Estate in *Skermisdale* called *Sand,* late belonging to *Peter Latham,* deceased; distributed every August Assize, by the Trustees of the said Peter Latham, or their order j paid by Messrs. Greaves and Co. of Preston--------

By the Will of *William Edmondson,* of Outhwaite, half the rent of a field in Scotforth, purchased by the money left for such purpose by the said Will; paid by the County Treasurer in bread. N. B. This field is now, (October 1805), in the tenure or occupation of Mr. G. Marshall, at the yearly rent of five pounds; and the other half of the rent is paid to the Prisoners at *Preston* -------2 10 0

From Mrs. *Abigail Rigbrfs* Executors, paid by the Mayor of Lancaster. every St. Thomas's Day-------------20 0. "

A spirit of restlessness had at one period introduced itself into this, as well as many other Prisons, by forming *Committees of Association,* or *Secrecy,* as they termed it; and by correspondence with others, equally misadvised; by which they were led to believe that a Gaoler had no controul, and might even be set at defiance. It was unfortunate to be thus unwise, and even, for a time, occasioned an abridgement to the Debtors, of some of those comforts, which the liberality of the County had provided for them; and which their errors and distresses failed not to claim, from the humanity of the virtuous and more fortunate part of mankind.

In the excellent management of this Prison, which, from its situation in a very populous and maritime County, is seldom without atrocious offenders, there is the most clear and demonstrative proof how much more *Humanity* and *Firmness* operate to promote penitence and reformation, than *Harshness* and *Severity;* which last, as I have often witnessed, make the Criminal only more desperate, and tend rather to harden the heart, than reform the manners. Of the 90 Felons, &c. at my visit here in 1802, not one was in irons; although amongst them was one committed for a double Murder, but of which he was afterwards acquitted. At my next call, in October 1805, not one of the 58 was in irons. They were all usefully and peaceably at work. In short, no Criminal was ever fettered at any time when I have been here. There are irons indeed, provided for the refractory, *in terrorem,* but

I never saw any *used*. Such is the force of well-tempered authority, the influence of example, and the impressive weight of steady, calm, and active attention to duty.

The buildings for the convenience of this Gaol, have added much to the appearance of the *Castle,* and in some parts are singularly constructed, without either wood, plaister, or arches; the whole, both inside and out, being finished with hewn stone. The Architect, Mr. *Harrison,* (of whose professional abilities the Castle of *Chester* will stand a lasting monument) has here availed himself with much judgment of that fine material, which Nature has so plentifully provided in the neighbourhood; and of which is thus formed one of the strongest and most durable Felons' Gaols in this Country.

The halls and County offices at the West end of the Castle, in the style and utility of building, do credit to the taste of those Gentlemen who promoted them; and it is an addition, both to the convenience and safety of the Gaol, that the approach to them is now removed out of the Castle-Yard.

The front of these buildings is a beautiful and regular piece of Gothick Architecture; comprehending a County and Crown-Hall; Grand and Petty Jury, and Record Rooms, with offices for Prothonotary, "Clerk of the Crown, &c. all covered by connected roofs; and so contrived, that from them water is conveyed into the general reservoir in the Castle Yard, for the use of all the Prisoners.

In both Halls, the Bench, the Bar, and the Audience, are placed in full view of each other, as in every other Court of Justice they ought to be. This is effected by leaving an area behind the bar, and raising the Auditors one above another, upon broad steps, in the manner of the Greek and Roman Theatres: thus at once producing a general accommodation, and exempt, in a great degree, from that pressure of crowds, so constantly experienced in other Courts, where the bar and the floor are on the same level. This, I presume, likewise, in a great measure checks or prevents the noise and disturbance arising from the conversation too often carried on by those, who can neither see the Courts, nor hear the business of them; but are concealed from the view of the Bench, as in the old Halls, and most other Courts of Justice.

The *County Hall* is a hemi-polygon, ornamented with light handsome Gothick Columns, that support a groined roof; and capable of containing near sixteen hundred persons. The *Crown Hall* is a spacious oblong, likewise in the Gothick taste; and has a commodious gallery for the accommodation of Ladies. Great attention has been paid in both, to the conveniencies of light and air; and, as far as possible, to prevent any echo from confounding the voice. The *Grand Jury Room* is circular, large and convenient; and its windows command a fine view of that stupendous range of Westmoreland and Cumberland Mountains, which surround the Lakes. The New Terrace, also, while it forms one of the approaches to the Halls, affords the same grand and delightful prospect.

The County Hall is supported by massy pillars, forming a noble arcade; the foundations of which are 18 or 20 feet deep, where the moat anciently was, that surrounded the Castle. This arcade, especially in bad weather, at Assize-time, will be a very useful promenade for the many, who are then generally drawn together by curiosity, and not unfrequently crowd and disturb the Courts, which afford no other place of shelter than the Halls.

Within the arcade is an arched room, that may be made good use of as a guardroom, &c. for the County or other Militia. At present, both it and the room adjacent are occupied by the Joiners.

These excellent edifices, together with the *New Chapel, in* the Great Tower, ren-. der this one of the most complete and healthy of our County Gaols, as well as the finest groupe of Castle-building in the Kingdom. The style of the modern erections is very carefully adapted to the old parts of the structure, and to the manner of building at the period in which they were supposed to be done. And they have this advantage, likewise, over many of the same kind, that from the solidity of their construction without timber, they will be little liable to injury from fire or time, the most rapidly or surely destructive of all agents.

The ground in front of the New Halls being laid open, very much improves this side of the Castle; and since the judicious liberality of the Magistrates has so far improved the venerable pile, it is most ardently to be wished that it may be extended to a removal of those old houses and unsightly cottages, which so much block up and disgrace that magnificent specimen of Gothick Architecture, the *Gate-way Tower,* as well as other parts both of the old and new buildings.

Since my visit in October 1S05, a *new Tower* has been built here, between the Well-Tower and the Felons' Wards. It has on the ground-floor an excellent kitchen, fitted up with suitable conveniences, and a set of boilers on a new con-r struction. Over it is a spacious day-room, with a fire-place, a pump, and watercloset; and above this room are ten airy and well-ventilated sleeping-cells, eaoh 9 feet by *6,* and 9 feet high. This last-mentioned compartment of the Prison is intended and used as a place of separation for those Criminals, who are committed and detained as King's evidence: But at my last visit, in 1809, it was occupied by two of the most unruly of the five *Lunaticks,* who had been here for some time; and concerning whom I shall presently add a few observations, not unworthy, I hope, of attention, from their evident importance.

The *Rules* and *Regulations* for the government of the Criminal Side of this Prison do great credit to their composers, and are printed and stuck up in different parts of the Gaol. Convicts for Transportation */tave not* here the King's allowance of *c2s. 6d.* per week.

§£3'' I cannot omit to mention, that at the request of the Magistrates of the County of Lancaster, and with the ready consent of the Sheriff, in the year 1784, Fees for Debtors were abolished, and a more adequate Salary was liberally granted to the Keeper in their stead.

Of the 116 *Debtors* that were here at my last visit, six I found had been comButted by the Manchester Court of Requests; and Manchester being 55 mile distant from Lancaster, the Court allows the Serjeant escorting them *2l. 15. con'duct money* for each. This expence, together with the Costs, are payable by *the* Creditor; so that, in some instances, the amount of the original Debt is exceeded in a triple degree. In the case of one *Nancy Evans,* whose Debt was but *twelve shillings,* I learnt that the Costs, &c. were *3l. 8s. 2d.* A more than flyefoM exceeding of the original demand!

The worthy Chaplain is empowered, at the expence of the County, to purchase Bibles and Common Prayer Books, and distribute them at his discretion for the instruction of the Prisoners.

Mr. *Baxendale,* the humane Surgeon, is frequent in his visits, and particularly attentive to the sick. He makes a regular entry of the state of his patients, in a book kept for that very useful purpose.

The Act for the Preservation of Health, and Clauses against Spirituous Liquors, are conspicuously hung up; and the Prison is kept exceedingly clean.

Excellent, however, as this Gaol is, there cannot but occur some alterations to the attentive eye, which would considerably improve it; and which I beg leave therefore respectfully to suggest.

I. A private avenue for the Gaoler, into his seat at Chapel, would be much better, for obvious reasons, than through the common door of entrance. This might easily be managed, by a slight change in the present distribution of the seats.

If. The place in the room under the Shire-Hall, where the boiler now stands, is dark and inconvenient. There is a large space of ground unoccupied, near the first Ward, which would admit of a good kitchen; with a *few* rooms for *Lunatichs,* or for work-shops, that might be aired by the kitchen flue. By this small addition, a greater degree of separation might also be obtained, for the work-folks, during their hours of labour.

III. And, though last, not of least importance, there is no suitable recess yet provided, where a person deranged in mind can be kept separate from other, *selfcreated* Prisoners. At my visit Oct. 1805, there were no less than *Jive Maniacs,* two of whom were furiously frantick. From the want of proper places to keep them retired, I could conceive that the personal safety of the Keeper and his Turnkeys may, at some time or other, be greatly endangered.

I am anxious to leave it on record, That to my mind it appears very desirable, that Beings of this most pitiable description should be kept either in *an Hospital,* or as similar to it as possible: I mean, irf some retired seclusion; where, by medical aid, and a continuation of suitable treatment, they might be rendered far more comfortable than the best Regulations, even of Lancaster Castle, can afford.

LANCASTER.
The Town Gaol.
Keeper, the Town Sergeant.

There were no Prisoners at my visits, 22d Sept. 1802, Oct. 24th, 1805, and,Npv, 7th, 1809.. 1 REMARKS.

This temporary place of confinement is a room under the stair-case of the Town Hall, in size, 15 feet 8 inches by 11 feet 5, and 8 feet 10 inches high. It has a fire-place, with a window about 3 feet square, and contains two barrack bedsteads.

The door has an aperture 12 inches square: and over it, on a stone Tablet, is inscribed, *"Executio Juris nullifacit Injuriam.*
1669."

Prisoners are sent hither before examination. When a Debtor is taken in custody 011 a Borough Process, the Officer is under the necessity of keeping his Prisoner in the Town Sergeant's house, until the business is settled.

LAUNCESTON. Cornwall.
The County Gaol for Felons.
Gaoler, *John Mules,* now *Christopher Mules.* Salary, 167.
Fees, 13. *Ad.'* Conveyance of Transports, 1$. per mile.

Chaplain, Rev. *Charles Lethbridge;* now Rev. *John Row. ..*
Duty, only once a week, yet sometimes omitted. Salary, 20l.
Surgeon, Mr. *Roe.* Salary, *16l:*
Number of Prisoners, Oct. 18th, l8C, One. Sept. 27th 1S06, Three.

Allowance, twenty ounces of brown bread daily, (one gallon of bran only being taken out of a bushel of wheat,) *cut from the Keeper's loaf.* Half a pound of meat on Sundays, and every morning a pint of skimmed milk, which costs a half-penny. The Mayor sends weekly to the Prisoners one shilling's worth of best wheaten bread; the weight of which, in October 1803, was six pounds and a half. The County humanely allow coals for the common day-room.
REMARKS.

This Gaol, for Felons only, belonged formerly to the Constable of the Castle of Launceston: But it has since been purchased by the County; and in the year 1779, the sum of 500/. was, by the King's bounty, appropriated to it.

The building is small, the area within the boundary wall being only 100 feet by 50. On the left of the entrance are the Gaoler's apartments; on the right is a room about 37 feet square, with a fire-place, and two glazed windows. This is called the *Old Gaol,* and is assigned for Women Prisoners; who have in it three sleepingcells, the largest 7 feet 6 inches square, the two others of the same length, by 4; feet 6, and 7 feet 6 inches high. Divine Service, when performed, is in a room in the Keeper's house.

The Men's Gaol is down eleven steps: their day-room, 17 feet square, has a flagged floor, with benches to sit on, a large iron-grated window, and a fire-place, to which the County considerately allow.coals; but it is, notwithstanding, very damp..'

A passage, 27 feet long, and 5 feet G inches wide, opens into the day-room, and contains four sleeping-cells, of 8 feet by 6 feet 6, and 8 feet 4 inches high. All the cells have boarded floors, laid with straw, two blankets, and a rug.

Close to, and communicating with the above day-room, is the court-yard, 50 feet by 30, laid down in grass, with a pump, and sewer.

The Women Prisoners have also a court-yard, about 37 feet square, with a sewer; but, having a mud bottom only, and unsupplied with water, this court-yard is seldom, if ever used.

Ducks and fowls were kept in both courts, at my visit in September 1S0(7; an accompaniment, which, in a Prison, might always much better be avoided: It occasions dirt and negligence, as I have experienced, and sometimes noticed, in several other Gaols.

The Dungeons of the Old Gaol were filled with lumber when I made my visits; and there was no appearance of their having ever been used since the new cells were built.

No Memorial in the Gaol, of the Gift of Bread allotted weekly, and sent in regularly by the Mayor.

The Prison is kept clean. A woman is always hired to wash the Prisoners' linen. Transports here have the King's Allowance of *2s. 6d.* per week. The Act for Preserving the Health of Prisoners is *not hung tip*; nor the Clauses against their use of Spirituous Liquors.. $3 Although Chapel Duty here is but once a week, I was concerned to hear that in repeated instances it had been passed by, not for weeks only, but for several months together. That there were only *three Prisoners* in 1806, was not, surely. a ground for omission; and as the Gaoler also, and his family, were ever present, and could not quit the Gaol, they ought at least to have had the Prayers read, for which a due consideration is allowed. I neither make, nor can make any apology for noticing a remissness, which a sense of duty forbids me to conceal.

LAUNCESTON. *Cornwall.*
The Town Gaol.
Gaoler, the Town Sergeant. No Salary. No Fees. I have not met with any Debtors here at my several visits; and in 1806 the three Criminals were out upon Bail. Allowance, two-pence a day!
REMARKS.
This Gaol, called very appropriately " *The Dark House"* stands over the South Gate; and the ascent to it is by a flight of steps.

Debtors are sent hither by process issuing out of the Borough Court, for sums to any amount: a Court is held every three weeks.

The Prison is in a most filthy and dilapidated state. About a fortnight before my visit in 1803, a Debtor had made his escape very judiciously; and none have have been sent there since. Upon asking the Keeper when it had been cleaned and white-washed, I well remember his telling me " that he had frequently applied to the Mayor of Launceston to have it done; but the answer was, 'The *blacker* it is, the *better*: It has more the appearance of a *Gaol*""

The room over the gateway, 15 feet by 11, for *Criminals,* has an iron-grated window towards the street, with an inside shutter; and two sleeping-cells, which open into the room, each about 7 feet square, and 8 feet high; *the doors only Jour feet high, andfifteen inches wide.*

Over this room is another, 22 feet by 18, assigned as a Gaol for *Debtors 1* the only light it can possibly receive is from two opposite apertures in the wall, of about 3 feet by Q inches. And that light, as if envied the *quondam* inhabitants, almost totally annihilated, by an iron bar placed lengthwise; just enough to tantalize the insolvent victim of such obscurity! Straw lies scattered over the floor; and *fiere is a fire-place,* butno *fuel is allowed.* To recompense such denial of luxury, however, a half tub effectually supplies the place of a necessary.

No court-yard. No water! but the Constable brings it, when wanted, thrice a day.

LAUNCESTON. *Bridewell.* Keeper, the Master of the Work-house. Salary, *6I.*
It stands in the Work-house Yard; and consists of one room, and two sleeping-cells, for Women, and for Men; with straw on the boarded floors., The Allowance for Prisoners here is the same as for the *poor.* They are not permitted the use of the court-yard. No water accessible. The Prison very dirty.
LEEDS. *Vorkshire.*
The Town Gaol.
The Keeper is the Town Constable, and lives distant. Salary, 5/. 5.

1802, Aug. 17th, Prisoners, Three.
REMARKS.
This Gaol is for temporary confinement. It stands nearly in the centre of the Town; and consists of four rooms, about 12 feet long by 9 j and a small one, with barrack beds, and iron-grated windows, which front the street.
No fire-places: No court-yard: No water: No sewer.
LEICESTER. *The County Gaol.*
Gaoler, *John Simons;* afterwards *James Staples;* now (lSll) *Christopher Musson.* Salary, *130L*
Fees, as per Table. Besides which the Under-Sheriff demands *6s. 8d.* for his *liberate!* Felons' Fee of 13$. *4d.* each is paid by the County. For Conveyance of Transports, 8/. each.
Garnish, though prohibited, is generally exacted from a new comer.
Chaplain, Rev. Mr. *Anderson.* Salary, 60/.
Duty, Prayers four days in the week; Sermon on Sunday.
Surgeon, Mr. *Maule,* now Mr. *Laid lam.*
Salary, for Debtors and Felons, both in the Gaol and Bridewell, *25I.*
Number of Prisoners, Debtors. Felons, &c.
1800, March 28th,------18-------13.
1802, Jan. 20th, 4-------1 1803, Aug. 23d,------12--*11* 1805, Sept. 26th, 8-------12 1807, July 30th,-11 8 18og, Aug. 22d,------13-------17.
Allowance. One pound six ounces of bread, sent from the Baker's every other day, in loaves of two pounds twelve ounces each; and one quart of small daily.
REMARKS.
This COUNTY GAOL looks as it should do. It has a Prison-like appearance. The ingenious architect, Mr. *Money penny,* has shewn his knowledge of grand design bordering on the terrifick.

The noble stone face of the building extends 120 feet in front of the street, and near to it is the Free-School. The Gaoler s house is at one corner; and the Turnkey's lodge, which adjoins it, leads both to the Men-Felons' court-yard, and likewise, by a passage, to that of the Debtors.

It was first inhabited in 1703, and has four airy court-yards, with water in all; and a day-room to each. The court for Debtors is 74 feet by 32, and the day-room 29 feet by 13 feet *6* inches. For those on the Master's-side there are ten rooms, which the Keeper supplies with beds at *2s. 4d.* weekly for a single bed; and if two sleep together, l. *6d.* a week each. Common-side Debtors have a Free Ward, with ten good-sized sleeping-rooms over the Men-Felons' cells, to which they furnish their own beds. One room is set apart for an Infirmary, 30 feet by *16,* with opposite windows, and a fire-place.

The Men-Felons' court-yard is 59 feet by 30, with a day, or common mess-room, 23 feet by 13, which has a fire-place, a large table, and benches to sit on. They have also four sleeping-cells *on the ground floor,* each 8 feet by 4 feet 11; one cell of double the size, for Convicts under Sentence of Death, which is likewise occasionally used for refractory Prisoners; and, at the back of these, and separated by a narrow passage, are five other cells, of equal dimensions. The cells upon the ground floor are boarded, but much out of repair, and dirty. Several of them had ashes heaped up in the corners. The Felons, for bedding, have two straw mats and two blankets each.

One side of the court-yard is occupied by a room with a cold bath; and another adjoining, for Prisoners to undress in, with a boiler for warm water.

Behind these buildings is another court-yard for less-atrocious Felons, 38 feet square; a day or mess-room (fitted up as above) 18 feet 4 inches by 11 feet *9;* an Infirmary-room *16* feet square over it; and on the ground floor are five sleepingcells, exactly similar to those already mentioned.

Women Felons have a court-yard, a day-room, an Infirmary, and three sleepingcells; another room having a cold bath, and one adjoining it, with a boiler, like those before described. The Women's bath had not been used, nor is there any water to supply it.

The Chapel is a square building in the centre of the Prison; and has at each corner a door of entrance for the respective classes, who are seated in the area, separated from each other by partitions *6* feet 6 inches high.

Over the rooms that contain the baths are two spacious *Iiifirmaries,* 30 feet each by 16', with large opposite casement windows, and fire-places: But some of the Infirmary windows have been injudiciously stopped up. These rooms open into the gallery of the Chapel, which is partitioned off for the sick. The Chapel is open to the top, with a large sky-light, and fan sash-window.

The cells of this Gaol have boarded floors, with arched roofs, and are fitted up with three mats and two blankets each. The door-ways, being only 22 inches wide, are both too narrow to admit the introduction of a bedstead, and too few in number for so populous a Prison; so that two Prisoners are generally locked up in each cell, affording a space of 2 feet 5 inches only for each Prisoner. The courtyards here are not kept clean: I found grass growing between the flag-stones: But they are well supplied with water, and the sewers are not offensive. The Keeper appears humane; and the Prison is as clean as its present construction will admit. It is much to be regretted, however, that the plan originally proposed by so able an Architect was not adopted. There would then have been *no cells on, a ground-Jloor,* which are incommodious, unhealthy, and insecure.

Those Prisoners who work receive all their earnings, but no County Allowance of bread. It has always given me pleasure, at my several visits, to find some of them weaving stockings, others making shoes, &c.

"Table Of Fees,
To be taken by the Keeper of this Gaol.
£". s. dl "For lodging of every Prisoner, per week--------02 4
For Gaol-Fees on Discharge of every Prisoner------O 13 1
For the Turnkey-020
For the Copy of every Warrant or Commitment------0 10
For signing the Certificate, in order to obtain a *Supersedeas*--0 1 0 *Thomas a Beckel Sessions.*—10th July, 1759..

"We, his Majesty's Justices of the Peace for the County of Leicester, do hereby allow of the above Fees.
W. Wright. J. Danvers.
Ch. Hutchinson. W. Cant. "We, the Judges of Assize, have reviewed, and do confirm the above Table ofT Fees, this 17th day of August, 1759.
T. Parker. Ja. Hewitt."

Formerly there used to be an annual collection for the Prisoners, by a kind of voluntary brief. The Gentlemen of the Grand Jury recommended it to the Clergy, who promoted the good work in their respective parishes. A Table was kept, of the sum received from each parish; a list of Debtors clothed or discharged; and an account of the expenditure of the remainder, in. feeding and warming all the Prlsoners, during the inclement season. The collection in 1774 amounted to 74/. In 1779, only to 12/. 5s. *6d.* In 1780, to *6I. is. 9d.;* and in 1781, to 3/. 18$. Mr. Gregory informed me, by letter, dated 28th August 1803, that no collection had been made for several years; that from 1795 to 1803, the whole amount was but 5/. 1. *6d.* and that the balance then in his hands was 32/. *6s. l id.*

No firing is allowed by the County. Neither soap nor towels for Prison cleanliness. No Rules and Orders! Here, as in too many other Gaols, is an *useless tub;* and two cold baths, that are never used.

Prisoners are discharged from hence in *a morning;* but without money, or the allowance of bread. For eight of them, therefore, (who were 20 miles distant from home,) a stranger, present at the time, left one shilling each.

The Clauses against the use of Spirituous Liquors are properly painted on the same board as the foregoing Table of Fees. But the Act for Preserving the Health of Prisoners was not hung up.

LEICESTER.
The County Bridewell.
Keeper, *Daniel Lambert;* now *William Phillips.*

Salary, 52/. 10. He is also allowed mops, brooms, pails, soap, and every requisite for Prison cleanliness.

Chaplain, none: But at my visit in

1807, the Keeper told me his Prisoners regularly attended Prayers three times a week; and also Prayers and Sermon on Sundays, in the Chapel of the County Gaol.

Surgeon, Mr. *Maule;* now Mr. *Ludlam.* Makes a Bill.

Number of Prisoners, 1803, Aug. 23d,----7. 1 1807, July 30th,----17. 1805, Sept. 26th,---15. 1809, Aug. 22d,---17.

Allowance, one pound six ounces of bread per day, sent in loaves of 2lbs. 12oz. every other day from the Baker's; and one pint of small beer daily.

REMARKS'.

This *New Bridewell,* first inhabited in 1804, is situate inTree-School Lane, and adjoins to the *County Gaol;* in the wall of which there is a door of communication for the Prisoners, who go thither, as above noticed, to Chapel; where the sexes are properly placed in separate divisions, out of sight of each other.

Here are two court-yards, for the Men and Women, with dust-pens to receive ashes, which in the County Gaol are much wanted. To each court-yard there is a day-room.

A *Reception-room* is provided, for Prisoners to be examined by the Surgeon, previous to their admission into the interior of the Prison. In the centre of the Men's court is a small detached building, which contains a *bath.* Their sleepingcells are nine,, all on the ground-floor; and each 8 feet by 5, with arched roofs and boarded floors. They are all supplied with two straw matresses; lighted by an iron grating above each door, having an inside shutter; and all opening into the courtyard, in which there are two convenient sewers.

The Women's court is of the same size as the former, and has four sleeping-cells attached to it on the ground floor, fitted up in the same manner as those for the Men. Three other such cells are also building (1S03) on the Women's side, and over them a large work-room. The sewers are all judiciously placed, and not offensive.

Above stairs are two rooms, set apart as *Infirmaries,* which have each a large iron-grated and glazed window, with a fire-place. Also two large work-rooms, with similar windows, spinning-wheels, stocking-frames, &c.

Those Prisoners who work for themselves, and are not committed for hard labour, pay to the Keeper 2. 6d. in the pound out of their earnings; and such have no County allowance of food. Those committed for hard labour, and who can earn more than ten shillings per week, have the overplus for themselves.

Prisoners discharged from hence are sent away *penniless.* At least, therefore, it is hoped, that they are dismissed *in a morning.*

Here are no books provided, for the visiting Magistrates to enter their remarks; a deficiency, which it would be highly useful to supply.

Neither the Act for Preserving the Health of Prisoners, nor the Clauses against Spirituous Liquors, are hung up. §3 The Keeper shewed me a bottle of *Gin,* which he had taken from a person, who was bringing it into the Prison.

At my visit to the *Old County Bridewell,* in 1803, the Keeper of it was the celebrated Mr. *Daniel Lambert,* who afterwards exhibited himself for the gratification of the metropolis. He is said to have weighed in 1805, forty nine stone, twelve pounds (or 6"98 lbs) which exceeds, by nearly ninety pounds, the corpulency of Mr. *Edward Bright,* of Maldon, in the County of Essex . Some few years since, Lambert is said to have been very active; and, considering his bulk, was of singular vivacity in the year 1807....

From the well-known print of Mr. Bright, (engraved by M'Ardell, after a painting by Osborne) it appears that he died on the 10th of November, 1750, aged 29 years: and weighed, while living, forty three stone, seven pounds, which amount to 609 pounds.

In 1805, I found at *Leicester* both a new Prison and a new Keeper. The sedentary habits of Mr. Lambert, we are told, had rendered him so much attached to his late employ, that it was with reluctance he heard the business of the *Bridewell* was to be transferred to the County Gaol; and himself, obliged, like some other great men, to retire upon a pension.

Mr. Lambert, it seems, had an invincible objection to have his weight ascertained. It was at length, however, effected by the following contrivance: Going one day to Loughborough, the carriage that conveyed him was designedly drawn over a weighing engine; and thus, to his great vexation, he was informed of the fact, which he had so assiduously wished to avoid.

His brief historian, in a vein of irony observes, that " had this fat man studied a thousand years, he could not have thought of a *profession* better calculated to suit his constitutional propensity to ease."

It is hoped that the wit and humour of the above shrewd remark outweigh its scrupulous conformity to matter of fact; and yet, even Gaolers, possibly, like the Pilot *Palimirus* of ancient times, may now and then be found nodding on the post of duty. To name instances might be deemed sarcastic, or insidious.

A tolerably executed etching of Mr. Lambert has been in circulation. He died in June 1809, *Obruit mole sud;* and his weight then was fifty two stone, eleven pounds, (or 739 lbs.!) He is spoken of as a humane, benevolent man.

LEICESTER. *The Town Gaol.*

Gaoler, *Welborn Owston.* Salary, 37/. 10.

Fees, for Debtors, 15. 4f.; besides which the Under-Sheriff demands 6s. Sd.

for his *Liberate!* Felons, 13. 4d. Bridewell Prisoners, 2s. 6d. For Conveyance of Transports, 10/. each. Garnish abolished.

Chaplain, Rev. *Thomas Robinson.* Salary, *lol.*

Duty, Prayers and Sermon once a month.

Surgeon, Mr. *Maule;* now Mr. *Ludlam.* Makes a Bill.

Number of Prisoners, Debtors. Felons. &c. Assaults. Deserters.
1803, Aug. 23d,---5-.-12--. 0---3
1805, Sept. 26th,--.4--. 2---0
1807, July 30th,---2---1-2---0---0
1809, Aug. 22d,---4---9---0---1.

Allowance, one pound six ounces of bread, sent from the Baker's every other

day, in loaves of 2 lbs 12 ounces.
REMARKS.
This Gaol was built in 1793, and has on each side a narrow slip of ground, partitioned off by open iron palisades, and divided into court-yards for the different classes of Prisoners.

The court-yard for *Debtors,* is 32 feet by 16, with a day-room of 13 feet by 12; And up stairs are eight lodging rooms, to which the Debtor who brings his or her own bed, pays sixpence per week. If the Keeper furnishes a single bed, he is paid 2. *Ad.* a week; and if two sleep together, 1. arf. each. One room is set apart for the sick Women on the Debtors' side; and all the apartments above stairs are appropriated to Debtors.

In the centre of the Prison is the Chapel; very small, and the Prisoners are not properly separated.

The Felons' court-yard, on the Debtors' side of the Gaol, is 40 feet by 10; and to prevent conversation with the Debtors, a vacancy, 8 feet wide, is left between the palisades of the two court-yards.

The other slip is divided into three court-yards by similar iron palisades.

The *bottom court,* assigned for *Women Felons,* is 34 feet by 20, and has a dayroom, and five sleeping-cells. In this Female Felons' court-yard is stationed *a coop to fatten fowls in!* Such protectors, in such a place, are indeed the most eligible; but such an accommodation is very unsuitable, and must be attended with dirt, and other inconveniencies. Poultry should never be admitted amongst Prisoners.

The *middle court,* for *Deserters,* is 21 feet square, and has three sleeping-rooms. The *upper,* or *top court,* assigned to *Men Felons,* 41 feet long by 12, has six sleeping-cells. All criminals sleep here upon the ground floor.

Every cell is 12 feet long, by *6* feet 2 inches, and 9 feet 4 inches high, to the crown of the arch; and has a crib bedstead, with two sedge-mats to sleep on. At my visit in 1803, each cell contained a cast-iron privy: but in 1805 I had the satisfaction to find them removed, and instead of them, sewers were distributed in the court-yards. These cells are all on the ground floor; but above stairs there are sleeping-rooms, for those Prisoners who can pay for beds.

One room belonging to this side of the Gaol is set apart for an *Infirmary.* Such care and humane attention towards the sick is surely ever laudable, and a bounden duty. But the matter should not rest here. The healthy and the diligent also equally require some consideration.

Yet, really, instead of encouraging Industry, the very disposition to it seems here to be most 'Unaccountably repressed, by a curious mode of pains and penalties. Every Prisoner, *Debtor* or *Criminal,* that procures for himself the means of labour, in the Town Gaol of *Leicester,* has not only his *County allowance of bread stopped,* and withheld, but is even obliged to *pay the Gaoler* one shilling, and sometimes two shillings per week, for *permission to work.'* A novelty of this kind is undoubtedly severe; and such as I have only once met with elsewhere, in my wide perambulation of the Gaols.

The number of commitments for Trial, from Aug. l8oo, to Aug. 1809, was 423.

A bath was heretofore provided, as an excellent accommodation for every place of incarceration, whether previous to admission, or during the state of confinement: But I am informed it-has never been used here; and at my visit in 1809, /*found the bathing room converted into a stable for the Keeper's horse.*

The Prison is seldom visited, but it is kept clean, and water plentifully supplied. No Rules and Orders. Formerly there was a *Table of Fees,* signed by the Magistrates, and confirmed by the Judges of Assizes; but none has been exhibited in the Gaol for many years. Neither the Act for Preserving Health, nor the Clauses against Spirituous Liquors, are hung up.

LE1TH. Scotland.
The Town Gaol.
Gaoler, *James M'Kenzie;* Town-officer. No Salary.
Fees, none. No religious attentions. No Surgeon.

Number of Prisoners, 24th Sept. 1809, Three Debtors. Two Criminals,

Allowance, to Debtors as alimented; generally 1. per day. Felons, &c. *6d.* a day.
REMARKS.
This Gaol is above the Council Chamber, and on the first story is a room for Criminals, about 12 feet square, with one small grated window. No fire-place; a.wooden bedstead, straw-in-ticking bed, a blanket, and a rug.

The next floor in ascent has one room of the like dimensions with that described, and has bedding of the same quality, with a fire-place, but no coals allowed. Nearly adjoining to it is a large room for Debtors, with two windows, and a fire-place.

Between the two rooms last noticed is a place called the *Black Hole,* which has no bedding, and is totally dark, being appropriated for temporary confinement.

Tubs, which are emptied every three days, supply the place of sewers. No court-yard. Water, as wanted, is brought by the Keeper, from a pump in the: Street.

LENTON, /ate BASFORD. *Nottinghamshire.*
Gaoler, *George Wombwell.* No Salary. Has a Licence for Wine, Beer, and *Spirituous Liquors.*
Fees, 13. *4d.* by the Court-Roll. No Table.
Garnish, one shilling, spent in Liquor.
Number of Debtors, 1805, July 20th, 1. 1809, Aug. 26th, 0.
Allowance, formerly none; but now three pence a day, in bread, REMARKS.

This is his Majesty's Gaol of the Court of Record for his Honour of Pevehex, and additional limits of the same, in the Counties of Nottingham and Derby. Henry Lord Middleton, by Grant from Queen Anne to his Ancestor, Sir Thomas Willoughby, in Fee, is the High Steward of this Honour and its limits.

The Prison, formerly at *Basford,* in this County, was afterwards removed to Lenton: but, being in a decayed state, a new Gaol was built in the back yard of the Keeper's publick house, and first inhabited in 1805. It consists of a court-yard 30 feet by 16 feet 6 inches, paved iwith broad flag-stones; and in it area pump, and a sewer.

There are two sleeping-rooms below, and two above, each 14 feet 6 inches by 12 feet 6, and 7 feet 3 inches high; with a fire-place, and an iron-grated glazed window in each. To these the Keeper furnishes beds at 2. per week, or at l. 6d. each, if two sleep together. Here is also a work-room, of 12 feet 6 inches by 9 feet 6, with a window the whole length of the room.

The Judicial practice of this Court of Record is Trial before Judge and Jury, similar to the superior Courts in Westminster Hall, but most resembling the Common Pleas; proceeding by *Capias,* &c. and the suits are, in like manner, carried on to judgment and execution, except that every Tuesday throughout the year is a Court Day, or Term; so that the proceedings are quickly dispatched, unless the Defendant files a Plea, or Demurrer; in which case the business is argued before Mr. *Balguy,* Barrister, the Steward and Judge, and a respectable Jury, at two General Courts in the year, which Mr. *Balguy* appoints to be held about Michaelmas and Easter. The Debt and Costs are from forty shillings up to fifty pounds.

LEOMINSTER. *Herefordshire.*
The Town Gaol.
Gaoler, *James Morgan,* the Town Crier. Salary, 67. Fees, none.
Prisoners, 3d June, 1802, and 24th Aug. 1803, None.

Allowance. Debtors, if poor, have three shillings per week, on application made to the Magistrates. Criminals, Sixpence a day.
REMARKS.
This Prison consists of two upper rooms, about 20 feet by 14; one of which is for Debtors, the other for Criminals. Here is a small court, about 14 yards square; but Prisoners have no use of it, except by the indulgence of their Keeper.

LEWES. *Sussex.*
House of Correction,
For the *Eastern Division* of the County . Keeper, *William Cramp.*
Salary, 60l. and allowed 14. per week for a Turnkey. Fees, none.
Chaplain, Rev. Mr. *Dale.*
Duty, on Sunday, Prayers; on Wednesday, Prayers and Sermon. Salary, 25/.
Surgeon, *Mr. Crockford.* Salary, 20/.
Number of Prisoners, 1804, Sept. 20th, 35.
Allowance, two pounds of best wheaten bread daily. For the Sick, better or other nourishment is ordered by the Surgeon, at his discretion.
REMARKS.
The boundary wall encloses above an acre Of ground, in the centre of which are the Gaoler's house, and the Chapel. Here are four spacious court-yards; in one of which is a forcing pump, that amply supplies every part of the Prison with excellent water.

The two wings of the building are over arcades, and two stories high. On each story are sixteen cells, 9 feet 2 by 6 feet 4, and 9 feet 9 inches high, to the crown of the arch. Each cell has a wooden bedstead, straw-in-sacking bed, two blankets, and a rug. They have double doors, the outer one iron-grated, and a glazed window, with a casement.

The lobbies are 5 feet wide, and well ventilated, with water-closets at the end. A kitchen, supplied with leaden sink to wash in; and a day-room, to which the For the *Western* Division, see Petworth.

County *now* humanely allows *coals,* as it had been sometimes the practice for the Prisoners even to *sell their bread,* in order to purchase so necessary an article.

On the ground-floor are four solitary cells, of the same size with those before mentioned; but to each of these is a water-closet, with a sink to wash in, well supplied with water. In one of them it is customary to confine a foul Prisoner till the occasion is removed, and the County clothing put on; when he is admitted into the interior part of the Prison. In these cells are likewise confined the refractory, till *they have submitted to proper Government, which a seclusion from Society soon effects.* They seldom continue above 24 hours before promises of amendment procure a release, that *again restores them to the World!*

Their employment consists in the compounding of whiting, carding wool, and beating hemp. In the first branch of work each Prisoner can earn eight pence a day, over and above the divisional shares of the County and the Keeper, which are five shillings in the pound upon the nett proceeds: this, however, can only be done in the seven Summer months. In carding of wool, the Prisoner receives a halfpenny per pound, and the County has the same. Beating of hemp is charged 4. 6d. for four dozen of *Punnies,* (about 3lbs. weight;) half of which goes to the County, and the Prisoner receives the other half.

Here is a cold bath, with a bathing-tub, and an oven for purifying the Prisoners' clothes at their first admission.

LUDLOW. *Shropshire.*
The Town Gaol.
Gaoler. The Corporation appoint three persons, as Sergeants at Mace; who attend them to execute Processes, and are alternate Gaolers, to whom a Salary is allowed by the Corporation. Fees, on discharge, 13s. 4d.
Surgeon, when wanted, from the Parish.
Prisoners, 3d June 1802, None.
Allowance, sixpence a day.
REMARKS.
This Gaol stands in the street named "August Fee," and is usually called Gauvet's Tower. It consists of one room, 24 feet by 18, and three others, 18 feet square. No bedding provided. Straw was found by the then Gaoler, *Joseph Scott.*

The persons committed hither are chiefly for small offences, and take their Trial at the Quarter Sessions held in the Town.

LICHFIELD. *Staffordshire.*
The City and County Gaol, and Bridewell.
Gaoler, *John Pricket.* Salary, 50/.
Fees, Debtors and Felons, 13. *Ad.* each. And the Under-Sheriff demands 2s. 6d. from every Debtor for his *Liberate!* Garnish, not yet abolished, *Is.*
Chaplain, none statedly appointed; but the Rev. Mr. *Proby* attends when

one is desired.

Surgeon, when wanted, from the Corporation.

Number of Prisoners, Debtors. Felons, &c.
1803, Aug. 24th,--2---2. 1805, Oct. 31st,--0.

Allowance, *Debtors,* none; unless Paupers, who, have *6d.* a day. *Felons,* the same, in bread. *Bridewell Prisoners,* a three penny loaf; but if they earn 32. by their labour, it is allowed them additionally in bread.

REMARKS.

Here is one court-yard only for all descriptions of Prisoners, 42 feet by 30, with a pump of excellent water in it, and a sewer. Above stairs are two rooms for Debtors, to which the City supplies bedsteads, but no bedding. If a Debtor brings his own bed and bedding, he pays nothing; if the Keeper furnishes a bed, and two sleep together, they pay 1. per week each. Debtors are allowed the use of the Keeper's kitchen, or else find their own coals in their apartments.

Those Bridewell Prisoners who are *not committed to hard labour,* receive two pence out of every shilling they earn.

For Felons here are three cells, which open into a passage or lobby 3 feet 4 inches wide, near the Keeper's kitchen. Each cell has an iron grating, of 24 inches by 4, over the door, and is 11 feet by 5, and *6 feet 6* inches high, with wooden bedstead, straw-chaff beds, two blankets, and a rug. One cell for Vagrants, and one for Deserters.

Here are likewise two Dungeons, totally dark, 7 feet by *6,* and 8 feet high; planked with oak on the bottom, top, and sides. The bedding, like that in the cells. The three parishes of Lichfield allow *thirty shillings* a year, at 10. each, for coals, and the Corporation grants twenty shillings per annum for straw.

Neither the Act nor Clauses hung up. The Gaol whitewashed once in two or three years.

LINCOLN CASTLE.
The County Gaol.
Gaoler, *John Merrytceather.*
Salary, 300/. out of which he provides three Turnkeys; and a *Caterer,* who attends daily at nine o'clock, and three, to purchase in the City whatever the Prisoners may want, liquors excepted. He also supplies eight chaldrons of coals yearly, together with straw, mops, tubs, buckets, &c. for the use of the Prison; and is allowed one shilling a mile for the removal of Transports, and other Convicts.

Fees, abolished. But the Under Sheriff demands *6s. 8d.* for his *Liberate,* from every Debtor, except those discharged by Proclamation, or under the Lord's Act; who pay no Fee.

Garnish, also abolished.

Chaplain, Rev. *George-Davies Kent.* Salary, 50/.

Duty, Prayers and Sermon on Sundays; Prayers twice a week; and to attend those daily, who are under Sentence of Death.

Surgeon, Mr. *Charles Franklyn;* who is required to attend all the Felons and certificated Debtors. Salary, 30/. for both Debtors and Felons.

Number of Prisoners, Debtors. Peloiw.
1800, March 26th,-----14 12 1801, Nov. 20th,-----16 13 1802, Aug. 12th,-----11 9 1805, Jan. 17th,-----36-------Ifl 1809, Sept. 5th,--,--24-------8.

Allowance. Debtors, obtaining a *Certificate* of their having no visible estate or effects (given under the hands of the Minister, Church-Wardens, and Overseers of the Parish in which they last lived,) are allowed by the County a pound and half of good household bread per day, and one pound of good beef, without bone, per week. The bread is delivered three times in the week, in loaves of three pounds and a half each; the 'whole furnished by contract Also four chaldrons of coals every year, which are distributed half-quarterly.

Those Debtors who receive their sixpences, have no County Allowance of food. To Felons, the same Allowance as to Certificated Debtors, and an equal quantity of coals. In cases of illness, the Surgeon, when it is necessary, takes off the County Allowance; and orders, at the charge of the County, such diet and nursing as he thinks proper.

REMARKS.

This excellent Gaol, for the County of Lincoln, is situate in the Castle-Yard, which contains about seven acres of land, enclosed by a high wall. Here, previous to proceeding in my usual narrative, I shall throw in some historical matter; which is not only curious, but may prove a relief to the Reader of the subsequent ample delineation.

Of the Castle of Lincoln, which was built by the Conqueror, little now survives the devastations of Time. The few remaining vestiges convey a similar idea of original Norman Architecture to that of York Castle, erected nearly at the same

The entrance to it is on the Eastern side, through an arched gateway, under a large square Tower. In the North-East angle of the wall is a curious small edifice, appearing from without the walls like a round Tower. It is called Cobb's Hall, and is believed to have been originally used as a Chapel; having a fine old vaulted roof, richly ornamented, and supported by pillars, with a crypt underneath, and adjoining to it a small Chapel. The pillars are so placed against the loop-holes, that they are said to have proved a defence against missile weapons.

Before the erection of *The New Prison,* this building was occasionally made use of by the Military, for the confinement of Deserters; but since that time, has very properly been discontinued. The first part of it is now, with the leave of the Gaoler, used by such joiners, cabinet-makers, &c. as can procure work from the Town; and this has proved a very considerable aid to many poor families. A Debtor of that description was working here, at my last visit, in 1809.

Near the North-Western angle are the reliques of an elevated turret, erected over the ancient arch of the Sally-Port, which has a groove adapted for a Portcullis. This part, being within the line of an old Roman wall, might have belonged to a still more ancient building, or been occupied as a gateway to the old Roman City, which lay on that side of the Castle.

About the middle of the South wall

is the large *Keep,* or Tower, raised on a very high mound of earth, and standing half within, and half without the Castle walls, which ascend up the sides of the Hill, and join to the Great Tower. The form of the Keep is nearly circular; covering the summit of the Mount, and thereby rendered tenable with or without the Castle.

At the South-Eastern angle there is a lesser Keep, or Tower, placed also upon an artificial Mount; and thus a communication was kept up between the two Towers, by a covered-way on the wall; a part of which yet remains.

The Well, for supplying the Great Tower with water, stands on the top of the wall adjoining to it; but is now nearly filled up with rubbish. The whole of the walls, upon an average, are 10 feet thick at the top, about 14 feet at the bottom, and 25 feet period high. The premises here attempted to be described, are held by lease from the *Dutch/ Court of Lancaster,* for a term of thirty years, at the annual rent of *Ten Shillings.*

The *New Gaol* has been erected about two and twenty years, and is a good brick building, with stone facings. The front of it, containing the Gaoler's and the Debtors' apartments, is about 46 yards long; having nearly two acres of grass-plat lying before it, fenced off for the use of the Debtors, who enjoy the happy privilege of walking there during the day-time. It is supplied with a well of good water.

One *half* of the building is occupied by the *Male Debtors,* and has three day-rooms for those of the Master's-side, of the average size 20 feet by 15 feet *6,* and 12 feet 9 inches high: also one room for Common-side Debtors, 21 feet by 16, and of the same height as the former. .

On *the flrst floor* are five lodging-rooms, of about 17 feet by 15 feet *6,* and 11 feet high; with an airy passage communicating to them. On the *second floor* five other lodging-rooms, of the same dimensions, with a similar passage; and one of them is set apart for the Common-side Debtors.

N. B. In this Prison no communication whatever is at any time permitted between *Debtors* and *Felons;* and the Sexes are completely separated both by day and night.

The-other half of this building is occupied by the Gaoler's house, excepting two attick rooms for *Female Debtors;* one a day-room, the other a night-room, in size 16 feet 9 inches by *i*6 feet, and each 10 feet high. In this story are also two large Infirmary-rooms, 20 feet each by 10, and 12 feet high.,

The *Chapel,* 31 feet by 28, is neatly pewed. The Debtors and Felons are properly separated by a high framing, and the Women, during Divine Service, placed out of view of the Men. All the Prisoners, Debtors or Felons, are obliged to attend Chapel; and one Prisoner from time to time officiates there as Clerk; of which he receives a double allowance of provisions.

The *Common Prison* is so built, from the centre 'of the whole edifice on the South side, as to enjoy the benefit of sun and air in the court-yards. The passage down it lies in a line with the front-entrance door; and is arched above, 10 feet high by 5 feet wide. The lower end of it is laid open, with an iron grating; by which means the ventilation can never be obstructed.

This Common Prison comprizes, on the ground-floor, first, a " *Strong Room,"* for refractory Debtors; another room opposite, containing a bath and oven; and next to these, three night-cells, of 10 feet by 8 feet 6, and 11 feet high, each set apart for two Prisoners, with wooden bedsteads, fastened to the floors.

Four day-rooms, with fire-places, are here also assigned to Prisoners of different descriptions; viz. No. 1, of 20 feet by 11, and 11 feet high, for Male Prisoners before Trial. No. 2, of 11 feet by 10, and 11 feet high, for Females in the same circumstance. No. 3, of 17 feet by 9, and 11 feet high, has Male Convicts under Sentence of Transportation: and No. 4, of 12 feet by 10, and the same height, is for those who are convicted for smaller offences. These day-rooms have each a court-yard, 45 feet by 30, communicating to them; and are all private with respect to each other; being separated by walls twenty-four feet high. The courtyard of No. 2 has pumps, from which a supply of excellent water, both hard and soft, is at all times accessible to the Prisoners. And in the centre of the yard is a wash-house, with copper, tubs, &c.

Next to the above rooms are six *night-cells,* for single men, each 9 feet by 5 feet 9, and 11 feet high; with bedsteads as mentioned before. The night-cells on the ground floor are arched above, with strong oak boarding to the walls and floors; and the windows, looking into the court-yards, and double barred, have wooden shutters, to keep them close and warm at night. Every Felon in this Prison has straw-inticking for his bed, with three blankets, and a rug.

The *upper story* contains seven other night-cells, and also the Turnkey's sleepingroom; the average size of them 10 feet square, and 12 feet high. Here are likewise two larger apartments, of 20 feet each by 10 feet, and the same height as the former, for Male and Female *Infirmaries.* All the cells above stairs have glass windows, and arched roofs.

Adjoining to the building already described there have since been added four other *solitary cells;* two on each side of the passage, with fire-places and glass windows. Each cell is 13 feet finches by 8 feet 9, and 11 feet high, and communicates respectively with separate court-yards, of 23 feet by 12. Over these four cells is the *Chapel,* beforementioned.

The worthy Magistrates of this County are not only in a very *humane* degree, but also very *religiously* attentive to the comforts of the Prisoners. They have accordingly directed, that any sum, not exceeding Five Pounds *per annum,* shall be laid out, at the discretion of the Chaplain, in the purchase of *Religious Tracts,* for the common use of all. These, carefully numbered, and entered into a book as delivered out, are called in once a week, and then re-delivered in the same manner: by which means they have a change of readers; and their being lost or destroyed is prevented, by the regularity with which it is done.

By long practice I consider myself as able to form some tolerably good judgement of a *Gaoler,* from the countenance of his *Prisoners.* Complacency, submission, and good order, were visible in every part of this well-regulated Gaol; a sure proof that the Keeper is intelligent, active, and humane.

The County does not allow bedding to the poor, or certificated Debtors; but two large apartments, a day and a night-room, are set apart, free of rent, or any charge whatever, for the use of those Debtors who choose to find their own bedding.

Masters-side Debtors, or such as can afford it, may go into rooms furnished by the Gaoler; for which, if two sleep together, they pay 1. *6d.* per week each. But if a Debtor has a bed to himself, it is 2. *6d.* weekly.

The *Number of Debtors* committed to Lincoln Castle in the last ten years, up to the 31st of December, lS0o, was 518. The Number of Actions against them was 577; of which 212 were for Sums from Ten to Twenty pounds; 197 from Twenty to Fifty Pounds; and 168 for Fifty Pounds and upwards. Strange as it may appear, out of the whole number so imprisoned, *two hundred and sixty two Debtors* were absolutely *discharged, without their Plaintiff's obtaining one Farthing, either of Debt or Costs;* a proof of the extreme folly of being so stimulated by their passions, as to go to Law with fellow Creatures, too poor and miserable to afford them any prospect of payment; for such, surely, those must be, who are *certificated* as Paupers! Of the remaining 256 otherwise variously discharged, here, as in every Prison for Debt, a very great proportion obtain their Liberty from Plaintiffs, *not by paying them the Debt,* but by *giving new undertakings for discharging it and Costs, by Instalments;* from which, very seldom, if ever, is any thing obtained. Second Actions thereon are very rarely brought; the Plaintiffs having suffered sufficiently by the first experiment, from the immense addition of Costs, so frequently transcending the original Debt.

The County, as yet, furnishes *no Employment* within the Gaol; but Prisoners of handicraft trades have permission to obtain it on their own account, and generally procure work by an application to the Town.

Several houses of Correction where work is furnished, are to be found in each District and Division of the County of Lincoln. That established at *Kirton* for the Division of *Lindsay* (comprizing half the County) is a newly-erected and convenient building, under good Regulation, and the employment there is in the woollen line. Another House of Correction is also begun at *Louth,* for the same Division of Lindsay; but I understand it is undergoing many alterations and additions. The rest are at *Folhingham,* for the Parts of *Kesteven;* at *Spalding,* for the Holland Division, &c.

The Male Convicts of this Gaol wear a County Uniform, of blue and drab-coloured cloth. Assize Convicts, under sentence of Transportation, have the King's allowance of 2. *6d.* per week, instead of the usual County Allowance.

From hence, two Guineas are annually paid by the Clerk of the Peace to poor Prisoners, both in the *King's Bench* and *Marshalsea.*

This Prison is perfectly dry. The whole is white-washed twice a year, and the day-rooms oftener, as they may happen to require it.

Of Legacies and Benefactions to Lincoln Castle Gaol, the following is the best statement I am enabled to give: 1. Mrs. *Rebecca Hussey,* by her Will, proved in London, 10th of May, 1715, bequeathed the *Interest of One Thousand Pounds,* to release poor Debtors from this Castle. But,

No Debtors have received the benefit for many years past. 1 could get no farther account of-this Legacy; and by some singular occurrence, or want of attention, it seems to be entirely lost 2. Mr. *Thomas Heselden,* by his Will, proved the 21st of September, 1720, bound his Estate called *Works-Chantry* (being a house in Lincoln, now in the occupation of Mrs. *Mary Culleri)* with the payment of *Three Pounds a Year,* for the better maintenance of the poor Prisoners in the Castle*;* and this Legacy is regularly paid half yearly, at Lady-Day and Michaelmas.

3. In the Will of *Thomas-Robert Jenkinson,* late of the City of Lincoln, Esq. deceased, dated the 23d of October, 1770, and proved at Lincoln, the 13th of February 1772, there is contained the following Clause:—" Also I give and bequeath to the said *Alexander Hunter,* and *George Dealtry,* the sum of One Hundred and Twenty Pounds, to be paid within twelve Months after my decease; upon this special Trust and Confidence, that they, the said *Alexander Hunter* and *George Dealtry,* or the survivor of them, or the Executors or Administrators of such Survivor, do and shall place the said sum of One Hundred and Twenty Pounds upon some publick or private security or securities; and call in and re-invest the same at interest as often as there shall be occasion, in order to fulfil the trusts hereinafter declared concerning the same. And upon this further trust, that they, the said Alexander Hunter and George Dealtry, or the Survivor of them, or the Executors or Administrators of such Survivor, do and shall from time to time forever hereafter, pay the Interest and yearly Proceed of the said Sum of One Hundred and Twenty Pounds, as the same shall arise, on *Easter Monday* in every year, to and amongst such Prisoners who shall be confined for Debt in the Common Gaol in and for the County of Lincoln, and who shall be willing to accept their proportion thereof. Provided, and I do hereby Will and Direct, that if there shall be, on any such yearly day of payment, any one Prisoner, who can, within fourteen days then next ensuing, procure his Discharge out of Custody for all the Interest that is on such yearly day directed to be distributed as aforesaid, that then, and in such case, the same shall that year be paid and applied for the procuring the Discharge of any such Prisoner, at the discretion of my said Trustees, or the Survivor of them, or the Executors or Administrators of such Survivor."

The Trustees under the Will were Dr. Hunter, and Mr. Dealtry, of York. From the above Bequest, five pounds a year is payable out of a Farm at Ripham, in the neighbourhood of Lincoln, (now in the tenure of William Glossop) left by Mr. Jenkinson, the Testator, to John Harrison, Esq. of Norton-Place, in this County; and the Legacy is paid by Mr. Harrison, who came into possession of the bulk of the property of the said Thomas-Robert Jenkinson, esq.

LINCOLN. *The City Gaol, and House of Correction.*

Gaoler, *Thomas Drewry.* Salary, 40/. Fees, Debtors & Felons, 6y. *Bd.* on discharge. Chaplain, none yet appointed.

Surgeon, Mr. *Swan.* Salary, none. Makes a Bill.'

Number of Prisoners, 1S09, Sept. 5th, Debtors, 0. Felons, &c. 9.

Allowance, four-pence halfpenny each per day, in money.

REMARKS.

A handsome new-built Sessions House fronts the Road; and the Gaol, (first inhabited in 180S,) is immediately behind it. The Keeper's house is at the SouthWest corner; and his windows command a view of the Debtors' court only, which is 27 feet by 21, and has their day-room, of 18 feet by 11, opening into it.

On the *Chamber Story* are two sleeping-rooms, with fire-places, and grated glazed windows. One of these rooms holds two beds, the other holds five; and they are supplied with feather-beds, bedding, and suitable furniture.

Close to the boundary wall is an inspecting walk, 5 feet wide, Which encircles the whole Prison; and the several court-yards are separated from it by an open wood palisade, 12 feet high. A flagged passage, 60 feet long and 6 feet wide, runs through the centre of the Gaol, and has three iron-palisaded doors of separation.

On the *Ground Floor* are two day-rooms, of 18 feet by 11 each, with separate court-yards, 27 feet square, for Male and Female *Felons;* and two others, of the same size, for Petty Offenders.

For *Vagrants* here is a room of 11 feet by 8; with a court 27 feet by 9. Also one solitary cell of 11 feet by 8, to which a small court is attached, of about the same size as the former.

Felons, and other Criminal Prisoners, have nine sleeping-cells, 10 feet each by 8; and are allowed a wooden bedstead for two, with straw-in-ticking bed, two blankets, a bolster, and a rug. The windows of these cells are double-grated, and have inside shutters.

The six day-rooms, and two *Infirmaries,* are 17 feet 6 by 10 feet, and have fireplaces. The court-yards are all gravel-bottomed, and have gratings in the centre, to carry off rain and wet. Every court is supplied with spring water; and there is a reservoir provided, from which the whole Prison has soft water, laid on by pipes.

The loathsome Prison at the *Stone Bow Gate,* and the House of Correction, that so long disgraced this City, were fully described by me, and truly, in the Gentleman's Magazine for March 1805, p. 198. I am glad to find they have been dis-, continued as Prisons, since the building of the above New Gaol.

LIVERPOOL. *Lancashire.*
The Borough Gaol.

Gaoler, *Edward Frodsham;* now *William Frodsham.* Salary, 130/. For Conveyance of Transports, one shilling per mile.

Fees, Debtors and Felons, on discharge, 4. *6d.* But see Table.

Garnish, 4. *6d.*

Chaplain, Rev. *George Monk.* Salary, 31/. 10s.

Duty, Prayers and Sermon on Sundays, and Prayers on Wednesday. $3 Nothing can exceed the slovenly manner in which Divine Service was performed, when I was here present on Sunday 12th Nov. 1809; a short Prayer, and Sermon, to which no attention was paid by 24 Prisoners, out of *fifty seven,* who stood up all in one corner. They have a short Prayer only on Wednesdays, with no forms or benches to sit on, or to kneel at.

Surgeon, as wanted, is sent from the Dispensary; and 12/. per annum paid by the Corporation, who furnish Medicines.

Number of Prisoners, Debtors. Felons, &c.

1802, Oct. 11th, 71 38. 1805, Oct. 24th,-34-4. 1809, Nov. 12th,------35 19. And Five Deserters.

Allowance, to very poor *Debtors,* a threepenny loaf per day, weighing only 13 oz. Nov. 1809. Also a dinner from the Mayor every Christmas Day. See " Legacy," in the Remarks. To Felons, &c. a threepenny loaf daily. Convicts have *6d.* a day in money and bread.

REMARKS.

The Castle of Liverpool, built by Roger de Poictiers, was pulled down in the reign of George the Second. But the Earl of Derby's castellated mansion has been for many years used as the Borough Gaol, and stands at the bottom of Water Street. Here is only one court-yard, of 60 feet by 30, for all descriptions of Prisoners, Men and Women; it is paved with brick, and has in it a pump of excellent water, and two sewers. In the court-yard are kept fowls, ducks, &c. suffered to run about; and a large dunghill, that cannot but be offensive, and is only cleared away once a month. Attached to it are five day-rooms, three of which were originally intended for the Men Debtors, for the Women, and the fifth for the Criminal Prisoners; but they are now used indiscriminately by all. Firing is allowed to every day-room by the Corporation. Here is also one small room set apart for tire sick.

Common-side Debtors have seven rooms in one of the Towers separately partitioned off, and these are *Free Wards,* to which the Corporation allows straw for bedding. In the other Tower are three rooms for Debtors on the Master's-side, furnished with beds by the Keeper at one shilling per week each; and two sleep together.

At my visit in 1805, there was a narrow passage, or gallery, built in the Chapef, into which tire doors of live new sleeping-eel Is opened, each 7 feet G by 6 feet, and 7 feet 6 inches high; these were intended for Men Debtors, and1 supplied with beds by the Keeper, at *Is.* per week each. They had no light or ventilation, but what vras received through the grated apertures over the doors, and I was obliged to have lighted candles at noon-day to inspect them. Also three new rooms, over what is called the *Pilot's Office,* for Women Debtors, two of them holding three beds each; the other a single bed, with fire-places and glazed windows. To these rooms Prisoners furnish their own bedding, or hire it from the Town.

Table Of Fees.
For the Debtors in *Liverpool Borough Gaol.*
"Debts from *10l.* to 20/. 7. d. 20/. to 30/; *Ws*. 30/. to 40Z. 12». *6d.* 40/. to 50/. 15. from 50/. to 60/: *ITs. 6d.* 60/. to 100/. 1/. 100/. to 200/. *ll. 5s.* 200/. and upwards, 1/. 10"

To this Gaol are taken all persons arrested for Debt, by process issued out of the Borough Court of Liverpool.

The Felons Gaol: Down ten steps under ground are seven gloomy cells, or more properly *Dungeons,* within a passage of 11 feet wide, each of them *6 feet 6 inches by 5 feet 9, and 'six feet only high.* The grated vent-holes in these doors are of 11 inches only by 6 inches, and so barred, as almost to shut out every ray of light. When I was here in 1802, no less than 28 Prisoners were locked up at night, four in each of these wretched receptacles, which could not allow more than *twenty-two inches* space for each Prisoner; and in a larger one adjacent, 23 feet by 16", and 13 feet high, were lodged the Ten other Criminals. This last is chiefly set apart for *Deserters;* of whom, I was informed, that Forty at a time had been there immured for three or four days together, and *without being suffocated!* It is ventilated and lighted by a treble iron-barred and grated window, that looks towards the Street.

At my visit on the 12th of November, 1S09, eight Felons slept in two of the cells or dungeons, and nine in the three other dungeons. Two Women slept in another, and one was empty. Not having been changed for four months, the straw was short and dirty; and the brick floors being very damp, the Prisoners complained sadly about it, for they were neither stocks nor stones. Flesh and blood should meditate on these things!

From the promiscuous association and licentious intercourse between the Sexes in this Gaol, I could not but imagine that little attention was paid to the officiating Minister; and having therefore requested Mr. *Staniforth,* an able and active Magistrate of the Borough, to accompany me to the Chapel, I found that on the 14th of October 1802, *six Prisoners only,* out of the 10Q, attended Divine Service.

The probable great importance of the following document will be my best apology for giving it; as obligingly communicated to me by Mr. Brounker, the worthy Mayor of this respectable Borough.

"Abstract Of A Deed,
In the *Old Church* at *Liverpool,*
Respecting the Distribution of certain Legacies of 200/. and 300/. left by Mrs. *Ann Molyneux,* in the year I727, to poor Prisoners for Debt, &c. in the
Borough Gaol; and also to poor Sailors and Sailors' Widows, especially those in the Alms-houses.

"This Indenture, quadripartite, &c. made the 9th day of October, in the year 1732, between *Ralph Williamson,* of Liverpool, &c. Merchant, and *Robert Whittle,* of Knowsley, &c. Gentleman, executors of the last will, &c. of *Ann Molyneux,* late of Liverpool, &c. widow, of the first part; *George Tyrer,* of Liverpool, &c. Merchant, of die second part; *Hannah Tyrer,* of Low Hill, &c. widow, of the third part; and *Riclutrd Gildart,* Mayor for the time being, *John Stanley,* and *TJwmas Raldwin,* Rectors of the Parish, &c. of the fourth part. Whereas the said *Ann Molyneux,* being charitably disposed, by her last Will, &c. dated the 19th day of January, in the year 1727, gave, devised, and bequeathed, to the said Mayor and Rectors, the sum of 200/. for the support and maintenance of poor Prisoners for Debt (or otherwise) in the Gaol or Prison for the Borough of Liverpool; and it was also declared to be her will and mind, that the said Mayor and Rectors should place the said sum of 200/. out at interest, upon land security, if such could be had, and dispose of the said interest yearly, for the support and maintenance of the said Prisoners."

In a subsequent part of her Will, as referred to in the said Indenture, she also bequeathed to the said Rectors for the time being, the sum of 300/. the interest of which was directed to be distributed by the said Rectors to poor Sailors and Sailors' Widows, especially those in the Almshouses.

It is afterwards mentioned, in the said Indenture, that with the said sums of 200/. and 300/. were purchased three closes of land in Mosslake, containing seven acres of land, of the large measure; which were subjected to the payment of two fifth parts of the rents and produce to the said Mayor and Rectors, for the support and maintenance of the said poor Prisoners for Debt (or otherwise) in the Borough Gaol; and the remaining three fifth parts of the rent and produce were to be paid to the Rectors, and distributed yearly to the said poor Sailors and Sailors' Widows, especially those in the Alms-houses, by the said Rectors.

The foregoing statement was faithfully abridged and extracted from the original Deed, kept in the vestry of St. Nicholas's Church, in Liverpool, the 5th day of July, in the year 1798, by *R. H. Roughsedge.*

Amount of the produce of the Poor's Fields in Mosslake, Liverpool, in 1802.
From Mr. *Carson,* as Tenant 76'.
From Mr. *Whitlow,* as Tenant, 41.

Clear Rent, per annum, The above Legacies appear to have been most judiciously laid out, so as best to answer the pious intentions of the Donor; and from the local situation of the land, so contiguous to the Town of Liverpool, it will, in all probability, be soon built upon, and produce an immense revenue.

Debtors of the Borough Gaol receive also the benefit of a Legacy of Forty Pounds a year from some other source; which is paid into the hands of the Mayor and Bailiffs of the Corporation, and by them applied yearly at Christinas to the discharge of Insolvent Debtors. But no Memorial of it appears on record in the Prison.

The Act for preserving Health, and the Clauses against Spirituous Liquors, are both hung up. I am informed that the Gaol built by Mr. Blackburn is now fitted up, and nearly ready, for the reception of Prisoners; and that the wretched Prison just described, and the old House of Correction, are no longer to be continued as places of confinement.

LIVERPOOL. *Lancashire.*
The New Borough Gaol, and House of Correction.
Gaoler, *Thomas Amos.* Salary, 300/. and four Turnkeys, 60/. each.
Fees, of every kind, very laudably prohibited.

Chaplain, Rev. *George Monk.* Salary, not fixed.
Duty, Prayers and Sermon every Sunday.

Surgeon, from the Dispensary; to whom a Salary is paid for attendance, and
Medicines furnished by the Corporation.

Allowance. See the Borough Gaol.
REMARKS.
This Gaol, built by Mr. *Blackburn* 1787, is in a fine situation, a little way out of the Town, on which the *Corporation* have spared no expence. It is formed upon a *ven/ large scale,* with a proper separation of the different classes and sexes; and for security, health, reformation, and convenience, appears to be one of the best Gaols in the Kingdom. Unluckily, however, it was let to Government many years, and used as a place of confinement for French Prisoners; who wantonly and deliberately damaged the building, to so shameful a degree, that it was not repaired and fitted up for the reception of Prisoners before 1811.

It is surrounded by a boundaiy wall, 20 feet high. In the front is the Turnkey's lodge, with suitable apartments for his residence. A wash-house, and baths, and reception-rooms for Prisoners, until they are examined by the Surgeon, previous to their admission into the interior. A bell at the top serves equally for the Chapel, and in case of any alarm.

The Gaoler's house is detached from the six wings of the Prison, and 50 feet distant from the Turnkey's-lodge.

On the ground floor it has a convenient room for the Visiting Magistrates, and several others for the Keeper. At the back part is a very large room, nearly circular, and 23 feet in diameter, intended.as a General Inspection-Room; the windows having, very properly, a command of the several court-yards.

The *First floor* has three rooms for the Gaoler, and a large *Chapel,* 23 feet in diameter; to which there is a communication by means of stone bridges, from the different Prisons, into their several divisions or classes.

On the Second, or *Attick Story,* is a large room, well calculated for a General tnfirm&ry; and three other rooms, for the Surgeon's Dispensary, the nurse, and convalescents; with the leaden roof, prepared and set apart for their taking air and exercise.

The wing, No. 1, has, on the ground-floor, 17 single working-cells; of which two' are dark, assigned for refractory Prisoners. The lobby or passage is 5 feet wide, with arcades in the middle, for Prisoners to take the air in wet weather; and at each end is a day, or work-room, 25 feet by 22, with fire-places, and glazed grated windows.

Every single work-room or sleeping-cell in this Prison is 8 feet by 6 feet 6, and 9 feet high, to the crown of the arch; lighted and ventilated by a grated and glazed window made to open, and also by a circular aperture, 12 inches in diameter, over the door; with this only exception, that the grated windows of the Male Felons or Criminals are not glazed, like those of the other Prisoners.

The first story contains twenty-two sleeping-cells, with a day-room at the end of the lobby, which is of the same size as those below; and the second or attick story is in every respect similar.

The wing No. 2, has on the ground-floor 14 single working-cells, and one large work or day-room. And of the first and second story of this wing, each contains eighteen sleeping-cells, and a large work-room.

The wing No. 3, is similar on the ground-floor to No. 2. The first story of it has seventeen sleeping-cells, and two large work-rooms, of 42 feet by 21, and 24 feet by 22; with two fire-places in each.

The wing No. 4, has on the ground-floor twenty single working-cells, and a day or work-room, 95 feet by 22, with two fire-places. On the first floor of this wing there are 30 cells, and a day or work-room; and the attick story has eighteen sleeping-cells, and two day or work-rooms, of 25 feet by 22, with two fire-places in each of them.

No. 5, the wing intended for *Debtors,* has on the ground-floor twenty workingcells, and a day-room 25 feet by 22, with two fire-places. The second, or attick story, is exactly similar.

The wing No. *6* is also intended for Debtors; and has seventeen single workingcells on the ground-floor, with a day-room at each end, of 25 feet by 22. The first story contains twenty-two sleeping-cells, and two large day-rooms. The second or attick story is similar.

In each of the above six wings, and of which two are appropriated for House of Correction Prisoners, here is a leaden sink, with conveniencies for washing; and.Water is laid on by a pipe and cock, from cisterns at the top of the building, which are filled by a forcing pump, and thus supply the whole Prison.

The six court-yards appropriated to the wings are irregular polygons, enclosed with an open Wood paling; which, being distant about 36 feet from the boundary wall, affords a convenient garden for the growth of vegetables; and the sewers are judiciously placed.

In eacrh wing there are two dark cells for the refractory. The sleeping-cells of the two wings intended for the Debtors, and that Which is assigned for the Women Criminals, have boarded floors; but all the rest are of stone. Each wing has arcades, for the use and exercise of the respective Prisoners in wet weather.

All the day-rooms are fitted up with benches, tables, and utensils for frugal cookery. Coals are allowed by the Corporation, and cupboards to secure provisions. The Debtors' sleeping-cells are furnished with iron frame bedsteads, sacking bottoms, two blankets, two sheets, and a quilt: those for Felons, and other Criminal Prisoners, have wOod plank bedsteads, a paillasse, two blankets, and a rug.

The following is a Summary of the

various Apartments comprehended in the new Gaol of Liverpool:
    Single Work-Rooms-----------102
    Very large ditto----------8
    Sleeping-Cells-------------*249*
    And of very spacious Day? or Work-Rooms----18 '. Total, 377.

LIVERPOOL. *Lancashire.*
The Bridewell.
Keeper, *Robert lValton;* now *John Hart.* Salary, 57/. 14. and two Turnkeys, at 15s. per week each. Fees, None.

No Chaplain, nor religious attentions. J

Surgeon, as wanted, sent from the Dispensary.

Number of Prisoners, 1S02, Oct. nth, 28. 1805, Oct. 25th, 8. 1809, Nov. 13th, 13.

Allowance, three-pence each per day.

REMARKS.

The ancient Bridewell was formerly a Magazine, belonging to the Old Castle, ancf" consisted of two cells, one of them 12 feet by 7 feet 6, the other 18 feet by 12; both eight steps under ground, and damp; lighted and ventilated by one iron-barred and grated window in each, with fire-places. Also two rooms above stairs, the one 18 feet by 10, the other 10 feet by *9*; and two other cells, totally dark, of only 5 feet by 3 each, and 6 feet high! No straw, or other bedding whatsoever, was allowed. No employment provided. No court-yard. No water accessible to the Prisoners; and the Corporation only allowed them firing. In short, it laboured not merely under the infirmities of deserted age, but had several great and radical defects, which time and skill only could remove.

It was pulled down, accordingly, at my visit in 1805; and the present building, as a place of *temporary* confinement, having been got ready, was first inhabited *26* Dec. 1804.

This new Bridewell nearly adjoins the Town-Hall, or Sessions House. From the basement story there is a subterraneous passage, through which the Prisoners are conducted, either for examination or trial. It opens by a trap-door into the bar of the Sessions House; and thus the Prisoners are remanded, when necessary, without being exposed to public view. It also prevents occasional crowds, and disorderly conduct, during the removal of the Prisoners.

The front entrance, or first floor, consists of the Porter's Lodge, 21 feet by 14, and 11 feet high. This room has a fire-place, and glazed windows, and is fitted up with chairs and benches for the Turnkey, and Assistant Constables of the night. A lock-up room, intended for *disorderly Females,* 23 feet by 15, and 11 feet high, with a fire-place, is fitted up with wooden benches, and a sewer attached to it. Here are also two other cells, for Prisoners to be kept separate; each 9 feet by 8, and 10 feet high, fitted up with cast-iron bedsteads; to each of which the Town furnishes straw-in-sacking beds, two blankets, a bolster, and a rug. The remainder of this floor is occupied by the Keeper.

The basement story before-mentioned, (to which the descent is by 17 steps,) is surrounded by an open area, from which the rooms are ventilated; and consists of one room, 23 feet by 15, and 10 feet high, with a fire-place, and wooden benches. Here are also two sleeping-cells, of the same size, and fitted up like those above described, with a convenient sewer attached. These rooms are set apart for the reception of refractory Prisoners, or those who are under charge for offences of a more serious nature. The stair-cases are of stone; and all the rooms in which Prisoners are confined, are arched with brick, and have flag-stone floors.

The second story, ascended by *22* steps, is appropriated for the reception of Prisoners of a more decent appearance, committed for slight offences; and contains a large room, and two sleeping-cells, of the same dimensions, and fitted up in like manner as the former.

The remainder of this story, also, is occupied by the Keeper, except one room over the Porter's lodge, which is reserved for Prisoners of respectable connections. Should there be more Prisoners than the cells will accommodate, they must sleep irt their clothes, upon benches *2* feet wide.

The sexes are separated. Coals and candles are furnished by the Corporation. But here is no allowance for food, which must be purchased by the Prisoners, or supplied them by their friends. The Prison is well accommodated with excellent water, brought in by pipes. No employment is yet provided; nor any room set apart for the sick. The Act for preserving Health, and Clauses against Spirituous Liquors, not hung up.

LIVERPOOL. *Tlte House of Correction.*
Keeper, *Henry Widdowes.* Salary, 84/. with firing and candle; and a Turnkey, at 10. per week, who also has fuel for his apartment.

Chaplain, none; nor any religious attentions whatever.

Surgeon, when wanted, sent from the Dispensary.

Number of Prisoners, 1802, Oct. 14th, 76. 1805, Oct. 25th, 39. 1809, Nov. 13th, *62.*

Allowance, to Convicts, sixpence per day: to other Prisoners, a three-penny loaf, and one pennyworth of potatoes.

REMARKS.

This Prison was. built in 1776, on an eminence adjoining to the Work-house. The Men and Women have separate rooms and court-yards.

For t;he Men, here are four rooms below, and four above; for the Women, six rooms, both below and above. They are each 12 feet by 10, and nearly 9 feet high; all supplied with three bedsteads, straw-in-sacking beds, two blankets, and coverlets. They are all, however, too close; having no windows, but only an aperture in the doors, about 9 inches square, and an iron plate near the ceiling, perforated with-five small holes. At the end of the passage is a room for the refractory, of 7 feet by 4 feet 10 which is totally dapk, and without ventilation.

In_the Men's court-yard is a work _shop, which originally was of 20 feet by 17 feet 9, but since divided into two; where Men and Boys were employed in picking oakum. Their average earnings were two-pence half penny per day; but now there ia seldom any employment, and Prisoners are allowed no share of their earnings.

At a subsequent visit I found that one room from the Men's-side, and another

LQSTWITHYELL, or LESTWITHIEL. Cornwall.
Gaol for Debtors.

Keeper, *Barnard Westlake;* now *William Blewitt,* Blacksmith, and Town Sergeant. Salary, none. Fees, 13. *Ad.* No Table.

Prisoners, 1803, Oct. 9th, 0. 1806, Sept. 29th 0. Allowance, None.

REMARKS.

This is a *Stannary* or Tin-miner's Prison for Debtors; the property of His Royal Highness the *Prince,* Duke of *Cornwall,* and Lord of the Stannaries. It is a Prison for Debtors only. Adjoining to it are two court-yards, not supplied with water, which the Prisoners have from the Keeper's house.

The room which is now denominated "The Prison," is spacious, 42 feet by 18, and 7 feet 6 inches high; and has four iron-grated windows looking to the street, with inside shutters, a fire-place, and straw on a tarras-floor, for men. Above it are three rooms for Women Debtors. Besides these there are several small sleeping rooms, to which the Keeper furnishes beds, at 1. per week. They were used one year as a "Sheriffs ward," for the County: Some of them have been since inhabited by the Keeper, and others are a deposit for wine. Over the old Prison is a board, on which is painted, " *Dealer in Spirituous Liquors* f1

A large vaulted room below is called *The Dungeon,* and has two iron-grated windows toward the street. At my visit in 1806, it was filled with lumber; and over it is a large room, in which Prisoners for the Midsummer and Christmas Session are detained for trial.

Five sleeping-rooms are in the upper part of the Prison; of which one is furnished with a wooden bedstead, and an old chaff bed, left by the late Keeper.

The last Debtor confined here was *Salathiel Harris;* committed the l6th of July 1805, and liberated the 14th November following, in consequence of his Plaintiff's being non-suited. During the period of his four months confinement, his Wife and Children were thrown for subsistence on his parish, of St. Agnes; and as no allowance whatever is granted to the Prison, this poor Man received the indulgence of being brought down from his room to an iron-grated window next the street; there to solicit the casual charity of passengers, by means of a *shoe,* suspended by a cord, which the Keeper had humanely provided for him!

There formerly were, and I believe still are, certain *Rules,* or free boundaries to this Prison, somewhat like those of the King's Bench and Fleet; which are said to extend over the whole Borough, and a Prisoner was indulged with them, ou giving security.

The Lord Warden of the Stannaries holds his Court here four times a year, and has his *Office of Cuinage;* explained to me, as signifying the Process of making up the Tin into Pigs or Blocks. See under *Helston,* page 265.

This Prison is very dirty, not having been white-washed for near 20 years.

LOUTH. *Lincolnshire.*
The House of Correction.

Gaoler, *Richard Cox.* Salary, loOl. No Fees.

Chaplain, Rev. Mr. *Benson.* Salary, 20l. Duty, Prayers once a week.

Surgeon, Mr. *William King.* Salary, none. Makes a Bill.

Number of Prisoners, 1810, Jan. 1st, 32. 1811, May 5th, J7.

Allowance, eight pence per day, paid to the Keeper.

REMARKS.

This Prison, at Louth, for the Eastern Division of Lindsay, is an old building, which has been lately repaired and considerably improved. It consists of a comfortable dwelling-house for the Keeper, and four Wards for Prisoners. No. I, for Felons and Vagrants, has a court-yard, 32 feet by 21, and a day-room, 14 feet by 10, the floors of which are paved with Yorkshire flagging. On the ground-floor are two sleeping-cells, 10 feet by 9, with two beds each, and two others, 10 feet by 6, with one bed each: they are raised 2 feet from the ground, to keep them dry; and above stairs are two others, of the same size, for Felons. Ward No. 2, is for Prisoners convicted of small offences, and *Debtors* from the *Court of Conscience:* they have a court-yard 36 feet by 21, and a day-room 14 feet square, with flagged floors. Above stairs are three sleeping-rooms, two of which are 14 feet square, and the other 22 feet by 12. Ward No. *3,* for Women Felons and Vagrants, and Ward No. 4, for Women convicted of small offences, have day-rooms, court-yards, and sleeping-rooms, nearly similar to those before described; and in the attick story are rooms set apart for the sick. The sleeping-rooms have boarded floors, and all have glazed windows, except the four cells on the ground-floor of No. 1, which have wooden shutters. There is a sewer and pump in every court, to which the Prisoners have access in the day-time. Each Class is kept separate, and they never see each other, except at Divine Service, which is performed in the Gaoler's house. A strike, or bushel, of coals is allowed weekly to each day-room. Those sentenced to hard labour are allowed one third of their earnings: the remainder is equally divided between the Keeper and the County; but a full supply of work cannot be obtained.

LYDD. *Kent.*
The Town Gaol.

Keeper, *John Leper,* Town Serjeant. Salary, none. Fees, 6s. 8d.

Surgeon, when wanted, sent from the Town.

Number of Prisoners, 1804, Aug. 27th, 1806, Aug. 9th, 1807, Sept. 1lth,—None.

Allowance, sixpence per day.

REMARKS.

This Prison, built in 1792, is under the Town-Hall; and has a court-yard, 20 feet by 12, surrounded by a wall about 15 feet high, with a sewer in the corner. Two rooms, or sleeping-cells, 10 feet by 9 each, and 8 feet 6 inches high; with wooden bedsteads and loose straw to lie on: an iron-grated window to each, of about 2 feet square, with inside shutters opening to the court-yard. No water: the Keeper carries it three times a day. The Gaol has never been whitewashed.

LUDGATE. *London.* Gaoler, *John Teague.* Salary, loo/. *i. d.*
Fees. To the Keeper, on entrance----------10

To the Clerk of the Papers of one of the Compters, for making out a *Ducifacias* (as it is called) if in execution------26

To ditto, if on Mesne Process-----------14

To the Officer for his Conduct Fee--------50

Every Debtor, on his entrance, pays to the Steward of the Prison-6 0
Which is'disposed of as follows; viz. to the Secretary, for entering his name, &c. in the book, *6d.*; and the remaining *Ss. 64.* is applied to the Fund for supplying the Prison with coals, candles, oil for the lamps, &c

Every Debtor contributes weekly, during confinement, to the said Fund I 0

Every Debtor pays the Keeper, on discharge--------20

To the Turnkey-IO

To the Keeper, every week during confinement------03

To the Clerk of the Papers of Giltspur-street Compter----3 8

To ditto of the Poultry Compter-----38

To the Secondaries of London-----------54

To ditto, for every other Action, (if more than one)-----34

To the Messenger--------------10.

Chaplain, Rev. *John Rose.* Duty, Prayers and Sermon on Sundays. Salary 50/.

Surgeon, Mr. *Hodgson.*

Salary, looi. and *20l.* for medicines to Ludgate, and the two Compters.

Number of Debtors'.
1800, April 15th,-28 1804, Sept. 6th, --*9* 1808, June 28th,--*26* 1801, Sept. 16th,-12 1805, Nov. 13th,--26 1809, May 22th,--30 1802, March 14th, 22 1806, May 23d,--26 1810, April 19th,--14 1803, Nov. 12th,-25 1807, Feb. 16th,--23 1811, April 15th,--27.

Allowance. A loaf of bread, weight 20 oz. every other day to each Prisoner, and 1 lk of rice, 3 lbs of beef, and 5 lbs of potatoes weekly, to each.

REMARKS.

This Prison was formerly one of the Gates of the City of London, and then situated on Ludgate-hill, near the spot where the London Coffee-house now stands.

Those Debtors who are too poor to pay the 6. on entrance have to that amount of their dole stopped, oat of the first Quarterly distribution of Charity Money.

It is at present appropriated for the reception of Debtors, being Freemen of London; Clergymen, Proctors, Attornies, or such other Persons as the Court of Lord Mayor and Aldermen shall from time to time think fit to be removed hither. It is believed to have formerly had the privilege of permitting Prisoners to go out (with a Keeper) for the purpose of calling upon their several creditors, to compromise their debts, or otherwise obtain their discharge: But that custom, whatever might have been its origin, was many years since discontinued, and cannot now be traced.

About fifty years ago, when old Ludgate (to which the Table of Fees, and Rules and Orders for its Government, were adapted) was pulled down, the Prisoners were removed to the London Work-house, in Bishopsgate-street; a part whereof was fitted up for that purpose, and Ludgate Prisoners continued to be received there, until the year 1794; when they were removed to the present Prison of Ludgate, adjoining to, and partly encircled by, the Compter in Giltspur-street.

Ludgate has one small yard, 25 feet by 10; containing a pump, which supplies spring-water from a well in the Compter; another, affording soft water from the river Thames; and a shed, under which is a bathing tub.

The yard leads to eight rooms; *viz.* the Hall, fitted up with benches and tables, for the general accommodation of all the Prisoners, as a sitting-room in the day-time, and until they usually retire to rest. It is the custom of this Gaol for the Prisoners to have access to the yard at all times, either by day or night. The Hall has one fire-place, which is supplied by a Subscription from the Prisoners, of six shillings at their entrance, and seven pence weekly afterwards; aided by charitable donations, the surplus of which, after payment of certain salaries hereafter described, is divided quarterly among such Prisoners, as have been in custody for the space of one month before the same became due.

The next is a long room over the Hall, which will conveniently contain six persons, as a bed-room. The room over the long room will contain two persons, exclusive of two little rooms, partitioned from it, for the use of the sick.

There is a small room over the Chapel (which is on the ground-floor;) and this, together with another room over it in the second story, are convenient bed-rooms for three persons each. Here are also two closets, which are used as bed-rooms for one person each.

Two other rooms are upon the ground-floor on the other side of the yard; one of which is the bed-room of the steward and secretary, and the other a chamber for three Prisoners. The Women's ward, over the Steward's room, will contain three persons. There are fire-places in the rooms, to which two chaldrons of coals a year are given by the Lord Mayor and Sheriffs.

All the prisoners here find their own beds, and bedding, except one rug yearly, which the City allows to such as need it.

At Christmas every Debtor receives one pound of beef, onejpint of porter, and one loaf, value three halfpence, or potatoes in lieu of it. On New Year's day, at Easter, and on some uncertain day after, the same gift is made by the Lord Mayor and Sheriffs, who also occasionally give coals, according to their discretion. Michael Angelo Taylor, Esq. M. P. on Christmas-eve gives eight pounds of beef, a halfpeck loaf, and a sack of coals, to each Prisoner; and the same to the Turnkey.

There are also certain established donations, of bread and meat, at stated periods, besides some private gifts. Money is likewise paid by several of the City companies, and others, for the release of Debtors from this and other Prisons; which is most frequently applied towards the discharge of such

Prisoners, as cannot obtain the same without *undertaking to pay some further sum*, in addition to the money raised by such donations; and who are thereby prevented from availing themselves of the Bounty of the Honourable and Benevolent Society for Relief of Debtors, held in Craven Street in the Strand: Of which description are, the legacies of Mr. *Humble,* (paid by the Leathersellers' Company to the amount of eight pounds *per annum,)* and others. The legacy of Lady *Rich* is usually applied in aid of the legacies of Mr. *Humble,* or any other benevolent Donor, for the release of Prisoners, at one moiety by each legacy; and if the sum of twenty-four pounds has not been advanced for such release, before the payment of Lady *Rich's* legacy, then the remainder is divided among those Prisoners who were in Gaol on the Christmas-day preceding, and still remain in custody.

A List of Benefactions to Ludgate Prison.
Christmas Quarter.
  When paid.
  Yearly-
  Ditto-
  Ditto- (Quarterly
  Half-Yearly
  Yearly-
  Ditto--
  Half-Yearly
  Ditto-
  Ditto- (Quarterly-
  Half-Yearly
  Yearly-
  Quarterly
  Yearly-
  Quarterly
  Ditto -
  Yearly-
  Ditto-
  Quarterly
  Yearly-
  Donors' Names.
  Fishmongers Company---
Sir Thomas Kneesworth--
Mrs. Lettice Smith----
Sir Thomas Gresham, Knt.
Mr. Middleton-----
Sir John Kendrick, Knt.--
Sir Stephen Peacock, Knt.
  Mr. W. Parker

Mr. John Wooler---
Lady Maurice and Mr. Bennett
Mr. Peter Blundell----
Sir William Home, Knt.--
Mrs. Cook------
Mr. Peter Blundell---
Mr. James Hodgson---
Mr. Meridith------
Mr. John Draper---
Mr. Thomas Dawson---
Mrs. Holligrave-----
Sadlers Company---

Archbp. of Canterbury- The Society for the Relief and Discharge of Persons confined for Small Debts admit of no sucb. undertaking, but always require a receipt in full from the Creditor.
je?.6 11 4. Being the produce, or interest, of 45J. 4«. Id. Old South Sea Annuities. *Extract of Ike Will of Thomas Cottle, dated March* 17, 1556.—" My very Will and Mind is, that immediately after my decease, at or about the end of erery quarter of the year for evermore, with sixteen shillings, parcel of the same Rents and Profits, arising, coming, growing, and to be received of the same Messuages or Tenements, with the Appurtenances, the Churchwardens, for the time being, of the Parish of Saint Dunstan, in the East, shall bay and provide one quarter of good beef, and one peck of oatmeal; and the same quarter of beef and peck of oatmeal, so by them bought and provided, they shall give and distribute, or see to be given and distributed, truly and faithfully, at or about every quarter's end as aforesaid, to and among the poor Prisoners in the Prison Houses of Newgate and Ludgate in London, the King's Bench, and the Marshalsea in Southwark, according to this my Mind, Intent, and Will, in that behalf; that is, to wit, That the poor Prisoners, in every of the same four Prison Houses, shall have given and distributed amongst them yearly for ever, after my decease, of my Gift and Bequest, one quarter of good beef, and one peck of oatmeal as aforesaid; that is to say, a quarter of beef and one peck of oatmeal to the one Prison House, at one quarter of the year's end; and at the next quarter's end, another quarter of beef, and another peck of oatmeal, to another of the said four Prison Houses, to the Prisoners in the same being; and so at every quarter's end to change, to the intent that the Prisoners in every of the same Prisons, once in the year, for ever, be relieved by my said Gift and Bequest."

Sir *Stephen Peacock,* Knt. by his Will, dated 3d November 1535, gave the Haberdashers1 Company certain Lands in the Parish of St. Sepulchre without Newgate, London, on condition of bestowing *(inter alia)* "Two loads of charcoal, for the Prisoners of Newgate and Ludgate, of 12j. more or less, at the Warden's direction, to be delivered three or four days yearly." For many years *11.* 10. each was paid to the Prisoners in Newgate and Ludgate; but, on a recent investigation of this and other Charities, the Company thought that two loads of Charcoal might be fairly computed at 4/. and therefore directed that each of the Prisons should receive that sum yearly, commencing from Christmas 1809.

Lady North gave yearly, in bread, thirteen pence every Friday for ever, out of the King's

Head Tavern, near Newgate; and twelve loaves every quarter. This is sent from the bakers, in threepenny loaves, every fortnight. Mrs. *Margaret Dane,* widow, gave yearly for ever eighteen stone of beef, and five dozen of bread, value one pound, by the Ironmongers' Company, to be paid at Allhallows-tide,

Michaelmas quarter.

Mr. *Robert Rogers,* Leatherseller, gave yearly, by the Leathersellers' Company, twenty shillings, to be paid quarterly in bread. Mrs. *Margaret Symcott,* every eighth week for ever, by the Chamber of London, sixty-five penny loaves. This is *Eleanor Gwynris* Gift, under that name. Mrs. *Frances Ashton,* by will, dated 30th March 1727, gave one Annual Rent Charge of

One Hundred Pounds *per annum* " To be issuing and payable to them my said Trustees.

and their heirs, by and out of all and singular my lands, tenements, and hereditaments, situate and being in the county of Bedford, Bucks, and Hertford., or any of them, other The nett Receipt of St. Dunstan's Parish for the year 1809, from, the Premises whence the Legacy is payable, was 59. than such as are hereinbefore given or limited for charity; Upon the trusts, and to and for the uses, intents, and purposes hereinafter mentioned, (that is to say,) As for and concerning Ninety-five Pounds *per annum,* part of the said One Hundred Pounds *per annum,* to be by my said Trustees last-mentioned, and the survivor of them, and the heirs of such survivor annually, in the month of January in every year, paid, applied, and disposed of for and towards the discharging out of Prison such or so many poor Prisoners, as then shall be Prisoners in the Prisons of Ludgate, and the Compters in London, and the Marshalsea in Southwark, whose respective sums, for and towards such respective discharges of such respective Prisoners, shall not amount to more than the sum of Five Pounds a-piece." Probate granted in London, 27th April, 1809.

Mr. *Richard Jacob,* Vintner, gave yearly for 257 years, by Joseph Howell and Susannah his wife, their heirs, executors, and assigns, out of five tenements situate in Lincoln's-InnFields, two pounds, payable at Easter. Will dated Oct. 13th 1612. This is subject to land-tax. See the foregoing List of Benefactions, in page 366.

Mr. *Thomas Stretchley,* by his Will dated August 6, 1678, gave for ever forty shillings, to be paid every three years, by the Treasurer of Christ's Hospital. This is regularly paid.

The Chamber of London, in lieu of 250/. being the gift of Mr. *Middleton,* payable at Christmas and Midsummer, 3/. 2. 6d. See List of Benefactions, pp. 365, 366.

George Humble Esq. gave to the Company of Leathersellers "the Sum of Two Hundred Pounds in money, to be laid out and bestowed by them (with what convenient speed may be), in the purchasing of so much freehold lands and tenements, as far as the same will extend; To this intent and purpose, that out of the rents and profits arising of such lands and tenements so to be bought as aforesaid, there may yearly and every year for ever be acquitted and released out of the Prison of Ludgate, London, three, four, or five poor Men who shall lie in there for Debt, (those that be free of the said Company of Leathersellers being preferred before others in this my Gift.)" The money does not appear to have ever been laid out; but 8/. *per annum* is paid to discharge Prisoners, by the Leathersellers' Company. Mr. Humble's Will is dated 20th Sept. 1638.

Lady Rich gave yearly, for ever, towards the relief and release of the Prisoners, thirty pounds, payable at Christmas: this is subject to land-tax, six pounds. If the money has not wholly or in pari been appropriated to release Prisoners, the remainder is divided among as many Debtors as were in confinement at Christmas, and not discharged on Lady-day. Twenty-four pounds were divided the 6th April 1807 among ten Prisoners, 2/. 8s. each, who had remained in custody since the preceding Christmas; no person having, in the course of twelve months prior to the payment thereof, been released thereby. This legacy is paid on Lady-day old style, by Mr. *John Roberts* of Oakingham, Berks, attorney at law.

Mrs. *Elizabeth Misson,* gave by Will dated 23d May, 1770, the produce of Fourteen Hundred Pounds, in three per Cent. India Annuities, in the manner therein directed; that is, the produce of 200/. of the same Annuities, for the use of the sick and lame in the Middlesex Hospital; likewise the produce of 200/. for the sick and lame in the Westminster Infirmary, and the produce of 200/. for the use of the sick and lame at Mile End; likewise the produce of 100/. to the Asylum for poor deserted Children: Also for the use of the Charity Children of Saint Mary-le-bone, she gave 50/.; and to fifty poor families in

Saint Mary-le-bone, I leave *SOL.*; twenty shillings to each. I also give, of the produce of the same Annuities, to the *Debtors of Ludgate Prison Two Hundred Pmnds,* and also the produce of 200/. to the Debtors only of the Fleet Prison, and also 200/. to the Debtors only of Newgate Prison.——There has lately been some irregularity and great reluctance in the payment of this legacy.

Legacies not received.
Hugh Offley 5s. John Symonds 4j. Lady *Carew* 405. John Jackson *ZOs.* Sir *Ralph Freeman* 5/. *John Hobby,* Esq. 22/. annually, for ever, for the release of eleven poor prisoners, at 4-oj. each.

Excellent Rules and Orders, for the governmt.it of this Prison, were made on the 6th November 1808, signed by the Lord Mayor and Sheriffs, and approved by Lord Ellenborough and Sir Archibald Macdonald, 5th March 1810.

The accounts of Receipts and Disbursements of this Prison are kept with great accuracy; and th3 order and decorum observed in it do much credit to Mr. Teague, the Keeper.

LUDLOW. *See page $43.* LYDD. *Seepage 362.* LYNN REGIS. *Norfolk.*

The Town Gaol, and House of Correction.

Gaoler, *William Hawes.* Salary, 35/. for both.

Fees, Debtors, *6s. 8d.* Felons, &c. 5. *6d.*

Chaplain, none. Surgeon, from the Workhouse, if wanted.

Number of Prisoners. Debtors. Felons, &c.

1802, Jan. 28th,------3-1 1805, Aug. 30th, 1 4 1810, Sept. 5th,------1--1 assault.

Allowance, none, except to Paupers; and that varies, according to the price of provisions. In August, 1805, it was eight-pence a day each. In September 1810, nine-pence a day each, in money.

REMARKS.

The Town Gaol is nearly opposite to St. Margaret's Church, and was built in 1784, as appears by the Inscription in front. The ground-floor is occupied by the Keeper; and the Gaol is separated by two iron-grated doors, within a passage 4 feet wide.

, The Gaoler's kitchen commands a view of the court-yard, which is 82 feet by 15, for the common use of all descriptions of Prisoners. On the left-hand is the only day-room in the Prison, 19 feet by 13, with a fire-place, and stone sink.

At the end of the court-yard, and under arcades, are two sleeping-cells, about 8 feet square, arch-roofed; lighted and ventilated by two iron-grated windows in each, and furnished with crib-bedsteads, straw, and two, three, or four coverlets, as the weather may require. Poor Debtors and petty Offenders sleep in these cells, and if they bring their own bedding, pay sixpence a week.

At the end of the day-room is a staircase, leading to two Infirmary rooms, which have each a fire-place, and two glazed windows, with crib-bedsteads, straw, and coverlets..

On the attic-story, and in front of the Keeper's house, are three good sized rooms, about 16 feet by 11, and 0. feet high, for Master's-Side Debtors, with glazed sash windows, and fire-places in two of them. To these the Gaoler furnishes a single bed at 2s. per week; or if two sleep together, 1. 6d. each.

Over the day-room is the Women-Felons' apartment, 26 feet by 14, and 8 feet high, which has two beds in it, a fire-place, and three glazed windows. The dungeon yard here is a passage of 18 feet by 4 feet wide, in which are three dungeons; two of them about 12 feet square, with arched roofs, crib bedsteads, straw, and coverlets; the third, called the *Long Dungeon,* is about 10 feet by 4, with a crib-bedstead and straw: The only light and ventilation which they receive is from a small iron-grated aperture, nearly over each door. The Long Dungeon has no light, but through an opening of 10 inches by 4; and being now stopped up, is converted into a military depot.

Debtors from the Courts of Conscience are sent hither, and have the same allowance as the other Prisoners. It decreases, however, on a second commitment of this class; and a watch-maker, who had been confined here before, received only sixlence a day.

I found the Act and Clauses both hung up. Here is a pump of excellent springwater; and soft water also is laid on by a pipe.

The House of Correction adjoins to the Town Gaol, and has four large iron-grated windows fronting the street, with inside shutters; and two rooms with arched roofs, 27 feet by 11, and 10 feet high. Into one of these, Prisoners were heretofore permitted to come: but, in consequence of disorderly behaviour, it is now denied them; and the apartments are used only as store-rooms.

The Prison consists of four rooms: the first is 12 feet square; the next has been partitioned off into two; in one of which is a sewer. That which they call the *Large Room,* is 22 feet by 12, and furnished with three crib-bedsteads; and the *Dungeon,* which formerly opened into it, as well as the place called *Little Ease,* are now topped up. The iron-grated windows to these last-mentioned rooms have outside shutters, and are all of them under the Town-Hall. Here are hemp blocks, and beetles for pounding of tile sherds, and brick-dust was lying pounded in one corner.-Debtors from the Court of Conscience are sent hither for any sum less than forty shillings. Offenders are also sent here, for trial at the Quarter Sessions, from Swaffham. Felons are tried at this Borough by the Recorder, at the Sessions, four times in the year; and the Court here has the power of life and death. Prisoners of this Bridewell have the accommodation of going hence into Court for trial, without the painful circumstance of coming through the street.

An old Table of Fees, and Rules and Orders, dated 1st Mach 1729, signed *John Goodwyn,* Mayor, and *Robert Undericood,* Town Clerk, are kept here; and both the Act for preserving Health, and Clauses against Spirituous Liquors, are properly hung up.-.

MACCLESFIELD. *Cheshire.*
The Town Gaol.
Gaoler, *Maurice Jones;* now *James Stott.* Salary, none.

Fees, 7. 6d. No Table. Garnish, not yet abolished, 2. 6d.

Number of Debtors, 1808, Jan. 4th,----3.
1809, Feb. 24th,----4. 1800, March 30th,----1. 1802, Feb. 17th,----1. 1805, Sept. 15th,----1.

Allowance, none whatever.
REMARKS.
This Prison, for the Liberty of the Hundred, Manor, and Forest of Macclesfield, in the *Pinfold,* or Pound, of that Hundred, is the property of the Earl of Derby, who holds a Court twice in the year; viz. in *April* and *October.*

Debtors are committed hither for indefinite sums, from one shilling up to any amount: and as they cannot obtain their *Sixpences,* by virtue of the Statute, called "The Lord's Act," before the holding of the Court next after their commitment, it may be their hard lot to be immured in this dreary abode for several months together, without a chance of speedier deliverance.

Here is a court-yard, or area, of 24 feet by 18. The Prison consists of four rooms, two on the ground-floor, about 11 feet square, and two of about *6* feet square.

No bedding: not even straw is allowed. The Keeper furnisher those-Prisoners, who can pay, with a day-room, bed-chamber, and fire,, at three shillings and sixpence per week each.

The old Dungeon, which is seven steps down in size 111. feet by Q-, and lighted by a window only 6 inches square, was formerly used for the confinement of Deserters; but at my visit in 1805, it was, happily, in a state of total ruin, and' 6 inches deep in mud.

The Gaoler, who is a Bailiff, or Sheriff's Officer, keeps the Eagle-and-Child (the *Derby Arms)* Publick House, and pays *26l.* annual rent, with all taxes. He told me that one Isaac Wylde was confined here *six months,* for a Debt of *Jive shillings and three, pence!*

Of the three Debtors, (all Women,) who have been here confined subsequent to the first of October, 1807, the names and circumstances areas follow:
1. *Elizabeth Gosling,* widow, aged 48, a Washerwoman, who g. s. d. has two Children under 14 years of age. Her Debt was for

Linen and Cotton Goods-----------1 10 6

Costs, *9l.*3«. *3d,* Prison Fees, *ll.* 15,-- ----1018 3

Total, .12 8 9

Committed to Macclesfield Gaol, 2d Oct. 1807. -- 2. *Mary Marsland,* widow, aged 65, and incapable of gaining a livelihood. Debt, for Linen and Cotton Goods--0 7 0 Costs, *9l. 15s. lid.* Prison Fees, *l/*-15.-----11 10 11

Total, 11 17 11 Committed to Macclesfield Gaol, 23d December, 1807..

3. *Margaret Ashton,* widow, aged 56, a Cotton-Weaver, Debt, for Flour, Cheese, and Butter--074
Costs, *9I. 15s. 11 d.* Prison Fees, *2l.10s.* -----12 5 11

Total, 12 13 s 3; Committed to Macclesfield Gaol, 21st Nov. 1807..

The three Debts together, *2/. 4s. lod.* Costs and Prison Fees, 34/. 14. *id.* Total, 36V-*lSs.lld!*

These are facts verified, which need no comment.

How desirable then must it be, in such very extreme cases of Poverty and Woe, of Female Poverty, and Female Woe, if the Legal Execution of British Law could so operate, as to attach upon the *Goods* only, not on the *Person,* of helpless widowed Debtors !

I should have mentioned, that Elizabeth Gosling's Debt, *ll. 10s. 6d.* was accepted from the Society for Discharge and Relief of Persons imprisoned for small Debts, and she was soon discharged, after presenting her Petition at the Office in Craven Street. Mary Marsland, and Margaret Ashton, were ordered two shillings and sixpence per week, for their support in Prison, till the Committee should hold their next monthly meeting.

All these poor Women had excellent characters given of them respectively; which renders the consideration of their distresses doubly painful. Marsland has a son, who should have been her greatest helper, "To rock the cradle of declining age:" But he enlisted for a soldier. Her goods had been seized and sold for rent; and, having no allowance' in Gaol, misery must have sunk her there, but for the incidental charity of some well-disposed persons, (of whom one was a gentleman actually in the Gaol, as a fellow Prisoner at the time,) who felt for her accumulated Trials.

From one of the Plaintiffs (a Woman also,) the Society received a Letter, dated the 17th of March 1809, which is pointedly expressive. "I could not," says the writer, " make up my payments; therefore was obliged to sue some, to make others pay me; but *little thought what the expence would be.* I have since been told the Macclesfield Court are allowed very liberal Fees. When I went to Macclesfield, on *Goslings* account, I saw this Woman Marsland, and'was very'much shocked at her appearance. The weather being extremely cold, and having little to eat, sh£ had been very ill; but some of her neighbours had subscribed 8. and sent her; and Mr. *Jones* (the Gaoler) has been very humane to her1, ih'giving her a little broth now and then; for there is no allowance, not even fire, nor so much as straw for a bed-f-."

There is every reason to hope, as it is sincerely to be wished, that a radical and very beneficial change will ere long take place in the Town Gaol of Macclesfield.

Neither the Act nor Clauses hung up. The Prison-rooms are dirty, and out of repair.

See my Remarkstn Penzance Prison, in a following page; which is now humanely d0n6 away by Lord Arundel, and the wretched place turned into an innocent milk-cellar. f Mary Marsland vas discharged the 4th May 1808, by a Rule of Court, under the Lord's Act, without payment of Debt or Costs. Margaret Ashtoh was discharged the 12th May. The Plaintiff's Attorney, 00 being served with notice of Petition, and Schedule For Relief, under the Lord's Act, consented to discharge her without putting her to the expence of presenting a Petition to the Court. MAIDSTONE. Kent.

The County Gaol.
Gaoler, *Thomas Watson;* now *William Cutbush.* Salary, 300/.

Fees, see Table; and for Conveyance of Transports one shilling per mile each. Garnish, 2. *Sd.* exacted by the Prisoners. :

Chaplain, Rev. Mr. *Lloyd;* afterwards Rev. Mr. *Evans:* now Rev. Mr. *Shelton.* Duty, Prayers and Sermon to Debtors, Felons, &c. and that, heretofore, only on *alternate Sundays.* But see Remarks, and the Note in page 376. Salary, 50/...

Surgeon, Mr. *Coleman.*
Salary, 75/. for this Gaol, (Debtors included,) and for the Bridewell. Number of Prisoners.

Debtors. Felons, &c. Debtors. Felons, &c.
1801, Sept. 22d,--30--70 1804, Sept. 26th,--23--35 1806, Aug. 14th,--26--54 1807, Sept. 8th,--29--' 38 1808, July 14th,--51--57 1809, July 19th,--39--56 1810, Aug. 22d,--23--53 1811, May 23d,--51--50.

Allowance, a half-quartern loaf every other day, and one quart of small beer daily, for Prisoners of all descriptions. Whatever the Baker's bill amounts to weekly for bread, one half of that sum is allowed for *table beer:* But, when a Debtor has obtained his Sixpences, the allowance of bread is discontinued.

REMARKS.

From the Inscription, " *C. Sloane,* Architect," on a stone in front, it appears that this Gaol was erected in 1746. The Keeper's house separates the Debtors' Prison from that of the Felons; but he has no proper view of the Prison at large.

At the top of the Gaol is an alarm-bell.

For Men Debtors here are two courtyards. The upper one, 43 feet by 38, is paved with flag-stones: the lower, which is 96 feet by 48, has a hard gravelled bottom. They have likewise a common day-room, of 26 feet by 19.

The Women Debtors have no courtyard, and only one room, 13 feet by 10.

On the first floor are eight spacious rooms for Debtors, opening into a lobby, 6 feet 2 inches wide. Masters'-Side Debtors pay 1. *2d.* per week: Those who have, a room to themselves pay *2s. 6d.* and here is one handsomely furnished, for which a Prisoner has paid five shillings per week.,

The Common-Side Debtors have two rooms, of *26* feet by 19 each, called, by a singular fancy, the " *Pennyless Wards,"* because each poor Debtor who sleeps there pays one penny per week.

The Debtors are allowed by the County three chaldrons of coals a year; and *child-bed-linen* is also provided at the County expence.

The *Infirmary* has two rooms; one 20 feet by 18, the other 15 feet by 12; which are, very improperly, built in the

Common-Felons' court-yard, in the *centre* of the Prison. The lower room had a barrack bedstead; the upper was used as a storeroom for bedding, &c. and both have glazed windows, and fire-places.

At my visit, in 1S09, I found that the following alterations had taken place in the Infirmary. The lower part is now converted into a *reception-room* for unclean Prisoners, and supplied with a copper for warm water, and a tin slipper-bath: The upper room is furnished with beds and bedding, proper for sick persons; and both apartments are well lighted and ventilated by three large windows.

Here is *no regular Chapel;* for want of which, the Debtors have Divine Service performed to them in a lobby room. Of the *Felons* I shall speak presently.

Master's-Side Felons have a courtyard, 42 feet by 18, and a day-room of 16 feet by 13; with eight sleeping-rooms, nearly the same size; two of which front the street. They are furnished with wooden bedsteads without curtains, feather-beds, and bedding, at *2s. 6d.* per week, and have two or more beds in each room. But, if a Prisoner has a room to himself, the charge is five shillings per week.

§3 The wall being three feet thick, the light and air are still further obstructed at the windows, both of Debtors and Felons, by wooden bars, three inches and a half broad, instead of single iron bars.

The Common-Side Felons' courtyard is 47 feet by 29. They have also a dayroom, 15 feet 6 inches by 12 feet 6. Their sleeping-wards, on the ground-floor, are six rooms, of the average size of 14 feet by 12; and each contains a barrack bedstead, for five Prisoners, which are judiciously made to turn up, as is done every morning; not only to give a fresher circulation of air, but for the purpose of sweeping and washing the rooms. These Prisoners are allowed a straw-in-sacking bed each, with two blankets, and a rug.

The Women-Felons have a courtyard, of about 18 feet by 12, with a pump, and a sewer in one corner; and arcades for air and exercise. Also a day-room, 20 feet by 16, and two lodging rooms, about the same size. The bedding here is like that on the Male-Felons' Side, for such as pay 2'. *6d.* per week. Those who cannot pay for beds have straw-in-sacking, with two blankets and a rug each.

Felons are allowed by the County thirteen chaldrons of coals yearly. Convicts, under sentence of transportation, in addition to the County Dole, have the King's Allowance of 2. *6d.* per week, till their removal.

In this Gaol there are two horrid *Dungeons,* of 12 feet square, and totally dark, assigned for the Condemned Prisoners; the descent to which is by eleven steps: And here it was, that in almost all my visits, (not likely to be soon forgotten,) I found men confined, for robbing their Fellow-prisoners in the Gaol! At my last visit there were two, of this very depraved description, shut up together; nor do I indeed recollect to have ever been here without seeing some one so detained. Surely this nust seem to argue some reprehensible degree of neglect, as to matters of religious attention.

Tlje duty of Divine Service, for many years past, has been generally performed to Debtors and Felons on alternate Sundays. I have been informed that at some times, previous to the appointment of Mr. *Evans,* the late Chaplain, no such service, no mental guardianship whatsoever, had taken place for sis weeks or *two* months together.....

And, even now, in what a manner, and whsre is the solemn business performed? Prayers are read, and a Sermon delivered by the Chaplain of this County Gaol, upon he landing of the staircase, to the *Criminals,* who are *stationed within Hie Iron Gate*; but scarce one-third of them can either see the Minister, or hear the SerT vice. The Women Eejons tyave long had no religious attentions of any kind paid to them, nor any opportunity of joining in the service, although some are confined here for years together. Nay, even those Convicts, who lie under sentence of death, are brought forth into a small open court-yard, and the Minister prays by them from the Keeper's back-room. Yet, this is the populous Prison of a most respectable and opulent County;— and thus I exonerate my mind upon the subject *f,*

The Common-Side Felons, &c. of this Gaol are some of the most miserable beings imaginable, squalid, dirty, and in rags. No discrimination of turpitude is duly observed. The Prisoners here frequently rob each other; and particularly those Deserters, who occasionally stay but a few days, are sure to lose any money they may have about them. One of this description lost ten pounds, and another had a pair of new shoes taken from him. Young Novices in transgression, and notorious Offenders, are blended in a mass of mutual and inevitable injury to each other. In short, the Prison in question is a discredit to the County; and I hope I am assured upon good grounds, that a *New Gaol* is intended to be soon built; which, like that just finished at Canterbury, may obliterate the remembrance of its Predecessor, and do honour to all who shall be concerned in so beneficial an improvement.

The following is a copy of the old Table Of Fees, hung up in the Gaol.
Kent, to wit,
A Table of Fees, to be taken by the Gaoler at *Maidstone;* settled at the General
Quarter Sessions, holden on Thursday the 12th day of July, in the 22d Year of George II. and in the year 1750, pursuant to the direction of the statute in that behalf provided.,
For the discharge from the said Gaol of every Prisoner committed for *s. d.*
treason, felony, or any offence against his Majesty's Peace, to the Gaoler or Keeper-----------------13 4
Since the drawing up of my short statement of Maidstone Gaol for the last edition, in 1S08, of my ", Account of *Prisons* for *Debtors,"* I have recently been informed, by a letter from the Gaoler, that Divine Service is at present performed every Sunday morning at nine o'clock, to the *Criminals,* in which the *Women,* have an opportunity of joining; and likewise, that to the *Debtors* it

is performed every Sunday evening, at seven o'clock; so that the Sapred Duty is now regularly attended to in the *Gaol* twice on every Lord's day.

d.

To the Turnkey, on Commitment of every such Prisoner-----1 o

To ditto, on the Discharge of every such Prisoner-------10

On the Commitment, or coming into Gaol, of every Prisoner in any Civil Action, to the said Gaoler or Keeper----------30

On the Discharge of every such Prisoner, to the said Gaoler or Keeper-7 10 And to the Turnkey--------------_ _ 1 6

For the use of bed, bedding, and sheets, for each of the said last-mentioned

Prisoners, on the Master's-Side of the said Prison, for the first night, to the said Gaoler or Keeper------------0 6

And for every night after the first------------03

And if two such Prisoners lie together in one bed, then each----0 *2*

For every such Prisoner, as shall chuse to be on the Master's-side, for the use of the bed, bedding, and sheets, the first night------06

For every night after the first-------------O S

But, if two such Prisoners lie together, then two-pence each---0 4 If any such Prisoner, through poverty, can only provide a couch, then to the said Gaoler or Keeper for chamber-rent, per week ----0 1

July 12th, 1750, Seen and allowed by us,

Wm. Turner. P. Boteler. Ed. Austen. Herbt. Palmer. Jas. Calder. Wm. Champness.

Here were, till 1809, no Rules and Orders. No employment is now furnished: no Regulations as to the quantity of liquors, which Prisoners may receive by sinister means. No books were heretofore provided for the Visiting Magistrates, Chaplain and Surgeon to enter their Remarks in, for the better ordering of their important concern; but, in my last visit, I found this deficiency properly supplied. The Surgeon now regularly sets down the name and disease of every sick Prisoner, together with what medicines, extra diet or clothing, are necessarily administered, according to his discretion.

Cupboards have lately been put up in the Debtors' rooms, to secure their provisions; and an alarm-bell is fixed in the Women's Ward, in case of sudden illness, or fire. A night-chair also is placed in each of the Debtors' wards, and one room is now set apart for their Infirmary.

Weights, scales, and measures, have been recently provided; so that each Prisoner may see that the allowance of bread, beer, &c. is fairly dealt out to them.

To this Gaol, the Earl of Romney and his family have annually, for thirty years past, given five guineas at Christmas, for the benefit of the Prisoners in general.

The High Sheriff also gives two guineas, and his Under-Sheriff one guinea, at each Assize.

Called the *Pennyless Ward.*

Prisoners are discharged from hence in a morning; bat have no money, to carry them home, and thus prevent an immediate recurrence to such acts of depredation, as may speedily consign them back to their late abode.

The Gaoler appears to be a humane Man; and every beneficial tendency to an improved arrangement, cannot but render the execution of his arduous office more respectable in itself, and infinitely more comfortable to the many under his care.

The Act for preserving the Health of Prisoners is not hung up: but the Clauses against their use of Spirituous Liquors are duly exhibited, in the entrance of the Gaol.

It is with pleasure I can inform my Readers, that since these pages were written, it has been determined upon to build a New Gaol, House of Correction, and Courts of Justice, upon a very large plan, every way worthy of so opulent and respectable » County: and that Fees and Garnish are then to be abolished.

MAIDSTONE. *The House of Correction.*

Gaoler, *John Downe;* afterwards *Daniel Kingsnorth;* now *Thomas ORill.* Salary, 50/. and five chaldrons of coals yearly for the Keeper's house, and the Prison.

Fees, Felons, 13. 4. Misdemeanors, *6s. 8d.* Faulty Servants, *4s.6d.* No Table, Garnish, not yet abolished, 2.

Chaplain, none. Divine Service never performed here, nor any religious attentions paid whatever; although Prisoners are sometimes committed hither for so long a term as two years.

Surgeon. *Mr. Coleman.*

Salary, for this Prison, and the County Gaol, 75/.

Number of Prisoners, 1801, 22dSept. 32. I804, 26th Sept. 20. 1807, 8th Sept. 14.

1808, 14th July, 29. 1809, 19th July, 35. 1810, 22d Aug. 52.

Allowance, a half quartern loaf each, in two days, to those who do not work; and to those who work, five half quartern loaves per week, No beer.

REMARKS.

The Men's court-yard in this Bridewell is 54 feet by 42, paved with flag-stones. ; and has a pump in it, with a sewer in one corner. Their day or mess-room is 12 feet by 8; with a fire-place, benches to sit upon, and shelves for provisions.

They have also two sleeping-rooms on the ground floor: one, called the Upper Ward, 22 feet by 16, has straw-in-sacking beds on the floor; no bedding whatever; and two iron-grated windows, which look into the court. Eleven Prisoners slept in this room.

The Lower Ward, 19 feet by *16,* has barrack beds, with straw-in-sacking, but no bedding. The iron-grated windows look into a narrow passage, 5 feet wide, and 21 feet long. In this twelve Prisoners slept.

The Men's Infirmary, which is likewise on the ground floor, and in size 15 feet by 12, has two wooden turn-up bedsteads, with flock beds, two blankets, two sheets, and a rug each.

The Women have a court-yard, paved with flag-stones, 42 feet by 36; the door of which has a cylinder, and opens into the narrow passage above described. Their day or mess-room is 8 feet by 7, with a fire-place and copper. Their sleeping-room, 21 feet by *16,* has straw-in-sacking laid on the floor, but no bedding. Six Women slept here.

Their Infirmary room is up stairs, above the Men's Infirmary, and of the same size, with two grated and glazed windows, and afire-place. When this room is not occupied by the sick, the barrack beds are furnished by the Keeper with bedding, for those who can pay him 2. *4d.* a week.

If a Prisoner is sick, the Surgeon has a discretionary power to order a better regimen, or clothing, as he deems needful; which is humanely allowed by the County.

In the Women's court-yard, (and seven steps under ground,) are two *loathsome Dungeons,* 15 feet by 10, and *6 feet 6' inches high,* totally dark, for confining the refractory. They give, indeed, no inadequate idea of *Penitentiary Retirement.*

Nine Prisoners, and a little boy just sent in, were *heavily ironed,* at one time when I was here. Upon my enquiring the cause of such unusual rigour, the Keeper informed me "that he made it a constant practice to put every new-comer into irons; which, if they behaved well for some time, he took ofT." At my visit in 1804, few were either manacled or fettered: but in 1807 I found they were all again in irons; and amongst them, 1 recollect, was one man committed for bastardy.

The Gaoler's house, till lately, commanded no view of any part of the Prison. If this were the cause of his official rigour, it is hoped that a remedy has been provided; for in 1S0S, I found a window made, through which the Keeper has a oommand of the Men's court. Indeed, the whole Prison is now put under better regulation; and lenity, in some degree, has supplied the place of severity.

For many years a great part of this Prison has been rented of the Keeper by Mr. Blundell, a Weaver in the Town, at *lol.* per annum; and here he has a work room, of 2S feet by 16, the three windows of which look into the Men Criminals' court. In this room are nine hemp-blocks, and the Prisoners are occasionally employed in beating hemp, making sacks, and picking oakum; but they receive no part of their earnings. Above stairs are store-rooms, the whole length of the Prison, in which Mr. Blundell deposits the rough materials used in his business.

This Bridewell is white-washed twice a year; and the whole Prison kept clean.

Prisoners are discharged in a morning, but have no money issued, to carry them safely home.

The Act for Preservation of health is not hung up; but the prohibitory Clauses against Spirituous Liquors are placed in the Keeper's house.

$Gf Since writing the above account, the Keeper by letter acquaints me, That "a *new Chapel* is taken from what is here called the *Long Warehouse,* where the Rev. Mr. Skelton attends Service once a week. A new sleeping-ward, and likewise an hospital is provided for the Women. The Men's work-room is now divided into two sleeping-wards; and the walls of the court-yards have been white-washed." MALTON. *Yorkshire.*
The Town Gaol.
Keeper, the Constable. No Salary.
REMARKS.

This Gaol, called by some " *The Black Hole,"* is a small, narrow-arched place, of about 17 feet by 6' feet 3 inches.

The Men and Women are kept separate during confinement here, and are brought from the North-Riding House of Correction to the Sessions in this Town, which are held once in two years. The Keeper furnishes his Prisoners with victuals from the Publick house adjoining.

The only ventilation which the rooms of this Gaol can receive, is through an iron grating in each door, about 7 inches square. They have barrack bedsteads, which are supplied with straw every three or four months. On the 31st August, 1802, I found no Prisoners here.
MANCHESTER. *Lancashire.*
The New-Bailey.
Gaoler, *William Dunslan.* Salary, 300/. with coals and candles.

Task-Master, *Thomas Hutton.* Salary, 50/. and a-sixth of the Prisoners' earnings.

Turnkeys, three; at one guinea each per week.

These Salaries to the different Officers are paid by the Hundred of
Salford.
Chaplain, Rev. Mr. *Cheek;* now Rev. Mr. *Dallis.* Salary, 30/.
Duty, Prayers and a Lecture on Tuesdays, and Fridays.

Surgeon, Mr. *Richard Nanfan.* Salary, 40/. and Medicines provided by the
Hundred of *Salford.*

Number of Prisoners, 1802, Oct. 4th, 164. 1S05, Oct. 23th, 71. 1809, Nov. nth, 79. And
One Lunatick.

Allowance, Every day, Breakfast and Supper, a quart of oatmeal porridge, and half a pound of bread each at meal to every Prisoner.

Sunday, Dinner, half a pound of boiled beef, half a pound of bread, and one pound of potatoes, or other vegetables.

Monday, Ditto, a quart of vegetable, or pease soup, from the beef of Sunday.

Tuesday, four ounces of cheese, and half a pound of bread.

Wednesday, a quart of rice and oatmeal porridge, and half a pound
of bread.

Thursday, the same as Sunday.
Friday, the same as Monday.

Saturday, ox-head, and shin-bones, made into a stew.
REMARKS.

The New-Bailey Prison was first inhabited in the year 1788. It is properly surrounded by a boundary wall, 100 yards square; which stands at such a distance, as to afford a convenient Kitchen Garden, to supply the Prison with vegetables.

The Turnkey's lodge, in front, has four reception-rooms for Prisoners, and another room, with a warm and cold bath; in which they are washed, the County clothing put on, and their own clothes purified, ticketed, and hung up. Over this lodge in front, is the Examining-Magistrates' room, which opens into a very neat Sessions-house, or *New-Bailey Court-house;* in the front pannel of which is "The Magistrates' Oath," painted in golden letters.

The Reverend *W. R. Hay* is the appointed Chairman of the Quarter Sessions, with a Salary of 400/. per annum.

In the centre of the Prison is the Gaoler's house. There are nipe airy court-yards: viz. two for Men Felons before their Trial; two for Men Felons after Trial; two for Male Bridewell Prisoners; one for Women Felons; one for Female Bridewell Prisoners; and one for convicted Female Felons.

On the ground-floor are fourteen solitary cells, 8 feet by 6, and 7 feet 10 inches high; each having a small aperture over the door, for the admission of a glimmering light, and air. At each end, and down 10 steps, is a Dungeon, 8 feet by *6* feet 8, and 7 feet 10 inches high: These have each an iron-grating over the door, of 21 inches by 14; and double doors, the outer one iron-grated, the inner of wood. This range of cells is separated from the court-yard by a lobby 4 feet wide, and they have a warming flue running through them.

In the different court-yards are *sixty-six Workshops;* where all the Prisoners are employed in weaving, batting of cotton, carding, &c. &c.

On the first story of the building, the Chapel is in the centre: into which four Wards respectively open; so that the sexes are completely separated, and out of sight of each other.

In each ward are eleven sleeping-cells, 8 feet by 6, well ventilated, and divided each from the others by a passage or lobby 5 feet wide: at the end of which there is a plentiful supply of water, with soap and towels for the use of the Prisoners, who are required to wash themselves before each meal; and, if they come dirty, are sent away without it.

On the second story are four wards, with eleven cells in each, the same as those below them, already noticed. Three rooms also are set apart for the sick, of 24 feet by 18, with three beds in each, and a Dispensary furnished with Medicines. Each Prisoner has a *separate bed;* the frame of which is *iron,* with a wooden frame upon it, a hair mattress, a sheet, (changed every other week,) two or three blankets, and rugOn a detached part of the *Neva Bailey* there are fourteen work-cells, added since the Prison was first built. The total number of sleeping-cells is one hundred and thirty.

The hours of work are from six in the-morning to six in the evening, during the Summer, and from eight to eight in the Winter; allowing half an hour to breakfast, and one hour for dinner. Each Prisoner has one-third of the earnings gained, upon producing a certificate of his or her good behaviour to the Magistrates, signed by the *Keeper* and *Chaplain:* and some of them have received from ten to fifteen pounds each; part of which is laid out in purchasing such articles of wearing apparel as the Prisoner stands in need of.

The amount of earnings is, upon an average, nine pence per day: their diet stands in about six pence halfpenny a day, and the overplus is accounted for to the Treasurer. The expence of maintenance, and of earnings, from the 27th of April to the 19th of July, 1803, was as follows:

Expence Of Maintenance.
Butcher's Bill-38
Bakers Ditto---163
Meal, Peas, and Salt---------*6l*
Rice, Soap, &c.-----------14
Cloth, for Clothing 18 18
Vegetables from the Garden--------6 7

Exceeds in Earnings----------91 7 *d.* ti 0 0 0 0 8

The Statement for 1805, is added, to introduce the explanation given of it.

The reason assigned by Mr. *Dunstan,* the Gaoler, for the earnings being less than the maintenance, was the stagnation in the Cotton Manufactory at that time.

Here is an excellent kitchen, fitted up and furnished with every article for simple frugal cookery. A Man Cook dresses the provisions, and serves out each Prisoner's allowance. There is water over the three boilers, and in each court-yard, to which every Prisoner has access. The sewers communicate with the common drain.

The Act for the Preservation of Health, and Clauses against Spirituous Liquors, are conspicuously hung up. The whole Prison is white-washed twice a year, or oftener, if required; and the Gaoler seems very attentive to promote cleanliness, industry, and good order.

The humanity and liberality of the gentlemen in the opulent and respectable Hundred of Salford, is conspicuous in every department of the Prison Police.

And here, (perhaps for the last opportunity in my very uncertain life,) let me repeat, that I beg the Magistrates of Manchester and its vicinity will please to accept my grateful acknowledgements for the honour done me, in paying such attention to my former Remarks on the Workhouse, and Lunaticks there; and for the great improvements which, in consequence, have been so liberally and humanely ordered.

MUSSELBURGH. Scotland.

Gaoler, *William Robertson;* keeps a PuWick-House.

Salary, 5. per week, from the Town. Fees, *4d.* per night. No Table.

Surgeon, from the Town, when wanted.

Number of Prisoners, Debtors. Criminals.

1802, Sept. 17th,------0-------1. 1809, Sept. 23d,------*1* -------1.

Allowance, Debtors, *9d.* to 1. *6d.* a day. Criminals, *6d.* a day.

REMARKS.

This Prison is over the guard-house, and has on the first floor a large room for Debtors, with two iron-barred windows towards the Street. At the end is a room for Criminals, about *9* feet by *6,* with straw on the floor, and lighted by a pane of glass in the roof. Over these is a room the length of the building; the boarded floor very rotten and unsafe. It has four iron-grated windows, and an offensive sewer.

No court-yard. No water. Very dirty; never whitewashed. The Act and Clauses not hung up.

Over the door of the Magistrates' room is this Inscription:

"Magistrates! do Justice in the Fear of God.

He that God doth fear,

Will not to Falsehood lend an Ear."
MARLBOROUGH. *Wiltshire.*
The County Bridewell, and Town Gaol.
Gaoler, *William Alexander.* Salary, 70/.
t. Chaplain, Rev. Mr. *Tucker.* Salary, 20/. Duty, Prayers and Sermon on Sundays.
Surgeons, Messrs. *Pinghenny* and *Morris.* Salary, 10/.
Number of Prisoners, 1801, Dec. 13th, 19. 1806, Oct. 16th, 16.
Allowance, one pound twelve ounces of best bread per day each, in loaves sent from the Baker's; which I have regularly found to be of full weight.
REMARKS. This Prison was first inhabited in 1787.
For men here is a court-yard, of 72 feet by 36; and two day-rooms on the ground floor, about 21 feet by 9, with a fire-place in each, and two iron-grated windows; and two sleeping-rooms above them, of the same size. One of these is used as a *Chapel,* and has *two beds in it;* the other has six beds laid on the floor, with straw-in-sacking cases, and one blanket each.
For Women here is also a court-yard, 29 feet square; a day-room, 29 feet by 15, with fire-place, &c. and a room above, of the same size, divided into two, for sleeping-rooms, supplied with straw-in-sacking beds, and a blanket.
In 1791, a new court-yard was added, and six cells were built over arcades, in the area of it; each cell 10 feet by 6, and 8 feet 9 inches high, with an iron-grated window, of 30 inches by 18, and an aperture in each door, 6 inches by 4; ventilated also by a circular grating in the floor, and another in the cieling of each. These cells have iron-framed bedsteads, with straw-in-ticking bed, and a blanket to each. A small stone trough is in one corner of each cell, to which water is laid on by a pipe and cock.
. At my visit in 1801, three Men-Prisoners were in the above cells, very ill of a typhus fever; and, what I could not but think improper, two of them were in one cell, although several of the other cells had no Prisoners at the time.
The *arcades* underneath are very convenient for them in wet weather. A large tub, for a bath, had been usually placed there; but, on my visit in 1806, I found it very judiciously removed to a room over the Women's day-room.
There is a sewer in every court yard, and the whole Prison is well supplied with water, and kept very clean.
The Act for Preserving Health was not hung up; and the Clauses against Spirituous Liquors were so defaced, as to be scarcely legible.
No employment is provided; but when any can be procured, the Prisoners who work receive one half of their earnings..
... MARSHALSEA. *Southwark, London.*
Knight-Marshal, Sir *James-Bland Burgess,* Bart. Salary, 500/.
Substitute, Mr. *William Jenkins.* Salary, *60I.* Fees, 10. lorf. See Table.
Licence for beer, ale, and tobacco. Spirituous Liquors are prohibited, and an
Order to that effect is painted on the door. The *Tap* is let. Garnish, called " Ward Dues," for coals, &c. 1. *4d.*
Chaplain, Rev. *Arthur William Trollope,* A. M. who officiates by his
Deputy, Rev. Mr. *Webster.*
Duty, Prayers only, orice every Sunday.
Salary, Mr. Webster receives one shilling from every *Debtor,* on discharge. See Table. The amount of his stipend, for the last three years, has only been 34/. 7. Admiralty Prisoners pay nothing.
Surgeons, Messrs. *Saumarez* and *Dixon;* now Mr. *Phillips.*
Salary, one shilling on the discharge of every Debtor. See Table. Admiralty Prisoners pay nothing.
Number of Prisoners,
Allowance, to *Debtors,* none whatever. But see *Remarks* on Legacies, &c. Admiralty Prisoners, if Officers, have one shilling a day: Foremast Men, sixpence a day, paid in money, on petition to the Admiralty; and likewise clothing, if wanted.
REMARKS.
To this very ancient Prison of the Court of the Marshalsea, and of the King's Palace-Court of Westminster, are brought Debtors, arrested for the lowest sums, any where within twelve miles of the Palace, except in the City of London.
King Charles 1. in the sixth year of his Reign, by his Letters Patent, erected a New Court of Record, called the *Curia Palatii,* or " Palace-Court," to be held before the Steward of the Household, *Xhe* Knight-Marshal, and the Steward of the Court, or his Deputy; with Jurisdiction to hold Plea of all manner of Personal Actions whatsoever, which may arise between parties within the above-said distance from his Majesty's Palace at Whitehall.
This Court, together with the ancient Court of Admiralty, is now held once a week; namely, on every Friday, in King-street, within the Borough of Southwark. And, as the nature of it cannot be matter of general notoriety, I avail myself of the following detail, which has been given me by a well-informed friend.
"These Courts are chiefly useful, as affording a ready and expeditious Jurisdiction for the recovery of Debts *under ten pounds;* But they may hold plea of Actions above that sum, to any amount, and have jurisdiction in all personal Actions, as Debt, Trespass, Assault, &c. They are both of them Courts of Record, and were formerly held separate; but are now united, and the Process from them issues in the name of the *Palace..'*
Actions from this Court are generally brought in the following Cases: 1. When the Debt or Damages to be recovered are not thought considerable enough to warrant the parties incurring the expence of bringing them in the superior Courts; as in actions *not amounting to five pounds,* , 2. Where the Plaintiff wishes to avoid delay, particularly during the vacations of the superior Courts: for *here,* the continuances are from week to week, without any vacations; and judgment is generally had in three or four weeks., 3. In Actions of *Trespass,* or *Assault,* where the Plaintiff' wishes to avoid the risk of paying Costs, for in this Court he is entitled to his Costs, upon obtaining a verdict even for the smallest sum. The Statute of 22d and 23d Car. II. Ch.Q. which takes away

Costs in those Actions, unless the Jury shall give forty shillings damages, does not extend to inferior Courts, and was enacted for the purpose of confining small actions to those inferior Courts.

4. When it is apprehended that several other writs may have been issued against a Defendant, which altogether he may not be able to pay or bail; as a Defendant, arrested by process from this Court, may be discharged, on paying or bailing the Debt for which he is arrested, without being subject to other detainers.

The proceedings in this Court are, in other respects, nearly the same with those in the Court of King's Bench. The Jurisdiction, however, does not extend beyond twelve miles from Whitehall, nor into the City of London; but comprehends Westminster and South wark, and actions may be brought for sums to any amount. If the Debt or Damages laid in the Declaration, be *above ten pounds,* the Defendant may, if he thinks proper, remove the Record into any of the superior Courts; which, however, is seldom done, unless in cases of importance, as the removal is attended with considerable expence to the Defendant. But if the Debt or Damages be *under ten pounds,* the cause cannot be removed, unless the Defendant shall become bound, with two sufficient Sureties, by a *recognizance of Jifty pounds each,* (in the nature of bail in error,) to pay the Debt and Costs recovered; nor are the Bail at liberty to surrender the Defendant in their discharge, but must absolutely pay the money, on judgment being obtained; and where the Debt or Damages in the Declaration *do not exceed five pounds,* the cause cannot by any means be removed from this Court. «/

In ordinary cases, the *Taxed-Costs* allowed to the parties in this Court, are the full Costs incurred: And if an Action be commenced here, and then removed by *Habeas Corpus* or *Certiorari* into the Courts of Westminster, the Plaintiff shall have full Costs, although the Damages are under forty shillings.

If a cause should proceed to trial, the *common Costs,* (on verdict for the Plaintiff, where the Defendant has been served with a Copy of Process, and the General Issue pleaded,) *are about Jive or six pounds.*

The *Juries* in this Court are selected from *Westminster,* and the four adjoining Counties, viz. *Middlesex, Essex, Kent,* and *Surrey;* and are changed every fortnight.

The *Counsel* and *Attornies* hold their places for life, and practice in the Courts of Westminster; in which it is necessary they should be admitted, before their admission into the Marshalsea and Palace Court.

Actions are not tried in this Court *for Debts under forty shillings;* and a Writ of Error lies from hence to the Court of King's Bench.

But, if the cause be of any considerable consequence, it is usually removed (on its first commencement, together with the custody of the Defendant,) either into the King's Bench or Common Pleas, by a Writ of *Habeas Corpus, cum causd.*

The inferior business also of this Court has of late years been much reduced, by the introduction of the *New Courts of Conscience,* erected within the environs of London: In consideration of which, the four Counsellors belonging to the united *Marshalsea* and *Palace Court* had Salaries granted to them for their lives, by the Statute of 23 Geo. II. Cap. 27."

This Prison is under the particular custody of a " *Substitute?* whose appointment is from the Knight-Marshal of the King's household for the time being. The great abuses practised under a Predecessor of this vicarious Officer, were reported to Parliament by the well-remembered " Gaol Committee," in 1729 .

« The *Generous Band,* '"
Who, touch'd with human woe, redressive search'd
Into the Horrors of the gloomy Gaol!
Unpitied, and unheard, where Misery moans,
Where Sickness pines; where Thirst and Hunger burn,
And *poor Misfortune feels the lash of Vice!* .

O great Design! if executed well,
With patient care, and wisdom-temper'd zeal...
Ye sons of Mercy! yet *resume the search:*
Drag forth the legal Monsters into light:
Wrench from their hands oppression's iron rod,
And bid the cruel *fed the pains they give* /"-Thomson, *Winter.* . For some time the Marshalsea was held under lease by Mr. Cracklow, a *Surveyor,* Already one half of the structure had fallen into rums; and of the remainder it might be almost said, with our great Bard, that
"The Castle toppled o'er the Warder's Head."

It is not now let on lease, having been sold to Mr. Davis, a Back-maker; from whom it is rented, until the new Prison is built.

The court-yard is spacious, and contains near fifty rooms, six of which only are for *Common-Side* Debtors. If more of this description are here than the six rooms can receive, at three in a room, others are allowed to accommodate them, from the Masters-Side. There are two or three rooms for Women; but, as here is only one court-yard, Men and Women mix together in the day-time.

No *Pirates* Irave been committed to this Prison since the year 1789; but several persons have been and still are committed in execution, under sentence of CourtsMarshal, to suffer imprisonment for a limked time; and they are sent hither by the Lords of the Admiralty,, pursuant to such sentence. Of this description I have found fromybur to *seventeen,* at my several visits within the last twelve years.

Here is no Infirmary. The court-yard is well supplied with water. The Prisoner sometimes employ themselves in cutting pegs for the Brewers, and are paid two shillings per thousand.

The *Tap* within the Prison, which heretofore was let to *William Matthews, a Prisoner,* at forty shillings per week, is now let at two guineas per week to *Hezekiah Denby,* . .... , ...

There are twenty new rooms,-about 11-feet-by 10, and *1* feet high, built in the centre of the Prison, and also three somewhat larger, under the Court-House.:For refractory Prisoners here are three strong cells, the middle one 10 feet 10 by 8 feet 4; and the two others, 8 feet 4 by 4 feet 10, with wooden bedsteads, raised about 2 feet 6 inches from the floor. To these cells is attached a small court-yard, 28 feet 9 inches by 16 feet, and separated from the Debtors by a 'brick-waft.

The average number of Prisoners, about thirty years ago, was 200, as appears by the books: But since the Act of *19* Geo. III. Cap. 70, it has been reduced to 50.

The object of the Act for restraining Arrests under *10l.* is, "That no person shall be held to bail, or taken to. Prison in the first instance, unless his Debt amount to *ten pounds*" But a Creditor may still sue out a Writ for any sum *above two pounds,* prosecute his action against the Debtor to a Judgment, and then take-him in execution for Debt and Costs, be that sum under or above ten pounds.

It is not necessary, where there is a Judgment obtained, that the sum should exceed *lot.*: If it W;ere so, a person having five or Bix pounds due to him would be without a remedy.---'.

If an action be originally brought in the Marshalsea Court, and removed tor any other" by the *Debtor,* (for the *Creditor* cannot remove it,) the PlamttfTmust foLlow the removal, or lose his Debt: and when the said Creditor, or Plaintiff, has obtained Judgment, the Debtor cannot be imprisoned in the Marshalsea, but in the Prison of that Court where the Judgment was obtained.

Mr. Henry Allnutt, who was many years since a Prisoner here, had, during his confinement, a large estate bequeathed to him. He learned sympathy from his sufferings; and left *One Hundred pounds a year* to discharge such poor Debtors from hence, the payment or the composition of whose debts does not exceed *four pounds.* As he bound his Manor of Goring, in Oxfordshire, for charitable uses, this is called " *The Oxford Charity."*

In 1786, there was a delay in the distribution of this Charity. The Court of Chancery, on application made, gave its directions. The arrears were paid up; and I have not heard of any complaint since. The present Trustees are *Henry Hard ing,* Esq. of Abingdon, and Mr. *Henry Morland,.* , List of Legacies
To the Prison of the *Marshalsea* and *Palace Courts. per Annum.*
1. The legacy of *Henry Allnatt,* Esq. for the release of Debtors, whose *jg. s. d.* respective Plaintiffs will accept of a small sum, in full satisfaction for *Debt* and *Costs*------------100 0 0
2. There is paid by the Treasurer of every County-town and Place

Corporate in England and Wales, the sum of *20s.* on the first day of Trinity Term; which *is* advanced monthly, at *5l.* per month:
out of which 10$ per month are deducted by the receiver, as a remuneration for his trouble---r, -65 0 0
3. The legacy of *Frederick Ashfield,* Esq. to provide 2 lbs. of meat per week, for from ten to twenty Prisoners, is paid by Mr. *IV. Jlaillon,*
of Clifford's Inn. The meat is sent regularly every Saturday;
and if there be any overplus of money at the end of the year, it is laid out in coals------------50 00
4. The legacy of Mrs. *Frances Ashton* is *95l.* per annum. (See the
Extract of her Will, " Ludgate Prison," page 367.) 5. The legacy of Dr. *John Pelting* is regularly paid by Messrs. *Hoare,*
Fleet-street--------------900 6. The legacy of Sir *Thomas Gresham,* paid quarterly, by the Cham berlain of London, at per quarter, 2/. Ioj.-------10 00 7. The legacy of Mrs. *Margaret Symcott,* paid by the Chamberlain of London, is 65 penny loaves every eight weeks, (Eleanor Gwynn's gift).
8. The legacy of Mr. *Jacob,* left in 1609, is paid yearly, by the pro prietors of the Grainge Inn, Carey-street, at Easter----200 9. The legacy of Mr. *John Marks* is, per annum, *Ii,* and the interest of 21/. 18$. lOd. S. S. Stock, paid by the Company of Mercers-1 13 1 Per I
10. The quantity of *bread* and *money* sent by the Company of Lea thersellers, is, at the rate of 6$. *ad* quarterly----- 11. The legacy of *Robert Rampston,* Esq. is paid at Christmas by Mr. *Ruckeridge,* Orchard-street, Portman-square----- 12. The gift of *W. Roper,* Esq. paid by the Company of Parish Clerks, yearly---------------- 13. The legacy of Mr. *John Gaythomct* by the Company of Cutlers, at Christmas-----_ _--------0 14. The legacy of Mr. *T. Dawson,* paid by the Churchwardens of St. Ethelburgh, Bishopsgate-----------0 15. The legacies of Mrs. *Lettice Smith* and Mr. *Arthur Mouse,* by the

Company of Fishmongers-----------0 16. The Company of Salters send annually--------0 17. The Gift of Mr. *Thomas Cottle,* paid by the Churchwardens of St.

Dunstan in the East, at Lady-day, yearly, is a *quarter of beef, and*
a peck of oatmeaL (See an Extract of the Will, "Ludgate
Prison," page 367.)
1807, 48 stone, 4 lbs. and a peck of oatmeal.
1308, 48 stone, and ditto. 1809, 39 stone, 4 lbs. and ditto. 1810, 20 stone, and ditto. 18. The Company of Drapers send yearly sixty three *penny haves.* (Legacy of Mr. *John Stokes.)* 19. The Gift of Mr. *Ralph Carter,* is a quantity of beef, at Christmas, paid by the Churchwardens of St. Andrew Undershaft. But see an Extract of the Deed, "Giltspur-street," page 234,
line 23—25.
1801, 80 lbs. 1805, 102 lbs. 1809, 100 lbs. 1802, 84 lbs. 1806, 72 lbs. 1810, 100 lbs. 1803, 90 lbs. 1807, 100 lbs. 1804, 461 lbs. 1808, 50 lbs. 20. The Company of Ironmongers send yearly, on the 15th November, a quantity of beef and bread, the Gift of Mrs. *Dane. Annum s. d.* 6 8 0 0 0 0 15 0 9 0 6 8 6 9
The Petition is signed by the Prisoners, and beef and bread, are sent in propor iou to the number.

THE following Voluntary Donations have *generally* been paid yearly.
Her late Royal Highness the Duchess of Gloucester used to send at £. *s. d.*
Christmas, yearly, two chaldrons of Coals: now discontinued, or forgot. '

His Grace the Archbishop of Canterbury, whose Donation is sent for to Lambeth, *at Christmas* ------------10 0

The Lord Steward of bis Majesty's Household, *per annum,* regularly paid by Mr. *Coster,* at St. James's----------55 0

The Steward, Deputy Prothonotary, Council, and Attornies of his
Majesty's Palace Court 536
Henry Thornton, Esq. M. P. for the Borough of Southwarfc---3 3 0

Table of Fjbes to be taken at the Marshalsea Prison, on any Civil Aotion,
Settled 17 th May, *1765...*
To the Knigbt-Marshal, upon the discharge of every Prisoner charged *s. d.* with one or more Actions-------------- 1 8

To the Keeper, for his care and safe custody of every Prisoner, upon the discharge of such Prisoner, on the first Action-------48

To the Keeper, upon the discharge of such Prisoner, charged with one or more Actions, after the first-------------,J 8

To the Surgeon, or Apothecary, on discharge of every Prisoner, charged with one or more Actions------------10

To the Chaplain, on the like discharge----------1 0

To the Turnkey, upon the discharge of every Prisoner, on the first Action 1 G

To the Turnkey, upon the discharge of every Prisoner, charged with one or more Actions after the first----------10

To the Clerk, for entering the discharge of a Prisoner, 011 one or more
  Actions-------------------10

To the Keeper, for the use of a bed, bedding, and sheets, for every Prisoner, if found by the Gaoler at the Prisoner's request, for the first night, on the Master's-side of the said Prison--------0 6

And every night after the first night---------03

And if two lie in a bed, *2d.* each------------0 4

No other fee for the use of chamber, bed, bedding, or upon the discharge or commitment of any Prisoner on any Civil Action.

W. RrcHARDsoN. MANSFIELD.

Elliot Bishop. C.PRATT.
Leonard Howard. T. PARKER.

THE NEW MARSHALSEA PRISON,

Is situate in High-street, in the Borough of Southwark, near St. George's Church, and was formerly the Gaol for the County of Surrey. The entrance-gate fronts the street, and a small area leads to the Keeper's house. Behind it is a brick building, the ground-floor of which contains fourteen rooms in a double row, and the three upper-stories the same number; making in the whole 56 rooms, about 10-i. feet square, and 8-i-feet high, with boarded floors, a glazed window and fire-place in each, intended for Male Debtors. Nearly adjoining to this is a detached building called the Tap, which has, on the ground-floor, a Beer Room, and another called the Wine Room, for prisoners' and their friends' occasional resort.

The first floor is intended for the Tapster, and one Turnkey, from whose room the window looks into the court-yard of the Admiralty Prisoners. The upper-story has three rooms for Female Debtors, similar to those for the men.

Between this building and the Admiralty Prison there are two solitary cells, 9 feet by 6 feet 6, and 7 feet high, for refractory Debtors; and the iron gratings in the doors look into a small court-yard.

Admiralty Prisoners are here separated from the Debtors: they have a court-yard, 28 feet by 23, with sewers conveniently placed; and two large rooms are to be made into sleeping-cells. Here is a very good bath, with a large copper for warm water.

At the extremity of this long range of building is a neat Chapel, with pews and forms for Debtors, separate from the Admiralty Prisoners.

The Prison is well supplied with water, but the Debtors' court-yard is too small for the numbers generally confined here; the whole area being only 177 feet by 56, and the centre of it occupied by the Debtors' Prison and the Tap, so as to leave no more than a narrow slip on each side, for air and exercise. It is in contemplation, however, to make an addition to it, by the purchase of some land adjoining.

MELTON MOWBRAY. *Leicestershire.*
The Bridewell.

Keeper. *Robert Gould.* Salary, *4l.* Fees, is.

Allowance, a threepenny loaf to each per day.

The Keeper has a small house, consisting of a room, a kitchen, pantry, and three sleeping-rooms above; of which two are over the Bridewell. This contains two small rooms, of U feet by 9 feet *6,* and 7 feet 6 inches high. They have no fire-place, but crib bedsteads, straw mat, and a rug each; and are lighted and ventilated by an iron-grated window, 2 feet 10 inches by 2 feet, with a hemp-block fixed in them. The court-yard, or slip, is of 21 feet by 5..

There were no Prisoners at my visit in 1S65, Sept. 28th.

MIDDLEWICH. *Cheshire.*
The County House of Correction.

Gaoler, *William Harrison;* now *Samuel fVhitaker.*

Salary, 150/. Fees, none.

Chaplain, Rev. *George Leigh.*

Duty, Sermon on Sunday; Prayers on Wednesday, and Friday. Salary, 25/.

Surgeons, Messrs. *Beckett and Son.* They make a Bill.

Number of Prisoners, 1801, Nov. 20th, 21. 1805, Oct. 13th, 26.

Allowance, six pounds of best wheaten bread, sent from the Baker's in loaves of that weight every Thursday; and one sixth of the value in bread to be given each week in potatoes. Also 18/. per annum in coals, amongst the Prisoners, which in 1805 would purchase 29 tons.

REMARKS.

The entrance to this Prison is from a narrow street, called Dog-Lane; and the small court in front, about 64 feet by 21, is well flagged with broad stones.

The Keeper's house is placed in the centre of the area, between the court-yards No. 1, and 2; having a window pointing to each yard, by which means he commands a full view, not only of all the Male Prisoners, but also of the cells, and of the Women's court-yard, No. 4, which is destined for *old offenders.*

I shall here describe them in their order.

No. I. On the North-West side of the Keeper's house is a yard for *Male Prisoners,* about 47 feet by 40, well flagged, on an inclined plane; in which are two working or day-rooms, with five-places and glazed windows, and in one of them are four looms for the Prisoners to work at. Over these are two sleeping-rooms, with iron bedsteads, straw-in-sacking, a bolster, and three blankets, the upper one brown. In the centre of the yard is a pump, supplied from a spring.

No. II. On the South-East side of the Keeper's house is another yard, likewise for Male Prisoners, of 72 feet by 36; with three sleeping-rooms on the ground floor, which is paved with flag stone, and furnished with oaken barrack bedsteads, raised about 2 feet from the floor, and with loose straw, and four blankets for two persons. Each room is well ventilated by an iron grating, about 2 feet square, with inside shutters, and adapted to contain nine Prisoners. Over these sleeping-rooms is the Infirmary, lofty and airy, with opposite windows, for giving a free circulation.

At the upper end of the yard, near the Keeper's house, is a day or work-room, about 30 feet by 21; at the bottom of which is a Shop, or Store-room; and above these a lodging-room, for such Prisoners as are allowed a bed; and for which they pay two shillings per week each.

At the lower end of the same yard is an apartment, formerly used as the Chapel, but now a work-room; over which is a laundry for the Keeper's domestick use. There is also in this yard a leaden cistern, which is not only too small, but frequently without water in dry weather; and a pump near it, supplied from a well of excellent water in Dog-Lane.

This last-mentioned yard is, about two thirds of it, partitioned off by a brick wall 7 feet high, with cast-metal palisades *9* feet long; at the top of which are iron spikes, projecting about 3 feet inwards. This is a judicious and well-executed contrivance, for keeping the court-yard and house both airy and healthy. The other part of the fence is of brick, 15 feet high, coped with stone, and surmounted with iron spikes.

No. III. On the other side of the last-mentioned yard are six *solitary cells,* with a well-flagged court, 43 feet by 21, and an excellent bath, lined with lead, *6* feet in length, 3 feet *6* inches wide, and 5 feet deep, supplied from the cistern. Each cell has a small area, of 15 feet by 7, and is itself 7 feet 10 by 6 feet 8, and 8 feet high; lined with strong oak planks 2 inches thick; and, by the same means, each bedstead is raised 18 inches from the floor.

No. IV. At the upper end of the court, and adjoining Nos. 2 and 3, is a yard for *female veteran offenders,* about 56 feet long by 18, with a day or work-room, 24 feet by 18; at the end of which is a Dungeon, or sleeping-cell, on the ground-floor, with an iron-grated window and inside shutter. This contains three bedsteads, and will, upon occasion, accommodate nine Prisoners. Over these are three rooms, generally occupied by sick Women, with fire-places and glazed windows. In the court are a pump and sewer.

No. V. On the South side of the Prison is a court-yard for Women, 61 feet by 44, and a large working or day-room, over which are two sleeping-rooms with glazed windows; and in the centre of the court a pump, supplied with spring water by pipes, or wooden layers.

At the end of this court-yard is the *Chapel,* of about 14 feet by 22; with a gallery for the Women, very neat and airy. The Men sit at the bottom of the Chapel on forms or benches; but the sexes are not out of sight of each other during Divine Service.

The Chapel is likewise made use of at the Petty Sessions for the Hundred of *Northwich.*

The *Employment of the Prisoners* consists of weaving, shoemaking, picking of oakum, batting cotton, and spinning jersey; and all of them, who formerly had but one third, have now one half of their earnings; and the other half is accounted for to the County.

When a Prisoner comes in ragged and dirty, he is stripped, and undergoes ablution in the bath; the County clothing is then put on, his own clothes washed, boiled in alum and water, mended, and laid by for him till he goes out.

The whole Prison is whitewashed at least twice a year; the sleeping and day-rooms, oftener; and good water is accessible at all times. Every part of the building is consequently very clean: Scales and weights are provided by the County; and I found the loaves supplied to the Prison of full weightAll the court-yards here are well paved with flag-stone; and being on an inclined plane, soon become dry after wet weather, and are easily kept clean.

The humane and very attentive Constable of Chester Castle was for many years the Keeper of this Gaol. His faithful conduct, at length, has raised him to the important trust which he now meritoriously discharges, as an excellent example to his successors. Its influence here remains. The present Keeper of this County Bridewell is both intelligent and active, and appears in all respects well calculated for his situation.

Every attention is here paid by the considerate Magistrates, which the sorrows and sufferings of wholesome confinement can require. The average number of annual commitments to this Gaol appears to have been, From 1785 to 1795,. 137.

MONMOUTH. *Town Gaol.*

Gaoler, *James Walkman* afterwards *William Jarratt;* now *William Jones;* a Sheriff's Officer, and Serjeant at Mace. Salary, *9l.* No Fees.

Number of Prisoners, 1802, Nov. 15th, 0. 1803,Sept. 4th, 2. 1806, Sept. 11th, 0.

Allowance, four-pence a day in bread.

REMARKS.

This Gaol consists of two small rooms on the first floor, and a large one above, very dirty: the straw on the floor worn to dust: an offensive sewer in one corner, which the Keeper told me was emptied once a quarter. The whole Prison quite filthy.

MONMOUTIT. *The County Gaol, and Home of Correction.*

Gaoler, *Thomas Phillips;* now his Widow. Salary, 105/.

Fees, none; but the Under-Sheriff demands from every Debtor 10,v. 6d. for his *Liberate!*

For the Conveyance of Transports, 7*l.* each. Garnish abolished.

Chaplain, Rev. *John Powell.* Salary, 30/.

Duty, Prayers and Sermon on Wednesday; and Prayers on Sunday.

Surgeon, Mr. *William Powell.* Salary, 20*l.*

Number of Prisoners, Debtors. Felons, &c. Debtors. Felons, *ht.* 1801, Nov. 11th,--7--6 1802, Nov. 15th,--3--11 1803, Sept. 5th,--1--12 1806, Sept. 11th,--3--12. Lunatick, 1.

Allowance, to *Debtors,* who are paupers, one pound and a half of bread per day, and one penny per day in money. To *Felons,* the same allowance.

To House of Correction Prisoners, the like proportion of bread daily, and one fourth of their earnings.

Those who are imprisoned for a term have the one pound and half of bread per day only. The bread is sent in from the Baker's every other day, in loaves of 3 lbs. weight.

Convicts under Sentence of Transportation have the King's allowance of 2*s.* 6*d.* which is given to them in a threepenny loaf every day, and nine pence a week in money.

REMARKS.

This two-fold Prison has much the appearance of a Castle. It is situated on a fine eminence. The boundary wall incloses about an acre of ground, given by the Duke of Beaufort. The outer gate has on one side the Turnkey's lodge, and a small room. On the other side are the wash-house and oven, and cistern for soft water.

Up stairs are three cells, used as day-rooms for Prisoners under Sentence of Death, 7 feet 6 inches each by *6* feet 6, and 9 feet high, well lighted and ventilated; and a room for the Turnkey to sleep in. Over these is a flat roof, where Criminals are executed. The Gaol is in the centre of the area, and the Keepers court-yard and house front the Turnkey's lodge.

On the ground-floor are the Visiting Magistrates' room, two rooms for the Keeper, and twelve sleeping-cells, 8 feet o by *6* feet, with glazed windows: five of these cells are for Common-side Debtors; to whom, as also to Criminal Prisoners, the County allows a wooden bedstead, a straw-in-sacking bed, a pair of clean sheets once a month, a blanket, and a rug; and in the Winter an additional blanket, or rug. Five other cells are for solitary confinement; and two, totally dark, for the refractory.

The Masters'-side Debtors have a court-yard, 57 feet by 45; a day-room, 28 feet by 19; and above, a sleeping-room of the same size, with four wooden bedsteads; to which, if the Debtor brings his own bed, he pays one shilling per week; or else the Keeper furnishes the beds at 2*s.* 6*d.* per week each, for two sleeping together. If any Debtor has a bed in the Keeper's house, he pays five shillings per week.

Mr. *James Gabriel,* a most worthy character in this town, (who died 26th March, 1754, at the age of 75) had been very kind to the Prisoners in his lifetime; and at his death left them 100/. which is vested in the Turnpike Security, and from which each Prisoner, every quarter-day, receives a sixpenny loaf. A memorial of this legacy is fixed up in St. Mary's church.

Here are four court-yards for Criminal Prisoners, each 57 feet by 45, all well supplied with water, and a sewer; and four very small circular day-rooms, one at the bottom of each *Tower,* for such it seems to be. The court-yards, not being paved nor bottomed with gravel, are, from the nature of the soil, very damp, dirty, and at times rendered almost useless.

In the centre of the building is the Chapel, to which the Prisoners come from their respective divisions to the seats appropriated for them; and all are required to attend Divine Service. On the first story are twelve sleeping-cells, three on each side the passages or lobbies, of 5 feet wide. Each cell is 8 feet o. inches by 6 feet, with arched roofs, plank bedsteads, and double doors, the outer ones of wood, the inner iron-grated; and all well ventilated, with a window half glazed, and inside shutters to every cell.

At the end of each lobby or passage is a circular room, intended for Prisoners to undress in, on going to bed; and above these are twelve other sleeping-cells, exactly similar to those above described, with iron-grated windows, inside shutters, and sloping blinds. In the attick story are two good-sized Infirmaries, one for Men, the other for Women; and on the top four circular rooms, one in each Tower, of 12 feet diameter, and 7 feet high, totally dark, with straw on the floor, for refractory Prisoners.

The space between the court-yards and boundary wall is from 15 to 30 feet, and affords the Keeper a garden; but the soil appears unfavourable for the growth of vegetables.

Rules and Orders printed, but not exhibited; nor are the Act for Preservation of Health, and Clauses against Spirituous Liquors, hung up.

The Prisoners in the *House of Correction,* and Female Felons, are sometimes employed in spinning of coarse cloth, and making tobacco-pipes; and receive one half of their earnings: but materials can seldom be procured. The Men Felons have no employment.

Here is a cold bath, and County clothing for the use of the Prisoners: They have monthly, fresh straw, with a change of sheets, and clean linen once a week.

Prayer Books are supplied to those who can read.

The Magistrates now visit frequently, as appears by their entries in the book. The County allows firing to all parts of the Prison, when used with discretion.

The Gaol is kept very clean. I weighed the bread sent in, and found every loaf full weight.

At my visit in Sept. 1805, I was informed that the Gaoler was dead. The Magistrates continued his Widow in that situation, with an Assistant, at 50/. per annum, and likewise allowed *9s.* weekly to a Turnkey; to which Mrs. Phillips had added 3s. per week.

MONTROSE. *Scotland.*

Gaolers, The four Town's-officers; who

officiate weekly in turn, but have no Salary as Gaolers.

Fees; for Felons, none. Debtors pay fourpence a night.

No religious attentions.

Surgeon, when one is wanted, ordered by the Magistrates.

Number of Prisoners, 29th Sept. 1809, Criminals, 0. Debtors, 2.

Allowance, to Felons, &c. fourpence in bread per day, and the same in beer. Debtors are alimented at the discretion of the Magistrates.

REMARKS.

This Gaol occupies one end of the old Town-Hall; and on the first story, (to which the ascent from the Street is by 12 steps,) there are two large rooms for Debtors, with boarded floors, lighted and ventilated by a large grated window, that has an inside shutter; a fire-place, but no coals are allowed, nor is any bedding whatever provided. No water, but what is fetched by the Keepers. No sewer, but a tub instead, requiring a more close attention, for health and comfort.

For Criminals here is a large room, of 21 feet by 12, on the ground-floor, having grated windows facing the Street: for bedding, loose straw scantily thrown upon the mud floor.

Debtors here are not allowed to work, even if they can procure it of themselves. No court-yard. The Keepers live at a distance. The whole Prison very dirty.

MONTGOMERY. *North Wales.*
The County Gaol.
Gaoler, *John Davies.* Salary, 35/.

Fees, Debtors, 8. *Ad.* Besides which the Under-Sheriff demands 7. *6d.* for his *liberate!* Felons pay no Fees. For conveyance of Transports, one shilling per mile. Garnish abolished.

Chaplain, Rev. *Charles Williams.* Salary, 20J.

JJuty, every Sunday, Prayers and Sermon; and daily visits those who are under Sentence of Death.

Surgeon, Mr. *Stephens;* now Mr. *Jones;* for *Felons only.* Salary, *8I.*

Number of Prisoners, Debtors. Felons, &c. Lunaticks.

1800, Apr. 5th,----5-----(J--_ 0 1802, Jan. 30th, ----6-----10---'--1 1803, Sept. 8th,----3-----10-----3.

Of the latter, three Lunaticks, one was *Aaron Bywater,* committed for murder; but acquitted on the ground of insanity. He had killed a Fellow-Prisoner here. See Remarks.

Allowance, sixpence per day each in bread.

REMARKS.

This Gaol is finely situated, on a rising ground. Here is one court-yard for Men and Women Debtors, 44 feet by 32, with a sewer in it; a day-room, 14 feet square, and a small room adjoining, fitted up with a bath, and boiler.

Above stairs they have also eight good-sized rooms, three of which are *Free Wards.* The County allows no bedding, except straw on the floor. The Keeper furnishes beds, at J . *6d.* per week the single bed; but 2. a week, if two sleep together.

The Men Felons have a small court-yard, and a day-room, with six sleeping-cells on the ground-floor, the average size about 8 feet *6* inches by 7 feet, and 9 feet *6* inches high. Also up stairs two sleeping-rooms or cells. The Women Felons have likewise a small court-yard; a day-room, with one sleeping-cell on the ground floor, and two rooms above-stairs: to all which the County allows wooden bedsteads, with straw, two blankets, and a rug.

A large room, over the entrance door of the Gaol, is used as a *Chapel,* but not partitioned off so, as to keep the classes, Male and Female, distinct from each other.

The three *Lunatichs,* at the time of my visit in 18o;j, were in the Felons' courtyard. One of them seemed melancholy, and made me no reply. This man was not *tethered.* The second had shewn marks of insanity, which was assigned to me as the reason for his confinement. He was young and hale, and conversed with me so very rationally, that I was induced to examine his breast-bone, (which he shewed me) by opening his shirt-neck: it was red, and appeared to have been galled by the iron collar which encircled it, and was attached to a strong chain, about eight yards long.

The next morning, after breakfasting with Mr. *Lloyd,* an active Magistrate, he accompanied me back to the Gaol, when the above collar was ordered to be taken off; and for this the poor young man was most warmly thankful.

The third maniac, *Aaron Bywater,* kept walking quickly about, backwards and forwards, as far as his chain-tether would permit: But there was something in his eyes so highly ferocious, that, *being alone,* I did not like to speak to him, or come within the length of his tether; bearing in mind the situation I once brought myself into at Glasgow, in the year 1802. This pitiable man, I was next day informed, had been heretofore committed on a charge of Murder, but was acquitted at the Great Session, as being insane; and since his confinement here, had killed a Fellow Prisoner, who was a Convict for Transportation: But, having received the King's pardon, was dressing himself to leave the Gaol, when Bywater came behind, struck him a violent blow, and then dispatched him.

In my late visit to Scotland I was informed that a Woman Lunatick in the Gaol at Banff, had formerly murdered one of her own Children; but afterwards recovering her senses, was permitted to return home to her husband. After living twelve years with him, she became again insane, and destroyed another of her progeny; for which she was then in confinement.

Another instance I met with at York Castle, in 1802, of a gentleman of very large fortune, (W. Medhurst, esq.) who in a fit of phrenzy murdered his wife. He was tried at York in July 1800, and found Insane. Soon after I saw him at the Castle in 1802: The Gaoler had removed him to Brooke House, Upper Clapton, under the care of Dr. Monro, where I believe he now remains, in 1811.

I have dwelt the more fully on the circumstance of *Bywater,* from a clear conviction of the absurdity, the danger, and the cruelty, of admitting such unhappy objects into the association of a Gaol. It is hazardous to all, and capable of being made very injurious to the poor frantick wretch, exposed, as he or she must be, to various inconveniencies. I sincerely hope this narrative may tend to do away entirely the sad Practice—I might call it justly the inhuman Custom, of sending Maniacs to common Gaols; where they have the worst chance of becoming, not 3 F furiously only, but incurably mad; of endangering the Keepers, and destroying all order and decorum. If they prove *simple* and *idiotick,* they but too often become the butt and sport of the unfeeling Criminals around them; and thus furnish a most affecting proof, how much lower than the lowest of all created Beings is Man, *devoid of reason!*

One Wing in the *House of Industry,* near this Town, might, I apprehend, be well appropriated for the comfort, the safety, and the only probable restoration of *Lunaticks.*

A small room is set apart for an Infirmary. The well for the Prisoners was out of repair; and no water accessible.

The Rev. *Thomas Powell,* formerly Chaplain to this Prison, left by his Will *the Interest of Twenty Pounds,* to be laid out every Winter in *coals,* for the use of the Gaol Prisoners.

A *Memorial* of this deserves to be kept in remembrance, but I did not find k recorded in the Gaol.

MONTGOMERY.
The House of Correction
Keeper, *Henry Lloyd.* Salary, 12/. 13s. 4d.

Fees, *2s. 6d.* Garnish, not yet abolished, is *one shilling.*

Surgeon, if wanted, is sent from the Town.

Prisoners, 8th Sept 1803, Two.
Allowance, fourpence a day in bread.
REMARKS.

Here is only one court-yard for all descriptions of Prisoners; with a dungeon 13 feet by 9 feet 3 inches, to which the descent is by nine steps, and within it is fixed a whipping-post.

/On the ground-floor are two middle-sized rooms, with four wooden bedsteads, and loose straw. Seven persons at a time had been confined in the Dungeon, and.as many also in the two rooms.

The employment for the Prisoners is spinning.

MORPETH. *Northumberland.*
The County Gaol.
Gaoler, *John Blake.* Salary, 90I.

Fees, Debtors and Felons, 13. *4d.* each. (No Table.) Besides which the Under-Sherin0 demands of every Debtor a Fee of 2. *6d.* for his *liberate;* and if upon a Supersedeas, *6s. 8d.* Transports, the expence of conveyance. Garnish, *(not yet abolished,)* is a gallon of ale, or porter, from Debtors upon coming in, and another on being discharged from Prison.

Chaplain, Rev. *Edward Nicholson.* Salary, 40/.

Duty, Prayers and a Sermon every Sunday afternoon; and daily attendance on persons under Sentence of death.

Surgeon, *Mr. Douglas Sands.* Salary, none; but makes a Bill.

Number of Prisoners. Debtors. Felons, &c.
1802, Sept. 9th,----ii-2 1809, Sept. 17th,----18--8.

Allowance. Those Debtors who are poor, and petition the Magistrates, obtain the same allowance as the Felons, of *Jburpence* per day in money.
REMARKS.

In the centre of this building is a small court, about 25 feet square, with a pump in it, which is principally used for the Debtors to wash themselves; and is likewise a passage to the Keepers large garden, of which the Debtors have the daily use. In this court are five sleeping-cells, two below, (which, on account of their dampness are not used,) and three above; each 9 feet by 6 feet 7 inches, with arched roofs. On the *left entrance* to the house is the Debtors' day-room, 23 feet by 19, and 12 feet high. This is also the Chapel.

The middle Tower, over the Dungeon hereafter described, is about 23 feet square, and occasionally used both by Debtors and Felons, but not at the same time. It has a fire-place in it, and a sewer. The two windows, glazed and iron-grated, are of 3 feet 7 inches by 3 feet; and in the door is an aperture about 8 inches square.

On the Debtors' side of the Prison there is, on the first floor, one room for Women, about 14 feet square, and another of 18 feet by 15. The second story has five rooms, to which the Keeper furnishes beds, at from two shillings to one shilling per week. The upper story has two rooms; the largest of which, 18 feet square, is used as a free Ward, whenever the middle Tower is occupied by Felons. The other room, used as an Infirmary, is 14 feet by 10, having a large closet, well lighted and ventilated.

On the *right hand entrance* to the house, two steps below ground, lies " the Black Hole," or Dungeon for Felons, 21 feet 4 inches by 19 feet 2, with a boarded floor; straw, two blankets and two rugs for each Prisoner: an offensive sewer in it, and the windows are only 18 inches by 9.

Over the Middle Tower is that called the *High Tower,* which is divided into two apartments: the one 24 feet 10 inches by 15 feet 8, having two grated windows; the other of 14 feet by .6 feet 10, with one window; a fire-place and a sewer in each.

Water is accessible at all times to the Debtors; and it is carried, as wanted, to the Felons, who have a day-room, 21 feet by 12.

Here is no Uniform Clothing; but the County, where requisite, allows what is suitable to the poor and needy.

It was intended, at the next General Quarter Sessions, to represent the want of a proper Infirmary, with a bath and oven, for the Prisoners.

I found this Gaol kept as clean as the bad construction of it would permit.

MORPETH. *Northumberland.*
The Bridewell.
Gaoler, *John DoxJ'ord*; now *Nicholas Henderson.* Salary, 30/.

Fees, 13. *Ad.*; for Misdemeaners, *$s. Ad.* No religious attentions.

Surgeon, Mr. *Sands;* who makes a Bill.

Number of Prisoners, Sept. 9th, 1802, Four. Sept. 18th, 1809, Five.

Allowance, four-pence a day. At my visit, in 1802, those who were committed to hard labour, and in health, had only their earnings to subsist on: But, in 1809, the workshop was sold, and there had been no employment since.

REMARKS.

This Prison, near the South-end of the Bridge, is at the back of the Keeper's house; and a covered passage, 16 yards long, and *6* feet 3 inches wide, leads to the Bridewell, which has twelve sleeping-cells on the ground-floor, divided by a passage *6* feet wide.

Each cell is 8 feet by *6,* and 8 feet high, to the crown of the arch, and fitted up with crib-bedsteads for a single person, loose straw, and 3 blankets or coverlets; a stool to sit on, and lighted and ventilated by an iron-grated and glazed window, 17 inches by 15. A small tub, used as a sewer, is emptied every morning. An inspecting wicket in each cell door, about 9 inches square.

Above stairs is a day and working-room for the Men, and another for Women, each 17 feet by 15, with flagged stone floors, fire-places, and grated and glazed casement windows in each: And into these rooms open four cells; one of which is used as an Infirmary, of 13 feet by 8, with fire-place, beds and bedding: The others are sleeping-cells.

The Women's court-yard, 45 feet by 18, and laid down in grass, has a sewer in the centre. That for the Men is about the same size in front, with a pump to supply the Prison, and a dust-pen. The lower cells are damp; and, to render them less unhealthy, might be warmed by the tube of a German stove running through them.

The Prisoners have no employment assigned them; nor, if procured, do they obtain any part of their earnings. When discharged, they are allowed money, from one-shilling to ten shillings, according to their distance from home.

MUSSELBURGH; *See page* 384. NAIRNE. *Scotland.*

The County Gaol.

Gaolers, the two Town-Officers, who act in rotation.

Fees, for Criminals, none. Debtors, *4d.* a night.

Surgeon, from the Town, if wanted. No religious attentions.

Number of Prisoners, 7th October, 1809, Debtor, 1, Felon, 1. The latter was a Woman, with her infant Child! Both the Prisoners looked very squalid; and but too exactly exhibited that genuine " *Squalor Carceris,"* already noticed with Horror, in Page 241.

Allowance, Felons, &c. *6d.* a day Debtors, as alimented.

REMARKS.

This Tolbooth adjoins the Town-Hall. For Criminals here is a black, dirty room, about 16 feet by 10, with a fire-place, and a grated glazed window. A wooden bedstead nearly filled up the whole apartment; and upon it was spread a ragged blanket, in which slept the Woman Criminal and her Child. Over this is the room for Debtors, which had a fire-place, but no grate. The Debtor here confined was in the Woman Felon's room, warming himself by a small fire, which somebody had charitably afforded her, the weather being very cold.

No bedding: not even straw allowed. No coals: no water, but as brought in by the Keepers.

NANTWICH. *Cheshire.*

Prison for Debtors.

Keeper, *Humphrey Topkam;* a Sheriff's Officer.

Salary, none. He pays rent, six pounds, and all Taxes.

REMARKS.

This Prison, for the Manor or Barony of *Wich-Malbank,* otherwise Nantwich, is the property of the Earl of Cholmondeley; and consists of four rooms in the Keeper's house, with a work-shop. The court-yard here is insecure, but has a pump in it of excellent water. At my visit on the 30th of October 1802, here were *three Lunatichs;* one of them, a poor Woman, frantick, and chained to her bed! On the 29th of October 1805, I found *two* Lunaticks.

The Keeper informed me that no Debtor had been confined here these twenty years.

NANTWICH *Town Gaol.*

Gaoler, *Henri/ Robinson.* Salary, 8/. a suit of clothes, hat, shoes, and a load of coals.

Number of Prisoners, 1802, Oct. 20th One. 1805, Oct. 29th, Two. Allowance, none.

REMARKS.

This " *Round House,'* as it is usually called, was built by the County in 1782. It consists of two rooms and a kitchen for the Gaoler. Here is a room for Prisoners, of 12 feet 3 inches by 10 feet 2 inches, arched with brick, which has an iron-grated window, and is supplied with a barrack bedstead, and straw; but no fire-place.

Down eleven steps are *two Dungeons;* the largest 17 feet by 10, the other 12 feet by 10, with iron-grated apertures, 12 inches by 9; brick-floored, and damp. Only *one Jire-place,* and that in the Gaoler's kitchen. Here is an adjacent courtyard, about 34 feet square; but of which the Prisoners have no use. It is occupied by the Gaoler, and in one corner of it is a sewer. No water laid on.

The Gentlemen hereabout, and in the adjacent Counties, seem to have overlooked a Clause in the Act of 14 Geo. III. cap. 43, " To prevent Prisoners being kept under-ground, whenever they can do it conveniently;" for amongst those Prisons which have been *lately built,* I observe very few that have not a *Dungeon.*

Since my visit in 1802, I find that water is now prevented from getting into the Dungeons, which rendered them uncomfortable, and even dangerous to their pitiable inhabitants.—Whatever is both needless and injurious, may well be laid aside.

NEWARK-UPON-TRENT. *Nottinghamshire.*

The Town Gaol, and Bridewell.

Gaoler, *William Cropper.* Salary, lol. out of which he is to provide straw for the
Prisoners.

Fees, Debtors, 4. Felons, 13$. *Ad.* No Table. Surgeon, when wanted, from the Workhouse. Allowance, *three-pence* a day!

Number of Prisoners 1803, l8th August, One. 1809, 2d Sept. One.

REMARKS.

This House of Correction adjoins the Workhouse. It has two rooms above, and one below, of about 22 feet by 12; with arched roofs, flagged floors, a fire-place, and one double-bar iron-grated and glazed window to each, for light and ventilation. Here is a small courtyard, 26 feet by 10, with a pump in it, but no sewer; a halftub in each room being substituted.

Without the prison-wall is one room, about 15 feet by 8, in which Women Prisoners are occasionally confined; and for the admission to it of light and air, there is a circular grating over the door. The Corporation allows to every Prisoner two blankets and a rug.

Below, within the Gaol, is a *horrid Dungeon*, of about 22 feet by 12. The descent to it is by fourteen steps: totally dark. The only possible light or ventilation it can ever receive, is from a wicket in the door, of about *6* inches by 4, which heretofore was opened — *to give the Prisoner his Food!* The flooring is of damp mud. On enquiry, I learned from the Keeper, that sometimes, in Winter, the water in this subterranean cavern had been *sixteen inches deep!* N. B. The vile old dungeon is now happily turned into an oil-cellar.

No employment. The rooms and staircases very dirty; not having been whitewashed for five years (1805). The only Prisoner, at my visit in 1800, was a Man for Bastardy, who had been here *Jive months!* $3 Above *thirty* years ago, my illustrious Predecessor, Mr. Howard was here, and, in consequence of what he saw, uttered the following Ejaculation: "Among the ' various Improvements that are making in this town, I hope the Corporation *u will think of a better Prison"* What might he not have said *now?* NEWBURY. *Berkshire.*
The Corporation Gaol.

Keeper, *Thomas Allen.* Salary, 5*I.* Fees, *6s. Sd.* No Table.
Surgeon, when wanted, sent by the Parish.

Prisoners, lS0i, Dec. 14th, none. 1806, Oct. 16th, one. Allowance, 5f. a day.
REMARKS.
This Prison consists properly of two rooms, in a Public-house, the *Town-Arms,* kept by JohnTownsend, a Sergeant at Mace. The Keeper informed me that he had had thirty Prisoners in them at one time. The first is 13 feet by 9, and 8 feet high; lighted by two iron-grated windows, with a chaff-bed on the floor, a blanket over it, a piece of old sacking, two blankets and a rug, supplied by the County: The second room, 15 feet square, 10 feet high, with 3 iron-bar grated windows, and a fireplace, but *no grate.* Adjoining to this is a small room opening in it, which has a good sized bedstead, with sacking bottom, a feather bed, two blankets, and a rug.
NEWBURY. *The Bridewell.*
Keeper, *Frederick Arrowsmith;* now *William Hudson.*

Salary, as Keeper of the Bridewell, none; but for the Workhouse which adjoins it, 25/. No Fees. Prisoners, lS0i,Dec. 13th, One. 1806, Oct. 16th, Two. Allowance, as at the Workhouse.
REMARKS.
The Bridewell contains four rooms. The first; 8 feet square, lighted by a small iron-grating, and an aperture in the door; of *6* inches by 4. The second room is 16' feet *6* inches by 8 feet,, and 8 *feet* high, lighted by a glazed window. In it was a Woman Prisoner, ill in bed. The third, of nearly the same dimensions, is lighted by two large glazed windows. To these rooms the Corporation allows a bedstead, flock-bed, a coarse sheet, bolster, two blankets, and a rug. The fourth, is for the refractory, totally dark; size 10 feet by 8, and 8 feet high.

Men and Women Prisoners are here kept separate.

Like the Corporation Gaol, this has its privations. No water accessible; No firing allowed. No court-yard. *The Prisoners constantly locked up.* The whole Bridewell filthy, and very ill ventilated. Divine Service never read. No employment provided. The Act and Clauses *not* hung up!
NEWCASTLE-UPON-TYNE. *Northumberland.*
The County Gaol.
Gaoler, *John Gale;* now *Robert Gee;* who lives near the Prison. Salary, 100/.

Fees, for Debtors and Felons, 14. *4d.* each, of which one shilling is paid to the Turnkey. The Under-Sheriff demands 2. *6d.* on discharge of a Writ from the Court of King's Bench, or Common Pleas; and five shillings on a *Supersedeas!* No Table. For Conveyance of Transports, the expence. 7

Garnish, abolished. See *Remarks.*
Chaplains, Rev. Mr. *Perkins,* and Rev. Mr. *Heartley.*

Salary, *lol.* from the Corporation, and *lol.* from Sir *Walter Blackett.*
Duty, on Sundays, none; but on Wednesdays and Fridays, Prayers; and a Sermon monthly. The Chaplains officiate month and month alternately.

Surgeon, Mr. *fVUliam Fife,* Salary, none. He makes a Bill.

Number of Prisoners. Debtors. Felons, &c. Bastardy.

l802, Feb. 7th,----13----12----0.

Sept. 6th,----12----10----0.

1809, Sept. 16th, _--5----$-_ 3,
Allowance, to *Debtors,* two-pence a day, on Petition to the Mayor of Newcastle. *Felons,* five-pence per day.
REMARKS.
This Prison is conspicuous, being the Gate at the upper end of the Town, and in times past was a fortified Gateway. Here is no court-yard; but one might easily be made out of the vacant ground, which lies west of the Gaol, as the Town Wall stands on one side of it. It was once in contemplation to build six new-rooms, and an Infirmary at the West-end of the Prison, and to enclose the open spot alluded to, for a Debtors' court-yard, which must be a great improvement.

At my visit, in 1802, the vacant space above noticed had a pig-stye in it, with swine, ducks, &c. The offence, however, was in 180G removed; and there is now a cold bath constructed, which has a constant run of water; and where the Felons, one at a time, enjoy the fresh air, accompanied by the Turnkey.

On the right-hand of the stair-case, leading to the Debtors' Prison, is a miserable place, called "*The Black-Hole,*" measuring 24 feet by 8; with a vaulted roof, lighted and ventilated by a small grating under the gate, loose straw to sleep on, and a coverlet.

The *left-side* of the gateway is the Gaol for *Debtors;* On the tstair-case leading to whose apartments, is placed up the following Inscription, framed and glazed:

"Friends visiting the Debtors in this

Prison are to take notice, that the following are the hours of admission; which cannot be departed from, except on very particular occasions, viz.
u From eight to nine in the morning:.. _ "From twelve to one at noon: "From four to five in the evening. "Those who neglect to come out at the appointed hour, must remain till the next opening. "..

The Debtors have no court-yard, but walk on the battery at the top of the Gaol; which is a space of about 34 feet square, with a flagged floor, and a sewer in one corner; or else, on the flat leads, 40 feet square. To these two outlets for air and exercise they have access at all hours. Here is no distinction of Debtors.

The Corporation allow an iron bedstead, a ticking bed, filled with new chaff every three months, one under blanket, two upper ones, and two coverlets, (which are scoured quarterly) to Debtors, Felons, and all descriptions of Prisoners alike. The former have eight lodging-rooms assigned them, and each Debtor sleeps single, in case the Prison will admit of it. They succeed to the best rooms by seniority of confinement; and every one is required to attend Divine Service, unless prevented by illness, or professing himself to be of a different religious persuasion.

All the Prisoners are allowed as much fuel as they can expend without waste, together with mops, brooms, pails, &c. to keep the Prison clean. Any one who misbehaves is tried by a court held amongst themselves, at which the senior Debtor presides. The culprit, on conviction, is fined according to Rules laid down for preserving good behaviour in the Prison; and all communication with him is interdicted till the Fine is paid. If he conceives himself hardly judged, his appeal is to the Keeper; who examines into the matter, and settles it accordingly. This only relates to petty offences, committed against the peace of the Prison.

The present is one of those very few Gaols that have, what in London are termed ' The Rules." They here extend, South of the Prison, to a running water arched over, called Execution-Dock; and on the East of the Prison down High Fryer-street, about two hundred yards, to a rivulet called *Lork Burn* , now arched over with stone. As the Keeper cannot find by what authority these *Rules* were granted, no Debtors are indulged in the use of them, but those of good character, and who are confined for small sums.

The Debtors' day-room,—and in which Divine Service is performed,—is 27 feet by 21: but being on the other side of the Gateway, the Felons cannot attend. Here, "Lork Burn, up which, for a considerable way, the tide flowed formerly, made a division anciently in the lower part of the ' Side '—a street so called. This runnel of water was covered with stene, A. D. 1696." See Hutchinson's *Hut. of Durham.* '- painted on a board, is conspicuously hung up the following exemplary advertisement:

"Be it understood, that no Debtor on his entrance into, or departure from this 'Prison, shall be liable to the payment of any sum of money for the purchase of v beer, heretofore exacted under the title of *Garnish.*" "No money, under any pretence whatever, can be levied on the relations and "friends of Debtors visiting them in this Prison."

Every Debtor committed by process issuing out of the Mayor's or Sheriff's Court, for a Debt *exceeding ten pounds,* is entitled to his *Sixpences* in about six months; but, as he must employ an Attorney of the Court for this end, whose charge is *Jour guineas,* the benefit is seldom obtained. It is a pity, that in so respectable and opulent a town as Newcastle, there is not a Fund established for the purpose, like that at Winchester, Gloucester, &c. &c. If the Debt be *under* ten pounds, by serving the Plaintiff with fourteen days notice, he becomes entitled to his Sixpences at the first Sheriff's Court, which is held twice a week.

Debtors are sent hither from the Court of Conscience.

On the *right side of the Gateway* leading into the Gaol, opens a passage, of about 8 yards by 2, in which there is a water-cock to supply that part of the Prison; and adjoining to this is the *Condemned-Room,* the only one upon the ground-floor: all the others are up stairs, and both clean and airy. This Condemned-Room is about *6* yards by 4-J-, having a fire-place, and an iron-grated window that looks toward the street; but, to check conversation with passengers, and prevent files, or other mischievous utensils, being conveyed to them, a wall is erected at a little distance from the Felons' window. It is also called the *Cap-Room.*

There are four rooms within the Felons' Gaol; and no Prisoners here have fetters, unless they prove riotous or refractory.

Over the Condemned-Room is another of the same size, which also looks to the street. Just by is a small court, of 54 feet by 17, with a bathing tub in it; but the court not being deemed secure, the Felons have not the use of it.

The Act for the preservation of Health, and the Clauses against Spirituous Liquors, are conspicuously hung up in this Prison; and the whole is kept very clean.

NEWCASTLE-UPON-TYNE. *Northumberland.' The Castle-Garth. "' '.*

A Place of temporary confinement for Prisoners from Morpeth only. See page 402 for the Officers and other particulars of " Morpeth County Gaol."

Gaoler, *Ann Hardy.* Salary, 4/. 4s. 1802, Sept. 7th, 1809, Sept. 17th, no Prisoners. REMARKS.

In the very centre of Newcastle (dignified by *Camden,* as "the Glory of all the Towns of this Country,") is the curious Prison of *Castle-Garth,* or *Castle-Keep,* as the phrase is elsewhere used; so denominated, probably, in old time, from the close, area, or court-yard, by which it was formerly surrounded.

The Gaol Delivery for Morpeth, (about sixteen miles distant from Newcastle,) takes place once a year. The Assizes are held at Newcastle; and hither the Morpeth Prisoners are brought for trial. In the interim, however, the Felons, &c. of Morpeth are confined, Men and Women promiscuously,—and sometimes, we are told, for a whole week tog-ether,—in the Castle-Garth. This anciently formed, it seems, a part of the Castle; but is now merely a wretched, damp, dirty *Dungeon,* to which the descent is six steps below the level of the street.

Of this place, and its appendages, we have the following Records; which I recite, as being somewhat connected with the subject.

In a survey of the Castle, taken 29th October, 1649, the following item occurs. "There is an auncient building within, the inner-wall of the *Castle-Garth,* which is "commonly called or known by the name of ' *The Moote Hull,'* which is now "vested in the State; and is used by the Justices of the Assize Sessions and Gaole "Delivery, for the keeping of their Assize and Session for the County of Northum"berland."

July 3d, 173(, The King granted the Castle and *Castle-Garth, forjifty* years, to George Liddell, Esq. at 100 chaldrons of coals annually to Chelsea Hospital, and keeping all the buildings, as well as those excepted in the lease, as granted, in good repair..,

The *exceptions* are, "That strong building, used for a common Gaol for the County of Northumberland; and also the Hall, commonly called the Moot Hall; and all other buildings appertaining."

Nov. 19th, 1777. The King granted to Lord Ravensworth, for forty years and a half, to commence in July 1786, a lease of the Castle and *Castle-Garth,* with the like exceptions.

May 19th, 1779, the above lease was purchased by John Critchloe Turner, Esq. (now-Sir John) at auction; and by the said lease to Lord Ravensworth, the Lessee, for the time being, is bound to repair the Old Castle, Out-wails and Stairs, MootHall, Grand-Jury Room, and Gaoler's House.

When I applied for admission to Ann Hardy, the Keeper of Castle-Garth, (who lives at a distant part of Newcastle,) a Man was directed to attend me, with a shovel, to clear away the dirt and filthy rubbish about it; and at length I *was* admitted!

This "Durance, vile" has neither light nor ventilation, but, what » introduced through a small iron-grated window, that looks toward the pavement. There are iron rings fixed into the wall, to which the Men Felons are chained, and a small part of the Dungeon is partitioned off for the Women. These, however, (perhaps from motives of delicacy!) are even placed in a worse situation than the Males; being thus in *utter darkness,* and without any apparent means of ventilation that I could discover. The wet came pouring down the walls in every part, and the flooring was several inches deep in water; so that I could not find either patience or resolution to measure the dimensions. My visit was in the month of September, 1802.

In this horrid cavern are Prisoners confined for seven, and sometimes for eight nights together. The Man who accompanied me said he had known it two feet deep in water; and hence, at such times, the poor wretches must be obliged to take their station upon the inside-steps. The necessity for this seems, indeed, to have been foreseen by the Guardians of the place, as there is a flight of steps, on the *inside* of the Dungeon, as high as the street; so that whether the Prisoners could sit down, or must stand upon the steps, depended on the number thrust into it!

At the Assizes held '29th July, 1800, seven Prisoners were here for three nights,

A New Prison is now building; and this wretched place will be no longer continued as a living sepulchre for human misery.

NEWCASTLE-UPON-TYNE. *Northumberland.*
The Sessions Prison.
Keeper, *Richard Hill;* now *James Sapwith,* Town Marshal.
Salary, I5I. and for the Bridewell, 5/.
Fees, one shilling on entrance, and the same on discharge.
Number of Prisoners, 1802, Sept. 6th, Four. 1S09, Sept. 17th, none.
Allowance, three-pence a day, and coals.
REMARKS.
This *Old House of Correction* consists of two rooms; one of them for Men, the other for Women; and its dungeon is now used as a cellar. Straw on barrack bedsteads, with three blankets, and a coverlet each.

No court-yard. No water. No employment. Criminals are sent hither for trial at the Quarter Session, NEWCASTLE-UP-ON-TYNE. *The Bridewell.*
£eeper, *Edward Manners,* as Deputy to *Richard Hill.* Salary, 5/. and the profit of the Prisoners' work.
Chaplain, none. Surgeon, when wanted, sent from the Dispensary.
Number of Prisoners, 1802, Sept. 6th, 10. 1S09, Sept. 17th, 18.
Allowance, three-pence a day, and coals.
REMARKS.
Here is a room below for the Keeper; and one adjoining for the Women, whom I found employed in spinning.

In the New Buildings are four rooms with chimnies: three of them on the ground-floor, are 17 feet by 12, and arched with brick. In one room the Men, by a machine, beat hemp and flax; but none of those materials being to be procured when I was there, all the eleven were unemployed. There are two upper rooms; one for the Men, the other for Women.

The walls of the court not being secure, the Prisoners have no access to it; nor is any use made of the five small rooms that occupy it.

Water is laid on to the house by a pipe; but so ill supplied, that the Keeper told me he was frequently obliged to fetch it for his own domestick use.

Neither the Act for preserving the Health of Prisoners, nor the Clauses against Spirituous Liquors, hung up.
NEWPORT. *Isle of Wight.*
The Bridewell, and Town Gaol.
Gaoler, *James Reynolds;* Sergeant at Mace. Salary, 40/. Fees, none. burgeon, Mr. *Watersworth,* who makes a Bill.
Number of Prisoners, 1802, March 18th, Debtors,One; Felons, &c. none. 1807, Sept. 19th, Debtor, One; Felons, &c. Two.

Allowance, to all, sixpence per day, in bread or money.
REMARKS.
In this Prison Debtors are confined by process issuing out of the Borough Court, and their allowance is granted

them after two Court-days, which are generally held in a fortnight. Here is no court-yard, nor water accessible to the Prisoners. The Gaol consists of six rooms, about 14 feet each by 8; two of which are appropriated to Debtors, who pay *6d.* per night; and the other four are for Felons or Petty Offenders. Their bedding, *hulls of oats* in sacking, changed once a year, with two or three blankets, and a rug. The floors are boarded, windows glazed, and urinals emptied as required daily. All have the same bedding. The Prisoners here are chiefly Debtors from the Courts of Conscience; and the proceedings for five pounds, the same as in London. Neither the Act nor Clauses hung up. *t* NEWGATE. *London.*

Gaoler, *John Kirby;* now *John Addison Newman.* Salary, 450/.

Fees, for Debtors and Felons, &c. as per following Tables.

'Table *I. Debtors.*

London, Sc.

"A Table of Fees, to be taken by the Gaoler or Keeper of the Prison of *Newgate,* within the said City of London, for any.Prisoner or Prisoners committed or coming into Gaol, or Chamber-Rent there, or discharged from thence, in any *Civil Action:* Settled and established the 19th day of December, 1729.

Every Prisoner, on the *Master s-$ide* shall pay to the Keeper, for his En-*s. L* trance Fee------------------30

Every Prisoner, on the Master's-Side, shall pay for chambter-room, use of bed, bedding, and sheets, to the Keeper, there being two in a bed, and no more, each per week--------------13

Every Prisoner, on the said Master's-Side, who, at his own desire, shall have a bed to himself, shall pay to the Keeper for chamber-room, use of bed, bedding, and sheets, per week----------26

Every Debtor shall pay to the Keeper, for his discharging Fee---6 10 And to all the Turnkeys, 2j. and no more---------2 O.

No other Fee for the use of chamber, bed, bedding, or sheets; or upon the commitment or discharge of any Prisoner on any *Civil Action.*

Edw. Becher. ROB. RAYMOND.

Rob. Alsop. R. EYRE.

John Barnard. THO. PENCELLY.

The Fee to the Middlesex Sheriff's Office, for every Debtor's discharge, *s d.* for one Action, is----------------46

And for every additional Action, more 2 6."

But Messrs. BURCHELL, the present humane Deputy Sheriff, sometimes remit this Fee, upon the Keeper's Certificate of the Debtor's being poor, and unable to pay it. The Warrant of such discharge is given under the Hand and Seal of the Sheriff of Middlesex, and is called " *The Red Seal.* The Fee for a *London Debtor's* Discharge from the Sheriffs, is the same as before stated in my Account of *Ludgate Prison.* See Page 3113.

Or, tq any price, according to the quality of the Prisoner, and the nature of his or her accommodation. f A Seal, in which are quartered the Arms of both the Gentlemen appointed by the City to be Sheriffs, wTio, together, make one Sheriff of Middlesex. The impress of it is always placed after the names of the Sheriff upon the Warrant of Discharge in. *red wax,* and hence it obtained the name. Table II. *Felons,* ojfc.

Hung up, in several places, on the *Criminal* Side of Newgate.

£. t. d.

"For every Felon's discharge------------01810

For every Misdemeanour O 14 10

For every Felon's Entrance on the Master's-Side---..-0 10 6 For every Person admitted into the *Press-yard* ------. 330

For every Transport's discharge---..--.-.-014 10 For every Bailable Warrant-----------36 8.

Robert Wilmott,. ROB LADBROKE.

W« Barnard. SAMUEL PENNENT.

"And to the Clerk of the Peace, of Clerk in Court of the Session of Gaol Delivery of Newgate. *£. s. d.*

For every Felon's Discharge-----------062

For *every* Petty Larceny-------------04 10

For every Misdeamcanour-------------0 10 0."

Garnish, Debtors; on the *Cabin-Side,* a subscription of one Guinea, for coals, candles, mops, brooms, &c. at entrance, and a gallon of ale on quitting the Prison.

On the *Master's-Side,* a subscription of thirteen shillings and four-pence, for coals, &c. and a gallon of beer at entrance.

On the *Common-Side* a subscription of eight shillings and ten-pence for coals, &c. and a gallon of beer.

Those, who, from their poverty, cannot pay this last-mentioned sum, are to wash and clean the wards.

Felons, on the *Masters-Side,* pay about thirteen shillings Garnish, and those on the Common-Side, about eight shillings, according to the price of coals and candles; and those who, from their poverty, cannot pay the same, are required to afford a greater share of labour, in washing andcleansing the Felon-wards.

The above several sums are paid to the *Stewards* of the Wards on the *Debtors'-Side;* and to the *Gatesmen* and *Wardsmen* on the *Felons'-Side;* and laid out towards purchasing coals, wood, candles, mops, brooms, and other necessary articles.

The Stewards, Gatesmen, and Wardsmen entrusted with these respective charges, have each a double allowance of bread.

In a room, formerly the Tap, *Anne Sell,* a free Vintner, supplies the Criminal Prisoners with wine; and serves out the beer which is sent to the Prison from the Public Houses; for which she is allowed two-pence per gallon.

Chaplain, or Ordinary; The Rev. Dr. *Forde.*

Duty, Prayers and Sermon every Sunday Morning, and Prayers in the Afternoon: also Prayers every Wednesday and Friday Morning; and private Prayers, on Tuesday and Saturday, to those under Sentence of Death. After the Recorder's Report, he attends those Convicts who are to suffer, twice a day, and on the Morning of Execution; as does likewise a Catholic Priest, with those who are of the Romish Church. Salary, 200/. and a House adjoining to the Gaol. Also 67. *per annum,* from

Lady *Barnardutorts* Legacy, and *1ol.* a year, from an old Legacy, paid by the Governors of St. Bartholomew's Hospital. Over and above which, sundry sums have been occasionally presented to the Ordinary by the Court of Aldermen.

Surgeon, Mr. *William Box,* who visits the Prison daily.

Salary, 10O/. and Medicines, for Debtors as well as Criminals, paid for by the City.

There is no Surgeon's Book kept in Newgate. But I am informed he makes a regular Return to the Court of Aldermen, and another Return to the Court every day, during the Sessions at the Old Bailey, of the state of Health in the Gaol; together with a Certificate, that the several persons to be called on, are fit and able to take their trials, or otherwise. No Prisoner is ever brought to the Bar of the Old Bailey without such Certificate.

The Surgeon also attends the removal of Convicts, and others; who are never sent to any other place of confinement, without his Certificate of their being free from putrid or infectious fevers, and fit to be removed.

Number of Prisoners.
1800, June 14th, 1801, April 27th, 1802, April 3d, 1803, July 2d, 1804, Feb. 10th, 1805, April 22d,

Debtors. Felons, &c.
-*199 289.* -275--375 -221--418. -191 "-519. -204--317 -149--287. 1S06, May 24th, 1807, March 16th, 1808, March 12th,1809, June 16th, 1810, April 19th--184--347. 1811, Jan. 16th,--233--396.
Debtors. Felons, &c.
-198--205. -175--204. -197--182. -252--234. Of these, 84 were under Sentence of Death; and Eight Lunaticka.

There were in Newgate, at the following periods of passing the Insolvent Bill,

Allowance, to every *Debtor* fourteen ounces of the best wheaten bread, daily- f-. The Debtors on the *Poor* and *Wometis-Side* have eight stone (or sixty-four pounds) of beef, divided weekly amongst them, without bone, such as clods and stickings; which is paid for by the Sheriffs.

To the *poor Criminals,* ten stone of beef every Saturday; four stone every Tuesday, and four stone every Thursday; besides an allowance of mutton for the sick, and ten ounces of the best bread daily to each Criminal: Together also with a weekly allotment of rice, or potatoes,—and sometimes of coals, to the amount of about fourpence each Criminal; or (as nearly as may be) according to the then value of twenty-eight ounces of bread. The meat is paid for by the Sheriffs, and the bread, rice, &c. by the Court of Aldermen.

There are also sundry *Donations* to the poor Men and Women *Debtors,* payable at different periods; some of which are regularly paid, and others discontinued; as will appear by the following Lists. A List of Donations to the Poor Debtors confined in Newgate.

Lady-day Quarter. In Middlesex alone, between six and seven thousand persons are annually arrested on mesne process, and about half of them for debts under twenty pounds. The total number, in the kingdom, may be reckoned at 80,000i. And if all do not go immediately to the Common Gaols, tbey are, for a time, in the custody of Bailiffs, and in lock-up houses.

-J-There is a want of regularity and correctness in making the loaves of bread; many of which I have found, when weighed singly, to lie deficient two ounces, and some to be over-weight. There are, likewise, persons within the prison, who sell green-grocery and meat, witk measures, weights, and scales, not stamped. J Taylor, Grosvenor, &c. § And eight dozen of bread. II And five dozen of bread,
Yearly-
Ditto-
Ditto--
End of Term
Yearly--
Quarterly
Ditto-
Ditto-
Yearly-
Ditto-
Ditto-
Ditto-
Quarterly
Ditto-
Yearly-
Ditto-
Ditto-
Ditto-
Ditto-
Ditto-
Ditto-
Ditto-
Quarterly
Donors' Names.
Company of Parish Clerks--
Receiver General of Land-Tax
Sr John Kendrick----
Barons of Exchequer-
Sundry Persons J---
Mr. John Meridith---
Mr. John Draper---
Sir Tho. Gresham, Knt.--
Fishmongers Extra Bounty
Mr Thomas Kneesworth-
Mrs. Letitia Smith----
Sir Stephen Peacock-
Mr. Peter Blundell---
Mr. Peter Blundell---
Mr. William Parker--
Mrs. Margaret Crawthoro-
Mrs. Margaret Hargrave-
Archbishop of Canterbury-
Mr. John Gerrard--
Sir William Home-----I Ditto
Sir John Peachey-----Grocers Company----
Mr. Thomas Dawson----1 Church-wardens of St. Ethelburga
Mr. Robert Ramston----31, Orchard Street, Portman-Sqtt
Sadlers Company Sadlers Company----
By whom paid.
Brought to Prison, Nov. 1---
Auditor's Office, Palace-Yard--
Drapers Comany-----
Exchequer Office, Templeleathersellers Company---
Skinners ditto------
Ditto
Chamberlain of London---
Fishmongers Company---
Ditto
Ditto
Haberdashers Company--
Ditto
Merchant Tai lors ditto--
Ditto

Cutlers Company-----
Qothwwkers Company---
At Lambeth Palace----
Salters Company-----

Provisions, with additional Donations, and to what purpose they are applied.

Mrs. Margaret Dane, from the Ironmongers Company, 18 stone 6 lbs. of beef, and five dozen penny loaves, sent for to the Hall on the 5th of November. "The parish of St. Dunstan in the East, 20 stone of beef, and a peck of oatmeal, sent to the Prison on-Christmas-eve by the Churchwardens.. Legacy of Thomas Cottle;—see Ludgate, page 367.

Allhallows, Lombard-street, 175. laid out in beef every two years. Brought to prison.

St. Andrew Undershaft, 17s. laid out in beef every two years. Brought to prison.

St. Ethelburga, *9s.* laid out in beef every two years. Brought to prison.

Mrs; Margaret Simcott, 65 penny loaves, to be delivered every 56 days. Brought to prison.

Mrs. Fisher, executrix of Mrs. Eliz. Misson, 6/. yearly, in February, being the produce of 200/. India Annuities. Will, dated 23d May, 1770, proved at London, 9th March, 177+.—See Ludgate, page 369. This legacy is reluctantly and irregularly paid.

§£3 Through the exertions of the attentive Keeper of this Gaol, a very excellent arrangement took place in 1807; for the distribution of the Prison-Charities: By which all the Prisoners are equally benefited, and the monies arising therefrom *laid out in necessaries for their use,* instead of the quarterly distribution, as heretofore, in money; which, but too frequently, was spent in liquor, by those only who happened to be in Prison at the time the said Charities became payable.

The *Debtors* are also especially relieved by the humanity of the Society, held at No. 7, *Craven-street* in the *Strand,* who monthly vote large sums towards procuring their Discharge, and paying their Fees. For the same merciful purpose, money is likewise issued by some of the *City Companies;* by a liberal Society at *Mile End;* and, for unfortunate Inhabitants of *Christ-Church Parish,'* by the Common-Councilmen there

.

»

Twice in a year, the Debtors have, moreover, a share of *one hundred pounds;* laid out, first, by the Lord Mayor, and, secondly, by the Sheriff's, in the purchase of provisions and coals; and distributed to all the Prisoners in *Newgate, Ludgate,* and the *two Compters,* according to the number of persons in each of those Prisons.

Broken victuals are often sent by the Master of the London Coffee-house, by Mr. Alderman Birch in Cornhill, and by the Masters of the City of London Tavern: Of the two former of which the more distressed Debtors sometimes partake; and of the latter they have lately appointed a Collector, to attend daily, and receive them.

I should now proceed to my *Remarks,* but that the following Document seems previously to demand the present, as the most suitable place for its insertion. It is a *List,* very different indeed from those which have just preceded it:—a painful List, of what are called " *Courts of Conscience Debtors:"* of the *Debts* they had in See before, page 935.

curred: of the times of their commitment to Newgate; and of the charges accumulated against them for Costs, upon such very inconsiderable demands . It were easy to extend the melancholy detail; but I forbear:— Reverence for existing law precludes the saying more, than

"Pity it is, 'tis truer *Dale of Warrants. Defendants' Names. Debts. Costs.* 1797. s. d. s. d.

February 7, John Allen 3 5 8 8

May 11, William Gongh 3 10 8 10

October 15, Thomas Blackburn 2 0 6 lO

Ditto 1 5 6 10

December 14, Ann Jones 2 3 8 10 1798.

April 12, Charles Burnet, 3 10 8 10

September 20,-Thomas Blackburn 2 6....... 8 10

November i, Elizabeth Irvine 3 9 8 8 1799.

August 15 CalebOnly 3 9 8 10 22, Thomas Dobson 1 0 .... 8 10

September 1, John Hyder 3 10 8 8

October 1, Susannah Evans 2 2 6 8

17, William Owen 3 0 8 S 1300.

March 13, Abraham Slater 3 4 6 10

July 24, John Jones 3 0 6 10.

REMARKS.

Newgate, formerly one of the gates of the City of London, was first erected iu the reign of Henry the First, or of Stephen, his successor, for the conveniency of such, as had occasion to pass from the *North East part of the City to Hofljorn;* the passage at that period being much obstructed by the enclosing of ground for the building of *St. Paul's Cathedral: so* that the way became very circuitous and dangerous from thence *through Ludgate,* which had originally been the usual thoroughfare.

This *New-Gate,* after having, for upwards of six hundred years, been used as a Prison for Felons and other offenders, was, about 40 years ago, pulled down, and From the best accounts I could extract from the Books, there were One Thousand Three Hundred and Twelve *Debtors* committed to Newgate by the Court of Conscience, from the 1st of January 1797', to the 1st of January 1808. And the number of *Creditors,* who recovered Debt and Costs in consequence of such imprisonment, amounted to *One Hundred and Ninety-seven.* Wretched harvest, from barren soil!

the present Gaol erected; which, having been destroyed by the Rioters in 1780, has since been rebuilt, and appropriated, as before, for the reception of persons charged with offences committed in London and Middlesex; and also for the custody of all manner of persons committed by either House of Parliament, by the Secretary of State, by the Court of King's Bench, or either of the Judges thereof: by his Majesty's Judges of Assize; by the several Commissioners of Bankrupts, Customs, Excise, &c. and by the Magistrates in and for the City of London and County of Middlesex; as also of *Debtors* arrested by the Sheriff of Middlesex: no London Debtor being ever brought hither, without being likewise charged with some offence cognizable by a Court or Magistrate having Criminal Jurisdiction, or unless sent by the Sheriffs of London, from the Compters, or Ludgate, by *Ducifacias.*

The Mayor and Commonalty of London, or their Deputies, may also arrest and take Felons, Thieves, &c. who are found in the Borough of Southwark, and commit them to this Gaol of Newgate.

The Prisoners in this strong-hold are divided into two general classes; viz. *Debtors,* and *Criminals;* and those of the latter description into four other classes:

I. *Capital Convicts,* under Sentence of Death.

II. *Transports,* and *Respited Convicts.*

III. Persons under Sentence of *Imprisonment,* for certain determinate periods of time; or until they shall have paid certain Fines or Amercements: And IV. Prisoners detained for *Trial;* not so much distinguishing between the *magnitude* of the particular *Crimes* wherewith they stand charged, or of which they may be convicted, as between the *Habits of Life* of the individuals; many of whom are well known in Courts of Justice; and who, although at times they may be committed for crimes apparently or comparatively small, are yet of manners more likely to corrupt the morals of young offenders, than some of those Convicts who are under Sentence of Transportation, or Fine, or Imprisonment. The Males, too, of all the above criminal classes are kept separate from the Females of their class; and so, likewise, are the Capital Convicts from other Criminals.

This Gaol of Newgate is accordingly divided into *eight separate and distinct court-yard;* of which, two on the North-West angle are appropriated for Debtors, viz.

N. I. The Men Debtors' court, 49 feet long, by about 31 feet wide, leading to three Wards, called " The *Cabin-Side,-* " each Ward being 37 feet long by 144 wide, and having four cabins or small rooms in each, of about 7 feet and a half square, and capable of containing twenty-four persons within the three Wards, reckoning two to each cabin: also leading to two other Wards, called the *Master's Side,* being each 23 feet long by 14 wide, capable of containing about twenty persons; and to a day-room of the same dimensions, fitted up with benches and settles, after the manner of a tap-room in a public house; and also leading to eight other wards, called the *Common-Side,* one of which is 36 feet; six others, about 23 feet; and the one other 18 feet in length; all of these are about 15 feet wide, and together capable of containing about 90 persons.

No. 2. The Women-Debtors' court-yard, about 49 feet long by 16 feet wide, leads to two Wards; one of which is 36 feet long by 15 feet wide, and the other 18 feet long by 15 wide; and these are calculated to contain about 22 persons.

All the before-mentioned Wards are about 11 feet high. These yards are separated from each other by a stone wall 15 feet high, and both well supplied with water. The Debtors, who are enabled, all find their own beds and bedding; but the poor, as well Debtors as Criminals, are sometimes supplied with rugs by the City.

No. 3. The Capital Convicts'court-yard; which is also called the " *Press-yard,"* on account of a press having been, of old time, kept there, for the punishment of persons who *stood mute* through obstinacy, and refused to plead to the indictments found against them. The manner was this: the culprit being laid upon his back, a board was placed over him, on which was put a succession of heavy weights, until he either pleaded Guilty or Not Guilty to the indictment, or died through the extremity of pressure. This barbarous custom, however, has been justly abolished for nearly a century; nor is it now customary (as heretofore) for the Executioner to put a whip-cord round the thumbs of condemned Prisoners, when brought up to receive Judgment of Death; nor for the Bellman of St. Sepulchre's parish to go into the passage leading to the cells, to pronounce two exhortations to such condemned persons on the solemn night before their execution; their time, it is hoped, being much better employed in prayer, and preparation for so awful an event, assisted by some *pious Chris-* *tians, who frequently come from various parts of the Metropolis, and pray with them the whole of that night,* and until the *Ordinary* arrives in the morning, to attend them in their last moments, having administered to them the Sacrament the day before.

This court-yard is about 85 feet long, by 20 wide at one end, and about 15 at the other end, leading to the *Condemned Room.* This is a day-room for the Capital Convicts, and is about 35 feet by 18; behind which is the cold bath, and over it the Men's Infirmary, of the same dimensions, having five sash windows, and a fire-place. It is about 11 feet high, (like the former apartments) and furnished with eleven iron bedsteads, sacking bottoms, flock bed and bolster, three blankets, two sheets, and a rug to each.

The Press-Yard also leads to the *Condemned Cells,* fifteen in number; which are all vaulted, and nearly 9 feet high, to the crown of the arch. Those upon the ground-floor measure full 9 feet by *6*: those on the first story are a little larger, about 9 feet *6* inches by 6 feet, on account of a set-off in the wall; and the five uppermost are a little larger still, for the same reason. In the upper part of each of these condemned cells is a window, double grated, of 2 feet Q inches wide, bv 14 inches high. The doors are 4 inches thick; through each of which a circular aperture, of 2-f-inches diameter, was made by Mr. *Kirby,* the late worthy Keeper of this Gaol, for the purpose of admitting a free current of air; and in each cell is a barrack bedstead on the floor, without bedding.

The strong stone-wall is lined all round each cell with planks, studded with broad-headed nails.

No. 4-The *Chapel-I'ard* is about 43 feet long by 25; in which, as nearly as may be, are confined the Men Transports, and oldest offenders. It leads to five wards, of 20 feet by 15 each, and to one other ward of 15 feet square; all of them fitted up with barrack bedsteads on the floor, without bedding, and capable of containing about *Go* Prisoners. This yard, also, as its name indicates, leads on to the body of the Chapel; on the stair-case to which are two rooms, each 15 feet square, and used for the confinement of those accomplices in crimes, who are usually termed "*King's Evidence,*" and admitted to give testimony on the part of the Prosecution. Here, therefore, they are kept retired, and separate from the reach of the other joint offenders, who might otherwise be inclined to ill treat, or perhaps to murder them.

There are two other stair-cases to the galleries of the Chapel; one leading from a lodge on the Debtors" Side, the other from a lodge on the Felon Side of the Gaol.

No. 5. The Middle Yard, about 50 feet by 25, in which the less profligate are confined, leads on to five wards, each 38 feet long by 15; fitted up with barrack bedsteads on the floor, without bedding, and capable of containing about 120 persons. In this middle yard there is also an arcade under the Chapel, in which are three cells, for the temporary confinement of very refractory Prisoners.

No. *6.* The Men Felons' Master-Side yard, which also is about 50 feet by 25, and contains the more decent and better-behaved Prisoners, leads on to a room, in which are lodged those Prisoners called "*Gatesmen*whose business it is to direct the friends of the others in this Gaol to the different wards in which they are confined. It leads, likewise, to seven wards; one 38 feet long, four of about 20 feet, the other two of about 15 feet, and all of them nearly 15 feet wide. These are capable of containing about 90 persons; and are supplied with barrack-beds, and bedding on the floor, furnished by the Gaoler, at 2. *Gd.* per week each.

No. 7. The Women Felons' two court-yards, laid into one, adjoin each other at right angles; the one 40 feet, the other 20 feet long; and both about 10 feet wide. These lead to nine wards, three of which are about 30 feet by 15; the other six about i5 feet by 10; and all fitted up with barrack-bedsteads laid on the floor, except one large ward on the attick story, which is set apart for the *Female Infirmary.* This capacious apartment has four casement windows, and two fire-places; and, like all the other wards, is about 11 feet high. It is furnished with ten iron bedsteads, sacking bottoms, flock bed, bolster, &c. to each, exactly the same as in the Men Felons' Infirmary, already described under No. 3. The other eight wards can accommodate about 90 persons; and in this range all sorts of Female Criminals are confined, there being no other suitable means of keeping them distinct in their respective classes.

$£5" The Women's wards are generally, indeed, so crowded, as *not to admit a space of twenty inches* for each to sleep, on the bare boards, and without any bedding whatever!

No. 8th, and last, is the court-yard called the *State-Side,* about 40 feet long by 30; where such Prisoners are safeiy associated, whose manners and conduct evince a more liberal style of education, and who therefore are lodged apart from all other districts of the Gaol. This yard leads to twelve rooms; three of them about 21 feet by 15, the next three.about 18 feet by 15; three others nearly 15 square, and the rest about 11 feet square. These rooms are calculated to receive 30 persons, and furnished by the Keeper with bedsteads, bedding, &c. at seven shillings each per week.

All the several floors throughout this ample Prison have sewers, or water-closets, properly disposed. The eight courts above enumerated are well supplied with water; and dust-bins of stone are suitably distributed, to receive all the ashes and other dirt, which are taken away every week by the City Scavenger.

The two *lodges,* or first entrances to the Debtors' and Felons' Sides of Newgate, have each a small room adjoining, where one or more of the Turnkeys, like the eyes of *Argus,* keep watch and ward day and night. They have, likewise, staircases leading to the Chapel Galleries, like those before noticed; and also to two rooms, with two cells in each, which are set apart either for the temporary confinement of refractory Debtors, or for Female Convicts unhappily ordered for execution; no Woman Convict being ever, otherwise, confined in a *cell.* The same staircases lead also to the apartments of the servants belonging to the Prison.

On the Debtors' Side, and beyond the lodge, is a convenient room for the Turnkeys; and near it a grating, through which the Debtors receive their beer from the neighbouring publick houses. The Felons' Side has a similar accommodation; and this mode of introducing their beverage is adopted, because no publican, as such, can be permitted to enter the interior of this Prison .

The *Bar,* newly made, by which the quantity of liquor daily consumed is ascertained, proves to be a very good alteration, and, under proper restrictions, may prevent excess. Thus, also was prevented the frequency of Clubs, resorted to in consequence of cards sent out to persons who were not Prisoners. For instance: "Mr. Sueh-a-one's Public. Free and Easy Society, at No. "Mrs. So-and-so's Route. A Dance at No.

These took place generally twice, and sometimes three times in a week.

There is, likewise, a convenient room beyond the Felons' Side lodge, to accommodate the servants of the Gaol. This, formerly, (when the Keeper had permission *p* sell beer,) was the tap-room; and, near to it is another apartment, heretofore called the " *Wine Room"* with a copper, &c. fixed up, in order to cook the provisions humanely sent in by the Lord Mayor, the Sheriffs, and other friends. Into this apartment persons accused of Felony are now occasionally admitted; either to consult with their legal advisers, or to see such of their relatives or acquaintance, as may not be allowed to visit them in their own wards.

On the *top of the Gaol* are a watch-house, and a sentry-box; where two or more guards, with dogs and fire-arms, in addition to the Turnkeys below, watch all night.

Adjoining to the Felons' Side lodge is also the Keeper's office, where the Prison Books are kept; and his Clerk, called the *Clerk of the Papers,* attends daily, (Sundays excepted,) from ten in the morning till two in the afternoon, and from four till eight in the evening.

Here are also communications, from the Men Felons' Master Side Yard, and from that of the Female Felons, with the Sessions-House in the Old Bailey, by means of an arched passage, through which the Prisoners are led into Court to take their Triajs.

This Prison, though comparatively vast, is generally crowded. Newgate will conveniently accommodate *ninety-four* Men, and *sixteen* Women Debtors; also *three hundred* Men, and *eighty* Women Criminals; making a total of 490 persons. It might be rendered capable of containing about 750 persons in the whole, allowing a space of 7 feet *6* inches by 3 feet for every Criminal, and rather more for every Debtor, according to the size and shape of the room. The greatest number of Debtors ever confined here at one time, has been 285 Men, and 40 Women: and, astonishing as it may appear, I have been informed that there have been in it nearty *nine hundred Criminals* at the same time; making, in all, upwards of *twelve hundred* Prisoners!

scf An excellent opportunity was offered to the City, of building a *detached Prison Jor Debtors* on the side where Surgeon's Hall once stood: And, indeed, unless the Debtors be removed, to give room for a more effectual separation of Criminal Prisoners, I fear it will be very difficult to restrain that licentious intercourse, which every where presents itself in this peculiar region of Enormity; and which the utmost vigilance of the worthy Keeper cannot prevent, so long as an audacious spirit of prophaneness and vice shall continue to prevail in the lower classes of the people.

From the frequency of my visits to this much-interesting Gaol, I have so often witnessed the very distressful state of apparel, and filthy appearance of the poorer

Females, particularly Convicts, crowded together in few rooms, like sheep in a pen, that it was matter of surprize there should be, comparatively, so small a number on the sick list, or that the Gaol-Fever did not prevail! One half of the Prisoners, especially the *Women,* are miserably poor; and, having pawned or sold their ap_ parel, are covered, and scarcely covered, with rags. To prevent a circumstance so very offensive, every *Criminal,* at least, should be clad in some Uniform, that could not be disposed of; and their own clothes tied up in a bundle, laid aside during their stay, and then exchanged, upon their quitting the Prison. This, also, might be very beneficial to the more indigent *Debtors,* who, in any Prison, are with great difficulty to be kept in a state of cleanliness. 1

There were already two rooms set apart for the sick Felons, Male and Female: and lately a room, on the attick story, with four iron bedsteads and bedding, has been fitted up for the use of the *Debtors;* who, before, had no such accommodation, and were therefore necessarily obliged to be put into the *Felons' Infirmary.* There was something shocking in the idea; and upon this subject I had a conference with that truly philanthropick character, Dr. *Lettsom.* He accordingly accompanied me several times to Newgate; humanely visited the sick; examined every part of the Gaol; and gave it as his opinion, that an additional convalescent-room was absolutely necessary.

The want of a sufficiently *thorough* Air is a very great inconvenience to this Prison: and although, from its structure, the evil may in some measure be irremediable, yet, at the back part of the building, towards the East, there is a yard, or area, belonging to the *Royal College of Physicians,* which, if that learned and benevolent Body could be induced to part with, would be a great acquisition to Newgate. A space might thus be obtained for making a very practicable improvement to this important edifice. A wall, about *20* or 30 feet distant from that part of the Prison, might then be built; back windows might also be made in those Eastern Wards; and if some adjacent premises in Warwick Lane were likewise attainable, it would allow space sufficient for more ample Infirmaries, together with warm baths, and *another cold hath.* The present one is certainly very incommodious; since no person can use it, without first coming into the press-yard, amongst the *Capital Convicts* .

There are no established Rules and Orders hung up in this Prison for its government; the whole as it were resting with the Keeper. But I understand that the Worshipful Court of Aldermen have recently appointed a Committee, for the purpose of framing some *Rules* to be observed by the Debtors. In the mean time, An additional cold-bath might be made under the stairs of the South Wing of the Prison, where there is a space 10 feet by 8; and about 10 feet distant from a well, now flagged over, in which the water is 9 feet deep: or it maybe supplied from a cock close by, which lias New-River water laid on three days in the week.

several regulations have been judiciously adopted; and attended with such salutary effects, that the worthy Keeper says he has not now any complaint to make against the Debtors.

The Chapel is plain and neat; the Prisoners silently attentive: No noise in the court-yard; nor devotion interrupted or destroyed by opening and shutting the door during Divine Service, as too often happens in the King's Bench Prison.

Below is a pew belonging to the Chaplain; and adjoining to it a larger one for *Men Criminals;* opposite to which are three benches, enclosed with an iron railing, set apart also for men of that class,—Capital Convicts excepted, who sit in a pew about the middle of the Chapel, with a large table in it; whereon a *coffin* is placed, whenever any persons but *Murderers* are ordered for execution. Those sentenced for murder are always kept on bread and water, within their cells, where the Ordinary or other Minister attends them.

Facing the Communion Table are the reading-desk and pulpit. On the South side is a gallery for Debtors: on the North side another for Female Criminals; in which last-mentioned gallery, at the West end, and over the Chaplain's pew, is an enclosed seat for the Sheriff's.

The Chapel not being large enough to contain all the Prisoners in the Gaol, they are often left to their own option: those, however, who do not attend Divine Service on Sunday, are generally detained in their several Wards, to avoid hindering the edification of such as are sincerely and better disposed.

There seems to be a deficiency in the manner of conducting the sacred Service, from the want of a discreet and steady person, capable of leading the *Responses,* and setting and joining in the *Psalm.* This I should conceive to be a very essential business, and especially to be observed *in all Gaols;* inasmuch as the neglect of religious duties, both in principle and in manner, is generally the first fatal step towards a reprobate and dishonest course of life. Criminals in Gaols, being for the most part ignorant of their duty to their Creator, are often at a loss how to conduct themselves in Chapel, without having some person in the Lay-Clerk's desk, to whom they may look up as a guide for their proper demeanour; For want of which, they either irreverently sit down, when they ought to stand up or kneel; or else employ themselves in scribbling on the benches, or have their eyes, and of course their thoughts, wandering from their duty. This, indeed, I am informed, is a frequent cause of complaint by the Ordinary against them; whereas it is to be hoped, that a good pattern set them from the desk before-mentioned, might in a great measure be the means of bringing many to a sense, both of the sacredness of the place, and of what they all alike owe to the God and Saviour of all.

The danger, in point of Health, to the Prisoners, and to the City, has at times been very imminent, from the great number of persons crowded together in a space comparatively small. The number of Prisoners here in May 1802, was *eight hundred and sixty seven;* and the average number of some years previous, had been from six to seven hundred.

The number of deaths, between the first of January and the first of May, in the year 1803, was *forty-nine;* many of whom we may reasonably suppose to have died of putrid disorders, as I have been informed that some very hale and robust men, who had been removed from the Poultry Compter in a perfect state of health, but a few days before, were among the number just mentioned. Since, however, a more frequent removal of Convicts has taken place, the deaths have happened more amongst the Debtors than the Criminals; possibly, because the average number of their description has not been so much reduced (except immediately after the passing of an Insolvent Act) as that of the Felons; whose average has been reduced by nearly one half, and of whom two only appear to have died within the last two years; and of the whole Gaol-List, whether Debtors or Felons, not one died of putrid or infectious fever within the same period. Let me here also observe, that if all the Sheriff's Debtors in the vicinity of London were taken (as formerly) by *habeas corpus,* before a Judge, to be charged in execution, their average number in the common Gaols would be much reduced; as there would then remain none but those upon Mesne-Process, together with the Court of Conscience Debtors; and a still greater security from the danger of contagion might be expected.

Heretofore, the Gaol was not sufficiently supplied with soft water, to cleanse the court-yards, and the well of the pump frequently became dry: But the City have now (1807) caused the supply of water to be daily renewed, instead of three times a week; and have also erected an Engine, by which the water can easily be forced, through leaden hose, into every part of the Prison.

The Act and Clauses are conspicuously hung up; and the Gaoler is intelligent and humane.

Prisoners discharged from hence *by Proclamation,* are liberated in a morning, and have one shilling each given them. Others are dismissed as *acquitted on Trial,* in the day-time, or in the evening, *without any money* being given. This is the more to be regretted, as I am credibly informed that an instance has occurred, of a Woman's having been discharged *penniless* on one day, and brought in again on the next!

The number of Prisoners on Mesne-Process, for want of Bail, in Newgate, on the 4th May, 1807, for Debts *under 20l.* was *forty-eight,* having 85 Children.

The number, of the same description, for Debts *above* 20/. was, at the same time *twenty-five,* having 57 Children.

And the number for Debts above 30/. and under 40/. at the same period, was *thirteen,* having 25 Children.

The number of Prisoners on Mesne-Process for want of Bail in Newgate, on the 28th June, 1809, for Debts *under 20l.* was *66,* having 43 Wives, and 127 Children.

The number of the same description, for Debts *above* 20/. and under 30/. was at the same time forty-four, having 27 Wives and *69* Children.

And the number, for Debts above 30/. and under 40/. at the same period, thirty-two, having 21 Wives, and 63 Children.

$3" Since writing the above narrative of Newgate, I have been informed that the College of Physicians have determined to dispose of the whole of their premises in Warwick-lane. It is much therefore to be hoped, that so unlooked-for, and so excellent an opportunity, may not be lost by the City of London; as thus every means will be happily afforded, to *build a separate Gaol for the Debtors;* and thereby render that for the Felons far more commodious, unoffensive, wholesome, and secure. NEWPORT. *Essex.*

The Bridewell.

Keeper, *Robert Baker.* Salary, 60/. No Fees.

Chaplain, Rev. *Thomas Bell.* Salary, 20/.

Duty, Sunday, Prayers and Sermon; and Prayers Or Thursday.

Surgeon, Mr. *Ftsk.* Makes a Bill.

Prisoners, 21st Aug. 1805, Three. 23d Aug. 1807, Five. 29th Aug. 1810, One. Allowance, a pound and half of bread per day; and a quart of small beer, or one penny in money.

REMARKS.

This Prison was erected in 1775, and has a front both elegant and simple. In it are the Keeper's apartments, and a Committee Room for the Magistrates. Behind is the Men's court-yard, about 36 feet square; with a pump in the middle, of excellent water.

Before the Keeper's door is a latticed partition from the court-yard, of 5 feet by 4 feet 6; with iron spikes, to prevent the Prisoners from rushing out. On the farther side is a room, in which straw is kept for the use of the Prison. Also a large work-room on the ground-floor, 45 feet by 18, and 9 feet high, with a fire-place, and four large iron-grated and unglazed windows. In this latter, as the substitute for a Chapel, Divine Service is performed; and on my visit in Aug. 1807, it was impressively performed, and the Prisoners all very attentive and orderly.

Over the above are three lodging-rooms, well ventilated, which are supplied with wooden bedsteads, straw, and two blankets. Of the court-yard the Keeper has a good yiew from two of his back windows.

The Women's compartment is separated from that of the Men Prisoners by a wall. The access to it is through the Keeper's Brewhouse, the window of which overlooks the Women's court; and io this is a pump, from which that compartment is well supplied with water. They have also a small court-yard, of 21 feet by 6, well arranged; a day-room, with a fire-place, on the ground-floor; and above stairs, two sleeping-rooms, about 13 feet by 10, and S feet high, which have semicircular iron-grated windows, unglazed, but with shutters to keep them occasionally warm

Adjoining to the Women's Prison is a room set apart for faulty Boys, with a small lattice-partitioned court-yard.

Here is no Infirmary room. Firing is allowed in Winter. The Prison is white-washed once a year, and kept very clean. The sewers should have lime now and then thrown down them.

I could not learn that the Prisoners had any Employment whatever provided for them; and yet, in the Women's room I saw some spinning-wheels. At my visit in 1810, the Prisoner was picking oakum.

Here are scales for weighing the bread: But, in every Prison, I could prefer its being sent in from the Baker's, rather than cut from the Gaoler's loaf, however conscientious he may and ought to be.

Neither the Act hung up for Preserving Health, nor the Clauses against the use of Spirituous Liquors.

NEWPORT, *Iste of Wight; See page* 414.
NORTHALLERTON. *Yorhshire.*
The Bridewell.
Keeper, *Thomas Shepherd.* Salary, 100/. Fees, 2. each; and for the removal of Transports, one shilling per mile. Chaplain, Rev. Mr. *Wilkinson.* Salary, 20/. Duty, Prayers and Sermon on
Sundays.
Surgeon, Mr. *Dighton.* Salary, none. Makes a Bill.
Number of Prisoners, 1802, Sept. 4th, 16. 1809, Sept. 12th, 19; and one poor *Lunatick,* who had been here ever since the year 1782! Allowance, seven-pence a day each, paid to the Keeper, REMARKS.

This Prison, for the North Riding of the County of York, is removed hither from *Thirsk;* and has been built about twenty years.

The Sessions House, under which are the Gaoler's apartments, adjoins to this structure; the whole of which is nearly enclosed by a boundary wall; and the doors of entrance to it have each a small space, enclosed with iron palisades, to prevent Prisoners from rushing out.

The *Bridewell* has *A* double front; and facing each is a very spacious and airy court-yard, so that the sexes are completely separate. The front court, for Misdemeaners, is 114 feet long by 69, and now planted with vegetables. The back court, which is of the same size, is divided in the centre by a wall, for the above separation of Male and Female Criminals: that on the Men's side is paved; and the other, for the Women, is thrown into grass-plat.

At one end of the Prison is a small court-yard, having a wash-house and bath; and a door for Men and Women alternately. There is a convenient sewer in every court-yard.

On the ground-floor are twelve cells for the Men, each about 12 feet square; and two of them are *solitary,* with a cylinder in each door. They are severed from each other by a passage 6 feet wide, which has a window at one end. At the other end is a large work-room, used on Sundays as a *Chapel,* where the Rules and Orders for the Government of the Prison are conspicuously hung up. Here is likewise another work-room, 24 feet square. Most of the cells have fire-places, and in one corner a covered sewer. Firing is allowed throughout the year: a *German stove* in the passage, or lobby, conveys warmth to this part of the Prison; but, many years since, the stove had been out of repair, and was not mended at my second visit in 1809.

The windows of the cells are semicircular, with casements for ventilation.

On the upper story are two spacious rooms: the one to work in; the other, called the *bell-room,* is for the accommodation of the Turnkey. Here, also the Women Prisoners have five sleeping-cells, with a work-room, of the same size as those for the Men, and divided by a similar passage, 6 feet wide. These cells have arched roofs, and are but badly ventilated.

Here is a bathing-tub, and a stove also for purifying foul or infected clothes. If the Prisoners, on admission, are ragged, the County clothing is assigned them. The North Riding allows plank bedsteads, with straw-in-ticking beds, two blankets, and a coverlet.

The Employment here is combing and spinning wool, weaving serge, &c. Those who work receive one half of the nett produce of their earnings at their discharge. This, in the year 1809, ending at Midsummer, amounted to 24/. 13

I found this Prison very clean, and the whole is well supplied with water.

NORTHAMFrON. *The County Gaol, and Bridewell.*
Gaoler, *John Wright.* Salary, 200/. for both Gaol and Bridewell.

Fees, Debtors pay one shilling for a copy of Commitment to the Gaoler, and two shillings for signing a Certificate in order to obtain the Sixpences. Besides which the Under-Sheriff demands eight shillings and eight pence of every

Debtor for his *liberate!* Felons pay no Fees. For the conveyance of Transports, 1. per mile, if only three; but if exceeding that number, *6d.* a mile each.

Garnish is prohibited, but not yet abolished. If the Prisoner has money, 2. *6d.* isenerally exacted by his " *Brothers.* "

Chaplain, Rev. *John Watts.* Salary, 507.

Duty, Prayers twice a week, and Sermon on Sunday.

Surgeon, *Mr. Hardin.* Salary, *26l.* for all.

Number of Prisoners, Debtors. Felons, &c. DebtoFS. Felons, &.
1801, Aug. 18th,--10--31 1802, Jan. 31st,--10--38 1805, Sept. 26th,--6 --24 1807, July 24th,--13--21 1808, July 2Qth,--14--25 1809, Aug. 17th,--6--24 1810, Aug. 13th,--7--28

Allowance. To Debtors, none whatever, till lately; but, in cases of very great distress, the Magistrates *now* allow one pound and half of bread per day.

To Felons, 3. *2d.* each; viz. Three pence in bread daily; in meat, eight pence per week; the remainder in soup, potatoes, &c. Convicts for Transportation have the King's allowance of 2. *6d.* a week.

REMARKS.

This Gaol is also The County Bridewell. It adjoins to the Town Half. The Turnkey's lodge is in front, and the Grand-Jury Room on the first floor: also three rooms, each about 23 feet by 14, for Men-Debtors, on the second floor, and a smaller one for the Women Debtors. To these the Keeper furnishes beds and bedding, at 2. per week, two sleeping together. If the Debtor finds his own bed and bedding, he pays 1. per week. Common-side Debtors, if very poor, are sometimes allowed by the County a straw bed, a sheet, and a rug each.

Every Criminal Prisoner who comes in ragged, or dirty, is put into one of the reception-rooms. Their own apparel is then hung up, after being fumigated or purified in a most excellent stove, and the County clothing is put on. They have clean linen once a week, and all are directed to wash themselves daily, before they receive their bread. Here is fine water in every court-yard; and mops, brooms, pails, and soap are allowed, to keep the Prison clean.

On the ground-floor is a day-room for the Debtors, of about 28 feet by 20; and a work-room 15 feet by 10. The court-yard, for both Men and Women Debtors, is 51 feet by 42, and well supplied with water carefully laid on.

To the honour of this Gaol, and for the great benefit of all its inhabitants, *Debtors* and *Felons* are constantly kept *separate.*

The *Felons' Gaol and Bridewell,* is enclosed by a boundary wall, 15 feet distant from the court-yards.

The Keeper's house is stationed in the middle of the Prison; and has, on the first floor, the *Chapel,* of 31 feet by 25. But it is not properly *partitioned off,* according to the respective classes of Prisoners, so that they are here seated in sight of each other.

In the Chapel there is a gallery provided for the Town's People, and another for the Gaoler and his family. The Debtors and Felons sit opposite each other, on benches in the area below; and some of the Town's People are frequently placed in the centre. The Women have a small space pewed off, so high as to be entirely out of view of the Minister, but they are in sight of the Gaoler.

Over the Chapel are three small Infirmary-Rooms, supplied with iron bedsteads, that have *screws* in their construction, (which is very considerate and humane,) to *raise occasionally the head of the sick Prisoner;* and in two of these rooms is a fire-place. Also an excellent warm bath, a tub for a cold bath, and an alarm-bell in the centre of the building.

In this ample Gaol there are many peculiar advantages; viz. A spacious courtyard, with a cookery and wash-house, boilers, &c. A yard adjoining is for the drying of clothes; and nine others are appropriated for the due separation of the several classes of Prisoners, of the average size of 25 feet by 16; five day-rooms, of about 17 feet by 10 feet *6* inches; three working-rooms, about 28 feet each by 22; and seventy single sleeping-cells. Of these latter, Male Felons have twenty upon the first floor, and the same number on the second story, divided by lobbies or passages, nearly *6* feet wide.

The *Female Felons* have five cells on the first floor, and five on the second, which open into an iron-railed gallery, 4 feet wide. The other cells are for BridewellPrisoners, excepting twelve upon the ground-floor, which are set apart either as reception-rooms, or for separate confinement; and two dark cells for the refractory.

Each of the numerous cells before noticed, is 10 feet long by 7 wide, and 8 feet 10 inches high. They are alike fitted up with a plank bedstead, flock-bed, one blanket, and a rug each; and all well ventilated and lighted, by an iron-grated window, about 2 feet square, with a semicircular iron grating over each door; and in each door is a grated aperture, about 4 inches square.

That aweful part of this Prison which is appropriated to Convicts under Sentence of Death, and left for execution, consists of three cells, or day-rooms, of a similar size with those already described: they are airy, well ventilated, and to each of them is attached a small court-yard. It is a singular circumstance, and very striking, that when locked up for the night, the Prisoner ascends, by a ladder of fourteen steps, through a grated trap-door made in the cieling of his day-room, up to his sleeping-cell, which is of the same size.

I found, to my no small concern, that in this capital County Gaol, no Employment was provided either for Debtors or Felons. In some of the rooms, indeed, at my visit in 1801, I saw *looms,* with their work, like Penelope's Webbr half finished. It had an odd appearance to a stranger; but the lesson it inculcated was painfully instructive. Our *Hogarth* might have improved upon it.

It seems that the *profits* of an infant manufacture were found to be less than its *expenditure;* and therefore the County of Northampton was necessitated, or induced, to discontinue the only visible means of checking idleness, and of adding the comforts of diligence to the sad privations of imprisonment.

In a case like this, how was it possible not to ask, " And have they, in *Northamptonshire,* no domestick, no publick nurseries of-human infant debility? and do they there look for *Profit* only, whilst aiming at the attainment of *Health,* at the security of *Life,* and the consequent increase of *Vigour* and of *Happiness* P My own ideas could have suggested an answer; but it might be deemed intrusive to proclaim it. To my mind, however, its meaning has long since been fully summed up in that one comprehensive line of Doctor Young: "Do Good; and let Heaven answer for the Rest.

For the beneficial effects of *Regular Employment* in Prisons, let me again refer my Reader to *Dorchester,* (p. 163); to *Gloucester,* (p. 250); and various other Prisons, noticed, to their honour, in the prosecution of this work.

The *Dungeons* and *Condemned Room,* sunk to the depth of *eleven steps under ground,* were not stopped up at some of my former visits, neither are they now ,but Mr. *Wright,* the Gaoler, has assured me that they have nev.er of late been made use of This however is no security, that, under some less lenient Administration, they may not again be applied to aggravate the pains of incarceration.

I found very few of the Prisoners ironed; and the irons so used were comparatively light ones.

The Gaol is regularly visited every Saturday by the Magistrates, and the Surgeon; who enter their several remarks in books kept for so very useful a purpose. They would prove wholesome memoranda in every other Prison.

This is whitewashed once a year. No Prisoner in it ever received the Benefit of the Lord's Act, or *sixpences,* till lately; and the good office was effected through the exertions of Our Society for the Discharge and Relief of Debtors.

I do not find that there are any Legacies or Donations to these Prisons; and no money is given to Prisoners, at the time of their being discharged, to carry them safely home.

The Act for Preservation of Health, and Clauses against Spirituous Liquors, are neither hung up here, nor at the Town Gaol.

NORTHAMPTON.
The Town Gaol and Bridewell.
Gaoler, *Robert Roberts.* A Sheriff's Officer, and Bellman of the Town. Salary, *lol.*

Fees, for Debtors, 10. *6d.* on Commitment, and 13s. *Ad.* on Discharge. But if too poor to pay the Fees, they are humanely settled by the Corporation. For Felons, 13. *Ad.* paid by the Corporation. No Table.

Chaplain, none. See the *Remarks.*
Surgeon, Mr. *Blissard;* who makes a Bill.

Number of Prisoners, Debtors. Felon, &c. Lunaticka.
1801, Aug. 18th,----0----2----0. 1805, Sept. 26th,----0----4----1. 1807, July 24th,----0--3 0. 1808, July 2Qth,----1-- -2----1. 1809, Aug. 17th,----0----0----1.

Allowance, to Debtors, none. To Felons and Bridewell Prisoners, fourpence a day each.

REMARKS.
This Prison is situate in *Fish Lane,* and was built in 1792. The Keeper is a Tobacco-Pipe Maker. His house fronts the Street, and his windows command a view of the two court-yards for Criminal Prisoners, which are both 21 feet by 18, with cisterns for pump water, and a sewer in each.

Debtors are sent hither by Process issuing out of the Borough Court. They have no court-yard, but are sometimes indulged by the Keeper with the use of his garden. The single Debtor was walking in it, when I came hither in 1808.

The Bridewell Room is 15 feet by 7; and the Keeper furnishes beds at one shilling per week each, two sleeping in a bed.

Debtors and Criminals are here very properly placed, so as to be kept separate. The former, deprived of a court-yard, have only one room above stairs, of 14 feet by 11, and 9 feet high, adjoining to the Bridewell part: these have both fire-places, two iron-grated windows in each, and a sewer in the corners.

Poor Debtors are allowed by the Town a wooden bedstead, with straw laid on it, and one blanket.

Each of the Felons' court-yards before mentioned has two cells attached to it, of 10 feet by 7, and 9 feet high; which are fitted up with wooden bedsteads, loose straw, and a blanket for each Prisoner. They are lighted and ventilated by an iron-grated window over the doors, 3 feet high, 18 inches wide; and by a grated aperture in each door, of 6 inches by 5

The Bridewell Prisoners have but the one room above noticed; which is nearly of the same size with that for the Debtors, and fitted up in the same manner.

Here is no Infirmary, or Sick Room. The Gaol is white-washed once a year. As mops, brooms, or pails are not allowed to keep it clean, it can be no wonder that the cells are extremely offensive, being in want of proper drains.

Divine Service, heretofore, was occasionally and gratuitously performed by the Rev. *John Stoddart;* but that Gentleman falling blind, no religious attentions whatever have been paid to the poor Prisoners for several years.

The Keeper does not remember that any Debtor here has ever received the Benefit of the Lords' Act (or Sixpences) during the nine or ten years of his being in Office.

No *Employment* is provided; but those Prisoners who are of handicraft trades may procure work for themselves, if they can. No water accessible to the Debtors or Bridewell Class: it must be brought to them.

Prisoners are discharged from hence at all hours, without money being given to carry them home.

Neither the Act for preserving Health, nor the Clauses against Spirituous Liquors are hung up.

NORTHLECH. *Gloucestershire.*
The House of Correction.
Keeper, *Samuel McDowell.* Salary, 50/. No Fees.

Chaplain, Rev. *John Allen.* Salary, *20l.*

Duty, Prayers and Sermon on Sunday, and Prayers on Wednesday. Also enters in a book his attendances, and the number of Prisoners who attend Chapel.

Surgeon, Mr. *Thomas Child.* Salary, 10/. He visits the Prisoners twice a week; and, by entry in the book, reports the state of their Health.

Number of Prisoners, 1802, 22d Nov. Five. 1806, 31st Aug. Four.

Allowance, one pound and half of bread per day, and a quart of pease soup for dinner on Mondays and Fridays.

REMARKS.

This Prison,'in the Parish of Hampnel, is surrounded by a boundary wall, within side of which vegetables are raised for the use of the Prisoners.

The Keeper's house, in front, has a convenient kitchen and office below, two rooms above, and one for the Turnkey, which command every part of the Prison. The Magistrates have here also their Committee Room, in which the Sessions are held four times a year.

This excellent House of Correction is semicircular; and encloses seven court-yards, divided from each other by open wood palisades, with a stream of excellent water running through them.

On the ground-floor are seven working-cells, of about 7 feet by *6,* arch-roofed, which open into a lobby 20 yards long, and 3 yards wide, where the Prisoners were employed in picking wool; and above these are seven sleeping-cells, of the same size.

On the upper story is a large store-room for the goods manufactured, and also as a deposit for the Prisoners' clothes, &c.

On each side of the centre building are ten day-cells, upon the ground-floor; and above them as many sleeping-cells, opening into a stone gallery, skirted with an iron railing. Each sleeping-cell has a double door; the outer of iron, the inner one of wood; furnished each with an iron bedstead, straw mattress, hair-stuffed and quilted bed, two sheets, two blankets, a coverlet, and a night-cap.

The Women's wing of the Prison adjoins to one end of the last-mentioned cells, and has a kitchen and wash house on the ground-floor. On the first story six. sleeping-cells, three on each side of a passage, about *6* feet wide; and on the upper story is a large work-room.

The Men's wing is on the left, and has on the ground-floor a large day-room. Above, six sleeping-cells, divided by a passage, the same as on the Women's side. On the upper story are two Hospital-Rooms, and a small pne used as the Dispensary for Medicines. There are, in the whole, thirty seven lodging-cells, and the greatest number of Prisoners confined at one time has been 30.

Adjoining to the Men's wing are a cooking and provision room, two warm baths, a cold bath, and a fumigating-rooin.

The Chapel is on the second floor of the Keeper's house; to which the several classes of Prisoners enter, by different doors, to the seats set apart for them! where they are excluded from seeing each other, by a wooden screen in the centre of the arch.

The Prison is very compact, clean, and regularly visited by the Magistrates, Surgeon, and Chaplain.

The goods here wrought up for sale are garters, gloves, and bottle stands. Employment also comes from a Fell-monger in Northlech, who sends in wool, and pays two pence per pound for spinning, picking, and carding it. Prisoners before Trial have one half of their earnings; but if they can procure employment of themselves, they receive the whole profit.

At my visit in 180G, it unluckily so happened, that there was no Employment. The pavement of some of the cells was loose, and the court-yards wanted paving. The back part of the Keeper's house seemed to afford a too easy means of escape at the two corners, by the projecting stone work. This might be prevented, either by a *chevaux-de jnze,* or an extended coping. I found the Gaol well ventilated; plenty of excellent water in every court-yard. The sewers were all water-closets.

The plan of this Prison may justly be reckoned as one of the best in the whole Kingdom. Its situation, dry and elevated, has the singular advantage of a copious stream of excellent water, running through the centre; and its salubrity must be unquestionable: for it appears that during a period of eighteen years, not one Prisoner has died, though the Commitments exceeded eight hundred, nor has there been any specific or contagious disease within it. Such are the incalculable benefits resulting from cleanliness, and a free circulation of vital air: yet, in many Prisons, how seldom and how little are they thought of!

NORWICH CASTLE. *Norfolk.*

The County Gaol.

Gaoler, *John Johnson.*

Salary, 200/. He is also allowed two Turnkeys, to whom the County pays *10s.6d.* each per week; and for Conveyance of Transports, one shilling per mile. Fees and Garnish are abolished.

Chaplain, Rev. *Peter Hansell.*

Duty, Prayers and Sermon on Sunday; and Prayers on Tuesday and Friday.

Salary, 50/.

Surgeon, *Edward Righy,* Esq. Mayor of Norwich in the year 1805. Salary, 40/I for Debtors and Felons. And here let me seize the occasion of paying my respectful acknowledgments to the then worthy Chief Magistrate, for his politeness in accompanying me to the Prisons, Hospitals, and Workhouses of this City.

Number of Prisoners, Debtors. Felons, &c.

1800, April 1st,----30 34. 1805, Sept. 6th,----13 12. 1810, Sept. 7 th,----15 17, and 1 Lunatick.

Allowance, *to Debtors,* one pound and half of bread per day, and half a pound of cheese per week each. One bushel of coals to each room weekly in winter, and half a bushel in summer; to be increased or diminished at the discretion of the Visiting Magistrates.

To *Felons,* and other Criminal Prisoners, two pounds of bread daily, and half a pound of cheese per week each: with an allowance of coals, regulated according to their number in custody, so as to avoid superfluity, waste, and want.

REMARKS.

This Castle is seated on the summit of a lofty hill, and the Prison has of late been enlarged by additional buildings.

In 1806, an Act passed, enabling Ilis Majesty to grant the Castle of Norwich, with the Castle-hill and circumjacent ground, (consisting of six acres, one rood, and thirteen perches,) and to convey the same absolutely to the Justices of the Peace for the time being, acting in and for the County of Norfolk; free and discharged from all claim, right, and title of his Majesty, His Heirs and Successors.

Since the obtaining of this Act, the site above described has been fenced in or'inclosed by handsome iron-palisades, forming an area round the Castle of 100 yards in diameter; and affording the Citizens a most beautiful and healthy promenade.

While the Castle was merely a place of defence, the grounds adjacent were surrounded by a very wide and deep moat, with a bridge thrown across it: but, being now become dry, they are converted into a variety of gardens; and the whole being encircled by an elegant fence on Castle-hill, displays a view of scenery singularly cheerful and pleasing.

At the foot of the bridge are erected two stone-lodges; one of which is assigned for the residence of the Turnkey, and the other as a *Lazaretto,* or receiving room for Prisoners, until they have been examined by the Surg«on, and deemed proper for admission into the interior of the Castle. These additions and alterations, of recent date, give a noble appearance to the approach of entrance; and are well suited to the grandeur and magnificence of that venerable pile of buildings, which constituted the *Old Castle.*

The *defects* of this Prison, as they existed at the time of my visit in 1805, are so fully described by me in the Gentleman's Magazine for August 1808, as to preclude the necessity of any farther notice, than that, *now,* they are *happily done away.* Such, I trust, may have been the salutary effect of my entries in the Magistrates' Book at the Castle, where it is presumed they still remain on record. *Non omnis effusus Labor.*

The Gaoler's house isi, to the right of the entrance; and on the ground-floor are his parlour, and the Visiting Magistrates' Committee-Room. He has also four bedrooms, upon the first and second floors.

A small area, of 18 feet 6 inches by 15 feet, divides the Gaoler's house from the Turnkey's lodge, on the left: and over it stands the *Chapel;* in which the Gallery is appropriated to Debtors, and the lower part to Criminal Prisoners. The MastersSide Debtors, or those of the better order, who are on the Keeper's side of the Prison, have five rooms, of 12 feet by 7, with fire-places in each, and glazed windows; but of these the casements, being 20 inches only by 12, are far two small.

On the Chapel side are three rooms, ten feet square, with glazed windows, but no fire-place; and four others, 15 feet by 10, with fire-places, but windows scanty, like the former.

The *Debtors' court-yard* is 39 feet by 37, with an arcade 18 feet square, and a pump in it; which is supplied from another pump in the Felons' court-yard: and river water likewise is laid on.

Women Debtors, on the Master's-side, have three cells, each .9 feet by 7; with a day-room 12 feet square, having a fire-place in it, and glazed windows. Their courtyard is 17 feet by 7.

To all the above rooms the Keeper furnishes beds and bedding, at from 1a 6d. per week each to 4. The prices are painted on the doors; but none of these lodging-rooms have sufficient air to be wholesome.

Common-Side Debtors, Men and Women, have six sleeping-rooms, each g feet by 7; a day-room 12 feet square, with a fire-place; and all the windows are glazed. These rooms have each a bedstead, rush-mat, two blankets, or in winter three; and a rug also supplied by the County.

Male and Female Debtors *have only one day-room.*

The *Female-Felon Convicts* have a court-yard, 13 feet by 8. For some years they had two rooms only, of about 8 feet square, with glazed windows in both, and a fire-place in the lower-room: But *now;* a good lodging apartment, of 24 feet by 14, and 8 feet 6 inches high, is added for their accommodation, near their dayroom. They have, however, no water accessible, except what is fetched for them from the Debtors' pump.

The *Male Criminal Prisoners,* of all descriptions, are confined in the older part of the building, and have one courtyard only, 54 feet long by 32; 'on each side of which are arcades under the cells, for taking air and exercise in bad weather. Their cells are in all thirty-six, each 5 feet 6 inches by 8 feet; and furnished with an iron bedstead, wooden-bottomed; two mats, two blankets in summer, or three in winter, and a rug. The windows are not glazed, but have inside shutters. They have also seven day-rooms, of 14 feet each by 12, three only of which have fireplaces.

In each of the before-mentioned cells a tub is substituted for an urinal; and on every landing-place are sewers, which, from their construction, were heretofore rendered very offensive, but have since been greatly improved. The cells are all ventilated by a circular aperture over the doors, and likewise by a small kind of pothole placed in each door.

Felons are always divested of their own apparel, on being brought into custody, and the County.clothing put on: but when going to La tried, they have their own clothes given to them. After conviction, the County dress is always resumed. Their washing linen is all done out of the Gaol, at the County's expence. Misderneaners also, if received in a dirty, offensive state, are always stripped and washed, previous to being admitted into the interior of the Gaol.

Out of two of the Felon's-court arcades, two cells, of o feet by 7, have been constructed for *refractor/ Debtors.* In the same court-yard there is also an hospital: On the ground-floor is a bath, not used. On the upper floor are *two convalescent rooms;* one of 15 feet by 8, with a fire-place, the other without one,—and 10 feet by 6; both furnished with iron bedsteads, wooden-bottomed, and suitable bedding. Above these is the Hospital or *Infirmary-Room,* 17 feet by 14, with fire-place and glazed windows; ventilated by leaden pipes run through the roof, and fitted up with a wooden bedstead and hangings, bed, bolster, pillows, a regular change of linen, &c.

There seems to be no proper *store-room* in the whole of this Prison.

The general *employment* here consists of Taylor's work and Shoemaking; cutting, of pegs and skewers, and making various sorts of nets. *Debtors* are allowed to work, if they can procure the means from without, and they have all they can earn. Crir minal Prisoners have nine-pence in the shilling of their earnings; and the Keeper has the other three-pence, for furnishing them with implements and materials.

Many are the *co?nforts* here afforded by the considerate Magistrates, to alleviate the burthen, and soothe the sorrows of imprisonment. A nurse, or matron, is constantly retained, and paid six shillings per week by the County: Her duty is to attend the sick daily, whether Criminals or poorer Debtors, and to provide for them broth, gruel, milk-pottage, wine, extra diet, &c. by order of their Surgeon; of whose professional abilities, humanity, and assiduous attentions, the Hospital and Prison books bear ample record.

A Porter, or Errand-Man, also is employed, at 10. *6d.* per week by the County, to purchase articles of food, and other needful accommodations for all the Prisoners. Every Debtor is allowed to purchase one quart of ale or porter daily, but not more:. And no other liquor is permitted to be introduced, except by order of the Surgeon, in cases of sickness.

Bibles, Prayer-Books, and religious Tracts, adapted to their condition, are most humanely furnished by the County, and delivered out to the Prisoners, at the judicious discretion of their worthy Chaplain.

Mops, brooms, pails, towels, washing-bowls, coal-boxes, &c. are liberally sup-, plied by the Magistrates for their use; so that not their persons only, but all parts of the Prison may be kept in a state of cleanliness and comfort; and the orders given to this end I found literally obeyed by the attentive Keeper.

At my visit in 1810, not one Prisoner was found in irons; nor are those odious implements ever now used, except on the refractory, or those unhappy objects who are under sentence of death.

There is still a want of arrangement in the distribution of the building. The Gaoler's house commands but a very imperfect view of the whole Prison. The court-yards are small, and the air, of course, is rendered impure. Almost every chimney smokes miserably, when the wind is at west, south-west, and north-west; owing to an eddy which, under such an exposure, is unfortunately produced in those directions.

The lobbies, or passages, in this Gaol are scarcely wide enough for a single person": nor is there any convenience for a proper distinction or decent separation to be observed between the sex or classes of its inhabitants. Above all other considerations, however, this last, though little regarded, is in fact the most important, as it *affects the* Morals. Those who are guilty of atrocious crimes, and others, barely suspected of venial faults, should never be mixed together. In little, and far distant abodes of durance vile, it may, because it *must* be, seen and passed by, as locally irremediable; But never so, surely, in the Gaol, or the Bridewell of a large, opulent, and well-informed *County,* to which many others in the kingdom may look up for exemplary precedence in liberal regulation.

Legacies To Norwich Castle Gaol. 1. Mrs. *Frances Kempe,* (of whose Will I have ait Extract by me,) formerly bequeathed *three Pounds* to the Poor of Norwich and Heydon; viz. thirty shillings for preaching three Sermons in a year, and the like sum to the Prisoners in the *Hall* and *Castle-Gaols,* annually for ever. For the payment whereof she bound an Estate in Heydon, left her by *John Miagay,* Esq. her Father. The payment of these Legacies, so far as concerns the poor Prisoners, has for many years heen *cruelly withheld.* The Gaoler could furnish me with only one instance of *jive shillings* having ever been paid by the Parish of St Stephen.

2. *John Norris,* Esq. late of *Witton,* left by Will *Five Guineas* annually for ever, the Dividends of Three per Cent. Consols, to purchase religious books, for the use of *all Prisoners* of the *Cattle-Gaol* who can read; and ordained that any overplus of that sum should be distributed amongst the most needy and deserving *Felon-Prisoners,* or be laid out iu the weekly purchase of *beef,* for all the Felon-Prisoners indiscriminately, at the discretion of the Dean and resident Prebendaries. To this Legacy an addition was made in November 1797, by the purchase of Seventy-five Pounds *Three* per Cent. Consols; so that *Seve/i Guineas* are now allowed yearly by the Dean and Chapcr, to be expended as aforesaid, and they are regularly paid.

Every Prisoner in this place attended Divine Service at Chapel, when I was here on the 8th Sept. 1805, and 7th Sept. 1810. Tl»eir behaviour was orderly, and they were suitably attentive to a very appropriate and impressive discourse from the Rev. Mr. *Hansell.*

Here is now an alarm-bell. Abstracts from the Rules and Orders are duly exhibited in various parts of the Prison. The Clauses for prohibiting Spirituous Liquors are also conspicuously hung up in the Gaol; but, singularly enough, the Act for preserving the Health of Prisoners is placed in the Crown-Court of the Shire-Hall adjacent; and of course the Prisoners here have not a chance of ever seeing it.

Enquiry is made, on the discharge of every Prisoner; and, if not possessed of means of subsistence to his legal settlement, or if destitute of friends, he is supplied with money by the Gaoler, according to distance, or necessity; which is charged in his Bill at the General Quarter Sessions.

The Gaol-Delivery is once a year at Norwich, and once a year at *Thetford;* to which Gaol the Keeper of Norwich informed me he had *removed forty-two* Prisoners in 1805, when *three* more were sent from Wyndham, *three* from Aylsham, and *four* from Swaffham; making in all *Jifty-two;* who were confined for six nights in the dungeon and two cells of Thetford. At the Assizes in 1810, he sent from the Castle, 23; from Wyndham Bridewell, 2; from

Swaffham Bridewell, 5; and one from the Bridewell of Walsingham: And the whole thirty-one were then confined in Thetford Dungeon and its two cells for six nights!

The following is an enumeration, and the annual average, of Prisoners of all descriptions in *Norwich Castle Gaol*, for nearly twelve years, from the commencement of 1799, to September 1810; viz.

Number of Debtors---675. Average---56.

Felons 924. Ditto----77.

Misdemeaners--.--341. Ditto----28.

1940. 161. NORWICH. *NorfolTt.*
The City Gaol.
Gaoler, *Edward Sharpe*. Salary, 100/. and 25/. *per annum* for a Turnkey.
Fees, for Debtors; see Table. For Felons, 13s. 4Z. paid by the City. For the.
Conveyance of Transports, the Expence.
Garnish prohibited: But Debtors sometimes pay a gallon of beer on their entrance, which is called " *The Welcome Pitcher* and Felons, at coming in, a bushel of cosils.

Chaplain, Rev. Mr. *Millard*. Salary, 30/.

Duty, Prayers and Sermon every other Sunday, alternately, here, and at the Bridewell.

Surgeon, Mr. *Keymer.* Salary, Eight Guineas, for Debtors and Felons.

Number of Prisoners. Debtors. Felons, &c 1800, March 28th,-6 --------4.

1805, Sept. 4th,----7--3. 1810, Sept. 7th,----4--3

And one Lunatick.

Allowance, to Debtors, one pound and half of best wheaten bread; and to Felons, two pounds, sent in loaves from the Baker's; which I tried, and found them to be of full weight See also the Remarks.

REMARKS.

So long since as 1407, a New Guildhall of this City was built? the arches under which, being destined for Prisoners, are 45 steps down from the entrance door, and. were occupied in 1412.

The lower dungeon is about 36 feet by 21, furnished with barrack bedsteads, and strong iron rings, to which Prisoners were chained at night: The floor is of earth, and there is a sewer in it at one end. The upper dungeon is about 12 feet by *6,* and has an iron grating toward the street; to which the Prisoners come for fresh air. and to solicit charity.

In 15.97 an order was made, that these dungeons should cease to be used as Prisons after the 20th of October then next following; and that the Common Gaol should be kept in the house called *The Lamb*. This, at that period, was an Inn, and upon the site of it the City Gaol now stands. Notwithstanding the above order, however, it appears that the dungeons in question were used even so late as in the year 1771; a Prisoner, named *Plum,* having been confined there, until taken out for execution.

This City Gaol is erected opposite the Guildhall. The Gaolers house fronts the street, and his back windows command a full view of every court-yard. The gravel-walk and garden are now made into a court-yard, a day-room, and three sleeping-cells, for Prisoners before trial, which alteration reduces the size of the Debtors' court to 50 feet by 15. Here is a pump; and it is paved with pebbles, and separated from the court of the Female Felons by open palisades only.

Master's-Side Debtors have twelve good-sized airy rooms, ten of which have fireplaces; and these are furnished by the Keeper with beds and bedding, at from two to five shillings per week: the price of each room is painted on the door. Here are also two spacious and well-ventilated infirmary rooms, of 22 feet by 17 each, and 11 feet 8 inches high; with fire-places and glazed windows, iron bedsteads, and bedding.

Common-Side Debtors had heretofore a room, or, more properly speaking, a *cellar,* ten steps below their court-yard, of 17 feet by 13 feet 6' inches, and 7 feet high. It was lighted and ventilated by a small iron-grated window, of 24 inches by 22, with straw laid on the damp brick-floor.

This room, or cellar, has since been humanely discontinued; and over it the Common-Side Debtors have now a good day.-room, of 20 feet by 14, and 8 feet high. Also above it are a comfortable lodging-room, 19 feet by 14, and S feet 9 inches high; and a third room, 22 feet by 8-i-high, with glazed-windows. The three last-mentioned rooms are all Free-Wards, in case the Debtor brings his own bed: But if the Keeper furnishes one, he is paid 1. *6d.* per week for a single bed; and if two sleep together, one shilling each.

Female Debtors have a sleeping-room up stairs, of 24 feet by 13; with a fireplace, and very large glazed window, looking into the court-yard, which is common to all.

Painted on a Board, and hung up in this Gaol, is the following

"Table Of Fees,

To be taken by the Gaoler, as settled by order of the Justices at the Quarter Sessions, held the 1-th day of January, 1700, and confirmed and allowed by *Lord Loughborough,* and Sir *William Henry Ashurst,* two of His Majesty's Judges.

d.

"For the Commitment, or coming into Gaol of any Prisoner for Debt 3 4. For the Discharge of those in Execution----------3 5.

For the Discharge of those upon Outlawry--------_-3 4.

f or the Discharge of those committed on Common Process----3 0."

The *Old Chapel,* which was a room in front of the street, is now (1810) conveniently fitted up, and converted into a dwelling-house for the Keeper; and a New Chapel has been made at the upper-end of the court-yard, over a room called *Potter's Cellar:* it is 27 feet by 15, and 11 feet 8 inches high.

Prisoners before trial have a court-yard, 33 feet by 23; a day-room, 13 feet by 12, with a fire-place and glazed window; and three sleeping-cells, of 9 feet 6, by 7 feet C, and,9 feet high, lighted and ventilated through the perforations of a castiron plate, 26 inches by 24. These cells have boarded floors, iron bedsteads, strawin-sacking beds, two blankets, and a coverlet.

An open wood palisade separates the

above court-yard from that of the MaleFt Ions after conviction; which is about the same size, and has three sleeping-cells, about 8 feet square, and planked all over, to which the descent is by three steps below the ground: They are furnished similar to those already described, except that they have double doors; the outer one of wood, the inner, iron-grated; together with a double iron-grating as a window, of 21 inches by 18. At my visit, in 1805, a close wire-work was placed over this small window, and thereby light and ventilation were so excluded, that when the doors were shut, it was almost impenetrable obscurity, and inspired the gloomiest horror. These now, (in 1810,) are greatly improved by the Magistrates' having humanely ordered the wire-work to be taken away. Near the above cells is a day-room, of 13 feet 6 by 11 feet, and 7 feet high, with a glazed window and fire-place. The sewers in both court-yards are conveniently placed, and water is laid on.

Male Felons were formerly confined in two dungeons, that go down eleven steps: one of these, 12 feet by 10, and 8 feet high, has a boarded floor, and is called "The Nine-Foot Hole;" the other, called *Clay-Hole,* from its having an earthen floor, is nearly of the same size; and both of them are sadly deprived of light and ventilation. From a very careful examination, I have reason to believe that these have not been occupied for many years: However, upon expressing my wishes to preclude the possibility, the Magistrates in 1810 assured me, that they should be inaccessibly bricked up.;

Female Felons, heretofore, had a large dungeon, 38 feet long by 16 feet wide, and 9 feet four inches high, with a flagged-floor and fire-place, which I have already noticed as being named *Potter's Cellar;* and to which the descent is by twelve steps below the court-yard; also a sleeping-room, justly called " *Little Ease,"* being 10 feet long, 5 feet 6 inches wide, and *only* 4 *feet* 2 *inches high!* with a small iron-grated window, of 15 *inches square.* Straw is now (1S10) deposited in the former, and the latter is entirely done away. The Female Felons at present have a large day-room, with a fire-place and glazed window; adjoining to it is a comfortable sleeping-room, of 14 feet by 5 feet 6 inches, and 8 feet high, with bedding the same as the Men; and the doors of both these rooms open into the court-yard.

On my inspecting this Prison in 1805, the large room over the Potter's Cellar, (where straw for the Prisoners was deposited,) seemed to me well calculated for a New Chapel, in which the sexes might be distinctly seated during Divine Service: And I have since had the satisfaction to see that my idea has been candidly adopted; so as at once to avoid the noise and inconvenience of the former place assigned for that sacred purpose, and to answer those ends of devotion, decency, and decorum, which are peculiarly suitable to a *House of Prayer.*

The Rules and Orders of the Prison are now very properly and conspicuously hung up in this more commodious Chapel.

Convicts, under sentence of Transportation, have not here the King's Allowance of 2. 6*d.* per week. But Prisoners, when discharged, have money given them, according to their distance from home.

The City allows the Debtors and Felons of this Gaol two chaldrons of coal yearly; which are issued to them on the 20th of November, and 20th of January.

A begging-box is sent round the town to solicit Donations for their benefit, which averages about one shilling per day; and also a basket to receive broken victuals. The person employed for this purpose is a Pauper from the Workhouse; who has one penny out of every shilling so collected, and also one shilling per week from the City.

Ten shillings are annually paid on New Year's Day, as the Legacy of Mr. *BlacMiead,* of which a written Memorial is duly kept in the Gaol. The like sum is annually given by the Corporation, on the 29th May, 4th June, 22d September, 25th October, and 5th November; and also nine-pence to each Prisoner upon the Saturday before Shrove-tide, Easter, Whitsuntide, and Christmas. Every NewYear's Day five shillings are paid by the parish of *St. Stephen;* and the same on 'the 10th of May, by the parish of *St. John Sepulchre.* The latter had been discontinued for more than twenty-one years; and both seem to be the Legacy of Mrs. *Kempe.* See Remarks on Norwich Castle, p. 444.

Here"is an excellent cold and warm bath, and a wash-house, with coppers, &c. The Act and Clauses are conspicuously hung up, and the Prison is kept clean.

NORWICH. *The City Bridewell.*
Keeper, *Richard Mingay.* Salary, *6ol.* with coals and mops, brooms, pails, towels, and thirteen pence per week for soap, to keep the Prison clean. Fees, none: except for night-charges, or assaults; which are 2. each.

Chaplain, Rev. Mr. *Millard.* Duty, Sermon and Prayers every other Sunday. Salary, 30/. for Bridewell and City Gaol.

Surgeon, Mr. *Robinson.* Salary, *5l. 5s.*

Number of Prisoners, 5th Sept. 1805, Eleven; 10th Sept. 1810, Four.

Allowance, one pound and half of best wheaten bread per day, sent in loaves from the Baker's; which I examined, and found of full weight. Also seven pence in money per week: A tub of coals (about a peck) to each day-room; and the cinders from the Keeper's fire daily, from Michaelmas to Lady-Day.

REMARKS.

This Bridewell is situate opposite St. Andrew's Church; and in the front is the Keeper's house, the windows of which command the court-yard: This is 19 feet by 12, paved with pebbles; has two sewers in it, a pump with excellent spring-water, and soft-water also is laid on.

On the left-hand is the Men's day-room, 21 feet square, with a brick-floor, three lofty glazed windows, and a fire-place. Here are also three sleeping-cells, each 14 feet 9 inches by 6 feet, 10 feet 6 inches high; lighted and ventilated by a double iron-bar grated and glazed window, with double casement, 3 feet by 18 inches; opening into a lobby of 5 feet *6* inches wide, and communicating with the Men's day-room.

Over the Men's cells is the Women's day-room; which is also 21 feet square, and 10 feet high, with a fire-place, and three lofty glazed windows. Here is likewise a room up stairs, set apart for the sick, of the same size.

The Keeper's apartments open into the Chapel above stairs, which is 24 feet long by 17 feet 6 inches, and 10 feet 2 inches high. It has a pew for the Keeper, and seats are set apart for the Prisoners.

The *Dungeon* (to which from the court-yard is a descent of 15 steps) has, on its right-hand, a large vaulted sleeping-cell, with two wooden bedsteads, and straw; and is lighted by a small iron-grating from the court-yard. At the farther end of the dungeon just mentioned, are two other vaulted sleeping-cells; the first of which, 16 feet 6 inches long by 9 feet 4 inches wide, and 8 feet 6 in height, is called The *Light Dungeon,* from its receiving just sufficient to make darkness visible: the other, called *The Dark Dungeon,* is equally long and high, but 15 feet wide, and totally obscure! These gloomy caverns have brick-floors, vv ith straw; and I was given to understand they have not been inhabited these seven years. In each there is a wooden tube, to carry off foul air and noxious vapours very judiciously left open at the top of the building.

On the right-hand; are seven sleeping-cells, which communicate with a lobby, or passage, 39 feet long, 4 feet 6 inches wide; and each cell is 12 feet 10, by 6 feet 8, and 9 feet high. Above stairs is the same number of cells, with a lobby of like dimensions. Every cell is fitted up with a crib-bedstead, straw-in-sacking bed, a double blanket, and a coverlet.

The Prisoners all attend Chapel, or lose their bread allowance of the day: They are also required to wash themselves every morning, previous to their receiving it.

Their employment formerly consisted, in cutting wood for the dyers, and spinning; but none had been procured these seven years. No part of their earnings is assigned them; but, if their behaviour has been good under confinement, money is given to them on being dischargedi They have clean linen once a week.

Here are no Rules and Orders. No bath, nor oven. The Prison is whitewashed once a year, and kept very clean. The Act for the preservation of Health is hungup, but not the Clauses against Spirituous Liquors. The Number of Prisoners committed to this Bridewell, from June l804 to June 1805, was 380; and from the 10th September 1809, to the LOth of September 1810, 175.

NORWICH. *Prison for the Precincts ofthe Close.*
Keeper, *James Clahurne"* Salary, none. Fees, 1. *2d.*

There were no Prisoners, either on the 8th Sept. 1805, or 10th Sept. 1810.

Allowance, three penny worth of bread per day.

REMARKS.

This Prison belongs to the Dean and Chapter of Norwich. It consists of two rooms at the top of the Keeper's house, each about 13 feet square, and 9 feet high, separated by a wooden-grated door. Prisoners are committed hither for all offences within the precincts, and have straw to lie upon. I was informed that none had been sent here since 1806.

No Court. No sewer. No. water accessible to Prisoners.

NOTTINGHAM. *The County Gaol.*
Gaoler, *Joint Holt;* now *Tlwmas Wright.* Salary, 140/.

Fees, *for Debtors, 13s. 4d.* ; and to the Turnkey, 1#. *4d.* The Under-Sheriff has generally demanded four shillings for his *Liberate!* But Mr. *WilliamWillson Kent,* the present worthy Under-Sheriff, takes no such Fee.

For Felons, &.c. none; and for Conveyance of Transports he is allowed the expence. Garnish prohibited.

Chaplain, Rev. *William Gill;* now Rev. Dr. *Wood.*

Duty, Prayers every Thursday; and Prayers and Sermon every Sunday, Christmas-Day, and Good Friday. Salary, 50/.

Surgeon, Mr. *Partridge;* now Mr. *Bigsby.*

Salary, 30/. for Debtors and Felons, &c.

Number of Pr'isoners. Debtors. Felons, Sc. Bastardy.
1803, Aug. 24th,---7----8----0. 1805, Sept. 29th,---8----5 0. 1809, Aug. 26th,---8 ----6 ----s'.

Allowance, Debtors, 16 ounces of bread per day. Felons have the same Allowance in bread, with one penny per day each in money, and one penny per week for soap. I am informed by the Gaoler that Assize Convicts, under Sentence of Transportation, have the County allotment of bread, in addition to the allowance of *2s. 6d.* per week for their maintenance.

REMARKS;

This Gaol adjoins to, and stands on the South-side of the County, or" *Shire-Hall.* It is situate on the declivity of a hill. The entrance to it is doWh a passage from' the street, leading to the Turnkey's Lodge; and: close to this is the Debtors'courtyard, of 100 feet by 41, with a flagged terrace, and handsome iron palisades, commanding a view of three Counties.

On the *Eastside* of the Debtors' court is their day apartment or cbmmbn' messroom, 1.7 feet by 10; which has three tables-in it, chairs, shelves, arid cupboards, to secure their provisions; with a glazed' window, fire-place, and side oven. Here are also three good-sized sleeping-rooms.

On the *North-vide* are three other sleeping-rooms;' oneof which has been lately converted to its proper use out of the KeeperYstable, now disused; The average size *22* feet 8-inches by 11 feet.

Women-Debtors have a room 20 feet square, which has-1 a' flagged1 floor, with arched roof, a fire-place, and a large window, that very improperly looked into the Men's court. This window, however, has been made of *ground-glass,* by way of prevention; and the Women-Debtors have now a separate court-yard of their own, about 11 feet square, which is supplied with water by a pipe laid on.

To all the above-mentioned rooms the Keeper furnishes beds and bedding, at 3s. per week for a single person; or at *2s.* per week, if two sleep together. Such Debtors as provide their own bedsteads and bedding, pay *6d.* each per week.

Over the mess-room is a small *Chapel,* 23 feet by 20 feet 6 inches; which has four glazed casement windows. The sexes are placed separate, and all attended Divine Service when I was here. The Chapel is too scanty for the number of Prisoners; and the *casement construction* of its windows must at times render it uncomfortably close.

The *poor Debtors,* who cannot afford to pay for a bed, are most unpleasantly provided for in this County-Prison. Their descent is, by *twenty-eight* steps, to three miserable sleeping-rooms, called *"Free Wards"* The two largest, about 12 feet by 9, have fire-places; the third, which formerly was the *Condemned-Room,* or place for Convicts under Sentence of Death, is about 9 feet square, with a wooden bedstead in it; and all have a small iron-grated and glazed window. The Debtors here confined are obliged to furnish their own beds; which yet necessity only, in the extreme, can induce, or rather compel them to occupy. I feel a pleasure in being enabled to add, that these wretched and deep-sunk *dormitories* have not been used since the appointment of Mr. Wright, the present Gaoler.

A considerable part of the North-side of the Debtors' court-yard was once sadly encumbered by a large dust-hole 'and dung-hill, leading to arcades, under which were a capacious and convenient *bath,* with a *copper* to warm it when necessary; But, singular as it may appear, they were seldom used. At present, however, a decent covered *dust-bin* has succeeded to the hole, which was worse than unsightly; and within the former dung-plot, is now constructed an excellent *stove,* for purifying infected or filthy clothes.

There is no spring-water supplied or belonging to this Gaol: But, as the large bath became almost wholly useless for the purpose originally intended, it is now made to serve as an additional *reservoir;* which, as well as the Gaoler's house, and the whole Prison, are furnished, by means of two pumps and three cisterns, with soft water from the river *Leen.* It is sometimes muddy, and,

at other times, must be fetched from the bath reservoir, as the best resource.

In the Felons' old court-yard, near the Keeper's parlour, there is a well, which, if a pump were substituted, would amply supply the Prison with excellent springwater. But the well, I am told, was covered over in the year 1799; for which the only reason I could hear assigned was, that some of the Prisoners at that time had thrown improper things into it!

The *arcades* before mentioned, built under the County-Hall, are now made a repository for coals, wood, &c. but would afford good room for workshops, and comfortable *free-wards* for the poor Common-Side Debtors.

For Felons, at a descent of *forty steps!* here are two dark and damp dungeons, called "The Pits," cut out of the friable sandy rock. One of them, 23 feet long by 13, and 7 feet high, appears not to have been used for a long time: The other, occupied at the time of my former visits, is nearly circular, 12 feet in diameter, supplied with barrack bedsteads; and opposite to it, in a narrow passage, are three cells, each of them 8 feet by 5. All the light or ventilation these subterranean abodes can receive, is from two circular apertures over the doors, of 7 inches in diameter. Each has a wooden bedstead, with loose straw thrown upon them, and two rugs: the door-ways, only 4 feet 6 inches high, and 2 feet wide! The present Gaoler says, he has never put any Prisoners into the circular dungeon, or the three dismal cells in the narrow passage opposite to it; but I was sorry to find them all cleaned out, and made ready, as it were, for any occasion, instead of being inaccessibly bricked up, and consigned to merited oblivion.

The court-yard, appendant to the above cells, is that which heretofore had the well in it; and close to the Keeper's door is raised an open iron-palisaded fence, of 10 feet by 5, to prevent the Felons from rushing out. Their court-yard, of 39 feet by 28, is paved with flag-stone; and their day or mess-room, in the centre of it, is 15 feet by 10.

The *newly-built part* of the *Felons' Gaol* has a court-yard for the Men, 46 feet by 18, with a day or mess-room, 25 feet by 18. For the Women here are arcades, about lG feet square. Their day-room, in its original construction, was 22 feet by 10; but at my last visit in 1809, 1 found it divided into two. One part contained two beds, and near it was a narrow slip for *Vagrants,* who sleep on straw. To each day-room there is a fire-place, with side-ovens, and a table and shelf for provisions: And over the Women-Felons' day-room they have now three sleeping-cells, 9 feet each by 7. Every Felon, Male or Female, is here allowed a straw-in-ticking bed, three blankets and a rug; and each window of their rooms and cells has a casement of 16 inches by 12.

Over these apartments are eight sleeping-cells for Men, which open into a lobby 5 feet wide. Each cell is about 9 feet by 7, arch-roofed, with a semi-circular grated and glazed window, and a grating of like form over each door. They were heretofore only supplied with a wooden bedstead each, for two Prisoners, loose straw, and two rugs; but the considerate Magistrates have lately ordered a bed for every cell, and to these new cells have added a stove, to introduce warmth when needed. The doorways to the cells are 4 feet 6 inches high by 2 feet 6' wide, and cased with ironIn the New Gaol are twelve sleeping cells.

Upon Convicts being left for execution, it is customary to confine them, during the day-time, in a room 22 feet by 10, with three windows in it, a fire-place, and a table. Here they are duly supplied with religious books: they have tea twice a day, and a hot dinner; and are daUy attended by the Chaplain, or other Clergyman,.

$3 At the West end of the Shire-Hall, there is a very convenient and suitable place for the awful business of *Executions,* and where a platform might be occasionally or permanently fixed, as at Chelmsford, Reading, and many other places. Instead of which, at Nottingham, the poor wretches are dragged along through the Town, in a cart, to a place about *a mile distant;* to the preposterous gratification of unfeeling curiosity, that "knows no brotherly yearnings," and to the sad disgrace of civilized society! "When Criminals," says Dr. Moore, "are carried to execution with little or no solemnity, amidst the shouts of an unconcerned rabble, who applaud them in proportion to the degree of indifference and impenitence they display, and consider the whole scene as a source of amusement; how can such exhibitions make any useful impression, or terrify the thoughtless and desperate from any wicked propensity f If there *is a Country"* continues he, *f* in which great numbers of young, inconsiderate creatures are, six or eight times every year, carried to execution in this tumultuous, unaffecting manner, might not a stranger conclude that the view of the Legislature was to cut off guilty individuals in the least alarming way possible, that others *may not* be deterred from following their example?"

Some years since, the following singular incident happened with' respect to this Prison, which is vouched by good authority. On the loth of Feb. 1787, two women, *Mabel Morris* and *Elizabeth Morris,* were committed to this Gaol by virtue of a Bishop's Writ, and confined there until the 25th of February, 1799; when, some repairs being wanted at the Prison, their doors were thrown open. They sent fpr a cart, in which their goods were loaded in the day-time, and the women went out unmolested. Application was made to the then Sheriff, to know if they were to be brought back to Prison; but nothing was done; and at my visit in Sept. 1805, they resided at Calverton, in this County.

The sanction for the confinement of a Prisoner upon the above-mentioned Process runs thus: "Forasmuch as the Royal Power ought not to.be wanting to the Holy Church in its Complaint, You are commanded to attach the said by his or her Body, according to the Law and Custom of England; until he or she shall have made satisfaction to the Holy Church, as well for the contempt, as for the injury by him or her done unto it. " One cannot help wishing that the *Reformation,* or the *Revolution,* or any other adequate and legal interference, had tone away the *power* of such imprisonment.

See his *"View of Society and Manners in Italy."* Vol. I. 3d edit. p. 476.

List of Legacies and Donations. *Jehu Sherwin,*-Esq. of Nottingham, four pounds *per annum*; now' paid1 quarterly by *Jolin Longddii,* Esq. out of an Estate at Bramscote, purchased by Mr. Sherwin of the descendants of Henry Handle)', Esq. the Donor.

By *Samuel Smith,* Esq. M. P. for Nottingham, pursuant to the Will of Mr. Abel Collings, *four shillings monthly,* to the Prisoners, for coals.

John Elliott, Esq. of Nottingham, gives annually a sixpenny loaf, and a pint of ale to every Prisoner; and a buttock of beef amongst all.

The Rev. Dr. *Wood,* Chaplain, gives annually one pound of beef, and a pint of ale to every Prisoner.

The High Sheriffs send to each Prisoner a sixpenny loaf, one pound of best cheese, and a pi tit of die.

The *Crrand Jury,* at the Assizes, make a collection for the *Criminal Prisoners,* to the amount of from thirty to forty shillings.
.,,.4.

Here, as at *Derhf, Horsham,* &c. a Man goes round the country, about Christmas, and collects money at Gentlemen's hduses for the *Debtors.* I have ah account of the Christmas Collections from l8o1, of which the following yeafs are a specimen: £. s. d.

In 1806, Collection--59 16 6

Paid John Brandeiith the Collector, being out twelve weeks-----25 40

Nett amount--------34 J 2 6

Distributed as follows: £. si d. £. s. d. 1806, Dec. 24th, Four Debtors--3 3 10 each,--12 15 4' 1807, Jan. 14th, ditto ditto----I' 9' fl--5186 Feb. 11th, ditto ditto---2170--11 8 0 March 1st, ditto ditto _-129--4112 34 12 6 £. *s. d.*

In 1807, Collection 6840

Paid Collector, being out twelve weeks-----------25 40

Nett amount-------43 00

Distributed as follows: £. *s. d.* £. *s. d.* 1807, Dec. 24, Fourteen Debtors--1 0 0 each,--14 0 0 1808, Jan. 13th, ditto ditto---0 17 0--11 18 0 Feb. 4th, ditto ditto--0 14 0--9160 Feb. 25th, ditto ditto---0 10 5$--7 6 If *£.* 43 0 If *£. s. d.*

In 1808, Collection-71116

Paid Collector, being out twelve weeks-----------25 40

Nett amount------46 76

Distributed as follows: *£. s. d. £. d.* 1808, Dec. 24th, Sixteen Debtors--0 18 9 each--15 O 0 1809, Jan. 21st, ditto ditto---0 15 0--12 00

Feb. 11th, ditto ditto---0 14 0--1140 March 4th, Fourteen ditto---0118$--8 3 7 *£.* 46 7 7f *s. d.*

In 1809, Collection 70 16

Paid Collector, being out twelve weeks and four days-------26 120

Nett amount-------43 96

Distributed as follows: *£. s. d. £. s. d.* 1809, Dec. 23d, Nine Debtors--1 18 3 each,--17 8 0 1810, Jan. 13th, Twelve Debtors,--0 12 3§--776 Feb. 3d, ditto ditto--0 15 2f--926

Feb. 28th, Thirteen ditto- 0 14 8--9 11 6 *£.* 43 9 6

Here is no County clothing provided; but if a Prisoner be ragged, he is clothed at the County's expence.

The Surgeon has a discretionary power to order indulgences of extra clothing, linen, food, wine, &c. for the sick and infirm, as he finds it necessary.

Religious books are supplied for the use of the Prison. The Gaol has no fixed Infirmary; but if any Prisoners fall sick, they are removed to some separate room unoccupied.

Upon their discharge from hence, they have money granted, proportionably, to carry them home.

The Act for Preservation of Health, and Clauses against Spirituous Liquors, are hung up in the Debtors' mess-room.

I here beg leave to pay my respectful acknowledgements to William-Elliott Elliott, esq. of Gedling-House, late High Sheriff of this County, who humanely accompanied me to the Prisons, Hospital, and Work-houses: And also to the worthy Magistrates in general, for the polite notice they were pleased to take of my suggestions relative to the state of the Gaols at Nottingham and Southwell.

NOTTINGHAM. *The Town Goal.*

Gaoler, *Philip Bailey;* a Peace Officer

for the Town.

Salary, 70/. and 30/. per annum for a Turnkey.

Fees, for Debtors, 14. *Sd.* Besides which the Under-Sheriff demands four shillings for his *liberate!* For Felons, 13. *4d.* paid by the County. Conveyance of Transports, *lol.* each, whether to Woolwich or to Portsmouth. Garnish; one shilling is paid upon entrance to the Prison stock for coals.

Chaplain, none regularly assigned, but the Rev.'Mr. *Bryan,* a Calvinist, frequently attends the Prisoners here gratuitously; and many religious books are sent them.

Surgeon, Mr. *Basnett.* Salary, for Gaol-Felons only, and the House of Correction, 10/. 10.

Number of Prisoners, Debtors. Felons, &c.
1803, Aug. 24th,------5-*12.* 1805, Oct. 1st, 7-------10. 1809, Aug. 26th,------12-------14.

Allowance, for all descriptions, a threepenny loaf per day each, which in October 1805, weighed 1 lb. and 1 oz. When a Debtor has obtained his sixpences, he continues also to receive the County Bread. If a Debtor be very poor, and petition the Magistrates, he is allowed half a loaf in addition. Debtors likewise receive, as the benefit of a Legacy, one shilling per week for coals. Colonel Elliott gives annually, at Christmas, one pound of beef, a threepenny loaf, and a pint of ale, to each Prisoner; and the Mayor of Nottingham, for the time being, sends 1 cwt. of coals to every Prisoner at the same season.

REMARKS.

This Gaol is partly under the Guild-hall. The Keeper's house fronts the Street;: and his windows, as well as those of the Turnkey's lodge, command a view both of the Debtors' and Criminals' court-yards.

For *Debtors* here are two court-yards; the upper one of which, 33 feet long by 23, has a flagged floor, and is over what they call "The *Felons Pit"* which receives its light and ventilation from a circular iron grating, of 11 feet diameter, placed in the centre of this court-yard: the lower one is 38 feet *6* inches by 23 feet, and has a dust-hale and a sewer at the upper end. The Debtors have also nine good-sized sleeping-rooms, with fire-places, and glazed windows, all furnished by the Gaoler; for which, if two sleep in one bed, they pay 2. per week; or if the Debtor have a bed to himself, 3. weekly.

The Felons, before Trial, have a court-yard of 60 feet by 31, with a sewer, dusthole, and water laid on; a day-room 11 feet by 10, with a fire-place, and a small workshop.

After conviction they are confined in what is called " The Felons' Pit," which is sixteen steps down, a circular court, of 21 feet by 18, with a flagged floor; and derives its light from the circular iron-grating, of 11 feet diameter, in the floor of the Debtors' yard before-mentioned. Three sleeping-cells open into this court, each 10 feet by *6,* and 8 feet high, the doors of which are only 5 feet high and 22 inches wide. Here is also a passage 32 feet long and 4 feet wide, which has on each side of it three cells. One of them, damp and useless, is now suitably converted into a coal-hole; the other two have iron-grated windows, with inside shutters, and a grating over each door, 16 inches square. The other three cells, or dungeons, on the opposite side, have no other light orventilation than the small grating above-described. All of them are fitted up with wooden bedsteads, to provide straw for which the Keeper was allowed four guineas a year. At my last visit in 1805, the *Town* supplied a straw-in-ticking bed, with three blankets, and a rug.

The Debtors here are indeed locally and occasionally separated from the Felpns; but the sexes, in each class and division of so scanty a space, must necessarily be together iu the day-tme.

The *Employment* here consists in weaving, making shoes, cutting pegs, &c. and the Debtors thus usefully occupied, enjoy the whole of their earnings. Roth they and the Felons, ajje allowed to send for one quart of ale in the four-and-twenty hours.

A *Collection,* is charitably made every year throughout the Town, at Christmas, for the benefit of the Prisoners in general. In 1804 it amounted to *nine Pounds, si-x Shillings.;* out of which, after paying the Collector 14. for four days trouble, the remainder was distributed to the Prisoners, at *10s. gd.* each.

The Christmas annual collection, up to the time of my visit in August 180Q, amounted to between eight and ten pounds, and was distributed to all classes of Prisoners equally.

This whole Gaol is well supplied with river water; and in the Street adjoining is a pump, from which excellent spring water is daily fetched by the Keeper for the use of his Prisoners.

The Prison is whitewashed. The Clauses against Spirituous Liquors are hung up; but not the Act for the Preservation of Health.

On the whole this is a wretched Prison; and it gave me great pleasure to be informed, that the Grand Jury had presented it at the Assizes in 1809, and that a new one was to be built.

NOTTINGHAM.

The House of Correction.

Keeper, *Robert Machin.* Salary, 30/. Fees, 3. *4d.*

Chaplain, none. See the Remarks.

Surgeon, Mr. *Bennett,* for this house and the Town-Gaol.

Salary for both, *Debtors excepted* at the Town Gaol, *10I. 10s.*

Number of Debtors, 1805, Oct. 1st, 13. I809, Aug. 28th, 7;

Allowance, a threepenny loaf per day, weighing 1 lb. 14-oz. at my visit in 1805.

REMARKS.

This Prison, situate in St. John Street, was formerly St. John's Chapel. It has a boundary wall, and the Keeper's house, which is in the centre, commands the two court-yards. That for the Men-Prisoners is 54 feet by 36, paved with flagstone, and supplied with a pump and sewer. For the Women there are, below, four rooms with arcades, each about 9 feet square; and above-stairs are three others of the same size, with fire-places and glazed windows, that open into a gallery 27 feet long, and 3 feet wide; and *all look into the Men's court.*

The court-yard for the Women Prisoners is 33 feet by 19 feet 6, and is unsupplied with water They have also a day-room, opening towards the Men's courtyard.

In August 1807, an addition was made to this Prison for the separate confinement of the Women. On the ground-floor here is a day-roOm, about 14 feet square, with a fire-place, a large glazed window, and forms to sit on; two sleeping-rooms, with two beds in each; a room for the refractory, with borrowed light, arid without windows; and a spacious flagged court, with convenient sewer, a purrtpy and dust-pen.'

The *Jirst story* has three good-sized rooms; one of which is used as a Work-room, and the others have two beds each. The *second story* has also three rooms, two of which are appropriated for the sexes to hear Prayers, which are read every Sunday, alternately, by Mr. *Budger,* a hosier; Mr. *Hazard,* a linen-draper; Mr. *Simpson,* a rope-maker; and Mr. *Medlam,* a frame-work knitter. The *third story* has a very large work-room, and a 6leeping-room. The bedsteads are of wood, to contain two persons; with a straw-in-ticking bed, and four blankets to each, but no rug.

The Men's day-room below is nearly 18 feet square, with a fire-place; and up stairs they have three rooms, of about the same size, with fire-places and glazed windows. Each of these last holds two wooden bedsteads, to which the Keeper furnishes straw at 20. a quarter, with four blankets, allowed by the Town; but if he supplies a bed, and two sleep together, the charge is *2s.* each per week.

The two court-yards originally set out for this Prison were comparatively of little use, or beneficial consequence. There is but one pump in common betwixt them; and the intercourse of all sorts and classes was prevented only at night. Both these court-yards, in the old part of the Gaol, as well as the rooms formerly occupied by Women, are now appropriated to the Men. They have convenient sewers; and are supplied, not only with soft water from the river *Leen,* but with spring water also, by the pump above noticed.

No employment, as yet, is furnished by the Town; but, in common cases, those who can obtain it, have the benefit of their labour to themselves. Those whom I saw in 1805 were tambouring, running of lace, or weaving stockings. Now, if a frame-work knitter procures work, for a Man he pays one shilling per week; for a Woman, sixpence per week to the Keeper: and then they receive all their nett earnings, together with the Prison allowance of bread. At my last visit, in 1809, three out of the seven Prisoners were at work.

The *Commitments* hither, from 31st March 1807, to 31st March 1809, were *eight hundred and fourteen.*

Poultry were used to be kept in the court-yards; but at my last visit, I found that very offensive practice discontinued. It does not suit nor become a place of human confinement.

Coals are allowed to the day and work-rooms; and the sleeping-rooms, when needful, are warmed by the tubes of German stoves. No County clothing is supplied. No bath or oven, to purify foul and infected clothes.

The Keeper is furnished with mops, brooms, and pails, to keep the Prison in neat order; but no soap or towels are allowed for personal cleanliness; nor religious books distributed for the Prisoners' use, under guilt, sorrow, or sickness.

They have their usual allowance of bread given them when discharged.

Neither the Act for preserving Health, nor Clauses against Spirituous Liquors, are here hung up.

OAKHAM. *Rutlandshire.*
The County-Gaol, Bridewell, and Town Gaol.
Gaoler, *William Sewell;* now *George Gould.* Salary, 50/. Fees, 14. *lod.* for Debtors and Felons. Besides which the Under-Sheriff demands *9s. 2d.* of each Debtor for his *liberate 1* Garnish abolished.

Chaplain, Rev. *Richard Williams;* who attends Prisoners under Sentence of Death only; for which he receives a gratuity from the Treasurer of the County.

Surgeon, Mr. *William Keal.* Salary, 5/.

Number of Prisoners, Debtors. Felons, &c 1800, April 22d,------3-4. 1805, Sept. 27th,------0-------2.

Allowance, one pound of bread per day to Prisoners of all descriptions.
REMARKS.
The old Gaol, which was a thatched building, I have described fully in the Gentleman's Magazine for Nov. 1810, page 422. The present Gaol, finished in 1810, is situated a little way out of the Town, and the boundary-wall encloses about half an acre of ground. Here is no lodge for a Turnkey; the door of entrance opens into a room, which has in it a boiler and a sleeping-cell; and up stairs is a condemned cell, and a straw loft. The flat roof at the top is intended for the place of execution. The Gaoler's house is an octagon, centrally placed, with three wings for Prisons, the court-yards of which are commanded by his windows. Men Debtors have a court-yard 50 feet by 20; and a day-room about 14 feet square, with glazed and grated windows and fire-place; three sleeping-cells below, and five above, each *9* feet by 7, and 9 feet high. Women Debtors have a small court-yard 16 feet by 14, a dayroom like the Men's, and only one sleeping-cell, which is above stairs. Men Felons have a court-yard 40 feet by 23, a day-room 14 feet square, and above stairs three sleeping-cells. Women Felons the same.

The Bridewell part of the Prison has, for Men, a eourt-yard *46* feet by 27, a day and work-room on the ground-floor; above stairs five sleeping-cells; and the same for the Women. For slight offences here is a court-yard, day-room, and two sleeping-cells on the ground-floor, and three above. Here is one solitary cell, with a small court attached. The Chapel is in the Gaoler's house, and the Prison is supplied with water by an engine.

ODIHAM *Hampshire.*
The Bridewell.
Keeper, *William Brown,* a Sheriff's-Officer. Salary, 25/. Fees, *6s. 8d.* No Table. Surgeon, Mr. *Shibbear.* Salary, none. Makes a Bill. Number of Prison-

ers, 1802, March 20th, 0. 1803, Oct. 25th, 3. Allowance, 170Z. of bread per day.

Remarks. This Bridewell is at the back of the Keepers house, and separated from it by a court-yard, 55 feet by 28, with a pump and sewer in it.

Here is only one day-room, of 12 feet 3 inches by 11 feet 3. On the ground-floor a sleeping-room for Men, and one of 11 feet 8 inches by 7 feet, and *6* feet 10 inches high, for Women; with each a double iron-grated window, and loose straw on the floors. No firing allowed.

There is a large room in the centre of the building, which the Keeper has converted into his brewhouse, dairy, &c. In the house are two rooms for those who can pay 2. *d.* a week. No Rules and Orders. No employment. Prison dirty.

OKEHAMPTON. *Devonshire.*
The Town Gaol.
Gaoler, *William Partridge;* Sergeant at Maee. Salary, 3/. Prisoners, 19th Oct. 1803, None. Allowance, three-pence a day.

Remarks. This Gaol consists of two rooms, about 12 feet by 7; dark and dirty. In the lower room a privy. Each has an iron grating, that looks toward the Street. A bundle of straw, weekly, is supplied when wanted.

Formerly Debtors were kept in the upper room. Nineteen Prisoners have been confined here at a time, for a night or two. No water. No court-yard. It had been white-washed about nine years previous to my visit.

ORFORD. *Suffolk.*
The Borough Gaol, and Bridewell.
Keeper, *Joseph Lewcock,* Sergeant at Mace. Salary, 20s. per annum.
Allowance, a two penny loaf of bread, and a pint of small beer each per day. Sept. 13th, 1805, no Prisoners.

Remarks. The *Borough Gaol* is a room under the Town-Hall, of 11 feet 4 inches by 9 feet 5, and 8 feet high. The doorway only 4 feet inches high, and 2 feet 3 inches wide. Here is a fire-place, a wooden bedstead, loose straw, and one iron-grated window, 3 feet by 2 feet 9, opening towards the Street.

The *Bridewell* is also under the Town-Hall, 16 feet by 9 feet 10, and 7 feet 9 inches high; with fire-place, and two iron-grated windows, of 3 feet by 2 feet *6,* next the Street. Firing allowed by the Borough. No court. No sewer, nor water!

A New Bridewell is building, with two cells 10 feet by 8 feet each, having fireplaces. Also two small courts, 10 feet by 7 feet each, and supplied with sewers.

OXFORD. *TJie Castle Gaol, and County Bridewell.*
Gaoler, *Daniel Harris;* now *John Wyatt.* Salary, 200/. and for coals 30/.
Turnkeys, three. The Salary of the Upper Turnkey, 45/.; the two others have 40/. each; and 5/. *per annum* allowed to each Turnkey for coals. Fees and Garnish are abolished: But the Under-Sheriff continues to demand from each Debtor 3s. *6d.* for his *Liberate!* For Transports, the expence of Conveyance.

Chaplain, Rev. *Richard Graham.*
Duty, Sunday, Prayers and Sermon morning and afternoon; also on GoodFriday and Christmas-day; and Prayers every Wednesday and Friday. The Sacrament four times a year.
Salary, 50/. for the Gaol, and *20l.* for the Bridewell.

Surgeon, Mr. *Rawlins.*
Salary, 30/. for Debtors, Felons, &c. both of the Gaol and Bridewell.

Number of Prisoners, Debtors. Felons, &c. Debtors. Felons, &c.
1800, April 29th,--17--37. 1802, Nov. 23d,--16--28. 1803, Aug. 19th,--*14* --15. Allowance, to *Debtors.* "Every Debtor, producing a Certificate from the Minister, and some other known and respectable Inhabitant of the place of his usual residence, (not being his Creditor,) that he is not able to support himself, and that he is wholly destitute of friends to afford him support, shall receive from the County the same allowance of food and bedding as is allowed to Criminal Prisoners by the County: But such allowance shall cease, when the Debtor shall have obtained his Sixpences from his Creditor; in which he shall be assisted by the Gaoler, at the County's expence.

To *Felons,* &c. one pound and half of good wheaten bread, baked the day before; and one ounce and half of salt butter, or Cheshire cheese: Also two pounds and half of good oatmeal, and some salt every week, with such vegetables as can conveniently be furnished them out of the garden belonging to the Gaol.

And, as an encouragement to orderly and good behaviour, and to a due attendance on religious Worship, an extra Allowance shall be made on every Sunday, of half a pound of coarse beef, and a quart of broth, prepared with vegetables, to every Prisoner who shall have behaved well during the week preceding.

Weights and scales are provided, that all may see their Allowance fairly dealt out.

REMARKS.
This Gaol has a very castellated appearance. The boundary wall encloses about three acres of ground; and being at a considerable distance from the Prison, affords the Keeper a convenient garden, which supplies not only his family, but the whole Gaol, with sufficient vegetables. At the Outer-lodge, near the road, is a kind of cage, or watch-house, as a room for Vagrants, or others brought in at night, and for that night only.

On one side of the entrance is the Upper Turnkey's Lodge, about *16* feet square, with a room above for himself and Assistants to sleep in; also an office, and a store-room. On the other side, corresponding therewith, is a *reception-room* for Prisoners, when first brought to Gaol; and above it a *lazaretto.*

Here are likewise a warm and cold bath, a general kitchen and bake-house, for the use of the Gaol, and rooms above for the Prisoners' clothes, and the Gaol uniform. Above stairs is a remarkable neat *Chapel,* where the Prisoners are seated in classes, out of sight of each other. The flat roof over all is the place of Execution.

In the centre of the area is the Keepers house, which overlooks all the inner court-yards; also the Visiting-Magistrates' Committee-Room. The wing on the right hand of the Keeper's house is attached to the old Tower. The bottom part contains three day-rooms for *Debtors,* 16 feet by 12, with a fire-place in each, appropriated to the three classes; two for Males, and one for Females: also nine sleepingrooms, 11 feet by 8 each, with boarded floors and glazed windows.

The first story contains twelve sleeping rooms, similar to those below. The Debtors' part of the Gaol is divided into two Wards; first the *Governor's,* and second, the *Common Ward.*

No Debtor who desires to be confined in the Common-Ward has any thing to pay for his room; but if he chooses to be in the Governor's Ward, he has one shilling a week to pay for room-rent, and for which the Governor (or *Gaoler)* is accountable to the County. Every Debtor, if he pleases, may provide his own bedding, &c. But if he prefers it, the Gaoler will provide them; and he must pay to the Gaoler, for his own use, as the hire of the same, one shilling per week in the Governor's Ward, and nine-pence per week in the Common Ward.

At the East-end of this Prison is a circular bastion, 28 feet in diameter, and four stories high; each containing two rooms of a semicircular form, 30 feet by 15, with a fire-place in each: these are intended for working and sleeping rooms. No *Employment* is as yet furnished by the County; but any Debtor who can procure it from without, is allowed to work, upon paying to the Gaoler half the profits of his labour; which, however, is to be repaid him on his leaving the Gaol. But should such Debtor desire to receive the whole of his earnings (relinquishing all claim to allowance of food and bedding from the County), the whole is to be paid to him accordingly.

At the end of the building, and adjoining to the old Tower, are four cells, of 11 feet by 8 each; to which there is added a day-room, of an irregular polygon shape, and about 25 feet by 13. These are intended for the *separation of Prisoners,* 6uch as King's Evidence, the Refractory, &c.

The ground-floor of the old Tower is the *Dungeon,* 20 feet square, and 20 feet high; the floor of which is mud; and it receives a dull glimmering through a small treble-bar iron-grating, 15 feet high, just sufficient for " teaching light *to counterfeit a gloom."* This is used as a Black Hole, for the short confinement of those taken in an actual attempt to escape, or the very unruly and turbulent.

The first-floor contains a room of the same size as the dungeon below; It has a boarded floor, with one treble-bar iron-grated window, and is called "The Condemned Hole." The second and third stories contain each one room, of the same size as those below; but the Keeper assured me they had not been used these fifteen years. The upper room of this Tower is of the same size as the others: it has a boarded floor, one window, and a large lantern light; and is intended for the use of Debtors, (as formerly,) if found necessary. An Engine throws water into a leaden cistern, from which every part of the Gaol is well supplied. The sewers are conveniently constructed, and not offensive.

To the left of the Keeper's house is a detached wing, for Felons and Convicts, which consists of two divisions; *viz.* The first and second class of Felons, and first and second class of Convicts; each with a distinct court-yard, of about f?0 feet by 40, and a day-room, with a fire-place in each. The ground-floor of this wing contains 16 worksheds under arcades, about 9 feet by 7, and 10 feet high. These are divided by a lobby, or passage, 88 feet long, and 5 feet wide; at each end of which is a day or workroom; the one 25 feet by 15; the other circular, and 28 feet in diameter.

The first story contains seven cells for the first class of Felons, and eight cells for the second class of Convicts; separated by a lobby, and with a day-room at each end, the same as below.

The second story contains seven cells for the first class of Convicts, and eight cells for the second class; in every respect like those on the first story.

The third, or attick story, contains two *Infirmaries;* one, of 24 feet by 10, for Male Criminals; the other, of 16 feet by 10, for Females: and on each side of the Leads there is a flat, upon which Convalescents are separately permitted to take the air.

Each cell in the foregoing wing is rather *singularly fitted itp,* with a Yorkshire stone bedstead, 6 feet by 2, or an elm plank bedstead, 6 feet by 2 feet *6;* a mattress stuffed with hair, two blankets, a coarse sheet, and a rug; and the sheets are changed once a fortnight. These cells are well lighted, and ventilated, with an inside shutter to their iron-grated window. On the first and second story is 'A small room for the Watchman, or Inner Turnkey.

Behind the Keeper's house, and on each side, are separate buildings and yards, which now constitute the House of Correction, instead of those formerly occupied at Thame and Witney. i.'

They consist of two detached wings, for Male and Female. On the ground-floor are ten sleeping-cells, 8 feet by *6* feet 6, and 10 feet high, with arched roofs to each wing; also a day-room to each, 20 feet by 15, with a fire-place; and a court-yard, 40 feet by 25.

The upper-story has the same number of sleeping-cells and day-rooms; the whole forming four classes, according to the several descriptions of Prisoners. They are employed in sawing of stone or wood, or else in gardening; and have such a proportion of their earnings at the time of their discharge, as their good behaviour appears entitled to, in the opinion of the Magistrates.

Towels, soap, mops, brooms, and pails are provided, for personal comfort and prison cleanliness; and the Chaplain has a discretionary power to distribute amongst the Prisoners such religious books and tracts as he shall think fit.

Donations to the Castle Gaol. Mr. *Thomas Horde,* by Will, dated August 6th, 1709, left 24/. a year to be distributed amongst Prisoners of *both* sorts, at 2/. a mouth. For the Payment he bound an Estate in Oxfordshire: and to make up any deficiency of that Estate, he bound an Estate in Berkshire. But this Estate *having been recovered against the Charity since his death,* the Prisoners have *now* only thirty-three shillings a month, which is paid by the President of Trinity College.

Mrs?. *Catharine Mather,* of Headington in the County of Oxford, by her Will, dated the 4th of March 1805, (whereof an extract is subjoined,) left as follows:

"I give and bequeath to the Mayor and Aldermen of the City of Oxford, and their succesors for the time being, the sum of Four Hundred Pounds of lawful money of the United Kingdom of Great Britain and Ireland, current in Great Britain; upon trust to place out the same at Interest, upon Government, or such other security or securities, as they or the major part of them shall think proper, in their names: With power, from time to time, to call in and new-place out the same as often as they shall think fit, and pay and apply the interest, dividends, and produce thereof yearly and every year, or oftener, at their discretion for ever, in the following manner; that is to say, One moiety or half-part thereof in providing and furnishing necessaries for the Prisoners confined in the *County Gaol* of Oxford; and the other moiety or half-part thereof in furnishing and providing necessaries for the Prisoners confined in the *City Gaol* of Oxford." With the above sum, 421/. Is. Od. Stock in the Navy Five per Cents, was purchased in the names of Edward Lock, John Parsons, William Fletcher, and Christopher Yeates, the Mayor and Aldermen at the time of Mrs. Mather's decease.

Common-Side Debtors and Criminal Prisoners are supplied with coals throughout the year, from the above Legacies of Mr. Horde and Mrs. Mather, and also the Quarterly money (next mentioned) from Magdalen College; which, if not sufficient, is-made up by the County.

The next Bequest to Prisoners of both sorts is *Ss. 8d.* paid quarterly by Magdalen College: From which College also, in Lent, there is about forty shillings, called *Forfeitmoney.* Fram Merton College, sixpence per week in bread to Debtors.

Corpus Cbristi College, and other Colleges, send 7. *6d.* every month in bread, and a peck of oatmeal, for Debtors. Soup also is sent from the several Colleges frequently in the Winter, but at no stated periods.

Christ Church College sends fifty shillings every Christmas, and six pounds of mutton every Saturday, of which Debtors partake in common: and the Vice-Chancellor give annually thirty shillings at Christmas.

The Rev. Mr. *Swinton* (formerly Chaplain to this Gaol,) bequeathed the interest of one hundred pounds Three per Cent South-Sea Annuities, to be distributed in bread (threepenny loaves) every Sunday, while it lasts, to each Prisoner who regularly attends Chapel.

Every Prisoner attended Divine Service at my visit in August 1806; and their their behaviour was orderly and attentive.

It is pleasing to add, that this Gaol is in a continued state of improvement.
OXFORD.
The City Gaol.
Gaoler, *Thomas Wharton.* Salary, 52/. 10.

Fees, Debtors, *9s. 2d.* Misdemeaners, 3s. *4a1.* Felons, none. No Table.

Chaplain, Rev. Mr. *Penson.* Duty, Sunday Prayers and Sermon. Salary, 10/. 10s.

Surgeon, Mr. *Rawlins;* makes a Bill.

Number of Prisoners, Debtors. Felons, &c. Debtors. Felons, &c. 1800, April 29th,--1--4 1802, Nov. 23d, 0--6 1803, Aug. 19th,--0--10 1806, Aug. 30th,--1--6 1809, Nov. 2lst,--0--3. Allowance, for *Debtors,* none regularly established: But see the *Remarks, Felons,* and other *Criminal Prisoners,* have each eight pounds and eleven ounces of best wheaten bread per week, sent in twice weekly from the baker's, in loaves of 4 lbs. 5 oz. each. These I found to be very exact, there being weights and scales provided by the City, for the use of the Prisoners. Those who can procure Employment from without are allowed to work, and have the whole of their earnings, but not the City allotment of bread, as above. At my visit in 1806, I found all the seven Prisoners employed; but four of them, not being able to maintain themselves entirely, had the City bread.. j REMARKS.

This Gaol is surrounded by a boundary-wall, 20 feet high, inclosing about an acre of ground; and being at the distance of 25 feet from the Prison, the Keeper has a convenient garden within it, for the growth of vegetables.

There is an alarm-bell at the top of the Prison. The Gaoler's house, which is in the centre of the building, fronts the outer-gate, and has, on each side, a small flower-garden, 40 feet by 20, fenced in with open palisades. At the entrance is a small room, about 10 feet square, in which the Act for preservation of Health, and Clauses against the use of Spirituous Liquors, are conspicuously hung up.

In the above room, on an old door, and engraved on a brass plate, (as if *in perpetuam reimemoriam,)* is the following Inscription.

"This Door was at the entrance of a *Cell,* in the Old City Gaol Boccardq, "called 'The Bishops' Room wherein the Bishops *Cranmer, Ridley,* and "*Latimer* were confined; and from whence they were taken to suffer martyrdom in the Town-Ditch, behind the Houses opposite Baliol-College, in the Reign of "Queen Mary."

Over the Door are the Heads of the three Prelates, *burnt in wood.*

Here are five court-yards, each about 54 feet by 29, enclosed with open wood palisades; three are assigned for Criminals, and two for Male and Female Debtors. The two court-yards fronting the entrance have arcades, for shelter in wet weather, or for the Prisoners to work in. Every court has a sewer, and is well supplied with water.

The ground-floor of the Prison contains the Visiting Magistrates' CommitteeRoom; the Gaoler's Kitchen; also a place called *The Hall,* an irregular octagon of 23 feet diameter; and two day-rooms for Criminal Prisoners, one for Men, the other for Women; with fire-places, and shelves to deposit their provisions.

The Hall has on each side a lobby, 43 feet long, and 5 feet wide, with three working-cells, 8 feet by *6,* and 9 feet high to the crown of the arch. Both the lobbies terminate in a stair-case leading to the Chapel; which is on the first-floor, and of the same size with the Hall beneath it. The Chapel is open above to the top of the building, with a sky-light in the roof. The Prisoners are disposed according to their classes; the Debtors seated below, the Felons in the gallery; and all in full view both of the Chaplain and Gaoler.

On each side of the Chapel is a lobby, similar to those below, each containing eight sleeping-cells, with double doors; the outer one iron-grated, the inner of wood. They are 8 feet long by *6,* and 9 feet high to the crown of the arch; all well lighted and ventilated, and fitted up with elm-plank bedsteads on stone bearers, 6 feet long, 22 inches wide, and supplied with a sedge mat, and three blankets each.

Here are also two day-rooms for Debtors, about 14 feet square, with fire-places; and a sleeping-room, furnished with beds by the Keeper, at 1. *6d.* each per week. A Criminal Prisoner, in his proper department, is allowed to bring his own bed; or else hires one from the Keeper, at a shilling or eighteen pence per week.

Common-Side Debtors, who have not beds of their own, and cannot afford to pay, sleep in the cells above-mentioned.

The second, or attick story, contains two dark cells for refractory Prisoners; two Lazarettos, for those infected with cutaneous or other disorders, so as to render their admission amongst the other Prisoners improper; and sixteen sleepingcells. Also two Hospital-rooms, with fire-places, for the Men and Women, 15 feet square, with a water closet in each. The Dispensary is close to the Infirmaries, and from these a door opens into the Chapel gallery. Above the Dispensary is a large cistern, replenished with water by a forcing-pump, which is placed at the back of the Gaol, and plentifully supplies the whole Prison.

No Gaol uniform is here provided; but if any Prisoners, on entrance, are found ragged, or in offensive apparel, they are supplied with other, by an order from the Magistrates. Here is no oven to purify infected clothes; but towels, soap, &c. are allowed by the City, for Prison cleanliness.

Coals in the Winter, meat, and soup, are frequently granted by the Magistrates; and when a Prisoner is ill, the Surgeon has a discretionary power to order such food, and other accommodation, as he thinks necessary.

One Moiety of Mrs. *Catherine Mathers* Legacy, (mentioned in my Remarks on the Castle Gaol,) is appropriated for the supply of Coals to the Prisoners in this City Gaol; and any deficiency of that article is sent in by the considerate Magistrates; who visit here in monthly rotation, and enter their Remarks in a book kept for so very useful a purpose.

Here are seldom any Debtors; none being sent hither but by Writ issuing from the City Court.

Upon their discharge, and if they have behaved well under confinement, money is given to the Prisoners, according to their respective distances from home; and all of them are humanely discharged *in the morning.*

No *Rules* and *Orders.* The Prison is clean.

PAISLEY. *County of Renfrew, Scotland.* Gaolers, *William,* and *John Hart.* Salary, 45/. Fees, see Table.

Chaplain, none, nor any religious attentions.

Surgeon, as wanted, on application to the Magistrates.

Number of Prisoners, 26th Oct. 1809, Debtors, 8. Felon, 1. Petty-Offenders, 3.

Allowance, Debtors as alimented; generally 1. per day. Criminals, *6d.* a day.

REMARKS.

This Prison is in the centre of the Town, and the Court-House forms part of the building. On the first floor are the Gaoler's two tap-rooms.

The first story has two small rooms for Criminals, with grated and glazed windows opening to the Street, and stone floors. The Prisoners sleep upon boards raised from the floor about 6 inches, furnished with two blankets each, and a coverlet. No fire-places.

The second story has two rooms, of a similar description to those above-noticed; in one of which is fixed the *Gad,* or strong iron bar, for chaining by the leg the more atrocious Criminals. There are also on this story three small rooms for Debtors, with boarded floors and fire-places, grated and glazed windows; tables, and benches to sit on; but no fuel whatever, nor any bedding is allowed.

The attick, or upper story, has two rooms for Women Debtors and Criminals, with a grated and glazed sky-light. They sleep on the boarded floors, and have two blankets and a coverlet allowed them.

No coals are allowed for any part of this Prison. No water supplied, but as it is brought in by the Keeper.

In several of the rooms a tub is made to serve the purpose of a sewer; which being discharged into a stone receptacle on each flat, or roof, renders the whole Gaol extremely offensive.

Fees and Regulations To be exacted and observed in the Tolbooth of Paisley, as appointed by an Act of the Magistrates and Town Council, 24th Dec. 1800.

£. *s. d.* "I. Every Burgess incarcerated, shall, during his confinement, pay for Gaol Fee, for each night--------002 II. Every person not a Burgess-----------004 £. *s. d.* III. For every person imprisoned by virtue of an act of warding, the Gaoler shall be paid by the incarcerator------.010, IV. For every person imprisoned in virtue of a written warrant from a Magistrate, a Justice of Peace, or Sheriff, the Gaoler shall be paid by the incarcerator--..---.-0-12

V. For every person imprisoned by virtue of a Caption, Justiciary or Admiralty Warrant, the Gaoler shall be paid by the incarcerator, if the Prisoner is a Burgess--------026

VI. If an un-freeman------------050 VII. The Gaoler, on signing an attestation of a commitment, shall receive----------------010 VIII. And on delivery of diligence to persons neglecting to require the same, within eight days after the Prisoner's liberation, he shall receive---------.-----010

But if the Procurator Fiscal be concerned in any of the above diligences, he shall receive nothing.

IX. The Town Clerk shall be entitled, for keeping the records of each of the articles aforesaid, viz. Nos. 3, 4, 5, 6, for every person incarcerated, and to be paid to him by the Gaoler, as usual; and the warrants to be delivered by the Gaoler to him, so soon as the Prisoners are liberated---.---0 0 2 X. The Gaoler shall collect from each Prisoner liberated, and pay to the Clerk for his liberation----------00 2.

Rules to be observed by the Gaoler and his Servants.

I. The Gaoler shall not, by himself, or any of his Servants, directly, or indirectly, demand or receive from any Prisoner, or from any person in his or her name, at entry, or during his or her confinement, any sums of money, under the name of entry-money, garnishing, or any other denomination, separate from, and over and above the Fees stipulated as above. Further, the Gaoler shall not suffer any of the Prisoners to make demands of money, or drink, from persons newly incarcerated, on any pretence whatever.

II. The Prison shall be opened no sooner than nine in the morning, for the admission of visitors, and shall continue open for that purpose till three o' Clock in the afternoon, when it shall be shut, and again opened at five o'Clock in the afternoon; and shall continue open till nine o'Clock at night, and no longer, for the admission of visitors: Only on Sundays, the Prison shall be shut during public worship; and the Gaoler is always to keep the whole keys of the Prison in his own custody, while it is shut up, and not intrust them with any of his servants. III. The Gaoler shall, every morning and evening, at the opening of, and before shutting up of the Prison, personally visit every room and place therein, carefully inspect the windows, chimnies, and walls thereof, in order to prevent and discover all attempts to cut the iron stanchers, or to break through the stone Walls, joists, and floors of the Prison: And he shall take particular care that no instrument be conveyed to, or be in the possession of, any of the Prisoners, whereby they may effectuate their escape, or hurt one another. And in case the Gaoler shall, through indisposition, be prevented from the execution of his duty, he shall take care to employ some faithful person in his absence. IV. The Gaoler and his Servants are expressly prohibited from selling, or allowing to be brought in, to any of the Prisoners, spirits or strong liquor, whereby they may be in danger of being intoxicated; and they are to use their utmost endeavours to promote sobriety among those under their charge.

V. The Gaoler shall keep the Prisoners fof Debt in die best rooms, and separate from Criminals and disorderly person; and prevent, as much as possible, their associating and conversing together: and the friends and servants of Debtor's shall be allowed, at all convenient times, to bring in vivres for their support.

VI. In order to make the Prison more healthy and clean, the Gaoler shall, at his own exp«nce, cause pair and clean the stairs, sweep the rooms and passages, and remove and carry away all filth and nastiness, at least three times in the week. VII. The Gaoler, in the event of his exacting, by himself or his Servants, more Fees than are specified as above, or in the erent of his transgressing any of the rules or instructions aforesaid, shall be dismissed from his office, or otherwise punished, as the Magistrates for the time being, and Council, shall judge proper.

It is recommended to the Magistrates frequently to examine and enquire into the fidelity of the Gaoler and his Servants: and the Council hereby ordain these Fees and Regulations to be printed and published; and ordain the Gaoler for the time being to affix a copy thereof in the most publio part of the Tolbooth.

Extracted from the Records of the Magistrates and Town Council,

Alex. Gibson, Town Clerk."

The Provost, Magistrates, and Council of Paisley, were pleased to honour me with the Freedom of their Burgh; which I received at Glasgow, accompanied by a most polite letter from the Provost, and for which I beg to return my grateful thanks. tmi PEMBROKE. *Sonth Wales.*

This Gaol is completely a ruin. It formerly consisted of a room on the ground floor, and one above: the flooring of which, at my visit in 1807, had fallen in; and the lower room was used as a pig-stye. At high Spring-tides the water flows into it; therefore unfit for the confinement of any human being. Prisoners are now taken to Haverford West.

1 PENRHYN. *Cornwall.*
The Borough Gaol.

This consists of two rooms adjoining to the Town-Hall, about 7 feet 6 inches square each; with a chimney in both, and loose straw upon the floor. The Borough Constable is its Keeper, and Prisoners are confined here only till examined and committed to the County Gaol for trial, or else discharged by the Magistrates.

At my visits, 10th Oct. 1803, and 2d Oct. JS06, there were *no Prisoners.* One had broke out, and made his escape, the day before.

The Prison for Debtors, formerly St. Leonard's Chapel, I found was let out in tenements; and no Debtor had been confined there for ten years past.

PENZANCE. *Cornwall.*
The Borough Gaol.

This Prison has been built about seven years. It consists of two rooms, formerly the old School, at the end of the Oat-Market-House, 9 feet by 8, and 6 feet 5 inches high; with a grated and glazed window 2 feet square, and a small wicket, or pot-hole, in the door. Each room has an iron bedstead, with a straw mattress, and a covered sewer in one corner. No court-yard. No water, but as brought in by the Constable, who is the Keeper. Oct. 4th, 1806, No Prisoners.

At Penzance was also the Prison for Debtors, for the Hundred of *Penwith,* the property of Lord Arundel: but it has been discontinued as a place of confinement since the year 180G; when I found it turned into a milk-cellar. The Gaoler, *Humphrey Bridgeman,* informed me that he was not likely to have any more Prisoners, because execution is *now* issued against the *Goods,* instead of the *Person* of the Debtor.

This miserable Prison, and the old Gaol for the Borough, called the *Black Hole,* are fully described by me in the Gentleman's Magazine for March,

1804, pages 158, 199.

PERTH. *Scotland.*

Gaoler, *Thomas Carnaby.* Salary, 35/.

Fees, for *Felons,* none. But the County allows the Gaoler one half-penny per night for each, during Imprisonment. For *Debtors,* 5. on Caption, and *Is.* to the Town-Sergeant, paid by the Creditor.

Chaplain, noue; nor any religious attentions, except to those who are under Sentence of Death.

Surgeon, Mr. *George McLaren;* who makes a Bilr.

Number of Prisoners, 18th Oct. 1809, 4 Debtors, 8 Felons.

Allowance, to Debtors, as alimented; generally one shilling per day. To Felons,, half a quartern loaf of household bread per day, sent in from the Baker.

REMARKS.

This Prison is at the bottom of the High-Street, and built on the site of anantient Chapel, dedicated to the Virgin Mary.

On a stone tablet, m front of the building, is the following Inscription, copied *verbatim et literatim.* tt Think with thyself whilst thou art on the Vay

And take some course thy Creditor to pay

Lest thou by him befor a Judge be calld. And by ane officer be here inthralld.

Till utmost farthing shall by the be paid

Thou shalt be closs within this Prison staid."

On another stone Tablet is inscribed: "This House loves Peace hates. Knaves Crimes punisheth Preserves the Laws and good men honoureth."

A wooden door from the Street opens into a stone passage, 6 feet 3 inches wideband leads to three vaulted rooms. N. I. on the right of the passage, is 22 feet 6 by 19 feet *6,* and 12 feet *6* inches high. The iron gratings of the window almost exclude both light and air. In this room are two sleeping-cells, enclosed by boards, each 7 feet 5 by 4 feet *6,* and 8 feet high. N. II. on the opposite side of the passage, is 19 feet *6* by 10 feet *6,* and 12 feet high; has only one enclosed sleepingcell in it, 10 feet by 6, and 9 feet high; and is better ventilated, having a grated window towards the street. N. III. at the end of the passage, is 25 feet 3 by 19 feet *6,* and, 8 feet high, with a treble-iron-barred window. This room has two See St. Matthew's Gospel, ch. v. 25, 26. enclosed sleeping-cells, 9 feet 3 by 6 feet three, and 8 feet high. The narrow slip through which it should receive both light and ventilation, was filled up with dung, from an aperture of the stable adjoining, which is higher than the window itself. The floors of these three rooms are of stone, and without fire-places. The sleepingcells have boards raised about 10 inches above the floors, on which a little loose straw, scantily thrown, is the only bedding provided. They have no other light or ventilation, than what is introduced through a grated aperture, of 18 inches by 10.

On the first story is a room for Criminals, called the " *Low Iron House?* 24 feet *6* inches by 20 feet 9; which has four enclosed sleeping-cells, of 7 feet by 4 feet 6, similar to those already described.

Nearly adjoining to this is the *Low Burgher's Room,* for Debtors, 17 feet by 13 feet 9, and 8 feet high. This room has a fire-place; and a glazed window, which admits both light and ventilation. Here are two enclosed places to sleep in, but no bedding whatever.

On the upper story is the Women-Felons' ward, 25 feet 6 by 21 feet, and 16 feet high. In the centre is an enclosed sleeping-cell, 6 feet 9 by 5 feet, and *6* feet high. A Woman Lunatick was here confined with four Female Felons, one of whom had her son, about six years of age, with her. Felons in this Prison are permitted to work, and have all they earn. At the time of my visit three of the Women were spinning.

Adjoining to the Sheriff's Court-Room, there are two *Upper Burgher's Rooms, for* Debtors, each 14 feet 9 inches by 10 feet 3, and 9 feet *6* inches high, with fire-places, and well ventilated by glazed windows; but the floors were as black and dirty as a common coal-cellar. No bedding nor fuel here, or in any part of the Prison, which is never whitewashed.

The Criminals' rooms have none of them fire-places, although the floors are of stone. No water, except what is brought by the Keeper, who lives at a distance. Half tubs are made to supply the place of sewers.

After a very elegant entertainment, provided on the occasion of my visit in October, 1809, the Provost, Magistrates, and Council, were pleased to honour me with the Freedom of the City; rendered more highly gratifying, by the speech with which the Provost delivered it.

PETERBOROUGH. *Northamptonshire.*

Gaoler, *William Millwood;* a Sheriffs-Officer. Salary, 30/.

Fees, 6s. *8d.* and to the Turnkey, 1. The Table neither signed nor dated. Transports, 8/. *8s.* for one; but if more, *6I. 6s.* each.

Chaplain. None regularly established; and, properly speaking, Peterborough Gaol has no regular attentions paid to matters of religion. But the Borough Court, having the power of Life and Death, when a Prisoner lies under Capital Sentence, the Vicar of St. John the Baptist, for the time being, is required to attend him. Salary, none.

Surgeon, Mr. *Beetham;* who makes a Bill.

Number of Prisoners. Debtors. FeloHs, &c.

1802, Jan. 28th,----1--------0.

Aug. 9th,----0--------2.

Allowance, to Debtors, none. To Felons, &c. *6d.* a day.

REMARKS.

This Gaol, for the liberty, called the *Soke,* which comprises thirty two Towns, is the property of the Marquis of Exeter. It is now also the Prison of the Dean and Chapter of the Cathedral Church of the Borough of St. Peter, otherwise Peterborough.

Here is one court-yard only, for Debtors, Felons, and every description of offenders, in size *63* feet by 21, with a pump and sewer; and a day-room, 19 feet 6 inches by 13 feet *6.*

The Master s-side Debtors have a spacious good room above stairs; for which, if the Keeper furnishes a bed, they pay 2. *4d.* a week each; if the Debtor finds his own bed, he pays I, per week.

Here are also three Dungeons, about 12 feet square each. Two of them are four steps below the ground; the third, two steps only; with stone floors, and no fireplace; all built beneath the arches of the Old Minster.

One of these Dungeons is called "the Gaol Room;" and the window being stopped uj), there is only an iron-grated aperture in the door, of 13 inches by 7, for the admission of light and air. The other two Dungeons have each an iron grating over the door. The boards on which Prisoners sleep, are raised two feet above the floor; which otherwise would be very damp, there being no fire-place.

The Soke allows straw, two blankets, and a rug to each Prisoner. As there is but one court-yard, the two Prisoners, a Man and Woman, were together in it, when I made my visit.

No employment provided. The Gaol was very clean.

PETERBOROUGH. *TJie Bridewell.*
Keeper, *John White.* Salary, 8/.

Fees, on Commitment, 3. *6d.* No Table.

Surgeon; if wanted, Mr. *Beetham* attends.

Prisoners, 1802, Aug. 9th, Three. Allowance, six-pence a day.

REMARKS.

This wretched place has, on the ground-floor, a room about 21 feet by 7, formerly a work shop, which opens into a narrow slip, or court, 9 feet 4 inches wide. This being deemed insecure, the Prisoners are always locked up, and have no use of it.

The two sleeping-rooms are 9 feet by 6, close, and ill ventilated. The Soke here, as in the Gaol, allows straw only, with two blankets and a rug to each Prisoner.

No employment; and, indeed, the place is too dark to admit of any. When an offender is committed to hard labour, he beats hemp in a dirty room that leads to the Prison.

No sewer. No water accessible to the Prisoners. No religious attention. Neither the Act nor Clauses hung up.

The whole Bridewell must be more unhealthy, and is not much cleaner, than a pig-sty. It did not appear to have been whitewashed for many years.

PETWORTH. *Sussex.*
County Bridewell, for the Western Division.
Keeper, *William Phillips.* Salary, 50/. and 13. per week for a Turnkey. No Fees..

Chaplain, Rev. *Thomas Vernon.* Salary, 20/.

Duty, Prayers every day, and Sermon once a week.

Surgeon, Mr. *Robert Blagden.* Salary, 15/.

Number of Prisoners, 1804, Sept. 18th, Six.

Allowance, two pounds of bread per day, sent in loaves of one day old".

REMARKS.

This Prison, in an airy situation, has four good court-yards. The enclosed ground is about one acre, and well supplied with water. The Keeper's house is detached, and has only one closet window, looking towards the Gaol. The rooms are on two stories, over arcades, sixteen on each floor, 13 feet 3 inches by 10 feet, and 9 feet high. Each room has two doors, one of them iron-grated; with an iron bedstead, straw-mattress, and bolster, two blankets and a quilt.

The stair-cases are of stone, with iron rails, and the windows not close glazed, but made to open: Each room has a large semicircular iron-grated window.

Here are two Infirmaries on each floor; and these are the only rooms that have chimnies.

The Chapel is in the centre of the building, and has thirty-two pews, each 3 feet by 2 feet 10; with sides so lofty, that the Prisoners cannot see each other, though they are all in view of the Chaplain.

There is no Employment for the Prisoners.

Every Prisoner, excepting Deserters, or for bastardy, is on his entrance undressed, washed, and the County clothing put on him; his own are purified, laid by, and returned to him at his discharge. The privies here are all water-closets.

There are many excellent Rules and Orders in the Keeper s book, which I hope will be printed and hung up.

Mr. Blagden, the Surgeon's, Remarks do honour to his judgment and humanity. The Prison is frequently visited by the Magistrates, and great good order is preserved throughout.

PLYMOUTH. *Devonshire.*
The Town Gaol.
Gaolers, *Thomas Tatam, Geo. Pardon, Thomas Totcton,* Serjeants at Mace.
Salary, 15/. each *per annum.*

Fees, Debtors, on arrest, 15s. on discharge, 15. *Ad.* No Table. Conveyance Transports paid, according to the expence incurred.

Chaplain, none.

Surgeon, Mr. *Richardson:* makes a Bill.

Number of Prisoners, Debtors. Felons, &c.
1803, Oct. 9th,-------1 8. 1806, Oct. 10th,-------0--9.

Allowance; Debtors, a threepenny loaf per day, upon Petition as Paupers: weight, in Oct. 1806, lib. 50Z. Felons, and other Criminals, the same.

REMARKS.

This Gaol adjoins to, and is partly under the Guild or Town-Hall. A door from hence opens into it; through which the Prisoners are brought into Court for trial, by a flight of seventeen steps.

Here are three rooms on an upper-story, for Debtors, with a *fire-place in each;* but *no firing is allowed:* Their accommodation is straw-in-sacking on crib-bedsteads, one blanket, and two rugs. They have also the use of the attic-story, which is 1Q feet by 1-2, and 7 feet high; and likewise of the flat-roof, 21 feet by 12, to walk on, and take the air. It is carefully enclosed by a wall 14 feet high, and topped with a wooden *chevaux de jrise.*

Below, on the ground-floor, are three cells for Felons, of *9* feet by 5, with arched roofs, and two iron-grated and opposite windows: one of which looks toward the Corn-market; the other into a lobby or passage, 3 feet wide, which has a grated window opening toward *Bowl-Hill.* The next story has two cells, about

12 feet by 10, and 7 feet high. The story above this is called the *fVomen's Gaol,* containing *two rooms,* with boarded floors, glazed windows, and m each a fire-place: Yet, at the time of my visit, the three wretched Prisoners were put together in *one* of the rooms, although one of them had a young child; another had the itch; and the third said, that the straw of her bed (the only bedding they are allowed) had not been changed in seven months: it was indeed, literally, worn to dust.

The Prisoners hold a constant communication with the street; and by letting down a hat, or a canister, receive the casual charity of passengers, in money, &c. Convicts under Sentence of Transportation have not the King's allowance of 2. *6d.* a week.

The whole Prison is dirty in the extreme: the lowermost cells were filthy beyond conception, with urine and excrement. The Gaolers live distant from their charge, to which they can hardly pay more than a divided attention, whose effects are too glaring. Here is no day-room; No court-yard; and the Gaol is but ill supplied with water. No firing.

The respectable Mayor of Plymouth politely accompanied me; and from him. fc learned " that it was in contemplation to build a *new Prison."*

No Employment provided. The Act and Clauses are both hung up.

PLYMOUTH.
The Dock Gaol.
Gaoler, *William Cock;* now *Hugh Tregonan.* No Salary. He lives at a distance, and keeps a Publick House, the Queen's Head. Fees, none.

Surgeon, from the Workhouse, when wanted.

Number of Prisoners, 1803, Oct. ath, Nine. 1806, Oct. 9th, One.

Allowance, a pound of bread, milk porridge, or broth, as at the Workhouse.
REMARKS.
This Prison is under a room where the Petty Sessions are held, and adjoins the Poor-House. It'has Four cells on the ground-floor, 10 feet 8 by 9 feet 6 each, with arched roofs: two of them have crib-bedsteads with straw, and open into a passage 4 feet *6* inches wide; the other two have straw on the floor only to sleep on, and open into a passage, 6 feet 10 inches wide. The only light or ventilation they receive is through a wicket in the door, 9 inches by7. Nocourt. No sewer. Water not accessible.

PONTEFRACT. *Yorkshire.*
The Town Gaol.
Gaoler, *Francis Fryer.* He is also Sergeant at Mace, and a Sheriff s Officer;
lives distant, and keeps a Publick House. Salary, One Guinea,
Fees, Debtors and Felons, 13. each. No Table,

Surgeon, if wanted, is sent in from the Town....

Number of Prisoners, 1802, Aug. 16th, one Debtor.

Allowance: Debtors have none. Felons and Criminal Prisoners, eightpence a day.
REMARKS.
This Prison is under the Town-Hall. The *passage to the Felon's cells* is 33 feet long by 12 wide, with a fire-place at one end; but no firing allowed. It is lighted and ventilated by three very small iron-grated windows, nearly at the top of the lofty roof: And this is called "*The Room for Debtors* /"

The single Debtor I found here in 1802, was a shoe-maker. The debt for which he suffered confinement was of his Son's contracting, for whom he had been a surety. His case was much commiserated in the town. He had constant employment; and the Corporation humanely allowed him to work in one corner of the TownHall, the stone-passage below being too dark.

Without these indulgences he must have been in a miserable state: especially if the Gaoler should have been from home, on *a caption,* or other business, so as to have forgot him; as he could neither see nor be seen by any person, for relief.

Debtors are sent hither by process issuing out of the Borough Court, for any sum, great or small.

The *Felons* have two cells, each 12 feet by 9; the windows of which look towards the street, and the doors open, as before-mentioned, into the *passage,* or "Debtor's Room." They have straw only laid upon the floor to sleep on; and the cells are very offensive, from each of them having a sewer in one corner. The roofs are of stone, arched and lofty, and must be very cold in winter. The windows being towards the street is another inconvenience, in consequence of the facility thereby afforded to introduce Spirituous Liquors: But this is the only light or ventilation which these cells can receive, as there is no court yard. No water accessible.

POOLE. *Dorsetshire.*
The Town Gaol.
Gaoler, *William Arney.* Salary, 8. per week. Fees, *1%s.4d.* No Table.
Prisoners, 22d Oct. 1803, Debtors, none. Felon, one. Allowance, *6d.* a day.

For Debtors here is a court-yard, 51 feet by 47, and a day-room, 11 feet by 9. Above stairs are four sizeable sleeping-rooms, for which Debtors pay one shilling per week each. The Town allows firing, from November till May.

Felons have a court-yard, of the same size as that for the Debtors, but no day-room; and two sleeping-cells, 9 feet by 5 feet 10, and 8 feet 10 inches high, with wooden bedsteads, straw, two blankets, and a rug.

Both courts are well supplied with water, and the Prison is clean. Neither the Act nor Clauses hung up.

POOLE. *The Bridewell.*
Keeper, *William Hosier,* Master of the Workhouse. Salary, for both, 50/. The Prisoners, 22d Oct. 1803, were Five; one a Vagrant, without a shirt, and four *Lunatichs I* Allowance, the same as in the Workhouse. This Prison stands in the back-yard of the Workhouse. It has two dark, close, offensive cells, with wooden bedsteads, feather-bed, two blankets, and a rug: also three old cells, and two new ones lately built. The grated window of the Vagrants' cell, and the wicket in the door, were both shut, so as to render it not only quite dark, but destitute of ventilation.

PORTSMOUTH. *Hampshire.*
The Town Gaol.
Gaoler, *George Luscombe;* now *Edward Hunt,* Sergeant at Mace.
Salary, 200/. and 80/. *per annum* for a

Turnkey.

Fees, Debtors, gs.6d. Felons, &c. 15. lod. Out of both which 3. 6d. is paid to the Town Clerk. See Table. Chaplain, none. Surgeon, when wanted, is sent from the Parish.

Number of Prisoners,

In the *Old Gaol.* Dtbtors. Felons, &c. Misdemeaners.
1800, March 30th,----5----13----15.
1802, March, 17th,--.-5----20----12.
1807, Sept. 18th,-12--.-23.
In the *New Gaol.* 1810, May 27th, 6----16----2.

Allowance, to every description, a threepenny loaf per day. Also every Wednesday, one pound of meat, and vegetables; and seven pence in money per week, called "*Prize Money.*" $C£ Formerly the Keeper received from the Borough *sixpence per day,* for the support of each Prisoner. It is now raised to sevenpence per day, 4. *id.* per week: And out of it he furnishes them with the above articles, and a fire to each day-room.

REMARKS.

The wretched Old Gaol, which so long remained a disgrace to the Borough, and in which the *unfortunate* shared a common fate with the *infamous,* being pulled down, and the present *New Gaol* previously got ready, the Prisoners were removed into it on the 15th of July, 1808.

This modern structure is situate in *Penny-street,* and extends 160 feet in front. It has four court-yards, with a day-room in each. The entrance, which is in the centre, leads into a Hall, about 11 feet square; on the right of which is the Gaoler's office, and on the left, a room for the Turnkey.

From the Hall is a stair-case to the chamber-story, and common to all the upper apartments of the building. On each side of the Hall is a lobby, or passage, 3 feet wide, leading to the Men-Felons' court-yard, which is *60* feet by 27; also to the court-yard of the Men-Debtors, and of those committed for slight misdemeanors, which is 54 feet by 24. To each of the above court-yards belong ten sleeping-cells; five on the ground-floor, of *9* feet by 6, and 12 feet high to the crown of the arch, opening into the passages before mentioned; and five above, of the same dimensions. Each cell is lighted and ventilated by two iron-grated windows, and those that open to the court-yards are glazed.

Returning to the Hall of entrance, there is, by the side of the stair-case, a passage leading to the court-yards of the Female-Debtors and Female-Felons, and also to the Gaoler's sitting-rooms: And on each side of the passage is a room for the Prisoners before examination,-with fire-places and glazed windows in each.

The court-yard for Female Felons is *46* feet by 20, in which is a store-room, and sixteen sleeping-cells; eight on the ground-floor, of 9 feet by *6,* lighted and ventilated by opposite windows, two feet in diameter; and eight above, of the same size, all opening into passages 4 feet wide.

The Female-Debtors' court-yard is 31 feet by 26, with a sleeping-room on the ground-floor; adjoining to which are two day-rooms, and two sleeping-cells, for the better sort of Criminal Prisoners, opening into a passage 4 feet wide, and common to both Sexes. For the last-mentioned class of Prisoners here is no court-yard; but the Female-Criminals are occasionally allowed the use of the Women-Debtors' court-yard, and the Male-Criminals, that of the Men-Debtors.

The Keepers parlour and kitchen are at the back-part of the Prison, and open into a hall, or passage, which communicates with St. Nicholas-street. His sleepingrooms are over the Turnkey's apartment, and the Men-Felons' day-room is in the front of the building. The above apartments of the Keeper afford scarcely any command either of the court-yards or of the Prison apartments. The plan, indeed, is not a good one; and care must be taken to keep the cells and court yards clean, for otherwise the Prison cannot be healthy.

The court-yards above mentioned are laid down with fine gravel. In each of them are a pump and sewer; and in the Men-Felons' is also a bath, with a copper for heating water.

On the chamber-story is the Sessions House, for the trial of Prisoners; and adjoining to it a room for the Grand Jury, an office for the Clerk of the Peace, and a Record-room: Also two sleeping-rooms for Men-Debtors, and two Infirmaryrooms for the sick; with boarded floors, fire-places, and glazed windows to each.

All the cells, passages, and day-rooms, on the ground and chamber-floors, are boarded; and the cells are fitted up with a mat, blanket, and coverlet to each.

As yet there is no *Employment* for the Prisoners in this New Gaol.

A Table of Fees, written on Paper, is stuck up in the Prison.

s. d. "Debtors, on Caption, 3s. 4/.; on Discharge, 6s. 2d.----9 6
Felons and Misdemeaners, on Commitment 1510
(Of which 3j. 6d. each is to go to the Town-Clerk.)
Stephen Barney, Town Clerk."
This continues to be taken in the present Gaol.

§d I cannot help remarking, that a Gaoler ought never to *farm* his Prisoners per head, nor be any way interested in the means or manner of their support. He should be excluded from all concern in the Prisoners' Allowance; from all possibility of profit, directly or indirectly, arising from the sale of their bread, or other food. Whoever distributes it should be free from every motive to fraud, and subjected to a strong check. Scales, weights, and measures should be provided in all places of confinement, that so the Prisoners may eee that they have their due allowance. Too much cannot be said upona subject like this; for a fortune, thus acquired, must have been drawn from the bowels of misery; and particularly from sailors, who being least aware of imposition, are therefore the most liable to oppression.

POULTRY COMPTER. *London.*

Gaoler, *John Teague;* now *Edward Kirby.*

Salary, 250/. paid by the Court of Aldermen, and 30/. by the Common Council. Fees, as per following Tables.

Table I. *Debtors.* s. d.

Master's-Side Debtors pay, on coming in, *5s.* to the Keeper, and *2s.* to the Turnkeys---------------070

Common-Sde Debtors pay nothing on coming in-000

Common-Side Debtors pay, on Discharge, *twenty shillings and eightpence,* disposed of as follows. To the Keeper, 7s.; at the Sheriff's Office, Poultry, 3s. 8d-; at the Sheriff's Office, Giltspur-street, *Is.;* at the Secondary's Office, Lothbury, *6s.*; to the Turnkeys, *Is.;* and Messenger, *Is.* --------------108

Master's-Side Debtors pay on Discharge *Is.* more than Common-Side Debtors------------1 18

Master's-Side Debtors pay for the use of a room, bed, bedding, sheets, &c. per week------------026

Table II. *Felons,* &c.

Every Felon who goes on the Common-Side pays Entrance---0 0 0 To the Keeper, on Discharge, 2s. Cd.; to the Turnkey, *Is.* ... 0 3 6

Every person who, at his own desire, shall go on the Master's-Side-0 14 8 For the use of a bed, per week------------036

For every Commitment after first Examination discharged, or bailed-0 14 8 For every Night-Charge, who shall be discharged before a Magistrate 0 3 6 If, at their own desire, they have a bed, first night »---#.-020 Every night afterwards-------------010

Master's-Side Felons pay for bed, bedding, and sheets, the first night 0 2 0 For every other night, unless committed for trial------001

When fully committed, to the Keeper 0 12 8

To the Turnkeys---------------0 2 0

And for every other night-------------00 6.

Garnish, *6s. 2d.* called " *Ward Due's;"* paid for coals and candles to the Steward.

Chaplain, Rev. Mr. *Davis.*

Duty, Sunday, Prayers and Sermon. See Remarks.

Salary, 50/. and a yearly Freedom of the City; voted by the Court of Aldermen, and valued at 25/.

Surgeon, Mr. *Hodgson.*

Salary, 100/. and 20/. for Medicines, at the two Compters and Ludgate, both for Debtors and Felons.

Number of Prisoners, Debtors. Felons, &c. Debtors. Felons, &c.

Allowance, to poor Debtors, Felons, &c. ten ounces of bread, and one pound of potatoes, daily. Also six stone (48 lbs.) of beef, divided amongst them every Saturday. For *Legacies* and *Donations,* &c. See Remarks.

REMARKS.

In my former octavo publication, I spoke of this *ruinous receptacle* for Debtors, Felons, and other Criminal Prisoners, as it once stood, in spite of age and debility. Its whole history is most singular; and it must, hereafter, become incredible, whenever its locality is considered to have been in the centre and very heart of the British Metropolis! How long before the fire of London this Compter had been a Prison, cannot easily be ascertained. There is reason, however, to believe it to be quite as ancient as the other Compters. It first appears in the reign of Edward the Sixth, when the keeping of it was an office of no small consideration; for, at that period, one John Seymour, at the special recommendation of the King, had a lease granted to him of this Compter, for a term of years; and in the year 1554 the Keeper of the other Compter was Robert Smarte, the City's Sword-bearer, who had the keeping thereof granted to him for life, he obeying the Orders of the Court with respect to its management. In the year 1600, certain buildings and alterations of this Compter were finished, at an expence of upwards of six hundred pounds; and in the year 1614, the Compter was again partially rebuilt, and repaired with oak. After the Fire of London, in the year 1666, two of the City Gates, *Aldgate* and *Bishops-gate,* were converted into Prisons, in lieu of the two Compters, (which were both destroyed in that general conflagration,) until New Compters could be built. For this purpose an order was passed in the year 1669, and executed accordingly. Since then the *Wood-street Compter* has been pulled down, and a new one erected, as described in its proper place: But the old Poultry Compter still remains; and, until the alteration hereafter mentioned, was appropriated for the reception of Prisoners, in the manner following.

For Masters-Side Debtors, heretofore, there were fifteen rooms betwixt the inner and outer gates; for the use of which each Prisoner, paid as per Table. For Common-Side Debtors six wards, within the inner gate; two of them on the groundfloor, called the *King's Ward,* and the *Prince's Ward;* in the former of which, Nov. 12, 1803, were seven Debtors, and in the latter, the same number.

On the first-floor, or story, was the *Women's Ward,* with two Debtors; the *Middle Ward* (so called, as I conceive, from its being betwixt the Women's and Jews' ward) containing six Debtors; and the *Jews' Ward,* in which were two Jew Debtors, with a separate staircase leading to it. This, let me pointedly observe, is the only Prison I ever visited, in which persons of their persuasion were allowed to have the generous, humane, and just indulgence, of being kept intirely distinct from the other Prisoners: And very sincerely do I hope, that, in the projected change and improvement of this building, some similar allotment will be assigned, of a place of retirement, security, and comfort, for Debtors, or others, of their peculiar description. Reason suggests the motive for such a hint; and Christian principle sanctions its adoption. It may easily be done, as no great space will be requisite.

On the second-story, or floor above, were also the *Queen's Ward,* which had ten Debtors; and a small room adjoining to it, for the sick.

The 34 Debtors whom I found here at my visits, had ten wives and fifteen children living with them in prison. All are allowed one rug each by the City, but are expected to provide their own beds.

To each ward there is a fire-place. In one of the rooms on the second floor, called the *Pump-room,* the Debtors had the convenience of water. The court-yard here is very small, paved with flag-stones, and had water continually running through it. In the passage-court was a day-room for Felons, and a small one adjoining to it for Debtors. They have iron-grated windows, opposite the *public house,* kept *within the gates of the Prison;* and from which they were constantly supplied with liquor.

Men-Felons slept in two " *Strong Rooms,"* planked with oak, and studded with large broad-headed nails, on boards raised about three feet from the ground; having each a rug allowed them: And up stairs was another large room for Men, and one for Women.

The *Chapel,* which was below, had a gallery for Master's-Side Debtors; and the Felons, and other Criminals, were seated on forms or benches in the area beneath.

At the top of the whole building are spacious leads, where the Master's-Side Debtors were occasionally allowed to take the air. The Keeper, however, or Turnkey, was always with them; because the adjacent houses were thought capable of furnishing the ready means of escape.

SUCH *was* this Prison in the year 1803: But the building being in a very dilapidated state, and in many parts shoared up with props, it became at length so dangerous, not only to the lives of Prisoners, but of other persons resorting thither, that in July 1804, an Act passed, (with a degree of uncommon expedition, suited to the supposed pressure of the occasion,) for the removal of " all the Debtors and

"Prisoners here in custody, to the *Gilt-spur Street Compter,* or to such other *safe,* "*secure,* and convenient place within the City, as should be approved of by the Lord "Mayor, Aldermen, and Commons thereof, in Common Council assembled." It was also ordained to " be lawful for the Sheriffs, from time to time, and until the "*Poultry Compter* shall have been rebuilt, or made *secure,* and *jit,* and *commodious "for the reception of Prisoners,* or another Compter shall be provided, to receive, "keep, and detain them in such place of intended removal." This took place in consequence without delay, and Prisoners continued to be received in Gilt-spur Street Compter till the 20th May 1805;

when the very crowded state of that temporary receptacle occasioned a necessity of sending all the *night-charges* to their old place of destination in the *Poultry.*

Nor was this step sufficiently adequate; for in August 1S06, the Gilt-spur Street Compter not being found large enough to contain the *Criminal Prisoners* of both Gaols, *they* likewise were reconsigned to the Poultry. This ruinous and tottering pile, therefore, (so long before deemed hardly tenable) has now, for above eighteen months, been made the only place of confinement for Criminals of the two Compters; and the *Chapel* of the present, being turned into a *sleeping* room, for want of space, no Divine Service is performed there.

The result is, that *Gilt-spur Street Compter* is now wholly appropriated to the confinement of the *Debtors only* belonging to both prisons, until a *new Poultry Compter* shall be provided, or the old one rendered "*safe"* for we can hardly say, "*fit,* and *commodious* for the reception of Prisoners.'

More than five years have now elapsed: The circumstances above narrated are matter of notoriety; and yet, how little, if any thing, is done!!!

The two rooms already mentioned, as fronting the public house, the one set apart for Debtors, the other for Felons, are at present both shut up: and the *Queen's Ward,* with nearly the whole East end of the Prison, have been taken down, to prevent their falling with instant destruction on the helpless Inhabitants!

Masters-Side Felons, or those who can pay for beds, sleep in strong-rooms above stairs; to which the access is from the Keeper's house.

Common-Side Felons have, within the wooden gate, a small court, paved with flag-stones, and a miserable room, called the *Rat Hole,* with an iron-grated unglazed window: also two *dismal cells* to sleep in, upon boards raised about a yard from the floor, with *a rug or two each,* according to their number;—but *no straw.*

One of these cells is for four Prisoners, and the other for two: Above which

are two rooms, of a similar description. The Chapel, since its conversion into a Dormitory, has barrack bedsteads laid on the floor.

The Women-Felons are shut up in a dreary place below, called the *Mouse Hole.* This will hold sixteen Prisoners, and is fitted up in the same manner as the above are for the Men. Over it is that, which was formerly called the *Jews' Ward* for Debtors, but now set apart for the sick.

List Of Legacies And Donations To The Poultry Compter.
Christmas Quarter.
When paid.
Half-Yearly-
Ditto--
Yearly--
Ditto-
Ditto--
Half-yearly-
Yearly-
Ditto-
Ditto-
Ditto-
Ditto-
Ditto--
Ditto
Quarterly
Yearly--
Every 3 years
Quarterly
Ditto--
Ditto--
Donors' Names.
Mr. Peter Blundell
Ditto....
Sir James Peachey
Mr. Ralph Carter
Sir John Kendrick, Knt.-
Sir William Middleton, Knt.
Sir Robert Rampson-
Archbishop of (
Mr. John!
Mr. Thomas Dawson-
Mrs. Mary Holligrave-
Mr. James Hodgson-
Mr. William Parker-
Mr. William Peake--
Mr. John Wooller--
Mr. Thomas Strelchly-
Mr. John Meridith--
Sundry Persons f--
Dilto

By whom paid.
Drapers Company-----
Fishmongers Company-
Excise Office-------
('Churchwardens of St. Andrew Undershaft & Allhallows, one I year beef, & the other money J
Drapers Company-----
Chamberlain of London---
Mr. Buckeridge, 13, Orchard-street, Oxford-Road--J
At Lambeth Palace-----
Cooks Company----
Churchwardens of St. Ethelburgh
Clothworkers Company---
Churchwardens of St. Sepulchre's
Merchant Taylors Company--
ll. 10s. Mr. Dunnage (pays") land-tax, *6s.)* ----J
Merchant Taylors Company--
Christ's Hospital-----
Skinners Company-----
Leathersellers Company---
Ditto, 7 dozen penny loaves.

Annually, on the 5th of November, the Gift of Mrs. Margaret Dane, one quarter of beef, and five dozen penny loaves, sent by the Ironmongers Company.

Lady-day Quarter. Mr. Dunnage lives in Gloucester-street, Hoxton. f Taylor, Darnel, Firebras, &c.

% Mrs. Starling lives in Carey-street, near Chancery-lane. § Taylor, Firebras, Grosvenor, &c.

The Drapers' Company up to forty shillings each, annually fourteen pounds for the discharge of Small Debts, included, the gift of Mr. John Kendrick.

Michaelmas Quarter.

Sheriffs' Court, two-pence each judgment, from the Clerk of the Judgments, Mr. Higden, Curriers Hall, at Christmas.

The Prisoners receive 65 penny loaves every eight weeks, as the gift of Mrs. Margaret Symcott; but which is *Eleanor Gwymfs* Gift, under that name.

N. B. Master's-side Debtors partake of no Charity, except it be particularly ordered by the Donor.

The Public House within the passage leading to this Prison, is rented from the City, at Thirty Pounds *per annum.* 1 was constantly assured that it had nothing to do with the Compter, although I as constantly saw, that the iron-grated rooms of the Debtors and Felons were supplied from thence with liquors, the windows of both being opposite to it. It is worthy of remark, that this public-house was shut up, as soon as the Poultry Prisoners were removed to Giltspur-Street Compter, but was opened again immediately on their being returned hither.

Taylor, Firebras, Grosvenor, &c.

On my examining the books it appears, that from the first of January 1800, to the 1st of January, 1807, there were *Four hundred and twenty-Jive* Debtors committed to this Prison from the Court of Conscience; and yet, the Number of Creditors who received Debt and Costs, in consequence of such Imprisonment, was no more than *seventy-eight.* Scanty fuel this, for the Spirit of Litigation!

PRESTEIGN. *Radnorshire, South Wales.*
The County Gaol.
Gaoler, *Robert Lewis.* Salary, 20/.
Fees, Debtors, *6s. Sd.* Felons, 10. If discharged by Proclamation, *6s. fid.*
No Table. Conveyance of Transports, the expence. Garnish abolished.
Chaplain, Rev. Mr. *Smith.* Salary, 10/.
Duty, Prayers once or twice weekly, as required: A Sermon four times a year!
Surgeon, Mr. *Cooksey.* For Felons only. Salary, *lOl.*
Number of Prisoners, Debtors. Felons, &c.
1801, Nov. 14th,-5------4. 1803, Sept. 9th, 3------2.
Allowance, to all, a sixpenny loaf every other day.
REMARKS.
This Gaol adjoins the County Bridewell. Here is only one court-yard, of 66 feet by *46,* for Men and Women. Debtors, Felons, and all descriptions, are promiscuously mixed together.
Beside the Keeper's apartments, there are five rooms for Debtors, about 12 feet square; to which the Keeper furnishes beds, at 1. *6d.* per week, and if two sleep together, I, each. Also a day-room, or hall, *22* feet by 14, which is used as a *Chapel.* Here is a cell for Criminals, 11 feet 6 by fj feet, with another day-room: and, three steps down, a damp Dungeon.

The Gaoler here is a Sheriff's-OfHcer. At the time of my visit he was out upon a *Caption,* six miles off.

, $3" Two other rooms are wanted for Criminals; and an Infirmary, or Sick Ward. Also a separate court-yard, which might be taken out from the ground adjoining.

Common-Side Debtors have a Free-Ward, and straw to lie upon, furnished by the County. No water accessible. An useless tub is kept, instead of a bath. The Act and Clauses are hung up. The whole Prison very dirty, out of repair, and seldom visited.

PRESTEIGN.
The County Bridewell.
Keeper, *Tliomas Sirrel.* Salary, *lol.* No Fees.

No Prisoners, at ray visit, 9th Sept. 1803.

Allowance, a sixpenny loaf per day.
REMARKS.
Here are two rooms below, and three above. A small court-yard; and. in it a pump, which had been dry for a month. The Keeper furnishes beds, at two-pence per night each. To the still poorer Prisoners are supplied wooden bedsteads and straw. Their employment is knitting, and they have all their earnings.

PRESTON. *Lancashire.*
The House of Correction.
Keeper, *William Halstead.*
Salary, 250/. out of which he pays 50/. per annum to a Turnkey. He has also a plot of ground, worth 30/. per annum.
Fees, none. For the conveyance of Prisoners to Lancaster, Wigan, and Ormskirk, one shilling each per mile.
Chaplain, Rev. Mr. *Myers;* now Rev. Mr. *Harrison.*
Duty, Prayers and Sermon on Sunday mornings.
Salary, 20/.; and l0/. as Auditor of Accounts.
Surgeon, Mr. *Birdsworth.*
Salary, *42I.* and Medicines furnished by the County.

Task-Master, *Thomas Houghton*.

Salary, *60l.* and ten per cent, on the gross earnings of the Prisoners. He has a Man to assist him, to whom the County allows 14«. a week.

Number of Prisoners, Men. Women. 1802, Oct. 1st,-115 45 1S05, Oct. 24th,----"--, 42;------70 1806, Sept. 2d,--- ,-- 42------48 1809, Nov. 9th, *46-- --26*.

Allowance, every day, breakfast and supper; 7 oz. of bread, 2 oz. of oatmeal, and £oz. of salt at each meal, boiled into gruel.

Sunday and *Thursday,* half a pound of beef, with the bone; seven ounces of bread, with one pound of potatoes; and water to drink. *Monday* and *Friday,* seven ounces of bread each; and one quart of peas, with other vegetables, to ten Prisoners. *Tuesday* and *Saturday,* a stew of cow-head and shins. *Wednesday,* seven ounces of bread, and four ounces of cheese each. REMARKS.

This Prison stands a little way out of the Town of Preston, near the Church-Gate Bar; and is surrounded by a boundary wall; which being at a distance from the house, the Keeper has within it a convenient garden.

On one side of the entrance is the Turnkey's lodge; on the other is the office of the Clerk of the Peace. Up stairs are two reception-cells, where Prisoners are examined before they are admitted into the interior of the house. There are, likewise, rooms for the Turnkey's family. For Prisoners there are six airy courts, about 22 yards by 12 each; four of which are for Men, and two for Women, with water, and a sewer in each. To every court-yard there is a day-room, the average size about 5 yards square.

On the ground-floor are eighteen sleeping-cells, 7 feet *6* inches by 6 feet 6; with vaulted roofs. There are also sixteen other cells; but, being very damp, they were not used for the confinement of Prisoners, Upon the same floor likewise, are 48 workshops, in which, when I was there, thirty-one pair of looms were employed.

On the first story are 52 sleeping-cells, of the size of those below; and on the upper story 53 of the same kind. Each cell is fitted up with a wooden bedstead, straw-in-sacking, two or three blankets, and a quilt; and ventilated by an aperture over the door, with an iron-grated window opposite. Here is an excellent kitchen, fitted up with every convenience for frugal cookery; and a room with a bath, in which every Prisoner is washed previous to trial.

Each Prisoner has clean linen every Sunday; and all are required to attend Divine Service, unless prevented by sickness.

The Chapel, which is in the centre of the building, has a cupola on the top; and is so partitioned off, that the Men and Women cannot see each other.

There are two large work-rooms up stairs, in one of which were six pair of looms for weaving, and the other is used for the batting of cotton. Two rooms are set apart for Infirmaries; but, as there were no sick Prisoners at the time of my visit, shoe-makers and taylors were at work in one of them.

The Rules and Regulations for the Government of the Prison are conspicuously stuck up in various parts. The Court, or Session House, is within the walls; and convenient passages lead into it, for Prisoners on Trial. The Act for Preservation of Health, and Clauses against Spirituous Liquors, are both hung up. The Prison is clean.

It being their dinner-hour when I made this visit, I was much pleased with the *Order and Regularity of the Prisoners' Behaviour, and the Attention with which it was served.* The Keeper was out on business: it could not, therefore, be accidental, but the pursuance of method: and, indeed, Mr. *Halstead* appeared to me, on both visits, to be well calculated for so important a trust.

The full amount of *Earnings* and *Disbursements,* from Easter Sessions L808» to Easter Sessions 1803, was as follows, viz:

Disbursements. *£. s. d.*

Total amount paid to Prisoners discharged----362 6 2

Ditto, necessaries for manufactory, oil, batting-sticks, &c. 506

Ditto, Cash advanced to Prisoners, and entered to their accounts--------------32 16 o£.

Ditto, of Salary for an Assistant in the Manufactory-30 12 0

Ditto of per-centage allowed the Task-Master---73 11 1

Ditto, of Cash paid to Mr. Threlfall, the Inspector--*966* 15 5 147T 2 0. '.

Earnings.

Total amount of cotton-picking--------686 17 0'

Ditto, Ditto, of weaving----615 2 0

Ditto, joiners, taylors, shoe-makers, &c.-----169 3 0 *t£.* 1471 2 *(k*

The Keeper, however, has informed me, that since the above annual period, to Easter, 1803, several obstacles had occurred, that in future were likely to prevent the Earnings by joiners, taylors, shoe-makers, &c. from being so ample as before Till that time Prisoners of their description had been permitted by the *Magistrates* to obtain work out of the Prison; which, soon after, was by order discontinued, so as materially to reduce the amount of earnings; and trade also had declined, whether from that circumstance, or other causes.

The accounts are examined and signed by Mr. Threlfall, the Inspector; and laid before the Magistrates at each Quarter Session, with the vouchers from the several employers, for their respective sums.

gg. s. d.

Amount of Earnings from 4th October 1804, to 9th

October, 1805------8ll 14 0

Disbursements for the above period- 305 18 4

Cash paid by Mr. Threlfall, the In-1 spector--------50$ 0 7§ _— _——— —
—._

S11 14 0.

The Prisoners here have the other moiety of the Legacy of *William Edmondson,* which I have mentioned in my list for Lancaster, page 326. It now amounts to 2/. 10. per annum, and is the only benefaction to this Prison. It is distributed as' follows:

Every New-Year s day, each Prisoner receives a loaf of fine bread, value three half-pence; six ounces of cheese, and a pint of ale; and what the Legacy falls short of that allowance is made up out of the earnings.

They have, likewise, a *Holiday every New-Year's day,* in the afternoon. Debtors arrested by process out of the Borough Court, for sums under ten pounds, are sent hither.

In October 1802, I had remarked a total neglect of Cleanliness in the courtyards of this Prison; and, for want of a drain, the uncovered deposits were extremely offensive. In some places dunghills, up to the very windows of the work-shops; in another part a hog-sty: and I was sorry to observe that no alteration had taken place at my visit in Oct. 1805. It was said to be intended that the cess-pools in the court-yards should be vaulted or covered over during the next Summer; but I thought the nuisance could not be effectually done away, without regular drains were made for a place so crowded; and that then it would be an excellent Prison.

What I had thus noticed, and wished for, is since achieved. Mr. Halstead, by letter in Jan. 1806, told me it was intended, in the course of the Summer, to do something effectual: and by a second letter, of 2d Sept. 1806, he informed me " that the dunghills were removed, and the other inconveniences to be shortly done away: that his Prisoners, Men and Women, were well employed; they had plenty of work, though wages were rather low; and if I should ever again be enabled to visit his charge, he hoped it would be found that every defect was supplied, agreeably to my ideas on the subject." Accordingly, at my last visit, in Nov. 1809, I found six cess-pools had been dug, to receive the night-soil; and being covered over, the Keeper told me they were not offensive, until emptied. I am still fully of opinion, however, that a regular *drain* would be much better, and quite effectual, as the ground is on an inclined plane, so as to carry off whatever might otherwise offend.

$3" The advantages arising from the *Employment of Prisoners,* in Bridewells and Houses of Correction, cannot, I conceive, be more fully demonstrated, than by the very exemplary Prison above described: and devoutly is it to be hoped, that such an instance will rouse our Magistrates to exert those salutary powers, which the Acts of 19 Cha. II. and 12 Geo. III. have sanctioned and authorized. Idleness is, indeed, the root of unbounded evil; and yet, how many Bridewells and " BetTering Houses" are there among us, in which no *Employment whatever* exists, even for those offenders who are expressly *committed to hard labour I*

I do not think it a difficult matter so to encourage Industry, as to make Idleness become just as *irksome* and *odious,* as hitherto it has been palatable. And this opinion, (which only requires calm reflexion,) is absolutely formed in my mind from frequent conversation, even with Prisoners, at various times and places.

READING. *Berkshire.*
The County Gaol.
Gaoler, *George Knight;* now *George Eastaff.*
Salary, 200/. for the Gaol and Bridewell.
Fees; Debtors, see Table. The Under-Sheriff, for each Debtor's *Liberate,* demands a Fee of 3. 6d. which is painted up, and affixed to a board in the Debtor's court-yard, by Order of the Magistrates! Felons pay no Fees.
For the removal of Transports, the expence of Conveyance.
Garnish, abolished.
Chaplain, Rev. Mr. *Hodgkinson.* Salary, *50L*
Duty, Prayers and Sermon on Sunday, and Prayers on Wednesday and Friday. Surgeon, Mr. *Bulley.* Salary, 30/. for Gaol and Bridewell. Number of Prisoners. Debtors. Felons, &c.
1800, March 24th, 10------21. 1801, Dec. 12th,------_ 12-1Q. 1806, Oct. 16th,-------8-25.

Allowance. This, in 1801, was ten ounces of bread, half a pound of rice, or two pounds of potatoes, to each Prisoner daily, on proof of his being a Pauper, and willing to work. But, on my subsequent visits, I found it altered to a contract with the Gaoler; who now receives fivepence per day, and fourpence per week each; for which he supplies the Prisoners, on *Monday, Tuesday,* and *Wednesday,* with one pound and half of bread: *Thursday,* half a pound of meat, and a pound and half of potatoes, made into soup: *Friday* and *Saturday,* one pound and a half of bread; and on *Sunday* (for which the additional *fourpence* is granted) with a dinner of offal meat, made into soup, with vegetables.
REMARKS.

This Gaol and Bridewell, placed in a very healthy situation, a little way out of the Town, is enclosed by a boundary-wall, 210 feet in length, and 327 in depth; which being about thirty feet from the Prison, the Keeper has within it a very convenient garden, for the growth of vegetables. The wall is about 28 feet high, and has a small *Chevaux dej'rise,* about four feet from the coping. The Keeper's house, in the centre, has an alarm-bell at the top, and the Visiting-Magistrates' CommitteeRoom fronts the Entrance Gate.

The *Men-Debtors* have two courts: The front is fjo feet by 57; the back-yard, 28 feet by 9, with arcades to both. They have also a Hall, or common day-room, with two iron-grated glazed windows, a fire-place, seats, two tables, and proper conveniences for frugal cookery. Here are likewise two day-rooms, for such Debtors as can maintain themselves; over which are six sleeping-rooms, fitted up with wooden bedsteads, and sacking bottoms; a straw-in-sacking bed, a sheet, blanket, and two rugs, supplied at the County cost.

To those Debtors who furnish their own beds, no charge for room-rent is made; and in the Gaoler's house accommodations are provided, for those who can pay as per Table.

Every Debtor inclined to work may be employed, on application to the Keeper, who is allowed one third of his earnings. But if the Debtor can procure work from without, he receives the whole of what he earns.

Women-Debtors have a small garden to walk in, about 14 yards square; and a sleeping-room, of J 6 feet by 9, fitted up like the Men's: Or, if they can pay as per Table, they may also be accommodated by the Keeper in his house, as before mentioned.

At the back of the Keeper s house, and

in the centre of a spacious court-yard, is the Chapel; a very neat building, and well adapted for its sacred purpose. Here the Debtors are seated in the galleries; the Felons and other Criminal Prisoners are placed below; and all who receive the County-allowance are required to attend Divine Service. Above the Chapel are rooms furnished by the Keeper with beds, at 2. 6d. per week each; out of which the County receives 1. 6d.

The worthy Chaplain is empowered to purchase books of religious or moral instruction, and distributes them at his discretion to the Prisoners.

Men-Felons have a very spacious court-yard, at the back-part of the Prison, 150 feet by 75; with a pair of large double gates opening into it, for the admission of rough timber. Within it are three double saw-pits, where those who can learn are instructed to saw; and to whom a daily additional allowance of ten ounces of bread is given, when they leave work in the evening. On Sunday they have a dinner of meat, broth, and vegetables; on Thursday, the same; on Wednesday and Saturday a quarter of a pound of bacon; and on Monday morning every working Man receives eight-pence in money, who has properly conducted himself through the preceding week.. ,,

In the Gaol-yard are two ranges of Gallery, 3 feet 3 inches wide, one story above the other; and Prisoners under Sentence of Death are executed on a platform at the West-end of the Gaol, to which the upper gallery leads. Each of these is divided in the middle by an arch, so as to form four galleries, into which the doors of eight sleeping-cells open. Each cell is 10 feet by 7 feet 6, and 7 feet 6 inches high; cased throughout with iron, and furnished with a straw-bed, in canvas case, a blanket and rug, at the County cost, each Prisoner sleeping single. These cells are ventilated by a small iron-grating over the door, and a tube, of about 3 inches diameter, in the opposite end of. the cell. The aspect being South, the late Keeper said they were excessively hot in the summer, and the sewer of each, placed in one corner, useless for want of water; so that half-tubs were substituted, and emptied once a day.

They have arcades in the court-yard, and a mess or day-room, with a fire-place, a large table, wooden stools, or benches, to sit on; a cast-iron pot, frying-pan, gridiron, &c. for plain cooking: and earthen-ware for their provisions; the window glazed and iron-grated.

Here are also four wards, with a court-yard to each, about 30 fet square, and well supplied with water. One is appropriated to Women-Felons; another to Gaol Prisoners detained for trial; a third, to Bridewell Prisoners in the same predicament; and the fourth is for Prisoners after conviction. Attached to each ward is a common day or mess-room, with a fire-place, copper, and washing-tubs, for the Women; and the County allows five chaldrons of coals yearly to the whole Prison. For Bridewell Prisoners, Men and Women, there are two rooms above stairs; each containing three beds for two persons in each, and furnished as the others above mentioned.

In the passages leading to these wards, and on the ground-floor, are eight solitary cells, with a small court to each; and six cells for Refractory Prisoners, with wooden bedsteads and bedding as in the other cells; and in each a sewer. In the different courts belonging to these cells are arcades paved with flag-stones.

All the Gaol and Bridewell Prisoners wear the County uniform: their own clothes are purified, numbered, and deposited in the wardrobe, until the time of their trial, or discharge.

Excellent Rules and Regulations are drawn up and printed for the good government of this Prison. The 42d Article ordains clean straw, or chaff, for mattresses, to be allowed as often as needful, and clean linen once a week. The 57th enjoins, that all Prisoners who receive the County allowance shall be kept to work: those sentenced to hard labour are entitled to receive 20 *per Cent*, of their nett earnings; those who are not so sentenced, to have 50 *per Cent*, agreeably to the Act of 22 Geo. III. Cap. *64*; and the remainder to be equally divided between the County and the Gaoler. The Prisoners' share of earnings is to be given them in clothes, or in money at their discharge, after deducting therefrom the cost of any wearing apparel issued for them, or any *extra allowances of provisions,* that may have been given to them during confinement.

The Gaoler's house commanding a view of but a small part of this ample Prison, the Turnkey formerly slept in the Chapel; but now he has a room which effectually commands the Felons' court-yard.

Men-Felons are clean shirted and shaved every week. Convicts under sentence of transportation have not here the King's allowance of 2. 6d. weekly, but the Prison allowance continued to them instead of it. Every Prisoner who has behaved well, is decently clothed at the time of discharge, and also receives a sum of money, not exceeding ten shillings, according to the distance from home.

Petty Offenders, in this Gaol, beat hemp, cut pegs, &c.: the Women spin. But the most productive branch of employment is the sawing of timber, by which means the Prisoner gains a new source of support, when discharged from custody. The earnings, from Michaelmas Sessions 1805, to Michaelmas l8oo', amounted to about *Two hundred pounds.*

Statement of the various Divisions into which the Prison is distributed.
1. Men committed on charge of Felony. 2. Ditto ditto on charge of Misdemeanour. 3. Men convicted of Felony. 4. Ditto ditto of Misdemeanour. 5. Men committed summarily for a time. 6. Witnesses; or (if not wanted for *them)* Men convicted summarily.. 7. Women committed for Felony and Misdemeanour. 8. Women convicted of ditto. Table of Fees, and Charges,
To be paid by the Debtors in the County-Gaol of *Berkshire,* at Reading.
s. d. "For discharging every Action upon Process, *Capias, Latitat,* or Execution 2 6 For the Certificate of a want of a Declaration, in order to sue out a Writ of *Supersedeas* ---__------------26

N. B. The above demandable of the Prisoner" For receiving every Declaration against a Prisoner in custody----10

For each Copy of the three first Warrants against a Prisoner----1,Q.
s. d.
And for every other........... 04

N. B. To be paid by persons making the Declaration, or demanding the Warrant.

Attending upon every Prisoner to give bail, special bail, *Habeas,* or other attendance out of the Gaol, as directed by Statute, per mile 1 0

Table of Charges for Lodging, Bedding, &c.

Every Person confined in the Sheriffs' or Magistrates' Ward, finding his own bedding, per week--------------10

Every person confined in the Sheriffs' or Magistrates' Ward, with bedding allowed by the County-------------26

Every Prisoner occupying a room in the Keeper's house, shall pay per week------------------26

Signed by the Judges of Assize, A. Macdonald.
J. Heath."

Extract from the Rules and Orders, settled by the Magistrates, 4th July, 1796.

"Every Prisoner who, during his confinement, shall have submitted to the Regulations with a decent respect and attention; and who has not been guilty of swearing or drunkenness, of any attempt to acquire more liquor than is allowed, or of other disorderly practices, shall receive a certificate of such good conduct from the Chaplain, or any one Visiting Justice, or the Chaplain and Governour: Which Certificate shall be a Discharge of all and every Fee payable to the Keeper or Gaoler, except those for extra bedding, and for the room in the Keeper's house."

Mrs. *Elizabeth Deane,* widow, who died on the 5th of July 1787, by her Will bequeathed 150/. to the Corporation of Reading, upon trust, to procure fire-wood for supplying this County GaoL Accordingly, on the 24th November 1787, with this Legacy, 156/. lis. 3d. was purchased in the 4 *per Cents.*; the Dividends whereof are to be laid out in fire-wood, "for the sole use and benefit of Prisoners, who shall from time to time be confined in the *u* County-Gaol of Berkshire, situate in Reading."

This is regularly received and appropriated according to the Will of the Donor.

In the Gaol are a warm and cold bath, and four separate Infirmary rooms.

At my last visit I weighed seven loaves, as sent from the Baker's, and found six of them deficient in weight

The Act for preserving Health, and Clauses against Spirituous Liquors, are conspicuously hung up: The court-yards well supplied with water; and the Prison clean.

READING. *Berkshire.*
The Town Bridewell.
Keeper, *John Shailer.* Salary, *lol.* No Fees.

Divine Service never performed here.
Surgeon, Mr. *Bulley;* makes a Bill.
Number of Prisoners, 1801, Dec. 13th, three; l8o6, Oct. 16th, three.
Allowance, was sixpence each; now only fourpence each per day.
REMARKS.

This Prison was built out of the ruius of an ancient Church. Here is a court-yard for the Men, 48 feet by 27, and under an arcade are two hemp-blocks. They have no day-room, but four sleeping-cells, of 15 feet by *9,* and 8 feet high, which open into a small court-yard, *6* feet *9* inches square, and are lighted by a little iron-grating over each door. In one of these was the Male-Prisoner confined. No firing or candle allowed by the Corporation: Straw only for bedding on the floors.

Opposite to those cells is another court-yard, 17 feet by 9; in which is a fifth sleeping-cell, of *9 feet by 7 feet 6* inches, entirely dark, except what light is occasionally thrown in through a pot-hole, or small aperture in the door, of 8 inches by 5. Over this cell is an ascent by a fifteen-step ladder, to another room of *9 feet 6 by 6 feet 6,* and 8 feet high, lighted by a small iron-barred window.

The Women's court-yard is 27 feet square; with a draw-well in the centre, and a sewer. Their day-room, 12 feet by 10 feet 6 inches, has a bricked floor, a glazed window, and a fire-place, but *no grate.* Their sleeping-room adjoining is 16 feet by 10, and 6 feet 4 inches high, with straw on the floor, but no light, except as admitted by a small iron-grating in the door, of 13 inches by 11. The two Women Prisoners were lodged here.

Water, heretofore inaccessible to the Prisoners, is now properly supplied. Whatever be their employment, they have the produce of their earnings.
READING.
The Town Gaol, or Compter.
Two rooms in a Publick House (the Three Maidens Heads) belonging to the Town. The Keeper, a Sergeant at Mace. Salary, 9/. Fees, 4. *4d.* No Table. Dec. 12th, 1801, and Oct. l6th, 1806", no Prisoners.
RENFREW. *Scotland.*
Gaoler, *John Reid;* a Town's Officer. Salary, 8/.

Fees, Criminals, none. Debtors; if a Burgess, *is. 6d.*; if not a Burgess, *2s. 6d.* on Caption, paid by the Incarcerator. Also, from a Burgess, *2d.* a night, and if not a Burgess, *4d.* a night, during Incarceration. No Religious Attentions.

Surgeon, if wanted, is sent from the Borough.

Prisoners, 26th Oct. 1809, None.

Allowance, Criminals, sixpence a day. Debtors, as alimented by the Magistrates; generally one shilling, or eighteen-pence a day.
REMARKS.

This Prison is in the centre of the Town, and adjoins to the Court-House.

Up a flight of steps, there is one sizeable room for Criminals, with boarded floors; a large wooden bedstead for two Prisoners; loose straw, a blanket and rug; a fireplace, and grated and glazed window opening to the Street.

Above this is another room, similar in every respect; and adjoining to it a very large room, (formerly the Town-Hall,) with three large sash windows, and fife-places, for the better sort of Debtors, Male or Female.
RICHMOND. *Yorkshire.*
The Liberty Gaol; for Debtors only.
Gaoler, *Robert Wright.* Salary, 5/. Fees, *6s. 8d.*

Number of Prisoners, 1802, Feb. 13th, 4. Sept. 4th, 3. 1809, Sept. 12th, 1.

Allowance, one shilling per week to those who are certified as Paupers.

REMARKS.

This Prison, for the very extensive Liberty of *Richmond* and *Richmondshire,* was formerly the property of Lord Holderness; afterwards of Sir Thomas Dundas, and now belongs to the Duke of Leeds. It is solely appropriated to *Debtors.*

It consists of two courts; the outer, of 87 feet by 39, is occupied by the Keeper's garden; the walls but *6* feet high; so that those only who are detained for small sums, and in whom the Gaoler places confidence, can be indulged with the use of so beneficial an accommodation.

The inner court is 63 feet by 24, and has a well in it. The Prisoners have a day-room, 15 feet by 12 feet 6, with a fire-place, a small grated and glazed window, a table, and chairs. Their sleeping-room, which adjoins, is 21 feet by 15, with two glazed casement windows: this is a Free Ward, for which they pay nothing; but must find their own beds. Both rooms have flag-stone floors, in a very decayed state. There is likewise a Free Ward for Women Debtors in the Keeper's house.

Master's-side Debtors have good rooms in the house, to which the Keeper furnishes beds at 2. 6d. per week; or, if the Prisoner finds his own bedding, he pays 2. per week.

The poorer class have beds supplied by the Keeper, at 1. *6d.* per week; and all have the use of the Gaoler's fire. The County allows no fuel, and it is therefore a very fortunate circumstance, that the Keeper is compassionate and humane; for his Salary is evidently not adequate to provide coals, even for his own consumption.

Formerly Criminals were sent here, and confined in two dark loathsotne *Dungeons,* at a descent of five steps; each 15 feet by *6,* and 6 feet 8 inches high. The aperture in the doors is only 6 inches by 3: But I am informed that none of this description have been sent hither these fifteen years.

RICHMOND. *Korkshire.*
The Corporation or Borough Gaol.
Gaoler, *Thomas Redford;* now *Thomas Close.* No Salary.
Fees, Debtors, *6s. 8d.* Criminals, *2s.* No Table.
Number of Prisoners, 1802, Sept. 4th, None. l8oo, Sept. 12th, One.
Allowance, to Debtors, none. To Criminals, Sixpence a day.
REMARKS.

This Gaol is likewise the *Poor-House;* and placed in a pleasant situation, with a fine field in front.

For Debtors here are two good rooms above stairs, with fire-places, and casement windows. These *now* have greatly improved the ventilation, which before was much wanted. They are Free Wards, in case the Debtor finds his own bed; but if the Gaoler furnishes one, his charge is 2. per week.

To this Prison all those Debtors are consigned, who are arrested by Process from the Borough Court.

For Felons there are two cells, heretofore ill-ventilated, of about 12 feet square, with straw to sleep on. The floors which covered these cells are now taken up, and the cells are opened to the roof. The semicircular windows have a casement added, which has rendered the rooms less offensive. But, the descent to these miserable places of rest is still by the seven-step ladder, which I before complained of. This is drawn up and let down by the Keeper, when he is disposed to indulge the Prisoner with a mouthful of fresh air in the court-yard. Here, at the upper end, is placed a sewer; and in the cells is a fire-place, and covered tub instead of a sewer: But no straw to sleep on, unless paid for by the Prisoner.

RIPON. *Yorkshire.*
The Liberty Gaol.
Keeper, *Robert Braithwaite;* now his Widow. No Salary.'
Fees, for Debtors, 10. *6d.;* for Felons, 3. *Ad.* No Table.
Surgeon, when wanted, is ordered by the Mayor, and paid by the *Liberty.*
Prisoners, 1802, Sept. 3d, None. 1809. Sept. 12th, Six Soldiers. See Remarks.

Allowance, Debtors, none. Felons, sixpence a day.
REMARKS.

This Gaol is the property of the Archbishop of York, by Charter from King Edward IV. His Court adjoining is called "The Court Military." The *Liberty* includes twenty-four parishes.

For Debtors there are four good rooms in the Keeper's house, and a very large room where the Grand Jury meet; the ascent to which is by a flight of twelve stone steps. This is called the *High Gaol.* No Free Ward.

If the Debtor furnishes his own bed, he pays one shilling per week: If the Keeper provides one, the Debtors pay per week two shillings.

On the ground-floor, called the *Low Gaol,* are two cells for Felons, both dark, damp, and offensive: one of them is 15 feet by 7 feet *6,* lighted and ventilated by a small iron-grating in the door; the other, about 13 feet *6* inches square, has a small iron-grated and glazed window. Straw laid upon the floors. No sewer: No water.

This Gaol is in a most dilapidated state: Great part of the gable-end tumbled down: The Debtors' rooms out of repair, and the windows broken.

A Court of Requests for the recovery of Small Debts is held in the Court Military every three weeks. The Grand Jury now meet also in the Court Military.

The Low Gaol for Felons is latey rented at 2. per week by the Military, for the confinement of Soldiers: There were six in it at my last visit. They have barrack beds, and large grated windows looking towards the *court-yard.*

The spacious area, of 240 feet by 150, has been recently converted into a bowlinggreen; for which the Keeper receives eight guineas a year. This, together with 2. per week from the Military, constitutes the whole of the Keeper's Salary: But Widow *Braithwaite* shewed me an Order of Session, 6th Oct. 177, which says, "It is ordered that the Treasurer for the *Liberty* do pay the Gaoler 10/. 10. for "his annual Salary, due the 10th instant." At a General Quarter Session, held Friday 5th Oct. 1798, it appears that this Order was repeated; but the

Widow said her Husband had only once received *seven guineas,* which were paid him the first year, though he had kept the Gaol twelve years; and she was not willing to quit the ruinous premises before the arrears were paid.

The Act for preserving Health, and Clauses against Spirituous Liquors, are conspicuously hung up.

RIPON. *Yorkshire.*
The Canon-Fee Court Gaol, and House of Correction.
Gaoler, *George Idle;* now *Thomas Thwaites;* who is also Bailiff for the Liberty, and a Stocking-Weaver. Salary, *21l.*
Fees, for Debtors, 15. *4d.*; for Criminals, 1.

Surgeon, when wanted, is ordered in by the Mayor.

Prisoners, 1802, Sept. 3d, none. 180Q, Sept. 12th, one.

Allowance, to *Debtors,* none whatever; to *Criminals,* fourpence a day, which the Gaoler receives, and likewise their earnings; for which he maintains them.
REMARKS.

This Prison belongs to the Dean and Chaper of Ripon; and is not only a *Gaol* for the *Canon-Fee Court,* but a *House of Correction* for the *Liberty.* The courtyard is 30 feet by 13, and Prisoners are permitted to be out for air and exercise, an hour or two in the day time, at the pleasure of the Keeper.

Here are three upper rooms for *Debtors,* but no Free Wards. If a Debtor provides his own bed, he pays 6*d.* a week: if the Keeper furnishes a bed, each Debtor pays weekly 1. *6d.* a

The *Bridewell,* or House of Correction part, consists of two rooms on the ground-floor, of 8 feet by 7. One of them has an aperture toward the court, 24 inches by 5 inches, with an iron stancheon running up the middle; and on the outside a small iron door, so as *to shut out this glimmering light altogether 1* The other Bridewell room has no other light than what is transmitted through a small hole in the door.

No bedding is here provided: The Keeper is allowed two guineas a year for straw; and at the time of my visit he had lent the Prisoner an old rug. Above stairs are two cells, destitute of Furniture, lighted and ventilated in the same wretched manner as the former.

The whole Prison very dirty. No water accessible. No sewer, but a covered tub.

Neither the Act for preserving Health, nor the Clauses against Spirituous Liquors, hung up.
ROCHESTER. *Kertt.*
The City Gaol, and Bridewell.
Gaoler, *Edward Wright;* now *Edmund Baker.*
Salary, none. But as Serjeant at Mace, 30/.
Fees, for Misdemeaners and Assaults, 13. *44-*No Table.

Chaplain, none, nor any religious attentions whatever.

Surgeon, Mr. *Thompson:* makes a Bill.

Number of Prisoners, Debtors. Felons, &c.
1800, April 21st,------1-------2, 1801, Sept. 20th,------0-------3 1804, Sept. 2jth,------1-.....-5. 1808, Aug. 16th,------1-------3 1809, July 10th,------1-------2. 1810, July 8th,--2 9

Allowance, Felons and Criminal Prisoners, sixpence a day in money. Debtors from the Court of Requests, *3d.* from their Plaintiff per day.
REMARKS.

This Prison is situated behind the Court-House, and there is a private passage, through which Prisoners are brought for Trial. The two cells below, now called "The *Bridewell,"* seem to have been co-eval with the court above, built, as appears by the date, A.D. 1687.

The City Bridewell was formerly two rooms down eight steps, in the basement story of a house appointed for the Reception of six poor Travellers. It has long been discontinued as a Prison; but the old barrack bedsteads still remain there. The design of this Charity may be seen from the following singular Inscription, placed over the door:

"Richard Watts, Esq. by his Will, dated 22dof August, 1579, founded this "Charity, for six poor Travellers, who, (not being Rogues, or *Proctors,)* may re"cerve *gratis,* for one night, Lodging, Entertainment, and four-pence each.''

Application is made to the Mayor, who gives an order of admission. I have always found some of the rooms occupied, and they are kept clean.

In the City Gaol are two close offensive cells, on the ground floor, 15 feet long by 5 feet 6, with a bedstead in each, that almost fills up half the space. In front of these cells there is a small area, enclosed by iron palisades, about 11 feet by 6, where the Prisoners of each sex stand tb receive their dole of provisions, and get a mouthful of air. Here are no sewers; buckets supply the purpose. No water, but what is brought in by the Keeper; who told me he has had six Men and three Women locked up there for two months together.

At my visit in 1804, I found a Woman Debtor in one cell, and three Felons in the other: a Woman with a Child at her breast, and a Boy, were confined in the Keeper's house; and in 1810 the Friends of one of the Debtors, a Woman, had engaged to pay the Gaoler for a bed in his house, to prevent her being associated with Felons, &c.

William Henry, convicted of keeping a disorderly house, and sentenced to three months imprisonment, and until he also paid a fine of 20/. was confined in one of these cells upwards of three years, before he paid the demand. These cells are called The *Bridewell.*'

In 1809 an addition was made to this miserable place of confinement, and it is called The *Gaol.* The ground floor has two slips of day-rooms, about 15 feet 6 by 8 feet *6,* and near 12 feet high; one for Men, the other for Women, with flagged floors, and cast-iron stoves; but no coals are allowed. To each there is a convenient enclosed water-closet, and a leaden sink, well supplied with water.

There is a door of communication from the Women's day-room, to that of the Men, and through which they must pass, to go to their sleeping-cell above. The grated windows of both day-rooms are 5 feet *6* by 5 feet; and look into a plot of ground, 34 feet by 26, with a pump in it; which it is intended to enclose as a court-yard: But at present (1810) they have not the use of it.

On the chamber story are three sleeping-cells, 13 feet by *6,* with a small solitary cell of *6* feet by 5; and to these the Corporation have furnished two iron bedsteads, with sacking bottoms. Those who occupy the others, sleep on straw, laid upon the floor, with a blanket, or as they can. There being three Felons to each cell, besides the poor Man Debtor, from the Court of Requests, he must necessarily associate with theni.

ROMNEY. *Kent.*
The Town Gaol.
Gaoler, *Adam Hammond;* Sergeant at Mace. No Salary. Fees, *6s. 8d.* No Table.

Prisoners, 1804, Sept. 24th, none. 1806, Aug. Qth, none. 1807, Aug. 24th, none. 1808, July 16th, one Felon.

Allowance, to Debtors, none. To Felons, *6d.* a day..

REMARKS.
This Gaol was built in 1750. Here are two roems; one on the ground-floor, 12 feet by 9 feet 6: the other, called " The *Dungeon,"* to which the descent is by nine steps, stands level with the Keeper's cellar, and has a small iron-grated aperture toward the Street.

Behind the Prison is another large room, with a fire-place, formerly used as a Bridewell; but now occupied by the Keeper as a wash-house.

ROTHWELL. Near *Leeds, Yorkshire. West Riding.*
Prison for Debtors only.
Gaoler, *William Carrett,* who is also Chief Bailiff of the Honour of Pontefract.

Salary, none. Being obliged to provide a Prison for Debtors, he rents the present building from Mr. Wilson, of Loftus, in this Parish, at eighteen pounds per annum.

Fees, on Commitment, a. *Ad.;* on Discharge, 18s. *4d.*
Garnish, each Debtor, *six shillings and twopence,* which is *spent in Liquor!*

Chaplain, JNone,
Surgeon, J
  Surgeon,
Number of Prisoners, who are principally Mechanicks and Manufacturers, from
  Leeds and Huddersfield.
1804, Jan. 18th,---30
1807, March 17th,--32.
1800, May 18th,---31
1802, Aug. 16th,---30
, Dec. 20th,---49
The average annual number in confinement, is about 34

Allowance, none whatever.
REMARKS.
This Prison appertains to the Liberty of the Honour of Pontefract, in the Dutchy Court of Lancaster.

Here is only one court-yard, of about 90 feet by 42, for both Men and Women, which has a mud surface, with a pump in it, and a sewer.

The Master's-side Debtors have a day-room about 18 feet square, and six rooms up stairs. Beds and bedding are furnished by the Keeper, and each Prisoner pays *2s. 4d.* per week.

The Common-side, or poor Debtors, have also seven rooms, five above stairs, and two below; with a day-room, about 15 feet square. To these the Keeper supplies bed and bedding, for which each pays *ij-d.* per week.

There is one room up stairs for Women, with two beds. No firing is allowed; nor any employment provided; which can seldom be procured by the Prisoners. "Every Debtor, thus immured, becomes a loss to the body politick; not only in the diminution of a certain portion of productive labour, but also in an additional pressure on the community, by the necessary support of the Debtor and his family." $3" The Regulations of this Prison, and its very curious Table Of Orders, being exactly similar to those of Halifax Gaol, I must refer the Reader to my Remarks upon them, under that head, in page 258 s and which, of courseware equally applicable to the present Gaol of Rothwell. Is it not singular, that the *WestRiding* of the largest County in England should be the only district of that respectable County, or in Great Britain, where a degree of rigour and authority so very peculiar is countenanced and maintained?

RUTHIN. *Denbighshire; North Wales.*
The County Gaol, and Bridewell.
Gaoler, *Humphrey Jones;* now *David Williams.* Salary, 50/. and 7/. in lieu of Fees. For Conveyance of Transports a Bill is made.

Garnish, (not yet abolished) Debtors, *2s. 6d.* Felons, 1.

Chaplain, Rev. *Richard Jones.* Salary, 30/.

Duty, every Sunday morning, Prayers and Sermon.

Surgeon, Mr. *Nichols.* Salary, 30/.
Number of Prisoners, Debtors. Felons, &c. Bridewell Prisoners.
1S00, Mar. 31st, 1802, Oct. 29th,----4----5----1. 1809, Nov. 18th,----8----4----O.

Allowance, to Debtors, Felons, and Petty-Offenders, 2s. per week each.

REMARKS.
This Gaol is also the County Bridewell. In front are the Gaoler's apartments. Backwards, on the ground-floor, is a day-room for Debtors, 27 feet by 15, and another of the same size, for Criminals. For the latter, only four cells, 7-J-feet by 6-f, two on each side of a passage, but 3 feet wide. The cells are arched with brick, and lined with oak-plunks. In each is a bedstead, with two blankets, and a coverlet. A window in each, 3 feet by 1.

In both the Debtors' and Felons' day-rooms are eight cupboards, with separate locks and keys, that each may secure his provisions. Above, are nine rooms for, Debtors, of about 13J feet by and a neat Chapel.

At the Denbigh Sessions, 10th July, 1802. "Ordered: — That the Keeper of the House of Correction at Ruthin bring his Prisoners, every Sunday, to attend Divine Service in the Chapel of the County Gaol; and that the Gaoler do give notice of the time of Service, and be aiding and assisting in bringing those Prisoners there and back.

"Ordered: That all Prisoners, who shall receive the County Allowance in the Gaol and House of Correction at Ruthin, do attend Divine Service in the Chapel every Sunday; and that every Prisoner refusing, except for some reasonable cause, be stopped his or her Allowance."

The above-mentioned nine rooms for Debtors, are all *free wards,* the County allowing to the Keeper 1. per week for room-rent; But, if he furnishes a bed, each Debtor pays 1. weekly for the use of it. In each of the Debtor's rooms are an *iron bedstead,* two chairs, and a table. Here are separate courts for the Debtors, and the Criminals, of about 2Q yards by 14; in each a pump, with excellent water, a bathing room, with a copper, &c.; but no Infirmary. Men and Women Debtors, and Men and Women Felons, associate together in the day-time, but are separate at night.

The Act for Preservation of Health, and Clauses against Spirituous Liquors, are both hung up. The Gaol is clean, and white-washed once a year. The Great Session is held here twice a year.

To the honour of the County, this Gaol is undergoing very considerable improvements. New apartments are building for the Gaoler; a separate kitchen, rooms, and court-yard for Female Debtors; a separate kitchen, rooms, and court-yard for Female Felons; a hospital, or sick-ward, with rooms above, for Males and Females; a room for Fines; three penitentiary-cells, each 10 feet by 6; and work-rooms for the Prisoners; all which, when finished, will make it a very good Gaol.

In the front of it, on an oval white marble, is this Inscription: "The Magistrates,
sensible of the miserable state of the antient Prison,
in Compassion to the Unfortunate,
caused this building to be erected in the year
M,DCC,LXXV.
J. Turner, *Architect"*
RUTHIN.
The House of Correction. Adjoins the County Gaol. Keeper, *Robert Jones.* Salary, *20l.*
Prisoner, 29th Oct. 1S02, One. Allowance, Two shillings per week.

Here are two court-yards, separate. For Men, a spacious day-room on the groundfloor, and a large sleeping-room above, with four iron bedsteads, sacking-flock-beds, two blankets, and a coverlet. For Women, a large room below, two above, and two in the garret; with beds and bedding, the same as for the Men.

No employment. Neither the Act for preserving Health, nor Clauses against Spirituous Liquors, hung up. The rooms well ventilated, and the Prison clean. The following is inscribed over the door:
"County Workhouse,
for
Industry, or Correction." RYE. *Sussex. The Town Gaol.*
Gaoler, *James Small;* Sergeant at Mace. Salary, *4l.* Fees, *3s. 4d.* No Table.'
Prisoners, 1804, Sept. 22d, Nine, Frenchmen. 1807, Sept. 12th, None.
Allowance, sixpence a day.
REMARKS.

This Gaol is in a very old square building, not far from the Cliff, called *Ypres Tower;* and contains five rooms. One below, is about 16 feet square, totally dark, denominated the *Condemned Room;* and close to it, a small one, nearly circular, about 5 feet 6 inches in diameter.

Above stairs is another large room, of the same size with the first; and adjoining are two small ones, nearly circular, like the second, and 6 feet 9 inches in diameter. Each of these is lighted solely by an unglazed small double iron-grated window, of about 15 inches by 13. In the larger room above, a fire-place, but *no grate.* The three circular rooms have floors of mortar, but the two larger ones are boarded; and of the lower one the flooring is very rotten, and unsafe.

Here is no court-yard; nor any water, except what is brought daily by the Gaoler. Loose straw on the floors, (changed once a fortnight, when used,) is the only bedding for the wretched inhabitants. The two sewers are, one below, the other, in the upper part of the Tower.

Before the front door and grated window, is a small piece of ground, enclosed in, to prevent people from handing Liquors to the Prisoners in such a Gaol. It is seldom, if ever, visited by any Magistrate, or other of the Corporation. No firing allowed. Never has been whitewashed, and very dirty.
SAFFRON-WALDEN. *Essex, The Town Gaol, and Bridewell.*
Gaoler, *William Mynott,* Town Cryer. Salary, 4/. 4.

Prisoners, 1805, Aug. S2d, 1807, Aug. 29th, l810, Aug. 29th, None.

Allowance, fourpence per day, in money.

Those confined in the Bridewell have one pound and a half of bread daily, sent in loaves from the Baker, and a quart of table beer.
REMARKS.

The Gaol occupies two rooms under the Court-House. The entrance is by a lobby, paved with flag-stones, and guarded by iron palisades, which separates the Prisoners from the Street. The rooms are about 13 feet each by 10, and 8 feet 6 inches high, with a fire-place, and a covered sewer in each; lighted and ventilated by an iron-bar grated window, 2 feet 2 inches square, and both looking towards the Street. They have straw for bedding, laid on the boarded floors.

No firing is supplied. Water is brought in by the Gaoler. Although the Allowance is more liberal at the Bridewell, Prisoners generally prefer being confined here, on account of such Donations as they casually receive from persons in the Street.

The Bridewell consists also of two rooms, in the Workhouse yard; which, at my visit in 1S05, were in a very ruinous state, but rebuilt in 1807. Each is about 10 feet long by 8 feet 6 inches wide, and 8 feet high; with a fire-place, a covered sewer, and iron-grated windows.

Wooden bedsteads are laid on the floors, with straw, and two blankets to each. Water, when wanted, is brought by the Keeper's wife; who is also mistress of the work-house, which is kept extremely clean.

At my several visits here were no Prisoners. Those who are committed to hard labour, in case of finding employment, have only what they earn to subsist on.
SAINT ALBANS. *Hertfordshire. The Borough Gaol.*
Gaoler, *James Deayton.* Salary, 20/. Fees, Debtors, none. Felons, *13s. 4d.*

Number of Prisoners, 1801, Aug. 15th, One. 1804, Sept. 8th, Three. 1807, July 31st, None.

1808, Aug. 1st, One. 1810, Aug. 12th, None. Allowance. To Debtors, none. To Felons, and other Criminal Prisoners, one pound of bread per day, eut from the Keeper's loaf. REMARKS.

Those Debtors who can pay, have very good lodging-rooms, adjoining to the Town-Hall; and, sometimes, the use of the Hall to walk in: for here is no court-yard.

Debtors from the Court of Conscience are confined in two very dirty, close, and offensive rooms below, with an iron grating towards the Street. In the same rooms Felons also are confined. These have no frre-place.

Debtors, however, fortunately remain here but a very short time. I have not met with one, at my several visits, in the course of *the last six years*.

The Men and Women Felons have tio other day-rooms than those above described. At one of my visits, I recollect, that a *shoe* was suspended from the irongrated windows to solicit charity; and the Prisoners were conversing with persons in the Street.

They have two close offensive night-rooms, or *cells,* separated only by an open wooden-bar partition. The largest of these is 7 feet by *6* feet 5 inches, and 8 feet 3 inches high; the other, *6* feet 8 inches by 4 feet 5 inches, and 7 feet 10 inches high. They have loose straw on the boarded floor, and one blanket each.

SAINT ALBAN S.
The Liberty Gaol .
Gaoler, *Samuel Lines;* now *John Cooke.* Salary, 50/.

Fees; Debtors, none. Felons, &c. *lgs. 4d.* For conveyance of Transports a Bill is made.

Chaplain, none; nor any religious attentions.

Surgeon, is ordered in, when wanted, by the Mayor.

Number of Prisoners, 1801, Aug. 15th, Five. 1802, Feb. 4th, Four. 1804, Sept. 8th, Two.

1808, Aug. 1st, Two. 1810, Aug. 12th, Five. Allowance, To Debtors, none whatever. To Criminals, one pound of bread per day, cut from the *Keepers loaves,* and which he *furnishes out of his Salary!* REMARKS.

This "Liberty Gaol," for twenty-two parishes, is the property of the Marquis of Salisbury.

Here is one court-yard, of 36 feet by 30 feet *6* inches, with a flag-stone floor, a pump and sewer, and a day-room, of which the Gaoler's room commands a full I was informed that a late Keeper of this Gaol had been dismissed, for cruelly treating, and halfstarving the Prisoners.

view. Also a spacious airy room for Debtors, with a fire-place, but *no bedding allowed, not even straw!* No room is set apart fpr the sick.

For Men-Criminals here is a small day-room, about 12 feet square; and four dark sleeping-cells, the size of the largest 12 feet by 8, with straw on the boarded floors, a blanket and a rug for each Prisoner.

The Women Criminals have a large room above stairs, with two sleeping-cells, 9 feet by 7 feet 6 inches.

Under the gate-way are two very offensive sleeping-rooms, the pne totally dark; the other has a post fixed up in it, to which refractory Prisoners are chained.

Here is no employment. Some years since, *Lady Spencer,* with her accustomed benevolence and humanity, had ordered a Mill to be fixed here; but sqme.Frejich Prisoners, who had been confined for but a night or two, just previous to my visiting the Gaol in 1804, had wantonly destroyed or spoiled it.

SAINT ALBAN S. *The House of Correction.*
For the *Liberty,* and the *Borough.*
Keeper, *Ann Twitckell;* now *John Deayton.*

Salary, from the Liberty, 38/. From the Borough, *2l.*

Fees, for Bastardy, and Assaults, 13. *4d.* No Table.

No religious attentions whatever.

Surgeon, sent by the Borough, when wanted.
t
Number of Prisoners, 1804, Sept. 8th, One. 1807, July 31st, Six. 1808, Aug-1st, Six. 1810, Aug. 12th, None.

Allowance, *four-pence* a day; but when bread was very dear, it was *sixpence* a day. The money is issued to the Keeper, who out of it furnishes daily one pound of bread, and straw for the use of the Prisoners.

REMARKS.

This Bridewell adjoins to the Liberty-Gaol, the entrance to both being on opposite sides of the gateway.

The Keeper's room, or lodge, is on the ground-floor, and the ascent to the apartments is by a flight of twenty-four stone steps. Above these rises a staircase of sixteen steps, leading to the Prison, which consists of two very spacious and lofty rooms. At one end of these, loose straw is laid on the boards, and each Prisoner has two blankets, and a rug.

In one of these ample rooms, there is a*fire-place;* but *no fuel is allowed.* The sewers are convenient, and not offensive.

Here is also a third room, with several spinning-wheels. Employment was formerly furnished to the Prisoners; but, unhappily, not *being found productive,* it has been *discontinued.*

I observed that the same wanton injury had been done to this Prison, by French miscreants received here, as I before mentioned to have taken place at the Liberty Gaol, during their temporary, and very short confinement.

Here is no court-yard. No water, but what is fetched from a pump in the Liberty Gaol, over the way. Neither the Act for Preserving Health, nor the Clauses against Spirituous Liquors, hung up in any of the Prisons here. No Rules and Orders.

SAINT BRIAVELS GAOL.
Forest of Dean; *Gloucestershire.*
Gaoler, *William Closs.* No Salary. No Fees.

Number of Debtors, 1804, Oct. 21st, One. 180G, Sept. 9th, Twe.

Allowance, none whatever.
REMARKS.

This Gaol, *for Debtors only,* is part of the old Castle, within the Forest of Dean, The Castle is the property of the Crown; and was formerly surrounded by a moat, which enclosed about a quarter of an acre of ground. It is now held by lease, as I am informed, granted to Lord Berkeley, who is chief Ranger of the Forest, and Constable of the Castle.

Over the Prison gateway is a painted board, inscribed "The Castle Inn: *Spirituous Liquors."* Company resort to it as to a common ale-house.

Here is one dismal room for Men-Debtors above stairs, 17 feet 10 inches by *16* feet 8; and another for the Women; both greatly out of repair. No bedding allowed, not even straw to sleep on: but the Gaoler furnishes beds, at *Is.* per week, to those who can afford to pay for them.

Of the two poor objects, both sickly, whom 1 found here in 1806, one was *Richard Jordan,* a labourer, who told me he had a Wife and seven Children; and that, since his confinement, three of them were sent to the Workhouse. His Debt was for Rent, *6I. $s.*; Costs of prosecution 5/. lls.6d.; *Levy-pence, 19s. 8d.*; and bringing to Gaol, 5. So that the expence exceeded the debt by *eleven shillings and two-pence I* Such cases cannot be known to *Earl Berkeley,* who I understand seldom, if ever, visits the town.

This is the only Gaol remaining in the respectable County of *Gloucester,* that, for construction and polity, is *not worthy of imitation.* It is without the controul of the excellent County Magistrates: But I have hopes that, through the humane exertions of the great presiding genius of reform here, Sir George Paul, the dreary abode in question will ere long be abolished.

No court-yard. No water, but what is brought by the Gaoler.

Neither the Act for the preservation of Health, nor the salutary Clauses against the use of *Spirituous Liquors,* are here hung up. The whole Prison very dirty.

SALISBURY. *Wiltshire.*
The County Gaol, and Bridewell.
Keeper, *James Weight;* now *John Willis.* Salary, 150/.

Fees, as per Table: Besides which the Under-Sheriff demands *6s. 8d.* for his Liberate! For Conveyance of Transports, Five Guineas each. Garnish, for Debtors on the Master s-Side, 2.; on the Common-Side, 1.

Chaplain, Rev. *John Malham;* now Rev. Mr. *Harrison.*
Duty, Prayers and Sermon on Sundays. Salary, 50/. See the *Remarks.*
Surgeon, Mr. *Still;* now Mr. *Fisher.*
Salary, *21I,* for Felons and Common-Side Debtors.
Number of Prisoners, Debtors. Felons, &c. Debtors. Felons, &c. l800, June Qth,--17--21. 1802, Jan. 1st,--12--24. 1803, Oct. 26th,--16--24. 1806, Oct. 6th,--14--ii. 1807, Sept. 25th,-14--30.

Allowance, formerly to Debtors, none. See *Remarks.* But in 1804, the Magistrates humanely granted to the Poor, or Common-Side Debtors, one pound and a half of bread each per day; and at the Easter Sessions they increased it to one pound and three quarters. It is sent, in loaves to that amount, from the Baker's, and I have found them to be of full weight.

Felons and Petty Offenders have a loaf daily of best wheaten bread, weighing one pound and ten ounces. REMARKS.

This Prison, called *Flskerton-Anger Gaol,* takes its name from the Parish in which it stands, near a fine stream; and is also one of the County Bridewells.

On the duter-gtitej towards the street; is painted, *Pray remember the Poor bettors' Box.*

The Debtors' court-yard, which is separated from that of the Felons, by a double iron palisade, (placed at such a distance as to prevent their conversing with each other,) is sufficiently large to admit of the Debtors' playing at Tennis, Fives, &c. There is no day-room either for them or Felons; but two might very conveniently fefe made, where a cart-house and stables now stand.

For Master's-Side Debtors there are four rooms in the Keeper's house: one of which, 11 feet square, has a fire-place in it, and four beds at 2. *6d.* per week, two sleeping in a bed: But if any Debtor have a room and bed to himself, he pays 5. per week.

Common-Side Debtors have only one room to eat and sleep in, of 20 feet by l6 It was formerly without bedding, or even straw: but in 1804, the County kindly allowed a straw-in-canvas bed, and two blankets, to every poor Debtor *gratis.* Here is a fire-place, but no *firing allowed.* The room was extremely dirty, not having been white-washed for many years. Over this are two rooms, (to which the ascent is by a stone stair-case from the court-yard,) set apart for *Infirmaries:* These have also fire-places, but were equally dirty as the former, and filled with lumber. In the smaller room Women Debtors are occasionally confined. At my last visit, in 1807, I found this room clean, and a Woman in it.

The Felons' court-yard is separated from that of the Debtors, on one side by a wall, and on the other by palisades, as above noticed. It is 65 feet by 34; and at the upper end of it are four small arches, for the Prisoners to stand under, if it be rainy when they are let out.

Their sleeping-wards are close to the river, and consist of three stories: That on the ground-floor has twelve cells, of about 10 feet *6* inches by *9* feet 6, and) feet high to the crown of the arch. Each cell has two wooden doors; the inner one, with an iron-grated aperture, of 7 inches by 4; and on the opposite side of the cell is an iron-grated window, with inside shutters. Every cell contains a wooden bedstead, straW-in-'sacking bed, and one or two blankets. The floors are of brick, and all the cells open into a narrow passage, hardly 3 feet wide.

The next story contains sixteen cells, and the upper story has the same number. In the centre of each story is a sewer, with a water-pipe well supplied, to prevent its being offensive. On the two upper stories the Turnkeys have their sleepingrooms; and at the top of the whole building is an alarm-bell.

The *Chapel* is on the Debtors'-Side of the Prison, and has a pew for the Gaoler, but no gallery. The Debtors are placed on one side; the Felons on the other; and the Women in the middle of the area, in sight of, and almost close to each other. Any Debtor refusing to attend Chapel is locked up during Divine Service; and it is the custom here, to lock up every Debtor in his room, from two o'clock on Sunday till four, that the Turnkey may go to Church. Ever since the accession of the late Chaplain, Mr. *Malham,* in 1796, and the appointment of Mr. *Harrison,* his immediate successor, the sacred Service has been regularly performed. Previously, however, great complaints were made of sad remissness in this respect; which (exclusive of other considerations) was doubly cruel, as it deprived the Prisoners of wholesome air, by thus being locked up the whole day.

In fact, this Gaol has received little improvement since Mr. Howard visited it in the year 1788; and "it still retains all the *severities of* the *Old School."* This, however, is the more to be wondered at, as I am assured that the Gaol is frequently visited by the Magistrates. The old Keeper, (now dead,) paid no attention to my Remarks, in the several visits I made for years together. Security from escape, by main force, seemed to be his chief, and indeed his only object .

At my last visit his Widow said, *"*that during the whole time her Husband kept the Gaol, which, I think, was six and twenty years, there had not been *one Escape."* From what I had seen, this did not surprise me; but I was never able to learn the number of deaths within its walls; nor, indeed could I procure any book or account relative to it. There were no Rules and Orders; and it was with much difficulty that, in l802, I could make out the following useful document, which is now *not "*Table Of Fees. *£. s. d. "*For entering and discharging every Action on process, *Capias,* or *Latitat* ------------------1 0 0

Entering and discharging of every second Action------Oloo

Entering and discharging every *Capias utlegat. ------*Oloo

To the Under-Keeper, or Turnkey, each Action or Writ----0 10

Felons' Fees are abolished."

There does not appear to be any Examination made either into Receipts or Disbursements in this Gaol; the whole seems to rest with the Keeper. I could obtain no account of the several monies arising from *Donations to the Prison,* since my visit in 1802 to the last. The Gaoler said they were lost, or destroyed.

The learned Editor of Hale's History of the Pleas of the Crown, declares that "Fetters ought not "to be used, unless there is just reason to fear an escape; as where the Prisoner is unruly, or makes an ' attempt to that purpose: otherwise, notwithstanding the common practice of Gaolers, it seems alto"gether unwarrantable, and contrary to the mildness and humanity of the Laws of England, by which. "Gaolers are forbidden to put their Prisoners to any pain or torment."

From the only book extant I copied as follows: *£. s. d.* 1806, Dec. 31, Dec. Balance due to the Prisoners-----18 0 2f 1807, Collected by the Turnkey's box 10 86

Rev. Dr. Ekins, Dean of Sarum--------110

A Lady unknown------------110

Interest of Mrs. Smith's Legacy--------1150

Grand Jury, Lent Assize----------1136

Mr. Beeby, Espences of a Prosecution--------110

John Paul Paul, Esq. High-Sheriff, 1806 5 5 0 7th May. Members for the County, 5/. 5s. Ditto for the County *Si. 5s.* 10 10 0

Grand Jury, Summer Assize--------- 156 £. 52 0 8

Of the Chaplain's Salary of 50/. twenty pounds *per annum* is paid by Lord Weymouth, as the Bequest of Thomas Thynne, Esq. who long since bound for the payment the Manor of Wrobly and Ross, in the County of Hereford. The Bequest was recognized by his Lordship in a Deed of Settlement, dated 2d November, 17oQ. The Bishop of Salisbury sends every Christmas forty shillings worth of meat, and twenty shillings worth of bread. The Earl of Pembroke pays a Legacy of Five Pounds a year out of the Manor of Swallow-Cliff in this County; part to the Chaplain himself; *viz.* a guinea for a hat; and the remainder to be by him distributed amongst all descriptions of Prisoners. The one pound fifteen shillings, being the interest of fifty pounds, left by Mrs. Smith of Salisbury, is likewise divided amongst them.

No Memorial of any Legacy is displayed or hung up in the Gaol. Every Christmas, one of the Turnkeys goes through the City, and adjacent parts, with the box before-mentioned. The Collection, when I was here in 1802, amounted to 9/. 18s. *4d.* and it is regularly laid out by the Keeper, as he informed me, in purchasing meat for the Felons.

I cannot close this narrative without a few Remarks on the *Felons' Gaol.* Their cells are very damp, and the lobbies, or passages, only three feet wide. Young Novices in vice, and inveterate Offenders, Vagrants and faulty Servants, are alike promiscuously confined here; and when let out for airing, it is *but for one hour only* out of the twenty-four. I happened to be there during that hour in the wintry month of January, 1802. There was a heavy fall of snow, sleet, and rain; it was extremely cold; and yet, upon opening their door, the Prisoners (seventeen Felons, and seven for Misdemeanors) rushed out into the midst of it, eagerly gasping, as it were, for a mouthful of fresh vital air. Some of them were cruelly ironed with a sort of fetters, called *Bolts* and *Sheers*; Under the former of these the Prisoner cannot move either foot four inches before the other: the latter having a joint in the middle, he may walk, though with difficulty; but his feet, both night and dayr are kept 13 inches asunder.

I saw here *no proportion of punishment* for the several offences, and, consequently, no suitable distinction of guilt. A run-away apprentice, only 13 years of age, was amongst those let out for air and exercise; and, like the rest, associated with a number of the worst description.

Prisoners under Sentence of Death are executed in the Gaol-Yard, and the Church bell tolls. The *Felons* are brought out of their cells, and placed in the Chapel, in full view of the awful ceremony; and the *Debtors* are locked up till it is over.

No County clothing is yet allowed; and of course I found the Prisoners miserably ragged and dirty. No bath supplied, although one might so easily be made from the adjacent river of fine water. No oven to purify infected or offensive apparel. I understand the Earl of Radnor has determined to bring the subject of clothing before the next Quarter Sessions.

The Debtors' lodgings are very highly charged, at 2. 6d. per week, for two sleeping in a wretched old bed, destitute of curtains; and four beds in one room.

Since the appointment of the present Gaoler, the Clauses against Spirituous Liquors are stuck up, but not the Statute for Preserving the Health of Prisoners.

It has given me great pleasure to find by the papers, that this abominable Gaol is to be presented as a nuisance; and that the County intend soon to erect a *new one;* for whose Government it is devoutly to be hoped, that good *Rules and Orders* will be not only established, but enforced.

SANDWICH. *Kent.*
The Gaol and Bridewell.
Keeper, *Nathaniel Bradley.* No Salary.
Fees, for Felons, 13. *Ad.*; for Bridewell Prisoners, 6s. 8d.

Chaplain, none appointed; but the Rev. Mr. *Conant* officiated occasionally in 1806; and the Rev. Mr. *Bunce* now attends those who are committed for heinous offences, or are desirous of spiritual comfort.

Surgeon, Mr. *Curling;* who makes a Bill.

Number of Prisoners, 1S04, Sept. 24th, Three. 1806, Aug. 10th, None.

Allowance, *four-pence* a day, or *six-pence,* according as bread is dear or cheap.

Court of Conscience Debtors are sent here for twenty days, but *never exceeding twenty eight days confinement;* during which the Plaintiff is obliged to allow *3d.* per day; so that few of this description are confined here new..

REMARKS.
This Prison is situate in *Jail Street,* and on the ground-floor fronting the Street has one room, 18 feet by 16, with boarded floor, an iron-grated window, and fixed sloping blinds; a crib bedstead, straw, and two blankets for each Prisoner.

Above stairs are two rooms, about 18 feet square; one with a fire-place; an irongrated window in each, opening toward the Street, with fixed Venetian blinds.

In the court-yard are two other rooms, called *The Bridewell,* supplied with crib bedsteads; but no fire-places. On a stone Tablet over them in front, is inscribed: "This House Of Correction was built in the year 1756, in the Mayoralty of Joseph Stewart, Esq. at the Joint Expence of the
Parishes in *Sandwich,* the Parish of *Walmer,*
and the Vills of *Ramsgate* and *Sarr."*

Hemp blocks are fixed in the Bridewell; but *no Employment, though Prisoners are here committed to hard Labour!*

Any Prisoner is permitted to work, however, if he can procure the means from without; and has, in this case, the whole of his earnings, but not the Gaol Allowance.

There is no water accessible to the Prisoners; and the court-yard being deemed insecure, they have not the use of it.

The SAVOY. *Strand, London.*
Prison exclusively appropriated for the Military.
Keeper, Captain *Bass.* Salary, 150/.
Surgeon, Mr. *Beckitt.* Salary, 20. per day.

Number of Prisoners, 3d July, l811, Nine.
(Three of the Guards; Five of the Line; and one from the Militia.)

Allowance, nine-pence a day each, paid to the Keeper.
REMARKS.
The once very interesting structure so called, derived its name from Peter, Earl of *Suvoy* and Richmond, whose sister Beatrix is recorded to have been the Mother of Five Queens. It was originally built by this Nobleman, about the year 1245, and he afterwards gave it to the Monks of Mountjoy. From them his niece, Queen Eleanor, wife of Henry III. , and one of the daughters of Beatrix, purchased it for her son Henry, Duke of Lancaster; by whom it is said to have been enlarged and beautified, at no less an expence than 52,000 Marks.

In 1357, John, King of France, resided here in captivity for some years; and again occupied it on his magnanimous return hither in 1363, until his death ; at which period it was considered as *one of the finest palaces in this Country.*

It was burnt to the ground in 1381, by the rebellious insurgents of Kent and Essex, who had taken some dislike to John of Gaunt, Duke of Lancaster, the then Proprietor. It was afterwards rebuilt by King Henry VII., for a *Hospital;* together with a handsome *Chapel,* first dedicated to Jesus Christ, his Mother, and St. John the Baptist; and he also purchased lands in maintenance of it, for the relief of one hundred poor people. Over the door fronting the Street stood once the following Inscription:

"1505.

"Hospitium hoc, inopi Turbe, Savoia vocatum,

"Septimus Henricus fundavit ab imo Solo."

'' r Itirfc '1

The *Palace* in question had often been destroyed by fire, and undergone many changes, as may be seen more at large in our City Historians, and other respectable Writers-J. The *Hospital* was at length suppressed; and its revenues, in Queen Elizabeth's time, were finally given to the Metropolis, in aid of the hospitals of Bridewell, Christ Church, and St. Thomas. The Chapel has since been con stituted a rectorial parish church for the Precinct; and is reckoned, in the Bills of Mortality, as one of the seven parishes of the City and Liberty of Westminster, by the name of *Saint Mary le Savoy.*

This Prison, for the *Military,* now consists chiefly of the old buildings, as distinguishably composed, in the antient style, of free-stone and flints. It has a spacious court-yard, paved with flag-stones, and is well supplied with water. A large day-room opens into it, which is furnished with tables, benches, and a fire-place; and coals are allowed for it throughout the year. One small room is set apart for This memorable event affords a most striking Lesson for Princes. The Terms of the Treaty between the conqueror, Edward III., and the Court of France, were indeed rigorous and severe; but John possessed such Fidelity and Honour, as determined him, at all hazards, to execute them on his part, in spite of every personal inconvenience. His Council endeavoured to dissuade him from so rash a design as his coming back to England; But John's repl) (too glorious ever to become trite) imposed silence on every hearer; nor could they resist the unanswerable argument which he advanced on that trying occasion: "Although good Faith," said he, "were banished from the rest of the earth, yet she ought still to retain her habitation in the breasts of Kings." f See Stowe's Survey; Weever's Funeral Monuments; Newcourt's *Repertorium*; Maitland; Nor thouck; Entick i and Pennant.

the refractory; another, called the *Guard-room,* is supplied with barrack-beds for twelve Prisoners; a third has the same accommodation for sixteen; and above these is a very large barrack apartment for forty.

The *Black Hole,* (above stairs,) is well ventilated, though gloomy; and the Prisoners there are allowed either a rug or a blanket in the Winter season. The spacious Infirmary has two large sash windows, looking toward the Thames; and close by it is a room for the nurse. Here are also a stove to purify infected or foul clothes, a copper for warm water, and a tub, which is used as a bath. In this irregular mass of building there are likewise two store-rooms, and several others, which I pass over; but the whole are lofty, well ventilated, and clean. The bedding provided for the whole Prison, except the Black Hole (to which a rug or blanket only is allowed in Winter,) consists of a paillasse, and bolster, filled with long wheaten straw, two blankets, two hempen sheets, and a rug.

On the whole, the condition of this Prison is greatly improved, since it was honoured by the visits of my Predecessor, Mr. Howard; particularly in the years 1776, and 1779, when it began to be safe, and wholesome.

SCARBOROUGH. *Yorkshire.*
The Town Gaol.
Gaoler, *Mary Grant.* Salary, 20/. Fees, Debtors, *6s. 4d.*; Felons, *6s.*
Number of Prisoners, 1800, Aug. 10th, Debtors, Four. 1802, Aug. 28th, Two. No Criminals.

Allowance, none, except certificated as Paupers: and then, the same as the poor of their respective parishes.
REMARKS.
This Gaol is over the Newborough Gate, at the entrance into the Town. The apartments below are occupied by washer-women, employed by the Gentry visiting this place; and the small court-yard is used to dry clothes in; so that the Debtors have no use of it! The only place they have to walk in is a lobby, about 9 yards long, and 4 feet wide.

Debtors have four well-ventilated and airy sleeping-rooms, to three of which the Keeper furnishes a bed, at *3d.* per night each; the fourth is for those who find their own bed, and pay *6d.* a week. No water accessible to the Prisoners, nor any to the Gaol, but what is brought. The Felons' Prison is upon the ground-floor, on the other side of the gateway; and consists of four cells, about 9 feet square, and 7 feet high. Two of these are Dungeons, four steps below the ground, with straw on plank bedsteads, very damp and dirty; but whitewashed while I was there. The iron-grating of the farthest Dungeon is just over an open and very offensive drain. A small court for the Felons might be made from the waste ground adjoining; and the common sewer's being arched over would make this part of the Prison more healthy...

The Clauses against Spirituous Liquors were hung up, and underneath written:
"Ordered, by the Bailiffs, that the Gaoler do provide fresh water for the Prisoners every morning, and that the same be placed in such convenient part of the Gaol as the Prisoners may have access to. That such of the Prisoners as are unable to work, or cannot find employment, and have no other means of subsistence, shall, on application to the Magistrates, be supplied with provision from the poor-house. John Travis, Town Clerk." SELKIRK. *Roxburghshire, Scotland.*
The Town Gaol.
Gaoler, *Gurney Tuck.*

Allowance, Criminals, Sixpence a day.
REMARKS.
This Gaol was finished in 1806, and, except that of Dumfries, is the only one in Scotland which has *court-yards* for the Prisoners. It stands on a rising-ground, and its boundary wall encloses about half an acre.

The Keeper's house has a proper reception-room, 11 feet by 7, and a Committeeroom, 11 feet square. It is detached from the Gaol in front of it; and a small garden, of about 30 feet, intervenes.

The centre building, which is the Gaol, has a day-room or kitchen for Debtors, 14 feet square, with a fire-place; to which a court-yard adjoins, of 66 feet by 4, with a convenient sewer.

In the chamber-story are three sleeping-rooms, with boarded floors, which have iron bedsteads and mattresses. Debtors are here alimented, as in the other Gaols of Scotland, according to the discretion of the Magistrates.

For *Felons* there is a court-yard, about 18 feet square; and for lesser Criminals another, about 16 feet square; a small day-room, with a fire-place; four work-rooms, 8 feet 6 by 6 feet 6; and a kitchen, 14 feet 6 by 8 feet 6.

In the chamber-story are three sleeping-cells for Felons, &c. stone-floored, and furnished with iron bedsteads, hair mattress, two blankets, and a rug each. For Women Criminals here is a court-yard 16 feet square; with two work-rooms and two sleeping-rooms, fitted up like those for the Men. The sewers of this Prison are inoffensively and conveniently placed.
SHEFFIELD. *Yorkshire.*
The Town Gaol.
It occupies the *lobbies* under the Town-Hall; and consists of three dark cells, which open into a narrow passage, the largest 8 feet square, and 6 feet high: each of their doors has an aperture, for ventilation and light, of 6 inches diameter! Here are plank bedsteads, with straw on the floors, and an offensive sewer in the corner of each wretched cell.

When the Quarter Sessions are held

in this Town, Offenders, as a sample of discomfort, are locked up for a night or two in this dreary Prison. In August 1802, though in the day-time, I went into it with a lighted candle. Prisoners at that time, none.

SHEFFIELD.
Eccleshall Gaol.
Gaoler, *William Needham.* No Salary.

Fees, on Discharge, Sixpence. Garnish, 1. *2d.*

Prisoners' allowance, and regulations, the same as for the *Low-Court Debtors* in the Town.

REMARKS.

This Prison, for the Manor of Eccleshall, is the property of Earl Fitzwilliam, and was built about twenty years since.

Here is a court, 18 yards by 15, with a pump in it. Adjoining are a large day-room, about 14 yards square, in which the Debtors work; and two lodging-rooms, each 18 feet by Q, with two large glazed windows in both. The latter rooms are partitioned off, to receive six Debtors in each, singly; who find their own beds, or straw.

The average number of Prisoners here is five; but there were none at my visit on the 14th of August, 1802.

&Cf" In no one of the Sheffield Prisons was the Act hung up, for preserving the Health of Prisoners, nor the Clauses against Spirituous Liquors. Neither did I find any religious care taken of them. It was therefore with less surprize, that I noticed Debtors busily employed in sifting cinders openly on a Sunday. How forcibly does that sentence in our Burial Service for the Dead, "*Ashes to Ashes, Dust to Dust*" strike home upon the anticipative and reflecting mind!

SHEFFIELD. Forks/lire.
The Debtors' Gaol.
Gaoler, *Godfrey Fox.* Salary, none.

Fees, in the High Court, *ll. 5s.* In the Low Court, *sixpence*.

Garnish, (not yet abolished,) for High-Court Debtors, 2. *6d.*; Low-Court ditto, 1. *2d.* This, however, I understand, is expended in coals, candles, and soap, for mutual benefit.

Chaplain, none; nor any religious attention paid to the Prisoners.

Surgeon; Mr. *Moorhouse* attends the Sick in Prison, as Surgeon for the Overseers of the Poor; from whom he has a Salary.

Number of Debtors, High Court. Low Court.
1801, Nov. 14th,------4-------14. 1802, Aug. 14th,------5-17. 1805, March 13th,------7-------15.

Allowance, none; but casual relief, from the Overseers of the Poor, to those who cannot work: in which case, High-Court Debtors have per week, 3s. and Low-Court Debtors, 2.

REMARKS.

This Gaol, for the Liberty of Hallamshire, is the property of the Duke of Norfolk, Chief Bailiff of that Liberty, and Lord of the Manor of Sheffield. It is appropriated to Debtors only; and these are of two descriptions, commonly called *HighCourt* and *Low-Court* Prisoners.

The High-Court Prisoners are detained for Debts above ten pounds, by process from the Courts at Westminster, directed to the Chief Bailiff of the Liberty of Hallamshire, &c.; and are entitled to the same legal privileges as the Prisoners in Yorkcastle. They have a day-room, about five yards square, which has two windows that look into the street; and four rooms up-stairs, two for Men, and one for Women to sleep in: the fourth is a work-shop. The Keeper furnishes beds at 10-rf. per week each, and two sleep in a bed.

The Low-court Prisoners are detained for Debts under 40. by virtue of a process from the Court-Baron of the Manor of Sheffield, held under a particular Act of Parliament obtained for that purpose; directing that three months imprisonment shall discharge the Prisoner from Debt and Costs, if the same be not sooner paid or satisfied. They have two rooms, about 5 yards by 4 each, with fire-places, and iron-grated windows looking into the court; and "in these rooms they work and sleep, which makes them filthy beyond description. Four rooms were lately added, at the top of the house, one of which is for the Women at night. Prisoners find their own straw and firing. The court-yard has a damp earth floor, and is 12 yards by 6. It is the only one, and where both sexes associate together. At my visit, Sunday, 15th August 1802, the Low-Court Prisoners were busy sifting sinders in it; the ashes of which they sell for three shillings per load. They had then about two cart loads, which were to be fetched away next day. Upon conversing with the civil and communicative Gaoler, I found their debts were frequently for the non-payment of ale-house-scores; and this I have observed to be the case in most large manufacturing towns, where idleness and drunkenness prevail. It would operate a good effect, if, in the Bills for the Recovery of *Small Debts,* there were a *clause to prohibit arrests for those contracted in public houses.* The actions entered in Sheffield Court every three weeks are on an average, *three hundred!* and, the Gaol being small, it frequently happens, that there are more warrants against the Persons of Defendants, than can be executed between court-day and court-day.

There is no difference, in the length of time of commitment, between one penny damages, and 39.V. lid.: to either of which the Costs are always added, and of the same amount, viz. *ll.gs. 6d.* on trial, and 17. *6d.* on enquiry.

Water is accessible to all during the da', and to fill their pitchers at night.

SHEFTON MALLET. *Somersetshire.*
The Bridewell.
Keeper, *Henry Shroll,* Sheriffs Officer. Salary, 75/. Fees, 13s. 4rf. SeeRemarks. Chaplain, none. Divine Service never performed.

Surgeon, Mr. *W. A. Goldsborough;* makes a Bill.

Number of Prisoners, 1801, Dec. 26th,Twenty-six. 1S06, Sept. 20th, Twenty-one.

Allowance, sixpenny worth of standard wheaten bread per day; which in 1801 I found to weigh two pounds five ounces the loaf.

REMARKS.

The Keeper's house commands a view of this Bridewell, in every direction. Here are no Debtors.

The Male-Felons have a spacious

court-yard, llC feet by 00; a day-room, 23 feet by *16,* and 10 feet high; also three lodging rooms; the first 16 feet square, and 10 feet high; but in which no one slept, it being made a depository of lime and rubbish. The second lodging-room is 24 feet by 12, of the same height as the former, and had eleven bedsteads in it. The third is of the same dimensions as the first, and contained ten bedsteads.

Here are likewise four cells for *solitary confinement,* each 12 feet by 10, and 8 feet high; in two of which a Man and a Woman were confined. These are supplied *now,* by the County, with a wooden crib bedstead, straw-in-sacking bed, and one blanket. The bedstead and blanket were added a few years since, (I think at the Easter Sessions in l8o1,) inconsequence of several Prisoners having suffered fatally from there being none.

In the Women's department is a smaller court-yard, 59 feet by 19; a day-room, 13 feet by 12, and 8 feet high; a sleeping-room, 25 feet by 12, 7 feet *6* inches high, with nine bedsteads, &c. in it, as in the Men's Ward; and two small rooms used as cells, 12 feet by 10, and 8 feet high: and in these are three bedsteads.

The cells above mentioned have all stone-floors, but no fire-places: Their irongrated windows, that formerly served as ventilators, were stopped up at the time of my visit.

There are two bathing-tubs here, but no oven. The Prisoners wear the County clothing from their first admission. The Male-Felons are washed and shaved once a week; and all have clean linen every week.

Fifteen shillings is allowed to the Keeper, for every Prisoner removed to Wells, four miles off; and the same also, if remanded hither, or conveyed on to the place of trial. At the Sessions in 1801, the number of Prisoners was 93.

Firing, for day-rooms, is allowed by the County, and straw, whenever wanted.

Here is *no Chapel:* nor any *Employment* provided. The Men and Women, I was informed, are kept distinct perpetually. This is decorous, and indispensably needful. But, it is painful to add, that of the males, young beginners, in error or in vice, and old offenders, are here promiscuously mingled together in perilous association. Unruly Apprentices, with Felons of experience, must surely feel far worse than the mere pressure of personal seclusion from the world at large. Imprisonment is bad enough: But what is this, compared with a daily exposure, amidst evil communications, to principles of depravity, and the horrid, the almost certain chance of infamy, acquired in a receptacle intended for moral reformation!

In the Men's court, were large loose stones lying scattered about, that seemed to call loudly for a removal. The Prison is, in general, very damp; yet no Infirmary for the sick. Water is constantly accessible to the Prisoners. They are all let out, I understand, early in the morning, and locked up again at dusk. The Prison is white-washed at least twice in the year. The Act for Preservation of Health, and Clauses against Spirituous Liquors, are very properly and conspicuously hung up. i . i '' SHREWSBURY. Shropshire.
The County Gaol.
Gaoler, *Richard Cartwright.* Salary, 300/.
For Conveyance of Transports, *Is.* per mile..
Fees, Debtors as per Table: But the Under-Sheriff demands a Fee of 7. 6d. upon discharge of a Common Writ; and from those under execution *Is.* in the pound, if under 100/.; but if above 100/. then *6d.* in the pound.
Felons, no Fees.
Garnish, abolished.
Chaplain, Rev. *W. G. Rowland;* now (1809) Rev. *Chas. Powlett.* Salary, 70/. Duty, Prayers every Thursday, and a Sermon every Sunday, Good Friday, and Christmas-day.
Surgeon, Mr. *William Thomas.* Salary, 50/. for Debtors and Felons.
Number of Prisoners, Debtors. Felons, &c.
1802, Nov. 3d,------*12* . v 58. 1803, Sept. 11th,------11--81. 1809, Nov. 20th,-.----12------45.

Allowance, Debtors, 1 lb. 8 oz. of wheat bread, which is made by the Female Convicts, and baked in the Gaol. Felons have the same allowance of bread, and one penny in cheese, or butter. Transports have the King's Allowance, of *2s. 6d.* per week.

REMARKS.
This Gaol, which is likewise the House of Correction, is near the Castle, and was first inhabited in 1793-The boundary-wall encloses two acres of ground, and is 16 feet high. The entrance in front is called the Porter's Lodge, and over the gate is a bust of Mr. Howard. In the door are two apertures to receive donations, *viz.* "To Debtors in a state of Industry," and "To Prisoners in a state of Reformation." The ground-floor, on the left, has the Turnkey's apartments, and his sleeping-rooms are above. On the right hand is the Lazaretto, with a hot and cold bath, and an oven to fumigate and purify Prisoners' clothes; which are taken from them on admission, and the Gaol Uniform put on.

Up-stairs are two reception-rooms, a room for the Irons, and a sitting-room (with a fire-place) for the Clergyman, who there performs his last offices to persons under sentence of death. They suffer on the flat roof above.

The court in front of the Keeper's house is about 20 yards square, and the Inner Turnkey's lodge adjoins. Master's-Side Debtors have a court-yard 36 feet square, a day-room 14 feet by 12, and eleven sleeping-rooms with boarded floors: they sleep single, and pay 4. per week for County furniture; but if they furnish their own beds, *2s.* per week. Common-Side Debtors have a court-yard, 70 feet by 39, a dayroom, 20 feet by 14, and fourteen sleeping-cells, 7 feet by *6,* with arched roofs and brick floors; to which the County allows a bedstead, a hair mattress, a pair of sheets, one blanket, and a rug in Summer, and two blankets in Winter. No firing is allowed, except the Debtor be very poor; but in severe weather they have frequently coals given them, the cost of which is only _d. per hundred weight. The name of every Prisoner who does not attend Divine Service is inserted in a book kept for that purpose. A Manufacturer, or Task-master, is employed by the County, with a Salary of 50/. *per annum,* who furnishes work, and deducts one-third of the. Prisoners' earnings, which is paid to the County-treasurer: but if the Debtor can have the means of labour brought to him from without the Prison, he receives the whole of his earnings. Female Debtors have a court-yard, with eight sleeping-room?, and are under the same regulations as the Men. Here are also two courts and rooms for Male and Female King's-Evidence, and two for Male and Female refractory Prisoners. Female Felons before trial have likewise a court-yard, and eight sleepingcells: After trial they are removed to another court-yard, which has twelve sleeping-cells.

Capital Male-Felons, before and after conviction, have each a spacious court, about 71 feet by 67, with day-rooms, and forty-four sleeping-cells. Petty MaleFelons, in the like circumstances, have courts of the same dimensions, and thirtyeight sleeping-cells.

Lewd Women aad Vagrants have a court-yard, with nine sleeping-cells. Male and Female disorderly Servants and Apprentices, have each their separate courts, and fifteen sleeping-cells: and Male Vagrants and Deserters have likewise a separate court, with sixteen sleeping-cells.

Besides all these, there is a detached Infirmary, with separate courts, two dayrooms, and four sleeping-rooms, for Male and Female Sick Prisoners, where extra food and wine are provided, by direction of the Surgeon.

Seventy-eight of the Felons' cells have double doors, the outer one iron-grated, and the inner of wood: Each cell has a brick floor, and is of 8 feet 8 inches by feet 7, and 8 feet 10 inches high: they have all arched roofs, and are fitted up with a bedstead, canvas or wadd-hair mattress filled with straw, a hempen sheet, two blankets, a rug, a leather or wooden bucket, and a stone chamber pot.

There are no sleeping-cells on the ground-floor.

The Chapel is in the centre of the building; and the several classes, who enter at different doors, are separated by partitions. Debtors are placed in the gallery.
3
T Table Of Fees,
To be paid by the Debtors in Shrewsbury County-gaol.

"For entering every Action whereon each Prisoner is brought into custody, either by Process, Capias, Latitat, or Execution----

For discharging every Action upon Process, Capias, Latitat, or Execution

For a Certificate of the want of a Declaration, &c. in order to sue out a Writ of *Supersedeas* ---------------

N. B. The following sums to be paid by persons delivering the Declaration, or demanding the Warrant respectively.

To the Turnkey, for receiving and entering every Declaration against a Prisoner in custody----------.----

For each of the three first Causes against a Prisoner

And for every other--------------

Attending every Prisoner to give bail, special bail, Habeas Corpus, or other necessary attendance, out of the Gaol, as directed by the Statute, *Is.* per mile.

And no greater or other Fee shall be taken by the Governor from or on account of any Prisoner."

On a level with the Chapel are six cells, for Prisoners under sentence of death, or solitary confinement. All the cells are well ventilated, and divided by lobbies or passages 6 feet wide. The whole Prison is well supplied with spring-water from a pump, and with river water thrown by a forcing engine into a large reservoir at the top. There are several work-rooms for Men and Women," with a store-house, store-rooms, bake-house, bread-room, and wash-house. A watchman goes round the Prison, and cries the hour, attended by a dog. There is a Committee-Room for the Visiting Magistrates, who are appointed at the Sessions. The Act for Preservation of Health, and Clauses against Spirituous Liquors, are conspicuously hung up.

The whole Prison is very clean, and has excellent Rules and Orders for its good government. When I attended Divine Service here, 11th Sept. 1803, all the Prisoners were present; their behaviour silent, and they were attentive to a very impressive discourse. The Employment of the Felons consists in making shoes, slippers, gloves, and bottle-stands: there are looms likewise for weavers.

1 0 1 0 0 4 SOUTHAMPTON. *Hampshire. The Town Gaol, for Debtors only.*
Gaoler, *Jeffery Truss,* Sergeant at Mace. Salary, 15/.

Fees, at entrance, *4s.* On Discharge, 20. for the first Action, 10. for the second and every other Action; and 2. to the Turnkey. No Table.

Surgeon, when wanted, sent by the Mayor.

Number of Debtors, 1802, March 19th, Four. 1803, Oct. 23d, One. 1S07, Sept. 22d, One.

Allowance, sixpence a day to Paupers, and a bushel of coals per week.
REMARKS.

This Gaol occupies a part of the old Tower, at the farther end of the Town. Here is a small court-yard, 46 feet by 36, not paved; and ducks, fowls, &c. are kept in it. Two rooms, with glazed windows and fire-places, of 16 feet each by 12, to which the Corporation allows a wooden bedstead, woollen mattress, two blankets, and a rug. A room at the top of the Tower is furnished by the Keeper, at 2. *6d.* per week. The Act and Clauses are not hung up, either here, or in the Felons' Gaol, or Bridewell. In 1803, I found the pumps out of repair, and for twelve months no water had been supplied to any of the three Gaols.

SOUTHAMPTON. *Tlte Felons' Gaol.*
Gaoler, *William Dymott,* a Taylor. Salary, 20/. and J 5/. as Sergeant at Mace. No Fees.

Surgeon, Mr. *Keele;* who makes a Bill.

Number of Prisoners, 1802, March 19th, Three. 1803, Oct. 23d, Four. 1807, Sept. 22d, One.

Allowance, sixpence a day, and a bushel of coals per week.
REMARKS.

This Gaol also is part of the old Tower, at the bottom of the Town; and has a narrqw slip, or court-yard, of 34 feet by 7, with a pump and stone sink, but frequently without water in a dry season: Four small rooms on the ground-floor for Prisoners, about 11 feet square, with iron-grated and glazed windows; and fire-places, furnished with a wooden bedstead, straw-in-sacking bed, two blankets, and a rug.

Over the Door of entrance is painted, "Pray remember the Poor Prisoners' Box!" SOUTHAMPTON. *Bridewell,*

Keeper, *Joseph Payne.* Salary, 2*l.* and 15/. as Sergeant at Mace. No Fees. Surgeon, Mr. *Keele:* makes a Bill.

Prisoners, 1802, March 19th, One. 1803, Oct. 23d, Two. 1807, Sept. 22d, One. Allowance, sixpence a day, and a bushel of coals per week.

REMARKS.

This Prison consists of a day-room about 15 feet square, and two sleeping-rooms, 12 feet each by 9; to which the Borough allows a crib-bedstead, straw-in-sacking bed, two blankets and a rug each. There is one room in the Keeper s house, furbished, for those who can pay 4. per week.

SOUTHWELL. *Nottinghamshire.*
The House of Correction, for the County.
Keeper, *James Nicholson.*

Salary, 100/. out of which, at bis option, he either pays the Turnkey 20/. a year, or maintains him.

Chaplain, Rev. *Richard Barrow.* Salary, 20/.

Duty, every Sunday, Christmas Day, and Good Friday.

Surgeon, Mr. *Hutchinson;* who makes a Bill.

Number of Prisoners, Men. Women. 1809, 1st September,-----21-------5.

Allowance, a loaf of 18 ounces good wheaten bread; and one penny, daily, in money, to each.

REMARKS.

The old Prison, (which I have fully described in the Gentleman's Magazine for February, 1807, page 106,) being pulled down, the present House of Correction was opened for the Reception of Prisoners on the 24th of June, 1808.

The whole building, with its several court-yards and areas, occupy about three quarters of an acre of ground. The boundary wall is a regular octagon, *69* yards in diameter, and 17 feet high; with several courses of loose bricks laid on the top, to prevent escapes. The entrance is through the Turnkey's lodge, which has a low.window, calculated for the purpose of general inspection. On the left is a room 14 feet by 11, with a capacious stone bath for the Prisoners; a conduit for spring water, and a pump for soft; a copper to warm the bath, and for washing; and an oven for purifying infected or foul clothes, &c.

On the right, leading to the first story, are two reception-cells for Prisoners, till they have been examined, or for those who arrive in the night; one of them 11 feet by 7, with a fire-place; the other 8 feet square. Also a bed-room for the Turnkey, 14 feet by 11; and under the stair-case a water-closet.

There is a passage through the lodge, leading to a walk flagged with stone, 10 feet wide, and a garden border on each side, about 12 feet wide; with a grass-plat, used for drying linen, similar in size to the other court-yards of the Prison.

The Keeper's house is an irregular octagon, and leads to a hall, which has an opening to the four doors belonging to as many rooms on the ground-floor. Of these, the first on the right is assigned to the Magistrates, and on the left, to the Gaoler. The others behind lead to the kitchen and scullery.

From the centre of the hall below, a circular staircase leads to the chamber story; 'in which is the *Chapel,* containing ten separate pews, four for the Keeper's family, and six for the Prisoners; who are so placed as to be seen by the Clergyman, the Keeper and his Turnkey, but not visible to each other.

The attick story is divided into bed-rooms for the servants, and store-rooms for depositing the various articles supplied by the County for Prison use.

The Prison consists of *three Wings,* which adjoin to the Keepers house, and are perfectly similar.

The first, or North Wing, contains two wards; the former of which is assigned to *Female Convicts,* and has a day-room 13 feet square, opening into the court-yard; *»* with a work-room of the same dimensions, in which, as a laundry, the Prisoners linen is dried and ironed after washing. From these a passage 12 feet 2 inches long, and 3 feet wide, opens to a solitary cell on the left, of 8 feet by *6*; with a water'closet, &c. under the stair-case.

A lobby, or passage of 41 feet 8, and 3 feet *6* inches wide, opens upon the left to a solitary-cell of 8 feet by *6*; with a moveable shutter to the window, for air and light occasionally. Also two cells of the same size, and a double cell, 13 feet by 8, for sick or infirm Prisoners, having two beds in each cell, and a fire-place.

At the extremity of the above passage, a door opens upon a bridge of excellent contrivance; by means of which the Prisoners enter the Chapel within the Keeper's house; and also, on the right hand, to a door leading to the Ward No. 2. This is appropriated to *Male Petty Offenders,* and its chamber-story and cells are exactly like those of No. I. A descending stair-case on the right hand leads back to the Keeper's house. The two wards of this wing are separated from each other by a brick partition wall, 14 inches thick; and each ward consists of a day-room, a working-room, and one cell on the ground-floor, 9 feet 6 inches high; also three solitary sleeping-rooms, and a double cell on the chamber-floor, each 8 feet *6* inches in height. All the passages and cells are arched, and well-ventilated, both by flues on the roofs, and grates in the floors.

In the West Wing, the ward No. 3, is for *Male-Felons* of the first class, and No. 4, for those of the second.

Ward No. 5, in the South Wing, is appropriated to *Male Petit/ Offenders* of the second class, and No. 6, for *Females* of the same description.

To every ward is attached a suitable court-yard, 50 feet long, by from 3,6" down to 10 feet wide, in consequence of the octagon construction of the building. Each court-yard has a stone seat, and stone washing bason: and the ends of them, next to, and farthest from the Keeper's house, are secured by iron palisades, 8 feet high; through which his window commands a complete view of the Prison, whilst the Prisoners are prevented from seeing each other by wooden palings in different places across the Keeper's area; yet so, as that they are always visible to him, though he himself is unseen by them.

The wall of each wing forms the boundary of the respective courts on one side; and a brick wall on the other side, 9 feet high, separates each court from that next adjoining.

A forcing pump, in the court of the ward No. 4, supplies water for the Keeper's house, the Prisoners, and the water-closets; and proper drains and cess-pools are so well constructed and disposed, as to carry off every thing offensive.

To the Keeper's house is attached an excellent garden, of near half an acre, for the growth of vegetables.

The work and day-rooms are all fitted up with grates, small side-ovens, and other accommodations for frugal cookery; a cupboard and shelf for each Prisoner; pegs for hats, a towell, pair of scales, and a quarter of a peck measure. Here is also fixed up an Abstract of *Rules*, with a *Table of Prices* for every article of diet: the latter is revised every Monday, and the purveyor is prohibited from demanding any other price than as specified in the Keeper's Table.

Each cell has an iron bedstead, screwed on bearers, with a straw-inticking case, two sheets, two blankets, and a rug; and every cell door has in it an Inspectingwicket.

Although, amongst the number here confined, some have been under Sentence of Death, and reprieved, *no Fetters are ever used;* nor is the general deportment of such Prisoners apparently different from that of other members of a numerous family, unless that they are more silent, tractable, and industrious. No noise is heard, save that of their implements of labour; and no punishment inflicted, except that of confining the refractory offender, without employment,

in a solitary cell; which, in a case of enormous offence, is totally darkened, by a shutter so constructed as to admit air, while it excludes light.

The means of inspection in this house are such, as render it difficult, if not impracticable, to offend without detection. A violation of the Rules, however comparatively slight, is never passed by with impunity. The Prisoner is ordered into a single cell, and denied the *Privilege* with the *Emolument* of *tVorhing*. Thus the certainty of a small punishment prevents the demand of severity; the irregular are rendered obedient, because they perceive that their superiors are as firmly bound as themselves by the Rules of the House; and thus, convinced that nothing is imposed merely to enhance their sufferings, but to reclaim their minds, they submit with a complacency, that wears more the appearance of gratitude, than of terror or moroseness.

No *Dietary* is here established; but every one purchases daily, out of the maintenance money allowed him, such articles of food, as come within the line of general regulations.

Southwell is not a place of Trade or Manufactory. The sources of Prison-Employment are therefore derived from a Cotton-Mill, about four miles off; and from Nottingham, the County Town, distant 14 miles from the Prison. The work done is for the wholesale traders, who furnish the machinery and implements at a settled rent, and the goods are weekly delivered at their warehouses. A profitable system is thus pursued, both without the need of a capital, and unexposed to the hazard of loss, or the fear of disappointment.

The following Statement is very interesting; and shews, first, the *Nett Profit* arising from the *Employment* of Prisoners in the Nottinghamshire House of Correction at Southwell; together with the *General Expence* of the Prison; from the 24th of June, 1808, to the 24th of June, 1809.

«£. ». d.
Total nett profit from the labour of 147 Prisoners employed 2(1 14 4
County's Share---71180
Keeper's ditto--------43 1 9
Prisoners' Common Share-----57 7 51
Extra Ditto-89 7 if
County's Allowance of Bread and Pence daily, to the Prisoners-----191 11 8
Extra Maintenance, in Sickness---4 6 4£
Ditto Money to Prisoners employed--36 6 3f
Thus the nett'profit from the Labour of *Prisoners employed*
exceeds the whole Expence of maintaining *all the Prisoners in Citstody*, by--„«-» .-»».:» r 3d 10 o£
General Expence of the County Prison at Southwell. sS s. a.
The Keeper's, Chaplain's, and Turnkey's Salaries--120 0 0
County allowance of bread and pence; extra maintenance
in sickness, and extra money to Prisoners employed-232 4 4
Keeper's four Quarterly Bills of Sundries-----98 3 3
Surgeon's Bill-------------38 12 0
Conveyance of Prisoners----------33 00
Total _---Jg.l 19 8.

SPALDING. *Lincolnshire.*
The Bridewell, for the Division of Holland.
Keeper, *Thomas Ives;* now *John Chapman.* Salary, 48/. Ss, Fees, 5. as per Table, hung up.
Surgeon, Mr. *Vyse.* Salary, *12l.*
Number of Prisoners, 1802, Aug. 11th, Four. 1809, Sept. 4th, Three; and Mary Allam, a Lunatick, who had been confined there *jour and twenty years.*
Allowance, sixpence a day. When the Prisoners work they receive three-fourths of their Earnings, and the Turnkey has the remainder.

REMARKS.
The ascent to this Prison is by 12 steps, and the doors open into a boarded gallery. The eight upper rooms (the work-room being divided into two), are 13 feet by 10; chimnies in two of them: all airy, and well ventilated. The eight under rooms are vaulted, 124-feet by 94-, and 7 feet high. The entrance to

four of them is by a trap-door from the upper rooms: The doors of the other four open into the court, in which there is a pump; but, not being secure, the Prisoners have no access to it.

The County allows straw on boarded floors, two blankets, and a rug, to each Prisoner. If the Keeper furnishes a bed, he receives (as *per Table*) *4d.* per night from each, if one only; or, if two sleep together, the same.

The Court of Requests for the Hundred of Elloe, send their Prisoners hither; and the Costs sometimes *exceed the original Debt I'*

The Clauses against Spirituous Liquors are conspicuously hung up, as is also the Act for preserving the Health of Prisoners,, neatly painted on a smallboard. The Prison clean, and excellent Rules for its government are painted and fixed up.

STAFFORD.

The County Gaol and House of Correction.

Gaoler, *John Harris.*

Salary, *2ol.* with three Turnkeys, at 45-each per annum, paid by the County. Fees, for Debtors, see Table. For Felons, 1. *6d.* each copy of Warrant. For Conveyance of Transports a Bill is made. Garnish abolished.

Chaplain, Rev. *Henry Rathhone.* Salary, 35/.

Duty, Prayers every Wednesday; and Sermon every Sunday, Christmas Day, and Good Friday.

Surgeon, Mr. *Hughes.* Salary, 42/.

Number of Prisoners, Debtors. Felons, &c. Debtors. Felons, &c. 1801, Nov. 19th,--18 83. I 1805, Oct. 30th,--r 20--53. 1802, Nov. 1st, 20 55. I 1810, June 23d, 30--95.

Allowance, "Ordered, that the following be the Dietary of Convicted Prisoners, *when in a course of Labour.*

Every morning, for breakfast, each one ounce of oatmeal, one third of a pint of new milk, and one eighth of an ounce of salt, made into porridge with water. Three half pints to each.

Supper, every evening the same as the breakfast.

Dinner, *Sunday,* each half a pound of bacon, and ten ounces of beef, before cooked; and one pound of potatoes, or one pound of cabbage, stripped from the stalk, and fit for boiling.

Monday, soup, two ounces of Scotch barley, two ounces of peas, half a pound of potatoes, one ounce of onions, a quarter ounce of salt each, with the proportion of 20 middle-sized turnips, 10 carrots, 10 parsnips, a handful of parsley and thyme, and a spoonful of pepper, for forty. The potatoes to be boiled in a separate copper, put into the cups, and three half-pints of the soup poured on them. *Tuesday,* two pounds of potatoes each. *Wednesday,* soup, as Monday. *Thursday,* meat, as Sunday. *Friday,* soup, as Monday. *Saturday,* potatoes, as Tuesday.

Each Prisoner one pound of bread every day, and one ounce of salt each every week, to eat with the meat and potatoe dinners.

N. B. Those who do not behave orderly, to have no Sunday dinner; and such as do not perform a given quantity of work, at the discretion of the Governor, to have a potatoe dinner on Thursday, instead of a meat one.

That such Prisoners as have the above Allowance, be not suffered to purchase any article of food whatever.

That the Debtors, and Felons, and other Prisoners, *not in a course of labour,* have each the following allowance of food, viz.

Monday, potatoes, each four pounds. *Tuesday,* two pounds of bread; half a pound of cheese. *Wednesday,* as Monday. *Thursday,* two pounds of bread. *Friday,* as Monday. *Saturday,* three pounds of bread, and half a pound of cheese.

In all cases the potatoes are considsred in the rough, and full grown; a proportionate reduction must be made, when young potatoes are served. The sick to have no allowance of food, but what is ordered by the Surgeon. (Signed.) Harrowby.

John Sparrow. George Talbot." Debtors, who receive the sixpences from their Plaintiffs, have no 'County allowance of food. Such Debtors as are poor, and have no work, have meat and vegetables on Sundays.

i REMARKS.

This Prison is surrounded by a boundary wall, inclosing three acres of ground. The entrance at the Turnkey's lodge, has, on the right hand, a room for the Turnkeys; on the left, a reception-room, for Prisoners to be examined as to their health, before they are admitted into the interior. Here are a warm and cold bath, with an oven for fumigating and purifying their clothes, which are taken from them, and the Prison uniform put on. Above are four reception-cells, 7 feet by 0', and 8 feet high; a store-room for the Prisoners' clothes, and two sleeping-rooms for the Turnkeys. Over these, upon the lead flat, is the place of execution.

In the centre, detached by a neat garden of 30 yards in length by 14, is the Gaoler's house, through the hall of which lies the passage to every part of the Prison.

On the ground floor is the apartment for the visiting Magistrates, the Gaoler's parlour and office, and a small room, used by the Debtors, to see their families and friends, no one being permitted to go into their day-room, or court-yard.

Behind the Keeper's house is the inner court, 65 feet by 40, which leads to the Men-Debtors' day or mess-room, 30 feet by 26, fitted up with two fireplaces, coppers, &c. for the purposes of frugal cookery; and on each side are eight small work-rooms, and two small spaces or slips, where, at stated times, the relations and friends of the Prisoners are allowed to see them. The Men Debtors have a spacious court, of 56 yards by 30, the greater part of which they are allowed to cultivate for their own use; and there are arcades for their accommodation in wet weather. Near this are fifty sleeping-cells, each of *9* feet by 8 feet 6 inches, with arched roofs, well ventilated, and divided by passages, or lobbies, *6* feet wide. To each cell there is an iron bedstead, a straw mat, three blankets, and a coverlet, allowed by the County.

Female Debtors have a separate court-yard, 90 feet by 24; a day-room, 24 feet by 15; and over it a sleeping-room of the same size. They have a like allowance of bedding as the Men, only that instead of iron, their bedsteads are of wood, with sacking bottoms.

For Criminal Prisoners there are fourteen separate courts; the smallest of which, assigned for thirteen Prisoners, is of 13 yards by 11; four are of 35 yards by 18; and the average of the rest, 30 yards by 10.

The Male Felons, before Trial, are divided into two classes, with each a separate court and day-room. They sleep in separate cells, of which there are, twenty-six, of the same size with those for the Debtors. Irons are here used only on Prisoners under Sentence of Death, Transportation, old Offenders, or for refractory behaviour in Prison. The Female Felons, before trial, have also a separate court and day-room, and thirteen separate sleeping-cells.

Male Prisoners, after Conviction, are divided into two classes; each class has its separate court and day-room, and the cells are the same in size and number as those of the Felons before Trial. So likewise the Female Prisoners, after Conviction, are divided into two classes, with work-rooms and cells, the same in number and dimension as those previous to their Trial.

The Male House of Correction Prisoners form also a distinct class, and have a large day-room, which is used as their work-room, and 13 cells, exactly like those / before described. The Female Convicts of the House of Correction are included in the second class of Female Prisoners, after Conviction. The cell of every Convicted Prisoner is fitted up with an iron bedstead, a straw mattress, two blankets, and a coverlet; and in size is 7 feet by 6, and S feet 6 inches high, with arched roofs and double doors, the outer one iron-grated, and the inner of wood. There are no sleeping-cells on the ground floor.

On the first story is a neat *Chapel*, properly partitioned and pewed off, to separate both the sexes, and the different classes confined. Close to which are four large day-rooms, for the several orders of Prisoners, and eightyfour sleeping-cells, divided by well-ventilated lobbies, 5 feet wide.

There are four dark solitary cells set apart for the refractory, and six for those under sentence of death.

The upper story has the same number of day-rooms, and sleeping-cells, together with two store-rooms.

Each class of Prisoners have a stone gallery, with iron railing, which leads to a door opening into their several divisions in the Chapel; where all the Prisoners are bound to attend Divine Service, or, otherwise, punished by an abridgement of their diet.

In the Keeper's house, on the second story, are two large rooms set apart for the Sick, and two store-rooms. The cells are the same throughout the Gaol, except that those for the Debtors have glass windows, and the others wooden shutters.

Here is a room built over a large water engine; adjoining to which is a day-room for Vagrants, and over it a sleeping-room. Deserters, when upon their march, sleep occasionally on straw in the upper room.

The Gaol is well supplied with water, and a sewer is placed in every court-yard.

Transports have the King's allowance, of 2. 6d. a week. All convicted Prisoners are obliged to work; and receive one sixth of their earnings.

There are about three acres of ground without the walls, cultivated with vegetables for the use of the Prison, by those who are sent to the House of Correction.

Many parts of this Gaol are sometimes very damp. The considerate Magistrates therefore humanely allow to the Men-Debtors two hundred weight of coals weekly, from the 1st of October to the 1st of April, and half the quantity per week during the rest of the year: But, if the number of Debtors exceed twenty, they are allowed the above quantity to each fire-place in the room. Female-Debtors are allowed one hundred weight per week all the year round. Felons, before trial, have one hundred weight and a half to each fire, from 1st October to 1st April; one hundred weight for the residue of the year; and convicted Prisoners have one hundred and a half weight weekly to each fire, from the first of October to the 1st of April only. The Sick, whilst in the Infirmary, have always such firing and food as the Surgeon thinks pruper..

The Rui.es and Orders of this Prison, which are excellent, direct "that a *Journal shall be kept by the* Chaplain *and* Surgeon, in books prepared for that purpose, stating the times of their attendance, and their observations when there:" But I was sorry to remark, at my visit in 1S05, that no such minutes had been entered for *ten years,* and the like neglect prevailed in 1810. I should be happy to see the same exemplary attention paid here to the Rules and Orders as I found prevail at *Gloucester;* where these important regulations are punctually observed.

So small a portion of the court-yards is paved, as to prevent this Gaol from ever being kept properly clean.

It appears that on the 11th of October 1796, there was a Balance of 171/. 5,?. remaining in the hands of the County Treasurer, out of a sum which had been subscribed for the benefit of the unfortunate Prisoners, at the time when a fever raged in the Old Gaol: on which day Mr. Wright, the late County Treasurer, bought 300/. in the *Three per Cent. Consols,* in the name of Mr. Hinckley, Clerk of the Peace. The Dividends thereon have been regularly received, and applied to the use of the Prisoners, under the direction of the Visiting Magistrates.

On the 14th of March 1793, it was ordered by the Magistrates, and confirmed by his Majesty's Judges of Assize, that the Fees to be paid by the Debtors in Stafford Gaol, should be as follows.

"Table Of Fees, s. d.

For entering an Action wherein each Prisoner is brought into custody on any Writ or Process---------------106

For every second or other Action-----------60

For the Certificate of a Declaration not having been delivered, in order to sue out a Writ of Supersedeas-----------68

The above deuiandable of the Prisoner. For receiving and entering every Declaration against a Prisoner in custody-----------20

For each Copy of a Warrant against a Prisoner-------34

These to be paid by the persons delivering the Declaration, or demanding the Copy of the Warrant.

For attending on every Prisoner to give bail, or special bail, as on a Habeas Corpus, or on any other necessary occasion out of the Gaol, as directed by the statute, *per mile* -----------10

That no greater or other Fee shall be taken by the Keeper of the Gaol, for or on the account of any Prisoner in his custody: And that all Fees hitherto demandable by law, or custom, by the said Keeper from the County, shall totally cease and determine.

That all the said Fees (except for the Keeper's attendance out of the Gaol) when paid by any Prisoner to the Keeper, shall be accounted for by him to the Publick Fund, in aid of the Debtor's maintenance.

That every Prisoner, who, during his confinement, shall have duly submitted to the Regulations, and who has not been guilty of swearing, drunkenness, or other disorderly conduct, shall receive a Certificate of good behaviour from a Visiting Justice, or from the Chaplain and Governor; which shall be a discharge from all Fees payable to the Keeper or Gaoler.

That the following Charges for lodging, bedding, &c. be allowed.

Table Of Charges For Lodging, &c.
s. d.

Every Person confined in the Sheriffs Ward, finding his own bedding, per week-----------------1 0

Every person, with bedding allowed by the County-------26

Every Person occupying a room in the Keeper's house shall pay per week 2 6 ff with bedding furnished by the Keeper---_----40

The foregoing Rules and Regulations for the Government of the *New Gaol*, for the County of Stafford, were approved and confirmed; and the Chairman was requested to lay the same before the Judges at the next Assizes.

(Signed,) J. Sparrow, Chairman; (Allowed by us,) J. WILSON.
N. GROSE."

The following Order was also made and confirmed at the ensuing Assizes.

"That Debtors shall be permitted to send for, or have brought to them, at seasonable hours, any victuals or clothing: But, in respect to Liquor, no Prisoners shall be allowed either to send for, or to drink more than one pint of wine, or one quart of beer in one day, or twenty-four hours. And if any Prisoner shall be detected in making use of the name of any other Prisoner, for the purpose of obtaining any greater quantity of wine or beer, the Prisoner consenting to lend his name, and the Prisoner using it, shall be incapable of receiving a Certificate of good behaviour; and the Gaoler shall be required to remove them into the Sheriff's or Common Ward." *Stafford, 1st August,* 1793. Allowed by us, KtNYON.
N. Gi.ose."

Account of the Maintenance and Earnings of the Prisoners, from Michaelmas, 1801, to Michaelmas 1802.
£. d
Ordinary County Allowance of Food--
-------293 10 9 *Deduct* the King's Allowance of 2s. 6d. per week to Convicts, under

Sentence of Transportation----------
55 ISO 237 15 9

Extra Expence of food-------------82 14

Total Maintenance-------£.319 17 1

Earnings, by picking Cotton-----------118 84

Ditto by making shoes-------------6138

Ditto by cutting a Drain in the Foregate-Field, Stafford--3 13 0

Sundry other Earnings in the Gaol--------9 85

Total Earnings-£. 198 3 5

From Michaelmas 1802 to Michaelmas 1803.
£. s. d.
Ordinary County Allowance of Food---------26 587 *Deduct* the King's Allowance of *2s. 6d.* per week to Transports--53 5 0 212 3 7

Extra Expcnce of Food-------------74 139

Total Maintenance-------£. 28« 17 4
£. s. d.
Earnings, by picking Cotton-----------11383

Ditto by making Shoes-------------28 142

Sundry other Earnings in the Gaol---------0 3 8

Total Earnings--------£, 202 6 1

From Michaelmas 1803 to Michaelmas 1804.
£. s. d.
Ordinary County Allowance of food--------259 13 3 *Deduct* the King's allowance of *2s. 6d.* per week to Transports--S3 15 0 225 is 3

Extra Expence of food-------------48 50

Total Maintenance-------.£.274 3 3

Earnings, by picking Cotton-----------91 3 7

Ditto by making Shoes-------------24 16 4

Sundry other Earnings in the Gaol---------54102

Total Earnings i. 170 10 I

In the Entrance Door of this Gaol are two apertures to receive Donations. Over the one is is painted

"For Poor Debtors."

Over the other,

"For the Encouragement of Penitence,,

and orderly Behaviour, in

Criminal Prisoners."

STAMFORD. *Lincolnshire.*
The Town Gaol.

Keeper, *Charles Rogers.* Salary, for the Gaol and Bridewell, 31/.; of which *24I.* paid by a Rate, and 7/. by the Corporation Treasurer.

Fees, Debtors and Felons, 10a each. Table hung up, but not signed.

Surgeon, if wanted, is sent by the Mayor.

Number of Prisoners, 1802, Aug. 10th, One.

Conveyance of Transports, if only one, 8/. 8.: if more, *6I. 6s.* each. Allowance, to Debtors, none; to Felons, eightpence per day.

REMARKS..,..

This Prison, built at the Town-hall, has one good room for Debtors in the Keeper's house. I was glad to be informed that none had been committed hither for ten years.

Here is a small court-yard for all descriptions of Prisoners, the use of which for exercise is now permitted them, the walls being raised to a height sufficient for security.

For Criminals, here are two offensive and unhealthy cells, 10 feet by 8, and 7 feet 6 inches high, to which the only admittance of light and air is through a niche in the wall, 3 feet long, 5 inches wide, and an aperture in each door, about 8 inches square.

The Bridewell room is 16 feet by 8, and has only one small window, 2 feet by 20 inches; a perforated door, and in each room a sewer. Water is laid on by a pipe, for which the Gaoler pays ten shillings a year.

Here is no Employment for the Prisoners, and the Bridewell room is too dark to admit of it. The Act for preserving Health, and Clauses against Spirituous Liquors', not hung up.

STIRLING. *Scotland.*
Gaoler, *John Macdonald.* Salary, 50/.

Fees, Felons, none. Debtors, 1. on Caption.

Chaplain, none, nor any religious attentions.

Surgeon, when wanted, sent from the Town.

Number of Prisoners, Debtors. Felons. 180Q, Oct. 21st,-------6 4.

One Man for Bastardy, and two faulty Apprentices.

Allowance, Debtors, as alimented; generally eight pence a day. Felons, three pence a day.

REMARKS.. This Prison, newly built, is on the South side of the Criminal Court in Broadstreet. Under the arches on which it is constructed, there are six sleeping-cells; three of which are 16 feet by 10, and the other three, 12 feet by 8, with flag-stone floors, fire-places, and large grated and glazed sash-windows, which turn on a pivot.

The Main Gaol has on the ground floor five rooms for Criminals, each about 18 feet by 15; with vaulted roofs, and large grated and glazed sash-windows, flag-stone floors, and fire-places.

The «tory above this is for Debtors, and consists of four rooms; one of which is 28 feet by 16, and the other three, 19 feet by 12, with large grated and glazed sash-windows, and fire-places, and to each of these rooms there is a wooden bedstead, furnished by the Town.

The second story has four rooms for Felons, similar to those before-mentioned.

The upper story has two large rooms for Women Criminals, each 28 feet by 26; with fire-places, and grated and glazed windows.

To no part of this Prison is there any article of furniture yet supplied, excepting a wooden bedstead to the Debtors' rooms already noticed. No fuel, no bedding, nor even straw to lie upon. Half tubs serve the purpose of sewers; and no water, but what is brought by the Gaoler.

Here is a small court-yard, indeed; but the Prisoners are not indulged with the use of it.

STOCKPORT. *Clieshire.*
Gaoler, *Thomas Barratt.* Salary, 5/.
Number of Prisoners, 1S09, Nov. 15th, Seven.
Allowance, one pound of bread per day.
REMARKS.

This Prison is for temporary confinement, and has, on the ground-floor, the Keeper's kitchen, parlour, &c. On the right hand, entering the house, is a day-room, 13 feet 10 by 6 feet 9, and 8 feet high; and another day-room adjoining, 14 feet by 9, and 7 feet 6 inches high; with fire-places in both, and iron-grated windows, about 2 feet square.

Above stairs are two rooms for those Prisoners who can pay 1. per night for beds. Others sleep in the two Dungeons, each 9 feet by 6, and 11 feet high, cut out of the rock, to which the descent is by 17 steps. They have wooden bedsteads, loose straw, two blankets, and a rug each; but are both damp, and very offensive.

The Keeper informed me by letter, 23d June, 1810, that no Prisoners sleep in the Dungeons now. Here is no court-yard, but the Prison is supplied with excellent water from a pump. The annual number of commitments is about four hundred.

SUDBURY. *Suffolk.*
The Borough Gaol and Bridewell.
Gaoler, *Richard Wright;* a Baker.
Salary, none. Fees, *4s.* No Table.
Prisoners, 1801, Oct. 17th, and 1810, Sept. 24th, none.
Allowance, Sixpence per day.
REMARKS.

This is a miserable place, for the imprisonment of inferior delinquents, or for their confinement until fully committed for Trial.. (.

It consists of two rooms on the ground floor, about 13 feet square, fronting the Street; having each a fire-place, and iron gratings, through which to breathe, and beg the casual charity of passengers.

Of these rooms, one, called "The *Toll*" has a wooden bedstead, raised about 12 inches from the floor, with loose straw to sleep on. The other, which has also an iron grating towards the Street, contains two sleeping-cells, of about 9 feet by 6, with straw only on the floor; and, as a glaring instance of filthy negligence, a bar of wood laid across one corner of each room, with a little straw underneath it, is the vile substitute for a privy!.

For Women, here is one wretched room, above stairs, equally destitute of furniture, and in a very dilapidated state. They are sometimes, however, indulged by the Keeper with the use of a small court-yard, leading toward his bake-house.

SWANSEA. *Glamorganshire. The Town Gaol. ...*
Gaoler, *David Thomas.* Salary, 5/. 5. Fees, 6s. *8d.*
Number of Debtors, 1803, Oct. 3d, Three. Criminals none.
-Allowance, none; except to such Debtors as are Paupers.
REMARKS.

Here is a small court, with three rooms up a flight of steps in the old Castle, and two above them, for Debtors, who are obliged to find their own beds. For Felons and other Criminal Offenders, a dark room, called the Black Hole, under the Town Hall; where they are confined for a night or two, till committed to the

County Gaol. It has an iron-grated aperture in the door, but no window.

The Sessions for the County are held as follows:

Epiphany Sessions, at Cardiff.—Easter ditto, Cowbridge.—Thomas a Becket ditto, Neath.—Michaelmas ditto, Swansea SURREY.

The County Gaol and Bridewell.

Gaoler, *James Ives.*

Salary, 300/. and in case the Debtors' Fees should not amount to an additional hundred pounds *per annum,* the County make up to him the deficiency. Also for the *Bridewell,* 50/. For the Conveyance of Transports he makes a Bill, and is allowed the expence incurred.

Fees; See Table. Felons here pay no Fees. Garnish, abolished.

Chaplain, Rev. Mr. *Winkworth;* now Rev. *William Mann.*

Duty, Prayers and Sermon on Sunday; and Prayers on Tuesday and Thursday. Salary, 50/.; and 30/. as Secretary to the Visiting Committee.

Surgeons, Messrs. *Saumarez* and *Dixon.*

Salary, 75/. for Prisoners of every description in the Gaol and House of Correction: And five pounds for his travelling charges, to report at the quarter Sessions the state of the Prisoners' health, &c.

Allowance, heretofore *one pound of bread* (but, on the 7th of May 1810, increased to *one pound and a half)* per day, for Prisoners of all descriptions; excepting those Debtors who receive the Sixpences from their Plaintiffs.

REMARKS.

This noble building does honour to the County. It is situate in an open and airy part of Horsemonger-lane, in the Parish of St. Mary, Newington, in the County of Surrey. The boundary-wall encloses about three acres and a half of ground. The Sessions House adjoins it, to which there is a communication from the Prison; and a housekeeper is appointed to keep it clean, with a suitable Salary, and apartments for her use.

The Gaol, which is likewise the County Bridewell, was first inhabited on the 3d of August 1798, and has in front the Turnkey's Lodge: On the ground floor of which is a day-room; another room with a cold bath; and a third is the washhouse, with an oven, &c. Over these are four rooms, of 18 feet by 15, for the Turnkeys to sleep in; and at the top of all is a spacious lead-flat, where Criminals are executed.

After passing through the Lodge, an avenue, paved with Yorkshire stone, leads to the Keeper's house; which is in the centre of the Prison, and from which the several court-yards are inspected.

For Master's-Side Debtors there is a court-yard paved with flag-stone, 75 feet by 30, enclosed by handsome iron palisades, so that a thorough air is admitted; and arcades, paved in the same manner, 31 feet by *26,* under which to walk in wet weather. Close to these is a day-room, 27 feet by 20, with a fireplace; and they have likewise sixteen sleeping-rooms, each 14 feet *6* inches by 9 feet 3, with an irongrated and glazed window. For these they pay as per Table subjoined, which 1 found printed, and put up on the Master's-Side, for the inspection of all persons whatever.

Common-Side Debtors have also a court-yard, with arcades, a day-room, and twelve sleeping-rooms, the same as those on the Master's-Side: But they sleep in hammbcks, and findlheir own bedding.

Women-Debits have a court-yard, about 20 feet square; a day-room, 18 feet square; and four sleeping-rooms, of the same size as the Men's: with wooden bedsteads, to which they also find their own bedding, and pay nothing.

The Men-Felons are of four classes; each of which has a spacious court-yard, neatly paved with Yorkshire stone, and in size about 87 feet by 30, for the Prisoners to take air and exercise in fine weather; or, if it be otherwise, they walk under arcades paved with flag-stone, of about 48 feet by 27. Also a day-room for each class, 27 feet by 20, to dress their victuals in.

Each Felon has a cell, 8 feet 3 inches by 6 feet 9; with iron-grated window 4 feet by 2, a wooden inside shutter, a circular ventilator, of 18 inches diameter in the middle of each cell, a wooden inside door, and an iron-grated one to each. They are all furnished with an elm-plank bedstead, only 22 inches wide, a flock-bed, and pillow, two blankets and a rug: The bedding is shaken and rolled up, and the cells are cleaned every morning.

Here are likewise four day-rooms, with boarded floors, occasionally used for Convicts under sentence of death; each about 26 feet by 18, with a tire-place, a table and benches, and three windows, 6 feet by three, iron-barred and glazed.

The Women-Felons have also a court-yard, about 70 feet by 30, with arcades, day-room, cells, furniture, and accommodations, the same as for the Men-Felons.

The lobbies of this Prison are all well ventilated, and 6 feet 3 inches wide.

Pumps are fixed in all the court-yards; Thames-water is laid on; and at the top of the four corners of the Gaol is a reservoir, each containing about eight hundred gallons of water, supplied from a well by a forcing pump.

Here are four spacious airy rooms, each 25 feet by *16,* set apart as Infirmaries, fitted up with flock-beds, blankets, pillows, and rugs; and adjoining to them are court-yards, 30 feet square, for convalescents to walk in: Also two rooms for nurses, another for the Surgeon, and a fourth with a warm bath.

The *Chapel* is a very neat structure, where the Prisoners are seated in their different classes; and all are required to attend Divine Service who receive the County allowance.

There are in this excellent Prison no less than four cold baths, one warm bath, and an oven for purifying infected or offensive clothing. Of sleeping-cells there are on the ground-floor, 15; first story, 82; and second-story, 80. Total 177.

"Table Of Fees,

"To be taken by the Gaoler of the County of Surrey, from the Debtors of the said

Gaol.

f. d.

For the Discharge of every Prisoner for Debt--------1010

For his Conduct Warrant on his attendance with Prisoners, on-returns of Habeas Corpus by the Sheriff---------- 106

For attending with Prisoners by Rule or Order of Court, or otherwise, to be bailed, or receive Judgement---------- 106

For the use of bed, bedding, and sheets, for every Debtor on the Master's Side of the Prison, for the first night----- __ --06

For every night after the first---------- ---03

For a room, bed and bedding, per week----------3 6."

Debtors committed hither from the King's Bench for any offence, pay no Fees whatever now, as was formerly the custom.

Convicts here, under Sentence of Transportation, do not receive the King's Allowance of *2s. 6d.* per week.

"A List Of Legacies and Donations "To the poor Debtors, on the Common-Side of the County-Gaol, Surrey, heretofore known by the name of ' *White-Lion Prison.*' £. s. d. "A Gift of the Archbishop of Canterbury, to be applied for, every

Christmas, at Lambeth Palace---------- --100 *Thomas Dawson,* a Legacy, paid every Christmas, by the Churchwardens of St. Ethelburga------------090 *Arthur Mouse* ditto, paid by the Fishmongers' Company----0 13 4 *Joan Hackett* ditto, paid by ditto-----------034 *John Stokes* ditto, in bread, yearly paid by the Drapers' Company, between All-saints and Christmas-----------050
Richard Jacobs ditto, every Easter; payable formerly at the Grange-Inn, near Lincoln's-Inn, but now (1810) by Mrs. Ann Starling, of Carey-street, Chancery-lane----------- 200

Margaret Dane ditto, 5th of November, four stone three quarters of beef, and two dozen loaves of bread. The beef is sent in by

Mr.Willson; and the bread by the Fishmongers' Company, who make enquiry, a few clays previously, of the then number of Prisoners,
and the Gaoler applies for the loaves.

The Parish of St. Andrew Undershaft sends, at Christmas, a quantity of beef, the gift of Mr. Ralph Carter. The Leathersellers' Company sends every quarter, 5s. in bread, and *2s.* in money. *Eleanor Gwynrts* Legacy, sixtyfive penny loaves every eight weeks, is sent from the Chamberlain's office. The *Dutchess of Gloucester* used to send one chaldron of coals yearly, during her life; but it seems to beinowdiscontinued, or forgotten."
Whatever money is collected in *Chapel,* at what are cal led the *Condemned Sermons,* is paid into the hands of the Chaplain; and by him laid out for the benefit of the Prisoners, in coals, meat, and other necessaries, at his discretion.

It once was customary for the Executioner to demand, and, by some means or other, to procure six shillings and eightpence, from the Criminal, on his way to execution. This inhuman practice was very properly discontinued on the 16th of July, 17Q9.

Excellent Rules and Orders are made for the Government of this Gaol, which are fixed up in four different parts of it, and signed,

Grantlet, KENYON.
Wm. Russel. Ad MACDONALD.
Leslie. Judges of Assize.

The Magistrates visit the Prison in regular monthly rotation: Their Remarks are entered in a book; and every time the Committee meets, the Surgeon also enters in his book the state of health in which he finds the Prisoners.

All of them are discharged in a *morning,* after breakfast; and have from one shilling to five shillings given them, according to their distance from home.
See an Abstract of the Deed, Giltspur-street Compter, page 334. . The Lent Assizes for the County of Surrey are always held at Kingston; and during that time the Prisoners of this Gaol are confined at the *Stock-House,* and the House of Correction. The Summer Assizes are once in two years at Guildford, and the Prisoners then kept at the House of Correction there. Every other summer they are held at Croydon; and during the time were confined heretofore in stables, now properly converted into a large room, suitable for the purpose. See P. 116.

The Act for Preservation of Health, and the Clauses against Spirituous Liquors, are conspicuously hung up; and the whole Prison is remarkably clean.
The Surrey *Bridewell, or House of Correction,*
Formerly situate in St. George's Fields, is now enclosed within the boundary-wall of the *County Gaol.*

Keeper, *John Spreadbury.*

Salary, 507.; and a share in the Prisoners' earnings, as hereafter mentioned.

He is under the controul of the Gaoler; but receives his Salary from the
County; and the Magistrates only have the power to dismiss him.

Fees, none.

For the Men-Prisoners here are two spacious airy court-yards, paved with Yorkshire flag-stone, about 37 feet each by *29,* for exercise in fine weather; and two arcades, each 27 feet by 23, paved with flag-stones. Also one large workshop, 37 feet square, for those Male-Prisoners, who are employed in picking oakum and knotting yarn. Each Prisoner has a cell, 8 feet 3 inches by 6 feet *9*; with an iron-grated window, 4 feet by 2, a wooden inside shutter, circular ventilator, 18 inches in diameter, double-door, bedsteads and bedding provided, and taken care of, and cell cleaned every morning, the same, in all respects, as those in the County Gaol for the Felons.

The Women-Prisoners have one spacious and airy court-yard, of about 27 feet by 23; together with workshop, cells, bedding, &c. the same, and their employment also, as the Men-Prisoners.

The following is an Account of the Receipt and Nett Profit of the Prisoners' Earnings, from Michaelmas 1802, to Michaelmas 1803.
s. d. g. s. d.
Earnings------------121 1 1

Expences attending the same-----33 90 87 12 1

Deduct Allowance of one third to Superintendant---*29* 4 »

Nett Profit, to Balance----"g.j8 8 1

The average number of Prisoners,

during the above year, was 50. Of the Balance thirty pounds were laid out, under the direction of the Rev. Secretary and Chaplain, in meat, coals, &c. and the remainder distributed as the Visiting Committee thought proper.

Earnings from Michaelmas 1803 to Michael-s. d. gg. s. d. mas 1804---------i11 15 8

Expences attending the work done---24 11 3 87 4 5

Deduct the Superintendent's one third-------29 15

Nett Profit, to Balance----£58 3 o

During the above year the average number of Prisoners was 45. Thirty pounds of the Balance were, as before, laid out in coals and meat by the Rev. Secretary; and the remainder in sundry articles for their use, under the direction of the Visiting Committee....

#3 For the following years to Michaelmas 1810, I have been furnished with similar accounts. The two statements already given might suffice, as the Distribution is similar, and the Balance nearly equal to the foregoing. But, as the insertion will take but little room, and may not only be satisfactory, but exemplary, it is here subjoined. g£. s. d. s£. s. d.

Earnings from Michaelmas 1804, to Michael mas 1805-----91 17 3

   Expences----20 2 10 71 14 5

   Deduct Superintendent's Third-------_ 23 18 1

Ditto, from Michaelmas 1S05 to Michaelmas 1806--------_ 8l 19 4

   Expences 15 n g 66 7 8

   Deduct Soperintendant's Third----.--22 26

Ditto, Michaelmas 1806 to Michaelmas 1807 100 9 11

Expences 15168

84 13 3

   Deduct as above '---------_ _ 28 4 5

Nett Profit .56 8 10

Every Prisoner *committed to hard labour* in this Bridewell, receives one third of his or her Earnings; the Keeper one third; and the residue goes to the County. Every other description of Prisoner receives one half of the Earnings, the Keeper one quarter, and the County has the rest.

When the Sessions are held at Ri/*egdtc*, the Prisoners sent from hence are confined there, generally, for two days in *The Cage:* The lower part of which, for the Men, is about 30 feet square; the upper, for the Women, of the same size; and they have loose straw only to sleep *oiu*

I avail myself with pleasure of this opportunity, to pay my acknowledgments to the Right Honourable Lord Leslie, to Sir Thomas Turton, Bart. *u. p.* for the Borough of Southwark, and to the Visiting Magistrates, who did my worthy friend Dr. Lettsom and myself the honour to accompany us over every part of this wellTegulated Gaol. The cleanliness and good order that prevail throughout it, I have not failed to notice in my Publications on Prisons and imprisoned Debtors, and to it, most probably, may be ascribed its singular healthiness: twelve persons only having died by illness since the 3d of August 1798, when it was first inhabited, although the average number of Prisoners in it is, and has been annually, from 15Q to 200.

SWAFFHAM. *Norfolk.*

The Bridewell.

Keeper, *David Raven.*

Salary, 70/. and one-fourth part of the Prisoners' earnings. No Fees.

Chaplain, Rev. Mr. *Chapman;* now Rev. *Win. Johnson Yonge.* Salary, 30/. Duty, Prayers three times a week, and Sermon on Sundays.

Surgeon, Mr. *Law;* now Mr. *Ross;* who makes a Bill.

Number of Prisoners, 1805, Sept. 2d, Seventeen. 1810, Sept. 5th, Seventeen.

Allowance, on Sunday, two pounds and two ounces of bread, with ox-cheek and soup for dinner.

Monday, two pounds two ounces of bread. *Tuesday,* one pound and one ounce of bread, with a quart of peasesoup.

Wednesday, lhursday, Friday, and *Saturday,* the same as on Tuesday.

REMARKS.

The Keeper's house fronts the Street, having behind it a court-yard *60* feet square, with a well in the centre, and two sewers and other conveniences on one side. The Keeper's rooms have a full view of the Prison in every part.

On the ground-floor of one side is a lobby, 42 feet long and 4 feet wide, into which open five cells; and at the end of the lobby is a small neat Chapel, of 18 feet by 12. The upper-story also has five cells; and at the end of the lobby is a workroom, of the same size as the Chapel.

The opposite side of the building has the like number of cells, opening into lobbies of the same dimensions with those before described; and also two end rooms set apart for Infirmaries. Each of the cells is 12 feet long by 7, with arched roof, and 9 feet 6 inches high; fitted up with crib bedsteads, straw-in-sacking, two sheets, two blankets, and a rug. They have spinning-wheels in them, and hemp-blocks; and are lighted and ventilated by an iron-grated window, 28 inches square, with inside shutter, and a small aperture in each door, for the convenience of the Keeper.

The Rules and Orders are printed and hung up; but neither the Act for Preserving Health, nor the Clauses against Spirituous Liquors.

Those committed to hard labour have no part of their earnings. Those for Assaults, Bastardy, and Poaching, have one half. The average of annual Earnings is *about forty pounds.*

Employment, beating and dressing hemp, and spinning. The Prison very clean, and whitewashed once a year.

SWANSEA, *Glamorganshire; See page* 546. TAUNTON. *Somersetshire.*

The County Bridewell.

Keeper, *William Coggan;* now *James Turle.* Salary, 55/. No Fees.

Chaplain, none; nor any religious attentions whatever.

Surgeon, Mr. *Buncomb,* who makes a Bill.

Number of Prisoners, 1803, Oct. 5th, Twelve. 1806, Sept. 21st, Eighteen.

Allowance, a half quartern loaf per day; and a dinner of meat and vegetables once a fortnight.

REMARKS.

This Prison, called " *Wilton Gaol"* from the Parish in which it stands, has two spacious court-yards, one for Men, 64 feet by 47; the other for Women, nearly the same size, well supplied with water, and a sewer in each.

On the ground-floor are two sleeping-cells, 6 feet by 5 feet 6 inches; and two others, totally dark, of 8 feet by 6, with straw upon the floors.

Here is also a large day-room, 36 feet by 17, with a fire-place, for the Men; on the wall of which is painted, "Whoever plays Ball,
or writes upon the Wall,
to'pay one Shilling,
or be put in the Cells for a Week."

The Women's day-room was formerly the *Chapel,* and on the wall there still Temains, painted, the Lord's Prayer. A Chaplain had been appointed, both here and at Shepton Mallet, with Salaries of 50/. generously granted by the Magistrates: but, whether from *neglect of duty* or of *attendance,* both have been discontinued.

Adjoining to the Men's day-room, is a large one, spread with straw, of 24 feet by 20: above it are three sleeping-rooms, one of which has four beds, the other has three, and the third is a small room, with one bed. The Women have two rooms over their day-room; in one of these were three beds, and in the other, straw only. In this latter, however, was one Woman, sick, yet lying on straw upon the floor. Those Prisoners who have beds pay one shilling per week.

Two bathing tubs are here provided; and also a Gaol-uniform, for such Prisoners as come in with ragged or offensive apparel. Coals are allowed to their respective day-rooms. The upper part of the windows in this Bridewell is glazed, and the lower part a sliding shutter.

Here is no employment whatever. I found many of the Prisoners were in irons, and amongst them a very little boy, committed for two months, had heavy irons on him. It is painful thus to see young beginners, and old adepts in vice associated unavoidably together. The Act for Preserving Health is conspicuously hung up, but not the Clauses against Spirituous Liquors.

The *Old Town Gaol,* now the Red-Lion Publick-house, is »sed only as a Lock-up house for a night. The *Constable* is the Keeper of it.

THETFORD. *Norfolk.*
The Town Gaol.
Gaoler, *John Penteny.* Salary, *1ol.* Fees, Debtors, *6s. 8d.* Felons, *1%t. 4d.*

Chaplain, Rev. Mr. *Manning* Salary, *lol.*

Duty, to attend the Condemned Convicts every day.

Surgeon, sent by the Mayor, as wanted.

Number of Prisoners, 1805, Aug. 31st, None. 1810, Sept. 17th, None.

Allowance, threepence a day, and a peck of coals per week each.
REMARKS.
On the front of the building is the following Inscription: "This Gaol was repaired, and enlarged,
in the Mayoralty of 'william Holmes, esq.'
1781."

The Gaoler's apartments front the Street; and adjoining to them is the MenPrisoners' day-room, 21 feet by 15, and 10 feet high, with a fire-place, brickfloor, benches to sit upon, and a sewer. It has two large semi-circular iron-grated windows, one of them looking towards the Street, and an aperture in the door, of.0 inches by *6.*

In the above room all Male Prisoners are kept together, during the day. At night the Men *Criminals* sleep in a large *Dungeon,* nine steps down, to which a trap-door opens from the floor of the Keeper's kitchen; its dimensions 18 feet by 9, and 8 feet high, lighted and ventilated by a small iron-barred and grated window, looking toward the court-yard, or garden, and in size 20 inches by 14!

The court-yard, converted into a little garden-ground, is 42 feet by 35; with a pump in it, and a privy. The wall is hardly 10 feet high, and deemed insecure.

There are two sleeping-cells on the ground-floor; one of which looks to the Street, *9* feet long by 8 feet *6,* and 8 feet high: it has a flag-stone floor, with a bench to sit upon; and the admission of light and air is through a circular iron-grating, 18 inches in diameter.

The other room adjoining, is of about the same size with the former; lighted in the same manner by a grating towards the garden. Straw only upon the floors to sleep on.

Women Prisoners are confined above stairs. Their day-room is 21 feet by 12, and 8 feet high; with a fire-place, and glazed window. Their sleeping-room, 13 feet *6* by 10 feet, and 8 feet high, has glazed windows and blinds.

A Table of Fees, Rules, and Orders, is hung up, but not being signed, I do not transcribe them.

The Gaol-Delivery for this County is held twice in the year; once at Norwich, and once a year at Thetford; to which, in the year 1805, the Gaoler informed me that forty-two Prisoners were removed from Norwich; three from Wyndham; fbnr from Swaffham; and three from Aylesham: Total, 52.—And were all confined six nrghts in the Dungeon and two cells of Thetford Town-Gaol! In 1810 twenty-three Prisoners were removed from Norwich Castle; two from Wyndham; five from Swaffham; and one from Walsingham; and were all confined six nights in the Dungeon and two cells. The Gaoler told me it was more than twenty years since any Debtor had been detained here. Neither the Act nor Clauses hung up. The Prison clean.

TIDESWELL. *Derbyshire.*
The House of Correction.
Keeper, *William Sheldon.* Salary, 20/. Fees, *2s. 4d.* Prisoners, 11th Oct. 1805,

Two; *vis.* One for Bastardy, in *double irons:* the other a Woman. Allowance, fourpence a day.
REMARKS.
The Keeper's house fronts the street, and the back of it constitutes this wretched Prison. It consists of a room, 13 feet by 11, and 7 feet high, with an iron-grated window and a fire-place. Also two sleeping-cells, each 7 feet by 3 feet 3 inches, and six feet high, without either light or sensible ventilation.

The court-yard, going down nine steps, is only 10 feet by 7 in extent; has a mud surface, and dung was laid in it.

Up stairs is a room for Women, of 13 feet by 10, and 9 feet high, with a fire-place and glazed window. Their sleeping-cell is of the same size as those of the Men below. No water; no sewer; no Employment.

I felt for the Keeper's severity; and therefore exercised a painful duty, in representing it to the Magistrates.

TIVERTON. *Devonshire.*
The Town Gaol.
Gaoler, *John Needes,* the Town Sergeant.
Salary, as Gaoler, none. Fees, *$s. 4d.*

Prisoners, 1803, Oct. 20th, None. lS0fj, Sept. 26th, Two.

Allowance, none to Debtors, except certificated as Paupers; But Felons have *6d.* a day.

REMARKS. ,: ,-,: , *'j.--'"'* v.;':.. *c 's* ft'.- ,*tr.* ,z1oi'«

Here are two rooms under the Town-Hall. One for Debtors, 18 feet by 17, and 9 feet high, supplied with two wooden bedsteads, straw, and two blankets. Nofire-place: an iron-grated window opens from it into a small courtyard, but of which the Prisoners have no use.,

The other room is called "The *Back Gaol,"* of about half the size of the Debtors apartment; and where the Felons are confined. Here is one bedstead, with straw and two blankets; and the iron-grated window looks into an *useless court,* like the former.

Debtors are sent hither for sums exceeding ten pounds, up to any amount, by process issuing out of the Borough Court; and after the holding of five Courts, a Debtor is entitled to receive his *Sixpences.* A Court is held every fortnight. Both rooms are supplied with sewers and water. The two little court-yards are angular, of about 18 feet in the widest part.

TIVERTON. *The Town Bridewell.*
Keeper, *Ann John.* Salary, I/. 8. Fees, 3s. 4/.

Surgeon, Mr. *Smith.* Makes a Bill.

Number of Prisoners, 1803, Oct. 20th, Five: viz. one Woman Transport, and four Frenchmen. 1806, Sept. 26th, Two Women; one of whom was the Female Transport I had seen here in 1803!

Allowance, fourpence each per day, in money.

REMARKS.

This Prison, in St. Andrew's Street, was built about thirty years since, and is partly enclosed by a boundary wall. In front is the Keeper's garden, and at the back the Prisoners' court-yard, about 84 feet by 56, in which are a pump and sewer; with the waste water from the pump so directed, as constantly to run through the latter.

On the ground-floor is the Men's kitchen, 15 feet square, with a fire-place, boiler, cupboard, benches, a glazed iron-grated window, looking into the courtyard, and another window, semi-circular, in the front, with iron bars and a shutter. The whipping-post also makes part of its furniture.

Within a passage of 3 feet 6 inches wide, are three sleeping-cells, 9 feet *6,* by 8 feet, and 8 feet *6* inches high, to the crown of the arch. They have a semi-circular iron grating at each end, for ventilation, with inside shutter, and a pot-hole in the door, about 7 inches square: each cell is furnished with a single crib bedstead, straw, one sheet, and one blanket.

Above stairs is the Women's day-room, in which are two looms for weaving, and two spinning-wheels. It has a fire-place, and two semi-circular glazed windows; one fixed, the other to be put up occasionally, if any Prisoner is sick: also three sleeping-cells, exactly like those for the Men below.

Beds are here supplied by the Keeper, at 1. *6d.* and 1. per week, to those wjio can afford it.

There is no Chaplain; but when I made my visits, the Prayers were read every Sunday by *John Hill,* a Shoemaker of the Town. For this purpose a Bible, with the Common Prayer-Book Service, is kept; on the first page of which is written as follows:

"*Tiverton, Devon. Septr.* 25, 1802. This Bible was sent to Tiverton Bridewell, by Beavis Wood, esq. TownClerk, on the very purpose for the confined Prisoners to hear read the order for Morning and Evening Prayers, on Sundays, and on all other occasional times, as shall or may be most convenient. And this Book is to be deposited into the care of the Keeper of the said Bridewell or Prison, to be kept decent and clean. As Witness my Hand, by Order of Beavis Wood, esq. TowuClerk.

John Hill, the present Reader, of the Established Order."

The Prisoners here have two thirds of their earnings, and the rest goes to the Keeper.

TOTHILL-FIELDS. *Westminster.*
The Bridewell.
JO. s. d.
Gaoler, *Alexander Fenwick;* now *Henri/ Bothwell.* Salary --400 0 0
Head Turnkey, One Guinea and Half per week-----81180
Three Under-Turnkeys, at One Guinea per week each---163 lG 0
Three Assistants from the Public Offices of Bow-street, Marlborough-street, and Queen's-square, at 7. per week each-54 12 0
Fees, as per Table: See Remarks. Garnish, 1. *2d.*

Chaplain, Rev. Doctor *Bennett.* Salary, *20L:* he officiates by his Deputy, the
Rev. Mr. *Evans,* to whom he pays 16/. Duty, Sunday, Prayers and a Sermon.
Surgeon, Mr. Henbury. Salary, 30/.

To this Prison were committed In the Year Debtors. Criminals. In the Year Debtors. Criminals.

Allowance, to Debtors, none; to Criminals, one pound of bread per day.

REMARKS. Over the Gate is this ancient Inscription:

"There are several Sorts of *Work* for the Poorof this Parish of *Saint Margaret's* "*Westminster,* as also the County, according to Law: And for such as will *beg,* "and *live idle,* in this City and Liberty of *Westminster.*"

Anno 1655,.."

At the entrance into the Prison is a room, on the left hand, called " *The Turnkey's Shop*in which there is a cage, or place for bonnets, and other articles of Female clothing, taken from the Women-Prisoners on their commitment, and deposited here.

The room over the gate-way, is called "*Newgate Ward*and contains five beds: for the use of which each Prisoner must pay sixpence a night, two sleeping in a bed. If the Prisoner has a bed singly, the charge is one shilling per night. Adjoining to this is the Turnkey's sleeping-room.

Almost the whole area of this Prison is engrossed by the Keeper's melon and cucumber gardens; and on the sides of it are four narrow court-yards, rendered, close and uncomfortable, especially in summer, when air and space become most desirable.

The first of these court-yards is for *Felons,* and has a day-room, with a fire-place: Also two rooms, which are *free wards,* furnished with barrack bedsteads, and one or two blankets to each, as the weather is mild or severe: The doors open into the court, and the iron-grated windows are not glazed.

The second yard, called " *The Sick Court,"* is very small, and into it opens the Door of the Men's Infirmary. This room (about 20 feet by 11, and 6 feet 8 inches high,) has a fire-place, and two iron-grated, unglazed windows, with barrack-beds, straw-mattress, and two or three blankets each. Of so miserable a room as this, the sick inhabitants must exist in a continual state of disturbance.

The third court-yard is for *Vagrants,* who have a day-room, and two sleeping-rooms on the ground-floor: one of them, about 25 feet by 12; the other, 18 feet by 12; and both have barrack bedsteads, to which blankets are allowed in winter.

The fourth is assigned for *Men-Debtors,* and those who are committed for *Assaults,* or *Bastardy.* Three sleeping-rooms open into this court-yard, and are *free-wards,* each supplied with barrack-beds, loose straw, and a blanket. Prisoners of the above descriptions, who can afford to pay sixpence per night for a bed, sleep in a part of the Gaol called the " *Old Bridewell;"* in which there are two good rooms, with three beds each.

Women-Debtors have the narrow passage to walk in, that leads to the Keeper's house; and, being separated from the Felons' court by low paling only, they are thus, very injudiciously, enabled at all times to converse with them. At my visit here, on the 11th of April 1805, the only two Debtors were in the Men-Felons' court; and on the 7th Nov. 1S0S, Three Fern ale-Debtors were confined with the FemaleConvicts. The Women-Debtors have also a small day-room, with a fire-place. Such of them as cannot afford to pay for bedding, sleep in the solitary eell;i; and to each of these a blanket only is allowed.

For *faulty Apprentices* here are four solitary cells, on the ground-floor, about 9 feet 7, by 6 feet 9, and 6 feet 9 inches high. Of these cells the upper and lower door pannels are iron-latticed, and open into a lobby, paved with flag-stones, about 3 feet 11 inches wide, which separates them, with great propriety, from the other parts of the Prison. Above these are four other cells, with iron-grated windows and wooden blinds, to prevent looking into the adjacent court-yards. A blanket is allowed to each Prisoner of this description.

At the Northeast corner of the building, Women have a comfortable room above stairs, set apart for an Infirmary. It has a fire-place, and two glazed' windows; and iB supplied with barrack-beds, straw-mattress, and two or three blankets for each

Invalid: and adjoining to this are two sleeping-rooms, with glazed windows and, two beds each, at 3. *6d.* per week.

The Chaplain's access to his desk is by an awkward avenue from the top of the stair-case; and he has a full view of the two rooms in which the Men and WomenPrisoners are assembled to hear Divine Service. A better Chapel is much wanted, and could not fail to produce a salutary effect.

Fees allowed for the Keeper of Tothill-fields Bridewell, as by order of Court, January Sessions, *17J2. . £. s. d.*

For Commitment and Discbarge of a Prisoner by Warrant---0 4 2

    For the Turnkey----------010

    Copy of Commitment--------------014

    For a night charge---------------010

    Signed in open Court, by J. Fielding. George Ried.

    George S. Bradshaw. Aaron Lamb.

The Old Gate-house, Westminster, (originally a Prison, the property of the Dean and Chapter,) having been some years since taken down, another Prison, as its substitute, was erected in Tothill-Fields, adjoining to the Bridewell, and first inhabited in the year 1789. It is now entirely set apart for Female Criminal-Prisoners; and has two spacious airy court-yards, of about 57 feet by 42, with three rooms, for dressing provisions, &c. about 15 feet by 10. To these courts belong four *free-wards,* nearly 20 feet square, supplied with barrack-beds, and to each one blanket is allowed during the winter.

'To both the above Prisons seven chaldrons and a half of coals are allowed; over and above which, coals have occasionally been sent, by the Rev. Dean and Chapter of Westminster, arising from a Legacy of Mrs. *Lcetitia Cornwallis.* This charitable Lady's Will bears date 13th December 1731; and through the politeness of a Friend I have been favoured with the following valuable Document.

"1797, June 9th, Received, at the Bank, eight half-year's Dividends of *Five pounds seven shillings and sevenpence* each, (ending 5th January 1797) on three hundred and fiftyeight pounds fifteen shillings and threepence, *Three per Cent. Consoh,* being the produce of the Legacy of *One hundred pounds,* given by the Will of Laetitia Cornwallis, spinster, dated 13th December 1731; the Interest whereof to be for ever applied, on the seventh of November, either in *Discharge* of, or for other *Relief* of such poor Prisoners in the Gatehouse Prison, Westminster, as the Dean of Westminster, for the time being, shall think fit: which said sum of 353/. 15s. *id.* was transferred by the Accountant General of the High Court of Chancery, by order of the said Court, to the Dean of St. Peter's, Westminster, and the Chapter of the same Church; who by Deed poll, under their Common-Seal, dated 25th January 1786, acknowledged to have accepted the said Stock, in trust for the" purposes mentioned in the said Will: Which said sum of 358/. 1 *5s. 'id.* standing in the Transfer Books, under the title of the Dean of St. Peter's, Westminster, &c. and under the Letter P. occasioned divers searches, before the same was found; and, therefore, in order to prevent the like trouble in future, it was transferred, on the 2d of June 1797, by Anthony Gell, Esq. the present Receiver, by power of Attorney, from the present Dean and Chapter of Westminster, from and out of the name of the Dean of St. Peter's, Westminster, into the name of the Dean of the Collegiate Church of St. Peter, Westminster, and the Chapter of the same Church."

"1804, July 20th, Received half-year's Dividend on Four hundred and fifty-eight pounds, fifteen shillings and threepence, *One hundred pounds Slock* having been bought 22d January 1804." jj£f

It is hardly to be conceived what ingenuity of low artifice has sometimes been practised on the very excellent and pious intention of the above Bequest. In consequence of a day being specified (the 7th.of November annually) for the application of its Christian Bounty, plans have been formed by worthless Characters, and but too successfully executed, *to have Prisoners ready in the Gate-house aJew days before,* under the pretext of real Debts, in order to avail themselves of a benefit, that could never be in the contemplation of the Donor; and of the abuse and misapplication of which the respectable Trustees could have had no idea.

Here is plenty of water at all times; and the whole Prison is washed twice a week; for which mops, brooms, pails, &c. are allowed by the considerate Magistrates.

It is said to be in contemplation to enlarge the Bridewell from some waste ground adjoining to the Premises: But I would submit to the Magistrates superintending so important a concern, whether it might not be better to erect a new Bridewell, on such a construction, as that the Keeper's house may have a full command of the different courts, &c

The TOWER. *London.*

The Tower is a strong fortress, and the only Prison in England for State Delinquents of rank. The care of it is committed to an officer called the Constable of the Tower, who has under him a Lieutenant, a Deputy Lieutenant, called the Governor, and many other officers; among whom are 40 Warders, whose uniform is the same with the Ring's Yeomen of tbeCuards. Nineteen of these Warders have separate houses, well furnished, in any of which, as the Governor is pleased to order, the State Delinquents may be confined; and the custom has been to assign them two of the best rooms on the first floor; with iron bars affixed to their windows by the Board of Works. Sometimes they are committed to close confinement; but in general they are at liberty to walk in the area of the Tower, attended always by a Warder.

When there are any Prisoners here, they are soon brought to a legal trial, and consequently their confinement can never be long. Six shillings and eightpence a day are allowed by Government for their subsistence; but they seldom accept this Allowance.

Sir Francis Burdett, Bart, was the last who went out, on the 21st June, 1810.

In this Fortress, besides the houses just mentioned, there are several public offices and store-houses; such particularly, as the office of Ordnance, the Jewel Office, the Mint, and buildings for holding artillery, arms, &c.

TOWER-HAMLETS GAOL. *Wellclose Square.*

This Prison is at the King's Arms publick house, kept by *William Morris,* who is the Gaoler. There is a court-room, in the House where the Ouarter Sessions for the Tower Hamlets are held. The Prison consists of two rooms, 16 feet by 10: one of them has a barrack bedstead in it; both are in a very ruinous state, and filled with straw and lumber.

The last Prisoner here was one *Fletcher,* committed under the Hair-Powder Act in 1801. Since that time Prisoners have been sent to the House of Correction in Cold Bath Fields.

TRURO. *Cornwall.*

The Town Gaol.

In front of the Street here are two houses for the two Sergeants at Mace, who are the Keepers, at a Salary of Forty Shillings each. No Fees. Prisoners, 1S03, Oct. 10th, One. 1806, Oct. 2d, One. Allowance, sixpence a day.

The Gaol is at the bottom part of the Keeper's garden, and consists of four convenient rooms; the largest 14 feet by 10 feet; the three others about 10 feet square. The two rooms now more constantly in use, are vaulted; one of them has a chimney, and to each there is a large iron-grated window. The two lower rooms are damp, with loose straw on the floors, and a half tub in each, as a sewer.

No water. The Keepers fetch it, even for their own use, from a quarter of a mile off. No court-yard; though one might be made out of the Keeper's garden; and a well also sunk, to supply the Prison and house.

Prisoners are brought hither from Bodmin; the Easter Sessions being held here.

TYNEMOUTH. *Northumberland.*
The House of Correction.
Keeper, *Robert Robson.* Salary, 30/. and six loads of coals. Fees, *l$s. 4d.*

No religious attentions.

Surgeon, Mr. *Ti-otter.* Makes a Bill.

Number of Prisoners, 17th Sept. 1809, Four Men.

Allowance, four-pence a day.

REMARKS.

This Prison, first inhabited in 1792, has on the ground-floor two apartments for the Keeper, divided by a passage 5 feet 10 inches wide, which leads to the Men's sleeping-cells; four on one side, and three on the other, separated by a lobby of like dimensions. Each cell is 7 feet by 6, and 8 feet high, to the crown of the arch; entirely built of stone, and furnished with crib bedsteads for one person in each; loose straw, and three coverlets; a covered sewer, emptied twice a day; a corner seat with a shelf for provisions. They are all lighted and ventilated by an irongrated and glazed window, 18 inches by 14, and an aperture into the lobby, of *20* inches by 3, with an inspecting-wicket in each door.

Here are two court-yards: that for the Women, about *60* feet square, has a sewer in the centre. The Men's court, of nearly the same size, has in it a kitchen, 1 6 feet by 10, and conveniences for boiling the Prisoners' clothes, moistening junk, &c. and a stone cistern, through which passes a constant stream of excellent water, that supplies the Prison. The Prisoners are let out singly for one hour in the day, accompanied by the Keeper.

The upper story is appropriated for the Women, and exactly similar to the one already described.

In wet and cold weather the Prisoners work in the lobby; which is flagged, and has an iron-grated window at the end, for ventilation.

When a Prisoner is brought in ragged or filthy, his clothes are boiled in soap lees and allum. Their employ consists in picking of oakum, knitting stockings, sewing and spinning. None are suffered to be idle here; and Prisoners have one half of their earnings, which is given them on discharge.

Religious books are supplied to them by the Magistrates; and the silence and decorum observed throughout this real House of *Correction* must greatly tend to *a* wholesome reformation of Morals.

The annual average number of Commitments, is about 40.

WAKEFIELD. *Yorkshire.*
The House of Correction.
Gaoler, *Charles S. V. Straubenzee.*

Salary, 250/. an excellent house to live in; coals allowed, and taxes paid by the County: also two Turnkeys. See Remarks.

Chaplain, Rev. Mr. *Brown.* Salary, 50/.

Duty, on Thursday, Prayers; on Sunday, Prayers and Sermon.

Surgeon, Mr. *Walker;* who makes a Bill.

Number of Prisoners, Men. Women. 1802, Aug. 15th,------50-------29. 1804, Dec. 28th,------56-------30.

Allowance, breakfast, every day, one quart of oatmeal pottage, and half a pound of bread. Supper, daily the same.

Dinner, Sunday and Thursday, half a pound of boiled beef, and one pound of potatoes, or other vegetables.

Monday and Friday, one quart of broth, from beef of the preceding days, with herbs, and half a pound of bread.

Tuesday, a quarter of a pound of cheese, and half a pound of bread.

Wednesday, one quart of rice and oatmeal pottage, and half a pound of bread.

Saturday, one quart of the stew of heads and bones.

§Cf This stew is made of shin-bones and heads, clean washed, after the proportion of two bullock's heads and two shin-bones for 120 Prisoners, with half an ounce of rice per head. It is made over night, by a slow fire, with onions, leeks, and salt, in a boiler which confines the steam, in the manner of a digester. The rice must be steeped in cold water all night, and put into the stew in the morning.

Breakfast is delivered at eight o'clock in Summer, and nine in Winter. Dinner at twelve. Supper at eight in Summer, and six in Winter.

The *Table of Diet* is printed and stuck up in the Gaol.

REMARKS.

This admirable Prison is built of stone, and does honour to the West Riding of Yorkshire. 1 he Gaoler's house fronts the Street, and is separated from the Prison by an area, containing nearly half an acre of ground, of which the Gaoler has a completely commanding view.

Two Turnkeys are allowed; the first at one guinea, the second at sixteen shillings per week; and a Porter also, at 20/. per annum. These are supplied each with a house and coals free, and live within the walls. They are entirely under the Keeper's direction; may be continued or dismissed at his pleasure; and are paid by the Keeper, who receives the money from the County Treasurer.

The Task Master, or Manufacturer, who superintends the Prisoners employed, is chosen by the Magistrates, who allow him 100/. a year. He, likewise, is under the Keeper's direction, and obliged to assist him; but the Keeper has no power to dismiss him.

The Prison consists of a centre, and two wings. The West wing has fiftyone cells, being seventeen on each of the three floors. Women Prisoners are here confined; and each has a separate cell.

The centre has two large rooms on the ground-floor; one for Felons, the other for Misdemeaners; and also 17 sleeping-cells, in which Men Felons are confined separately, unless their number exceeds that of the cells; in which case two sleep together.

The East wing has forty-five cells, fourteen on the first and second floor each, and seventeen on the upper story. All of them have arched roofs; are 7 feet 9 inches long by 6 feet 9 wide, and are fitted up with iron bedsteads, and a straw mattress, two blankets, a sheet, and a rug each. The lower range is warmed by the tube of a German stove passing through, and the cells are thoroughly ventilated. Each door has a cylinder for conveying provisions, &c. to the Prisoners. The upper stories of the house are like the lower, except that the windows of the latter are glazed. The lobbies or passages are very spacious and airy, supplied with plenty of water, and in each lobby is a judiciously and well-contrived sewer.

Amongst the cells are six, for *solitary confinement* of the Refractory; the doors of which have a cylinder, like the former, to admit Provisions, but no light, except what is received through a small circular perforation.

The Men's Infirmary has three sleeping-rooms, and three beds in each, with a sitting-room adjoining. 1 he Women's Infirmary consists of two sleeping-rooms, each three-bedded, and a sitting-room, like the former.

The Cook's kitchen has a small room attached to it, with two beds for servants.

There are within the Prison one hundred and thirteen cells, and seventeen beds in different rooms.

In the *Chapel* the Men are placed on one side, and the Women on the other; all in view of their Minister, but entirely unseen by each other. The Sick are seated, with like discrimination, in the Gallery, but can see and be seen by the rest of the Prisoners.

Each Prisoner, on Commitment, and previous to admission, is stripped and washed; and such part of their chess as is worth preserving, after undergoing fumigation, is ticketted and hung up, to be given them when discharged; together with such additional articles of apparel as their several necessities may require.

The County clothing assigned them, instead of their own, is a black and yellow alternately striped cloth, and a pair of wooden clogs. When I was there in 1802, a large capital letter was sewed upon each Prisoners' coat, denoting his offence; for during that one hour of the day wherein Felons are allowed to walk in the area, they mix and associate with the other Prisoners. In some Gaols the latter are, very prudently, separated during that short time of recreation.

At the back of this Prison there is an enclosed plot of ground, nearly three acres, in which are eighty-five work-cells; but, with the exception of four only, they appear much too small; their cielings are low, and the cells but 8 feet long by 6 feet and 1 inch wide. The remainder of the plot is occupied by a kitchen garden, which produces more vegetables in general than the whole Prison can consume. Its boundary wall is 1Q feet high.

If the earnings of the Prisoners do not amount to what they cost the County, it is perhaps because they too frequently want the means of Employment. *Men,* after the first fourteen days, will generally earn more than is sufficient for their subsistence, provided they are in health, and have work to do. Sawing of wood seems here the most productive; and by this kind of work, the profit of each Prisoners labour may be estimated at from half a guinea to fourteen shdlings per week. Women are often very deficient in this respect; many of them have helpless children; some are cripples; the younger Women, on their admission, are too often so afflicted with a certain disorder, that a great portion of their time is expended in obtaining a cure. The Employment of Females here is spinning of worsted, and picking of wool.

The respectable Magistrates of the West Riding have humanely directed that every Prisoner's subsistence shall be reckoned at six-pence a day. Of all above that sum, which the Prisoner shall have gained by his labour, he is to receive one half and the other half goes to the County. A noble example of liberality, and worthy of imitation! as, from the best calculation that can be made, each Prisoner stands, the County in one shilling a day.

The Quarter Sessions are held, as follows:

In the Spring, at Pontefract only; in the Summer, at Skipton, Bradford, and Rotherham; in Autumn, at Knaresborough, Leeds, and Rotherham; and in Winter, at Weatherby, Wakefield, and Doncaster.

The irons used in this Prison are of the very lightest kind1, being, as I conceive, not more than five or six pounds in weight. But I saw here one pair, that weighed *Jifty-two* pounds and which the Turnkey told me a refractory Prisoner had on for a fortnight, *by way of punishment.*

The Act for Preservation of Health, and Clauses against Spirituous Liquors, are conspicuously hung up: The whole Prison is whitewashed four times in the yeart and is as clean, in every part, as any private house.

WAKEFIELD.
The Town Gaol.
This, which is also by the vulgar jocosely called "the *Kidcotts,"* is a new Prison, built in 1800.

The *Constable* is its Keeper. It consists of two lofty rooms, about four yards square, with each an iron bedstead and straw. The floors are of flag-stone, dry, and well ventilated by iron-grated windows, looking into the passage which separates the rooms.

Prisoners are seldom detained here above a night or two. I met with none, at my visit, 16th August, 1802.

The liberal and humane spirit of the Magistrates will not suffer even this small place of confinement to escape their attention.

The sewers are judiciously constructed, and communicate properly with the drains.

August 1802, on my arrival at this place, (Wakefield) just as Divine Service had begun, I was surprized at not seeing a single Beggar or Vagrant, nor even an idling Lounger, about the Streets. The Church was filled within, and peace and good order equally prevailed without. I was pleased on being informed that "this was *not a casual circumstance,* for that I should always find it so, whenever I visited the place on a Sabbath Day." I had conceived the Police to be so regulated, that some of its respectable inhabitants must have perambulated the Streets alter nately; as, otherwise, it seemed hardly possible to keep so large a Town in such decent observance of the Sabbath.

In another part of this District I recollect finding some Low-Court Debtors in their Prison, on a Sunday, as black as chimney-sweepers, and as busy as ants or bees-They were sifting cinders, in order to make up a profitable "two loads of ashes, which were to be fetched away the next morning." : WALSALL. *Staffordshire. The Town GaoL*

Gaoler, *William Mason.* No Salary. Fees, 3. 4d. and 2. to the Town-Clerk 1802, Nov. 2d, no Prisoners..

Allowance, to Debtors and Felons, twopence per day.

REMARKS.

This Prison consists of two rooms under the Town-Hall: that for Debtors has a fire-place: it is down five steps, and has an iron-grated window to the Street, but not being glazed, and having no inside shutters, it is extremely cold; and there i& straw only, on the damp brick floor, to sleep upon. A door opens out of this room into a dark Dungeon for Felons, about 9 feet square

Adjoining to the Debtors' room is one for Felons, with an iron-grated window towards the Street, and two dark Dungeons, with straw to sleep on.

No court! No sewerT *No water!* The Beadle told, me he brought it to the grating for the Prisoners. Those for petty offences remain here till the Quarter Sessions. No Debtors are confined here for less than ten pounds.

WALSINGHAM. *Norfolk.* 1
Gaoler, *William Wright.* Salary, 50/. No Fees.

Chaplain, none; but the Rev. Mr. *Warner* reads Prayers gratuitously every week.

Surgeon, Mr. *Bulcoch;* now Mr. *Ad-*

coch. Salary, 10/.
Prisoners, 1805, Sept. 2d, Five. 1810, Sept. 6th, Nine.
Allowance, a half-quartern loaf per day, sent from the Baker's.
REMARKS.

On the ground-floor are four cells, 12 feet 6 by 6 feet *6,* and *9* feet high, fitted up with crib bedsteads, straw-in-sacking beds, two blankets, two sheets, and a coverlet. Each cell has an iron-grated window, 3 feet square, with an inside shutter. There are glazed windows also, to put up in cold weather; and an aperture, or pothole, in each door, 8 inches by *6.* Thq cell door opens into a lobby, or passage, 4 feet wide, 33 in length; at the end of which is the Chapel, 18 feet by 9, and 9 feet high, with a fire-place.

Above stairs are four other cells, of like dimensions, and fitted up in the same manner; with an Infirmary-room at the end, of the same size as the Chapel; and a small store-room.

The court-yard not being secure, the Prisoners are only permitted the use of it once a day, to clean their pots, and wash themselves; for which soap and towels are provided by the County..

The whole Prison is well ventilated, and very clean. Act and Clauses not hung up.

No Rules and Orders. No Employment for the Prisoners.

WARRINGTON. *Lancashire.*
The Town Bridewell.
Keeper, *J. Boardman,* who is also Master of the Workhouse.

Number of Prisoners, 1802, Oct. 10th, Four. 1809, Nov. 11th, None.

Allowance, one shilling each per day.
REMARKS.
This Prison is a detached building, consisting of two rooms, or cells, in the Workhouse Yard, of about 9 feet by G, with vaulted roofs, and stone-floors. Each has a wooden bedstead, with loose straw, and two rugs. A tub supplies the place of a sewer. The only light or ventilation is from a circular aperture, about 2 inches in diameter, made in the wooden door of one cell, and a wicket 6 inches square in the iron door of the other.

No water accessible, but as brought in by the Keeper. He informed me that Prisoners were sometimes confined here a fortnight, and never permitted to come out of their wretched and offensive cells, except when the Town Constable thinks proper, and finds it convenient to attend them J WELLS. *Somersetshire.'*
The Town Gaol.

The Prison here building is very conveniently situated near the Sessions-house, and intended for the Reception of Prisoners from Taunton, Shepton _Mallet, and Bridgewater, during the time of the Assizes being held here.

On the ground-floor is a room on each side of a lobby, or passage, 9 feet wide; and two other rooms above them, about 15 feet square, with two iron-grated windows in each, and a fire-place.

The Assizes are held at Wells every other year. My visit was the 21st Sept. 1806.
WARWICK. *The County Bridewell.*
Keeper, *Joseph Chaplin.* Salary, 80/. No Fees.

Chaplain, Rev. *Hugh Laugharne.* Duty, Prayers and Sermon once a week. Salary, 50/. for this Prison, and the County Gaol. Surgeon, Mr. *Birch.* Salary, for Bridewell and Gaol, 40f.

Number of Prisoners, Males. Females. 1803, Aug. 20th,------54 19. 1808, July 31st, 34--21. 1809, Aug. 19th,--*i, 7,- 'Jk.* ------31.

Six Children, and a Lunatics:.

Allowance, one pound and half of bread per day.
i REMARKS.
The Keeper's house has his garden in front, and commands a view of the two court-yards. That for Men is 99 feet by 36; that for Women, 87 feet by 15 and both are well supplied with hard and soft water.

Here are likewise two courts for Male and Female Vagrants, of about 21 feet by 12, with a sleeping cell in each, about 10 feet square.

On the basement story of the Men's-Side is a weaver's shop, containing a loom, six spinning wheels, a carding machine, and a twisting mill; and close to it, a combing and sorting room. In another room, above stairs, are seven other looms, ten spinning wheels, a small carding machine, and a warping mill. On the basement story also, in a new adjacent building, are a dye-house, with stoves, and a wash-house, with a staircase at each end.

On a second and principal story is a spinning room, extending the whole length of the building; and capable of containing about thirty spinning wheels, of which fifteen were at work when I made my last visit. The upper or attick story has a room for depositing the manufactured goods, and an Infirmary for li-he Women.

The centre-building, on the basement story, has a warm and cold bad), an oven and boiler; with pipes to convey water from the reservoir. The principal story has two day-rooms, one for the Men, the other for the Women, which open into their several court-yards; and to each of which the County allow one hundred weight of coals per day in the winter, and half that quantity in the summer months. Likewise a room set apart for Male-Convalescents, to which firing is allowed; and one solitary cell, about 7 feet square.

Over these is the Chamber story; in which are *the Chapel,* three sleeping-cells, and a sleeping-room, about 15 feet square: And on the same floor, two other lodgingrooms for Women, of about *16* feet by 14, and two cells, 7 feet square. The Gaoler supplies those Prisoners who pay 1. *6d.* per week with a bed, sheets, blankets, and a rug.

The attick-story, on the *Meiis-Side,* has a sleeping-room, of 30 feet by 16', with partitions on the floor; and a sick room, 16 feet by 14, furnished with wooden turn-up bedsteads, chaff-beds, and two rugs each. Adjoining to the latter room is a small one, about 7 feet square, with a fire-place, to prepare and warm their victuals.

The Women's-Side contains two rooms, of 16 feet by 14 each; and a smaller, like that for the Men, 7 feet square.

The Chapel is partitioned off for the Sexes but is too small for so populous, and sometimes crowded, a Prison. The Prisoners are all required to attend Divine Service, unless prevented by sickness.

The County allows to each Prisoner a chaff-bed, or sacking filled with straw, changed every quarter, and two rugs.

The Men have their Barber weekly, and clean linen once a week, which is Washed and mended by Women Prisoners. The County supplies soap and towels for all. lu sickness the Surgeon orders whatever is proper, at the County expence.

The Women are generally supplied with clothing from the Prison Manufactures; which is given to them when discharged.

The following Documents are worthy of record, and highly exemplary.

"Various Articles manufactured in the *House of Correction* at *Warwick.* 'The Combing of Wool: Carding ditto; spinning it'; and also Jerseys and Linen from Flax: Weaving of Carpets; Linsey for Petticoats; Tammies and Linen Cloth; Horse-girth Webbing; Horse clothing, rugs, and blankets." ,.. Earnings, and Rewards

Earning from Jan. 1st, 1803, to 18«4 »--..-- lt«T M& A,£ia Rewards ditto---- ----30 1 &

Nett Benefit---.£.115 a *9 £. s. d.*

Earnings, Jan. 1st, 1804 to 1805 213 17 H

Rewards-----37 7 6

Nett Benefit---£. 176 10 5

Earnings, Jan. 1st, 1805 to 1806------ --255 15 9

Rewards---42 18 2

Benefit----£. 212 17 G£

Earnings, Jan 1st, 1806 to 1807------- -278 14 9

Rewards----------------49 0 5

Benefit----.£.229 14 3£

Earnings, Jan. 1st, 1S07 to 1808------ --320 13 4

Rewards----------------51 9 2

Benefit----£.269 4 1

Earnings, Jan. 1st, 1S08 to 1S09------ --319 19 1

Rewards----------------54 13 0

Benefit----£. 265 6 1

The average number of working hands is about *fifty.* All Prisoners who work have twopence or threepence in a shilling out of their earnings, which is paid them weekly

The *Number of Commitments,* for seven years, was as follows: From 1st Jan. 1802 to 1803--265. 1 From 1st Jan. 1806 to 1807--216".
1803 to 1804--249 1804 to 1805--200. 1805 to 1806--204. 1807 to 1808--238. 1808 to 1809--259.

'When a Prisoner is discharged, a Donation is issued, according to the distance from home, and behaviour during confinement: and one or two shirts or shifts, a pair of shoes, or a jacket, are presented to such as have been six months imprisoned, and conducted themselves properly.

The Act for Preservation of Health, and Clauses against Spirituous Liquors, are «xemplarily hung up. The Prison is white-washed once a year, and kept very clean. There were seven Prisoners on the Sick List in 1809, when I made my last visit WARWICK.

The County Gaol.

Gaoler, *Henry Tatnall.* Salary, 300/.

Fees, *Debtors,* see Table. Felons pay no Fees. For removal of Transports, the Expence of Conveyance. Garnish abolished.

Chaplain, Rev. *Hugh Laugharne.*

Duty, Sunday and Friday, Prayers and Sermon.

Salary, 50/. for Gaol and Bridewell.

Surgeon, Mr. *Birch.* Salary, 40/. for Gaol and Bridewell,

Number of Prisoners, Debtors. Felons, &c.
1800, March 25th, 3-66 1802, March 23d,------19-71. 1803, August 20th, 15-36 1808, July 31st,--24------25 1809, August 19th,------11 29

Allowance, one pound and half of bread daily, to every description of Prisoners. It is sent in loaves from the Baker's; and I have always found them full weight. See in the Remarks, *Donations to Debtors.* , REMARKS.

At the entrance is the Turnkey's Lodge; the room over which, denominated the *Dead-Room,* is so called from the Executions which take place out of it. A small court-yard fronts the Gaoler's house, which is nearly in the centre of the building.

Master's-Side Debtors have a court-yard, 82 feet by 37; a day-room, 20 feet by *16;* and nine lodging-rooms, about 10 feet square, for which they pay as per Table. Above stairs are eighteen rooms, of about the same size, and opening into passages only 3 feet wide.

Common-Side Debtors have also a court exactly similar to the former; a dayroom about 14 feet square; and three sleeping-rooms above stairs, furnished with chaff beds, and two rugs each on the floor, for which they pay nothing .

Women Debtors have two rooms, the largest about 20 feet square, and the smaller, 16 feet by 9, with bedding the same as the Men; and are allowed wooden bedsteads, with sacking bottoms: they have likewise a smaH court-yard'.

Too poor, perhaps, to *pay any thing.* I could not but consider their circumstances as very pitiable; and I find that a stranger, of similar sentiments, sent these Common-side Paupers, as follows, at the time of one of my visits; viz. Four iron bedsteads, with sacking bottoms; four brown Holland flockbeds and pillows; four pair of blankets, and four quilts.

Besides the stated allowance, Debtors, receive, from a Legacy, eight threepenny loaves twice a month, of which here is no Memorial. They are regularly sent by Bernard Dewes, Esq. of Welshbourn in this County, who likewise gives annually one ton of coals to the Debtors, and one ton to the Felons, at Christmas. Debtors ska receive *JXonations.* at Christmas yearly;, which amounted, in 1798, to about 28/. in money, meat and coals; in 1799, to 26/.;. iul8oo, 26%; in lSoi, 24/.; in 1802, 25/.; in 1803, to 18/.; in 1804, *16I.*; in 1805, *III. 16s.$* in 1806, 52/. 12.; in 1807, 35/. 2.; and in 1808, to 49/. 7. *4%d.*

Table Of Fees,

As settled by his Majesty's Justices of the Peace at the General Quarter Sessions held at *Warwick,* the 30th day of July, 1759.

1 s. d.

Every Prisoner that lies on the Keeper's-side, if he has a bed to himself, pays by the week----------------26

Those Prisoners on the Keeper's-side who have a bed between two, pay each by the week--------------- 1 %

For entering every Action against each Prisoner--------30

For discharging every Action against each Prisoner-------10 6

To the Under-Sheriff for every Discharge----,----40

For receiving and entering every Declaration--------10

For a Copy of each Warrant against each Prisoner-------10

For every Certificate of the Cause of a Prisoner's being detained in Prison, *in* order for being discharged-.----..-..-30

"F. Stratford, Wm, Huddesfoud, J. Bird.

"We, the Judges of Assize for the County of *Warwick,* have received, and do hereby confirm, the above Table of Fees. Given under our hands this 24th August, 1759.

"T. Parker. J. Hewitt."

The Chapel is so partitioned off, that the Sexes are out of sight of each other. All the Prisoners attended Divine Service when I was here in 1803, and 1809. Below the Chapel are two work-rooms, in one of which the Men weave; and eight looms were employed: in the other the Women spin, and mend and wash for the Men-Prisoners.

The Male-Felons' court-yard is *96 feet by 54;* and that of the Females 51 feet by 21; both well supplied with hard and soft water. The Men have two day-rooms on the ground-floor, each 31 feet by 19 feet *6* inches; sixteen sleeping-cells, and three solitary ones, each 9 feet by *6,* and 9 feet high, with arched roofs, divided by a passage 5 feet wide. On the first story are twenty-eight cells of the same size, separated by a wall, and a passage on each side, of 5 feet wide. The second, third, and fourth stories have each the same number of cells divided in like manner, and of the same dimensions. In the whole, therefore here.are 103 cells, of which twenty four are called *double cells,* as being twice the size of the rest, and adapted to receive two Prisoners. Two large cells, with fire-places and glazed windows, are set apart for the sick.

The Women-Felons also have, on the ground-floor, one day-room, of 18 feet by 14; a wash-house and two sleeping-cells; and on the upper story, two sleep-ingrooms, of the same size as their day rooms; and an infirmary-room, with fire-places and glazed windows.

Felons are here allowed cast-iron bedsteads, covered with wood, chaff-beds, and two rugs to each. Every cell has a double door; the inner of wood, the outer one iron-grated. I must observe, that if the passages, numbered 3, 4, 7, and 8, on the Felon's-side of this Prison, had circular apertures at the end, it would greatly improve the ventilation. It is intended to have a separate court-yard for young Offenders, with a large room and a workshop, which are very much wanted.

Here is a room for depositing the irons, and a warm and cold bath. The old dungeon (a descent of 21 steps) in this Gaol, is made use of for *Deserters;* and adjoining to it is a subterraneous passage, through which the Prisoners are brought into Court for trial, and cannot but feel the awfulness of such a transit!

The Act for Preservation of Health, and Clauses against Spirituous Liquors, are conspicuously hung up; and the whole Prison is very clean.

Formerly, the Debtors in common were used to receive *thirty shillings* a year, from the rent of a house in the Town. This, I understand, was a Legacy; but am told it has been discontinued for many years. No Memorial of it is hung up in the Gaol.

In the Debtors court there is a Poor's Box, put up by Blackett Wise, Esq. , Sheriff, 9th January 1808; and on a board over it are the following original lines, which, for their excellent and scriptural pathos, have already been transcribed at *Dover-Castle.* See P. 171.

"Oh ye, whose hours exempt from sorrow flow,
Behold the seat of pain, and want, and woe!
Think, while your hands th' entreated alms extend,
That what to M ye give, to God ye lend.
"

This Gentleman likewise gave to poor Debtors in the last two winters, a joint of meat, a quantity of garden stuff, and one hundred weight of coals.

!. WELLINGTON. *Shropshire.*

Gaoler, *Edward Totige,* a Sheriff's Officer. No Salary. Fees, *js. 6d.*

No Prisoners, 4thNov. 1802, and 11th Sept. 1803.

Allowance, none, except as Paupers from the Parish.

REMARKS.

This Gaol, for the Hundred of Bradford, is, I am informed, the property of the Earl of Darlington, High Steward of that Liberty. It is for DebtorsonIy, and those of two descriptions, commonly called the High Court and Ldw. Court Prisoners,

Tne High Court Prisoners are detained for Debts from ten to twenty Pounds: The Low Court Prisoners are detained for Debts, not exceeding forty shillings.

The Gaol consists of five rooms in the Keeper's house, three of which are totally dark. The Gaoler, paying window-tax, has stopped them up. A little loose and dirty straw on the floor for bedding. No court-yard, or water, accessible to the Prisoners. Not white-washed for seven years together. The whole Prison is very nasty, and insecure.

Two Prisoners, who had been *here for as many years,* were released by the Insolvent Act. What a time is *two years* so spent!, WELLS. *Somersetshire; See Page* 572.

f WHITECHAPEL. *London.*

Prison For Debtors.

Gaoler, *John Simpson;* a Sheriffs Officer. Salary, none. Fees, 8. *id.* No Table.

Allowance; none whatever.

REMARKS.

This is a Prison for the Liberties and Manors of Stepney and Hackney. In it are confined those, whose debts are above 2l. and not exceeding 5/. There are four rooms fronting the road, two on each story, about 15 feet by 13, and 8 feet high. If a Debtor sleeps in any of these rooms he pays the Keeper, for the use of a bed, one shilling the first night, and six-pence per night afterwards. The court-yard is 40 fu:t by 20, in which is the Men's day-room, 12 feet by 10. From the courtyard the ascent is by a wooden stair-case to a gallery, in which are two sleepingrooms, and Women's-day-room, of equal size with that below. These are *free-wards.*

Bv the Act, 1781, 21 George III. entitled, "An Act for diminishing the Fees "payable, and altering the mode of proceeding, in the Court of Record, within the "Manors of Stepney and Hackney, &c." imprisonment is fixed, " for a time not "exceeding *one week,* for *every pound* of the total debt and costs." By virtue of this good Statute no Prisoners can be confined here more than five weeks.

The Court to which this Prison belongs does not proceed by Arrest, but by Summons; and no Prisoners are received, but in execution. The Costs are always 15. in every suit. Before Lord Beauchamp's Act I was told that fifty had been confined here at a tiqae; but since it passed, they have never exceeded three.

WHITEHAVEN. *Cumber/and.*
The House of Correction.
a
Keeper, *Thomas Curry.* Salary, 20/. No Fees..
Chaplain, none; but the Rev. *Richard Armistead* frequently attends.
Surgeon, none.
Allowance, two shillings a week.
REMARKS.

This Prison, built in 180S, is situate in a high and healthy part of Queen-street. The Keeper's house is in front; separated from the Prison behind it by an area of 56 feet by 23, and solely for the Keeper's use. Out of this area are two iron-grated doors of entrance to the Prison; one for Men, the other for Women; and opening into their respective court-yards; both of which are 43 feet by 12 feet 6, with sewers conveniently placed.

On the ground-floor each have a day or mess-room, 13 feet by 12 feet *6,* and 8 feet high; a work-room 17 feet by 12 feet *6,* and a sleeping-cell for Felons, J 2 feet by 9, of the same height: the floors are flagged; a small iron-grated hole gives light and ventilation to each cell, which has a cast-iron bedstead, with wooden bottom, straw-in-sacking bed, two blankets, and a rug. The day

and work-rooms have likewise flagged floors; but they are lighted and ventilated by grated and glazed casement windows, 4 feet 2 inches by 2 feet 6, and have fire-places; but coals are not furnished by the County.

On the chamber-story are four sleeping-rooms, about 12 feet square, and two infirmary-rooms, 12 feet by 9, with boarded floors: four of them have fire-places; and all have grated and glazed casement windows, and are fitted up with wood bedsteads, and bedding as before described The sexes are completely separated, and allowed to take the air in their court-yards during the day. The greatest number of Prisoners confined here at one time has been twelve. WINCHESTER. *Hampshire.*
The County Gaol.
Gaoler, *John Wldte.* Salary, 200/.; and Two Guineas *per annum,* for keeping a check-account of bread delivered. Fees, for *Debtors,* see Table: besides which the Under-Sheriff demands a Fee of *6s. Sd.* and also one shilling to his Clerk, for his *Liberate?*

For *Felons,* no Fees. For Conveyance of Transports the Gaoler makes a Bill, and the Expence is allowed him. Garnish, abolished.

Chaplain, Rev. *Nicholas Westcomb.*
Duty, Prayers and Sermon on Sunday; and Prayers on Wednesday and Friday. Salary, 70/. for Gaol and Bridewell.
Surgeon, Mr. *Giles Lyford.*
Salary, 100/. for Common-Side Debtors, Felons, and Bridewell Prisoners.
Number of Prisoners, Debtor. Felons, &c. Debtors. Felons, &o.
1800, March 30th--19--27. 1802, March 29th,--23--33. 1801, Jan. 10th,---42--59. 1803, Oct. 24th,--18--42. 1802, Jan. 3d, *26* --49-1807, Sept. 23d, 23--18.
Allowance, Masters-Side *Debtors,* none. Those on the Common-Side have each seventeen ounces of bread per day, in loaves, which, though two days old, I found to be of full weight: also a pound of mutton each, on Sunday.
Felons, seventeen ounces of bread, as to the Common-Side Debtors. And from Winchester College as follows:

Every Wednesday, four Sheep's *Hinges.* Saturday, a Bullock's Head.
Once a week twelve loaves, the same as used for the Collegians.
On Tuesday, Thursday, and Sunday, a basket of broken bread and meat; with six gallons of table beer three times a week, the same as used in College. Also two quarts of oatmeal, and one quart of salt once a week. The broken meat and bread are served out one pound per Man, or as far as it will go. Convicts, under Sentence of Transportation, have here the King's Allowance of 2. *6d.* per week.
REMARKS.
On a Tablet over the Entrance is the following Inscription:
"This County Gaol was erected in the Forty-fifth Year of the Reign of
His Majesty George the Third, &c.
and in the Year of our Lord,
M,DCCC,V.
Monevpenny, Architect."

To prevent encroachments, the ground recently purchased by the County extends about twelve feet beyond what is occupied by the Gaol. The Prison is enclosed on three sides by a low fence-wall, ten feet high; in the centre of which, on the East, or principal front, is the entrance. This is rendered very conspicuous by a noble and spacious gate, of the Tuscan order, constructed from a design of *Plgnola,* at the Farnese Gardens' Gate, or entrance into the Campo Vaccini; and adorned with rustick columns and pilasters, supporting a handsome entablature.

At sixty feet distance, on each side of the gate, are rustick piers, connected with the gate by an iron railing.. The principal front of this building is 220 feet in length, and is designed to form three advanced structures. The chief entrance is in the middle structure; and on each side are the publick entrances to the courtyard, with rooms for the Turnkeys adjoining.

The spaces between the advanced structures are ornamented with niches, finished in a style of chaste simplicity, and the angles are embossed with rustick quoins: The parts of which all are composed, are large, few in number, and of a bold relief, characteristick of the purpose of the building.

Over the niches are moulded square compartments, which give a simple and easy relief to the space between the crowning of the niches, and the beautiful Dorick cornice; which is a grand and striking object, imitated from the Theatre of Marcellus at Rome, excepting in the Dentil-band, which here remains uncut, and the soffit of the corona is divested of its ornaments.

The Keeper's house, a large and convenient dwelling, is in the centre of the building; and affords from each floor an entire communication, by arcades, all round the Prison, without the necessity of passing the courts. These arcades are likewise very commodious for the Debtors; giving them an easy and open avenue to their respective apartments, and a great accommodation for walking and exercise in bad weather.

The ascent to the floors of the arcades, which are paved with flag-stones, is by stone stair-cases, guarded by iron railing. Over each arcade, on the Master-Debtors' Side, are six sleeping-rooms, 16 feet square, and nearly 11 feet high; and a kitchen, or mess-room, 24 feet by 22, with a large fire-place, dining-table, shelves, and cupboards for provisions. They have also two rooms on the ground-floor, of the same size; one of which is a day-room, and the other for the Debtor to see his friends in. The bed-rooms are furnished with a wooden lath-bedstead, a straw-mattress, feather-bed, blanket, sheets, and a rug, at *2. 6d.* each per week.

The court for Common-Side Debtors is separated from that of the Master's-Side by an iron railing, and is of equal size, *viz.* 84 feet by 74. They have likewise three floors of arcades, that lead to their sleeping-rooms; three of which are on the ground-floor; three on the first story, with a mess-room, the same as on the Master's Side; and three on the attick-story, with an Infirmary. To these sleeping-rooms, which are similar to those on the Master's-Side, the County allows a straw-insacking bed, a blanket and coverlet, *gratis*.

In the Women-Debtors' court, which is So feet by 35, and situate on the Southside of the Prison, are four spacious rooms, of like construction with those for the other Debtors. One of these rooms is furnished by the Keeper, at *2 s. 6d.* per week; and the others have a straw-in-sacking bed, blanket, and coverlet, at the County's expenee. Every room has a bath-stove grate, an iron shovel and poker, and a coal-box, to hold two bushels. The recess on each side of the chimney has a shelf, 18 inches wide, for placing their provisions, &c. All the Debtors' rooms are boarded, with each a sash-window, 5 feet 6 by 3 feet *6,* and a grated, unglazed aperture over the door, of 3 feet by 18 inches. This court has no arcades, but a door out of it communicates with the Chapel.

Here is a reservoir, filled by an hydraulic pump from a well of fine water adjoining; which, being judiciously placed in the centre of the Men-Debtors' courts, is both convenient and ornamental, forming an elegant arcade beneath the cistern. Within this arcade are placed two large stone-troughs, with each a pipe and cock; so that the Debtors may enjoy all the use of a constant supply of water under cover from the reservoir. Pipes are also laid on to the Keeper's house, and to the court assigned for the Women-Debtors.,

The court-yard for Female-Felons is situate on the North-side of the New Build ings, and in dimension 105 feet by 45. On the ground-floor is a spacious dayraom, 24 feet by 22, and nearly 11 feet high, with iron-grated glazed windows, and paved with flag-stone. It is well supplied with water by a pipe and cock from the reservoir, which is placed in the Men-Debtors' court, and fitted up with fireplace, benches, table, and shelves 1 8 inches wide, in each chimney recess, for provisions; and a water trough.

Within the above court are three floors of arcades, containing three cells, or night-rooms on each floor, of 15 feet by 7, and nearly 11 feet high. The ascent to the upper-rooms is by a stone staircase, guarded by iron rails. These cells are well aired, by grated apertures over the doors, of 3 feet by 18 inches, without glass; and there is another aperture, through each partition-wall to the staircase, whereby a free circulation of air is obtained; and which, from the spaciousness of the rooms, cannot fail, with attention, to make this part of the Prison always healthy. There is also on the upper-floor an Infirmary-room, 24 feet by 22, with two sash-windows, and proper conveniencies for sick persons.

The Male-Felons' apartments in this Prison, as they stood in 1807, were erected upon a piece of ground that was purchased in the year 1788, adjoining to the old structure. A lobby, or passage, 28 feet long, and 6 feet wide, leads to the centre building; and on each side are two courts, of about *60* feet by 35- On the groundfloor in each-court-yard is a day-room, 13 feet square, with fire place, table, benches, shelves, a water-cock, and stone washing-trough; and also four sleeping-cells, each 9 feet by *6,* lined with oak plank, furnished with iron-grated, unglazed windows, 18 feet by 14, and inside shutters, each of which has a pane of knobbed glass.

In the centre of the building, on the ground-floor, is the Turnkey's lodge, and behind that his sitting-room. On the first story are 24 sleeping-cells, and a sleepingroom for each of the Turnkeys, which commands a view of the four court-yards.

On the second, or attick-story, are *16* sleeping-cells, and four infirmary-rooms.

The total number therefore of Men-Felons' cells is 56, with four day-rooms, and four infirmary-rooms. Each cell is 9 feet by 6, and fitted up with wheat-straw-incanvas bed, two blankets and a rug on the floor, and pewter chamber-utensils: And all, except those on the ground-floor, open into lobbies 4 feet wide.

The various sewers are placed at the end of the several wings of the Prison, on the outside of the stair-cases, the vaults of which are 60 feet deep. There are also adjoining the sewers, pens for ashes, &c. forming together little buildings, equally useful and ornamental.

The court-yards here are so extensive and open, that the paving of them entirely with flag-stones is thought unnecessary: yet, in order that Prisoners may enjoy the free use of them, spacious foot-paths of stone are laid out in various directions, and the intermediate parts are covered with fine gravel.

It is to be regretted, that when this addition was made to the Prison, a New Chapel also was not built. The present old one, of 2S feet by 25 only, and 12 feet high, is too low and inconvenient: And the sexes, though separated in the area of the Chapel, sit on benches, or forms, very near, and in full view of each other.

Debtors have the *option of attending Divine Service:* but, if they neglect, are locked up in their rooms till it is over. The Rev. *John Lee,* a Romish Priest, gratuitously attends those Prisoners who are of the same persuasion.

Underneath the Chapel is a large store-room, in which are deposited the fuel, &c granted for the use of the Prisoners.

The day-rooms have coals allowed, with kettles and other utensils for cooking, Common-Side Debtors have about forty bushels of coals for winter consumption.

Within the Gaol is hung up an Account of Fees, which, after a recital of the Preamble of the Statute enjoining it, is as follows: Table Of Fees,
For Debtors, in the County Gaol of Winchester.
£ s. d. "At the entrance of every Debtor; for cleansing the Gaol, and finding candle, and other necessaries----------0 + 0

Of every Debtor, for each week's lodging in the Gaoler's bed on the Master's-Side---------------0 26 £. s. d.

For each Debtor discharged, to the Gaoler--------100

Of him, for the second, and every other Action-------0 10 0

To the Turnkey, at the Discharge of every Debtor------020

To him, of such Debtor, for the second, and every other Action--0 I 0 For Copy of every Warrant for a Debtor __ __--_ o 10

Certificate, to obtain a Supersedeas---------034

"Hants, Lent Assizes, March 2d, 1790. "We have reviewed, and do confirm this Table of Fees.
"T. C. Shirley." "B. HOTHAM.
"J. Harrington. "R. PERRYN.
"T. Hall.
"Durnford, Clerk of the Peace." No Employment has hitherto been provided by the County: but Prisoners of handicraft trades are permitted to procure work from without, and have the whole of their earnings.

Saint Cross's Hospital *Bread,* called *"The Dole"* is a small loaf, given to each of the Prisoners six times a year; viz. Easter-Eve, Whitsun-Eve, May the 3d, August 10th, Oct. 31st, and Christmas-Eve. Upon sending thither the number of Prisoners in custody on each of those days, the same number of loaves is put by, and sent for the day following.

The Prisoners are obliged to wash their hands and face every morning: they have clean linen once a week, and are shaved twice weekly.

Mops, brooms, brushes, soap, and all other requisites for prison cleanliness are supplied to the whole Gaol by the considerate Magistrates; and every Prisoner must sweep his room, and wash it daily in summer, and weekly in winter.

Here is no Gaol-uniform provided; but if a Prisoner be ragged or filthy in apparel, he is furnished with suitable cloathing. A large tub is ready for a bath.

No Rules and Orders. The Act for the Preservation of Health, and Clauses against Spirituous Liquors, are conspicuously fixed up.

$3= All Prisoners are prudently discharged in a morning; and have money given them, according to the distance from their respective homes.

The Keeper is humane, intelligent, and attentive, and the Prison remarkably clean.

Through the singular exertions of that active and excellent Magistrate, the late Sir Henry St. John Mildmay, Bart. M. P. for the County , a Fund has been My kind Friend, and able Coadjutor in an Examination into, and Report of the State of Convicts in Portsmouth f and Langston Harbours; drawn up 16th March 1802, and hereafter inserted.

t The Keeper of Portsmouth Gaol, by Letter dated 27th May 1811, informs me, that every sleeping-cell is now furnished by the Corporation with an iron-bedsti'ad, and sacking bottom, a straw-bed, a pillow, two blankets, a coverlet, and pewter chamber utensil. Debtors, or others, who wish for better accommodations, are supplied with beds by the Gaoler, at from sixpence to one shilling per night. established here, for the relief of those poor Debtors, who are unable to sue for their Sixpences, Supersedeas, &c. and likewise for giving some pecuniary assistance, to enable them to return to their respective homes.

If similar institutions were set on foot throughout England and Wales, it would be productive of great advantage to the helpless Prisoner: in Wales, particularly, where many poor Debtors are confined for three or four pounds, and the expence of suing for their aliment is greater than the original debt.

WINCHESTER.
The City Gaol and Bridewell.
Gaoler, *William Foster.* No Salary.
Fees, for Debtors, *1l. 2s. od.*; for Felons, *6s. 8d.* No Table.
Surgeon, Mr. *Giles Lyford.* Makes a Bill.

Number of Criminal Prisoners, 1802, March 19th, Two. 1803, Oct. 24th, Three. 1807, Sept. 23d, One.

Allowance, to Felons, a *quart loaf* of bread every other day, which, in 1802, weighed two pounds four ounces.

REMARKS.
This Prison is a neat brick building, erected in 1800, during the Mayoralty of Joseph Barker Esq. Debtors, arrested on process issuing out of the Borough Court, may be here contined-for any sums great or small: but at my several visits I have not found any in custody.

A court-yard, paved with flag-stone, of about 20 feet by 14, and two rooms, about 13 feet square and 9 feet high, were at first set apart for Debtors. They are now however chiefly appropriated, the one to Petty Offenders, and the other to Female Criminals, or to Deserters.

The Felons have also two rooms, on the opposite side of the building, and below stairs, opening into their two paved court-yards, and of the same dimensions as those before mentioned. The four rooms, which have all of them boarded floors, with glazed windows and fire-places, are ventilated by iron-gratings over each door, and a small aperture in the doors, of 9 inches by 7. To each room the City allows a straw-in-sacking bed, without bedstead; a bolster, blanket, and rug. A bushel of coals also, per week, is granted in winter, for the common use of all.

At my visit in 1802, there being only one fire allowed, the two Prisoners, a Man and a Woman, were locked up together during the day time.

No Employment. No Rules and Orders. The Act and Clauses not hung up. The court-yards well supplied with water, and the Prison clean.

WINCHESTER. *The County Bridewell.*
Keeper, *Ricliard Page.* Salary, 100/. No Fees.

Chaplain, Rev. *Nicholas Westcomh.*
Duty, Prayers twice a week. Salary, 70/. for Bridewell and County Gaol.

Surgeon, Mr. *Giles Lyford.* Salary, 100/. for both.
i
Number of Prisoners, 1801, Jan. 13th, Fifty. 1802, Jan. 3d, Sixty-five. March 29th, Forty-nine. 1803, Oct. 24th, Sixty-three. 1807, Sept. 23d, Sixty.

Allowance, twenty-two ounces of best wheaten bread: I weighed several of the loaves, and found them good weight, though two days old. Also four, and sometimes five meals a week, during the winter, of meat boiled and broth together. The Keeper has a large garden, in which the Prisoners are occasionally employed; and from which, all the summer, the Bridewell is supplied with vegetables in season, and with potatoes during the winter, about one pound per day, to each Prisoner. (See the Remarks.) REMARKS.

This spacious Prison is a modern structure, and was finished in November 1787. It has four large court-yards, with a pump and 6ewer in each. The Keeper's house is in the centre of the building, but only commands the view of about one half of each court-yard.

Here are four day-rooms, three for Men and one for Women, in size, 26 feet by 16, and 9 feet 6 inches high; to each of which the County liberally allows *one faggot* of wood per day till Michaelmas, and *two* faggots from Michaelmas to Lady-day: also cooking utensils, tin dishes to eat out of; with mops, brooms, pails, towels, soap, and every article necessary for prison-cleanliness.

Of *sleeping-cells* there are forty-six; viz. Thirty-two, 10 feet by 6; four, 16 feet square; four, 16 feet by 10; and six, *16* feet by 12; all 9 feet *6* inches high.

Six of the above thirty-two are solitary cells; each having a door that opens into a small court-yard, of 14 feet by 9, with a sewer in the corner of each courtyard; (bur for the Men and two for the Women: There are likewise two tiers of cells, one above the other; the passage leading to which is about 4 feet wide. Also six rooms, 16 feet each by 13, and ten feet high; two of them on the first floor, and foHr on the second: in which are wooden crib-bedsteads, each for one person, with straw-in-ticking bed, bolster, blanket and rug. The like bedding (but without a bedstead) is also allowed to all the *cells* in this Prison.

The Chapel is in the centre of the building; and the Prisoners, seated on forms are distinctly partitioned off, according to their respective wards: The Men are placed in three compartments; the Women in the fourth; and they are all in sight of each other.

Previous to trial, each Prisoner has the alledged *offence* stuck upon the cell-door; and the *sentence,* in like manner, after trial.

They are all let out of their respective cells at six o'clock in *summer,* and again locked up at sunset: in *winter* they are enlarged as soon as it is light, and remanded at dusk. Each cell is cleaned out by about six in summer, and eight in winter; and the Prisoners are not allowed to go into their sleeping-cells during the day.

Over the Prison, and on each side of the Keeper's house, are very spacious and convenient work-rooms; in one of which was deposited junk for the Prisoners, and in the other several spinning-wheels. The Women were employed in reeling off raw-silk; and I was given to understand that they received the whole of their earnings, amounting to about *is. 6d.* per week. I was concerned however to hear, at my visit in September 1807, that this chief branch of their Employment, at least for the present, was discontinued, owing to a decay of trade in the article of silk; but Needle-work is pursued by them, when they can procure it.

Some of the Men-Prisoners are employed either in the garden-grounds, or about the building: All Handicrafts are allowed to work at their respective trades; and of the profits of their labour, after two-pence in every shilling is appropriated to those poor who cannot work, the remaining five-sixths belong to the Prisoner himself.

All the sleeping-cells are lighted and ventilated by iron-grated windows, with inside shutters: also an iron-grating over each door opens into a passage four feet wide, and thus produces a free circulation of air.

The *Infirmary* stands just behind the Chapel, from which it is detached by a court-yard. This room is pleasant and healthy, and looks over the spacious garden belonging to the Keeper's house.

Every Prisoner who comes hither in a filthy and ragged condition, is stripped at his entrance, and washed. He then receives the County-clothing, until his own is fumigated, or soaked in cold water, for six days at least, the water being changed every day.

The flag-stones in the lobbies of the ground-floor, being laid on chalk, are always damp in wet weather; as are also the floors of the day-rooms: But the boards of the cells, resting on what they call *rubley stones,* are pretty tolerably dry.

The Dean of Winchester, on Christmas-Day, sends a dinner of boiled beef to the Bridewell and County Gaol. The Chaplain also, and Surgeon, give a half-guinea each, to be laid out, at the same season, in meat for the poor Prisoners.

The Keeper's house Is a very good

one: The whole of the Prison particularly clean, and frequently visited by the Magistrates, who enter their Remarks in a book prepared for so good a purpose.

No Rules and Orders. The Clauses against Spirituous Liquors are hung up; but not the Act for preserving the Health of Prisoners.

The annual average of Commitments, within the last seven years, up to September 1807, exclusive of Vagrants and Deserters, was 150. *Six deaths* only had happened during 20 years, to that time!

Prisoners always have money given to carry them home, according to their respective distances; and are constantly discharged *in a morning.*

WIRKSWORTH. *Derbyshire.*
The Bridewell.
Keeper, *Thomas Mather.* Salary, 25/. No Fees.
Sugeon, Mr. *Anthony Goodwin.* Makes a Bill.
Prisoner, 1805, Oct. 12th, One.

Allowance, *none whatever; so* that the Keeper said many might starve, if he did not relieve them *at his own expence I* REMARKS.

This House of Correction is on Wash-Green, and was built in 1791. At the back of the Keeper's house are two court-yards, one for the Men, the other for the Women, of about 28 feet by 19 feet *6,* with a sewer in each.

Nine steps down, in the Women's court, is a damp Dungeon, 7 feet by *6* feet *6,* and 6" feet 4 high, to the crown of the arch. All the light or ventilation here received is by a grating through the door, six inches square.

On each side of the Keeper's apartment a door opens into a little day-room, 11 feet 9 inches by 7 feet, with afire-place in both. These are for the Men and Women; and each has attached to it two small sleeping-cells, 7 feet by 5 feet *6,* and 8 feet high; ventilated and lighted by iron grating over each door, 18 inches by 15, and by a square aperture in the door, of *6* inches. Wooden bedsteads only are provided by the County: straw-in-sacking and chaff-beds are furnished by the Keeper.

The Prisoner here was a shoe-maker, committed for bastardy: he was at work. No water, but what is fetched from a distance.

WISBEACH. *Cambridgeshire.*
The Town Gaol, and BridewelL
Gaoler, *John Beal,* a shoe-maker. Salary, 30/. No Fees.
Chaplain, was the Rev. Mr. *Stachall;* since deceased. Salary, 10/.
Duty, on Sunday, when there are Prisoners. But the above Gentleman dying in 1807, no Chaplain has been since appointed; so that Jiere are no religious attentions whatever.
Surgeon, Mr. *Skrimshaw;* now Mr. *Hardwich.*
Salary, none. He makes a Bill.
Prisoners, 1S02, Aug. 8th, One. 1810, Sept. 4th, Two.

Allowance, at my visit in 1802, it was sixpence in bread daily, sent in from the Baker's; but now reduced to fourpence a day.

REMARKS.

That miserable old Prison, which I fully described in the Gentleman's Magazine for October 1804, page 899, having been taken down, this new Gaol was first inhabited 27th April 1809. It is situate at the corner of Gaol-Lane, and adjoins the new Sessions-House.

The ascent to the Keeper's apartments is by a flight of eight stone steps. He has two rooms for his own use; and adjoining to them are two sleeping-cells; the largest 13 feet by 11, the other about 10 feet square, and 8 feet high; having each one double iron-grated window, of 3 feet by 2. They have no fire-place, but brick floors, a bench to sit on, and loose straw laid, with two blankets, and a rug for bedding.

These two cells are generally appropriated to Debtors committed hither by the Court of Requests, for sums not exceeding forty shillings, the jurisdiction of which Court extends eleven miles. The iron-grated windows have inside shutters, and a convenient sewer is provided.

On the basement story, which is level with the Street, are thirteen sleeping-cells for Criminals, their average size about 10 feet square, and 8 feet high, with windows and bedding as the former. They open into a lobby 4 feet wide, and must be cold and damp in the Winter. Adjoining to these cells is a very large room for *Prisoners of War,* of about 45 feet by 18; with three double iron-grated windows, and straw on the brick floor for bedding. At one end is a fire-place, and an adjacent sewer properly disposed.

Above stairs are six cells for Women, of about 12 feet square, with boarded floors, and in other respects accommodated in the same manner as those already described.

The room set apart for the Sick is about 14 feet square; and has a fire-place and grate, with a glazed sliding sash-window, but no furniture.

The room appropriated for Divine Service is of the same size as the above, with a glazed window.

No Rules and Orders. The Act and Clauses not hung up. It is in contemplation to make a court-yard, from the Keeper's garden behind the Prison.

Here is *no Employment,* although every convenience for it is at hand. The hemp and flax grown within the vicinity, furnish adequate materials for the industrious Prisoners at Swaffham, in Norfolk, above twenty miles from Wisbeach.

The Commitments to this Gaol in 1809, were 52.

WOLVERHAMPTON. *Staffordshire.*
The Bridewell.
Keeper, *George Roberts.* Salary, 80/. No Fees.
Surgeon, Mr. *Fowke;* who makes a Bill.
Number of Prisoners, 1802, Nov. 2d, Nine.
Allowance, seven pounds and a half of best wheaten bread, one pound of cheese,, and five-pence half-penny, in money or vegetables, per week, for each Prisoner.

REMARKS.

"This Prison," as we learn from Mr. Howard, " was once so greatly out of repair, and so insecure, that Prisoners, even for the slightest offences, were kept in irons." It was rebuilt in 1800. The Men Prisoners have a small flagged court-yard, about 33 feet by 18, furnished with a pump and sewer. Here is a day-room, with a fireplace; a work-room, and two solitary cells.

Up stairs are ten sleeping-cells, and an Infirmary room, with a fire-place. The Women Prisoners have also a day and working-room below stairs; a small courtyard, 27 feet by 18, with water laid on, and a sewer provided. Above stairs three sleeping-cells, and a sick-room with a fire-place; each cell 8 feet by 6, and fitted up with a rush mattress on the floor, two blankets, and a coverlet. The two rooms set apart for the sick have wooden bedsteads. The passage, or lobby, that separates the sleeping-cells from the court-yard, 4 feet 5 inches wide.

The Prisoners are employed in making sacks, nails, screws, &c. and receive two pence in every shilling of their earnings.

Here is a Magistrates' visiting-book, provided for entries; but none made of its being visited. The cells are well ventilated, and the Prison is clean.

WOODBRIDGE. *Suffolk.*
The Bridewell.
Keeper, *Robert Dowsing;* now *John Fisher.* Salary, 52/. 10. with coals and candles; also mops, brooms, pails, &c. to keep the Prison clean.

Chaplain, Rev. Mr. *Black.* Salary, 25.
Duty, Prayers and Sermon on Sunday, and Prayers on Wednesday and Friday.

Surgeon, Mr. *Ling;* who makes a Bill.
Number of Prisoners, 1805, Sept. 13th, One. 1810, Sept. 22d, Two.

Allowance, one pound and half of best bread per day, sent from the Baker's in loaves of that size, and weighed by the Keeper. In case of illness, the Surgeon has discretionary powers, with respect to the diet of his Patients.

REMARKS.
This House of Correction stands on an elevated and healthy spot, just out of the Town, and was first inhabited on the 11th of January, 1805. It consists of two wings, with the Keeper's house in the centre; on the ground-floor of which is the visiting Magistrates' room, and the Keeper's parlour: his rooms have a constant command of the whole court-yards.

On the right side of the entrance are five sleeping-cells on the ground-floor, for Men, and five also for them above stairs. On the left side three, and three more, in the same higher situation, for the Female Prisoners. The latter open into lobbies well ventilated, 31 feet long, and 3 feet 6 inches wide.

The Men's cells open into a lobby 52 feet long, and of the same width as the last mentioned.

Each cell is 11 feet by 7, and 9 feet high; fitted up with an iron bedstead, stravvin-sacking bed, two sheets, a double blanket, and coverlet, all lighted and ventilated by an iron-grated and glazed window, 28 inches square. One cell on each range has a fire-place, to be used as a sick-room in case of illness, at which time coals are allowed. The Prisoners' lobbies open into another passage, leading to the Chapel. This is over the Visiting Magistrates' room, 18 feet 8 inches long by 12 feet 10, and 9 feet high. Prayer-Books are allowed by the District, or Hundred, to all that are able to read.

The Men's court-yard is 52 feet 9 inches long, 39 feet wide; and that allotted to the Women, 39 feet by 31. These are separated by an area, of the width of the Keeper's house, viz. 36 feet 5 inches; and in it is a pump to supply the Prison with water. The courts are on an inclined plane, with gutters properly disposed; and all the water is so conducted, as to run through the sewers into a large receptacle without the Prison walls.

Water is introduced into every court-yard, and towels are provided for the Prisoners to wash, before they receive their bread: they also sweep and clean out their cells every morning. They have the use of their respective court-yards half an hour in the morning, one hour at noon, and half an hour again in the evening.

County clothing is allowed for those who have been convicted at the Assizes, or who come in offensive, or ragged: Their own clothes, are then cleaned, mended, and laid by, against their being discharged. An oven is provided, to purify foul or infected clothes, and a bathing-tub at hand, which is frequently used.

The Prisoners are shaved and clean shirted once a week; their linen is washed at the expence of the Hundred; and fresh straw is supplied to them monthly.

Their Employment in this Bridewell consists of spinning, and the making of garters and nets. Of their earnings one fourth goes to the Keeper, another fourth to the Prisoner during confinement, and the remaining half is paid on discharge; which provides them with immediate sustenance, as well as the means of reaching comfortably and honestly their respective homes.

On looking over the books I observed, that one working Prisoner had received *ggl. 14s. 3%d.*; another, *£1. 5. "id.;* and a third, *gg.l. Os. 2%d.*

The *Commitments* to this House of Correction, until my last visit in 1810, were as follow:

From April to....Arii'lfci''..-:--, r; 1 r-,- $th Oj 1806 to 867'*irX&t w&* 1807 to r 18,98 --,-.Tjj: 1808 to 1809 -70. 1809 to aid Sept. 1810 '--,,-/ r--.-. 0(1T Total-----337.

Scales and weights are judiciously furnished by the Magistrates of the Division; and, to the honour of the Baker, every loaf, at both my visits, was *considerably over weight.*

Here are printed Rules and Orders, approved by the Magistrates in Session, and confirmed by the Judges of Assize, in the year 1808.

The prohibitory Clauses against Spirituous Liquors are hung up, but not the Act for Preservation of Health. The whole Prison very clean.

WORCESTER.
Tlie City Gaol.
Gaoler, *James Griffiths,* the Parish-Clerk. Salary, 50/.

Fees, for Debtors, *9s. 2d.* The Under-Sheriff demands 2. *6d.* for his *liberate t* For Felons, 1. *4d.* on Discharge. No Table. Garnish abolished.

Chaplain, Rev. Mr. *Faulkner.* Salary, *lol.*
Duty, Prayers every Friday Morning.
Surgeon, Mr. *Rayment.* Salary, *6l. 6s.*
Number of Prisoners, Debtor. Felons, &c 1802, Nov. 8th,----2----4 & a De-

serter.
1803, Aug. 26th, --.g-.--2 & 2 run-away Apprentice'. 1806, Sept. 10th----4.---7 &a Deserter. 1808, Jan. 14th,----S----5. 1809, Nov. 21st,----0---.7.

Allowance, to Debtors, none; except they are extremely poor: then they have three-pence a day, the same as the Felons. N. B. No Prisoner arrested by Writ issued out of the Court of Pleas of the City of Worcester, has ever been able to derive any advantage under the Lord's Act REMARKS.

This Gaol, situate in Fryer-Street, is also the City Bridewell.

Debtors have a court of about 18 yards square, with a day-room 14 feet square; and there are five rooms on the Master's side, to which the Keeper furnishes beds at $s. per week, if single; if two sleep together, 2. per week each.

One large room, which serves as a Chapel, is the Debtor's Free Ward, to which the City allows straw and a rug each.

Criminal Prisoners have a small court-yard, a day-room, and a sleeping-room, on the ground-floor; to which straw and two rugs for each are allowed.

The Bridewell Prisoners have a small day-room up stairs, and a large sleeping room, separated off for Men and Women. No room set apart for an Infirmary.

The Gaol is well supplied with water.

The Prisoners procure work for themselves, and have all their earnings.

The Act and Clauses not hung up.
WORCESTER.
The Castle Gaol, and Bridewell.
Gaoler, *William Davis.*

Salary, 250/. for the Gaol, and the Bridewell which adjoins to it. Fees, for Debtors, as per Table. Besides which the Under-Sheriff demands *3s. 6d.* for his *liberate!* For Felons all Fees are abolished. The Gaoler is paid the expence incurred for the removal of Transports.

Chaplain, Rev. *William Faulhner.* Salary, 40/.

Duty, Prayers on Wednesdays and Fridays; and Prayers and Sermon on every
Sunday, on Christmas Day, and Good Friday.

Surgeon, Mr. *Rayment,* for the Felons only.

Salary, 20l. and is paid for Medicines.

Number of Prisoners, Debtors. Felons. Bridewell.
l802, Nov. 7th,----12----21----*23.* ,1803, Aug. 26th,----8----16----31.
J806 Sept. 10th,----14---.-10.---.-21.
1S08, Jan. 14th,----17----24----26.
1809, Nov. 21st,----8----23----27.

Allowance, to Debtors, none, except the Debtor, being very poor, applies to the Visiting Magistrates, and swears to his or her latest settlement; then, if the Parish be within the County of Worcester, they will make an order to allow the Prisoner a weekly sum: but if it be out of the Magistrates' jurisdiction, they cannot make an order. The utmost that the Keeper remembered to have been given in consequence, was *2s, 6d.* per week; and that only to one Man: But, since my visit in 1806, he informs me that the considerate Magistrates have ordered an Allowance to every Debtor having no property; and the Bill thus incurred is to be laid before them at every Quarter Sessions.,

To Felons, and other Criminal Prisoners, one pound of bread daily, and a quart of oatmeal gruel for every day's Breakfast. Dinner. *Sunday,* half a pound of meat, and one pound of potatoes. *Monday,* two pounds of potatoes. *Tuesday,* a quart of pease soup. *Wednesday,* two pounds of potatoes. *Thursday,* the same as Sunday. *Friday,* two pounds of potatoes. *Saturday,* a quart of pease soup. REMARKS.

The Castle Yard is spacious. The County Members are chosen in it; but the wood and iron-work of the entrance gate is so much decayed, as to render the courtyard very insecure and unsafe.

The Debtor's side of the Prison is separated from that of the Criminals by a brick wall, and divided into two classes; the Master's Ward, and the Common Ward. The ample court-yard allotted for the use of both, is one hundred and eleven feet by sixty five.

The Master's-Side Debtors have a day-room, 21 feet by 13 feet 3 inches; they pay 2a *6d.* per week for a single bed; but if two sleep together, 1. *6d.* each; and there are eleven good lodging-rooms in the Gaoler's house. The Common-side Debtors have a Free Ward, 18 feet by 17, to which the County allows straw, but no bedding, nor fuel. The cooking-room, common to both the classes, is 19 feet square.

Here is no distinct or separate apartment for Male and Female Debtors. They are confined together in one common Ward. Those Females who can afford to pay for a bed, sleep in the Gaoler's house.

The poor Debtors complained grievously, that, as they had *no Allowance,* and were both able and willing to work, there should be no attention paid to the *means of Industry:* (but which Mr. *Davis,* their compassionate Gaoler, told me he should find no difficulty to procure in this manufacturing City:) that they had also *no place or room to work in;* adding, that they were often penny-less, in a miserable state, bordering even on starvation; and that many of their description must have perished from want, had they not been relieved by *casual charity!* This shews how full of emphatical meaning is that malediction of the severe Creditor, who pronounced it as his Debtor's doom, "to starve, and rot in Gaol!"

There are, I think very improperly, two windows in this Ward, through which the Debtors may converse with the Felons, or even assist them with means of effecting an escape; (as has been practised at York, and other places;) and which inconsistency and danger the utmost attention of the Keeper cannot, under present circumstances prevent.

The Chapel is between the Gaol and the Bridewell.

The attendance of Debtors on Divine Service is, I find, optional. On my visit, 7th Nov. 1S02, only three out of the twelve Debtors were at Chapel; yet all the Felons and other Criminal Prisoners were there, and their behaviour was orderly and attentive.

The Sick Ward of the Male Felons is in the Debtors' court; and as it consists of (wo rooms which communicate with each other, the Males and Females are alike obliged to be put therein; because the other Ward, intended for sick Females, is both very remote from the house, and an insecure place for confinement. There is also but one sewer for the sick Debtors, and to which the Male and Female Felons likewise resort, whatever may be their disease.

The Gaoler's house itself, which forms a considerable part of the Prison, is not only insecure for custody, but in a very dilapidated and uncomfortable state to. reside in. Under all these circumstances, however, it is fortunate for the Prisoners,,, that their Keeper is a Man of Benevolence and Humanity, and accommodates them as well as he can.

The following is The Table Of Fees, To be paid by the *Debtors* to the Gaoler of Worcester Castle.

£. s. d. "For entering the Action wherein such Prisoner is brought into
Custody under any Writ or Process---------068
For entering every second or other Action-------03 4
For the certificate of a declaration not having been delivered, in order to sue out a Writ of Supersedeas--------034
N. B. The above are demandable of the Prisoner.
For receiving and entering every Declaration against a Prisoner in Custody,-.---------------034
For each copy of a Warrant against a Prisoner-------034 ?
N. B. These to be paid by Persons delivering the Declarations, or demanding the Copy of the Warrant.
For attending upon every Prisoner to give Bail, or Special Bail, or a *Habeas Corpus,* or on any other necessary occasion, out of the
Gaol, as directed by the Statute, per mile....... M D
That the following Charge&for the lodging, bedding, &c. of the Debtors be allowed:
Every person confined in the Sheriff's Ward, finding his own bedding, for a week---------_-----0 I 0i
Every Person who is found a lodging, and abed, bedding, and sheets, for a week--------------.-026
If two Persons in one bed, each for a week--_-_-_ 0l 6 For signing every certificate------o I 0."
Copy of every *Habeas Corpus,* and return thereof------0 5 Q.'

On the Crown Side of this Prison there are no reception-rooms for the Surgeon to examine Prisoners in, upon their confinement; or to fumigate, if needful, and purify their clothes, previous to their admission amongst the other Prisoners.

The court-yard is 127 feet by 80; where persons committed for, or adjudged guilty of Misdemeanors, those committed till trial for Felonies, the Convicted Felons, and Transports, with the Male Prisoners of every class, are obliged by day to *associate together;* contrary, as I conceive, to the Statute 31 Geo. I IK c. xlvi.

Here is a day-room, called the *Round-House,* 34 feet by 16; and on the same, side of the court are sixteen cells, 10 feet 2 inches by 7 feet 2, deep; but well ventilated. These, however, are not sufficient for keeping the Criminals separate from the rest, the Gaoler having at times been obliged to confine two, three, and sometimes more Prisoners at night in one cell. In the year 1801, sixty-two Male Prisoners slept in the above sixteen cells, that is nearly four persons, and, mostly, that number in each cell. Every cell has a *Boultin* (so called) of long wheaten straw, weighing about 15 or 16 lbs. laid on the boards, and two blankets each.

Female Felons have a separate court, of 31 feet by 19, and a day-room 19 feet by 12, with two sleeping-cells on the ground-floor; but, all the Female Criminals of every description associate together, as is the case with the Male Prisoners above described.

Here is no *separate place of confinement* for such persons as are intended to be examined on behalf of the Prosecution of any indictment for Felony; or for *Children* or *Youths* committed for Misdemeanors or Felonies; but such of the latter sort whether Witnesses or Youths, are confined in the day-time with the *Transport* or other Criminals, convicted and unconvicted; "forming," as Sir George Paul acutely and too justly observes, " one profligate Society; where the most ignorant may be initiated, and the novice ascend to the higher mysteries of infamy and vice."

Prisoners under Sentence of Death are here most uncomfortably provided for. They sleep in their cells at night; and in the morning they retire into the Debtors' cooking-room, formerly a Dungeon, but which has now a large glazed window, with a fire-place in it, and is a part of the Keeper's house. What a *retirement t* where the minds, and the devotions, (if possible,) of these hapless Beings, are in a state of continual disturbance and distraction; occasioned by the necessary and frequent passing of the Debtors and other Prisoners, close to the door of the room in which such Unfortunates are confined.

The Men and Female Felons are kept separate; but Male and Female Debtors and Male and Female Bridewell Prisoners sit together. The indiscriminate mixture of such various and discordant elements seems surely to call aloud for some different modes of arrangement. According to the opinion of that excellent Magistrate before quoted, and in which I most cordially join, the *Separations* indispensably necessary to preserve any idea of order and regularity, are these:. u I. Of *Sex,* through every species of Offenders.

II. Of *Debtors,* from every other Class of Prisoners. III. Of *accused* Persons, and Prisoners convicted: And IV. Of the *Notorious* and *Profligate,* from the less daring and atrocious."

The old Dungeon, in the Castle-Yard, which once lay twenty-six steps under ground, of a circular form, and supplied with barrack bedsteads, was afterwards more judiciously employed to keep potatoes in; and has since been consigned to a still better purpose. In October 1804 it was filled up entirely, and levelled with the court-yard, that the very remembrance of it may gradually drop from every humane mind.

Coals are allowed to Criminal Prisoners, by order of the considerate Magistrates, according to the season; and to the most necessitous Prisoners clothes are given upon their discharge, with money also, to carry them to their respective homes.

This Gaol i9 well supplied with water from the Severn by an engine, which the Prisoners work to convey it; and an Errand-Woman is retained, to fetch provisions from the Town.

A journal is regularly kept of daily occurrences; a correct account of each Prisoner's earnings; and *a Book in which the Visiting Magistrates make their R&marks.* The Surgeon likewise has a Book of entries, stating his visits, and the state of the several Prisoners' health. In short, a great and exemplary attention appears in every department of this miserable Gaol; a Prison, which I trust the humane Magistracy of a County so opulent and respectable, will never think of *repairing*; but raise, by the erection, of a new one, the noblest memorial of their humanity, and attention to the health and morals of its inhabitants .

Convicts under Sentence of Transportation have the King's allowance of 2s. 6d. per week.

The employment of the Prisoners consists of spinning, carding wool, making of bags, sacks, and gloves; beating hemp, pounding sand, and dressing leather.

Prisoners before Trial, if disposed to work, receive half their earnings, together with an extra allowance of food; otherwise they have only the Gaol bread to subsist on. But after Conviction, one sixth of the produce goes to the Prisoner, another sixth to the Gaoler, and the remaining four sixths to the County, paid weekly in money.

The total earnings of the Prisoners in the Gaol for the year 1804, amounted to 57/. 16s. _d. of which the Prisoners received 167. 15. jd.; the Gaoler, 7/. l6v. 11jrf. and the County 33/. 4. od. The Bridewell earnings were 91/. 19. 2d. Of this the Prisoners received 15/. lQs. 8frf. the Gaoler, 15/. 19s. 8frf. and the County 59'-1-8+£ '-.'

The total number of Prisoners committed to the Gaol in 1804, was 40; to the Bridewell, 61. ' '

Total Earnings of theGaol in 1805 were 55/. 12#. 5d.; Prisoners' share,14'. l8.5rf. the Gaolers share, *71. Ijs. 2d.* the County, 32/. 16s. 9§d. A new County Gaol is building, in a fine situation, a little way out of the City, and is now (1811) in great forwardness; so that the wretched Prison above described will be soon done away.

The Bridewell Earnings were 144/. 19. 3/-The Prisoners' share, 24/. 3. 0rf. Gaolers, 24/. 3. 0d. to the County, 0,67. 13. 2/.

Number of Prisoners com mi ted in 1805, to the Gaol, 30; to the Bridewell, 58.

The foregoing Remarks tend to confirm the truth of an opinion, which I have long since entertained; namely, That poor Debtors are often the most pitiable objects in our British Gaols. The same complaint, want of food, and of work whereby to earn it, still exists in many of our Gaols; whilst in others, to the honour of Philanthropy, a Generous Allowance is afforded. In some Prisons within or near the Metropolis, as well as in others far remote, the *Debtors* have no *Bread,* although it is granted to the *Highwayman,* the *House-breaker,* and the *Murderer;* and Medical Assistance, which is provided for the latter, is withheld from the former. Besides which, they suffer a variety of obstructions and hardships, to impede their discharge from custody, even after the Law has spent its force, or pitying Creditors have forgiven the Debts which had detained them.

WREXHAM. *Denbighshire. North Wales. The House of Correction.*
Keeper, *John Alcock.* Salary, 12/. No religious attentions.

Surgeon, Mr. *Griffiths;* makes a Bill.
Number of Prisoners, 20th Nov. 1809, Three.
Allowance, 2s. per week.
REMARKS.

This Prison stands at the end of Mount-street, and has a small court in front, with a pump, by which the Prisoners are supplied. „

On the ground-floor are four sleeping-cells, two on each side of a passage 4 feet wide. They are about 9 feet square, with arched roofs, but no fire-places; wooden bedstead in each, with loose straw, short and filthy, two blankets, and a coverlet. To each cell there is a small court, but not being flagged, they are damp, muddy and useless. The sewer is inconveniently placed.

Above stairs is the day-room, large, well-lighted and ventilated by three grated and glazed windows, with a fire-place; but no coals are allowed. For the Women there is a room below, 15 feet by 12, and another of the same size, above: these have fire-places also, but no fuel provided; bedsteads and bedding the same as for the Men..?

No court-yard. No employment. Neither Act nor Clauses hung up. The Prison dirty.

WYMONDHAM. *Windham. Norfolk. ..,-The County Brideicell. ,*
Gaoler, *Thomas Johnson.* Salary, 80/. Also for taking Prisoners to the Quarter Sessions at Norwich, *Is.* per mile; and the same on bringing them back j the distance, nine miles.

Chaplain, Rev. Mr. *Colman.* Salary, 30/.
Duty, Prayers and Sermon every Sunday.
Surgeon, Mr. *Cubit.* Salary, 20/.
Number of Prisoners,
I805, Sept. 6th, Nineteen. 1810, Sept. 12th, Eight.
Allowance, as per Dietary, viz:
Breakfasts, one pound of bread daily.
Dinners, *Sunday,* Hanway's soups, of ox-cheek, &c.
Monday, one pound of bread. *Tuesday,* potatoes. *Wednesday,* boiled peas. *Thursday,* one pound of bread. *Friday,* potatoes. *Saturday,* boiled peas. REMARKS.

This Bridewell is partly surrounded by a boundary wall; which being distant about 18 feet from the Prison, affords the Keeper a small garden, for the growth of vegetables.

The house, which has been newly built, occupies one side of the area; and the back windows command the whole court-yard, of about 82 feet by *66,* which has On each side a wing built for the use of the Prisoners, and a pump of excellent water in the centre. Here are likewise two sewers, a mill-house, a store-room, and the Keeper's stable; the door of which last opens at the outside.

The North West wing contains, on the ground-floor, the Turnkey's room, two eleeping-cells, the *Clink,* (a place in which the irons are deposited) and four other cells, called the Strong Wards, which open into a passage 4 feet wide, well ventilated. Here is also the Men's Infirmary, of 21 feet 6 inches by 9 feet 6'; having a fire-place, an iron-grated window of 3 feet by 2; a glazed window, with inside shutter, and two beds.

Up stairs is the *Chapel,* 17 feet by 14, and 10 feet high, with seats for the Prisoners; and a room for depositing peas, &c.: four sleeping-cells on this story open into a lobby, 4 feet 6 inches wide, well ventilated: and at the end of it is the Men's work-room, of the same dimensions as their Infirma/y, but with the chimney place stopped up.

The South-East wing has on the ground-floor a warping-room, and two sleepingcells, which open into a passage 4 feet 6 inches wide; likewise another repository for irons, called the *Clink;* four sleeping-cells, and an Infirmary, of the same size as those in the North-West wing.

The Women have four cells abovestairs, which open into a lobby of 4 feet 6 inches; and at the end of this is their work-room, and one apartment for an Infirmary. Each cell is 15 feet 6 by 6 feet 6, 9 feet 6 inches high; has an iron-grated glazed window, 3 feet by 2 feet 8; an inside shutter, with a pot-hole in each door, 8 inches by 7; and is fitted up with a crib bedstead, straw-in-sacking, and flock-bed, a double blanket, pair of sheets, and a coverlet. Eight of these beds are capable of having two to sleep together in each; and 1 found some Prisoners spinning in their cells. The Men's cells have blinds placed before the windows.

The mill-house already mentioned has in it a very excellent mill, worked by four or five men, who walk round its axis in the same manner as practised in a horsemill. The hopper, &c. are in the room above, to prevent their receiving injury from the Prisoners; who do not know what they are grinding, but are frequently in want of employment.

They have no other use of the large court-yard, than for washing themselves in the morning; and are allowed to rest half an hour at breakfast-time, an hour at noon, and a half hour, also, at three o'Clock.

No Liquor as beverage is permitted, but water, except in case of sickness, and when ordered by the Surgeon. The Prisoners have now no part of their earnings, which of later years have seldom exceeded twenty pounds per annum; one fourth of which is paid to the Keeper, and the rest goes to the County Treasurer, in Account..

Roth Felons and Convicts have the County clothing; clean shirt or shift once a week, and fresh sheets monthly. Towels are also supplied them.

The County allows firing to the Men's two rooms on a Sunday, and to one room for the Women, during the six Winter months. Religious books are very laudably distributed, and placed in every cell...

For all the washing in this Prison, the Keeper is allowed *lol.* a year; and is likewise furnished with mops, brooms, pails, and soap, to keep the whole clean: this is done effectually, and the Prison also whitewashed once a year.

Their provisions are cooked by the Keeper in the kitchen.

None of the Prisoners are put, or, at least, not kept in irons: Rut there is here one detestably curious pair, which came from the Castle, and is called " *The Fiddte."* The construction is an iron collar, to go round the Prisoner's neck, with a stiff projecting end, 20 inches in length; and two curvatures, to receive his hands, and hold them up, as in the attitude of prayer. It weighs seven pounds and a half, and 1 am told, was used on *John Cooper,* a refractory Prisoner, in April 1803.

The excellent Rules and Orders of this Prison are properly displayed; but, in express contradiction to Article xvi. the Act and Clauses of 24 Geo. II. c. 40, are *neither painted on a board, nor hung up.*

The Prisoners are discharged from hence in a morning, and have one shilling in money given them; after which the Keeper conveys them either to their respectivehome, or to their Parish.

On examining the accounts of" this House of Correction, it has been made to appear, that the earnings of the Convicts have every year exceeded the expence of maintaining them; and that heretofore, in the course of five years and a half, (17S3 to 1789) the Balance gained by the County, after defraying all charges, amounted to 262/. 18. It was likewise established as a Fact, that some, even of those

Convicts who once appeared to be the worst, became useful members of the Community; and supported themselves and their families, by the practice of that trade which had been taught them, during their confinement in the Bridewell of Wymondham.

$3 All this was effected by the unremitting attention of Sir Thomas Beevor, an excellent and active neighbouring Magistrate; at a period, when it afforded one of the best examples of the proper management of a House of Correction, so as tq render it a place of *Reformation* also, for the Idle and the Dissolute. 1 was sorry therefore to find, at both my visits, that the Prisoners are now left in a torpid state of idleness, and the working system almost totally abandoned: a sufficient, but melancholy proof, how liable any new regulation is to fall into neglect, if not constantly made the object of care and attention! For the Love of Virtue, and the Honour of Religion and Humanity, let us hope that the Family, or at least th« Spirit of the Beevors, is not wholly extinct at Windham.

YARMOUTH. *Norfolk.*
The Town Brideicell.
Keeper, *John Daniels,* who is Master of the Workhouse. Salary, 5/. 5
Fees, 2. *2d.* and *Jourpence a day,* during each Prisoner's confinement.
Surgeon, whoever attends the Poor.
Prisoners, 1802, Feb. 16th, and 1805, Sept. 9th, none; 1810, Sept. 13th, One.
Allowance, ten ounces of bread three times a day.
REMARKS.

The Bridewell stands in the Workhouse yard; and consists of four sleepfng-cells, about 10 feet by 8, and 8 feet high: a fire-place in one of them, lighted and ventilated by an iron-bar grated window, 2 feet 6 inches by 2 feet; having an outside,shutter, and fitted up with a wooden bedstead, straw-in-sacking bed, a blanket, and a rug.

On the floor of each cell is a strong iron staple, with a chain five feet long. This is fastened to the Prisoner's leg, and is sufficiently long to admit of his lying down on the bed; or going to-the grating to receive water three times a day, or the daily allowance of bread. Tubs are made to serve the purpose of a sewer, and are emptied when nearly full.

In this state of durance the Prisoners remain, till liberated by legal process!

Here is a small court-yard, of about 24 feet by 10, to which they have no access for air or exercise, though sometimes confined six months. At the end of the court is a room for the sick, 12 feet 3 by 7 feet 3, with a fire-place, and coals allowed.

One cell in this Prison, extremely dark, and called *The Dungeon,* 9 feet by 8, end 8 feet high, has a boarded floor: But no bedding; no straw on the floor. For ventilation it has an aperture in the door, 9 inches square; but the little *borrowed tight* it can possibly admit, is almost wholly obstructed by four iron bars. Com tnitments, from 30th August 1803, to the 30th Sept. l810, one hundred and fortyfour.

Court of Conscience Debtors may be carried either to the Common Gaol or to this Bridewell, where they have the same allowance as the other Prisoners.

YARMOUTH. *Norfolk,*
The Town Gaol.
Gaoler, *Richard Helsdon;* now *Thomas King.* Salary, 40/.
Fees, Debtors, 6s. 8d.; Felons, 13. 4d.

Chaplain, none; nor any religious attentions whatever.

Surgeon, whoever attends the Poor.

Number of Prisoners, Debtor. Felons, Sec. 1802, Feb. 16th, 2------3.
1805, Sept. 9th, 3 4. 1810, Sept. 13th, 4 8.

Allowance, one pound of bread each per day: the same also to Prisoners confined here from the Court of *Requests,* or of *Conscience.* REMARKS.

In the front of this Gaol is the Visiting Magistrates' room, or Keeper's parlour: His sitting-room has a full command of the court-yard.

Here is only one, 30 feet 6 inches long by 19 feet 6 inches wide, for all descriptions of Prisoners. It has a passage 18 feet long, 4 feet wide, which leads to the pump and sewer.

The Master's-Side Debtors have four rooms above stairs, to which the Keeper furnishes beds, at 2. 4l. and 3. 6d. per week; and 4d. per week to the *Turnkey,* from each Debtor of this description.

Common-Side Debtors have *ajreeward,* to which the Corporation supplies straw beds in sacking, two blankets, a pillow, and a rug. There is also a common dayroom for Debtors, Male and Female, of 10- feet by 9, to which a peck of coals per day is allowed throughout the year.

One room is set apart for the Sick Debtors, 20 feet by 12, but has no fireplace: The window large, iron-grated and glazed. Here are wooden bedsteads, wkh strawin-tickingbeds, two blankets to each, a pillow, and a rug.

Down a ladder of ten steps is the Felons' day-room, in size 15 feet by 12, with a fire-place, and one iron-grated and glazed window towards the court-yard, of 4 feet by 3.

Into that day-room opens the Women-Felons' sleeping-room, which is 13 feet by 6; with a window like the former, and outside shutter. No fireplace; but supplied with wooden bedsteads, straw-in-sacking beds, each having two blankets, a pillow, and a rug.

For the Men-Felons are four sleeping-cells, each 7 feet by 4 feet 6, and 9 feet 6 inches high; the door-way 5 feet 9 by 21 inches wide. In each of these cells sleep two Felons. They are ventilated by a small semicircular iron grating over each door, and one air-tube, which opens into the court-yard: there is a small aperture also in the door of each cell,.7 inches by 5, which has a bar in the middle; and each cell is supplied with wooden bedsteads, raised 14 inches from the stone-flooring, with straw-in-sacking beds, two blankets, a pillow, and a rug.

Here is likewise another room, of 20 feet by 12, for the Sick-Felons, having a large iron-grated and glazed window. It has no fire-place; but is furnished with bedsteads, straw-in-ticking, two blankets, pillow and rug, like the former.

Fresh straw is allowed monthly; and mops, brooms, pails, saucepans, kettles, gridirons, &c. are provided for the Prisoners of all descriptions.

It was formerly the custom here, for a Man to go about the Town once a week, to collect broken victuals for the Prisoners: But this has been discontinued many years, and in lieu of it.the Mayor for the time being allows them two shillings per week. A peck of coals per day is given to both Debtors and Felons, from Michaelmas to Lady-Day, from the same exemplary source.

On the next day after my visit in Sept. 1805, Mr. Reynolds, then Mayor, politely accompanied me to this Prison; where I pointed out to him, that by taking in the Publick-house close adjacent, the Bridewell might be properly consolidated, workrooms made, *the Sexes kept separate* in court-yards distinct from each other, and the loathsome cells bricked up. I was sorry, however, in Sept. 1810, to find my suggestions had been unavailing. No alteration had taken place with respect to the Females' sleeping-room, which opens into the Men's day-room; and the four Debtors, with the eight Criminals (two of them very young and decent looking Females) were all associated together in the small court-yard.

This Town-Gaol adjoins to the Tollhouse Hall; where Prisoners are tried by the Recorder of Yarmouth, and the Court has the aweful power of life and death.

Prisoners from the Court of Requests are committed hither for *any sum less than twenty shillings;* and confined twenty days. Above that sum, up to 40. cpnfinement is 40 days; but beyond the latter sum it has no power.

The Assize is held only once a year,

and upon no fixed day. In 1809 it was held on the 5th of July. One John Allen, upon *suspicion of Felony,* was committed hither on the 30th of August following. He lay in Prison until the 13th of Sept. 1810, and was then *acquitted,* at the Session which *happened* to be held during the time of my last visit.

Here is *no Employment for the Prisoners;* although plenty of it might be procured, if work-rooms were provided for the purpose.

The Prison is white-washed twice a year. No Rules and Orders. The Act for preserving Health, and the Clauses against Spirituous Liquors not hung up.
YORK.
The City Bridewell.
Keeper, *Edward Yeoman.*

Salary, 50/. and lol. for furnishing straw. Fees, two shillings each.

Chaplain, none; nor any religious attentions.

Surgeon, Mr. *Champneij.* Salary, 20/.

Number of Prisoners, 1802, Aug. 20th, Five. 1809, Sept. 11th, Fifteen.

Allowance, two shillings each per week, in bread, and one shilling ditto in money. Two chaldron of coals are annually sent in for Winter consumption, by the Corporation.
REMARKS.
Here are three spacious day-rooms; one for the Men, and the other two for Women-Prisoners, with a fire-place in each.

Over the Women's room is the *Infirmary,* which is light, and well ventilatedDetached from this building are seven sleeping-cells, of about *6* feet square, aud 7 feet high: two of which are totally dark, and the other five nearly so; having only one iron-grated aperture 1.5 inches by 12, for light and ventilation. Loose.straw only, laid on the floors, is supplied to sleep on, and there are uncovered tubs, as sewers. Also a room for faulty Apprentices, committed for a month. These have *no* allowance assigned them; but are employed in pounding cement, at five pence a bushel, which the Keeper sells at one shilling.

Here is xjne spacious court-yard, l8o feet long by 20, for Debtors, Male and Female; but not being deemed secure, the Prisoners derive no other advantage from at, than that of having their cells better ventilated than heretofore.

The *Employment* for Women here is spinning, and making laces; and they receive all they earn: The Men pound tile sherds, for which the Keeper pays then four pence per bushel, and then sells the dust at from ten-pence a bushel to one-shilling-: But as he had not disposed of a great stock on hand, when I was there in 1802, I found them making of list-shoes.

Neither the Act for preserving Health, nor the Clauses against Spirituous Liquors, hung up.
YORK.
St. Peter's Gaol.
Gaoler, *John Burnley;* afterwards *John Moiser;* now *Thomas Harrison;* who is also Sheriffs-officer for the Liberty of St. Peter.

Salary, 30/. out of which he furnishes straw.

Fees, Debtors, 6a-. *8d.;* besides which the Chief Bailiff demands 8. *Ad.* for his *Liberate!* Felons, no Fees.

Number of Prisoners, Debtors. Criminals.
1802, Aug. 20th, 2--------1
Sept. 2d,------2--------3

I805, Aug. 5th, 0 1 1809, Sept. 11th,-----0 1. This was a Woman for Bastardy, who had been here seven months, and by spinning, earned three-pence a day.

Allowance, none heretofore, unless certificated as Paupers: but at my last visit I found the Allowance was 2. per week; paid by Mr. Mills, the Dean's Proctor, in money, both to Debtors and Criminals.

This *poor,* but very decent looking young Woman, upon being informed I was a Magistrate, asked me, "why the Man who had seduced her was not imprisoned, as well as herself?" I replied, the ParishOfficers could best answer that Question. REMARKS.
This Gaol, near the Minster-Gate of York, for the Liberty of St. Peter, is-the property of the Dean; who holds his courts at this place, four time in the year.

Here is no court-yard for the use of the Prisoners. The Debtors have four sizeable rooms up stairs; to which the Keeper furnishes bed and bedding, some at *6s* others at 10. per month. But if a Debtor provides his own bed, he pays noftiing.

Eleven steps down are two Dungeons for Felons, of 19 feet by 8, and *6* feet high; each lighted and ventilated by an iron-grated window, which looks toward the Street. Lately, however, a small projecting space, of about 4 feet, has been palisaded off, so as to prevent communication with the Street. The above Dungeons had several loads of ashes and other filth in them, at one of my former visits, and which appeared to have Iain there a long time.

One of the Debtors, a shoemaker, who had his wife and four children with him, lived then in the room above, for which he paid half a crown per week. He complained to me of the offensiveness of the cells below, which, together with the crowded state of his own room, made it, in the hot weather of August lS02, most unbearable. The boards of his floor were rotten, and the roof of the cell beneath not being cieled, there was a fissure of communication about a foot long.

The next morning I waited upon the very Rev. Dean of York, Dr. *Marhham,* who politely accompanied me to the Prison; and, gave orders to the Gaoler, to take away the offensive rubbish immediately, and to whitewash and cleanse the whole Prison; which the Gaoler promised to set about the next day.

The only Prisoner in the cells at that time was a run-away apprentice, who wast employed in the pounding of tile-sherds.

On my return in September, I found nothing had been done; the Prison was in the same state of filth; two *lewd Women* were confined in the same cell with the Roy before-mentioned, and with them several persons in the Street were conversing. Fowls roosted every night in. one of the cells.

The Employment in the cells is pounding of tile-sherds, at four-pence a bushel,, which is sold by the Keeper at a shilling. The present Gaoler told me that *fVillinm Winterbum,* committed for drunkenness and assault, had pounded-sixty-five bushels during the nine weeks of his confinement.

If a Debtor procures work for himself, he has all he earns.

The Act for Preservation of Health was not hung up, but the Clauses against the use of Spirituous Liquors were. This, however, must be but of little effect, when Spirits can be so easily handed to Prisoners from the Street; an evil, which, be the Gaoler ever so vigilant or attentive, he could not prevent.

I could not help observing to *Burnley,* the former Keeper, the striking contrast there was between his face, which appeared as if capable of lighting a candle, and.

that of the poor Shoemaker, above stairs; in whose countenance there was a visible alteration since my last recent visit.

The Prison has been repaired and whitewashed, and a wooden bedstead, with loose straw, and two rugs, are allowed to sleep on.

Water is accessible to all the Prisoners; and there is now a sewer provided, with a stench pipe to prevent its being offensive.

In l8oi, Dr. *Fauntayne,* the former Dean, gave *100l.* and the four Residentiaries each *25/.;* making together, *Two Hundred Pounds,* for the benefit of this Prison. This Sum was invested in the Publick Funds, and the Dividends are directed to be applied towards the relief of the Debtors and Felons here confined, in such proportion as the Dean and Chapter for the time being shall think proper. There is also a Donation in Bread of twelve shillings per annum, given every Christmas amongst the Debtors and Felons of this Gaol.

Mr. Howard mentions " the having in his possession an old printed List of Parishes, Towns, and parts of Towns, which are in the Liberty of St. Peter, viz: within the City of York and Ainsty, nine Places. In the East Riding, sixty-two. West Riding, forty. North Riding, fifty-one. And there is," continues my great Predecessor, "*one Place* in each of the following Counties—Devonshire, Gloucestershire, Lancashire, Lincolnshire, Northumberland, and Hampshire; and in Nottinghamshire, *seven places"*

Of these places, however, I am unfortunate enough not to have obtained any ertain information, in consequence of my inquiries, nor to have procured the printed List to which Mr. Howard refers.

YORK. *Gaol for the City, and Ainsty .*
Gaoler, *George Rylah,* who is Sheriffs Officer for the City and Ainsty.
Salary, *150I.* out of which he pays 40/. to a Turnkey.
Fees, Debtors, *6s. Sd.* Felons, 13. *4d.* paid by the City. The Under-Sheriff 1 demands 7. *4d.* for his *Liberate!*

Garnish not allowed; but one shilling is generally exacted.

At the first view of my quotation from " *Howards* State of Prisons," Edit. 1777 4to, P-407, I had taken this word for " *County* 1" but find my Error corrected by *Camden,* in his Britannia, Edit. Gibson, 1C95, p. 72. Speaking of the West part of the County, "The City of *York,"* says he, "neither belongs "to this, nor any other part of the Shire; but enjoys its own Liberties, and a Jurisdiction over the "Neighbourhood, on the West-side called the Liberty of *Ansty ;,* which some derive from *Anciency,* to "denote its antiquity: Others, more plausibly, from the German word *Anstossen,* implying a bound, 01 "limit"

Chaplain, whosoever is appointed such to the Lord Mayor; and he officiates gratuitously.

Duty, Prayers and a Sermon on Tuesdays.

Surgeon, Mr. *Champney,* for Debtors and Felons.
Salary, 20/. for this Prison, and the Bridewell.

Number of Prisoners, 1809, Sept 11th, Debtors, Four; Felons, Four.

Allowance, to poor Debtors, on petition, 1. *6d.* per week in bread. To Felons, *is.* in bread, and *'jd.* in milk. See *Remarks.* REMARKS.

The horrid Gaol on the Ouse-bridge , which so long disgraced this very ancient and respectable City, being pulled down, and the new one I am about to describe, being got ready, Prisoners were removed to it in the year 1807. It is situated on an eminence, anciently termed *fetus Galium,* or, as it is now called, *Old Bail,* at the Southwest part of the City, and within its walls.

The boundary-wall encloses about three quarters of an acre of land. The front entrance is the Turnkey's lodge, which has two rooms below and two above, for his use.

The Gaol, which has a very handsome appearance, is entirely of hewn stone, and stands detached within the area. The court-yard for Debtors is about 200 feet long, and 60 wide, being the whole space between the Turnkey's lodge and the main building. The whole is a grass plat; and on a stone is inscribed "Debtors' Boundary." To convey an idea of this miserable place of human confinement, I will describe the Felon's-Side. It formed a part of the bridge; and level with the ground there was a room 30 feet by 14, with opposite and lofty windows, for Prisoners committed on suspicion of Felony. In the first passage, *down thirteen steps,* was a large cell, for those to work in who were sentenced to hard labour, 22 feet by 10, with one small window only. Near this were two horrid dungeons, 6 feet by 5 feet 3, and 7 feet 6 inches high,, totally dark. The Women-Felons' day-room was on the same floor as that of the Men, and separated from it by two wooden doors in the passage. It was 14 feet by 8, with a window and tire-place. There was also a door which led down *fourteen steps* to a large cell, 13 feet by 8, occasionally used for those who were under sentence of death; but commonly occupied as a *sleeping-room for the Women.* The door was iron-grated, and a small window in the passage opposite to it, throwing in a glimmering light, just sufficient to make darkness visible. One step lower than this cell were four other horrid caverns for Men-Felons, 6 feet 6 inches square, and 6 feet high, totally dark. They were dry at my visit, in August 1802; but the Gaoler's Son told me that in a high flood, the water has flowed into these cells *sixteen inch-*

es deep.

Surely our great Milton could have been no stranger to a scene, which seems capable of inspiring th« following lines. Par. Lost, IV. 76.

"And in the lowest deep, a *lower deep,* "Still threatening to devour me, opens wide!"

The Entrance to the Gaoler's house is under a double flight of stone steps, which form an arch, and lead to the Debtors' rooms on the first floor.

The ground-floor in front is wholly occupied by the Felons. On the right are eleven sleeping-cells for *Male-Felons,* each 7 feet 6 inches square, and 9 feet 9 high, to the crown of the arch; lighted and ventilated by an aperture, 22 inches by 4t guarded by a wire trellis, to prevent any thing improper being introduced. They have boarded floors, and six pair of rugs to sleep on; and the cell-doors open into a well-ventilated flagged passage, 6 feet 4 inches wide. The Male-Felons have also a day-room, 25 feet by 16, having a fire-place, a large grated and glazed sash-window, and furnished with a stone table, benches to sit on, and shelves for provisions, with a stone-sink for washing. The door of this room opens into a court-yard, 63 feet by 42, neatly paved with flag-stone; a sewer well contrived, dust-pen, and a place for coals.

Here is likewise a day-room for persons under sentence of death, 16 feet by 9; with a fire-place, grated and glazed sash window, and a covered sewer in one corner: a small room adjacent, with a bathing tub.

The *Women-Felons'* side is on the left, and corresponds in every respect with that for the Men; except that part of their day-room is used as a wash-house.

The windows of the Gaoler's apartments command a view of the different courts.

The handsome double flight of stone-steps before mentioned leads to the *Debtors' Prison,* which occupies the whole of the floor; and the doors of eight rooms open into a *Corridor,* or general Covert Gallery, 171 feet long, by 7 feet 9 inches wide, well lighted and ventilated, for the Debtors to walk in wet weather. They are entirely lodged on the first and second-floor; their rooms are 15 feet 6 inches square, and 10 feet high; having each a fire-place, and a large closet for meat, with a coal binn. Some of these rooms are very handsomely furnished by the Keeper, at from 10. 6d. to half a crown per week; but if Debtors bring their own bed, &c. they pay nothing. The gallery on the second-floor is 99 feet long, and 7 feet 9 inches wide; into which four rooms open, similar to those already described.

The Magistrates' Committee-room is on the first story, and over it a room, of the same size, used as a Chapel; where the Male and Female Prisoners are seated on forms, but not in pews, within view of each other.

A forcing-pump is used for throwing water into two cisterns, from which the whole Prison is well supplied.

In the centre of the building is a handsome turret, with a clock and bell.

§d" Debtors are allowed to send for two quarts of ale per day, and Felons for one quart, if they pay for it. The Felons are also allowed two chaldrons of coals yearly. If a Debtor can procure work, he has the full benefit of his earnings.

Mrs. Bowes's donation to the Prison is now discontinued.

The following is a Memorial *of certain Legacies,* heretofore put up in the Ousebridge Prison, and the benefit of which is now transferred to the present Gaol.

« LEGACIES.
"City Of York, to wit.
"Donations to the Prisoners in the Gaol upon Ouse-bridge, in the said City.
"Mrs. *Elizabeth Taylor,* by Will, dated 21st October 1580, gave three shillings and fourpence yearly, to be divided among the Prisoners on Lady-Day.
"The Corporation of York pay, yearly, *Peacock's Gift,* being three pounds four shillings, to be divided among the poor Prisoners.
"Mr. *William Edmonson's* Gift, being one pound six shillings, is distributed, weekly, in *bread* to the Prisoners."
YORK CASTLE.
The County Gaol.
Gaoler, *William Staveley.* Salary, 45 o/.

Fees, for Debtors, on coming into Gaol, *3s. 4d.*; on discharge, *8s. %d.*: Besides which the Under-sheriff demands of each Debtor 5. 4d. if discharged by the Plaintiff; and if by *Supersedeas, Js. 8rf.* Felons, and Crown-Prisoners here pay neither Fees nor Garnish. The Gaoler is allowed one shilling per mile, for the Conveyance of Prisoners of every description. Garnish; every Debtor pays a bag (containing a bushel) of coals, and a bag of turf to the room which he inhabits.

Chaplains, Rev. Mr. *Brown,* and Rev. Mr. *Richardson.*

Duty, Mr. *Brown,* Prayers on Monday, Tuesday, and Friday mornings; and Prayers on Sunday afternoon, during the Summer half-year. Also, twice a day, attends Convicts left for execution.

Mr. *Richardson,* Prayers and a Sermon every Thursday morning. Sacrament administered three times in the year. Salary, Mr. *Brown, 50I.* from the County. Mr. *Richardson, 2$l.* 15. from a Legacy. See the *Remarks.*

Surgeon, Mr. *Champney.*

Salary, none: He makes a Bill.

Number of Prisoners. Debtors. Felons, &c. Lunatick.
1800, March 31st,---73----43-----0.
1802, Aug. 23d,----60----38-----1. 1809, Sept. 10th,----50----39---_-0.

Allowance, to those *Debtors* who are certificated as Paupers, by the Parish to which they respectively belong, is allowed a *ninepenny loaf* every Tuesday and Friday. The weight of this loaf, 23d Aug. 1802, was three pounds ten ounces: On the 10th of Sept. 1809, it was two pounds fourteen ounces, and eleven drachms.

Criminals for trial, and *Misdemeaners,* have every morning a sixteen ounce loaf of fair wheaten bread, and two ounces of good cheese. *Transports,* convicted at the *Castle,* have the King's Allowance of *2s. 6d.* per week; *viz.* eighteen pence in money, and the remaining shilling in bread.. *Transports* from the *Quarter Sessions,* have two shillings per week; *viz.* one shilling paid in *money,* by that Riding of the County from which they were sent, and the other shilling in *bread.* REMARKS.

Within the spacious area, of about four acres, that surrounds this ancient castle, stands a noble County-hall; in which are the two Courts of Justice: one for the trial of Criminal Offenders; the other for *nisi prius,* or Civil Causes.

Opposite the Castle, and near the walls, is a very interesting structure, called "*Clifford's Tower.*" Favoured originally by good architecture, it is worthily and well kept in due preservation by the present owner, *Samuel Wilks Waud,* Esq. as a venerable piece of antiquity; and, let me add, highly to the honour of its respectable Protector. The *Times* want such *Recorders;* and much might be said on this subject.

In the centre of the area is the Prison for Debtors; to which, from a flagged terrace near their court-yard, (containing about an acre of ground) the ascent is by a fine flight of stone steps to an ample floor, on which are eight rooms, each *16* feet square, and twelve feet high.

Above these are twelve rooms for Common-side Debtors, which are *aUfree wards,* airy and wholesome; and the passage is through lofty and spacious lobbies. From these avenues however, in themselves very pleasant and commodious, and also from their sleeping-rooms, the *Debtors* have a full view into the court-yard and solitary-cells of the *Felons;* in consequence of which serious inconveniences have sometimes occurred: Dangerous implements have been conveyed to very improper hands, and the regularity and orderly conduct of the Gaol frequently disturbed. *Sloping boards,* in the manner I have seen them in other Gaols, if suitably placed before the windows, would effectually prevent so hazardous a communication.

The County furnishes neither bedsteads, bedding, nor even straw for Debtors. The Debtor who has a room to himself, pays for bedding and furniture three-pence per day: If a single bed amongst other Debtors, it is two-pence a day; and if two sleep in a bed, one penny each.

On the ground-floor of this Prison are the Gaolers apartments.

The Felons' court-yard, in front of the Castle, has a descent of five steps; and is separated from the area by a double-row of iron-palisades, enclosing a space of about 12 feet, to prevent all communication with strangers. It is chiefly defective in being too small, 54 feet only by 45. Soft water is *now* laid on; and just on the outside of the iron palisades is the pump, that supplies the whole Prison with excellent spring-water.

The day-room for Men-Felons, is 24 feet by 15, and has a fire-place. From this room there are two lobbies, containing nineteen sleeping-cells, of about six feet square; with lofty arched roofs, and boarded oaken floors, well ventilated, and dry.

Out of the Felons' court-yard is a passage leading to the Chapel, and in which are eight sleeping-cells, *9* feet by *6,* airy and dry like the former. Also another passage from the same court, which contains five sleeping-cells.

The room set apart for condemned Prisoners, called "Pompey Parlour," in size about 18 feet square, has a fire-place, and is sufficiently light to enable its unhappy tenants to read.

To each cell the County liberally supplies rugs for the Prisoners' bedding, from two pair even to six pair, according to the season of the year.

On the *West-side of the Gaol* is a court-yard of a semicircular shape, with a dayroom, for young Offenders, and capable of containing fifteen Prisoners.

At the back of the Indictment and Clerk of Assize Office there is a day-room, 24 feet by 15, for *Mistlemeaners,* with a fire-place, benches, &c. lighted by doublegrated and glazed casement windows, opening into a flagged-court, of 45 feet by 24, with sewers conveniently placed; and also four sleeping-cells. The first and second story have each a day-room, with the same number of sleeping-cells, and furnished in like manner.

The *South Wing* is appropriated to *Female-Felons;* on the ground-floor of which is a day-room, conveniently fitted up, and opening into a spacious flagged court, in which is a wash-house, boiler, &c. Also six sleeping-cells, the least of which is 12 feet by 10. The first story contains a day-room, with the same number of sleepingcells. The second, or attick-story has two *Infirmary-rooms;* one of which has a warm and cold bath, an adjoining dressing-room, and patent water-closets. All the Prisoners in this wing have wooden bedsteads, flock-beds, blankets, and rugs.

At the top of the building is a flat leaded roof, 45 feet by 25; secured by an ironrailing, 5 feet high, for convalescents to walk and take the air upon. From the dayroom of the first story the descent is by a flight of stone steps into the court-yard, 50 feet by 27.

The approach to the centre building of the South wing is by a flight of five stone steps; and four Ionic pillars, 26 feet 6 inches high, support the portico; exhibiting a noble and uniform appearance with the *Criminal* and *nisi prius* Courts on the opposite side of the area.

The back part of this building, in which there is a convenient *Sessions-House,* with lofty and opposite windows, is separated from the Prison by a lobby, *6* feet *6* inches wide, paved with flag-stones; in which are eight sleeping-cells, of 14 feet by 10; and two day-rooms, with fire-places, benches, tables, shelves, &c. each opening into separate court-yards, of 50 feet by 27, which are supplied with convenient sewers, and a pump in each, of excellent water.

The chamber-story contains nine rooms for *Debtors,* each 14 feet by 12 feet 3 inches, with glazed sash windows, and a fire-place in each. These rooms are set apart for the most respectable Prisoners of this class.

The Chapel is in the West wing of the Castle. The Women sit upon forms in the area, and in front of the pulpit: The Convicts, Felons for trial, and Misdemeaners, are placed on seats close to the wall, and nearly encircle the Chapel. The gallery is occupied by the Keeper's seat, in which are Debtors, and occasional Visitors. All are in view of the Minister. A pew is set apart, opposite the Keeper's seat, for those under sentence of death.

A Debtor officiates as Chapel Clerk,

for which he is paid sixpence a week by the Dean and Chapter. All the Felons, and many of the Debtors, attended Divine Service, when I was there on the 10th of Sept. 1809, and their behaviour was orderly and attentive.

On the whole, the design and execution of this County Gaol are highly commendable, and, I doubt not, will prove both the *Decus et Tutamen* of Yorkshire.

Its intelligent and active Keeper will thus enjoy the power of separating the Prisoners who are detained for *trial*, from those already convicted; as well as of keeping Misdemeaaers, and less injurious Offenders more safely to themselves. In short, every class of Prisoners will thus have its own district undisturbed; a convenience and a benefit, which the Gaol in question has so long wanted.

Every Prisoner who enters this Gaol in a ragged or dirty condition, is first clean washed; and then receives the clothing provided for such by the County. There are six *solitary-cells* here, with boarded floors, which are well ventilated; and to each of them is attached a small court-yard.

The County, as yet, provides *no Employment* for the Prisoners; but Mr. *Staveley,* the present humane Gaoler, is ever active in procuring it for those of handicraft trades; as taylors and shoemakers, weavers, wool-combers, sadlers, &c. And such as cannot, in a Prison, follow their own profession, soon learn to make laces, garters, purses, and other slight articles, which they expose for sale in the *Castle-yard:* and by these means many of them are enabled both decently to maintain themselves, and assist their pitiable families. As there is no working-room, however, for the purpose within their allotment of space, this manufacture, in rainy weather, is carried on in one or other of the lobbies, which are equally spacious, airy, and comfortable.

Mr. *John Watson,* Clerk to the Justices, attends all their Meetings held at the Castle; and regulates from time to time the weight of the Prisoners' bread, as issued to them in ninepenny loaves.

His Salary is Twenty Guineas *per annum*.

A *Table ofFees,* as settled by the Justices on the 14th of July 1735, is hung up in the passage of the Gaol; but seems to have become obsolete through time, as no other Fees than those before mentioned are now taken.

The Salary of the Rev. Mr. Richardson, as Co-Chaplain of the Gaol, for reading Prayers, and giving a Sermon weekly, originates as follows. Through the politeness of Mr. Gray I have been favoured with a copy of the Writing of Endowment; and as it is both curious and instructive, a full extract from it is here subjoined.

"16th, January," 1634 " 10 Charles I. Phineas Hodgson, D.D. Chancellor of the Cathedral Church of York, by his deed of that date, (after expressing his desire, out of his *Commiseration and Pity to the Souls of such Prisoners* as then were, or should be in the Castle of York, to provide that they, for ever afterwards, might be instructed in the Knowledge of God, to their eternal Bliss and Happiness, which he hoped would be, by providing some Godly Minister or Preacher of God's Word to preach unto them in the said Castle, which, *by reason of their Imprisonment, they were hindered elsewhere to hear;* and in regard that Richard" neile " then late Archbishop of York, did licence, or allow, that Godly Preachers for ever thereafter might be allowed to preach there to that purpose, *although there was no Church or Chapel;* Grants to *John Scott,* D. D. the then Dean, and to *George Stanhope,* D. D. and *Henry Wickham,* D. D. Prebend Residentiaries of the Cathedral of York, *a Yearly Rent-Charge of Thirty Pounds,* issuing out of a Messuage in Bempton, *alias* Benton upon the Woulds, in the County of York; and also out of the Chapel and Tithes of Bempton, *alias* Benton and Newsam, (parcel of the possessions of the late Monastery of Bridlington); and all the Lands and Tenements of the Grantor, in Bempton, *alias* Benton and Newsam; payable half-yearly, at Whitsuntide and Martinmas, at *Haxby's Tomb,* in the Cathedral Church of York,

with the usual Clauses of *nominepoenae,* and Distress on Default of Payment. In Trust, to pay *Twenty-five Pounds per annum,* parcel of the said Thirty Pounds, to such Minister or Preacher of God's Word, according to the True Religion then established in the Church of England, as should be nominated and appointed by the Grantor; and after his death, by the Dean and Chapter of the Cathedral of York, *to preach weekly, in the Castle of York,* to the Prisoners there for the time being; such Minister preaching there once every week throughout the year, except only in the Assize weeks, and at such times, by reason of any infection, or otherwise, as he shall be dispensed with by the Grantor, during his Life, or the Dean and Chapter after his Death. And to the intent that *Five Pounds,* residue of the Thirty Pounds, should be distributed weekly, by *Two Shillings a week, in Bread* amongst the pooorer sort of the Prisoners upon the Sermon Days, to such of them as should be present at the said Sermons; Hoping and Desiring that some others would attend to this pious and charitable work; and in time *increase the Allowance and Stipend;* and that the work might be acceptable to God, and profitable and comfortable to many distressed and poor Souls'."

The Instrument then goes on to make provision for continuing and perpetuating the Trust, on the Demise of the then Trustees.

Statement, and Application of the Legacy of the Rev. Chancellor Hodgson.

£. s. L

The Rent-Charge, now paid by the Representatives of the late

Robert Burton, Esq. of Hotham, in Yorkshire, as Owners of the

Estate and Tithes mentioned in the Deed, is------30 00

Out of which is deducted, and applied for the purposes directed by the Deed------*S o 0*

And for Land-Tax, on the 25l. per annum----150 6 5 0

Clear Receipt, paid to the Chaplain----*£.* 2 3 *is* 0

§CJ The above Writing, obligingly communicated to me, mentions, that

Mr. *William Hart,* a Merchant at York, had formerly bequeathed "One Hundred Pounds to the like use." Nothing certain, however, can now be obtained concerning this Legacy, which, probably, (like many others I have heard of in my perambulation of Prisons) is either lost, or diverted to some other purpose; and, from the lapse of time, it is not likely that any thing more can now be made out respecting it.

Account Of Charitable Donations to the Prisoners in his Majesty's Gaol, The Castle of York.

d. s. d. "The Lady Lumley; to be given yearly, on St. Thomas's Day. Formerly, 6/. 7 s. but since increased to *Ten Pounds,* paid to the Gaoler every Christmas; and ordered by the Trustees to be laid out in discharging poor Debtors out of Custody, in the same manner as the Money left in his (the Gaoler's) hands by the High Sheriff and

Gentlemen of the Grand Jury; and for which he produces proper vouchers at each Assize------------JO 00

The honourable and ancient City of York, weekly, in bread---026

Mrs. Frances Thornhill, for straw. The Lord Mayor has 30/. in his hands for the purpose; and the Thirty Shillings for *Straw* are now laid out in other articles for the good of the Prison, by the Clerk to the Justices 1 10 0

at?, *s. d. i* Doctor Phineas Hodgson; whose before-mentioned Legacy of *Si* per annum, is weekly distributed, at 2. per week, to all those Prisoners who attend Sermons in the Gaol----------5 o 0

Mr. Alderman White's Gift of *26s.* a year, and Mr. Bowes1 s of 20. a year, in bread, have long been discontinued." In the above Prison, as in some others, it is left as matter of *option* with the *Debtors,* whether to attend or absent themselves from Chapel Duty, and the Sermons; but why it is so permitted has never yet been satisfactorily accounted for.

®Cf" An omission of the following Legacies to CHESTER *New City Gaol* escaped my notice, till it was too late to supply the defect in my description, page 132. They should have been inserted thus:

"The sum of *ll. 13s. 4d.* at Midsummer, and of 3/. 3. at Christmas in every year, are distributed equally between the Debtors confined in the above Gaol; being Legacies left for that purpose."

CONCLUSION.

Animated with the hope of giving permanency and improvement to that reform in our Prisons which was so ably begun by my excellent Predecessor, Mr. Howard, I now send forth this Book, the labour of many years, as an important subject for publick consideration; and, however defective, deliver it to the World, with the spirit of a Man who endeavoured to do well, and at length enjoys the luxury o£ having lived to see his highest earthly wishes accomplished.

If it shall be found, as is very probable, that many things are omitted in this extensive work, which might greatly have added to its value, let it not be forgotten that much, likewise, is performed: that my numerous visits had not the patronage of Government to invigorate their ardour; that many Prisons proved to be difficult of access; that the information which I sought was not easily obtained; and that this massy collection of particulars is not published for general entertainment, but for the serious perusal of those distinguished Readers who have it in their will, no less than in their power, to soften the trials, and alleviate the sorrows of *Imprisonment.*

In Ireland, the Minister, or other respectable Gentleman of the district in which the Gaols are situate, is appointed the *Local Inspector,* with an humble Salary of Ten Pounds. His duty is to see that the TJiirteen Articles of *excellent regulation* , be duly observed; and to report upon each of them, and upon oath, at every Quarter Session. There is likewise an *Inspector General* constituted, with a Salary of Two Hundred Pounds; who is required to visit every Prison in that See Stat. 26s Geo. III. Cap. 27-Sect. 32. printed by Grierson, Dublin, 1804.

Kingdom, at least once within two years; and report also, in what manner, and with what effect, the Local Inspectors have discharged their interesting Trust.

The state, however, of the Prisons in question has been represented to me as extremely defective; and frequently have I been solicited to visit them. But, having failed in my application for *Authority* in this my native Country, I could entertain but little hope of success in a remoter sphere; where I might have to combat the opposition of those, whose interest was but too likely to prevent that reformation of abuses, on which their personal ease and emolument might depend.

List of County and City Gaols in Ireland; of their Local Inspectors, and the Gaolers; as given in the year 1808.

County. 1. Antrim---- 2. Armagh---- 3. Callow---- 4. Cavan----- 5. Clare----- 6. Cork 7. Cork City 8. Donegall---- 9. Down----- 10. Drogheda--- 11. Dublin-- 12. Dublin City, has 6 Gaols 13. Fermanagh--- 14. Galway---- 15. Galway Town-- 16. Kerry----- 17. Kildare 18. Kilkenny---- 19. Kilkenny City-- 20. King's County--41. Leitrim.---- 22. Limerick---- 23. Londonderry--- 24. Longford---- 25. Louth 26. Mayo 27. Meath 28. Monaghan--- 29. Queen's County-- 30. Roscommon-.- 31. Sligo---- 32. Tipperary--- 33. Tyrone 34. Waterford--- 35. Waterford City-- 36. Westmeath--- 37-Wexford 38. Wicklow

Local Inspectors:

Rev. Richard Dobbs.------

Rev. Mr. Ball.--

E. Fitzgerald, M. D.

Rev. Mr. Druitt."

Rev. Mr. Weldon.------

Rev. Mr. Kennedy.-----

Rev. Mr. Davis.------

Adam Gillespie, M. D.----

Rev. Mr. Ford.-------

Edward Fairlow, M. D.----

Rev. Mr. Baylie.------

Isaac Dejoncour, Esq.----

Rev. Mr. Johnston.------

Rev. Mr. Young.------

Rev. Mr. Shaw-------

Rev. Mr. Day.-------

Rev.Mr.Harrison,andDr.Johnson.--

Redmund Duffey, Esq.-----

Thomas Hutchinson, Esq.---

Mr. W. Ellis.-

Rev. Mr. Bennet.------

Sheppard, Esq. Gabbett, Esq.
Rev. Mr. Babington.-----
S. Duberdieu, Esq.----J-
Rev. Mr. Tinley.-----
Rev. Mr. Ashe.------
Rev. Mr. Wainwright.----.
Rev. Mr. Montgomery.---
William Pilsworth, Esq.---
Rev. Mr. Blakeney.-----
Rev. Mr. Armstrong.----
Rev. Mr. Stevenson.--—--
Rev. Mr. Stack.-----.-
  Rev. Mr. Frazier.-----
  Rev. Mr. White.-----.
  Rev. Mr. Dundas.-----
  Rev. Archd. Elgee.---
  Rev. Mr. Porter.----- *Gaolers.*
  William M'Claverty.
John Johnson.
Robert Kerevan.

William Stewart.
Anthony O'Laughlin.
J. Murphy, 1
John Walsh.
   Spearing.
   Isaac Simpson.
Edward Hamilton.
John Allen.
George Dunn.
Tresham Gregg.
George Gallogly.
Charles Eddington.
John Welch.
Francis Tuite.
Moorhead, and Ring.
Richard Elseworth.
William Montgorrwty
Thomas Simpson.
John Irwin.
.--- Hedderman,

Hugh Stevensou.
William Ridge.
Dennis Fitzpatrick.
Hen. Moran, Will. Keller.
James Hughes.
John Short.
John Clarke.
Edward Jones.
Anthony Sedley.
John Headon.
John O Brien.
James Wright.
Francis Carson.
Thomas Codd.
Joseph Gladwin.
Luke Ashmore.
   Foster Achkb, Inspector-General.—
1608.